In memory of Simon Katz and Lauren Erickson

Contents

CHAPTER 10
Language Processing and the Human Brain   444

CHAPTER 11
Computer Processing of Human Language   495

Preface

Well, this bit which I am writing, called Introduction, is really the er-h'r'm of the book, and I have put it in, partly so as not to take you by surprise, and partly because I can't do without it now. There are some very clever writers who say that it is quite easy not to have an er-h'r'm, but I don't agree with them. I think it is much easier not to have all the rest of the book.

A. A. MILNE, *Now We Are Six*, 1927

The last thing we find in making a book is to know what we must put first.

BLAISE PASCAL (1623–1662)

The tenth edition of *An Introduction to Language* continues in the spirit of our friend, colleague, mentor, and coauthor, Victoria Fromkin. Vicki loved language, and she loved to tell people about it. She found linguistics fun and fascinating, and she wanted every student and every teacher to think so, too. Though this edition has been completely rewritten for improved clarity and currency, we have nevertheless preserved Vicki's lighthearted, personal approach to a complex topic, including witty quotations from noted authors (A. A. Milne was one of Vicki's favorites). We hope we have kept the spirit of Vicki's love for teaching about language alive in the pages of this book.

The first nine editions of *An Introduction to Language* succeeded, with the help of dedicated teachers, in introducing the nature of human language to tens of thousands of students. This is a book that students enjoy and understand and that professors find effective and thorough. Not only have majors in linguistics benefited from the book's easy-to-read yet comprehensive presentation, but also majors in fields as diverse as teaching English as a second language, foreign language studies, general education, the cognitive and neurosciences, psychology, sociology, and anthropology have enjoyed learning about language from this book.

Highlights of This Edition

This edition includes **new developments in linguistics and related fields** that will strengthen its appeal to a wider audience. Much of this information will enable students to gain insight and understanding about linguistic issues and debates appearing in the national media and will help professors and students stay current with important linguistic research. We hope that it may also dispel certain common misconceptions that people have about language and language use.

Exercises (250) continue to be abundant in this edition, and more research-oriented exercises have been added for those instructors who wish their students to pursue certain topics more deeply. Many of the exercises are multipart, amounting to more than 300 opportunities for "homework" so that instructors can gauge their students' progress. Some exercises are marked as "challenge" questions: they go beyond the scope of what is ordinarily expected in a first course in language study. An **answer key** is available to instructors to assist them in areas outside of their expertise.

Chapter 1, "What Is Language?" continues to be a concise introduction to the general study of language. It contains many "hooks" for engaging students in language study, including "Language and Thought," which takes up the Sapir-Whorf hypotheses; the universal properties of languages including signed languages of the deaf; a consideration of animal "languages"; and the occasional silliness of self-appointed mavens of "good" grammar who beg us not to carelessly split infinitives and who find sentence-ending prepositions an abomination not to be put up with.

Chapter 2, "Morphology: The Words of Language," launches the book into the study of grammar with morphology, the study of word formation, as that is the most familiar aspect of grammar to most students. The subject is treated with clarity and an abundance of simple illustrations from non-English languages to emphasize the universality of word structure including the essentials of derivational versus inflectional morphology, free and bound morphemes, and the hierarchical structure of words.

Chapter 3, "Syntax: The Sentence Patterns of Language," is the most heavily revised chapter of former editions. Once it has introduced the universal and easily understood notions of constituency, syntactic categories (parts of speech), phrase structure trees, structural ambiguity and the infinite scope of language, the chapter delves into the now nearly universally accepted X-bar grammatical patterns for describing the deeper and more subtle syntactic structures of English and other languages. The topic is approached slowly and developed painstakingly so as to inform and not overwhelm. In particular, the current views on binary branching, heads and complements, selection (both C- and S-), and transformational analysis within the X-bar framework are carefully explained and illustrated. Formalisms are held to the bare minimum required to enhance clarity. Non-English examples abound in this chapter as throughout the entire book, and the weighty elements of theory are lightened by the inclusion of insightful examples and explanations, supplemented as always by quotations, poetry, cartoons, and humor.

Chapter 4, "The Meaning of Language," on semantics, has been more finely structured so that the challenging topics of this complex subject can be digested in smaller pieces. Still based on the theme of "What do you know about meaning when you know a language?" the chapter first introduces students to truth-conditional semantics and the principle of compositionality.

Following that are discussions of what happens when compositionality fails, as with idioms, metaphors, and anomalous sentences. Lexical semantics takes up various approaches to word meaning, including the concepts of reference and sense, semantic features, argument structure, and thematic roles. The most dramatic upgrade of this chapter is a newly expanded and modernized section on pragmatics. Here we discuss and illustrate in depth the influence of situational versus linguistic context on the communicative content of utterances, the significance of implicature in comprehension, Grice's Maxims of Conversation, presuppositions, and J. L. Austin's speech acts.

Chapter 5, "Phonetics: The Sounds of Language," retains its former organization and continues to embrace IPA (International Phonetics Association) notation for English in keeping with current practices, with the sole exception of using /r/ in place of the technically correct /ɹ/ when illustrating English. We continue to mention alternative notations that students may encounter in other publications.

Chapter 6, "Phonology: The Sound Patterns of Language," has been streamlined by relegating several complex examples (e.g., metathesis in Hebrew) to the exercises, where instructors can opt to include them if it is thought that students can handle advanced material. The chapter continues to be presented with a greater emphasis on insights through linguistic data accompanied by small amounts of well-explicated formalisms, so that the student can appreciate the need for formal theories without experiencing the burdensome details.

Chapter 7, "Language in Society," has been moved forward in the book from previous editions to emphasize its growing importance as a major subfield of linguistics. Growth in this area of study, even in the few years since the ninth edition, has been astronomical. We have strived heartily to present the established facts and principles of sociolinguistics while bringing up to date subjects such as banned languages (it's still happening); dead and dying languages (also still happening); gender differences; minority dialects such as Hispanic English ("Spanglish"); languages in contact such as pidgins, creoles, and lingua francas that may be found in linguistically heterogeneous areas; the use of computers in sociolinguistic analysis; second language teaching; and bilingual education, among others.

Chapter 8, "Language Change: The Syllables of Time," has been updated with the latest research on language families, language relatedness, and language typology. Also, in response to reviewers' requests, a detailed and more complex illustration of the application of the comparative method to two contemporary dialects to reconstruct their ancestor—often called "internal reconstruction"—is now part of this chapter.

Chapter 9, "Language Acquisition," has been thoroughly restructured and rewritten to enhance clarity since the ninth edition. In addition, much of what has been learned about second language acquisition (adult learning of a foreign language) has been folded into this chapter along with an entirely new section on "heritage languages," the learning of an intrafamily language after immigration to a country where that language is not spoken (e.g., Yiddish by Jews who emigrated from Russia).

Chapter 10, "Language Processing and the Human Brain," could well have been entitled "psycholinguistics and neurolinguistics" but that may have made the subject seem overly daunting. This chapter combines a straight-forward discussion of many of the issues that regard the psychology of language—what the mind does—with the neurology of language—what the brain does—during language usage. Dramatic changes in the understanding of the brain's role in language processing are occurring virtually every day owing to the rapid enhancement of the ability of neurolinguists to measure brain activity to tiny degrees of sensitivity at extremely precise locations. This chapter reports on those techniques and some of the results regarding language and the brain that ensue. The psycholinguistic portion of this chapter appeared as the first half of chapter 9 in the ninth edition; the second and greater portion of this chapter is an enlargement and updating of chapter 2 from the ninth and previous editions.

Chapter 11, "Computer Processing of Human Language," is an expansion into a full chapter of what was the second half of chapter 9 in the ninth edition. The fundamentals of computational linguistics are still covered and have been clarified and expanded, but the force driving the promotion of the subject into a chapter of its own is the astonishing progress in the application of computers to human languages, which has burgeoned to a degree hardly imaginable even as we wrote previous editions. Anchoring the extensive new material in this chapter is the introduction of the Culturomic Revolution in the computer processing of language, in which computers have analyzed billions (with a *b*) of lines of text with results that will astonish even the most blasé readers. Culturomics, which is concerned with published, written texts, is soon to be augmented by "twitterology," a study of "on-the-fly" language usage by billions of people (i.e., "twitterers") in thousands of languages, only beginning to be linguistically analyzed as the this edition goes to press. But those who wish to keep abreast of the power of computers applied to language will find this chapter indispensable.

Chapter 12, "Writing: The ABCs of Language," has undergone a mild re-writing to further improve clarity. Texting and twittering, while largely un-studied by linguists, are included in a new section adding a further dimension to what it means to write a language.

Terms that appear bold in the text are defined in the revised **glossary** at the end of the book. The glossary has been expanded and improved so that the tenth edition provides students with a linguistic lexicon of nearly 700 terms, making the book a worthy reference volume.

The **order of presentation of chapters 2 through 6** was once thought to be nontraditional. Our experience, backed by previous editions of the book and the recommendations of colleagues throughout the world, has convinced us that it is easier for the novice to approach the structural aspects of language by first looking at morphology (the structure of the most familiar linguistic unit, the word). This is followed by syntax (the structure of sentences), which is also familiar to many students, as are numerous semantic concepts. We then proceed to the more novel (to students) phonetics and phonology, which students often find daunting. However, the book is written so that individual instructors can present material in the traditional order of phonetics, phonology, morphology, syntax, and semantics (chapters 5, 6, 2, 3, and 4) without confusion, if they wish.

As in previous editions, the primary concern has been basic ideas rather than detailed expositions. This book assumes no previous knowledge on the part of the reader. An updated list of references at the end of each chapter is included to accommodate any reader who wishes to pursue a subject in more depth. Each chapter concludes with a summary and exercises to enhance the students' interest in and comprehension of the textual material.

Additional Resources

Linguistics CourseMate. *An Introduction to Language* includes Linguistics CourseMate, which helps students gain a deeper and more comprehensive understanding of the textual material.

Linguistics CourseMate includes:

- an interactive eBook, with highlighting, note taking and search capabilities
- interactive learning tools including:
  - Quizzes
  - Flashcards
  - Audio files
  - Web Links
  - and more!

Go to www.cengagebrain.com to access these resources, and look for this icon 🖥 to find resources related to your text in Linguistics CourseMate.

Answer Key. The Answer Key for *An Introduction to Language* contains answers to all of the exercises in the core text, and is available to instructors through the publisher.

Instructor Companion Web Site. This password-protected companion site contains useful resources for instructors—including chapter-level PowerPoint lecture slides, and a downloadable version of the Answer Key. Go to www. cengagebrain.com to access the site.

Acknowledgments

Our endeavor to maintain the currency of linguistic concepts in times of rapid progress has been invaluably enhanced by the following colleagues, to whom we owe an enormous debt of gratitude:

Natasha Abner	*University of California, Los Angeles*	American Sign Language
Byron Ahn	*University of California, Los Angeles*	Syntax
Susia Curtiss	*University of California, Los Angeles*	Neurolinguistics
Kyle Johnson	*University of Massachusetts, Amherst*	Syntax
Craig Melchert	*University of California, Los Angeles*	Historical linguistics
Robyn Orfitelli	*University of California, Los Angeles*	Language acquisition
Maria "Masha" Polinsky	*Harvard University*	Heritage languages
Jessica Rett	*University of California, Los Angeles*	Semantics
Erik Thomas	*North Carolina State University*	Sociolinguistics
Kie Zuraw	*University of California, Los Angeles*	Phonology

Brook Danielle Lillehaugen undertook the daunting task of writing the Answer Key to the ninth and tenth editions. Her thoroughness, accuracy, and insightfulness in construing solutions to problems and discussions of issues are appreciated by all who avail themselves of this useful document, including us, the authors.

We also express deep appreciation for the incisive comments of six reviewers of the ninth edition, known to us as R2 through R7, whose frank assessment of the work, both critical and laudatory, heavily influenced this new edition:

Anna Szabolcsi, Department of Linguistics, *New York University*

Kathryn Wolfe-Quintero, Department of World Languages, *University of South Florida*

Nicholas Sobin, Department of Languages and Linguistics, *University of Texas, El Paso*

Virginia Lewis, Department of Languages, Literature, and Speech Communication, *Northern State University*

Ulrike Christofori, Department of Humanities, Social Sciences, and Education, *San Joaquin Delta College*

Omer Silva-Villena, Departamento de Lenguas, Literatura, y Comunicación, *Universidad de la Frontera*, Chile

We continue to be deeply grateful to the individuals who have sent us suggestions, corrections, criticisms, cartoons, language data, and exercises over the course of many editions. Their influence is still strongly felt in this tenth edition. The list is long and reflects the global, communal collaboration that a book about language—the most global of topics—merits. To each of you, our heartfelt thanks and appreciation. Know that in this tenth edition lives your contribution:[1]

Adam Albright, Massachusetts Institute of Technology; Otto Santa Ana, University of California, Los Angeles; Rebecca Barghorn, University of Oldenburg; Seyed Reza Basiroo, Islamic Azad University; Karol Boguszewski, Poland; Melanie Borchers, Universität Duisburg-Essen; Donna Brinton, Emeritus, University of California, Los Angeles; Daniel Bruhn, University of California, Berkeley; Lynn A. Burley, University of Central Arkansas; Ivano Caponigro, University of California, San Diego; Ralph S. Carlson, Azusa Pacific University; Robert Channon, Purdue University; Judy Cheatham, Greensboro College; Leonie Cornips, Meertens Institute; Antonio Damásio, University of Southern California; Hanna Damásio, University of Southern California; Julie Damron, Brigham Young University; Rosalia Dutra, University of North Texas; Christina Esposito, Macalester College; Fred Field, California State University, Northridge; Susan Fiksdal, Evergreen State College; Beverly Olson Flanigan and her teaching assistants, Ohio University; Jackson Gandour, Purdue University, West Lafayette; Jule Gomez de Garcia, California State University, San Marcos; Deborah Grant, Independent consultant; Loretta Gray, Central Washington University; Xiangdong Gu, Chongqing University; Helena Halmari, University of London; Karin Hedberg, Sam Houston State University; Sharon Hargus, University of Washington; Benjamin H. Hary, Emory University; Tometro Hopkins, Florida International University; Eric Hyman, University of North Carolina, Fayetteville; Dawn Ellen Jacobs, California Baptist University; Seyed Yasser Jebraily, University of Tehran; Kyle Johnson, University of Massachusetts, Amherst; Paul Justice, San Diego State University; Simin Karimi, University of Arizona; Edward Keenan, University of California, Los Angeles; Robert D. King, University of Texas; Sharon M. Klein, California State University, Northridge; Nathan Klinedinst, Institut Jean Nicod/CNRS, Paris; Otto Krauss, Jr., late, unaffiliated; Elisabeth Kuhn, Virginia Commonwealth University; Peter Ladefoged, late, University of California, Los Angeles; Mary Ann Larsen-Pusey, Fresno Pacific University; Rabbi Robert Layman, Philadelphia; Byungmin Lee, Korea; Virginia "Ginny" Lewis, Northern State University; David Lightfoot, Georgetown University; Ingvar Lofstedt, University of California, Los Angeles; Giuseppe Longobardi, Università di Venezia; Harriet Luria, Hunter College, City University of New York; Jeff MacSwan, Arizona State University; Tracey McHenry, Eastern Washington University; Pamela Munro, University of California, Los Angeles; Tom Nash, Southern Oregon University; Carol Neidle, Boston University; Don Nilsen, Arizona State University; Reiko Okabe, Nihon University, Tokyo; John Olsson, Forensic

---

[1]Some affiliations may have changed or are unknown to us at this time.

Linguistic Institute, Wales, U.K.; Anjali Pandey, Salisbury University; Barbara Hall Partee, University of Massachusetts, Amherst; Fernanda Pratas, Universidade Nova de Lisboa; Vincent D. Puma, Flagler College; Mousa Qasem, Kuwait University; Ian Roberts, Cambridge University; Tugba Rona, Istanbul International Community School; Natalie Schilling-Estes, Georgetown University; Philippe Schlenker, Institut Jean-Nicod, Paris and New York University; Carson Schütze, University of California, Los Angeles; Bruce Sherwood, North Carolina State University; Koh Shimizu, Beijing; Dwan L. Shipley, Washington University; Muffy Siegel, Temple University; Andrew Simpson, University of Southern California; Neil Smith, University College London; Nancy Stenson, University of Minnesota, Twin Cities; Donca Steriade, Massachusetts Institute of Technology; Mel Storm, Emporia State University; Nawaf Sulami, University of Northern Iowa; Megha Sundara, University of California, Los Angeles; Robert (Bob) Trammell, Florida Atlantic University, Boca Raton; Dalys Vargas, College of Notre Dame; Willis Warren, Saint Edwards University; Donald K. Watkins, University of Kansas; Walt Wolfram, North Carolina State University; Maria Luisa Zubizarreta, University of Southern California.

Please forgive us if we have inadvertently omitted any names, and if we have spelled every name correctly, then we shall believe in miracles.

Finally, we wish to thank the editorial and production team at Cengage Learning. They have been superb and supportive in every way: Michael Rosenberg, publisher; Joan M. Flaherty, development editor; Daniel Saabye, content project manager; Erin Bosco, Assistant Editor; Janine Tangney, Media Editor.

Last but certainly not least, we acknowledge our debt to those we love and who love us and who inspire our work when nothing else will: Nina's son, Michael; Robert's children Zack and Emily together with a trio—soon to be a quartet—of grandchildren: Cedar, Luke, Juniper, and ?; our parents and siblings; and our dearly beloved and still deeply missed colleagues, Vicki Fromkin and Peter Ladefoged.

The responsibility for errors in fact or judgment is, of course, ours alone. We continue to be indebted to the instructors who have used the earlier editions and to their students, without whom there would be no tenth edition.

Robert Rodman
Nina Hyams

About the Authors

VICTORIA FROMKIN received her bachelor's degree in economics from the University of California, Berkeley, in 1944 and her M.A. and Ph.D. in linguistics from the University of California, Los Angeles, in 1963 and 1965, respectively. She was a member of the faculty of the UCLA Department of Linguistics from 1966 until her death in 2000, and served as its chair from 1972 to 1976. From 1979 to 1989 she served as the UCLA Graduate Dean and Vice Chancellor of Graduate Programs. She was a visiting professor at the Universities of Stockholm, Cambridge, and Oxford. Professor Fromkin served as president of the Linguistics Society of America in 1985, president of the Association of Graduate Schools in 1988, and chair of the Board of Governors of the Academy of Aphasia. She received the UCLA Distinguished Teaching Award and the Professional Achievement Award, and served as the U.S. Delegate and a member of the Executive Committee of the International Permanent Committee of Linguistics (CIPL). She was an elected Fellow of the American Academy of Arts and Sciences, the American Association for the Advancement of Science, the New York Academy of Science, the American Psychological Society, and the Acoustical Society of America, and in 1996 was elected to membership in the National Academy of Sciences. She published more than one hundred books, monographs, and papers on topics concerned with phonetics, phonology, tone languages, African languages, speech errors, processing models, aphasia, and the brain/mind/language interface—all research areas in which she worked. Professor Fromkin passed away on January 19, 2000, at the age of 76.

ROBERT RODMAN received his bachelor's degree in mathematics from the University of California, Los Angeles, in 1961, a master's degree in mathematics in 1965, a master's degree in linguistics in 1971, and his Ph.D. in linguistics in 1973. He has been on the faculties of the University of California at Santa Cruz, the University of North Carolina at Chapel Hill, Kyoto Industrial College in Japan, and North Carolina State University, where he is currently a professor of computer science. His research areas are forensic linguistics and computer speech processing. Robert resides in Raleigh, North Carolina, with his two rescued greyhounds Gracie and Shelby-Sue.

NINA HYAMS received her bachelor's degree in journalism from Boston University in 1973 and her M.A. and Ph.D. degrees in linguistics from the Graduate Center of the City University of New York in 1981 and 1983, respectively. She joined the faculty of the University of California, Los Angeles, in 1983, where she is currently a professor of linguistics. Her main areas of research are childhood language development and syntax. She is author of the book

Language Acquisition and the Theory of Parameters (D. Reidel Publishers, 1986), a milestone in language acquisition research. She has also published numerous articles on the development of syntax, morphology, and semantics in children. She has been a visiting scholar at the University of Utrecht and the University of Leiden in the Netherlands and has given numerous lectures throughout Europe and Japan. Nina lives in Los Angeles with her pal Spot, a rescued border collie mutt and his olde English bulldogge companion, the ever soulful Nellie.

What Is Language?

When we study human language, we are approaching what some might call the "human essence," the distinctive qualities of mind that are, so far as we know, unique to man.

NOAM CHOMSKY, *Language and Mind*, 1968

Whatever else people do when they come together—whether they play, fight, make love, or make automobiles—they talk. We live in a world of language. We talk to our friends, our associates, our wives and husbands, our lovers, our teachers, our parents, our rivals, and even our enemies. We talk face-to-face and over all manner of electronic media, and everyone responds with more talk. Hardly a moment of our waking lives is free from words, and even in our dreams we talk and are talked to. We also talk when there is no one to answer. Some of us talk aloud in our sleep. We talk to our pets and sometimes to ourselves.

The possession of language, perhaps more than any other attribute, distinguishes humans from other animals. According to the philosophy expressed in the myths and religions of many peoples, language is the source of human life and power. To some people of Africa, a newborn child is a *kintu*, a "thing," not yet a *muntu*, a "person." It is only by the act of learning language that the child becomes a human being. To understand our humanity, we must understand the nature of language that makes us human. That is the goal of this book. We begin with a simple question: what does it mean to "know" a language?

Linguistic Knowledge

Do we know only what we see, or do we see what we somehow already know?

CYNTHIA OZICK, "What Helen Keller Saw," *New Yorker*, June 16 & 23, 2003

When you know a language, you can speak and be understood by others who know that language. This means you are able to produce strings of sounds that signify certain meanings and to understand or interpret the sounds produced by others. But language is much more than speech. Deaf people produce and understand sign languages just as hearing persons produce and understand spoken languages. The languages of the deaf communities throughout the world are equivalent to spoken languages, differing only in their modality of expression.

Most everyone knows at least one language. Five-year-old children are nearly as proficient at speaking and understanding as their parents. Yet the ability to carry out the simplest conversation requires profound knowledge that most speakers are unaware of. This is true for speakers of all languages, from Albanian to Zulu. A speaker of English can produce a sentence having two relative clauses without knowing what a relative clause is. For example:

> My goddaughter who was born in Sweden and who now lives in Iowa is named Disa, after a Viking queen.

In a parallel fashion, a child can walk without understanding or being able to explain the principles of balance and support or the neurophysiological control mechanisms that permit one to do so. The fact that we may know something unconsciously is not unique to language.

Knowledge of the Sound System

When I speak it is in order to be heard.

ROMAN JAKOBSON

Part of knowing a language means knowing what sounds (or signs[1]) are in that language and what sounds are not. One way this unconscious knowledge is revealed is by the way speakers of one language pronounce words from another language. If you speak only English, for example, you may substitute an English sound for a non-English sound when pronouncing "foreign" words like French *ménage à trois*. If you pronounce it as the French do, you are using sounds outside the English sound system.

French people speaking English often pronounce words like *this* and *that* as if they were spelled *zis* and *zat*. The English sound represented by the initial letters *th* in these words is not part of the French sound system, and the mispronunciation reveals the French speaker's unconscious knowledge of this fact.

Knowing the sound system of a language includes more than knowing the inventory of sounds. It means also knowing which sounds may start a word,

---

[1]The sign languages of the deaf will be discussed throughout the book. A reference to "language," then, unless speech sounds or spoken languages are specifically mentioned, includes both spoken and signed languages.

end a word, and follow each other. The name of a former president of Ghana was *Nkrumah*, pronounced with an initial sound like the sound ending the English word *sink*. While this is an English sound, no word in English begins with the *nk* sound. Speakers of English who have occasion to pronounce this name often mispronounce it (by Ghanaian standards) by inserting a short vowel sound, like *Nekrumah* or *Enkrumah*, making the word correspond to the English system. Children develop the sound patterns of their language very rapidly. A one-year-old learning English knows that *nk* cannot begin a word, just as a Ghanaian child of the same age knows that it can in his language.

We will learn more about sounds and sound systems in chapters 5 and 6.

Knowledge of Words

Sounds and sound patterns of our language constitute only one part of our linguistic knowledge. Beyond that we know that certain sequences of sounds signify certain concepts or **meanings**. Speakers of English understand what *boy* means, and that it means something different from *toy* or *girl* or *pterodactyl*. We also know that *toy* and *boy* are words, but *moy* is not. When you know a language, you know words in that language; that is, you know which sequences of sounds relate to specific meanings and which do not.

Arbitrary Relation of Form and Meaning

> The minute I set eyes on an animal I know what it is. I don't have to reflect a moment; the right name comes out instantly. I seem to know just by the shape of the creature and the way it acts what animal it is. When the dodo came along he [Adam] thought it was a wildcat. But I saved him. I just spoke up in a quite natural way and said, "Well, I do declare if there isn't the dodo!"
>
> MARK TWAIN, *Eve's Diary*, 1906

If you do not know a language, the words (and sentences) of that language will be mainly incomprehensible, because the relationship between speech sounds and the meanings they represent is, for the most part, an **arbitrary** one. When you are acquiring a language you have to learn that the sounds represented by the letters *house* signify the concept 🏠; if you know French, this same meaning is represented by *maison*; if you know Russian, by *dom*; if you know Spanish, by *casa*. Similarly, ✋ is represented by *hand* in English, *main* in French, *nsa* in Twi, and *ruka* in Russian. The same sequence of sounds can represent different meanings in different languages. The word *bolna* means 'speak' in Hindu-Urdu and 'aching' in Russian; *bis* means 'devil' in Ukrainian and 'twice' in Latin; a *pet* is a domestic animal in English and a fart in Catalan; and the sequence of sounds *taka* means 'hawk' in Japanese, 'fist' in Quechua, 'a small bird' in Zulu, and 'money' in Bengali.

These examples show that the words of a particular language have the meanings they do only by convention. Despite what Eve would have us believe in Mark Twain's satire *Eve's Diary*, a pterodactyl could have been called *ron*, *blick*, or *kerplunkity*.

HERMAN®/LaughingStock Licensing Inc., Ottawa, Canada

As Juliet says in Shakespeare's *Romeo and Juliet*:

What's in a name? That which we call a rose
By any other name would smell as sweet;

This **conventional** and arbitrary relationship between the **form** (sounds) and **meaning** (concept) of a word is also true in sign languages. If you see someone using a sign language you do not know, it is doubtful that you will understand the message from the signs alone. A person who knows Chinese Sign Language (CSL) would find it difficult to understand American Sign Language (ASL), and vice versa.

Many signs were originally like miming, where the relationship between form and meaning is not arbitrary. Bringing the hand to the mouth to mean "eating," as in miming, would be nonarbitrary as a sign. Over time these signs may change, just as the pronunciation of words changes, and the miming effect is lost. These signs become conventional, so that the shape or movement of the hands alone does not reveal the meaning of the signs.

There is some **sound symbolism** in language—that is, words whose pronunciation suggests their meanings. Most languages contain **onomatopoeic** words like *buzz* or *murmur* that imitate the sounds associated with the objects or actions they refer to. But even here, the sounds differ from language to language and reflect the particular sound system of the language. In English *cock-a-doodle-doo* is an onomatopoeic word whose meaning is the crow of a rooster, whereas in Finnish the rooster's crow is *kukkokiekuu*. Forget *gobble gobble* when you're in Istanbul; a turkey in Turkey goes *glu-glu*.

Sometimes particular sound combinations seem to relate to a particular concept. Many English words beginning with *gl* relate to sight, such as *glare, glint, gleam, glitter, glossy, glaze, glance, glimmer, glimpse,* and *glisten.* However, *gl* words and their like are a very small part of any language, and *gl* may have nothing to do with "sight" in another language, or even in other words in English, such as *gladiator, glucose, glory, glutton, globe,* and so on.

To know a language we must know words of that language. But no speaker knows all the entries in an unabridged dictionary and even if someone did he would still not know that language. Imagine trying to learn a foreign language by buying a dictionary and memorizing words. No matter how many words you learned, you would not be able to form the simplest phrases or sentences in the language, or understand a native speaker. No one speaks in isolated words. And even if you could manage to get your message across using a few words from a traveler's dictionary, like "car—gas—where?" the best you could hope for is to be pointed in the direction of a gas station. If you were answered with a sentence it is doubtful that you would understand what was said or be able to look it up, because you would not know where one word ended and another began. Chapter 3 will discuss how words are put together to form phrases and sentences, and chapter 4 will explore word and sentence meanings.

The Creativity of Linguistic Knowledge

All humans are artists, all of us . . . Our greatest masterpiece of art is the use of a language to create an entire virtual reality within our mind.

DON MIGUEL RUIZ, 2012

ALBERT: So are you saying that you were the best friend of the woman who was married to the man who represented your husband in divorce?

ANDRÉ: In the history of speech, that sentence has never been uttered before.

NEIL SIMON, *The Dinner Party*, 2000

Knowledge of a language enables you to combine sounds to form words, words to form phrases, and phrases to form sentences. You cannot buy a dictionary or phrase book of any language with all the sentences of the language. No dictionary can list all the possible sentences, because the number of sentences in a language is infinite. Knowing a language means being able to produce and understand new sentences never spoken before. This is the **creative aspect** of language. Not every speaker can create great literature, but everybody who knows a language can create and understand new sentences.

This creative aspect of language is quite easy to illustrate. If for every sentence in the language a longer sentence can be formed, then there is no limit to the number of sentences. In English you can say:

This is the house.

or

This is the house that Jack built.

or

> This is the malt that lay in the house that Jack built.

or

> This is the dog that worried the cat that killed the rat that ate the malt that lay in the house that Jack built.

And you need not stop there. How long, then, is the longest sentence? A speaker of English can say:

> The old man came.

or

> The old, old, old, old, old man came.

How many "olds" are too many? Seven? Twenty-three?

It is true that the longer these sentences become, the less likely we would be to hear or to say them. A sentence with 276 occurrences of "old" would be highly unusual in either speech or writing, even to describe Methuselah. But such a sentence is theoretically possible. If you know English, you have the knowledge to add any number of adjectives as modifiers to a noun and to form sentences with indefinite numbers of clauses, as in "the house that Jack built."

All human languages permit their speakers to increase the length and complexity of sentences in these ways; creativity is a universal property of human language.

Our creative ability is reflected not only in what we say but also in our understanding of new or novel sentences. Consider the following sentence: "Daniel Boone decided to become a pioneer because he dreamed of pigeon-toed giraffes and cross-eyed elephants dancing in pink skirts and green berets on the wind-swept plains of the Midwest." You may not believe the sentence; you may question its logic; but you can understand it, although you probably never heard or read it before now.

In pointing out the creative aspect of language, Noam Chomsky, who many regard as the father of modern linguistics, argued persuasively against the view that language is a set of learned responses to stimuli. True, if someone steps on your toes you may automatically respond with a scream or a grunt, but these sounds are not part of language. They are involuntary reactions to stimuli. After we reflexively cry out, we can then go on to say: "Thank you very much for stepping on my toe, because I was afraid I had elephantiasis and now that I can feel the pain I know I don't," or any one of an infinite number of sentences, because the particular sentences we produce are not controlled by any stimulus.

Even some involuntary cries like "ouch" change according to the language we speak. Step on an Italian speaker's toes and he will cry "ahi." French speakers often fill their pauses with the vowel sound that starts their word for 'egg'—*oeuf*— a sound that does not occur in English. Even conversational fillers such as *er, uh,* and *you know* in English are constrained by the language in which they occur.

The fact of human linguistic creativity was well expressed more than 400 years ago by Huarte de San Juan (1530–1592): "Normal human minds are such that . . . without the help of anybody, they will produce 1,000 (sentences) they never heard spoke of . . . inventing and saying such things as they never heard from their masters, nor any mouth."

Knowledge of Sentences and Nonsentences

A person who knows a language has mastered a system of rules that assigns sound and meaning in a definite way for an infinite class of possible sentences.

NOAM CHOMSKY, *Language and Mind*, 1968

Our knowledge of language not only allows us to produce and understand an infinite number of well-formed (even if silly and illogical) sentences. It also permits us to distinguish well-formed (grammatical) from ill-formed (ungrammatical) sentences. This is further evidence of our linguistic creativity because ungrammatical sentences are typically novel, not sentences we have previously heard or produced, precisely because they are ungrammatical!

Consider the following sentences:

a. John kissed the little old lady who owned the shaggy dog.
b. Who owned the shaggy dog John kissed the little old lady.
c. John is difficult to love.
d. It is difficult to love John.
e. John is anxious to go.
f. It is anxious to go John.
g. John, who was a student, flunked his exams.
h. Exams his flunked student a was who John.

If you were asked to put an asterisk or star before the examples that seemed ill formed or ungrammatical or "no good" to you, which ones would you mark? Our intuitive knowledge about what is or is not an allowable sentence in English convinces us to star *b*, *f*, and *h*. Which ones did you star?

Would you agree with the following judgments?

a. What he did was climb a tree.
b. *What he thought was want a sports car.[2]
c. Drink your beer and go home!
d. *What are drinking and go home?
e. I expect them to arrive a week from next Thursday.
f. *I expect a week from next Thursday to arrive them.
g. Linus lost his security blanket.
h. *Lost Linus security blanket his.

If you find the starred sentences unacceptable, as we do, you see your linguistic creativity at work.

These sentences also illustrate that not every string of words constitutes a well-formed sentence in a language. Sentences are not formed simply by placing one word after another in any order, but by organizing the words according to the rules of sentence formation of the language. These rules are finite in length and finite in number so that they can be stored in our finite brains. Yet, they

---

[2]The asterisk is used before examples that speakers find ungrammatical. This notation will be used throughout the book.

permit us to form and understand an infinite set of new sentences. They also enable us to judge whether a sequence of words is a well-formed sentence of our language or not. These rules are not determined by a judge or a legislature, or even taught in a grammar class. They are unconscious rules that we acquire as young children as we develop language and they are responsible for our linguistic creativity. Linguists refer to this set of rules as the **grammar** of the language.

Returning to the question we posed at the beginning of this chapter—what does it mean to know a language? It means knowing the sounds and meanings of many, if not all, of the words of the language, and the rules for their combination—the grammar, which generates infinitely many possible sentences. We will have more to say about these rules of grammar in later chapters.

Linguistic Knowledge and Performance

"What's one and one and one and one and one and one and one and one and one and one?" "I don't know," said Alice. "I lost count." "She can't do Addition," the Red Queen interrupted.

LEWIS CARROLL, *Through the Looking-Glass*, 1871

Speakers of all languages have the knowledge to understand or produce sentences of any length. Here is an example from the ruling of a federal judge:

We invalidate the challenged lifetime ban because we hold as a matter of federal constitutional law that a state initiative measure cannot impose a severe limitation on the people's fundamental rights when the issue of whether to impose such a limitation on these rights is put to the voters in a measure that is ambiguous on its face and that fails to mention in its text, the proponent's ballot argument, or the state's official description, the severe limitation to be imposed.

Theoretically there is no limit to the length of a sentence, but in practice very long sentences are highly improbable, the verbose federal judge notwithstanding. Evidently, there is a difference between having the knowledge required to produce or understand sentences of a language and applying this knowledge. It is a difference between our knowledge of words and grammar, which is our **linguistic competence**, and how we use this knowledge in actual speech production and comprehension, which is our **linguistic performance**.

Our linguistic knowledge permits us to form longer and longer sentences by joining sentences and phrases together or adding modifiers to a noun. However, there are physiological and psychological reasons that limit the number of adjectives, adverbs, clauses, and so on that we actually produce and understand. Speakers may run out of breath, lose track of what they have said, or die of old age before they are finished. Listeners may become tired, bored, disgusted, or confused, like poor Alice when being interrogated by the Red Queen.

When we speak, we usually wish to convey some message. At some stage in the act of producing speech, we must organize our thoughts into strings of words. Sometimes the message is garbled. We may stammer, or pause, or produce **slips of the tongue** like saying *preach seduction* when *speech production* is meant (discussed in chapter 10).

What Is Grammar?

We use the term "grammar" with a systematic ambiguity. On the one hand, the term refers to the explicit theory constructed by the linguist and proposed as a description of the speaker's competence. On the other hand, it refers to this competence itself.

NOAM CHOMSKY AND MORRIS HALLE, *The Sound Pattern of English*, 1968

Descriptive Grammars

There are no primitive languages. The great and abstract ideas of Christianity can be discussed even by the wretched Greenlanders.

JOHANN PETER SUESSMILCH, in a paper delivered before the Prussian Academy, 1756

The way we are using the word *grammar* differs from most common usages. In our sense, the grammar is the knowledge speakers have about the units and rules of their language—rules for combining sounds into words (called *phonology*), rules of word formation (called *morphology*), rules for combining words into phrases and phrases into sentences (called *syntax*), as well as the rules for assigning meaning (called *semantics*). The grammar, together with a mental dictionary (called a *lexicon*) that lists the words of the language, represents our linguistic competence. To understand the nature of language we must understand the nature of grammar.

Every human being who speaks a language knows its grammar. When linguists wish to describe a language, they make explicit the rules of the grammar of the language that exist in the minds of its speakers. There will be some differences among speakers, but there must be shared knowledge too. The shared knowledge—the common parts of the grammar—makes it possible to communicate through language. To the extent that the linguist's description is a true model of the speakers' linguistic capacity, it is a successful description of the grammar and of the language itself. Such a model is called a **descriptive grammar**. It does not tell you how you *should* speak; it describes your basic linguistic knowledge. It explains how it is possible for you to speak and understand and make judgments about well-formedness, and it tells what you know about the sounds, words, phrases, and sentences of your language.

When we say that a sentence is **grammatical** we mean that it conforms to the rules of the mental grammar (as described by the linguist); when we say that it is **ungrammatical**, we mean it deviates from the rules in some way. If, however, we posit a rule for English that does not agree with your intuitions as a speaker, then the grammar we are describing differs in some way from the mental grammar that represents your linguistic competence; that is, your language is not the one described. No language or variety of a language (called a *dialect*) is superior or inferior to any other in a linguistic sense. Every grammar is equally complex, logical, and capable of producing an infinite set of sentences to express any thought. If something can be expressed in one language or one dialect, it can be expressed in any other language or dialect. It might involve different means and different words, but it can be expressed. (We will have more to say about dialects in chapter 7.)

Prescriptive Grammars

> It is certainly the business of a grammarian to find out, and not to make, the laws of a language.
>
> JOHN FELL, *Essay towards an English Grammar*, 1784

> Just read the sentence aloud, Amanda, and listen to how it sounds. If the sentence sounds OK, go with it. If not, rearrange the pieces. Then throw out the rule books and go to bed.
>
> JAMES KILPATRICK, "Writer's Art" (syndicated newspaper column), 1998

> Any fool can make a rule
>
> And every fool will mind it
>
> HENRY DAVID THOREAU, *journal entry*, 1860

Not all grammarians, past or present, share the view that all grammars are equal. Language "purists" of all ages believe that some versions of a language are better than others, that there are certain "correct" forms that all educated people should use in speaking and writing, and that language change is corruption. The Greek Alexandrians in the first century, the Arabic scholars at Basra in the eighth century, and numerous English grammarians of the eighteenth and nineteenth centuries held this view. They wished to *prescribe* rather than *describe* the rules of grammar, which gave rise to the writing of **prescriptive grammars**.

In the Renaissance a new middle class emerged who wanted their children to speak the dialect of the "upper" classes. This desire led to the publication of many prescriptive grammars. In 1762 Bishop Robert Lowth wrote *A Short Introduction to English Grammar with Critical Notes*. Lowth prescribed a number of new rules for English, many of them influenced by his personal taste. Before the publication of his grammar, practically everyone—upper-class, middle-class, and lower-class—said *I don't have none* and *You was wrong about that*. Lowth, however, decided that "two negatives make a positive" and therefore one should say *I don't have any*; and that even when *you* is singular it should be followed by the plural *were*. Many of these prescriptive rules were based on Latin grammar and made little sense for English. Because Lowth was influential and because the rising new class wanted to speak "properly," many of these new rules were legislated into English grammar, at least for the **prestige dialect**—that variety of the language spoken by people in positions of power.

The view that dialects that regularly use double negatives are inferior cannot be justified if one looks at the standard dialects of other languages in the world. Romance languages, for example, use double negatives, as the following examples from French and Italian show:

French:	Je	ne	veux	parler	avec	personne.
	I	not	want	speak	with	no-one.

Italian:	Non	voglio	parlare	con	nessuno.
	not	I-want	speak	with	no-one.

English translation: "I don't want to speak with anyone."

Prescriptive grammars such as Lowth's are different from the descriptive grammars we have been discussing. Their goal is not to describe the rules people know, but to tell them what rules they should follow. The great British Prime Minister Winston Churchill is credited with this response to the "rule" against ending a sentence with a preposition: "This is the sort of nonsense up with which I will not put."

Today our bookstores are populated with books by language purists attempting to "save the English language." They criticize those who use *enormity* to mean 'enormous' instead of 'monstrously evil.' But languages change in the course of time and words change meaning. Language change is a natural process, as we discuss in chapter 8. Over time *enormity* was used increasingly used to mean 'enormous,' and now that President Barack Obama has used it that way (in his victory speech of November 4, 2008) and that J. K. Rowling uses it similarly in the immensely popular *Harry Potter and the Deathly Hallows*, that usage will gain acceptance. Still, the "saviors" of the English language will never disappear. They will continue to blame television, the schools, and even the National Council of Teachers of English for failing to preserve the standard language, and are likely to continue to dis (oops, we mean disparage) anyone who suggests that African American English (AAE)[3] and other dialects are viable, complete languages.

All human languages and dialects are fully expressive, complete, and logical, as much as they were two hundred or two thousand years ago. Hopefully (another frowned-upon usage), this book will convince you that all languages and dialects are rule-governed, whether spoken by rich or poor, powerful or weak, learned or illiterate. Grammars and usages of particular groups in society may be dominant for social and political reasons, but from a linguistic (scientific) perspective they are neither superior nor inferior to the grammars and usages of less prestigious members of society.

Having said all this, it is undeniable that the **standard** dialect (defined in chapter 7) may indeed be a better dialect for someone wishing to obtain a

---

[3]AAE is also called African American Vernacular English (AAVE), Ebonics, and Black English (BE). It is spoken by some (but by no means all) African Americans. It is discussed in chapter 7.

particular job or achieve a position of social prestige. In a society where "linguistic profiling" is used to discriminate against speakers of a minority dialect, it may behoove those speakers to learn the prestige dialect rather than wait for social change. But linguistically, prestige and standard dialects do not have superior grammars.

Finally, all of the preceding remarks apply to *spoken* language. Writing is another story (see chapter 12). Writing follows certain prescriptive rules of grammar, usage, and style that the spoken language does not, and is subject to little, if any, dialectal variation. And writing is not acquired naturally through simple exposure to others speaking the language as spoken languages are (see chapter 9), but must be taught.

Teaching Grammars

I don't want to talk grammar. I want to talk like a lady.

G. B. SHAW, *Pygmalion*, 1912

The descriptive grammar of a language attempts to describe the rules internalized by a speaker of that language. It is different from a **teaching grammar**, which is used to learn another language or dialect. Teaching grammars can be helpful to people who do not speak the standard or prestige dialect, but find it would be advantageous socially and economically to do so. They are used in schools in foreign language classes. This kind of grammar gives the words and their pronunciations, and explicitly states the rules of the language, especially where they differ from the language of instruction.

It is often difficult for adults to learn a second language without formal instruction, even when they have lived for an extended period in a country where the language is spoken. (Second language acquisition is discussed in more detail in chapter 9.) Teaching grammars assume that the student already knows one language and compares the grammar of the target language with the grammar of the native language. The meaning of a word is provided by a **gloss**—the parallel word in the student's native language, such as *maison*, 'house' in French. It is assumed that the student knows the meaning of the gloss 'house' and so also the meaning of the word *maison*.

Sounds of the target language that do not occur in the native language are often described by reference to known sounds. Thus the student might be aided in producing the French sound *u* in the word *tu* by instructions such as "Round your lips while producing the vowel sound in *tea*."

The rules about how to put words together to form grammatical sentences also refer to the learners' knowledge of their native language. For example, the teaching grammar *Learn Zulu* by Sibusiso Nyembezi states that "The difference between singular and plural is not at the end of the word but at the beginning of it," and warns that "Zulu does not have the indefinite and definite articles 'a' and 'the.'" Such statements assume students know the rules of their own grammar, in this case English. Although such grammars might be considered prescriptive in the sense that they attempt to teach the student what is or is not a grammatical construction in the new language, their aim is different from grammars that attempt to change the rules or usage of a language that is already known by the speaker.

This book is not primarily concerned with either prescriptive or teaching grammars. However, these kinds of grammars are considered in chapter 7 in the discussion of standard and nonstandard dialects.

Universal Grammar

In a grammar there are parts that pertain to all languages; these components form what is called the general grammar. In addition to these general (universal) parts, there are those that belong only to one particular language; and these constitute the particular grammars of each language.

CÉSAR CHESNEAU DU MARSAIS, c. 1750

There are rules of particular languages, such as English or Arabic or Zulu, that form part of the individual grammars of these languages, and then there are rules that hold in all languages. The universal rules are of particular interest because they give us a window into the human "faculty of language" which enables us to learn and use any particular language.

Interest in language universals has a long history. Early scholars encouraged research into the nature of language in general and promoted the idea of *general grammar* as distinct from *special grammar*. General grammar was to reveal those features common to all languages.

Students trying to learn Latin, Greek, French, or Swahili as a second language are generally so focused on learning aspects of the new language that differ from their native language that they may be skeptical of the universal laws of language. Yet there are many things that all language learners know unconsciously even before they begin to learn a new language. They know that a language has its own set of sounds, perhaps thought of as its alphabet, that combine according to certain patterns to form words, and that the words themselves recombine to form phrases and sentences. The learner will expect to find verbs and nouns—as these are universal grammatical categories; she will know that the language— like all languages—has a way of negating, forming questions, issuing commands, referring to past or future time, and more generally, has a system of rules that will allow her to produce and understand an infinite number of sentences.

The more linguists explore the intricacies of human language, the more evidence accumulates to support Chomsky's view that there is a **Universal Grammar (UG)** that is part of the biologically endowed human language faculty. We can think of UG as the blueprint that all languages follow that forms part of the child's innate capacity for language learning. It specifies the different components of the grammar and their relations, how the different rules of these components are constructed, how they interact, and so on. A major aim of **linguistic theory** is to discover the nature of UG.

The linguist's goal is to reveal the "laws of human language," as the physicist's goal is to reveal the "laws of the physical universe." The complexity of language undoubtedly means this goal will never be fully achieved. All scientific theories are incomplete, and new hypotheses must be proposed to account for new data. Theories are continually changing as new discoveries are made. Just as physics was enlarged by Einstein's theories of relativity, so grows the linguistic theory of UG as new discoveries shed new light on the nature of human language. The comparative study of many different languages is of central importance to this enterprise.

The Development of Grammar

How comes it that human beings, whose contacts with the world are brief and personal and limited, are nevertheless able to know as much as they do know?

BERTRAND RUSSELL, *Human Knowledge: Its Scope and Limits*, 1948

Linguistic theory is concerned not only with describing the knowledge that an adult speaker has of his or her language, but also with explaining how this knowledge is acquired.

All typically developing children acquire (at least one) language in a relatively short period with apparent ease. They do this despite the fact that parents and other caregivers do not provide them with any specific language instruction. Indeed, it is often remarked that children seem to "pick up" language just from hearing it spoken around them. Children are language-learning virtuosos—whether a child is male or female, from a rich family or a disadvantaged one, grows up on a farm or in the city, attends day care or has home care, none of these factors fundamentally affects the way language develops. Children can acquire any language they are exposed to with comparable ease—English, Dutch, French, Swahili, Japanese—and even though each of these languages has its own peculiar characteristics, children learn them all in very much the same way. For example, all children go through a babbling stage; their babbles gradually give way to words, which then combine to form simple sentences and then sentences of ever-increasing complexity. The same child who may be unable to tie her shoes or even count to five has managed to master the complex grammatical structures of her language and acquire a substantial lexicon.

How children accomplish this remarkable cognitive feat is a topic of intense interest to linguists. The child's inexorable path to adult linguistic knowledge and the uniformity of the acquisition process point to a substantial innate component to language development, what we referred to earlier as Universal Grammar. Children acquire language as quickly and effortlessly as they do because they do not have to figure out all the grammatical rules, only those that are specific to their particular language. The universal properties—the laws of language—are part of their biological endowment. In chapter 9 we will discuss language acquisition in more detail.

Sign Languages: Evidence for Language Universals

It is not the want of organs that [prevents animals from making] . . . known their thoughts . . . for it is evident that magpies and parrots are able to utter words just like ourselves, and yet they cannot speak as we do, that is, so as to give evidence that they think of what they say. On the other hand, men who, being born deaf and mute . . . are destitute of the organs which serve the others for talking, are in the habit of themselves inventing certain signs by which they make themselves understood.

RENÉ DESCARTES, *Discourse on Method*, 1637

The sign languages of deaf communities provide some of the best evidence to support the view that all languages are governed by the same universal principles. Current research on sign languages has been crucial to understanding the biological underpinnings of human language acquisition and use.

The major language of the deaf community in the United States is **American Sign Language (ASL)**. ASL is an outgrowth of the sign language used in France and brought to the United States in 1817 by the great educator Thomas Hopkins Gallaudet.

ASL and other sign languages do not use sounds to express meanings. Instead, they are visual-gestural systems that use hand, body, and facial gestures as the forms used to represent words and grammatical rules. Sign languages are fully developed languages, and signers create and comprehend unlimited numbers of new sentences, just as speakers of spoken languages do. Signed languages have their own grammatical rules and a mental lexicon of signs, all encoded through a system of gestures, and are otherwise equivalent to spoken languages. Signers are affected by performance factors just as speakers are; slips of the hand occur similar to slips of the tongue. Finger fumblers amuse signers just as tongue twisters amuse speakers. These and other language games play on properties of the "sound" systems of the spoken and signed languages.

Deaf children who are exposed to signed languages acquire them just as hearing children acquire spoken languages, going through the same linguistic stages, including the babbling stage. Deaf children babble with their hands, just as hearing children babble with their vocal tracts. Neurological studies show that signed languages are organized in the brain in the same way as spoken languages, despite their visual modality. We discuss the brain basis of language in chapter 10.

In short, signed languages resemble spoken languages in all major aspects. This universality is expected because, regardless of the modality in which it is expressed, language is a biologically based ability. Our knowledge, use and acquisition of language are not dependent on the ability to produce and hear sounds, but on a far more abstract cognitive capacity.

What Is Not (Human) Language

It is a very remarkable fact that there are none so depraved and stupid, without even excepting idiots, that they cannot arrange different words together, forming of them a statement by which they make known their thoughts; while, on the other hand, there is no other animal, however perfect and fortunately circumstanced it may be, which can do the same.

RENÉ DESCARTES, *Discourse on Method and Meditation on First Philosophy*

All languages share certain fundamental properties, and children naturally acquire these languages—whether they are spoken or signed. Both modalities are equally accessible to the child because human beings are designed for human language. But what of the "languages" of other species: Are they like human languages? Can other species be taught a human language?

The Birds and the Bees

Teach me half the gladness
That thy brain must know;
Such harmonious madness
From my lips would flow,
The world should listen then, as I am listening now.

PERCY BYSSHE SHELLEY, 1792–1822, *To a Skylark*

Most animal species possess some kind of communication system. Humans also communicate through systems other than language such as head nodding or facial expressions. The question is whether the communication systems used by other species are at all like human language with its very specific properties, most notably its creative aspect.

Many species have a non-vocal system of communication. Among certain species of spiders there is a complex system for courtship. Before approaching his ladylove, the male spider goes through an elaborate series of gestures to tell her that he is indeed a spider and a suitable mate, and not a crumb or a fly to be eaten. These gestures are invariant. One never finds a creative spider changing or adding to the courtship ritual of his species.

A similar kind of gestural language is found among the fiddler crabs. There are forty species, and each uses its own claw-waving movement to signal to another member of its "clan." The timing, movement, and posture of the body never change from one time to another or from one crab to another within the particular variety. Whatever the signal means, it is fixed. Only one meaning can be conveyed.

An essential property of human language not shared by the communication systems of spiders, crabs and other animals is its **discreteness**. Human languages are not simply made up of a fixed set of invariant signs. They are composed of discrete units—sounds, words, phrases—that are combined according to the rules of the grammar of the language. The word *top* in English has a particular meaning, but it also has individual parts that can be rearranged to produce other meaningful sequences—*pot* or *opt*. Similarly, the phrase *the cat on the mat* means something different from *the mat on the cat.* We can arrange and rearrange the units of our language to form an infinite number of expressions. The creativity of human language depends on discreteness.

In contrast to crabs and spiders, birds communicate vocally and birdsongs have always captured the human imagination. Musicians and composers have been moved by these melodies, sometimes imitating them in their compositions, other times incorporating birdsongs directly into the music. Birdsongs have also inspired poets as in Shelley's *To a Skylark,* not to mention cartoonists.

Birds do not sing for our pleasure, however. Their songs and calls communicate important information to other members of the species and sometimes to other animals. **Birdcalls** (consisting of one or more short notes) convey danger, feeding, nesting, flocking, and so on. **Bird songs** (more complex patterns of notes) are used to stake out territory and to attract mates. Like the messages of crabs and spiders, however, there is no evidence of any internal structure to these songs; they cannot be segmented into discrete meaningful parts and rearranged to encode different messages as can the words, phrases, and sentences of human language. In his territorial song the European robin alternates between high-pitched and low-pitched notes to indicate how strongly he feels about defending his territory. The different alternations indicate intensity and nothing more. The robin is creative in his ability to sing the same song in different ways, but not creative in his ability to use the same units of the system to express different messages with different meanings. Recently, scientists have observed that finches will react when the units of a familiar song are rearranged. It is unclear, however, whether the birds recognize a violation of the rules of the song or are just responding to a pattern change.

Though crucial to the birds' survival, the messages conveyed by these songs and calls are limited, relating only to a bird's immediate environment and needs. Like the dog in Russell's quote above, birds cannot tell us their story,

MUTTS by Patrick McDonnell

Patrick McDonnell/King Features Syndicate

however beautifully they sing. Human language is different of course. Our words and sentences are not simply responses to internal and external stimuli. If you're tired you may yawn, but you may also say "I'm tired," or "I'm going to bed," or "I'm going to Starbucks for a double espresso." Notably, you also have the right to remain silent, or talk about things completely unrelated to your physical state—the weather, the movie you saw last night, your plans for the weekend, or most interesting of all, your linguistics class.

The linguists call this property of human language **displacement**: the capacity to talk (or sign) messages that are unrelated to here and now. Displacement and discreteness are two fundamental properties that distinguish human language from the communication systems of birds and other animals.

One respect in which birdsongs do resemble human languages is in their development. In many bird species the full adult version of the birdsong is acquired in several stages, as it is for children acquiring language. The young bird sings a simplified version of the song shortly after hatching and then learns the more detailed, complex version by hearing adults sing. However, he must hear the adult song during a specific fixed period after birth—the period differs from species to species; otherwise song acquisition does not occur. For example, the chaffinch is unable to learn the more detailed song elements after ten months of age. A baby nightingale in captivity may be trained to sing melodiously by another nightingale, a "teaching bird," but only before its tail feathers are grown. These birds show a **critical period** for acquiring their "language" similar to the critical period for human language acquisition, which we will discuss in chapters 9 and 10. As with human language acquisition, the development of the birdsongs of these species involves an interaction of both learned and innate structure.

An interesting consequence of the fact that some birdsongs are partially learned means that variation can develop. There can be "regional dialects" within the same species, and as with humans, these dialects are transmitted from parents to offspring. Researchers have noted, in fact, that dialect differences may be better preserved in songbirds than in humans because there is no homogenization of regional accents due to radio or TV. We will discuss human language dialects in chapter 7.

Honeybees have a particularly interesting signaling system. When a forager bee returns to the hive she communicates to other bees where a source of food is located by performing a dance on a wall of the hive that reveals the location and quality of the food source. For one species of Italian honeybee, the dancing may assume one of three possible patterns: *round* (which indicates locations near the hive, within 20 feet or so); *sickle* (which indicates locations at 20 to 60 feet from the hive); and *tail-wagging* (for distances that exceed 60 feet). The number of repetitions per minute of the basic pattern in the tail-wagging dance indicates the precise distance: the slower the repetition rate, the longer the distance. The number of repetitions and the intensity with which the bee dances the round dance indicates the richness of the food source: the more repetitions and the livelier the bee dance the more food to be gotten.

Bee dances are discrete in some sense, consisting of separate parts and in principle they can communicate infinitely many different messages, like human language; but unlike human language the topic is always the same, namely food. They lack the displacement property. As experiments have shown, when a bee is forced to walk to a food source rather than fly, she will communicate a distance many times farther away than the food source actually is. The bee has no way of communicating the special circumstances of its trip. This absence of creativity makes the bee's dance qualitatively different from human language.

As we will discuss in chapter 10, the human language ability is rooted in the human brain. Just like human language, the communication system of each species is determined by its biology. This raises the interesting question of whether it is possible for one species to acquire the language of another; more specifically, can animals learn human language?

Can Animals Learn Human Language?

It is a great baboon, but so much like man in most things. . . . I do believe it already understands much English; and I am of the mind it might be taught to speak or make signs.

ENTRY IN SAMUEL PEPYS'S DIARY, 1661

The idea of talking animals is as old and as widespread among human societies as language itself. All cultures have legends in which some animal speaks. All over West Africa, children listen to folktales in which a "spider-man" is the hero. "Coyote" is a favorite figure in many Native American tales, and many an animal takes the stage in Aesop's famous fables. Bugs Bunny, Mickey Mouse, and Donald Duck are icons of American culture. The fictional Doctor Doolittle communicated with all manner of animals, from giant snails to tiny sparrows, as did Saint Francis of Assisi.

In reality, various species show abilities that seem to mimic aspects of human language. Talking birds such as parrots and mynahs can be taught to faithfully reproduce words and phrases, but this does not mean they have acquired a human language. As the poet William Cowper put it: "Words learned by rote a parrot may rehearse; but talking is not always to converse."

Talking birds do not decompose their imitations into discrete units. *Polly* and *Molly* do not rhyme for a parrot. They are as different as *hello* and *goodbye*. If Polly learns "Polly wants a cracker" and "Polly wants a doughnut" and also learns to say *whiskey* and *bagel*, she will not then spontaneously produce "Polly wants whiskey" or "Polly wants a bagel" or "Polly wants whiskey and a bagel." If she learns *cat* and *cats*, and *dog* and *dogs*, and then learns the word *parrot*, she will not be able to form the plural *parrots* as children do. Unlike every developing child, a parrot cannot generalize from particular instances and cannot therefore produce sentences he has not been directly taught. A parrot—even a very verbose one—cannot produce an unlimited set of utterances from a finite set of units. The imitative utterances of talking birds mean nothing to the birds; these utterances have no communicative function. It is clear that simply knowing how to produce a sequence of speech sounds is not the same as knowing a language. But what about animals that appear to learn the meanings of words? Do they have human language?

Dogs can easily be taught to respond to commands such as *heel, sit, fetch,* and so on, and even seem to understand object words like *ball, toy,* and so on. Indeed, in 2004 German psychologists reported on a Border collie named

Rico who had acquired a 200-word vocabulary (containing both German and English words). When asked to fetch a particular toy from a pile of many toys Rico was correct over 90% of the time. When told to fetch a toy whose name he had not been previously taught, Rico could match the novel name to a new toy among a pile of familiar toys about 70% of the time—a rate comparable to that of young children performing a similar novel name task. More recently, a border collie named Chaser who lives in South Carolina is reported to understand the names of 1022 toys! Chaser was taught these names over a 3-year period. And like Rico he is able to connect a novel name to a new toy placed in a huge pile of toys whose names he already knows.

Rico and Chaser are clearly very intelligent dogs and their name recognition skills are amazing. It is unlikely, however, that Rico or Chaser (or Spot or Rover) understand the *meanings* of words or have acquired a symbolic system in the way that children do. Rather, they learn to associate a particular sequence of sounds with an object or action. For Chaser and Rico the name 'Sponge Bob,' for example, might mean something like 'fetch Sponge Bob'—what the dog has been taught to do. The young child who has learned the name 'Sponge Bob' knows that it refers to a particular toy or TV character independent of any a particular game or context. The philosopher Bertrand Russell summed up the dog rather insightfully, noting that ". . . however eloquently he may bark, he cannot tell you that his parents were honest though poor."

In their natural habitat, chimpanzees, gorillas, and other nonhuman primates communicate with each other through visual, auditory, olfactory, and tactile signals. Many of these signals seem to have meanings associated with the animals' immediate environment or emotional state. They can signal danger and can communicate aggressiveness and subordination. However, the natural sounds and gestures produced by all nonhuman primates are highly stereotyped and limited in the type and number of messages they convey. Their signals cannot be broken down into discrete units and rearranged to create new meanings. They also lack the property of displacement. Intelligent though they are, these animals have no way of expressing the anger they felt yesterday or the anticipation of tomorrow.

Even though primate communication systems are quite limited, many people have been interested in the question of whether they have the latent capacity to acquire complex linguistic systems similar to human language. Throughout the second half of the twentieth century, there were a number of studies designed to test whether nonhuman primates could learn human language, including both words (or signs) and the grammatical rules for their combination.

In early experiments researchers raised chimpanzees in their own homes alongside their children, in order to recreate the natural environment in which human children acquire language. The chimps were unable to vocalize words despite the efforts of their caretakers, though they did achieve the ability to understand a number of individual words. Primate vocal tracts do not permit them to pronounce many different sounds but because of their manual dexterity, sign language was an attractive alternative to test their cognitive linguistic ability. Starting with a chimpanzee named Washoe, and continuing over the years with a gorilla named Koko and another chimp ironically named Nim Chimpsky (after Noam Chomsky—and the subject of a major motion picture, *Project Nim*, released Aug. 2011), intense efforts were made to teach them American Sign Language. Though the primates achieved small successes such as the ability to string two signs together, and occasionally showed flashes of creativity, none remotely reached the qualitative linguistic ability of a human child.

Similar results were obtained in attempting to teach primates artificial languages designed to resemble human languages in some respects. Common chimpanzees Sarah, Lana, Sherman, Austin, and more recently, a male bonobo (or pygmy chimpanzee) named Kanzi, were taught languages whose "words" were plastic chips, or keys on a keyboard, that could be arranged into "sentences." The researchers were particularly interested in the ability of primates to communicate using such abstract symbols.

These experiments also came under scrutiny. Questions arose over what kind of knowledge Sarah and Lana and Kanzi were showing with their symbol manipulations and to what extent their responses were being inadvertently cued by experimenters. Many scientists, including some who were directly involved with these projects, have concluded that the creative ability that is so much a part of human language is not evidenced by the chimps' use of the artificial languages. As often happens in science, the search for the answers to one kind of question leads to answers to other questions. The linguistic experiments with primates have led to many advances in our understanding of primate cognitive ability. Researchers have gone on to investigate other capacities of the chimp mind, such as causality. These studies also point out how remarkable it is that within just a few short years, without the benefit of explicit guidance and regardless of personal circumstances, all human children are able to create new and complex sentences never spoken or heard before.

Language and Thought

It was intended that when Newspeak had been adopted once and for all and Oldspeak forgotten, a heretical thought—that is, a thought diverging from the principles of IngSoc—should be literally unthinkable, at least so far as thought is dependent on words.

GEORGE ORWELL, appendix to *1984*, 1949

The limits of my language mean the limits of my world.

LUDWIG WITTGENSTEIN, *Tractatus Logico-Philosophicus*, 1922

Many people are fascinated by the question of how language relates to thought. It is natural to imagine that something as powerful and fundamental to human nature as language would influence how we think about or perceive the world around us. This is clearly reflected in the appendix of George Orwell's masterpiece *1984*, quoted above. Over the years there have been many claims made regarding the relationship between language and thought. The claim that the structure of a language influences how its speakers perceive the world around them is most closely associated with the linguist Edward Sapir and his student

Benjamin Whorf, and is therefore referred to as the **Sapir-Whorf hypothesis**. In 1929 Sapir wrote:

> Human beings do not live in the objective world alone, nor in the world of social activity as ordinarily understood, but are very much at the mercy of the particular language which has become the medium of expression for their society . . . we see and hear and otherwise experience very largely as we do because the language habits of our community predispose certain choices of interpretation.[4]

Whorf made even stronger claims:

> The background linguistic system (in other words, the grammar) of each language is not merely the reproducing instrument for voicing ideas but rather is itself the shaper of ideas, the program and guide for the individual's mental activity, for his analysis of impressions, for his synthesis of his mental stock in trade . . . We dissect nature along lines laid down by our native languages.[5]

The strongest form of the Sapir-Whorf hypothesis is called **linguistic determinism** because it holds that the language we speak *determines* how we perceive and think about the world. According to this view language acts like a filter on reality. One of Whorf's best-known claims in support of linguistic determinism was that the Hopi Indians do not perceive time in the same way as speakers of European languages because the Hopi language does not make the grammatical distinctions of tense that, for example, English does with words and word endings such as *did, will, shall, -s, -ed,* and *-ing.*

A weaker form of the hypothesis is **linguistic relativism**, which says that different languages encode different categories and that speakers of different languages therefore think about the world in different ways. For example, languages break up the color spectrum at different points. In Navaho, blue and green are one word. Russian has different words for dark blue (*siniy*) and light blue (*goluboy*), while in English we need to use the additional words *dark* and *light* to express the difference. The American Indian language Zuni does not distinguish between the colors yellow and orange.

Languages also differ in how they express locations. For example, in Italian you ride "in" a bicycle and you go "in" a country while in English you ride "on" a bicycle and you go "to" a country. In English we say that a ring is placed "on" a finger and a finger is placed "in" the ring. Korean, on the other hand, has one word for both situations, *kitta,* which expresses the idea of a tight-fitting relation between the two objects. Spanish has two different words for the inside of a corner (*rincón*) and the outside of a corner (*esquina*).

That languages show linguistic distinctions in their lexicons and grammar is certain, and we will see many examples of this in later chapters. The question is to what extent—if at all—such distinctions determine or influence the thoughts and perceptions of speakers. The Sapir-Whorf hypothesis is controversial, but

---

[4]Sapir, E. 1929. *Language.* New York: Harcourt, Brace & World, p. 207.

[5]Whorf, B. L., and J. B. Carroll. 1956. *Language, thought, and reality: Selected writings.* Cambridge, MA: MIT Press.

it is clear that the strong form of this hypothesis is false. Peoples' thoughts and perceptions are not determined by the words and structures of their language. We are not prisoners of our linguistic systems. If speakers were unable to think about something for which their language had no specific word, translations would be impossible, as it would be to learn a second language. English may not have separate words for the inside of a corner and the outside of a corner, but we are perfectly able to express these concepts using more than one word. In fact, we just did. If we could not think about something for which we do not have words, how would infants ever learn their first words, much less languages?

Many of the specific claims of linguistic determinism have been shown to be wrong. For example, the Hopi language may not have words and word endings for specific tenses, but the language has other expressions for time, including words for the days of the week, parts of the day, yesterday and tomorrow, lunar phases, seasons, etc. The Hopi people use various kinds of calendars and various devices for time-keeping based on the sundial. Clearly, they have a sophisticated concept of time despite the lack of a tense system in the language.

The Munduruku, an indigenous people of the Brazilian Amazon, have no words in their language for triangle, square, rectangle, or other geometric concepts, except circle. The only terms to indicate direction are words for upstream, downstream, sunrise, and sunset. Yet Munduruku children understand many principles of geometry as well as American children, whose language is rich in geometric and spatial words.

Though languages differ in their color words, speakers can readily perceive colors that are not named in their language. Grand Valley Dani is a language spoken in New Guinea with only two color words, black and white (dark and light). In experimental studies, however, speakers of the language showed recognition of the color red, and they did better with fire-engine red than off-red. This would not be possible if their color perceptions were fixed by their language. Our perception of color is determined by the structure of the human eye, not by the structure of language. A source of dazzling linguistic creativity is to be found at the local paint store where literally thousands of colors are given names like *soft pumpkin*, *Durango dust*, and *lavender lipstick*.

by Jim Toomey

SHERMAN'S LAGOON © 2011 JIM TOOMEY

CLOSE ✖

The Whorfian claim that is perhaps most familiar is that the Eskimo language Inuit has many more words than English has for snow and that this affects the worldview of the Inuit people. However, anthropologists have shown that Inuit has no more words for snow than English does: around a dozen, including *sleet*, *blizzard*, *slush*, and *flurry*. But even if it did, this would not show that language conditions the Inuits' experience of the world, but rather that experience with a particular world creates the need for certain words. In this respect the Inuit speaker is no different from the computer programmer, who has a technical vocabulary for Internet protocols, or the linguist, who has many specialized words regarding language. In this book we will introduce you to many new words and linguistic concepts, and surely you will learn them! This would be impossible if your thoughts about language were determined by the linguistic vocabulary you now have.

In our understanding of the world we are certainly not "at the mercy of whatever language we speak," as Sapir suggested. However, we may ask whether the language we speak *influences* our cognition in some way. In the domain of color categorization, for example, it has been shown that if a language lacks a word for *red*, say, then it's harder for speakers to reidentify red objects. In other words, having a label seems to make it easier to store or access information in memory. Similarly, experiments show that Russian speakers are better at discriminating light blue (*goluboy*) and dark blue (*siniy*) objects than English speakers, whose language does not make a lexical distinction between these categories. These results show that words can influence simple percep-tual tasks in the domain of color discrimination. Upon reflection, this may not be a surprising finding. Colors exist on a continuum, and the way we segment into "different" colors happens at arbitrary points along this spectrum. Because there is no physical motivation for these divisions, this may be the kind of situ-ation where language could show an effect.

The question has also been raised regarding the possible influence of gram-matical gender on how people think about objects. Many languages, such as Spanish and German, classify nouns as masculine or feminine; in Spanish "key" is *la llave* (feminine) and "bridge" is *el puente* (masculine). Some psychologists have suggested that speakers of gender-marking languages think about objects as having gender, much like people or animals have. In one study, speakers of German and Spanish were asked to describe various objects using English ad-jectives (the speakers were proficient in English). In general, they used more masculine adjectives—independently rated as such—to describe objects that are grammatically masculine in their own language. For example, Spanish speakers described bridges (*el puente*) as *big, dangerous, long, strong,* and *sturdy*. In German the word for bridge is feminine (*die Brücke*) and German speakers used more feminine adjectives such as *beautiful, elegant, fragile, peaceful, pretty,* and *slender*. Interestingly, it has been noted that English speakers, too, make consistent judg-ments about the gender of certain objects (ships are "she") even though English has no grammatical gender on common nouns. It may be, then, that regardless of the language spoken, humans have a tendency to anthropomorphize objects and this tendency is somehow enhanced if the language itself has grammatical gender. Though it is too early to come to any firm conclusions, the results of these and similar studies seem to support a weak version of linguistic relativism.

Politicians and marketers certainly believe that language can influence our thoughts and values. One political party may refer to an inheritance tax as the "estate tax," while an opposing party refers to it as the "death tax." In the abortion debate, some refer to the "right to choose" and others to the "right to life." The terminology reflects different ideologies, but the choice of expression is primarily intended to sway public opinion. Politically correct (PC) language also reflects the idea that language can influence thought. Many people believe that by changing the way we talk, we can change the way we think; that if we eliminate racist and sexist terms from our language, we will become a less racist and sexist society. As we will discuss in chapter 7, language itself is not sexist or racist, but people can be, and because of this particular words take on negative meanings. In his book *The Language Instinct*, the psychologist Steven Pinker uses the expression *euphemism treadmill* to describe how the euphemistic terms that are created to replace negative words often take on the negative associations of the words they were coined to replace. For example, *handicapped* was once a euphemism for the offensive term *crippled*, and when *handicapped* became politically incorrect it was replaced by the euphemism *disabled*. And as we write, *disabled* is falling into disrepute and is often replaced by yet another euphemism, *challenged*. Nonetheless, in all such cases, changing language has not resulted in a new worldview for the speakers.

As prescient as Orwell was with respect to how language could be used for social control, he was more circumspect with regard to the relation between language and thought. He was careful to qualify his notions with the phrase "at least so far as thought is dependent on words." Current research shows that language does not determine how we think about and perceive the world. Future research should show the extent to which language influences other aspects of cognition such as memory and categorization.

Summary

We are all intimately familiar with at least one language, our own. Yet few of us ever stop to consider what we know when we know a language. No book contains, or could possibly contain, the English or Russian or Zulu language. The words of a language can be listed in a dictionary, but not all the sentences can be. Speakers use a finite set of rules to produce and understand an infinite set of possible sentences.

These rules are part of the **grammar** of a language, which develops when you acquire the language and includes the sound system (the **phonology**), the structure and properties of words (the **morphology** and **lexicon**), how words may be combined into phrases and sentences (the **syntax**), and the ways in which sounds and meanings are related (the **semantics**). The sounds and meanings of individual words are related in an **arbitrary** fashion. If you had never heard the word *syntax* you would not know what it meant by its sounds. The gestures used by signers are also arbitrarily related to their meanings. Language, then, is a system that relates sounds (or hand and body gestures) with meanings. When you know a language, you know this system.

This knowledge (**linguistic competence**) is different from behavior (**linguistic performance**). You have the competence to produce a million-word sentence but performance limitations such as memory and endurance keep this from occurring. There are different kinds of "grammars." The **descriptive grammar** of a language represents the unconscious linguistic knowledge or capacity of its speakers. Such a grammar is a model of the **mental grammar** every speaker of the language possesses. It does not teach the rules of the language; it describes the rules that are already known. A grammar that attempts to legislate what your grammar should be is called a **prescriptive grammar**. It prescribes. It does not describe, except incidentally. **Teaching grammars** are written to help people learn a foreign language or a dialect of their own language.

The more linguists investigate the thousands of languages of the world and describe the ways in which they differ from each other, the more they discover that these differences are limited. There are linguistic universals that pertain to each of the parts of grammars, the ways in which these parts are related, and the forms of rules. These principles compose **Universal Grammar**, which provides a blueprint for the grammars of all possible human languages. Universal Grammar constitutes the innate component of the human language faculty that makes language development in children possible.

Strong evidence for Universal Grammar is found in the way children acquire language. Children learn language by exposure. They need not be deliberately taught, though parents may enjoy "teaching" their children to speak or sign. Children will learn any human language to which they are exposed, and they learn it in definable stages, beginning at a very early age.

The fact that deaf children learn **sign language** shows that the ability to hear or produce sounds is not a prerequisite for language learning. All the sign languages in the world, which differ as spoken languages do, are visual-gestural systems that are as fully developed and as structurally complex as spoken languages. The major sign language used in the United States is **American Sign Language (ASL)**. The ability of human beings to acquire, know, and use language is a biologically based ability rooted in the structure of the human brain, and expressed in different modalities (spoken or signed).

If language is defined merely as a system of communication, or the ability to produce speech sounds, then language is not unique to humans. There are, however, certain characteristics of human language not found in the communication systems of any other species. A basic property of human language is its **creativity**—a speaker's ability to combine the basic linguistic units to form an infinite set of "well-formed" grammatical sentences, most of which are novel, never before produced or heard. Human languages consist of discrete units that combine according to the rules of the grammar of the language. Human languages also allow us to talk about things that are removed in time and space from our immediate environment or mental or physical state. These are the properties of **discreteness** and **displacement** and they distinguish human language from the "languages" of other species.

For many years researchers were interested in the question of whether language is a uniquely human ability. There have been many attempts to teach nonhuman primates to communicate using sign language or symbolic systems that resemble human language in certain respects. Overall, results have been disappointing. Some chimpanzees have been trained to use an impressive number of symbols or signs. But a careful examination of their multi-sign utterances reveals that unlike children, the chimps show little creativity or spontaneity. Their "utterances" are highly imitative (echoic), often unwittingly cued by trainers, and have little syntactic structure. Some highly intelligent dogs have also learned a significant number of words, but their learning is restricted to a specific context and it is likely that their "meanings" for these words are very different from the symbolic or referential meanings that would be learned by a human child.

The **Sapir-Whorf hypothesis** holds that the particular language we speak determines or influences our thoughts and perceptions of the world. Much of the early evidence in support of this hypothesis has not stood the test of time. More recent experimental studies suggest that the words and grammar of a language may affect aspects of cognition, such as memory and categorization.

References for Further Reading

Anderson, S. R. 2008. The logical structure of linguistic theory. *Language* (December): 795–814.

Bickerton, D. 1990. *Language and species.* Chicago: Chicago University Press.

Chomsky, N. 1986. *Knowledge of language: Its nature, origin, and use.* New York and London: Praeger.

___. 1975. *Reflections on language.* New York: Pantheon Books.

___. 1972. *Language and mind.* Enlarged ed. New York: Harcourt Brace Jovanovich.

Crystal, D. 2010. *Cambridge encyclopedia of language.* Cambridge, UK: Cambridge University Press.

Gentner, D., and S. Goldin-Meadow. 2003. *Language in mind.* Cambridge, MA: MIT Press.

Hall, R. A. 1950. *Leave your language alone.* Ithaca, NY: Linguistica.

Jackendoff, R. 1997. *The architecture of the language faculty.* Cambridge, MA: MIT Press.

___. 1994. *Patterns in the mind: Language and human nature.* New York: Basic Books.

Klima, E. S., and U. Bellugi. 1979. *The signs of language.* Cambridge, MA: Harvard University Press.

Lane, H. 1989. *When the mind hears: A history of the deaf.* New York: Vintage Books (Random House).

Milroy, J., and L. Milroy. 1998. *Authority in language: Investigating standard English,* 3rd ed. New York: Routledge.

Napoli, D. J. 2003. *Language matters: A guide to everyday thinking about language.* New York: Oxford University Press.

Pinker, S. 1999. *Words and rules: The ingredients of language.* New York: HarperCollins.

___. 1994. *The language instinct.* New York: William Morrow.

Premack, A. J., and D. Premack. 1972. Teaching language to an ape. *Scientific American* (October): 92–99.

Terrace, H. S. 1979. *Nim: A chimpanzee who learned sign language.* New York: Knopf.

Stam, J. 1976. *Inquiries into the origin of language: The fate of a question.* New York: Harper & Row.

Stokoe, W. 1960. *Sign language structure: An outline of the visual communication system of the American deaf.* Silver Spring, MD: Linstok Press.

Exercises

1. An English speaker's knowledge includes the sound sequences of the language. When new products are put on the market, the manufacturers have to think up new names for them that conform to the allowable sound patterns. Suppose you were hired by a manufacturer of soap products to name five new products. What names might you come up with? List them.

   We are interested in how the names are pronounced. Therefore, describe in any way you can how to say the words you list. Suppose, for example, you named one detergent *Blick*. You could describe the sounds in any of the following ways:

   bl as in *blood, i* as in *pit, ck* as in *stick*
   bli as in *bliss, ck* as in *tick*
   b as in *boy, lick* as in *lick*

2. Consider the following sentences. Put a star (*) after those that do not seem to conform to the rules of your grammar, that are ungrammatical for you. State, if you can, why you think the sentence is ungrammatical.

   a. Robin forced the sheriff go.
   b. Napoleon forced Josephine to go.
   c. The devil made Faust go.
   d. He passed by a large pile of money.
   e. He drove by my house.
   f. He drove my house by.
   g. Did in a corner little Jack Horner sit?
   h. Elizabeth is resembled by Charles.
   i. Nancy is eager to please.
   j. It is easy to frighten Emily.
   k. It is eager to love a kitten.
   l. That birds can fly flabbergasts.
   m. The fact that you are late to class is surprising.
   n. Has the nurse slept the baby yet?
   o. I was surprised for you to get married.
   p. I wonder who and Mary went swimming.
   q. Myself bit John.
   r. What did Alice eat the toadstool with?
   s. What did Alice eat the toadstool and?

3. It was pointed out in this chapter that a small set of words in languages may be onomatopoeic; that is, their sounds "imitate" what they refer to. *Ding-dong, tick-tock, bang, zing, swish*, and *plop* are such words in English. Construct a list of ten new onomatopoeic words. Test them on at least five friends to see whether they are truly nonarbitrary as to sound and meaning.

4. Although sounds and meanings of most words in all languages are arbitrarily related, there are some communication systems in which the "signs" unambiguously reveal their "meanings."

   a. Describe (or draw) five different signs that directly show what they mean. *Example*: a road sign indicating an S curve.

   b. Describe any other communication system that, like language, consists of arbitrary symbols. *Example*: traffic signals, in which red means stop and green means go.

5. Consider these two statements: I learned a new word today. I learned a new sentence today. Do you think the two statements are equally probable, and if not, why not?

6. An African grey parrot named Alex who was the subject of a 30-year experiment was reported to have learned the meanings of 150 words. There are many reports on the Internet about Alex's impressive abilities. In the light of evidence presented in this chapter, or based on your own Internet research, discuss whether Alex's communications were the results of classical operant conditioning, as many scientists believe, or whether he showed true linguistic creativity, as his trainers maintain.

7. A wolf is able to express subtle gradations of emotion by different positions of the ears, the lips, and the tail. There are eleven postures of the tail that express such emotions as self-confidence, confident threat, lack of tension, uncertain threat, depression, defensiveness, active submission, and complete submission. This system seems to be complex. Suppose that there were a thousand different emotions that the wolf could express in this way. Would you then say a wolf had a language similar to a human's? If not, why not?

8. Suppose you taught a dog to *heel, sit up, roll over, play dead, stay, jump,* and *bark* on command, using the italicized words as cues. Would you be teaching it language? Why or why not?

9. State some rule of grammar that you have learned is the correct way to say something, but that you do not generally use in speaking. For example, you may have heard that *It's me* is incorrect and that the correct form is *It's I*. Nevertheless, you always use *me* in such sentences; your friends do also, and in fact *It's I* sounds odd to you.

   Write a short essay presenting arguments against someone who tells you that you are wrong. Discuss how this disagreement demonstrates the difference between descriptive and prescriptive grammars.

10. Noam Chomsky has been quoted as saying:

    It's about as likely that an ape will prove to have a language ability as that there is an island somewhere with a species of flightless birds waiting for human beings to teach them to fly.

In the light of evidence presented in this chapter, or based on your own Internet research, comment on Chomsky's remark. Do you agree or disagree, or do you think the evidence is inconclusive?

11. Think of song titles that are "bad" grammar, but that, if corrected, would lack effect. For example, the title of the 1929 "Fats" Waller classic "Ain't Misbehavin'" is clearly superior to the bland "I am not misbehaving." Try to come up with five or ten such titles.

12. Linguists who attempt to write a descriptive grammar of linguistic competence are faced with a difficult task. They must understand a deep and complex system based on a set of sparse and often inaccurate data. (Children learning language face the same difficulty.) Albert Einstein and Leopold Infeld captured the essence of the difficulty in their book *The Evolution of Physics*, written in 1938:

    > In our endeavor to understand reality we are somewhat like a man trying to understand the mechanism of a closed watch. He sees the face and the moving hands, even hears its ticking, but he has no way of opening the case. If he is ingenious he may form some picture of a mechanism which could be responsible for all the things he observes, but he may never be quite sure his picture is the only one which could explain his observations. He will never be able to compare his picture with the real mechanism and he cannot even imagine the possibility of the meaning of such a comparison.

    Write a short essay that speculates on how a linguist might go about understanding the reality of a person's grammar (the closed watch) by observing what that person says and doesn't say (the face and moving hands). For example, a person might never say *the sixth sheik's sixth sheep is sick as a dog*, but the grammar should specify that it is a well-formed sentence, just as it should somehow indicate that *Came the messenger on time* is ill-formed.

13. View the motion picture *My Fair Lady* (drawn from the play *Pygmalion* by George Bernard Shaw). Write down every attempt to teach grammar (pronunciation, word choice, and syntax) to the character of Eliza Doolittle. This is an illustration of a "teaching grammar."

14. Many people are bilingual or multilingual, speaking two or more languages with very different structures.
    a. What implications does bilingualism have for the debate about language and thought?
    b. Many readers of this textbook have some knowledge of a second language. Think of a linguistic structure or word in one language that does not exist in the second language and discuss how this does or does not affect your thinking when you speak the two languages.

(If you know only one language, ask this question of a bilingual person you know.)

c. Can you find an example of an untranslatable word or structure in one of the languages you speak?

15. The South American indigenous language Pirahã is said to lack numbers beyond two and distinct words for colors. Research this language using the Internet with regard to whether Pirahã supports or fails to support linguistic determinism and/or linguistic relativism.

16. English (especially British English) has many words for woods and woodlands. Here are some:

    woodlot, carr, fen, firth, grove, heath, holt, lea, moor, shaw, weald, wold, coppice, scrub, spinney, copse, brush, bush, bosquet, bosky, stand, forest, timberland, thicket

    a. How many of these words do you recognize?
    b. Look up several of these words in the dictionary and discuss the differences in meaning. Many of these words are obsolete, so if your dictionary doesn't have them, try the Internet.
    c. Do you think that English speakers have a richer concept of woodlands than speakers whose language has fewer words? Why or why not?

17. English words containing *dge* in their spelling (*trudge*, *edgy*) are said mostly to have unfavorable or negative connotations. Research this notion by accumulating as many *dge* words as you can and classifying them as unfavorable (*sludge*) or neutral (*bridge*). What do you do about *budget*? Unfavorable or not? Are there other questionable words?

18. With regard to the "euphemism treadmill": Identify three other situations in which a euphemism evolved to be as offensive as the word it replaced, requiring yet another euphemism. *Hint*: Sex, race, and bodily functions are good places to start.

19. **Research project**: Read the Cratylus Dialogue—it's online. In it is a discussion (or "dialogue") of whether names are "conventional" (i.e., what we have called *arbitrary*) or "natural." Do you find Socrates' point of view sufficiently well-argued to support the thesis in this chapter that the relationship between form and meaning is indeed arbitrary? Argue your case in either direction in a short (or long, if you wish) essay.

20. **Research project**: (Cf. exercise 15) It is claimed that Pirahã—an indigenous language of Brazil—violates some of the universal principles hypothesized by linguists. Which principles are in question? Is the evidence persuasive? Conclusive? Speculative? (*Hint*: Use the journal *Current Anthropology*, Volume 46, Number 4, August-October 2005 and the journal *Language*, Volume 85, Number 2, June 2009.)

21. There are, very roughly, about half a million words in use in today's English language according to current unabridged dictionaries. However, if we reach back to the beginnings of the printing press and examine large amounts of published English we find an additional half a million words now no longer in use such as *slethem*, a musical instrument. (This matter is discussed in more detail in chapter 11 under the rubric "culturomics.") Write a short essay arguing one way or the other that the lexicon of the English language ought to be counted as containing one million or so words. Feel free, as always, to poke around the Internet to inform yourself further.

2

Morphology: The Words of Language

By words the mind is winged.

ARISTOPHANES (450 BCE–388 BCE)

A powerful agent is the right word. Whenever we come upon one of those intensely right words . . . the resulting effect is physical as well as spiritual, and electrically prompt.

MARK TWAIN

Every speaker of every language knows tens of thousands of words. Unabridged dictionaries of English contain nearly 500,000 entries, but most speakers don't know all of these words. It has been estimated that a child of six knows as many as 13,000 words and the average high school graduate about 60,000. A college graduate presumably knows many more than that, but whatever our level of education, we learn new words throughout our lives, such as the many words in this book that you will learn for the first time.

Words are an important part of linguistic knowledge and constitute a component of our mental grammars, but one can learn thousands of words in a language and still not know the language. Anyone who has tried to communicate in a foreign country by merely using a dictionary knows this is true. On the other hand, without words we would be unable to convey our thoughts through language or understand the thoughts of others.

Someone who doesn't know English would not know where one word begins or ends in an utterance like *Thecatsatonthemat*. We separate written words by spaces, but in the spoken language there are no pauses between most words. Without knowledge of the language, one can't tell how many words are in an utterance. Knowing a word means knowing that a particular sequence of sounds is associated with a particular meaning. A speaker of English has no difficulty in segmenting the stream of sounds into six individual words—*the, cat, sat, on, the,* and *mat*—because each of these words is listed in his or her mental dictionary, or lexicon (the Greek word for *dictionary*), that is part of a speaker's linguistic knowledge. Similarly, a speaker knows that *uncharacteristically*, which has more letters than *Thecatsatonthemat*, is nevertheless a single word.

The lack of pauses between words in speech has provided humorists with much material. The comical hosts of the show *Car Talk*, aired on National Public Radio (as reruns nowadays), close the show by reading a list of credits that includes the following cast of characters:

Copyeditor:	Adeline Moore (add a line more)
Accounts payable:	Ineeda Czech (I need a check)
Pollution control:	Maury Missions (more emissions)
Purchasing:	Lois Bidder (lowest bidder)
Statistician:	Marge Innovera (margin of error)
Russian chauffeur:	Picov Andropov (pick up and drop off)
Legal firm:	Dewey, Cheetham, and Howe (Do we cheat 'em? And how!)[1]

In all these instances, you would have to have knowledge of English words to make sense of and find humor in such plays on words.

The fact that the same sound sequences (Lois Bidder—lowest bidder) can be interpreted differently shows that the relation between sound and meaning is an arbitrary pairing, as discussed in chapter 1. For example, *Un petit d'un petit* in French means 'a little one of a little one,' but to an English speaker the sounds resemble the name *Humpty Dumpty*.

When you know a word, you know its sound (pronunciation) and its meaning. Because the sound-meaning relation is arbitrary, it is possible to have words with the same sound and different meanings (*bear* and *bare*) and words with the same meaning and different sounds (*sofa* and *couch*).

Because each word is a sound-meaning unit, each word stored in our mental lexicon must be listed with its unique phonological representation, which determines its pronunciation, and with a meaning. For literate speakers, the spelling, or **orthography**, of most of the words we know is included.

Each word in your mental lexicon includes other information as well, such as whether it is a noun, a pronoun, a verb, an adjective, an adverb, a preposition, or a conjunction. That is, the mental lexicon also specifies the **grammatical category** or **syntactic class** of the word. You may not consciously

---

know that a form like *love* is listed as both a verb and a noun, but as a speaker you have such knowledge, as shown by the phrases *I love you* and *You are the love of my life.* If such information were not in the mental lexicon, we would not know how to form grammatical sentences, nor would we be able to distinguish grammatical from ungrammatical sentences.

Content Words and Function Words

"... and even ... the patriotic archbishop of Canterbury found it advisable—"

"Found what?" said the Duck.

"Found it," the Mouse replied rather crossly; "of course you know what 'it' means."

"I know what 'it' means well enough, when I find a thing," said the Duck; "it's generally a frog or a worm. The question is, what did the archbishop find?"

LEWIS CARROLL, *Alice's Adventures in Wonderland*, 1865

Languages make an important distinction between two kinds of words—content words and function words. Nouns, verbs, adjectives, and adverbs are the **content words**. These words denote concepts such as objects, actions, attributes, and ideas that we can think about like *children, build, beautiful*, and *seldom*. Content words are sometimes called the **open class** words because we can and regularly do add new words to these classes, such as *Facebook* (noun), *blog* (noun, verb), *frack* (verb), *online* (adjective, adverb), and *blingy* (adjective).

Other classes of words do not have clear lexical meanings or obvious concepts associated with them, including conjunctions such as *and, or*, and *but*; prepositions such as *in* and *of*; the articles *the* and *a/an*, and pronouns such as *it*. These kinds of words are called **function words** because they specify grammatical relations and have little or no semantic content. For example, the articles indicate whether a noun is definite or indefinite—*the* boy or *a* boy. The preposition *of* indicates possession, as in "the book of yours," but this word indicates many other kinds of relations too. The *it* in *it's raining* and *the archbishop found it advisable* are further examples of words whose function is purely grammatical—they are required by the rules of syntax and we can hardly do without them.

Function words are sometimes called **closed class** words. This is because it is difficult to think of any conjunctions, prepositions, or pronouns that have recently entered the language. The small set of personal pronouns such as *I, me, mine, he, she*, and so on are part of this class. With the growth of the feminist movement, some proposals have been made for adding a genderless singular pronoun. If such a pronoun existed, it might have prevented the department head in a large university from making the incongruous statement: "We will hire the best person for the job regardless of his sex." Various proposals such as "e" have been put forward, but none are likely to gain traction because the closed classes are unreceptive to new membership. Rather, speakers prefer to recruit existing pronouns such as *they* and *their* for this job, as in "We will hire the best person for the job regardless of **their** sex." A convenient ploy used by writers is *s/he* or *she/he* pronounced "shee-hee" when read aloud, as in *If any student wishes to leave early, s/he must obtain special permission.*

The difference between content and function words is illustrated by the following test that has circulated over the Internet:

Count the number of F's in the following text without reading further, then check the footnote:[2]

FINISHED FILES ARE THE
RESULT OF YEARS OF SCIENTIFIC
STUDY COMBINED WITH THE
EXPERIENCE OF YEARS.

This little test illustrates that the brain treats content and function words (like *of*) differently. A great deal of psychological and neurological evidence supports this claim. As discussed in chapter 10, some brain-damaged patients and people with specific language impairments have greater difficulty in using, understanding, or reading function words than they do with content words. Some aphasics are unable to read function words like *in* or *which*, but can read the lexical content words *inn* and *witch*.

The two classes of words also seem to function differently in **slips of the tongue** produced by normal individuals. For example, a speaker may inadvertently switch words producing "the journal of the editor" instead of "the editor of the journal," but the switching or exchanging of function words has not been observed. There is also evidence for this distinction from language acquisition (discussed in chapter 9). In the early stages of development, children often omit function words from their speech, as in, for example, "doggie barking."

The linguistic evidence suggests that content words and function words play different roles in language. Content words bear the brunt of the meaning, whereas function words connect the content words to the larger grammatical context.

Morphemes: The Minimal Units of Meaning

"They gave it me," Humpty Dumpty continued, "for an un-birthday present."

"I beg your pardon?" Alice said with a puzzled air.

"I'm not offended," said Humpty Dumpty.

"I mean, what is an un-birthday present?"

"A present given when it isn't your birthday, of course."

LEWIS CARROLL, *Through the Looking-Glass*, 1871

---

[2]Most people come up with three, which is wrong. If you came up with fewer than six, count again, and this time, pay attention to the function word *of*.

Humpty Dumpty is well aware that the prefix *un-* means 'not,' as further shown in the following pairs of words:

A	B
desirable	undesirable
likely	unlikely
inspired	uninspired
happy	unhappy
developed	undeveloped
sophisticated	unsophisticated

Thousands of English adjectives begin with *un-*. If we assume that the most basic unit of meaning is the word, what do we say about parts of words, like *un-*, which has a fixed meaning? In all the words in the B column, *un-* means the same thing—'not.' *Undesirable* means 'not desirable,' *unlikely* means 'not likely,' and so on. All the words in column B consist of at least two meaningful units: *un + desirable, un + likely, un + inspired,* and so on.

Just as *un-* occurs with the same meaning in the previous list of words, so does *phon-* in the following words. (You may not know the meaning of some of them, but you will when you finish this book.)

phone	phonology	phoneme
phonetic	phonologist	phonemic
phonetics	phonological	allophone
phonetician	telephone	euphonious
phonic	telephonic	symphony

Phon- is a minimal form in that it can't be decomposed. *Ph* doesn't mean anything; *pho*, though it may be pronounced like *foe*, has no relation in meaning to it; and *on* is not the preposition spelled *o-n*. In all the words on the list, *phon* has the identical meaning 'pertaining to sound.'

Words have internal structure that is rule-governed. *Uneaten, undisputed,* and *ungrammatical* are words in English, but **eatenun, *disputedun,* and **grammaticalun* (to mean 'not eaten,' 'not disputed,' 'not grammatical') are not words because we form a negative meaning of a word by prefixing *un-*, not by suffixing it.

When Samuel Goldwyn, the pioneer moviemaker, announced, "In two words: im-possible," he was reflecting the common view that words are the basic meaningful elements of a language. We have seen that this cannot be so, because some words contain several distinct units of meaning. The linguistic term for the most elemental unit of grammatical form is **morpheme**. The word is derived from the Greek word *morphe*, meaning 'form.' If Goldwyn had taken a linguistics course, he would have said, more correctly, "In two morphemes: im-possible."

The study of the internal structure of words, and of the rules by which words are formed, is **morphology**. This word itself consists of two morphemes, *morph + ology*. The suffix *-ology* means 'branch of knowledge,' so the meaning of *morphology* is 'the branch of knowledge concerning (word) forms.' Morphology also refers to our internal grammatical knowledge concerning the words of our language, and like most linguistic knowledge we are not consciously aware of it.

A single word may be composed of one or more morphemes:

One morpheme	boy
	desire
	meditate
two morphemes	boy + ish
	desire + able
	meditate + tion
three morphemes	boy + ish + ness
	desire + able + ity
four morphemes	gentle + man + li + ness
	un + desire + able + ity
more than four	un + gentle + man + li + ness
	anti + dis + establish + ment + ari + an + ism

A morpheme may be represented by a single sound, such as the morpheme *a-* meaning 'without' as in *amoral* and *asexual*, or by a single syllable, such as *child* and *ish* in *child + ish*. A morpheme may also consist of more than one syllable: by two syllables, as in *camel*, *lady*, and *water*; by three syllables, as in *Hackensack* and *crocodile*; or by four or more syllables, as in *hallucinate*, *apothecary*, *helicopter*, and *accelerate*.

A morpheme—the minimal linguistic unit—is thus an arbitrary union of a sound and a meaning (or grammatical function) that cannot be further analyzed. So solidly welded is this union in the mind that it is impossible for you to hear or read a word you know and not be aware of its meaning, even if you try! These two sides of the same coin are often called a **linguistic sign**, not to be confused with the *sign* of sign languages. Every word in every language is composed of one or more morphemes.

The Discreteness of Morphemes

Internet bloggers love to point out "inconsistencies" in the English language. They observe that while singers sing and flingers fling, it is not the case that fingers "fing." However, English speakers know that *finger* is a single morpheme, or a **monomorphemic word**. The final *-er* syllable in *finger* is not a separate morpheme because a finger is not "something that fings." Similarly *butter* when not referring to goat-like behavior is monomorphemic food stuff, and *buttress*, to be sure, is neither a feminine form of *butt* nor has anything to do with locks of hair.

The meaning of a morpheme must be constant. The agentive morpheme *-er* means 'one who does' in words like *singer*, *painter*, *lover*, and *worker*, but the same sounds represent the comparative morpheme, meaning 'more,' in *nicer*, *prettier*, and *taller*. Thus, two different morphemes may be pronounced identically. The identical form represents two morphemes because of the different meanings. The same sounds may occur in another word and not represent a separate morpheme at all, as in *finger*.

Conversely, the two morphemes *-er* and *-ster* have the same meaning, but different forms. Both *singer* and *songster* mean 'one who sings.' And like *-er*, *-ster* is not a morpheme in *monster* because a monster is not something that "mons" or someone that "is mon" the way *youngster* is someone who is young. All of this follows from the concept of the morpheme as a *sound* plus a *meaning* unit.

The decomposition of words into morphemes illustrates one of the fundamental properties of human language—discreteness—a property that sets it apart from the animal communication systems discussed in chapter 1. In all languages, sound units combine to form morphemes, morphemes combine to form words, and words combine to form larger units—phrases and sentences.

Discreteness is an important part of linguistic creativity. We can combine morphemes in novel ways to create new words whose meaning will be apparent to other speakers of the language. If you know that "to write" to a DVD means to put information on it, you automatically understand that a *writable* DVD is one that can take information; a *rewritable* DVD is one where the original information can be written over; and an *unrewritable* DVD is one that does not allow the user to write over the original information. You know the meanings of all these words by virtue of your knowledge of the discrete morphemes *write*, *re-*, *-able*, and *un-*, and the rules for their combination.

Bound and Free Morphemes

Our morphological knowledge has two components: knowledge of the individual morphemes and knowledge of the rules that combine them. One of the things we know about particular morphemes is whether they can stand alone or whether they must be attached to a base morpheme. Some morphemes like *boy, desire, gentle,* and *man* may constitute words by themselves. These are **free morphemes**. Other morphemes like *-ish, -ness, -ly, pre-, trans-,* and *un-* are never words by themselves but are always parts of words. These **affixes** are **bound morphemes** and they may attach at the beginning, the end, in the middle, or both at the beginning and end of a word. The humor in the cartoon is Brad's stumbling over the bound morpheme *un-* in a questionable attempt to free it.

Prefixes and Suffixes

We know whether an affix precedes or follows other morphemes, for example that *un-, pre-* (*premeditate, prejudge*), and *bi-* (*bipolar, bisexual*) are prefixes. They occur before other morphemes. Some morphemes occur only as **suffixes**, following other morphemes. English examples of suffix morphemes are *-ing* (*sleeping, eating, running, climbing*), *-er* (*singer, performer, reader*), *-ist* (*typist, pianist, novelist, linguist*), and *-ly* (*manly, sickly, friendly*), to mention only a few.

Many languages have prefixes and suffixes, but languages may differ in how they deploy these morphemes. A morpheme that is a prefix in one language may be a suffix in another and vice versa. In English the plural morphemes *-s* and *-es* are suffixes (*boys, lasses*). In Isthmus Zapotec, spoken in Mexico, the plural morpheme *ka-* is a prefix:

zigi	'chin'	kazigi	'chins'
zike	'shoulder'	kazike	'shoulders'
diaga	'ear'	kadiaga	'ears'

Languages may also differ in what meanings they express through affixation. In English we do not add an affix to derive a noun from a verb. We have the verb *dance* as in "I like to dance," and we have the noun *dance* as in "There's a dance or two in the old dame yet." The form is the same in both cases. In Turkish, you derive a noun from a verb with the suffix *-ak*, as in the following examples:

dur	'to stop'	durak	'stopping place'
bat	'to sink'	batak	'sinking place' or 'marsh/swamp'

To express reciprocal action in English we use the phrase *each other*, as in *understand each other, love each other*. In Turkish a morpheme is added to the verb:

anla	'understand'	anlash	'understand each other'
sev	'love'	sevish	'love each other'

The reciprocal suffix in these examples is pronounced *sh* after a vowel and *ish* after a consonant. This is similar to the process in English in which we use *a* as the indefinite article morpheme before a noun beginning with a consonant, as in *a dog*, and *an* before a noun beginning with a vowel, as in *an apple*. The same morpheme may have more than one slightly different form (see exercise 6, for example). We will discuss the various pronunciations of morphemes in more detail in chapter 6.

In Piro, an Arawakan language spoken in Peru, a single morpheme, *-kaka*, can be added to a verb to express the meaning 'cause to':

cokoruha	'to harpoon'	cokoruhakaka	'cause to harpoon'
salwa	'to visit'	salwakaka	'cause to visit'

In Karuk, a Native American language spoken in the Pacific Northwest, adding *-ak* to a noun forms the locative adverbial meaning 'in.'

ikrivaam	'house'	ikrivaamak	'in a house'

It is accidental that both Turkish and Karuk have a suffix *-ak*. Despite the similarity in *form*, the two meanings are different. Similarly, the reciprocal suffix *-ish* in Turkish is similar in form to the English suffix *-ish* as in *boyish*.

Similarity in meaning may give rise to different forms. In Karuk the suffix *-ara* has the same meaning as the English *-y*, that is, 'characterized by' (*hairy* means 'characterized by hair').

aptiik	'branch'	aptikara	'branchy'

These examples illustrate again the arbitrary nature of the linguistic sign, that is, of the sound-meaning relationship, as well as the distinction between bound and free morphemes.

Infixes

Some languages also have **infixes**, morphemes that are inserted into other morphemes. Bontoc, spoken in the Philippines, is such a language, as illustrated by the following:

Nouns/Adjectives		**Verbs**	
fikas	'strong'	fumikas	'to be strong'
kilad	'red'	kumilad	'to be red'
fusul	'enemy'	fumusul	'to be an enemy'

In this language, the infix *-um-* is inserted after the first consonant of the noun or adjective. Thus, a speaker of Bontoc who knows that *pusi* means 'poor' would understand the meaning of *pumusi*, 'to be poor,' on hearing the word for the first time, just as an English speaker who learns the verb *sneet* would know that *sneeter* is 'one who sneets.' A Bontoc speaker who knows that *ngumitad* means 'to be dark' would know that the adjective 'dark' must be *ngitad*.

Oddly enough, the only infixes in English are full-word obscenities, usually inserted into adjectives or adverbs. The most common infix in America is the word *fuckin'* and all the euphemisms for it, such as *friggin*, *freakin*, *flippin*, and *fuggin*, as in *ri-fuckin-diculous* or *Kalama-flippin-zoo*, based on the city in Michigan. In Britain, a common infix is *bloody*, an obscene term in British English, and its euphemisms, such as *bloomin'*. In the movie and stage musical *My Fair Lady*, the word *abso-bloomin-lutely* occurs in one of the songs sung by Eliza Doolittle.

Circumfixes

Some languages have **circumfixes**, morphemes that are attached to a base morpheme both initially and finally. These are sometimes called **discontinuous morphemes**. In Chickasaw, a Muskogean language spoken in Oklahoma, the negative is formed by surrounding the affirmative form with both a preceding *ik-* and a following *-o* working together as a single negative morpheme. The final vowel of the affirmative is dropped before the negative part *-o* is added. Examples of this circumfixing are:

Affirmative		Negative	
chokma	'he is good'	ik + chokm + o	'he isn't good'
lakna	'it is yellow'	ik + lakn + o	'it isn't yellow'
palli	'it is hot'	ik + pall + o	'it isn't hot'
tiwwi	'he opens (it)'	ik + tiww + o	'he doesn't open (it)'

An example of a more familiar circumfixing language is German. The past participle of regular verbs is formed by tacking on *ge-* to the beginning and *-t* to the end of the verb root. This circumfix added to the verb root *lieb* 'love' produces *geliebt*, 'loved' (or 'beloved,' when used as an adjective).

Roots and Stems

Morphologically complex words consist of a morpheme **root** and one or more affixes. Some examples of English roots are *paint* in *painter*, *read* in *reread*, *ceive* in *conceive*, and *ling* in *linguist*. A root may or may not stand alone as a word (*paint* and *read* do; *ceive* and *ling* don't). In languages that have circumfixes, the root is the form around which the circumfix attaches, for example, the Chickasaw root *chokm* in *ikchokmo* ('he isn't good'). In infixing languages the root is the form into which the infix is inserted; for example, *fikas* in the Bontoc word *fumikas* ('to be strong').

Semitic languages like Hebrew and Arabic have a unique morphological system. Nouns and verbs are built on a foundation of three consonants, and one derives related words by varying the pattern of vowels and syllables. For example, the root for 'write' in Egyptian Arabic is *ktb*, from which the following words (among others) are formed by infixing vowels:

katab	'he wrote'
kaatib	'writer'
kitáab	'book'
kútub	'books'

When a root morpheme is combined with an affix, it forms a **stem**. Other affixes can be added to a stem to form a more complex stem, as shown in the following:

root	Chomsky	(proper) noun
stem	Chomsky + ite	noun + suffix
word	Chomsky + ite + s	noun + suffix + suffix
root	believe	verb
stem	believe + able	verb + suffix
word	un + believe + able	prefix + verb + suffix
root	system	noun
stem	system + atic	noun + suffix
stem	un + system + atic	prefix + noun + suffix
stem	un + system + atic + al	prefix + noun + suffix + suffix
word	un + system + atic + al + ly	prefix + noun + suffix + suffix + suffix

With the addition of each new affix, a new stem and a new word are formed. Linguists sometimes use the word **base** to mean any root or stem to which an affix is attached. In the preceding example, *system*, *systematic*, *unsystematic*, and *unsystematical* are bases.

Bound Roots

It had been a rough day, so when I walked into the party I was very chalant, despite my efforts to appear gruntled and consolate. I was furling my wieldy umbrella . . . when I saw her. . . . She was a descript person. . . . Her hair was kempt, her clothing shevelled, and she moved in a gainly way.

JACK WINTER, "How I Met My Wife" by Jack Winter from *The New Yorker*, July 25, 1994. Reprinted by permission of the Estate of Jack Winter.

Bound roots do not occur in isolation and they acquire meaning only in combination with other morphemes. For example, words of Latin origin such as *receive*, *conceive*, *perceive*, and *deceive* share a common root, *-ceive*; and the words *remit*, *permit*, *commit*, *submit*, *transmit*, and *admit* share the root *-mit*. For the original Latin speakers, the morphemes corresponding to *ceive* and *mit* had clear meanings, but for modern English speakers, Latinate morphemes such as *ceive* and *mit* have no independent meaning. Their meaning depends on the entire word in which they occur.

A similar class of words is composed of a prefix affixed to a bound root morpheme. Examples are *ungainly*, but no **gainly*; *discern*, but no **cern*; *nonplussed*, but no **plussed*; *downhearted* but no **hearted*, and others to be seen in this section's epigraph.

The morpheme *huckle*, when joined with *berry*, has the meaning of a berry that is small, round, and purplish blue; *luke* when combined with *warm* has the meaning 'somewhat.' Both these morphemes and others like them (*cran*, *boysen*) are bound morphemes that convey meaning only in combination.

Rules of Word Formation

"I never heard of 'Uglification,'" Alice ventured to say. "What is it?" The Gryphon lifted up both its paws in surprise. "Never heard of uglifying!" it exclaimed. "You know what to beautify is, I suppose?" "Yes," said Alice doubtfully: "it means—to make—prettier." "Well, then," the Gryphon went on, "if you don't know what to uglify is, you are a simpleton."

LEWIS CARROLL, *Alice's Adventures in Wonderland*, 1865

When the Mock Turtle listed the branches of Arithmetic for Alice as "Ambition, Distraction, Uglification, and Derision," Alice was very confused. She wasn't really a simpleton, since *uglification* was not a common word in English until Lewis Carroll used it. Still, most English speakers would immediately know the meaning of *uglification* even if they had never heard or used the word before because they would know the meaning of its individual parts—the root *ugly* and the affixes *-ify* and *-cation*.

We said earlier that knowledge of morphology includes knowledge of individual morphemes, their pronunciation, and their meaning, and knowledge of the rules for combining morphemes into complex words. The Mock Turtle added *-ify* to the adjective *ugly* and formed a verb. Many verbs in English have been formed in this way: *purify, amplify, simplify, falsify*. The suffix *-ify* conjoined with nouns also forms verbs: *objectify, glorify, personify*. Notice that the Mock Turtle went even further: he added the suffix *-cation* to *uglify* and formed a noun, *uglification*, as in *glorification, simplification, falsification*, and *purification*. By using the **morphological rules** of English, he created a new word. The rules that he used are as follows:

Adjective + ify	→	Verb	'to make Adjective'
Verb + cation	→	Noun	'the process of making Adjective'

Derivational Morphology

Macnelly/King Features Syndicate

Bound morphemes like *-ify*, *-cation* and *-arian* are called derivational morphemes. When they are added to a base, a new word with a new meaning is derived. The addition of *-ify* to *pure*—*purify*—means 'to make pure,' and the addition of *-cation*—*purification*—means 'the process of making pure.' If we invent an adjective, *pouzy*, to describe the effect of static electricity on hair, you will immediately understand the sentences "Walking on that carpet really pouzified my hair" and "The best method of pouzification is to rub a balloon on your head." This means that we must have a list of the derivational morphemes in our mental dictionaries as well as the rules that determine how they are added to a root or stem. The form that results from the addition of a derivational morpheme is called a **derived word**.

Derivational morphemes have clear semantic content. In this sense they are like content words, except that they are not words. As we have seen, when a derivational morpheme is added to a base, it adds meaning. The derived word may also be of a different grammatical class than the original word, as shown by suffixes such as *-able* and *-ly*. When a verb is suffixed with *-able*, the result is an adjective, as in *desire + able*. When the suffix *-en* is added to an adjective, a verb is derived, as in *dark* + *en*. One may form a noun from an adjective, as in *sweet* + *ie*. Other examples are:

Noun to Adjective	Verb to Noun	Adjective to Adverb
boy + -ish	acquitt + -al	exact + -ly
virtu + -ous	clear + -ance	
Elizabeth + -an	accus + -ation	
pictur + -esque	sing + -er	
affection + -ate	conform + -ist	
health + -ful	predict + -ion	
alcohol + -ic		

Noun to Verb	Adjective to Noun	Verb to Adjective
moral + -ize	tall + -ness	read + -able
vaccin + -ate	specific + -ity	creat + -ive
hast + -en	feudal + -ism	migrat + -ory
im- + prison	free + -dom	run(n) + -y
be- + friend		
en- + joy		
in- + habit		

Adjective to Verb

en + large
en + dear
en + rich

Some derivational affixes do not cause a change in grammatical class.

Noun to Noun	Verb to Verb	Adjective to Adjective
friend + -ship	un- + do	pink + -ish
human + -ity	re- + cover	red + -like
king + -dom	dis- + believe	a- + moral
New Jersey + -ite	auto- + destruct	il- + legal
vicar + -age		in- + accurate
Paul + -ine		un- + happy
America + -n		semi- + annual
libr(ary) + -arian		dis- + agreeable
mono- + theism		sub- + minimal
dis- + advantage		
ex- + wife		
auto- + biography		
un- + employment		

When a new word enters the lexicon by the application of morphological rules, other complex derivations may be **blocked**. For example, when *Commun* + *ist* entered the language, words such as *Commun* + *ite* (as in *Trotsky* + *ite*) or *Commun* + *ian* (as in *grammar* + *ian*) were not needed; their formation was blocked. Sometimes, however, alternative forms do coexist: for example, *Chomskyan* and *Chomskyist* and perhaps even *Chomskyite* (all meaning 'follower of Chomsky's views of linguistics'). *Semanticist* and *semantician* are both used for linguists who study meaning in language, but the possible word *semantite* is not.

Finally, derivational affixes appear to come in two classes. In one class, the addition of a suffix triggers subtle changes in pronunciation. For example, when we affix *-ity* to *specific* (pronounced "specifik" with a *k* sound), we get specificity (pronounced "specifisity" with an *s* sound). When deriving *Elizabeth* + *-an* from *Elizabeth*, the fourth vowel sound changes from the vowel in *Beth* to the vowel in *Pete*. Other suffixes such as *-y*, *-ive*, and *-ize* may induce similar changes: *sane/sanity*, *deduce/deductive*, *critic/criticize*.

On the other hand, suffixes such as *-er*, *-ful*, *-ish*, *-less*, *-ly*, and *-ness* may be tacked onto a base word without affecting the pronunciation, as in *baker*, *wishful*, *boyish*, *needless*, *sanely*, and *fullness*. Moreover, affixes from the first class cannot be attached to a base containing an affix from the second class: **need + less + ity*, **moral + ize + ive*; but affixes from the second class may attach to bases with either kind of affix: *moral + iz(e) + er*, *need + less + ness*.

Inflectional Morphology

Zits Partnership/King Features Syndicate

Function words like *to*, *it*, and *be* are free morphemes. Many languages, including English, also have bound morphemes that have a strictly grammatical function. They mark properties such as tense, number, person, and so forth. Such bound morphemes are called **inflectional morphemes**. Unlike derivational morphemes, they never change the grammatical category of the stems to which they are attached. Consider the forms of the verb in the following sentences:

1. I sail the ocean blue.
2. He sails the ocean blue.
3. John sailed the ocean blue.
4. John has sailed the ocean blue.
5. John is sailing the ocean blue.

In sentence (2) the *-s* at the end of the verb is an agreement marker; it signifies that the subject of the verb is third-person and is singular, and that the verb is in the present tense. It doesn't add lexical meaning. The suffix *-ed* indicates past tense, and is also required by the syntactic rules of the language when verbs are used with *have*, just as *-ing* is required when verbs are used with forms of *be*.

Inflectional morphemes represent relationships between different parts of a sentence. For example, -*s* expresses the relationship between the verb and the third-person singular subject; -*ed* expresses the relationship between the time the utterance is spoken (e.g., now) and the time of the event (past). If you say "John danced," the -*ed* affix places the activity before the utterance time. Inflectional morphology is closely connected to the syntax and semantics of the sentence.

English also has other inflectional endings, such as the plural suffix, which is attached to certain singular nouns, as in *boy/boys* and *cat/cats*. In contrast to Old and Middle English, which were more richly inflected languages, as we discuss in chapter 8, Modern English has only eight bound inflectional affixes:

English Inflectional Morphemes		Examples
-s	third-person singular present	She wait-s at home.
-ed	past tense	She wait-ed at home.
-ing	progressive	She is eat-ing the donut.
-en	past participle	Mary has eat-en the donuts.
-s	plural	She ate the donut-s.
-'s	possessive	Disa's hair is short.
-er	comparative	Disa has short-er hair than Karin.
-est	superlative	Disa has the short-est hair.

Inflectional morphemes in English follow the derivational morphemes in a word. Thus, to the derivationally complex word *commit* + *ment* one can add a plural ending to form *commit* + *ment* + *s*, but the order of affixes may not be reversed to derive the impossible *commit* + *s* + *ment* = **commitsment*.

Yet another distinction between inflectional and derivational morphemes is that inflectional morphemes are **productive**: they apply freely to nearly every appropriate base (except "irregular" forms such as *feet*, not **foots*). Most nouns take an -*s* inflectional suffix to form a plural, but only some nouns take the derivational suffix -*ize* to form a verb: *idolize*, but not **picturize*.

Compared to many languages of the world, English has relatively little inflectional morphology. Some languages are highly inflected. In Swahili, which is widely spoken in eastern Africa, verbs can be inflected with multiple morphemes, as in *kimeanguka* (ki + me + anguka), meaning 'it has fallen.' Here the verb root *anguka* meaning 'fall' has two inflectional prefixes: *ki*- meaning 'it' and *me* meaning 'completed action.'

Even the more familiar European languages have many more inflectional endings than English. In the Romance languages (languages descended from Latin), the verb has different inflectional endings depending on the subject of the sentence. The verb is inflected to agree in person and number with the subject, as illustrated by the Italian verb *parlare* meaning 'to speak':

Io parl**o**	'I speak'	Noi parl**iamo**	'We speak'
Tu parl**i**	'You (singular) speak'	Voi parl**ate**	'You (plural) speak'
Lui/Lei parl**a**	'He/she speaks'	Loro parl**ano**	'They speak'

Russian has a system of inflectional suffixes for nouns that indicates the nouns grammatical relation—whether a subject, object, possessor, and so on—something English does with word order. For example, in English, the sentence

Maxim defends Victor means something different from *Victor defends Maxim.* The order of the words is critical. But in Russian, all of the following sentences mean 'Maxim defends Victor' (the *č* is pronounced like the *ch* in cheese; the *š* like the *sh* in shoe; the *j* like the *y* in yet):

Maksim zašiščajt Viktora.
Maksim Viktora zašiščajet.
Viktora Maksim zašiščajet.
Viktora zašiščajet Maksim.

The inflectional suffix *-a* added to the name *Viktor* to derive *Viktora* shows that Victor, not Maxim, is defended. The suffix designates the object of the verb, irrespective of word order.

The grammatical relation of a noun in a sentence is called the **case** of the noun. When case is marked by inflectional morphemes, the process is referred to as **case morphology**. Russian has a rich case morphology, whereas English case morphology is limited to the one possessive *-'s* and to its system of pronouns. Many of the grammatical relations that Russian expresses with its case morphology are expressed in English with prepositions.

Among the world's languages is a richness and variety of inflectional processes. Earlier we saw how German uses circumfixes to inflect a verb stem to produce a past particle: *lieb* to **geliebt,** similar to the *-ed* ending of English. Arabic infixes vowels for inflectional purposes: *kitáab* 'book' but *kútub* 'books.' Samoan (see exercise 10) uses a process of **reduplication**—inflecting a word through the repetition of part or all of the word: *savali* 'he travels,' but *savavali* 'they travel.' Malay does the same with whole words: *orang* 'person,' but *orang orang* 'people.' Languages such as Finnish have an extraordinarily complex case morphology, whereas Mandarin Chinese lacks case morphology entirely.

Inflection achieves a variety of purposes. In English verbs are inflected with *-s* to show third-person singular agreement. Languages like Finnish and Japanese have a dazzling array of inflectional processes for conveying everything from 'temporary state of being' (Finnish nouns) to 'strong negative intention' (Japanese verbs). English spoken 1,000 years ago had considerably more inflectional morphology than Modern English, as we shall discuss in chapter 8.

In distinguishing inflectional from derivational morphemes in Modern English we may summarize in the table below and the Figure (2.1) that follows it:

Inflectional	Derivational
Grammatical function	Lexical function
No word class change	May cause word class change
Small or no meaning change	Some meaning change
Often required by rules of grammar	Never required by rules of grammar
Follow derivational morphemes in a word	Precede inflectional morphemes in a word
Productive	Some productive, many nonproductive

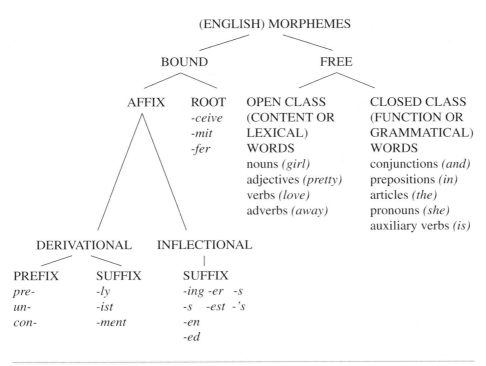

FIGURE 2.1 | Classification of English morphemes.

The Hierarchical Structure of Words

We saw earlier that morphemes are added in a fixed order. This order reflects the *hierarchical structure* of the word. A word is not a simple sequence of morphemes. It has an internal structure. For example, the word *unsystematic* is composed of three morphemes: *un-*, *system*, and *-atic*. The root is *system*, a noun, to which we add the suffix *-atic*, resulting in an adjective, *systematic*. To this adjective, we add the prefix *un-*, forming a new adjective, *unsystematic*.

In order to represent the hierarchical organization of words (and sentences), linguists use **tree diagrams**. The tree diagram for *unsystematic* is as follows:

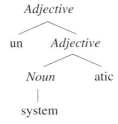

This tree represents the application of two morphological rules:

1. Noun + atic   →   Adjective
2. un + Adjective   →   Adjective

Rule 1 attaches the derivational suffix *-atic* to the root noun, forming an adjective. Rule 2 takes the adjective formed by rule 1 and attaches the derivational prefix *un-*. The diagram shows that the entire word—*unsystematic*—is an adjective that is composed of an adjective—*systematic*—plus *un*. The adjective is itself composed of a noun—*system*—plus the suffix *-atic*.

Hierarchical structure is an essential property of human language. Words (and sentences) have component parts, which relate to each other in specific, rule-governed ways. Although at first glance it may seem that, aside from order, the morphemes *un-* and *-atic* each relate to the root *system* in the same way, this is not the case. The root *system* is "closer" to *-atic* than it is to *un-*, and *un-* is actually connected to the adjective *systematic*, and not directly to *system*. Indeed, **unsystem* is not a word.

Further morphological rules can be applied to the given structure. For example, English has a derivational suffix *-al*, as in *egotistical, fantastical*, and *astronomical*. In these cases, *-al* is added to an adjective—*egotistic, fantastic, astronomic*—to form a new adjective. The rule for *-al* is as follows:

3. Adjective + al   →   Adjective

Another affix is *-ly*, which is added to adjectives—*happy, lazy, hopeful*—to form adverbs *happily, lazily, hopefully*. Following is the rule for *-ly*:

4. Adjective + ly   →   Adverb

Applying these two rules to the derived form *unsystematic*, we get the following tree for *unsystematically*:

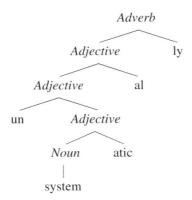

This is a rather complex word. Despite its complexity, it is well-formed because it follows the morphological rules of the language. On the other hand, a very simple word can be ungrammatical. Suppose in the above example we first added *un-* to the root *system*. That would have resulted in the nonword **unsystem*.

Unsystem is not a possible word because the rule of English that allows *un-* to be added to nouns is restricted to very few cases, and those always nouns that already have a suffix such as *un + employment, un + acceptance* or *un + feasability*. The large soft-drink company whose ad campaign promoted the *Uncola* successfully flouted this linguistic rule to capture people's attention. Part of our linguistic competence includes the ability to recognize possible versus impossible words, like **unsystem* and **Uncola*. Possible words are those that conform to the rules; impossible words are those that do not.

Tree diagrams make explicit the way speakers represent the internal structure of the morphologically complex words in their language. In speaking and writing, we appear to string morphemes together sequentially as in *un + system + atic*. However, our mental representation of words is hierarchical as well as linear, and this is shown by tree diagrams.

Inflectional morphemes are equally well represented. The following tree shows that the inflectional agreement morpheme *-s* follows the derivational morphemes *-ize* and *re-* in *refinalizes*:

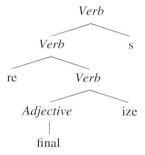

The tree also shows that *re-* applies to *finalize*, which is correct as **refinal* is not a word, and that the inflectional morpheme follows the derivational morpheme.

The hierarchical organization of words is even more clearly shown by structurally ambiguous words, words that have more than one meaning by virtue of having more than one structure. Consider the word *unlockable*. Imagine you are inside a room and you want some privacy. You would be unhappy to find the door is *unlockable*—'not able to be locked.' Now imagine you are inside a locked room trying to get out. You would be very relieved to find that the door is *unlockable*—'able to be unlocked.' These two meanings correspond to two different structures, as follows:

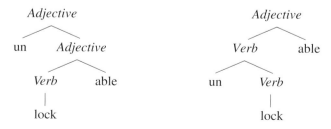

In the first structure the verb *lock* combines with the suffix *-able* to form an adjective *lockable* ('able to be locked'). Then the prefix *un-*, meaning 'not,' combines with the derived adjective to form a new adjective *unlockable* ('not able to be locked'). In the second case, the prefix *un-* combines with the verb *lock* to form a derived verb *unlock*. Then the derived verb combines with the suffix *-able* to form *unlockable*, 'able to be unlocked.'

An entire class of words in English follows this pattern: *unbuttonable*, *unzippable*, and *unlatchable*, among others. The ambiguity arises because the prefix *un-* can combine with an adjective, as illustrated in rule 2, or it can combine with a verb, as in *undo*, *unstaple*, *unearth*, and *unloosen*.

If words were only strings of morphemes without any internal organization, we could not explain the ambiguity of words like *unlockable*. These words also illustrate another key point, which is that structure is important to determining meaning. The same three morphemes occur in both versions of *unlockable*, yet there are two distinct meanings. The different meanings arise because of the different structures.

Rule Productivity

BABY BLUES © 2011 BABY BLUES PARTNERSHIP. KING FEATURES SYNDICATE

"Curiouser and curiouser!" cried Alice (she was so much surprised, that for the moment she quite forgot how to speak good English).

LEWIS CARROLL, *Alice's Adventures in Wonderland*, 1865

We have noted that some morphological processes, inflection in particular, are productive, meaning that they can be used freely to form new words from the list of free and bound morphemes. Among derivational morphemes, the suffix *-able* can be conjoined with any verb to derive an adjective with the meaning of the verb and the meaning of *-able*, which is something like 'able to be' as in *accept + able, laugh + able, pass + able, change + able, breathe + able, adapt + able*, and so on. The productivity of this rule is illustrated by the fact that we find *-able* affixed to new verbs such as *downloadable* and *faxable*.

The prefix *un-* derives same-class words with an opposite meaning: *unafraid*, *unfit*, *un-American*, and so on. Additionally, *un-* can be added to derived adjectives that have been formed by morphological rules, resulting in perfectly acceptable words such as *un + believe + able* or *un + pick + up + able*.

Yet *un-* is not fully productive. We find *happy* and *unhappy*, *cowardly* and *uncowardly*, but not *sad* and **unsad*, *brave* and **unbrave*, or *obvious* and **unobvious*. It appears that the "un-Rule" is most productive for adjectives that are derived from verbs, such as *unenlightened, unsimplified, uncharacterized, unauthorized, undistinguished*, and so on. It also appears that most acceptable *un-* words have polysyllabic bases, and while we have *unfit, uncool, unread*, and *unclean*, many of the unacceptable *un-* forms have monosyllabic stems such as **unbig, *ungreat, *unred, *unsad, *unsmall, *untall*.

The rule that adds an *-er* to verbs in English to produce a noun meaning 'one who does' is a nearly productive morphological rule, giving us *examiner, exam-taker, analyzer, lover, hunter*, and even *girlplayerwither*, as the cartoon illustrates, but fails full productivity owing to "unwords" like **chairer*, which is not 'one who chairs.'

The "other" *-er* suffix, the one that means 'more' as in *greedier*, also fails to be entirely productive as Alice's **curiouser* points out. The more syllables a word has, the less likely *-er* will work and we will need the word *more*, as in *more beautiful* (but not **beautifuler*) compared with the well-formed *nicer* or *prettier*.

Other derivational morphemes fall farther short of productivity. Consider:

sincerity	from	*sincere*
warmth	from	*warm*
moisten	from	*moist*

The suffix *-ity* is found in many other words in English, like *chastity, scarcity*, and *curiosity*; and *-th* occurs in *health, wealth, depth, width*, and *growth*. We find *-en* in *sadden, ripen, redden, weaken*, and *deepen*. Still, the phrase "**The tragicity* of Hamlet" sounds somewhat strange, as does "**I'm going to *heaten* the sauce.*" Someone may say *coolth*, but when "words" like *tragicity, heaten*, and *coolth* are used, it is usually either a slip of the tongue or an attempt at humor. Most adjectives will not accept any of these derivational suffixes.

Even less productive to the point of rareness are such derivational morphemes as the diminutive suffixes in the words *pig + let* and *sap + ling*.

In the morphologically complex words that we have seen so far, we can generally predict the meaning based on the meanings of the morphemes that make up the word. *Unhappy* means 'not happy' and *acceptable* means 'fit to be accepted.' However, one cannot always know the meaning of the words derived from free and derivational morphemes by knowing the morphemes themselves. The following *un-* forms have unpredictable meanings:

unloosen	'loosen, let loose'
unrip	'rip, undo by ripping'
undo	'reverse doing'
untread	'go back through in the same steps'
unearth	'dig up'
unfrock	'deprive (a cleric) of ecclesiastic rank'
unnerve	'fluster'

Morphologically complex words whose meanings are not predictable must be listed individually in our mental lexicons. However, the morphological rules must also be in the grammar, revealing the relation between words and providing the means for forming new words.

Exceptions and Suppletions

The exception gives Authority to the Rule

GIOVANNI TORRIANO, *A Common Place of Italian Proverbs*, 1666

The morphological rule that forms plural nouns from singular nouns does not apply to words like *child, man, foot,* and *mouse*. These words are exceptions to the rule. Similarly, verbs like *go, sing, bring, run,* and *know* are exceptions to the inflectional rule for producing past-tense verbs in English.

When children are learning English, they first learn the regular rules, which they apply to all forms. Thus, we often hear them say *mans* and *goed*. Later in the acquisition process, they specifically learn irregular plurals like *men* and *mice*, and irregular past tense forms like *came* and *went*. These children's errors are actually evidence that the regular rules exist. This is discussed more fully in chapter 9.

Irregular, or **suppletive**, forms are treated separately in the grammar. You cannot use the regular rules to add affixes to words that are exceptions like *child/children*, but must replace the uninflected form with another word. For regular words only the singular form need be specifically stored in the lexicon because we can use the inflectional rules to form plurals. But this can't be so with suppletive exceptions, and *children, mice,* and *feet* must be learned separately. The same is true for suppletive past tense forms and comparative forms. There are regular rules—suffixes *-ed* and *-er*—to handle most cases such as *walked* and *taller*, but words like *went* and *worse* need to be learned individually as meaning 'goed' and 'badder.'

When a new word enters the language, the regular inflectional rules generally apply. The plural of *geek*, when it was a new word in English, was *geeks*, not **geeken*, although we are advised that some geeks wanted the plural of *fax* to be **faxen*, like *oxen*, when *fax* entered the language as a shortened form of *facsimile*. Never fear: its plural is *faxes*. The exception to this may be a word "borrowed" from a foreign language. For example, the plural of Latin *datum* has always been *data*, never *datums*, though nowadays *data*, the one-time plural, is treated by many as a singular word like *information*.

The past tense of the verb *hit*, as in the sentence *Yesterday you hit the ball*, and the plural of the noun *sheep* as in *The sheep are in the meadow*, show that some morphemes have no phonological shape at all. We know that *hit* in the above sentence is *hit + past* because of the time adverb *yesterday*, and we know that *sheep* is the phonetic form of *sheep + plural* because of the plural verb form *are*.

When a verb is derived from a noun, even if it is pronounced the same as an irregular verb, the regular rules apply to it. Thus *ring*, when used in the sense of encircle, is derived from the noun *ring*, and as a verb it is regular. We say *the police ringed the bank with armed men*, not **rang the bank with armed men*. In the jargon of baseball one says that the hitter *flied out* (hit a lofty ball that was caught), rather than **flew out*, because the verb came from the compound noun *fly ball*.

Indeed, when a noun is used in a compound in which its meaning is lost, such as *flatfoot*, meaning 'cop,' its plural follows the regular rule, so one says *two flatfoots* to refer to a pair of cops slangily, not **two flatfeet*. It's as if the noun is saying: "If you don't get your meaning from me, you don't get my special plural form."

Making compounds plural, however, is not always simply adding *-s* as in *girlfriends* or *sheepdogs*. For many speakers the plural of *mother-in-law* is *mothers-in-law*, whereas the possessive form is *mother-in-law's*; the plural of *court-martial* is *courts-martial* and the plural of *attorney general* is *attorneys general* in a legal setting, but for most of the rest of us it is *attorney generals*. If the rightmost word of a compound takes an irregular form, however, the entire compound generally follows suit, so the plural of *footman* is *footmen*, not **footmans* or **feetman* or **feetmen*.

Lexical Gaps

United Feature Syndicate

The vast majority of letter (sound) sequences that could be words of English—*clunt, spleek, flig*—are not. Similar comments apply to morphological derivations like *disobvious* or *inobvious*. "Words" that conform to the rules of word formation but are not truly part of the vocabulary are called **accidental gaps** or **lexical gaps**. Accidental gaps are well-formed but non-existing words.

The actual words in a language constitute a mere subset of the possible words. There are always gaps in the lexicon—words not present but that could be added. Some of the gaps are due to the fact that a permissible sound sequence has no meaning attached to it (like *blick*, or *slarm*, or *krobe*). The sequence of sounds must be in keeping with the constraints of the language, however; **bnick* is not a "gap" because no word in English can begin with *bn*. We will discuss such constraints in chapter 6.

Other gaps result when possible combinations of morphemes never come into use. Speakers can distinguish between impossible words such as **unsystem* and **needlessity* and possible but nonexisting words such as *magnificenter* or *disobvious* (cf. *distrustful*). The latter are blocked, as noted earlier, owing to the presence of *more magnificent* and *nonobvious*. The ability to make this distinction is further evidence that the morphological component of our mental grammar consists of not just a lexicon—a list of existing words—but also of rules that enable us to create and understand new words, and to recognize possible and impossible words.

Other Morphological Processes

The various kinds of affixation that we have discussed are by far the most common morphological processes among the world's languages. But, as we continue to emphasize in this book, the human language capacity is enormously creative, and that creativity extends to ways other than affixation in which words may be altered and created.

Back-Formations

[A girl] was delighted by her discovery that *eats* and *cats* were really *eat* + *-s* and *cat* + *-s*. She used her new suffix snipper to derive *mik* (mix), *upstair, downstair, clo* (clothes), *len* (lens), *brefek* (from *brefeks*, her word for breakfast), *trappy* (trapeze), even *Santa Claw*.

STEVEN PINKER, *Words and Rules: The Ingredients of Language*, 1999

Misconception can sometimes be creative, and nothing in this world both misconceives and creates like a child, as we shall see in chapter 9. A new word may enter the language because of an incorrect morphological analysis. For example, *peddle* was derived from *peddler* on the mistaken assumption that the *-er* was the agentive suffix. Such words are called **back-formations**. The verbs *hawk, stoke, swindle, burgle* and *edit* all came into the language as back-formations—of *hawker, stoker, swindler, burglar* and *editor*. *Pea* was derived from a singular word, *pease*, by speakers who thought *pease* was a plural.

Some word creation comes from deliberately miscast back-formations. The word *bikini* comes from the Bikini atoll of the Marshall Islands. Because the first syllable *bi-* is a morpheme meaning 'two' in words like *bicycle*, some clever person called a topless bathing suit a *monokini* and a tank top with a bikini bottom a *tankini*. Historically, a number of new words have entered the English lexicon in a similar way, some of the most recent being the *appletini, chocotini, mintini* and *God-knows-what-else-tini* to be found as flavor additives to the traditional martini libation. Based on analogy with such pairs as *act/action, exempt/exemption,* and *revise/revision,* new words *resurrect, preempt,* and *televise* were formed from the existing words *resurrection, preemption,* and *television.*

Language purists sometimes rail against back-formations and cite *enthuse* and *liaise* (from *enthusiasm* and *liaison*) as examples of language corruption. However, language is not corrupt; it is adaptable and changeable. Don't be surprised to discover in your lifetime that *shevelled* and *chalant* have infiltrated the English language (from *disheveled* and *nonchalant*) to mean 'tidy' and 'concerned,' and if it happens do not cry "havoc" and let slip the dogs of prescriptivism; all will be well.

Compounds

[T]he Houyhnhnms have no Word in their Language to express any thing that is evil, except what they borrow from the Deformities or ill Qualities of the Yahoos. Thus they denote the Folly of a Servant, an Omission of a Child, a Stone that cuts their feet, a Continuance of foul or unseasonable Weather, and the like, by adding to each the Epithet of Yahoo. For instance, Hnhm Yahoo, Whnaholm Yahoo, Ynlhmnawihlma Yahoo, and an ill contrived House, Ynholmhnmrohlnw Yahoo.

JONATHAN SWIFT, *Gulliver's Travels*, 1726

Two or more words may be joined to form new, compound words. English is very flexible in the kinds of combinations permitted, as the following table of compounds shows.

	Adjective	Noun	Verb
Adjective	bittersweet	poorhouse	whitewash
Noun	headstrong	homework	spoonfeed
Verb	feel-good	pickpocket	sleepwalk

Some compounds that have been introduced fairly recently into English are *Facebook, linkedIn, android apps, m-commerce,* and *crowdsourcing* (the practice of obtaining information from a large group of people who contribute online).

When the two words are in the same grammatical category, the compound will also be in this category: noun + noun = noun, as in *girlfriend, fighter-bomber, paper clip, elevator-operator, landlord, mailman;* adjective + adjective = adjective, as in *icy-cold, red-hot, worldly wise.* In English, the rightmost word in a compound is the **head** of the compound. The head is the part of a word or phrase that determines its broad meaning and grammatical category. Thus, when the two words fall into different categories, the class of the second or final word determines the grammatical category of the compound: noun + adjective = adjective, as in *headstrong;* verb + noun = noun, as in *pickpocket.* On the other hand, compounds formed with a preposition are in the category of the nonprepositional part of the compound, such as (to) *overtake* or (the) *sundown.* This is further evidence that prepositions form a closed-class category that does not readily admit new members.

Although two-word compounds are the most common in English, it would be difficult to state an upper limit: Consider *three-time loser, four-dimensional space-time, sergeant-at-arms, mother-of-pearl*, *man about town, master of ceremonies*, and *daughter-in-law*. Dr. Seuss uses the rules of compounding when he explains "when tweetle beetles battle with paddles in a puddle, they call it a tweetle beetle puddle paddle battle."[3]

Spelling does not tell us what sequence of words constitutes a compound; whether a compound is spelled with a space between the two words, with a hyphen, or with no separation at all depends on the idiosyncrasies of the particular compound, as shown, for example, in *blackbird, six-pack*, and *smoke screen*.

Like derived words, compounds have internal structure. This is clear from the ambiguity of a compound like *top + hat + rack*, which can mean 'a rack for top hats' corresponding to the structure in tree diagram (1), or 'the highest hat rack,' corresponding to the structure in (2).

Meaning of Compounds

FAMILY CIRCUS © 2009 BIL KEANE, INC. KING FEATURES SYNDICATE

The meaning of a compound is not always the sum of the meanings of its parts; a *blackboard* may be green or white. Not everyone who wears a red coat is a

---

[3]From FOX IN SOCKS by Dr. Seuss, Trademark™ & copyright© by Dr. Seuss Enterprises, L.P., 1965, renewed 1993. Used by permission of Random House Children's Books, a division of Random House, Inc., International Creative Management, and HarperCollins Publishers, Ltd., UK.

Redcoat (slang for British soldier during the American Revolutionary War). The difference between the sentences "She has a red coat in her closet" and "She has a Redcoat in her closet" would have been highly significant in America in 1776.

Other compounds reveal other meaning relations between the parts, which are not entirely consistent because many compounds are idiomatic (idioms are discussed in chapter 4). A *boathouse* is a house for boats, but a *cathouse* is not a house for cats. (It is slang for a house of prostitution or whorehouse.) A *jumping bean* is a bean that jumps, a *falling star* is a star that (appears to) fall, and a *magnifying glass* is a glass that magnifies; but a *looking glass* is not a glass that looks, nor is an *eating apple* an apple that eats, and *laughing gas* does not laugh. *Peanut oil* and *olive oil* are oils made from something, but what about *baby oil*? And is this a contradiction: "horse meat is dog meat"? Not at all, since the first is meat *from* horses and the other is meat *for* dogs.

In the examples so far, the meaning of each compound includes at least to some extent the meanings of the individual parts. However, many compounds nowadays do not seem to relate to the meanings of the individual parts at all. A *jack-in-a-box* is a tropical tree, and a *turncoat* is a traitor. A *highbrow* does not necessarily have a high brow, nor does a *bigwig* have a big wig, nor does an *egghead* have an egg-shaped head.

Like certain words with the prefix *un-*, the meaning of many compounds must be learned as if they were individual whole words. Some of the meanings may be figured out, but not all. If you had never heard the word *hunchback*, it might be possible to infer the meaning; but if you had never heard the word *flat-foot*, it is doubtful you would know it means 'detective' or 'policeman,' even though the origin of the word, once you know the meaning, can be figured out.

The pronunciation of English compounds differs from the way we pronounce the sequence of two words that are not compounded. In an actual compound, the first word is usually stressed (pronounced somewhat louder and higher in pitch), and in a noncompound phrase the second word is stressed. Thus we stress *Red* in *Redcoat* but *coat* in *red coat*. (Stress, pitch, and other similar features are discussed in chapters 5 and 6.)

Universality of Compounding

Other languages have rules for conjoining words to form compounds, as seen by French *cure-dent*, 'toothpick'; German *Panzerkraftwagen*, 'armored car'; Russian *cetyrexetaznyi*, 'four-storied'; and Spanish *tocadiscos*, 'record player.' In the Native American language Tohono O'odham, the word meaning 'thing' is *haʔichu*, and it combines with *doakam*, 'living creatures,' to form the compound *haʔichu doakam*, 'animal life.'

In Twi, by combining the word meaning 'son' or 'child,' *ɔba*, with the word meaning 'chief,' *ɔhene*, one derives the compound *ɔheneba*, meaning 'prince.' By adding the word 'house,' *ofi*, to *ɔhene*, the word meaning 'palace,' *ahemfi*, is derived. The other changes that occur in the Twi compounds are due to phonological and morphological rules in the language.

In Thai, the word 'cat' is *mɛɛw*, the word for 'watch' (in the sense of 'to watch over') is *fâw*, and the word for 'house' is *bâan*. The word for 'watch cat' (like a watchdog) is the compound *mɛɛwfâwbâan*—literally, 'catwatchhouse.'

Compounding is a common and frequent process for enlarging the vocabulary of all languages.

"Pullet Surprises"

Our knowledge of the morphemes and morphological rules of our language is often revealed by the "errors" we make. We may guess the meaning of a word we do not know. Sometimes we guess wrong, but our wrong guesses are nevertheless "intelligent."

Amsel Greene collected errors made by her students in vocabulary-building classes and published them in a book called *Pullet Surprises*.[4] The title is taken from a sentence written by one of her high school students: "In 1957 Eugene O'Neill won a Pullet Surprise." What is most interesting about these errors is how much they reveal about the students' knowledge of English morphology. The creativity of these students is illustrated in the following examples:

Word	Student's Definition
deciduous	'able to make up one's mind'
longevity	'being very tall'
fortuitous	'well protected'
gubernatorial	'to do with peanuts'
bibliography	'holy geography'
adamant	'pertaining to original sin'
diatribe	'food for the whole clan'
polyglot	'more than one glot'
gullible	'to do with sea birds'
homogeneous	'devoted to home life'

The student who used the word *indefatigable* in the sentence

She tried many reducing diets, but remained indefatigable.

clearly shows morphological knowledge: *in* meaning 'not' as in *ineffective*; *de* meaning 'off' as in *decapitate*; 'fat' as in *fat*; *able* as in *able*; and combined meaning, 'not able to take the fat off.' Our contribution to Greene's collection is *metronome*: 'a city-dwelling diminutive troll; and *oxymoron*: 'a really stupid cow.'

Sign Language Morphology

Sign languages are rich in morphology. They have root and affix morphemes, free and bound morphemes, lexical content and grammatical morphemes, derivational and inflectional morphemes, and morphological rules for their combination to form morphologically complex signs. The affixation is accomplished by preceding or following a particular gesture with another "affixing" gesture.

---

[4]Greene, A. 1969. *Pullet surprises.* Glenview, IL: Scott, Foresman.

The suffix meaning 'negation,' roughly analogous to *un-* or *non-* or *dis-*, is accomplished as a rapid turning over of the hand(s) following the end of the root sign that is being negated. For example, 'want' is signed with open palms facing upward; 'don't want' follows that gesture with a turning of the palms to face downward. This 'reversal of orientation' suffix may be applied, with necessary adjustments, to many root signs.

In sign language many morphological processes are not linear. Rather, the sign stem occurs nested within various movements and locations in signing space so that the gestures are simultaneous, an impossibility with spoken languages.

Inflection of sign roots also occurs in ASL and all other sign languages, which characteristically modify the movement of the hands and the spatial contours of the area near the body in which the signs are articulated. For example, movement away from the signer's body toward the "listener" might inflect a verb as in "I see you," whereas movement away from the listener and toward the body would inflect the verb as in "you see me."

Morphological Analysis: Identifying Morphemes

Case study 1

As we have seen in this chapter, speakers of a language know the internal structure of words because they know the morphemes of their language and the rules for their combination. This is unconscious knowledge of course and it takes a trained linguist to make this knowledge explicit as part of a descriptive grammar of the language. The task is challenging enough when the language you are analyzing is your own, but linguists who speak one language may nevertheless analyze languages for which they are not native speakers.

Suppose you were a linguist from the planet Zorx who wanted to analyze English. How would you discover the morphemes of the language? How would you determine whether a word had one, two, or more morphemes, and what they were?

The first thing to do would be to ask native speakers how they say various words. (It would help to have a Zorxese-English interpreter along; otherwise, copious gesturing is in order.) Assume you are talented in miming and manage to collect the following forms:

Adjective	Meaning
ugly	'very unattractive'
uglier	'more ugly'
ugliest	'most ugly'
pretty	'nice looking'
prettier	'more nice looking'
prettiest	'most nice looking'
tall	'large in height'
taller	'more tall'
tallest	'most tall'

To determine what the morphemes are in such a list, the first thing a field linguist would do is to see whether some forms mean the same thing in different words, that is, to look for *recurring* forms. We find them: *ugly* occurs in *ugly, uglier,* and *ugliest,* all of which include the meaning 'very unattractive.' We also find that -*er* occurs in *prettier* and *taller,* adding the meaning 'more' to the adjectives to which it is attached. Similarly, -*est* adds the meaning 'most.' Furthermore by having our Zorxese-English interpreter pose additional questions to our native English-speaking consultant we find that -*er* and -*est* do not occur in isolation with the meanings of 'more' and 'most.' We can therefore conclude that the following morphemes occur in English:

ugly	root morpheme
pretty	root morpheme
tall	root morpheme
-er	bound morpheme 'comparative'
-est	bound morpheme 'superlative'

As we proceed we find other words that end with -*er* (e.g., *singer, lover, bomber, writer, teacher*) in which the -*er* ending does not mean 'comparative' but, when attached to a verb, changes it to 'a noun who "verbs,"' (e.g., *sings, loves, bombs, writes, teaches*). So we conclude that this is a different morpheme, even though it is pronounced the same as the comparative. We go on and find words like *number, somber, butter, member,* and many others in which the -*er* has no separate meaning at all—a *somber* is not 'one who sombs' and a *member* does not *memb*—and therefore these words must be monomorphemic.

Case study 2

Once you have practiced on the morphology of English, you might want to go on to describe another language. Paku was invented by the linguist Victoria Fromkin for a 1970s TV series called *Land of the Lost,* made into a major motion picture of the same name starring Will Farrell in 2009. This was the language used by the monkey people called Pakuni. Suppose you found yourself in this strange land and attempted to find out what the morphemes of Paku were. Again, you would collect your data from a native Paku speaker and proceed as the Zorxian did with English. Consider the following data from Paku:

me	'I'	meni	'we'
ye	'you (singular)'	yeni	'you (plural)'
we	'he'	weni	'they (masculine)'
wa	'she'	wani	'they (feminine)'
abuma	'girl'	abumani	'girls'
adusa	'boy'	adusani	'boys'
abu	'child'	abuni	'children'
Paku	'one Paku'	Pakuni	'more than one Paku'

By examining these words you find that the plural forms end in -*ni* and the singular forms do not. You therefore conclude that -*ni* is a separate morpheme meaning 'plural' that is attached as a suffix to a noun.

Case study 3

Here is a more challenging example, but the principles are the same. Look for repetitions and near repetitions of the same word parts, taking your cues from the meanings given. These are words from Michoacan Aztec, an indigenous language of Mexico:

nokali	'my house'	mopelo	'your dog'
nokalimes	'my houses'	mopelomes	'your dogs'
mokali	'your house'	ikwahmili	'his cornfield'
ikali	'his house'	nokwahmili	'my cornfield'
nopelo	'my dog'	mokwahmili	'your cornfield'

We see there are three base meanings: *house, dog,* and *cornfield.* Starting with *house* we look for commonalities in all the forms that refer to 'house.' They all contain *kali* so that makes a good first guess. (We might, and you might, have reasonably guessed *kal,* but eventually we wouldn't know what to do with the *i* at the end of *nokali* and *mokali.*) With *kali* as 'house' we may infer that *no* is a prefix meaning 'my,' and that is supported by *nopelo* meaning 'my dog.' This being the case, we guess that *pelo* is 'dog,' and see where that leads us. If *pelo* is 'dog' and *mopelo* is 'your dog,' then *mo* is probably the prefix for 'your.' Now that we think that the possessive pronouns are prefixes, we can look at *ikali* and deduce that *i* means 'his.' If we're right about the prefixes then we can separate out the word for 'cornfield' as *kwahmili,* and at this point we're a-rockin' and a-rollin'. The only morpheme unaccounted for is 'plural.' We have two instances of plurality, *nokalimes* and *mopelomes,* but since we know *no, kali, mo,* and *pelo,* it is straightforward to identify the plural morpheme as the suffix *mes.*

The end results of our analysis are:

kali	'house'
pelo	'dog'
kwahmili	'cornfield'
no-	'my'
mo-	'your'
i-	'his'
-mes	'plural'

Case study 4

Here is a final example of morphological analysis complicated by some changes in spelling (pronunciation), a bit like the way we spell the indefinite article "a" as either *a* before a consonant or *an* before a vowel in English.

Often the data you are given (or record in the field) are a hodge-podge, like these examples from a Slavic language:

gledati	'to watch'	nazivaju	'they call'
diram	'I touch'	sviranje	'playing (noun)'
nazivanje	'calling (noun)'	gladujem	'I starve'
dirati	'to touch'	kupuju	'they buy'
kupovanje	'buying (noun)'	stanovati	'to live'
sviraju	'they play'	kupujem	'I buy'

gledam	'I watch'	diranje	'touching (noun)'
stanovanje	'living (noun)'	stanujem	'I live'
diraju	'they touch'	gladovanje	'starving (noun)'
nazivati	'to call'	stanuju	'they live'
kupovati	'to buy'	gledaju	'they watch'
gladuju	'they starve'	svirati	'to play'
gladovati	'to starve'	sviram	'I play'
gledanje	'watching (noun)'	nazivam	'I call'

The first step is often merely to rearrange the data, grouping commonalities. Here we see that after (possibly considerable) perusal, the data involve seven stems, which we group by meaning. We also note that there are exactly four forms for each stem (infinitive, I (1st person singular), they (3rd person plural) and the noun form or gerund) and we fold that into the reorganization. We even alphabetize to emphasize the orderliness. Thus rearranged the data appear less daunting:

	touch	**starve**	**watch**	**buy**	**call**	**live**	**play**
Infinitive	dirati	gladovati	gledati	kupovati	nazivati	stanovati	svirati
1st, Sing.	diram	gladujem	gledam	kupujem	nazivam	stanujem	sviram
3rd, Plur.	diraju	gladuju	gledaju	kupuju	nazivaju	stanuju	sviraju
Noun	diranje	gladovanje	gledanje	kupovanje	nazivanje	stanovanje	sviranje

Now the patterns become more evident. We hypothesize that in the first column *dir-* is a stem meaning 'touch' and that the suffix *-ati* forms the infinitive; the suffix *-am* is the first-person singular; the suffix *-aju* is the third-person plural; and finally that the suffix *-anje* forms a noun, similar to the suffix *-ing* in English. We need to test our guess and the second column belies our hypothesis, but undaunted we push on and we see that the columns for 'watch,' 'call,' and 'play' work exactly like the column for 'touch,' with stems *gled-*, *naziv-*, and *svir-*.

But columns 'starve,' 'buy,' and 'live' are not cooperating. They follow the pattern for the infinitive (first row) and noun formation (fourth row), and give us stems *gladov-*, *kupov-*, and *stanov-* but something is awry in the second and third row for these three verbs. Instead of *-am* meaning 'I' it appears to be *-em*. (Yes, it could be *-ujem* or even *-jem*, but we stay with the form that's nearest to *-am*.) So the suffix meaning 'I' has two forms, *am/em*, again analogous to the English *a/an* alternation.

But horrors, something is going haywire with the stems in just these three cases and now our effort to rearrange the data pays off. We see fairly quickly that the misbehaving cases are all verbs ending in *ov*. And if we stick with our decision that *-am/-em* means 'I,' then we can hypothesize that the stem alternates pronunciation in certain cases when it ends in *ov*, kind of like English *democrat/democracy*. If we accept this we are forced into the decision that the third-person plural morpheme also has an alternate form, namely *u*, so its two forms are *-aju/-u*.

We may sum up our analysis as follows:

Stems *dir-*, *gled-*, *naziv-*, *svir-* take suffixes *-ati*, *-am*, *-aju*, *-anje*. The verbs ending in *ov* have stems *gladov-*, *kupov-*, *stanov-* when expressed as infinitives with *-ati*, and noun-forms with *-anje*; and stems *gladuj-*, *kupuj-*, *stanuj-* when expressed as 'I' with *-em* or as 'they' with *-u*.

Finally, if we discover in our field work, for example, that *razarati* means 'to destroy' then we immediately know that 'I destroy' is *razaram*, 'they destroy' is *razaraju*, and 'destruction' is *razaranje*. Or if we're told that *darujem* means 'I gift' then we deduce that the noun 'gift' is *darovanje*, the infinitive 'to gift' is *darovati*, and 'they gift' is *daruju*.

In chapter 6 we'll see *why* the "same" morpheme may be spelled or pronounced differently in different contexts, and that the variation, like most grammatical processes, is rule-governed. By following the analytical principles discussed in the preceding four case studies you should be able to solve the morphological puzzles that appear in the exercises.

Summary

Knowing a language means knowing the **morphemes** of that language, which are the elemental units that constitute words. *Moralizers* is an English word composed of four morphemes: *moral + ize + er + s*. When you know a word or morpheme, you know both its **form** (sound or gesture) and its **meaning**; these are inseparable parts of the **linguistic sign**. The relationship between form and meaning is **arbitrary**. There is no inherent connection between them (i.e., the words and morphemes of any language must be learned).

Morphemes may be free or bound. **Free morphemes** stand alone like *girl* or *the*, and they come in two types: **open class**, containing the content words of the language, and **closed class**, containing function words such as *the* or *of*. **Bound morphemes** may be **affixes** or bound roots such as *-ceive*. Affixes may be **prefixes**, **suffixes**, **circumfixes**, or **infixes**. Affixes may be derivational or inflectional. **Derivational affixes** derive new words; **inflectional affixes**, such as the plural affix *-s*, make grammatical changes to words. Complex words contain a **root** around which **stems** are built by affixation. Rules of morphology determine what kind of affixation produces actual words such as *un + system + atic*, and what kind produces nonwords such as **un + system*.

Words have hierarchical structure evidenced by ambiguous words such as *unlockable*, which may be *un + lockable* 'unable to be locked' or *unlock + able* 'able to be unlocked.'

Some morphological rules are **productive**, meaning they apply freely to the appropriate stem; for example, *re-* applies freely to verbal stems to give words like *redo*, *rewash*, and *repaint*. Other rules are more constrained, forming words like *young + ster* but not **smart + ster*. Inflectional morphology is extremely productive: the plural *-s* applies freely even to nonsense words. **Suppletive forms** escape inflectional morphology, so instead of **mans* we have *men*; instead of **bringed* we have *brought*.

There are many ways for new words to be created other than affixation. **Compounds** are formed by uniting two or more root words in a single word, such as *homework*. The **head** of the compound (the rightmost word) bears the basic meaning, so *homework* means a kind of work done at home, but often the meaning of compounds is not easily predictable and must be learned as individual lexical items, such as *laughing gas*. **Back-formations** are words created by misinterpreting an affix look-alike such as *-er* as an actual affix, so, for example, the verb *peddle* was formed under the mistaken assumption that peddler was *peddle + -er*.

The grammars of sign languages also include a morphological component consisting of a root, derivational and inflectional sign morphemes, and the rules for their combination.

Morphological analysis is the process of identifying form-meaning units in a language, taking into account small differences in pronunciation, so that prefixes *in-* and *im-* are seen to be variants of the "same" prefix in English (cf. *intolerable*, *impeccable*) just as *democrat* and *democrac* are stem variants of the same morpheme, which shows up in *democratic* with its "t" and in *democracy* with its "c."

References for Further Reading

Anderson, S. R. 1992. *A-morphous morphology.* Cambridge, UK: Cambridge University Press.

Aronoff, M. 1976. *Word formation in generative grammar.* Cambridge, MA: MIT Press.

——————, and Fudeman, K. 2005. *What is morphology?* Malden: MA: Blackwell Publishing.

Bauer, L. 2003. *Introducing linguistic morphology, 2nd ed.* Washington, DC: Georgetown University Press.

Haspelmath, M. and Sims, A. 2010. *Understanding morphology, 2nd ed.* USA: Oxford University Press.

Jensen, J. T. 1990. *Morphology: Word structure in generative grammar.* Amsterdam/ Philadelphia: John Benjamins Publishing.

Katamba, F. 2004. *Morphology: its relation to semantics and the lexicon.* Oxford, UK: Taylor and Francis.

Matthews, P. H. 1991. *Morphology: An introduction to the theory of word structure, 2nd ed.* Cambridge, UK: Cambridge University Press.

Pinker, S. 2000. *Words and rules: the ingredients of language.* New York: Harper Collins.

Stockwell, R., and D. Minkova. 2001. *English words: History and structure.* New York: Cambridge University Press.

Winchester, S. 2003. *The meaning of everything (The story of the Oxford English Dictionary).* Oxford, UK: Oxford University Press.

——————. 1999. *The professor and the madman.* New York: HarperCollins.

Exercises

1. Here is how to estimate the number of words in your mental lexicon. Consult any standard dictionary. (Note that Internet dictionaries may not work for this exercise.)
   a. Count the number of entries on a typical page. They are usually boldfaced.
   b. Multiply the number of words per page by the number of pages in the dictionary.
   c. Pick four pages in the dictionary at random, say, pages 50, 75, 125, and 303. Count the number of words on these pages.
   d. How many of these words do you know?
   e. What percentage of the words on the four pages do you know?
   f. Multiply the words in the dictionary by the percentage you arrived at in (e). You know approximately that many English words.

2. Divide the following words by placing a + between their morphemes. (Some of the words may be monomorphemic and therefore indivisible.)

Example: replaces = re + place + s

a. retroactive
b. befriended
c. televise
d. margin
e. endearment
f. psychology
g. unpalatable
h. holiday
i. grandmother
j. morphemic
k. mistreatment
l. deactivation
m. saltpeter

n. airsickness
o. bureaucrat
p. democrat
q. aristocrat
r. plutocrat
s. democracy
t. democratic
u. democratically
v. democratization
w. democratize
x. democratizer
y. democratizing
z. democratized

3. Match each expression under A with the one statement under B that characterizes it.

A

a. noisy crow
b. scarecrow
c. the crow
d. crowlike
e. crows

B

(1) compound noun
(2) root morpheme plus derivational prefix
(3) phrase consisting of adjective plus noun
(4) root morpheme plus inflectional affix
(5) root morpheme plus derivational suffix
(6) grammatical morpheme followed by lexical morpheme

4. Write the one proper description from the list under B for the italicized part of each word in A.

A

a. terroriz*ed*
b. un*civil*ized
c. terror*ize*
d. *luke*warm
e. *im*possible

B

(1) free root
(2) bound root
(3) inflectional suffix
(4) derivational suffix
(5) inflectional prefix
(6) derivational prefix
(7) inflectional infix
(8) derivational infix

5. Part One:

Consider the following nouns in Zulu and proceed to look for the recurring forms.

umfazi	'married woman'	abafazi	'married women'
umfani	'boy'	abafani	'boys'
umzali	'parent'	abazali	'parents'
umfundisi	'teacher'	abafundisi	'teachers'
umbazi	'carver'	ababazi	'carvers'
umlimi	'farmer'	abalimi	'farmers'
umdlali	'player'	abadlali	'players'
umfundi	'reader'	abafundi	'readers'

    a. What is the morpheme meaning 'singular' in Zulu?

    b. What is the morpheme meaning 'plural' in Zulu?

    c. List the Zulu stems to which the singular and plural morphemes are attached, and give their meanings.

Part Two:

The following Zulu verbs are derived from noun stems by adding a verbal suffix.

fundisa	'to teach'	funda	'to read'
lima	'to cultivate'	baza	'to carve'

    d. Compare these words to the words in section A that are related in meaning, for example, *umfundisi* 'teacher,' *abafundisi* 'teachers,' *fundisa* 'to teach.' What is the derivational suffix that specifies the category verb?

    e. What is the nominal suffix (i.e., the suffix that forms nouns)?

    f. State the morphological noun formation rule in Zulu.

    g. What is the stem morpheme meaning 'read'?

    h. What is the stem morpheme meaning 'carve'?

6. Sweden has given the world the rock group ABBA, the automobile Volvo, and the great film director Ingmar Bergman. The Swedish language offers us a noun morphology that you can analyze with the knowledge gained reading this chapter. Consider these Swedish noun forms:

en lampa	'a lamp'	en bil	'a car'
en stol	'a chair'	en soffa	'a sofa'
en matta	'a carpet'	en tratt	'a funnel'
lampor	'lamps'	bilar	'cars'
stolar	'chairs'	soffor	'sofas'
mattor	'carpets'	trattar	'funnels'
lampan	'the lamp'	bilen	'the car'
stolen	'the chair'	soffan	'the sofa'
mattan	'the carpet'	tratten	'the funnel'
lamporna	'the lamps'	bilarna	'the cars'
stolarna	'the chairs'	sofforna	'the sofas'
mattorna	'the carpets'	trattarna	'the funnels'

    a. What is the Swedish word for the indefinite article *a* (or *an*)?

    b. What are the two forms of the plural morpheme in these data? How can you tell which plural form applies?

    c. What are the two forms of the morpheme that make a singular word definite, that is, correspond to the English article *the*? How can you tell which form applies?

    d. What is the morpheme that makes a plural word definite?

    e. In what order do the various suffixes occur when there is more than one?

    f. If *en flicka* is 'a girl,' what are the forms for 'girls,' 'the girl,' and 'the girls'?

    g. If *bussarna* is 'the buses,' what are the forms for 'buses' and 'the bus'?

7. Here are some nouns from the Philippine language Cebuano.

sibwano	'a Cebuano'
ilokano	'an Ilocano'
tagalog	'a Tagalog person'
inglis	'an Englishman'
bisaja	'a Visayan'
binisaja	'the Visayan language'
ininglis	'the English language'
tinagalog	'the Tagalog language'
inilokano	'the Ilocano language'
sinibwano	'the Cebuano language'

    a. What is the exact rule for deriving language names from ethnic group names?
    b. What type of affixation is represented here?
    c. If *suwid* meant 'a Swede' and *italo* meant 'an Italian,' what would be the words for the Swedish language and the Italian language?
    d. If *finuranso* meant 'the French language' and *inunagari* meant 'the Hungarian language,' what would be the words for a Frenchman and a Hungarian?

8. The following infinitive and past participle verb forms are found in Dutch.

Root	Infinitive	Past Participle	
wandel	wandelen	gewandeld	'walk'
duw	duwen	geduwd	'push'
stofzuig	stofzuigen	gestofzuigd	'vacuum-clean'

    With reference to the morphological processes of prefixing, suffixing, infixing, and circumfixing discussed in this chapter and the specific morphemes involved:

    a. State the morphological rule for forming an infinitive in Dutch.
    b. State the morphological rule for forming the Dutch past participle form.

9. Below are some sentences in Swahili:

mtoto	amefika	'The child has arrived.'
mtoto	anafika	'The child is arriving.'
mtoto	atafika	'The child will arrive.'
watoto	wamefika	'The children have arrived.'
watoto	wanafika	'The children are arriving.'
watoto	watafika	'The children will arrive.'
mtu	amelala	'The person has slept.'
mtu	analala	'The person is sleeping.'
mtu	atalala	'The person will sleep.'
watu	wamelala	'The persons have slept.'
watu	wanalala	'The persons are sleeping.'
watu	watalala	'The persons will sleep.'
kisu	kimeanguka	'The knife has fallen.'
kisu	kinaanguka	'The knife is falling.'
kisu	kitaanguka	'The knife will fall.'

visu	vimeanguka	'The knives have fallen.'
visu	vinaanguka	'The knives are falling.'
visu	vitaanguka	'The knives will fall.'
kikapu	kimeanguka	'The basket has fallen.'
kikapu	kinaanguka	'The basket is falling.'
kikapu	kitaanguka	'The basket will fall.'
vikapu	vimeanguka	'The baskets have fallen.'
vikapu	vinaanguka	'The baskets are falling.'
vikapu	vitaanguka	'The baskets will fall.'

One of the characteristic features of Swahili (and Bantu languages in general) is the existence of noun classes. Specific singular and plural prefixes occur with the nouns in each class. These prefixes are also used for purposes of agreement between the subject noun and the verb. In the sentences given, two of these classes are included (there are many more in the language).

a. Identify all the morphemes you can detect, and give their meanings.

> *Example:*   -toto 'child'
>   *m-* prefix attached to singular nouns of Class I
>   *a-* prefix attached to verbs when the subject is a singular noun of Class I

Be sure to look for the other noun and verb markers, including tense markers.
b. How is the verb constructed? That is, what kinds of morphemes are strung together and in what order?
c. How would you say in Swahili:
    (1) "The child is falling."
    (2) "The baskets have arrived."
    (3) "The person will fall."

10. Part One

We mentioned the morphological process of reduplication—the formation of new words through the repetition of part or all of a word—which occurs in many languages. The following examples from Samoan illustrate this kind of morphological rule.

manao	'he wishes'	mananao	'they wish'
matua	'he is old'	matutua	'they are old'
malosi	'he is strong'	malolosi	'they are strong'
punou	'he bends'	punonou	'they bend'
atamaki	'he is wise'	atamamaki	'they are wise'
savali	'he travels'	pepese	'they sing'
laga	'he weaves'		

a. What is the Samoan for:
    (1) 'they weave'
    (2) 'they travel'
    (3) 'he sings'

b. Formulate a general statement (a morphological rule) that states how to form the plural verb form from the singular verb form.

Part Two

Consider these data from M'nong (spoken in Vietnam) with some simplifications for this exercise: (The ? is a sound called a glottal stop.)

dang	'hard'	da dang	'a little hard'
kloh	'clean'	klo kloh	'a little clean'
ndreh	'green'	ndre ndreh	'light green'
guh	'red'	go? guh	'reddish'
duh	'hot'	do? duh	'luke warm'
kat	'cold'	ka kat	'chilly'

1. What kind of morphological process do you observe to achieve the semantic effect of weakening an adjective?
2. If *thong* meant 'light,' how would M'nong express 'kind of light'?
3. If *khul* meant 'evasive,' how would M'nong express 'a little shifty'?
4. If *lo? luq* meant 'a little paunchy,' how would M'nong express 'fat'?
5. If *kho khot* meant 'a little crazy,' how would M'nong express 'crazy'?
6. Formulate a general statement (a morphological rule) of how M'nong speakers weaken certain kinds of adjectives. To be completely accurate and account for the given data, you will have to take spelling (pronunciation) into account.

11. Following are listed some words followed by incorrect (humorous?) definitions:

Word	Definition
stalemate	'husband or wife no longer interested'
effusive	'able to be merged'
tenet	'a group of ten singers'
dermatology	'a study of derms'
ingenious	'not very smart'
finesse	'a female fish'
amphibious	'able to lie on both sea and land'
deceptionist	'secretary who covers up for his boss'
mathemagician	'Bernie Madoff's accountant'
sexcedrin	'medicine for mate who says, "sorry, I have a headache"'
testostoroni	'hormonal supplement administered as pasta'
aesthetominophen	'medicine to make you look beautiful'
histalavista	'say goodbye to those allergies'
aquapella	'singing in the shower'
melancholy	'dog that guards the cantaloupe patch'
plutocrat	'a dog that rules'

Give some possible reasons for the source of these silly "definitions." Illustrate your answers by reference to other words or morphemes. For example, *stalemate* comes from *stale* meaning 'having lost freshness' and *mate* meaning 'marriage partner.' When mates appear to have lost their freshness, they are no longer as desirable as they once were.

12. **a.** Draw tree diagrams for the following words: *construal, disappearances, irreplaceability, misconceive, indecipherable, redarken.*

    b. Draw two tree diagrams for *undarkenable* to reveal its two meanings: 'able to be less dark' and 'unable to be made dark.'

13. There are many asymmetries in English in which a root morpheme combined with a prefix constitutes a word, but without the prefix is a nonword. A number of these are given in this chapter.

    a. Following is a list of such nonword roots. Add a prefix to each root to form an existing English word.

Words	Nonwords
_____	*descript
_____	*cognito
_____	*beknownst
_____	*peccable
_____	*promptu
_____	*plussed
_____	*domitable
_____	*nomer
_____	*crat

    b. There are many more such multimorphemic words for which the root morphemes do not constitute words by themselves. Can you list five more?

14. We have seen that the meaning of compounds is often not revealed by the meanings of their composite words. Crossword puzzles and riddles often make use of this by providing the meaning of two parts of a compound and asking for the resulting word. For example, infielder = diminutive/cease. Read this as asking for a word that means 'infielder' by combining a word that means 'diminutive' with a word that means 'cease.' The answer is *shortstop*. See if you can figure out the following:

    a. sci-fi TV series = headliner/journey
    b. campaign = farm building/tempest
    c. at-home wear = tub of water/court attire
    d. kind of pen = formal dance/sharp end
    e. conservative = correct/part of an airplane

15. Consider the following dialogue between parent and schoolchild:

    PARENT: When will you be done with your eight-page book report, dear?
    CHILD: I haven't started it yet.

PARENT: But it's due tomorrow, you should have begun weeks ago. Why do you always wait until the last minute?

CHILD: I have more confidence in myself than you do.

PARENT: Say what?

CHILD: I mean, how long could it possibly take to read an eight-page book?

The humor is based on the ambiguity of the compound *eight-page book report*. Draw two trees similar to those in the text for *top hat rack* to reveal the ambiguity.

16. One of the characteristics of Italian is that articles and adjectives have inflectional endings that mark agreement in gender (and number) with the nouns they modify. Based on this information, answer the questions that follow the list of Italian phrases.

un uomo	'a man'
un uomo robusto	'a robust man'
un uomo robustissimo	'a very robust man'
una donna robusta	'a robust woman'
un vino rosso	'a red wine'
una faccia	'a face'
un vento secco	'a dry wind'

   a. What is the root morpheme meaning 'robust'?
   b. What is the morpheme meaning 'very'?
   c. What is the Italian for:
      (1) 'a robust wine'
      (2) 'a very red face'
      (3) 'a very dry wine'

17. Following is a list of words from Turkish. In Turkish, articles and morphemes indicating location are affixed to the noun.

deniz	'an ocean'	evden	'from a house'
denize	'to an ocean'	evimden	'from my house'
denizin	'of an ocean'	denizimde	'in my ocean'
eve	'to a house'	elde	'in a hand'

   a. What is the Turkish morpheme meaning 'to'?
   b. What kind of affixes in Turkish correspond to English prepositions (e.g., prefixes, suffixes, infixes, free morphemes)?
   c. What would the Turkish word for 'from an ocean' be?
   d. How many morphemes are there in the Turkish word *denizimde*?

18. The following are some verb forms in Chickasaw, a member of the Muskogean family of languages spoken in south-central Oklahoma.[5] Chickasaw is an endangered language (see chapter 8). Currently, there are only about 100 speakers of Chickasaw, most of whom are over 70 years old.

---

[5]The Chickasaw examples are provided by Pamela Munro.

sachaaha	'I am tall'
chaaha	'he/she is tall'
chichaaha	'you are tall'
hoochaaha	'they are tall'
satikahbi	'I am tired'
chitikahbitok	'you were tired'
chichchokwa	'you are cold'
hopobatok	'he was hungry'
hoohopobatok	'they were hungry'
sahopoba	'I am hungry'

    a. What is the root morpheme for the following verbs?
        (1) 'to be tall'   **(2)** 'to be hungry'
    b. What is the morpheme meaning:
        (1) past tense
        (2) 'I'
        (3) 'you'
        (4) 'he/she'
    c. If the Chickasaw root for 'to be old' is *sipokni*, how would you say:
        (1) 'You are old'
        (2) 'He was old'
        (3) 'They are old'

19. The language Little-End Egglish, whose source is revealed in exercise 14, chapter 8, exhibits the following data:

kul	'omelet'	zkulego	'my omelet'	zkulivo	'your omelet'
vet	'yolk (of egg)'	zvetego	'my yolk'	zvetivo	'your yolk'
rok	'egg'	zrokego	'my egg'	zrokivo	'your egg'
ver	'egg shell'	zverego	'my egg shell'	zverivo	'your egg shell'
gup	'soufflé'	zgupego	'my soufflé'	zgupivo	'your soufflé'

    a. Isolate the morphemes that indicate possession, first-person singular, and second person (we don't know whether singular, plural, or both). Indicate whether the affixes are prefixes or suffixes.
    b. Given that *vel* means egg white, how would a Little-End Egglisher say 'my egg white'?
    c. Given that *zpeivo* means 'your hard-boiled egg,' what is the word meaning 'hard-boiled egg'?
    d. If you knew that *zvetgogo* meant 'our egg yolk,' what would be likely to be the morpheme meaning 'our'?
    e. If you knew that *borokego* meant 'for my egg,' what would be likely to be the morpheme bearing the benefactive meaning 'for'?

20. Here are some data from the indigenous language Zoque spoken in Mexico. (The **ʔ** is a glottal stop.) Hint: Rearrange the data as in the Slavic example at the end of the chapter.

sohsu	'he/it cooked'	cicpa	'he/it tears
witpa	'he/it walks'	kenu	'he/it looked'
sikpa	'he/it laughs'	cihcu	'he/it tore'
ka?u	'he/it died'	sospa	'he/it cooks'
kenpa	'he/it looks'	wihtu	'he/it walked'
sihku	'he/it laughed'	ka?pa	'he/it dies'

a. What is the past tense suffix?
b. What is the present tense suffix?
c. This language has some verb stems that assume two forms. For each verb (or stem pair), give its meaning and form(s).
d. What morphological environment determines which of the two forms occurs, when there are two?

21. **Research project**: Consider what are called "interfixes" such as -o- in English *jack-o-lantern*. They are said to be meaningless morphemes attached to two morphemes at once. What can you learn about that notion? Where do you think the -o- comes from? Are there languages other than English that have interfixes?

3

Syntax: The Sentence Patterns of Language

To grammar even kings bow.

J. B. MOLIÈRE, *Les Femmes Savantes, II*, 1672

It is an astonishing fact that any speaker of any human language can produce and understand an infinite number of sentences. We can show this quite easily through examples such as the following:

The kindhearted boy had many girlfriends.
The kindhearted, intelligent boy had many girlfriends.
The kindhearted, intelligent, handsome boy had many girlfriends.

.
.
.

John found a book in the library.
John found a book in the library in the stacks.
John found a book in the library in the stacks on the fourth floor.

.
.
.

The cat chased the mouse.
The cat chased the mouse that ate the cheese.
The cat chased the mouse that ate the cheese that came from the cow.
The cat chased the mouse that ate the cheese that came from the cow that grazed in the field.

In each case the speaker could continue creating sentences by adding another adjective, prepositional phrase, or relative clause. In principle, this could go on forever. All languages have mechanisms of this sort that make the number of sentences limitless. Given this fact, the sentences of a language cannot be stored in a dictionary format in our heads. Rather, sentences are composed of discrete units that are combined by rules. This system of rules explains how speakers can store infinite knowledge in a finite space—our brains.

The part of grammar that represents a speaker's knowledge of sentences and their structures is called **syntax**. The aim of this chapter is to show you what syntactic structures look like and to familiarize you with some of the rules that determine them. Most of the examples will be from the syntax of English, but the principles that account for syntactic structures are universal.

What the Syntax Rules Do

"Then you should say what you mean," the March Hare went on.

"I do," Alice hastily replied, "at least—I mean what I say—that's the same thing, you know."

"Not the same thing a bit!" said the Hatter. "You might just as well say that 'I see what I eat' is the same thing as 'I eat what I see'!"

"You might just as well say," added the March Hare, "that 'I like what I get' is the same thing as 'I get what I like'!"

"You might just as well say," added the Dormouse . . . "that 'I breathe when I sleep' is the same thing as 'I sleep when I breathe'!"

"It is the same thing with you," said the Hatter.

LEWIS CARROLL, *Alice's Adventures in Wonderland*, 1865

The **rules of syntax** combine words into phrases and phrases into sentences. Among other things, the rules determine the correct word order for a language. For example, English is a Subject–Verb–Object (SVO) language. The English sentence in (1) is grammatical because the words occur in the right order; the sentence in (2) is ungrammatical because the word order is incorrect for English. (Recall that the asterisk or star preceding a sentence is the linguistic convention for indicating that the sentence is ungrammatical or ill-formed according to the rules of the grammar.)

1. The President nominated a new Supreme Court justice.
2. *President the Supreme new justice Court a nominated.

A second important role of the syntax is to describe the relationship between the meaning of a particular group of words and the arrangement of those words. For example, Alice's companions show us that the word order of a sentence contributes crucially to its meaning. The sentences in (3) and (4) contain the same words, but the meanings are quite different, as the Mad Hatter points out.

3. I mean what I say.
4. I say what I mean.

The rules of the syntax also specify the **grammatical relations** of a sentence, such as **subject** and **direct object**. In other words, they provide information about who is doing what to whom. This information is crucial to understanding the meaning of a sentence. For example, the grammatical relations in (5) and (6) are reversed, so the otherwise identical sentences have very different meanings.

5. Your dog chased my cat.
6. My cat chased your dog.

In (7) we see that the phrase *ran up the hill* behaves differently from the phrase *ran up the bill*, even though the two phrases are superficially quite similar. For the expression *ran up the hill*, the rules of the syntax allow the word orders in (7a) and (7c), but not (7b). In *ran up the bill*, in contrast, the rules allow the order in (7d) and (7e), but not (7f).

7. (a) Jack and Jill ran up the hill.
   (b) *Jack and Jill ran the hill up.
   (c) Up the hill ran Jack and Jill.
   (d) Jack and Jill ran up the bill.
   (e) Jack and Jill ran the bill up.
   (f) *Up the bill ran Jack and Jill.

The pattern shown in (7) illustrates that sentences are not simply strings of words with no further organization. If they were, there would be no reason to expect *ran up the hill* to pattern differently from *ran up the bill*. These phrases act differently because they have different syntactic structures associated with them. In *ran up the hill*, the words *up the hill* form a unit, as follows:

He ran [up the hill].

The whole unit can be moved to the beginning of the sentence, as in (7c), but we cannot rearrange its subparts, as shown in (7b). On the other hand, in *ran up the bill*, the words *up the bill* do not form a natural unit, so they cannot be moved together, and (7f) is ungrammatical.

Our syntactic knowledge crucially includes rules that tell us how words form groups in a sentence, or how they are *hierarchically* arranged with respect to one another. Consider the following sentence:

The captain ordered all old men and women off the sinking ship.

This phrase *old men and women* is ambiguous, referring to either old men and to women of any age or to old men and old women. The ambiguity arises because the words *old men and women* can be grouped in two ways. If the words are grouped as follows, *old* modifies only *men* and so the women can be of any age.

[old men] and [women]

When we group them like this, the adjective *old* modifies both *men* and *women*.

[old [men and women]]

The rules of syntax allow both of these groupings, which is why the expression is ambiguous. The following hierarchical diagrams, also called **tree diagrams**, illustrate the same point:

In the first structure *old* and *men* are under the same node and hence old modifies *men*. In the second structure *old* shares a node with the entire conjunction *men and women*, and so modifies both.

This is similar to what we find in morphology for ambiguous words such as *unlockable*, which have two structures, corresponding to two meanings, as discussed in chapter 2.

Many sentences exhibit such ambiguities, often leading to humorous results. Consider the following two sentences, which appeared in classified ads:

> For sale: an antique desk suitable for lady with thick legs and large drawers.
> We will oil your sewing machine and adjust tension in your home for $10.00.

In the first ad, the humorous reading comes from the grouping [desk] [for lady with thick legs and large drawers] as opposed to the intended [desk for lady] [with thick legs and large drawers], where the legs and drawers belong to the desk. The second case is similar.

Because these ambiguities are a result of different structures, they are instances of **structural ambiguity**.

Contrast these sentences with:

> This will make you smart.

The two interpretations of this sentence are due to the two meanings of *smart*—'clever' and 'burning sensation.' Such lexical or word-meaning ambiguities, as opposed to structural ambiguities, will be discussed in chapter 4.

Often a combination of differing structure and double word-meaning creates ambiguity (and humor) as in the cartoon:

Hilary B. Price. King Features Syndicate

Syntactic rules reveal the grammatical relations among the words of a sentence as well as their order and hierarchical organization. They also explain how the grouping of words relates to its meaning, such as when a sentence or phrase is ambiguous. In addition, the rules of syntax permit speakers to produce and understand a limitless number of sentences never produced or heard before—*the creative aspect of linguistic knowledge.* A major goal of linguistics is to show clearly and explicitly how syntactic rules account for this knowledge. A theory of grammar must provide a complete characterization of what speakers implicitly know about their language.

What Grammaticality Is Not Based On

Colorless green ideas sleep furiously. This is a very interesting sentence, because it shows that syntax can be separated from semantics—that form can be separated from meaning. The sentence doesn't seem to mean anything coherent, but it sounds like an English sentence.

HOWARD LASNIK, *The Human Language: Part One*, 1995

Importantly, a person's ability to make grammaticality judgments does not depend on having heard the sentence before. You may never have heard or read the sentence

Enormous crickets in pink socks danced at the prom.

but your syntactic knowledge tells you that it is grammatical. As we showed at the beginning of this chapter, people are able to understand, produce, and make judgments about an infinite range of sentences, most of which they have never heard before. This ability illustrates that our knowledge of language is creative—not creative in the sense that we are all accomplished poets, but creative in that none of us is limited to a fixed repertoire of expressions. Rather, we can exploit the resources of our language and grammar to produce and understand a limitless number of sentences embodying a limitless range of ideas and emotions.

We showed that the structure of a sentence contributes to its meaning. However, grammaticality and meaningfulness are not the same thing, as shown by the following sentences:

Colorless green ideas sleep furiously.
A verb crumpled the milk.

Although these sentences do not make much sense, they are syntactically well formed. They sound funny, but their funniness is different from what we find in the following strings of words:

*Furiously sleep ideas green colorless.
*Milk the crumpled verb a.

There are also sentences that we understand even though they are not well-formed according to the rules of the syntax. For example, most English speakers could interpret

*The boy quickly in the house the ball found.

although they know that the word order is incorrect. To be a sentence, words must conform to specific patterns determined by the syntactic rules of the language.

Some sentences are grammatical even though they are difficult to interpret because they include nonsense words, that is, words with no agreed-on meaning. This is illustrated by the following lines from the poem "Jabberwocky" by Lewis Carroll:

'Twas brillig, and the slithy toves
Did gyre and gimble in the wabe

These lines are grammatical in the linguistic sense that they obey the word order and other constraints of English. Such nonsense poetry is amusing precisely because the sentences comply with syntactic rules and sound like good English. Ungrammatical strings of nonsense words are not entertaining:

*Toves slithy the and brillig 'twas
wabe the in gimble and gyre did

Grammaticality also does not depend on the truth of sentences. If it did, lying would be easy to detect. Nor does it depend on whether real objects are being discussed or whether something is possible in the real world. Untrue sentences can be grammatical, sentences discussing unicorns can be grammatical, and sentences referring to pregnant fathers can be grammatical.

The syntactic rules that permit us to produce, understand, and make grammaticality judgments are unconscious rules. The grammar is a mental grammar, different from the prescriptive grammar rules that we are taught in school. We develop the mental rules of grammar long before we attend school, as we shall see in chapter 9.

Sentence Structure

I really do not know that anything has ever been more exciting than diagramming sentences.

GERTRUDE STEIN, "Poetry and Grammar," 1935

Suppose we wanted to write a template that described the structure of an English sentence, and more specifically, a template that gave the correct word order for English. We might come up with something like the following:

Det—N—V—Det—N

This template says that a determiner (e.g. an article like *the* or *a*) is followed by a noun, which is followed by a verb, and so on. It would describe English sentences such as the following:

The child found a puppy.
The professor wrote a book.
That runner won the race.

The implication of such a template would be that sentences are strings of words belonging to particular grammatical categories ("parts of speech") with no internal organization. We know, however, that such "flat" structures are incorrect. As noted earlier, sentences have hierarchical organization; that is, the words are grouped into natural units. The words in the sentence

The child found a puppy.

may be grouped into [the child] and [found a puppy], corresponding to the subject and predicate of the sentence. A further division gives [the child] and then [[found] [a puppy]], and finally the individual words: [[the] [child]] [[found] [[a] [puppy]]]. It's sometimes easier to see the parts and subparts of the sentence in a tree diagram, as we did earlier to illustrate ambiguity:

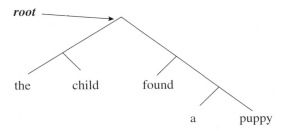

The "tree" is upside down with its "root" encompassing the entire sentence, *The child found a puppy*, and its "leaves" being the individual words *the, child, found, a,* and *puppy.* The tree conveys the same information as the nested square brackets. The hierarchical organization of the tree reflects the groupings and subgroupings of the words of the sentence.

The tree diagram shows, among other things, that the phrase *found a puppy* divides naturally into two branches, one for the verb *found* and the other for the direct object *a puppy.* A different division, say, *found a* and *puppy*, is unnatural.

Constituents and Constituency Tests

The natural groupings or parts of a sentence are called **constituents**. Various linguistic tests reveal the constituents of a sentence. The first test is the "stand alone" test. If a group of words can stand alone, for example, as an answer to a question, they form a constituent. So in response to the question "What did you find?" a speaker might answer *a puppy*, but not *found a. A puppy* can stand alone while *found a* cannot. We have a clear intuition that one of these is a meaningful unit and the other is just a list of words.

The second test is "replacement by a pronoun." Pronouns can substitute for natural groups. In answer to the question "Where did you find *a puppy*?" a speaker can say, "I found *him* in the park." Words such as *do* (which is not a pronoun per se) can also take the place of the entire predicate *found a puppy*, as in "John found a puppy and Bill *did* too." If a group of words can be replaced by a pronoun or a word like *do*, it forms a constituent.

A third test of constituency is the "move as a unit" test. If a group of words can be moved, they form a constituent. For example, if we compare the following sentences to the sentence "The child found a puppy," we see that certain elements have moved:

It was *a puppy* that *the child* found.
A puppy was found by *the child.*

In the first example, the constituent *a puppy* has moved from its position following *found*; in the second example, the positions of *a puppy* and *the child* have been changed. In all such rearrangements the constituents *a puppy* and *the child* remain intact. *Found a* does not remain intact, because it is not a constituent.

In the sentence "The child found a puppy," the natural groupings or constituents are the subject *the child*, the predicate *found a puppy*, and the direct object *a puppy.*

Some sentences have prepositional phrases in the predicate. Consider

The puppy played in the garden.

We can use our tests to show that *in the garden* is also a constituent, as follows:

Where did the puppy play? *In the garden* (stand alone)
The puppy played *there.* (replacement by a pronoun-like word)
In the garden is where the puppy played. (move as a unit)
It was *in the garden* that the puppy played. (move as a unit)

As before, our knowledge of the **constituent structure** of a sentence may be graphically represented by a tree diagram. The tree diagram for the sentence "The puppy played in the garden" is as follows:

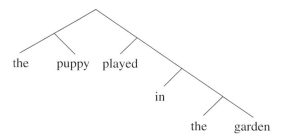

In addition to the syntactic tests just described, experimental evidence has shown that speakers do not mentally represent sentences as strings of words but rather in terms of constituents. In these experiments, subjects listen to sentences that have clicking noises inserted into them at random points. In some cases the click occurs at a constituent boundary, and in other sentences the click is inserted in the middle of a constituent. The subjects are then asked to report where the click occurred. There were two important results: (1) Subjects noticed the click and recalled its location best when it occurred at a major constituent boundary (e.g., between the subject and predicate); and (2) clicks that occurred inside the constituent were reported to have occurred between constituents. In other words, subjects displaced the clicks and put them at constituent boundaries. These results show that speakers perceive sentences in chunks corresponding to grammatical constituents.

Every sentence in a language is associated with one or more constituent structures. If a sentence has more than one constituent structure, it is ambiguous, and each tree will correspond to one of the possible meanings. For example, the sentence *I bought an antique desk suitable for a lady with thick legs and large drawers* has two phrase structure trees associated with it. In one structure the phrase [a lady with thick legs and large drawers] forms a constituent; it could stand alone in answer to the question "Who did you buy an antique desk for?" In its second meaning, the phrase *thick legs and large drawers* modifies the phrase [*desk for a lady*]; it could stand alone in answer to the question "What did the desk have?"

Syntactic Categories

"Very traditional. He's the noun. She's the adjective."

Each grouping in the tree diagrams of "The child found a puppy" is a member of a large family of similar expressions. For example, *the child* belongs to a family that includes *the police officer, your neighbor, this yellow cat, he, John,* and countless others. We can substitute any member of this family for the child without affecting the grammaticality of the sentence, although the meaning of course would change.

A police officer found a puppy.
Your neighbor found a puppy.
This yellow cat found a puppy.

A family of expressions that can substitute for one another without loss of grammaticality is called a **syntactic category**.

The child, a police officer, John, and so on belong to the syntactic category **noun phrase (NP)**, one of several syntactic categories in English and all languages. NPs may function as subjects or as objects in sentences. An NP often contains a *determiner* (like *a* or *the*) and a noun, but it may also consist of a proper name, a pronoun, a noun without a determiner, or even a clause or a sentence. Even though a proper noun like *John* and pronouns such as *he* and *him* are single words, they are technically NPs, because they pattern like NPs in being able to fill a subject or object or other NP slots.

> John found the puppy.
> He found the puppy.
> Boys love puppies.
> The puppy loved him.
> The puppy loved John.

NPs can be more complex, as illustrated by the sentence:

> The girl that Professor Snape loved married the man of her dreams.

The NP subject of this sentence is *the girl that Professor Snape loved*, and the NP object is *the man of her dreams*.

Syntactic categories are part of a speaker's knowledge of syntax. That is, speakers of English know that only items (a), (b), (e), (f), and (g) in the following list are NPs even if they have never heard the term *noun phrase* before.

1. **(a)** a bird
    (b) the red banjo
    (c) have a nice day
    (d) with a balloon
    (e) the woman who was laughing
    (f) it
    (g) John
    (h) went

You can test this claim by inserting each expression into three contexts: *What/who I heard was* _____, *Who found* _____? and _____ *was seen by everyone*. For example, **Who found <u>with a balloon</u>?* is ungrammatical, as is **<u>Went</u> was seen by everyone*, as opposed to *Who found <u>it</u>?* or *<u>John</u> was seen by everyone*. Only NPs fit into these contexts because only NPs can function as subjects and objects.

There are other syntactic categories. The expression *found a puppy* is a **verb phrase (VP)**. A verb phrase always contains a **verb (V)**, and it may contain other categories, such as a noun phrase or **prepositional phrase (PP)**, which is a preposition followed by an NP, such as *in the park*, *on the roof*, *with a balloon*. In (2) the VPs are those phrases that can complete the sentence "The child _____."

2. **(a)** saw a clown
    (b) a bird
    (c) slept
    (d) smart
    (e) ate the cake
    (f) found the cake in the cupboard
    (g) realized that the Earth was round

Inserting (a), (c), (e), (f), and (g) will produce grammatical sentences, whereas the insertion of (b) or (d) would result in an ungrammatical sentence. Thus, (a), (c), (e), (f), and (g) are verb phrases.

Lexical and Functional Categories

There are ten parts of speech, and they are all troublesome.

MARK TWAIN, "The Awful German Language," in *A Tramp Abroad*, 1880

Syntactic categories include both phrasal categories such as NP, VP, AP (adjective phrase), PP (prepositional phrase), and AdvP (adverbial phrase), as well as lexical categories such as noun (N), verb (V), preposition (P), adjective (A), and adverb (Adv). Each lexical category has a corresponding phrasal category. Following is a list of phrasal categories and lexical categories with some examples of each type:

Phrasal categories

Noun Phrase (NP)	*men, the man, the man with a telescope*
Verb Phrase (VP)	*sees, always sees, rarely sees the man, often sees the man with a telescope*
Adjective Phrase (AP)	*happy, very happy, very happy about winning*
Prepositional Phrase (PP)	*over, nearly over, nearly over the hill*
Adverbial Phrase (AdvP)	*brightly, more brightly, more brightly than the Sun*

Lexical categories

Noun (N)	*puppy, boy, man, soup, happiness, fork, kiss, pillow*
Verb (V)	*find, run, sleep, throw, realize, see, try, want, believe*
Preposition (P)	*up, down, across, into, from, by, with, over*
Adjective (A)	*red, big, happy, candid, hopeless, fair, idiotic, lucky*
Adverb (Adv)	*again, always, brightly, often, never, very, fairly*

Many of these categories may already be familiar to you. As mentioned earlier, some of them are traditionally referred to as *parts of speech*. Other categories may be less familiar, for example, the category **determiner (Det)**, which includes the articles *a* and *the*, as well as **demonstratives** such as *this, that, these,* and *those,* and "quantifiers" such as *each* and *every*.

Another less familiar category is T(ense), which includes the **modal** auxiliaries *may, might, can, could, must, shall, should, will,* and *would,* and abstract tense morphemes that we discuss below. T and Det are **functional categories,** so called because their members have grammatical functions rather than descriptive meanings. For example, determiners specify whether a noun is indefinite or definite (*a boy* versus *the boy*), or the proximity of the person or object to the context (*this boy* versus *that boy*). Tense provides the verb with a time frame, whether present (*John knows Mary*), or past (*John danced*). In English, T is expressed as a (sometimes silent) morpheme on the verb, except in the future tense, which is expressed with the modal *will*. Modals also express notions such as possibility (*John may dance*); necessity (*John must dance*); ability (*John can dance*); and so on. The modals belong to a larger class of verbal elements traditionally referred to as **auxiliaries** or helping verbs, which also include *have* and *be* in sentences such as *John is dancing* or *John has danced*.

Each lexical category typically has a particular kind of meaning associated with it. For example, verbs usually refer to actions, events, and states (*kick, marry, love*); adjectives to qualities or properties (*lucky, old*); common nouns to general entities (*dog, elephant, house*); and proper nouns to particular individuals (*Noam Chomsky*) or places (*Dodger Stadium*) or other things that people give names to, such as commercial products (*Coca-Cola, Viagra*).

But the relationship between grammatical categories and meaning is more complex than these few examples suggest. For example, some nouns refer to events (*marriage* and *destruction*) and others to states (*happiness, loneliness*). We can use abstract nouns such as *honor* and *beauty*, rather than adjectives, to refer to properties and qualities. In the sentence "Seeing is believing," *seeing* and *believing* are nouns but are not entities. Prepositions are usually used to express relationships between two entities involving a location (e.g., *the boy is in the room, the cat is under the bed*), but this is not always the case; the prepositions *of, by, about*, and *with* often have other than locational meanings.

Because of the difficulties involved in specifying the precise meaning of lexical categories, we do not usually define categories in terms of their meanings, but rather on the basis of where they occur in a sentence, what categories co-occur with them, and what their morphological characteristics are. For example, we define a noun as a word that can occur with a determiner (*the boy*) and that can (ordinarily) take a plural marker (*boys*); a verb as a word that can occur with an adverb (*run fast*) or modal (*may go, will dance*); an adjective as a word that can occur with a degree word (*very hungry*) or a morphological marker (*hungrier*), among other properties.

All languages have syntactic categories such as N, V, and NP. Speakers know the syntactic categories of their language even if they do not know the technical terms. Our knowledge of syntactic classes is revealed when we substitute equivalent phrases, as we just did in examples (1) and (2), and when we use the various syntactic tests that we have discussed.

Phrase Structure Trees

Who climbs the Grammar-Tree distinctly knows

Where Noun and Verb and Participle grows.

JOHN DRYDEN, "The Sixth Satyr of Juvenal," 1693

Now that you know something about constituent structure and grammatical categories, you are ready to learn how the phrases and sentences of a language are constructed. We will begin by illustrating trees for simple phrases and then proceed to more complex structures. The trees that we will build here are more detailed than those we saw in the previous sections, because the branches of the tree will have category labels identifying each constituent.

One of the striking things we observe when we consider the various phrasal categories discussed above is that they have a similar organization. Consider the following examples of each of the phrasal categories

NP: *the mother* of James Whistler
VP: *sing* an aria
AP: *wary* of snakes
PP: *over* the hill

As we noted in the previous section, the core of every phrase is a lexical category of its same syntactic type (italicized), which is its **head**; for example, the NP *the mother of James Whistler* is headed by the noun *mother*; the VP *sing an aria* is headed by the verb *sing*; the AP *wary of snakes* is headed by the adjective *wary*; the PP *over the hill* is headed by the preposition *over*. Loosely speaking, the entire phrase refers to whatever the head refers to. For example, the VP *sing an aria* refers to a "singing" event; the NP *the mother of James Whistler* to someone's mother.

A **complement** is defined as a phrasal category that may occur next to a head, and only there, and which elaborates on the meaning of the head. The complements are underlined: For example, the head N *mother* takes the PP complement *of James Whistler*; the head V *sing* takes the NP *an aria*; the head A(djective) *wary* takes the PP *of snakes*, and the P(reposition) *over* takes the NP *the hill* as complement.

In addition, a phrase may have an element preceding the head. These elements are called **specifiers**. For example, in the NP *the mother of James Whistler*, the determiner *the* is the specifier of the NP. In English, possessives may also be specifiers of NP, as in *Nellie's ball*. Similarly, in the PP *just over the hill*, *just* is the specifier. The specifier position may also be empty, as in the NP *dogs with bones* or the PP *over the hill*. Specifier is a purely structural notion. In English it is the first position in the phrase, if it is present at all, and a phrase may contain at most one specifier. APs and VPs also have a specifier position and their specifiers usually show up when the phrase is embedded in another sentence, as in:

a. Betty made [Jane wary of snakes].
b. I heard [Pavarotti sing an aria].
c. I saw [everyone at the stadium].

In (a) *Jane* is the specifier of the AP *wary of snakes*, in (b) *Pavarotti* is the specifier of the VP *sing an aria*, and in (c) *everyone* is the specifier of the PP *at the stadium*. We will have a bit more to say about this kind of embedded phrase later in the chapter.

These observations tell us that all of the phrasal categories, NP, VP, AP, and PP, have a similar 3-tiered structure, as follows:

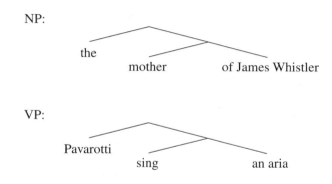

NP:

    the   mother   of James Whistler

VP:

    Pavarotti   sing   an aria

AP:

PP:

In each of the phrases the head and its complement are under the same **node** (a point in a tree where branches join), reflecting the fact that the complement has an important relationship with the meaning of the head. We refer to categories under the same node as **sisters**. Thus the complement is <u>defined</u> as the sister of the head, and the specifier is <u>defined</u> as the sister to the head + complement complex.

If we now label the branching points or nodes, the trees look like this:

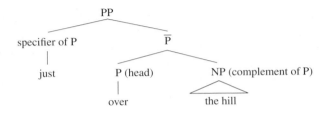

To capture the generalization that each phrasal category has the same internal structure, we substitute X in place of N, V, P, A and we get the following tree:

This 3-tiered structure, referred to as the **X-bar (X̄) schema**, is a template or blueprint that specifies how the phrases of a language are organized. The X-bar schema "stands for" the various phrasal categories given above (and others we will see later). The X-bar schema applies to all syntactic phrases.

The "bar" category is an intermediate level category necessary to account for certain syntactic phenomena that we'll see shortly. As noted above, the specifier of an NP may be absent or it may be a determiner (or a possessive). The complement, too, may be absent or may be a PP or even another phrasal category. The head N(oun) of the NP is obligatory, however, so a stripped-down NP composed solely of a noun actually has this structure:

The other phrasal categories follow suit. The specifier of VP may be absent, as may the complement; only the head is obligatory, so we may have structures as simple as:

The X-bar schema is hypothesized to be part of Universal Grammar. As such, all languages have phrases that consist of heads, specifiers, and complements that relate to each other as just described. However, the order of the head and complement may differ in different languages. In English, for example, we see that the head comes first, followed by the complement. In Japanese complements precede the head, as shown in the following examples:

Taro-ga	inu-o	mitsuketa.	
Taro-subject marker	dog-object marker	found	(Taro found a dog.)

Inu-ga	niwa-de	asonde	iru.	
dog-subject marker	garden-in	playing	is	(The dog is playing in the garden.)

In the first sentence, the direct object complement *inu-o*, 'dog,' precedes the head verb *mitsuketa*, 'found.' In the second, the NP complement *niwa*, 'garden,' precedes the head preposition *de*, 'in.' English is a VO language, meaning that the verb ordinarily precedes its object. Japanese is an OV language, and this difference is reflected in the head/complement word order. For Japanese the X-bar schema looks like this:

as opposed to English and VO languages in general with this $\overline{X}$:

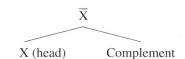

The X-bar schema captures a vast amount of syntactic knowledge in a concise way. If the hierarchical relationships that it expresses are universal (order aside), as many linguists believe, it reveals how children can quickly learn the abstract hierarchical structures associated with phrases in their language (see chapter 9). Given the X-bar schema, the Japanese child upon hearing *Taro-ga inu-o mitsuketa* (Taro dog finds) automatically knows not only that NP complements precede the verb in his language, but also that all other complements do so as well. For example, NPs precede their prepositional heads, as in *niwa-de* (garden in).

Let's now turn to the category S(entence). To keep matters simple—stepping away from the X-bar schema momentarily—we are going to let S have this structure:

This states that a sentence is a Noun Phrase (NP) followed by a Verb Phrase (VP). We are now able to provide a fully labeled tree diagram for entire sentences such as *The child found a puppy* by combining what we know of S, NP, and VP structures:

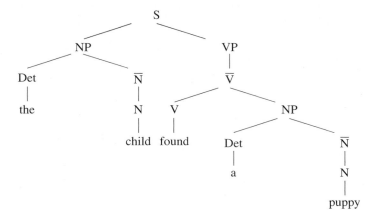

The tree diagram provides labels for each of the constituents of the sentence "The child found a puppy." These labels show that the entire sentence belongs to the syntactic category of S (because the S-node encompasses all the words). It also reveals that *the child* and *a puppy* belong to the category NP: that is, they are noun phrases, and that *found a puppy* belongs to the category VP or is a verb phrase, consisting of a verb and an NP. It also reveals the syntactic category of each of the words in the sentence.

In chapter 2 we discussed the fact that the syntactic category of each word is listed in our mental dictionaries. We now see how this information is used by the syntax of the language. Words appear in trees under labels that correspond to their syntactic category. Nouns are under N, determiners under Det, verbs under V, and so on. The larger syntactic categories, such as VP, consist of all the syntactic categories and words below that node in the tree. The VP in the tree above consists of syntactic category nodes V and NP and the words *found, a,* and *puppy*. Because *a puppy* can be traced up the tree to the node NP, this constituent is a noun phrase. Because *found* and *a puppy* can be traced up to the node VP, this constituent is a verb phrase.

A tree diagram with syntactic category information is called a **phrase structure tree** (PS trees, for short) or a **constituent structure tree**. The PS tree is a formal device that reflects the speaker's intuitions about the natural groupings of words in a sentence. It shows that a sentence is not simply a linear string of words but has a hierarchical structure with phrases nested in phrases.

PS trees represent three aspects of a speaker's syntactic knowledge:

1. The linear order of the words in the sentence
2. The identification of the syntactic categories of words and groups of words
3. The hierarchical organization of the syntactic categories as determined by the X-bar schema

Various relationships can be defined on PS trees. Every higher node is said to **dominate** all the categories that can be traced down the tree beneath it. S dominates every node; the NP under S dominates Det, $\bar{\text{N}}$, and N (but not, e.g., $\bar{\text{V}}$ or V), just as VP dominates $\bar{\text{V}}$ and the NP below it, but not the other nodes in the tree. A node is said to **immediately dominate** the categories one level below it. $\bar{\text{V}}$ immediately dominates V and NP, the categories of which it is composed, but nothing else. As noted earlier, categories that are immediately dominated by the same node are sisters. V and NP are sisters in the phrase structure tree of "The child found a puppy." PS trees are also useful for defining various grammatical relations in a precise way. For example, the **subject** of a sentence is the NP immediately dominated by S and the **direct object** is the NP immediately dominated by $\bar{\text{V}}$.

Selection

We noted that complements (and specifiers) are not always present in the phrasal structure. They are optional; only the head is obligatory. The parentheses included in the X-bar schema below indicate optionality:

Whether a head takes a complement or not depends on the properties of the head. For example, verbs select different kinds of complements: *find* is a transitive verb and requires an NP complement (direct object), as in *The boy found the ball*, but not **The boy found*, or **The boy found in the house*. Some verbs like *eat* are optionally transitive. *John ate* and *John ate a sandwich* are both grammatical. *Sleep* is an **intransitive verb**; it cannot take an NP complement:

Michael slept.
*Michael slept their baby.

Some verbs, such as *think*, may select both a PP and a sentence complement:

Let's think *about it.*
I think *a girl won the race.*

Other verbs, like *tell*, select an NP and a sentence:

I told *the boy a girl won the race.*

Yet other verbs like *feel* select either an AP or a sentence complement:

Paul felt *strong as an ox.*
He feels *he can win.*

Certain verbs, for example perception verbs such as *see* and *hear* and the causative verb *make* among others, select a particular kind of complement called a **small clause**. A small clause is an XP composed of an NP followed by a bar level category, for example:

as in the sentence:

I saw [John on the boat].

This sentence illustrates that the verb *see* selects a small clause PP complement. Similarly, the causative verb *make* selects an AP or VP small clause complement, as in:

The food made [John ill].
The wind made [the palm trees sway].

We see that small clause conforms perfectly to the X-bar schema, with the initial NP functioning as the specifier.

Categories besides verbs also select their complements. For example, the noun *belief* selects either a PP or a sentence, while the noun *sympathy* selects a PP, but not a sentence, as shown by the following examples:

the belief *in freedom of speech*
the belief *that freedom of speech is a basic right*
their sympathy *for the victims*
*their sympathy that the victims are so poor

Adjectives can also have complements. For example, the adjectives *tired* and *proud* select PPs:

tired *of stale sandwiches*
proud *of her children*

The information about the complement types selected by particular verbs and other lexical items is called **C-selection** or **subcategorization**, and is included in the lexical entries of the items in our mental lexicons. (C stands for "categorial.")

A verb also includes in its lexical entry a specification that requires certain semantic properties of its subjects and complements, just as it selects for syntactic categories. This kind of selection is called **S-selection**. (S stands for "semantic.") For example, the verb *murder* requires its subject and object to be animate, while the verb *quaff* requires its subject to be animate and its object liquid. Verbs such as *like*, *hate*, and so on select animate subjects. The following sentences violate S-selection and can only be used in a metaphorical sense. (We will use the symbol "!" to indicate a semantic anomaly.)

!Golf plays John.
!The beer drank the student.
!The tree liked the boy.

The famous sentence *Colorless green ideas sleep furiously*, discussed earlier in this chapter, is anomalous because (among other things) S-selection is violated (e.g., the verb *sleep* requires an animate subject). In chapter 4 we will discuss the semantic relationships between a verb and its subject and objects in far more detail.

The well-formedness of a phrase depends, then, on at least two factors: whether the phrase conforms to the structural constraints of the language as expressed in the X-bar schema, and whether it obeys the selectional requirements of the head—both syntactic (C-selection) and semantic (S-selection). The X-bar schema allows complements of any syntactic category (XP), but the choice of complement type for any particular phrase depends on the lexical properties of the head of that phrase.

Building Phrase Structure Trees

> Everyone who is master of the language he speaks . . . may form new . . . phrases, provided they coincide with the genius of the language.
>
> JOHANN DAVID MICHAELIS, *"Dissertation,"* 1739

The information represented in a PS tree and by the X-bar schema can also be conveyed by another formal device: **phrase structure (PS) rules**. Phrase structure rules instantiate the principles of the X-bar schema and can be used as a guide for building PS trees. A few of the PS rules needed to express the structures for S and for some of the phrases given above are:

1. S → NP VP
2. NP → Det $\bar{\text{N}}$
3. $\bar{\text{N}}$ → N
4. VP → $\bar{\text{V}}$
5. $\bar{\text{V}}$ → V NP

PS rules specify the well-formed structures of a particular language precisely and concisely. They make explicit a speaker's knowledge of the order of words and the grouping of words into syntactic categories. For example, in English an NP may contain a determiner (more generally, a specifier) followed by an $\bar{\text{N}}$ which itself may be a bare noun. This is represented by rules 2 and 3. To the left of the arrow is the dominating category, in this case NP, while the categories that it immediately dominates—that comprise it—appear on the right side, in this case Det and $\bar{\text{N}}$. The right side of the arrow also shows the linear order of these constituents.

The PS rules are general statements about a language and do not refer to any specific VP, V, or NP. In applying the rules to build trees certain conventions are followed. The S occurs at the top or "root" of the tree (remember that the tree is upside down). So first find the rule with S on the left side of the arrow (rule 1), and put the categories on the right side below the S, as shown here:

Continue by matching any syntactic category at the bottom of the partially constructed tree to a category on the left side of a rule, then expand the tree downward using the categories on the right side. For example, we may expand the tree by applying the NP rule to produce:

The categories at the bottom are Det, $\bar{N}$ and VP, and both $\bar{N}$ and VP occur to the left of an arrow. We may choose to expand either one; order doesn't matter. If we choose VP our work in progress looks like this:

Although not mentioned specifically in our five rules, certain verbs take a PP complement. According to the X-bar schema, then, the rule that we have just described can be written $\bar{V} \rightarrow V$ PP. Let's expand that along with $\bar{N}$ (applying rule 3) and complete lexical insertion for Det.

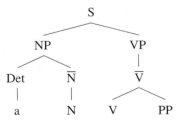

All that is left to expand is the PP, and then we'll fill in the remaining lexical items.

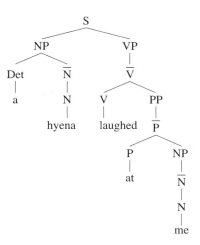

By following these conventions we generate only trees consistent with the X-bar schema and language-specific rules and hence only trees that conform to the syntax of the language. By implication, any tree not specified in this manner will be ungrammatical, that is, not permitted by the syntax. At any point during the construction of a tree, any rule may be used as long as its left-side category occurs somewhere at the bottom of the tree. By instantiating the different X-bar options with PS rules, we can specify all of the structures associated with actual English sentences.

The rules in (1)–(5) above certainly do not exhaust all the possible patterns of the X-bar schema. Below we list a few more rules. Recall that the X-bar schema allows any XP to function as a complement to a head. Rules (4) and (5) expand the VP to include an NP complement—a transitive verb structure such as *Every girl read some poetry*:

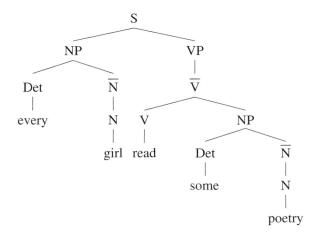

But as we've already seen, verbs also allow PP complements (*The boy biked to the store*), among others:

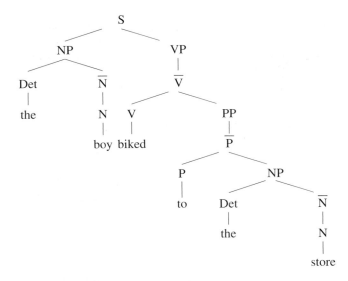

Similarly, nouns take complements, among which are PPs (*the father of the bride*):

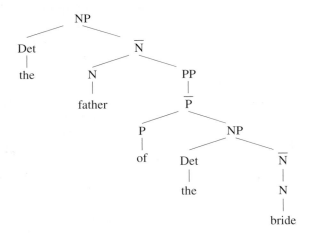

The following additional PS rules (6–14) illustrate these other options. (PS rules 1–5 are repeated for your convenience in following the derivation below.)

1. S → NP VP
2. NP → Det $\overline{\text{N}}$
3. $\overline{\text{N}}$ → N
4. VP → $\overline{\text{V}}$
5. $\overline{\text{V}}$ → V NP
6. $\overline{\text{V}}$ → V PP
7. $\overline{\text{V}}$ → V AP

8. $\overline{\text{N}}$ → N PP
9. PP → $\overline{\text{P}}$
10. $\overline{\text{P}}$ → P NP
11. AP → $\overline{\text{A}}$
12. $\overline{\text{A}}$ → A
13. $\overline{\text{A}}$ → A PP

By applying these rules in the manner prescribed, we can generate the phrase structure trees for such sentences such as *The majority of the senate became afraid of the vice-president*. In going about constructing such trees, a strategy of "divide and conquer" is in order. We'll first assemble the subtree for the NP subject, then the subtree for the VP predicate. Each level of the tree mentions the rule or rules (1–13, or LI for lexical insertion) that apply:

And now the VP:

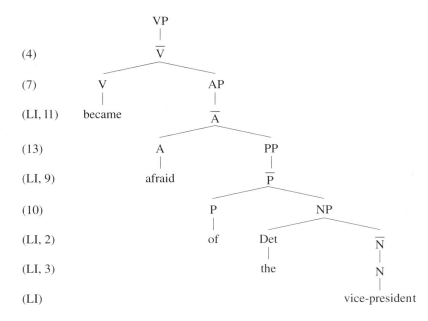

The final step (technically the first step) is to use rule 1 to expand the start symbol S into an NP VP into which the NP and VP that we just constructed can be inserted:

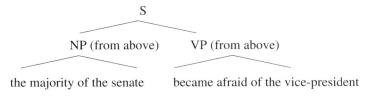

The Infinity of Language: Recursive Rules

So, naturalists observe, a flea

Hath smaller fleas that on him prey;

And these have smaller still to bite 'em,

And so proceed ad infinitum.

JONATHAN SWIFT, "On Poetry, a Rhapsody," 1733

We noted at the beginning of the chapter that the number of sentences in a language is without bound and that languages have various means of creating longer and longer sentences, such as adding an adjective or a prepositional phrase.

For example, an NP may contain any number of adjectives as in *the kindhearted, intelligent, handsome boy*. How do we account for this? Here is one reason that linguists posit the abstract category $\bar{N}$. To account for the potentially limitless number of adjectives we need a **recursive rule**—one that repeats itself—on $\bar{N}$:

14. $\bar{N} \to A\,\bar{N}$

By including this rule, that is, by permitting such structures to grow, we can easily represent the structure of the NP in question:

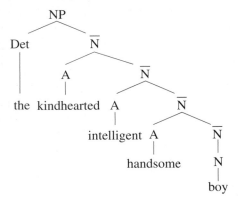

Without $\bar{N}$ we would be forced to have a recursive rule on NP such as NP→A NP, but although that would capture the recurring nature of the adjective, it would not work because it would allow the Det to show up in an impossible place as in *kind-hearted, intelligent, the boy*:

A similar kind of recursion occurs in this cartoon:

Newspaper Enterprise Association/United Features Syndicate

Another way speakers of English can "grow" structures of theoretically limitless size is by repeating the category of Intensifier (Int) within an AP. (Int functions as the specifier of $\overline{A}$.) The recursive rule looks like this and would not only handle Hattie's 100-word essay but also takes care of the more modest expression *really very pretty*:

15. $\overline{A} \rightarrow$ Int $\overline{A}$

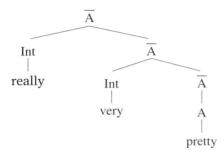

A slightly different form of recursion that also allows sentences of theoretically limitless length involves PP recursion, as illustrated by *she went over the hills, through the woods, to the cave.* . . . In this case the repeated category in the recursive rule on $\overline{V}$ occurs to the right of the barred category:

16. $\overline{V} \rightarrow \overline{V}$ PP

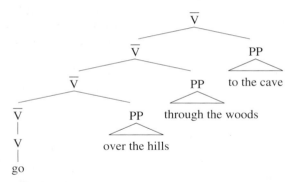

The X-bar schema gives us two ways of capturing this crucial aspect of speakers' syntactic knowledge, both of them being recursion on the $\overline{X}$ category, essentially structures (PS rules) of this form:

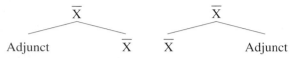

A phrasal category that is sister to an $\overline{X}$ and daughter of a higher $\overline{X}$, as in the above structures, is called an **adjunct**, and is distinct from a **complement**, which, as we've seen, is defined structurally as sister to the head X. And like complements, adjuncts may be of any phrasal type (XP). The first of the adjunct patterns above is reflected in the adjective and intensifier recursive rule (15) where the adjunct is the intensifier. It produces a right-branching structure, as you can see. The second pattern is reflected in the prepositional phrase recursive rule (16) where the adjunct is a PP and produces a left-branching structure.

Distinguishing between complements and adjuncts is not always straightforward. Structurally, the distinctions are unambiguous: complements are sisters to X; adjuncts are sisters to $\overline{X}$. But in analyzing sentences it is not always clear whether an addendum to a head is a complement or an adjunct.

We'll give a couple of "rules of thumb" for making the distinction, but an in depth discussion of the subject goes beyond the introductory treatment of our book.

PPs inside NPs are always complements if they are headed by *of*, while PPs headed by *with* are typically adjuncts. Thus in the NP *a patient of the doctor*, *of the doctor* is a complement, but in *a patient with a broken arm*, *with a broken arm* is an adjunct. When complements and adjuncts both occur, the complement must come first: thus *a patient of the doctor with a broken arm* is grammatical, but **a patient with a broken arm of the doctor* is ungrammatical. "One-replacement" provides a test: only nouns with adjuncts can be substituted for by *one*, as in *a patient with a broken arm and <u>one</u> with a broken leg*, but nouns with true complements do not allow *one*-replacement, so that **a patient of the doctor and one of the chiropractor* is not well-formed. Multiple adjuncts may be reordered without loss of grammaticality, so *a patient of the doctor with a broken arm from Kalamazoo* and *a patient of the doctor from Kalamazoo with a broken arm* are both well-formed NPs.

In verb phrases the direct object is always the complement and nearly every other addendum is an adjunct. As we have seen, *the puppy* in *found the puppy* is a complement, but *in the park* in *found the puppy in the park* is an adjunct. Complements precede adjuncts, so that *found in the park a puppy* is not grammatical.

In prepositional phrases, the NP object of the preposition is a complement, and in adjectives phrases (APs) an *of*-addendum is usually a complement, as in *jealous of Harry*.

Recursion is one of the defining characteristics of human language. Adjunction and complementation, expressed through the X-bar schema, are the sources of recursion or the infinitude/creativity of language that we have been emphasizing in this book.

17. $\bar{N} \rightarrow \bar{N}$ PP

The following structure for *the boat in the ocean white with foam from the gale* illustrates both NP and PP recursion:

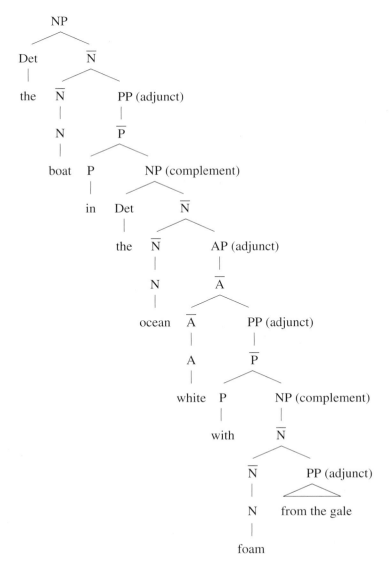

Our brain capacity is finite, able to store only a finite number of categories and rules for their combination. The embedding of categories within categories, common to all languages, places an infinite set of sentences at our disposal.

This linguistic property also illustrates the difference between competence and performance, discussed in chapter 1. All speakers of English (and other languages) have as part of their linguistic competence—their mental grammars—the ability to embed phrases within each other ad infinitum. However, as the structures grow longer, they become increasingly more difficult to produce and understand. This can be due to short-term memory limitations, muscular fatigue, breathlessness, boredom, or any number of performance factors. (We will discuss performance factors more fully in chapter 10.) Nevertheless, these very long sentences would be well-formed according to the rules of the grammar.

What Heads the Sentence

Might, could, would—they are contemptible auxiliaries.

GEORGE ELIOT (MARY ANN EVANS), *Middlemarch*, 1872

The structure of all phrasal categories follows the X-bar schema. One category that we have not yet discussed in this regard is sentence (S). To preserve the powerful generalization about syntax that the X-bar schema offers, we want all the phrasal categories to have a 3-tiered structure with specifiers, heads, and complements and/or adjuncts, but what would these be in the case of S? To answer this question we first observe that sentences are always "tensed." Tense provides a time-frame for the event or state described by the verb. In English, present and past tenses are morphologically marked on the verb:

John dances. (present)
John danced. (past)

Future tense is expressed with the modal *will* (*John* will *dance*). Modals also express notions such as possibility (*John* may *dance*); necessity (*John* must *dance*); ability (*John can dance*); and so on. A modal such as *may* says it is possible that the event will occur at some future time, *must* that it is necessary that the event occur at some future time, and so on. The English modals are inherently "tensed," as shown by their compatibility with various time expressions:

John may/must/can win the race today/tomorrow.
*John may/must/can win the race yesterday.
John could/would have tantrums when he was a child.
John could leave the country tomorrow.

Just as the VP is about the situation described by the verb—*eat ice cream* is about "eating"— so a sentence is about a situation or state of affairs that occurs at some point in time. Thus, the category Tense is a natural category to head S.

Using this insight, linguists refer to sentences as TPs (Tense Phrases) with the following structure conforming to the X-bar schema:

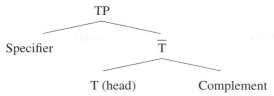

For sentences, or TPs, the specifier is the subject of the sentence and the complement of the TP is a verb phrase, or predicate, thus giving the sentence its traditional subject-predicate or NP VP form. Finally, the head T contains the tense (±pst) and modal verbs like *can* or *would*. This gives sentences, i.e., TPs, like the following:

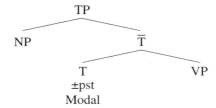

We are now able to represent the structures of such sentences as *The girl may cry* and *The child ate*:

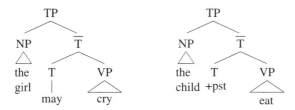

In these structures the T containing +pst and *eat* is ultimately pronounced *ate*. When there is no modal under T, the tense is realized on the verbal head of the VP.

Another way tense is expressed is by the tense-bearing word *do* that is inserted into negative sentences such as *John did not go* and questions such as *Where did John go?* In these sentences *did* means "past tense." Later in this chapter we will see how *do*-insertion works.

Structural Ambiguities

The structure of every sentence is a lesson in logic.

JOHN STUART MILL, Inaugural address at St. Andrews, 1867

As mentioned earlier, certain kinds of ambiguous sentences have more than one phrase structure tree, each corresponding to a different meaning. The sentence *The boy saw the man with the telescope* is structurally ambiguous. In the meaning in which the man has the telescope, the complement of *saw* is simply the NP *the man with the telescope,* with this structure:

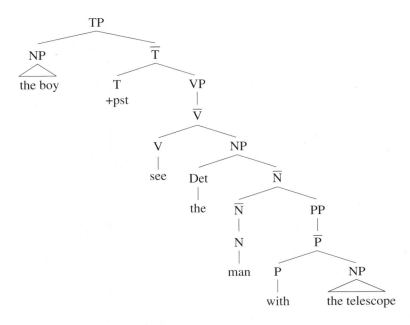

For the meaning in which the boy is using the telescope to see the man, we need to make use of recursive rule 16, name $\overline{V} \rightarrow \overline{V}$ PP, to produce this (slightly abbreviated) structure:

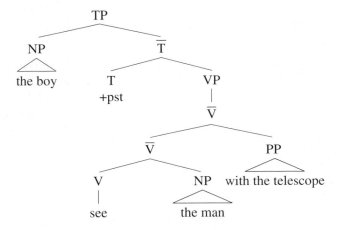

The different meanings arise from the fact that the PP *with the telescope* is sister to (hence modifies) *man* in the first case, but in the second case it is sister to, and hence modifies the $\overline{V}$ *see the man.* Thus, two interpretations are possible because the rules of syntax permit different structures for the same linear order of words.

More Structures

MacNelly/King Features Syndicate

Many other English sentence types are naturally accounted for by The X-bar schema. Consider this example:

The dog completely destroyed the house.

Adverbs are modifiers that can specify how an event happens (*quickly, slowly, completely*) or when it happens (*yesterday, tomorrow, often*). As modifiers, adverbs are adjuncts (sisters) to the $\overline{V}$ category just as adjectives are sisters to $\overline{N}$, as we saw in rule 4. This suggests the following rule:

18. $\overline{V} \rightarrow \text{AdvP } \overline{V}$

And this rule gives rise to the following structure:

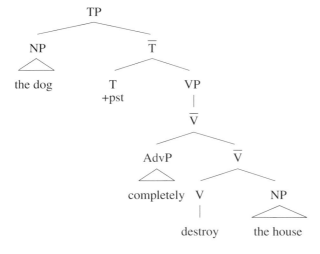

In the similar sentence *The dog destroyed the house yesterday* the structure must be different, as **The dog yesterday destroyed the house* is ungrammatical. We account for this with the following PS rule, expressing the fact that adjuncts may occur on both sides of the barred category, as we saw earlier in its X-bar schema on page 102:

19. $\overline{V} \rightarrow \overline{V}$ AdvP

Here, as with adjectival modification of the NP, the VP has a more deeply-tiered structure:

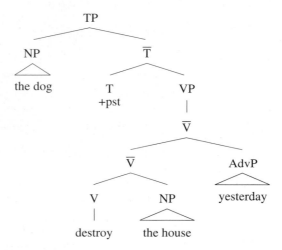

In the first of the two structures the adverb *completely* modifies the verb phrase by describing the extent of the destruction. In the second, the adverb *yesterday* adds information to the meaning of the VP by fixing the time of the event.

Most adverbs (e.g. *completely, often, suddenly*) can combine with a $\overline{V}$ using either rule 18 or 19: in other words, they can either precede or follow the $\overline{V}$. At the same time, some adverbs (e.g. *no longer, just, never*) can only precede $\overline{V}$, and some adverbs (e.g. *yesterday, fast, well*) can only follow $\overline{V}$. In all of these cases, the adverb follows our PS rules and is an adjunct (sister) of $\overline{V}$.

The joke in the "Shoe" cartoon is based on the fact that *curse* may take the NP *the day you were born* as a complement or as a temporal modifier—an adjunct—that is sister to $\overline{V}$ (similar to "cursed *on* the day"), leading to the structural ambiguity:

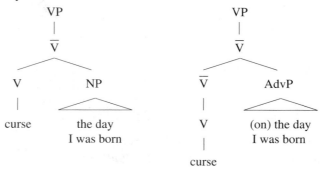

Interestingly, *I cursed the day I was born the day I was born*, with both the NP complement to the verb and the AdvP adjunct to $\overline{V}$ is grammatical and meaningful. (See exercise 23a.)

Transformational Analysis

I put the words down and push them a bit.

EVELYN WAUGH, quoted in *The New York Times*, April 11, 1966

We are able to characterize a limitless number of sentences via the phrase structure conventions outlined in the previous sections, which assemble words and phrases guided by the X-bar schema and constrained by C-selection and S-selection to satisfy lexical requirements. Nonetheless, phrase structure principles alone cannot account for the fact that certain sentence types in the language relate systematically to other sentence types, such as the following pair:

The boy will dance.   Will the boy dance?

These two sentences are about the same situation. The first sentence asserts that a boy-dancing situation will happen. Such sentences are called **declarative** sentences. The second sentence asks whether such a boy-dancing situation will occur. Sentences of the second sort are called **yes-no questions**. The only actual difference in meaning between these sentences is that one asserts information while the other requests it. This element of meaning is indicated by the different word order, which illustrates that two sentences may have a structural difference that corresponds *in a systematic way* to a meaning difference. The grammar of the language must account for this fact.

The standard way of describing these relationships is to say that the related sentences come from a common underlying structure. Yes-no questions are a case in point. They begin life as declarative sentences, or as TPs in the X-bar schema, for example:

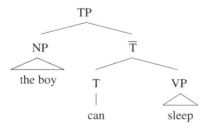

The head of the TP, namely T (the modal *can* in this example), is central to the formation of yes-no questions as well as certain other types of sentences in English. In yes-no questions, the modal appears in a different position; it precedes the subject. Here are a few more examples:

The boy will sleep.   Will the boy sleep?
The boy should sleep.   Should the boy sleep?

A way to capture the relationship between a declarative sentence and a yes-no question is to allow phrase structure principles to manipulate the underlying structure of the declarative sentence. A formal device, called **Move**, relocates the material in T before the subject NP. (Move is also called a **transformational rule** in traditional approaches to sentence relatedness.) For example, Move applies to

The boy must sleep

to derive

Must the boy ___ sleep

Yes-no questions are thus generated in two steps.

1. PS-rules implement the X-bar schema to generate a basic structure.
2. Move applies to the basic structure to produce the derived structure.

The basic structures of sentences, also called **deep structures** or **d-structures**, conform to the X-bar schema. Variants on the basic sentence structures are derived via the transformational operation Move. By generating questions in two steps, we are claiming that a principled structural relationship exists between a question and its corresponding statement. Intuitively, we know that such sentences are related. The transformational rule is a formal way of representing this knowledge.

The derived structures—the ones that follow the application of transformational rules—are called **surface structures** or **s-structures**. The rules of the language that determine pronunciation apply to s-structures (see chapter 6). If no transformations apply, then d-structure and s-structure are the same. If transformations apply, then s-structure is the result after all transformations have had their effect. Many sentence types are accounted for by transformations, which can alter phrase structure trees by moving, adding, or deleting elements.

Other sentence pairs that are transformationally related are:

active-passive

The cat chased the mouse.   →   The mouse was chased by the cat.

there-sentences

There is a bear in your closet.   →   A bear is in your closet.

PP preposing

Tom Dooley stabbed her with his knife.   →   With his knife Tom Dooley stabbed her.

An important question is: what do the *structures* of the derived sentences look like after Move applies? They *must* conform to the X-bar schema if we are to retain that crucial generality about syntax, but to do so requires an additional level of structure. In Appendix A to this chapter we'll show you how one could go about achieving this end.

The Structure Dependency of Rules

> Method consists entirely in properly ordering and arranging the things to which we should pay attention.
>
> RENÉ DESCARTES, *Oeuvres*, vol. X, c. 1637

The transformation Move acts on phrase structures without regard to the particular words that the structures contain, that is, it is **structure dependent**. When Move preposes a PP it moves any PP as long as it is an adjunct to $\bar{V}$, as in *In the house, the puppy found the ball*; or *With the telescope, the boy saw the man*; and so on.

Evidence that transformations are structure dependent is provided by the fact that the sentence *With a telescope, the boy saw the man* is not ambiguous. It has only the meaning 'the boy used a telescope to see the man,' the meaning corresponding to the second phrase structure on page 106 in which the PP is immediately dominated by the $\bar{V}$. In the structure corresponding to the other meaning, 'the boy saw a man who had a telescope,' the PP is in the NP, as in the first tree on page 106. Move as a PP preposing transformation applies to the $\bar{V}$–PP structure and not to the $\bar{N}$–PP structure.

Agreement rules are also structure-dependent. In many languages, including English, the verb must agree with the subject. The verb (in English) is marked with an *-s* when the subject is third-person singular and otherwise unmarked.

> This guy seems kind of cute.
> These guys seem kind of cute.
> Now consider these sentences:
> The *guy* we met at the party next door *seems* kind of cute.
> The *guys* we met at the party next door *seem* kind of cute.

The verb *seem* must agree with the subject, *guy* or *guys*. Even though there are various words between the head noun and the verb, the verb always agrees with the head noun. Moreover, there is no limit to how many words may intervene, or whether they are singular or plural, as the following sentence illustrates:

> The *guys* (*guy*) we met at the party next door that lasted until 3 a.m. and was finally broken up by the cops who were called by the neighbors *seem* (*seems*) kind of cute.

The (much abbreviated) phrase structure tree of such a sentence explains why this is so.

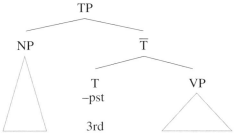

In the tree, "= = = = = =" represents the intervening structure, which may, in principle, be indefinitely long and complex. Speakers of English (and all other languages) know that agreement depends on sentence structure, not the linear order of words: agreement is between the subject and the main verb. As far as the rule of agreement is concerned, all other material can be ignored. (Although in actual performance, if the distance is too great, the speaker may forget what the subject was.)

A further illustration of structure dependency is found in the following declarative-question pairs:

The boy who can run fastest will win.
Will the boy who can run fastest win?
*Can the boy who run fastest will win?

The ungrammatical sentence shows that to form a question, Move applies to the modal dominated by the root TP, and not simply the *first* modal in the sentence as illustrated in this highly abbreviated structure. (See Appendix A for details):

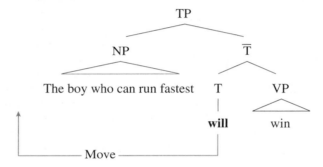

If the rule picked out the *first* modal, *can*, we would have the ungrammatical sentence *Can the boy who _ run fastest will win.* To derive a well-formed question, Move must refer to phrase structure and not to the linear order of elements.

Structure dependency is a principle of Universal Grammar, and is thus found in all languages. For example, in languages that have subject-verb agreement, the dependency is between the verb and the subject, and never some other NP such as the closest one, as shown in the following examples from Italian, German, Swahili, and English, respectively (the third-person singular agreement affix in the verb is in boldface and is governed by the boldfaced NP, not the underlined one, even though the latter is nearest the main verb):

La **madre** con tanti <u>figli</u> lavor**a** molto.
Die **Mutter** mit den vielen <u>Kindern</u> arbeite**t** viel.
Mama anao <u>watoto</u> wengi **a**najitahidi.
The **mother** with many <u>children</u> work**s** a lot.

Further Syntactic Dependencies

Sentences are organized according to two basic principles: X-bar schema derived constituent structure on the one hand, and the syntactic dependencies derived from the lexical properties of individual words (C-selection and S-selection). Constituent structure refers to the hierarchical organization of the subparts of a sentence, and transformational rules are sensitive to it. Syntactic dependencies mean that the presence of a particular word or morpheme can be contingent on the presence of some other word or morpheme in a sentence. We have already seen at least two examples of syntactic dependencies. C-selection is one kind of dependency. Whether there is a direct object in a sentence depends on whether the verb is transitive or intransitive, for example. More generally, complements depend on the properties of the head of their phrase. Subject-verb agreement is another kind of dependency between the features of the subject NP and the morphology on the verb.

Wh Questions

Whom are you? said he, for he had been to night school.

GEORGE ADE, "The Steel Box," in *Bang! Bang!*, 1928

The following **wh questions** illustrate another kind of dependency:

1. **(a)** What will Max chase?
   (b) Where should Pete put his dogbone?
   (c) Which toys does Pete like?

There are several points of interest in these sentences. First, the verb *chase* in sentence (a) is transitive, yet there is no direct object following it. There is a gap where the direct object should be. The verb *put* in sentence (b) is subcategorized for a direct object and a prepositional phrase, yet there is no PP following *his bone*. Finally, *does* in sentence (c) has the third-person singular *-s* morpheme though it is preceded by a plural noun.

If we remove the *wh* phrases, the remaining sentences would be ungrammatical.

2. **(a)** *will Max chase __?
   (b) *should Pete put his dogbone __?
   (c) *does Pete like __?

The grammaticality of a sentence with a gap depends on there being a *wh* phrase at the beginning of the sentence. The sentences in (1) are grammatical because the *wh* phrase is acting like the verbal object in (a) and (c) and the prepositional phrase object in (b).

We can explain the dependency between the *wh* phrase and the missing constituent if we assume that in each case the *wh* phrase originated in the position of the gap in a sentence with the corresponding declarative structure:

3. **(a)** Max will chase *what*?
   (b) Pete should put his dogbone *where*?
   (c) Pete likes *which toys*?

Phrase structure principles generate the basic declarative word orders in (3) (or more precisely the d-structure) with the *wh* expression in complement position, as required by the X-bar schema and the selectional properties of the transitive verb *chase*. Three transformational operations then occur: Move relocates the *wh* expression from its d-structure position to a structural position at the beginning of the sentence. A second occurrence of Move pre-poses the modal to precede the NP subject, and a transformational rule of *do-insertion* inserts the dummy verb *do* into T to carry the tense feature (which is realized as *does*), ultimately producing the s-structures in (1) at the beginning of this section. Appendix B illustrates these complex transformational processes.

A notable property of *wh* questions is that in this case Move can relocate the *wh* phrase outside of the clause in which it originates in d-structure if need be. Indeed, there is no limit to the distance that a *wh* phrase can move, as illustrated by the following sentences. The dashes indicate the d-structure position from which the *wh* phrases has been relocated.

Who did Helen say the senator wanted to hire __?
Who did Helen say the senator wanted the congressional representative to try to hire __?
Who did Helen say the senator wanted the congressional representative to try to convince the Speaker of the House to get the Vice President to hire __?

"Long-distance" dependencies created by *wh* movement are a fundamental part of human language. They provide still further evidence that sentences are not simply strings of words but are supported by a rich scaffolding of phrase structure trees. These trees express the underlying structure of a sentence as well as its relation to other sentences in the language, and as always are reflective of a person's knowledge of syntax.

UG Principles and Parameters

Whenever the literary German dives into a sentence, that is the last you are going to see of him till he emerges on the other side of the Atlantic with his Verb in his mouth.

MARK TWAIN, *A Connecticut Yankee in King Arthur's Court*, 1889

In this chapter we have largely focused on English syntax, but many of the grammatical structures we have described for English also hold in other languages. This is because Universal Grammar (UG) provides the basic design for all human languages, and individual languages are simply variations on this basic design. Imagine a new housing development. All of the houses have the same floor plan, but the occupants have some choices to make. They can have carpet or hardwood floors, curtains or blinds; they can choose their kitchen cabinets and the countertops, the bathroom tiles, and so on. This is more or less how the syntax operates. Languages conform to a basic design, and then there are choice points or points of variation.

All languages have structures that conform to the X-bar schema. Phrases consist of specifiers, heads, and complements; barred categories express recursive properties; sentences are headed by T, which is specified for information such as tense and modality; and so on.

However, languages may have different orders within the phrases and sentences. The word order differences between English and Japanese, discussed earlier, illustrate this interaction of general and language-specific properties. UG specifies the structure of a phrase. It must have a head and may take a complement of some type and have adjuncts. However, each language defines for itself the relative order of these constituents: English is head-initial, Japanese is head-final. We call the points of variation **parameters**.

All languages appear to have transformational rules such as Move for reordering elements to achieve certain purposes such as creating questions or emphasizing certain constituents. Move is found in Dutch, for example, in which the modal moves, if there is one, as in (1), and otherwise the main verb moves, as in (2):

1. Zal Femke fietsen? (from "Femke zal fietsen.")
   will Femke bicycle ride
   (Will Femke ride her bicycle?)

2. Leest Meindert veel boeken? (from "Meindert leest veel boeken.")
   reads Meindert many books
   (Does Meindert read many books?)

Main verbs in Standard American English do not move. Instead, *do* spells out the stranded tense and agreement features (see Appendix B). All languages have expressions for requesting information about *who, when, where, what,* and *how.* Even if the question words in other languages do not necessarily begin with "wh," we will refer to such questions as *wh* questions. In some languages, such as Japanese and Swahili, the *wh* phrase does not move. It remains in its original d-structure position. In Japanese the sentence is marked with a question morpheme, *no:*

Taro-ga	nani-o	mitsuketa-no?
Taro	what	found

Recall that Japanese word order is SOV, so the *wh* phrase *nani* ('what') is an object and occurs before the verb.

In Swahili the *wh* phrase—*nani* by pure coincidence—also stays in its base position:

Ulipatia	nani	kitabu?
you gave	who	a book

However, in all languages with *wh* movement (i.e., movement of the question phrase), the question element moves into the CP (complementizer phrase) (Appendix B). The "landing site" of the moved phrase is determined by UG. Among the *wh* movement languages, there is some variation. In the Romance languages, such as Italian, the *wh* phrase moves as in English, but when the *wh* phrase questions the object of a preposition, the preposition must move together with the *wh* phrase. In English, by contrast, the preposition can be "stranded" (i.e., left behind in its original position):

A chi hai dato il libro?
To whom (did) you give the book?
*Chi hai dato il libro a?
Who(m) did you give the book to?

In some dialects of German, long-distance *wh* movement leaves a trail of *wh* phrases:

Mit	wem	glaubst	du	mit	wem	Hans	spricht?
With	whom	think	you	with	whom	Hans	talks

(Whom do you think Hans talks to?)

Wen	willst	Du	wen	Hans	anruft?
Whom	want	You	whom	Hans	call

(Whom do you want Hans to call?)

In Czech the question phrase 'how much' can be moved, leaving behind the NP it modifies:

Jak	velké	Václav	koupil	auto?
How	big	Václav	bought	car

(How big a car did Václav buy?)

Despite these variations, *wh* movement adheres to certain constraints. Although *wh* phrases such as *what, who,* and *which boy* can be inserted into any NP position, and are then free in principle to move into the CP, there are specific instances in which *wh* movement is blocked. For example, a *wh* phrase cannot move out of a relative clause like *the senator that wanted to hire who*, as in (1b). It also cannot move out of a clause beginning with *whether* or *if*, as in (2c) and (2d). (Remember that the position from which the *wh* phrases have moved is indicated with __.)

1. **(a)** Emily paid a visit to the senator that wants to hire who?
   (b) *Who did Emily pay a visit to the senator that wants to hire __?

2. **(a)** Miss Marple asked Sherlock whether Poirot had solved the crime.
   (b) Who did Miss Marple ask __ whether Poirot had solved the crime?
   (c) *Who did Miss Marple ask Sherlock whether __ had solved the crime?
   (d) *What did Miss Marple ask Sherlock whether Poirot had solved __?

The only difference between the grammatical (2b) and the ungrammatical (2c) and (2d) is that in (2b) the *wh* phrase originates in the higher clause, whereas in (2c) and (2d) the *wh* phrase comes from inside the *whether* clause. This illustrates that the constraint against movement depends on structure and not on the length of the sentence.

Some sentences can be very short and still not allow *wh* movement:

3. **(a)** Sam Spade insulted the fat man's henchman.
   (b) Who did Sam Spade insult?
   (c) Whose henchman did Sam Spade insult?
   (d) *Whose did Sam Spade insult henchman?

4. **(a)** John ate bologna and cheese.
   (b) John ate bologna with cheese.
   (c) *What did John eat bologna and?
   (d) What did John eat bologna with?

The sentences in (3) show that a *wh* phrase cannot be extracted from inside a possessive NP. In (3b) it is okay to question the whole direct object. In (3c) it is even okay to question a piece of the possessive NP, providing the entire *wh* phrase is moved, but (3d) shows that moving the *wh* word alone out of the possessive NP is illicit.

Sentence (4a) is a coordinate structure and has approximately the same meaning as (4b), which is not a coordinate structure. In (4c) moving a *wh* phrase out of the coordinate structure results in ungrammaticality, whereas in (4d), moving the *wh* phrase out of the PP is fine. The ungrammaticality of (4c), then, is related to its structure and not to its meaning.

Constraints on *wh* movement are not specific to English. All languages that have *wh* movement show some kind of constraint on its operation. Like the principle of structure dependency and the principles governing the organization of phrases, constraints on *wh* movement are part of UG. These aspects of grammar need not be learned. They are part of the innate blueprint for language that the child brings to the task of acquiring a language. What children must learn are the language-specific aspects of grammar. Where there are parameters of variation, children must determine the correct choices for their language. The Japanese child must determine that the verb comes after the object in the VP, and the English-speaking child that the verb comes before it. The Dutch-speaking child acquires a rule that moves the verb to make a question, while the English-speaking child has a more restrictive rule regarding such movement. Italian, English, and Czech children learn that to form a question the *wh* phrase moves, whereas Japanese and Swahili children determine that there is no movement. As far as we can tell, children fix these parameters very quickly. We will have more to say about how children set UG parameters in chapter 9.

Sign Language Syntax

All languages have rules of syntax similar in kind, if not in detail, to those that we have seen for English, and sign languages are no exception. Signed languages have phrase structure (PS) rules that build hierarchical structures out of linguistic constituents and specify the word order of a given signed language. ASL is an SVO language. The signer of ASL knows that the first two sentences below are grammatical sentences of ASL, but the third is not. [The capitalized words represent signs.]

CAT CHASE DOG
'The cat chased the dog.'
DOG CHASE CAT
'The dog chased the cat.'
*CHASE CAT DOG

Unlike in English, however, adjectives can follow the head noun in ASL, as in Spanish, for example, and other spoken languages.

The PS rules also determine the grammatical functions of a sentence such as subject and object, so that a signer of ASL knows that while the first two sentences are both grammatical, they differ with respect to who is chasing whom. Finally, the PS rules of signed languages exhibit language-specific variation, just as those of spoken languages do. The grammatical sentences given above for ASL would not be grammatical for signers of Italian Sign Language (LIS or "Lingua dei Segni Italiana"), because LIS is an SOV language.

In ASL, as in English and other spoken languages, the basic word order can be modified by Move. For example, a direct object or other constituent such as a temporal adverb can be moved to the beginning of the sentence in a process called topicalization. This is done to bring attention to this constituent:

BOOK, JOHN READ YESTERDAY
YESTERDAY, JOHN READ BOOK

It is also possible for Move to apply iteratively, giving a double topicalization structure, as in:

YESTERDAY, BOOK, JOHN READ

Topicalization in ASL is accompanied by raising the eyebrows and tilting the head upward, marking the special word order, much as intonation does in English. The use of such non-manual markers is a salient feature of signed languages and something that distinguishes them from spoken languages. Spoken language may be accompanied by facial expressions and other non-manual gestures. But however expressive or informative such gestures are, they do not form part of the grammatical system of a spoken language as they do in signed languages.

Wh questions in ASL may also be formed via Move. In contrast to English, the movement is optional. In ASL *wh* phrases may remain in the d-structure position as in Japanese and Swahili. The ASL equivalents of *Who did Bill see yesterday?* and *Bill saw who yesterday?* are both grammatical. As in English and other spoken languages, *wh* movement in signed languages is constrained in various ways. For example, in ASL it is not possible to question one member of a coordinate structure:

*WHO JOHN KISS MARY AND ___YESTERDAY?
*'Who did John kiss Mary and yesterday?'

Similar constraints operate in topicalization. For example, a constituent cannot be moved out of the clause beginning with another *wh* phrase:

*MOTHER, I NOT-KNOW WHAT LIKE
*'(As for) Mother, I don't know what ____ likes.'

Wh questions in ASL are accompanied by an obligatory facial expression with a tilted head and furrowed brows. These non-manual markers are analogous to the special intonation that indicates interrogatives in many spoken languages.

Signed languages also have complex structural means to express notions such as tense, modality, and negation. For example, in ASL, as in English, there are several forms of negation, including NO, NOT, NONE, and NEVER, and they may follow different rules. The sign NOT, for example, can come at the end of an ASL sentence, quite unlike the behavior of the English word *not*. The structural rules for negation in ASL also require that the signer shake his or her head while producing a negative sentence, and even allow a signer to "shorten" or "reduce" the negation of a sentence to just a head shake, without producing the actual sign for NOT or NEVER. This is similar to how a speaker of English can shorten *not* to *n't*.

Thus, ASL and other sign languages show an interaction of universal and language-specific properties, just as spoken languages do. The rules of sign languages are structure-dependent, and movement rules are constrained in various ways, as illustrated earlier. Other properties, such as the non-manual markers and the use of space, are an integral part of the grammar of sign languages but not of spoken languages. The fact that sign languages appear to be subject to the same principles and parameters of UG that spoken languages are subject to shows us that the human brain is designed to acquire and use language, not simply speech.

APPENDIX A

The formation of yes-no questions comes from the transformation Move relocating the T from the corresponding declarative sentence:

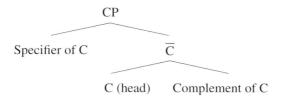

The boy will sleep   →   will the boy ___ sleep

But what is the structure of *will the boy sleep*? In keeping with the X-bar schema, linguists have proposed that the entire TP is actually a subpart of a phrasal category called a Complementizer Phrase or CP, which, of course, conforms to the X-bar schema:

```
                    CP
            _____|_____
           |                 |
     Specifier of C          C̄
                       _____|_____
                      |             |
                  C (head)   Complement of C
```

Putting the specifier aside for the moment, we see that TP occurs in this structure:

Thus, the TP is the complement to the complementizer phrase, while the head of the CP contains the abstract element +Q for questions or –Q for declaratives. The advantage of this analysis is that C provides a home for T when Move relocates it. The d-structure for questions is:

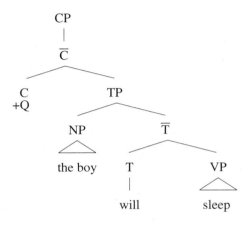

and the modal is moved to the front of the phrase:

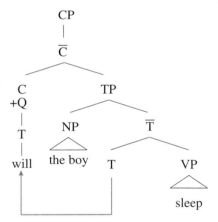

A further need for the complementizer phrase (CP) is provided by phrasal categories that take sentences (TPs) in their complements (underlined):

belief <u>that iron floats</u> (NP complement)
wonders <u>if iron floats</u> (VP complement)
happy <u>that iron floats</u> (AP complement)
about <u>whether iron will sink</u> (PP complement)

The words *that*, *if*, and *whether* are complementizers and the CP has a place for them under its head C, for example:

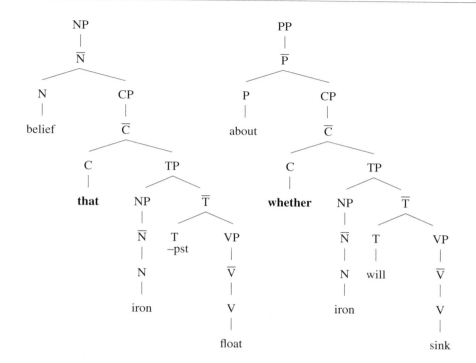

APPENDIX B

The d-structure for *What will Max chase?* is:

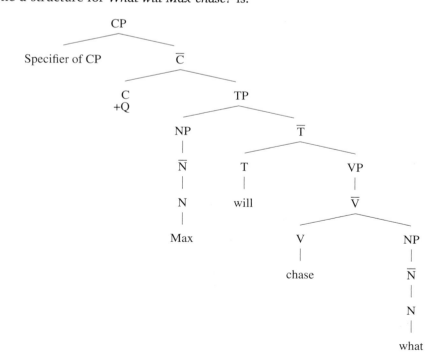

The specifier of CP is the "landing site" for the *wh* word *what,* while the head of CP will hold the T, as with yes-no questions. The result of the two applications of Move is:

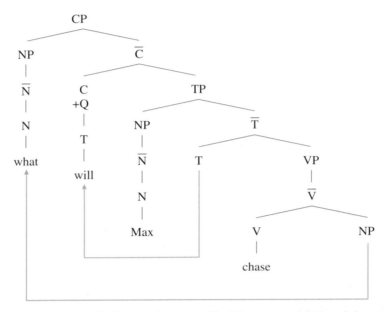

The derivation of *Which toys does Pete like?* has two additional features: The *which* is a determiner of *toys*; and when a derivation produces a T that lacks a lexical element AND is separated from the main verb by an NP, a rule inserts the "dummy" verb *do*. Here is the d-structure of *Which toys does Pete like?*

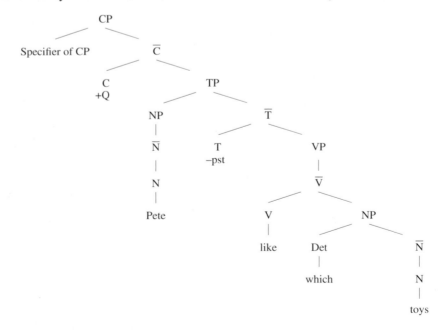

After Move has done its work we have this near s-structure:

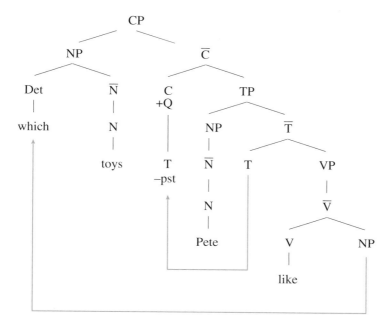

Although T lacks a lexical element, and carries only the present tense, Move moved it anyway because Move is *structure dependent* and not dependent on the presence or absence of a word. With T separated from the main verb by an NP, something is needed to carry the tense. That something is the "dummy" word *do*, and it is put in place by a transformational rule of *do-insertion*, yielding the final s-structure:

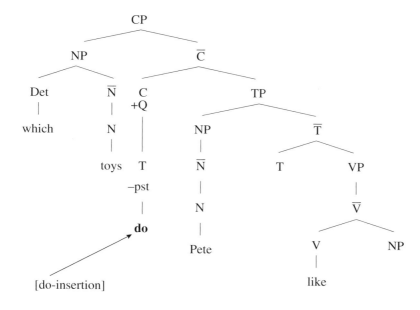

Do combines with [–pst] to yield the present tense *does*. Rules that convert inflectional features such as *past tense* or *third-person present tense* into their proper phonological forms are called **spell-out rules**. They apply to the syntactic output of s-structures.

Before concluding we should mention two other auxiliary verbs that participate in question formation in English. These are the auxiliaries *have* and *be* that we find in sentences such as:

1. Spot has chased a squirrel.
2. Nellie is snoring.

Like the modals, the auxiliaries *have* and *be* move to the position preceding the subject in both yes-no questions and *wh* questions.

Has Spot ___ chased a squirrel?
Is Nellie ___ snoring?
What has Spot ___ chased ___?

The question is: where do *have* and *be* originate in the d-structure? Note that *have* and *be* can occur in the same sentence with a modal:

Nellie may be snoring.
Spot must have found a squirrel.

We can conclude therefore that they do not originate in T (which may be occupied by a modal). Like other verbs in English, however, *have* and *be* inflect for tense (and agreement): *am, is, are, was, were, have, has, had*. Our analysis leads us to conclude that *have/be* originate under V in a recursive $\overline{V}$ structure, as follows. (An additional rule, 20. $\overline{V} \rightarrow$ V VP, joins rules 5, 6, and 7 in providing phrasal complements to the verb.)

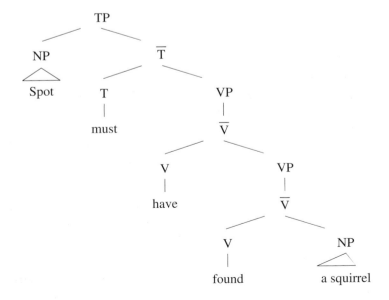

When there is no modal, T is occupied by a tense feature, which is realized on *have/be*, as would be the case for other verbs like *snore*:

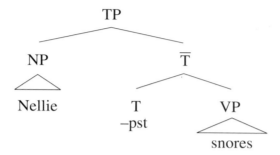

The auxiliaries *have* and *be* are special in one important respect, however. They can undergo a movement that is not available to other verbs: they can "raise" to T, and from this position they undergo a second movement to C to form a question. To illustrate this process, we have given several structural steps in deriving *What has Spot chased?* This derivation is shown below:

Here is the d-structure (from the X-bar derived phrase structure rules):

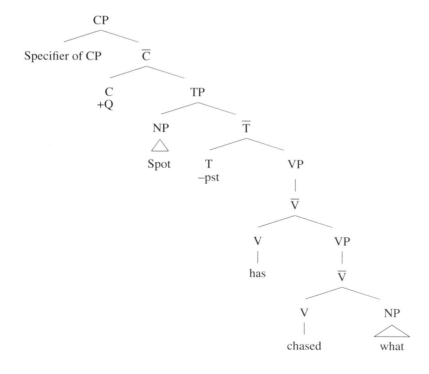

With T unoccupied by a modal and adjacent to *has* (if *has* were *is*, we'd be deriving *What is Spot chasing?*), the *has* is raised to T as shown in this tree:

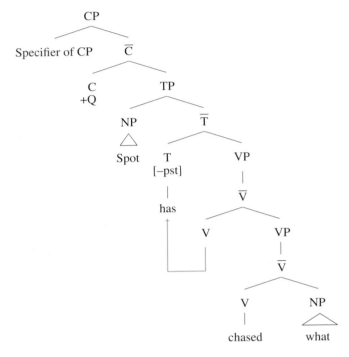

The transformational rule that raises V to T when V is *have* or *be* allows us to explain the unique behavior of *have/be* in English questions.

The transformational rule for questions now moves *has* to the front of the sentence into the head of CP position, C:

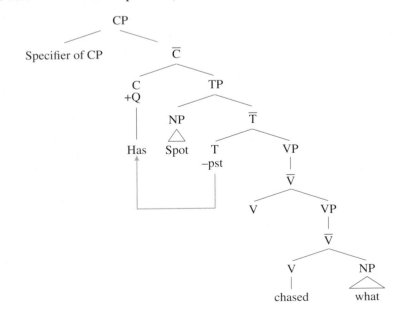

And finally, *wh* movement brings *what* to the front of the sentence into the specifier of CP position:

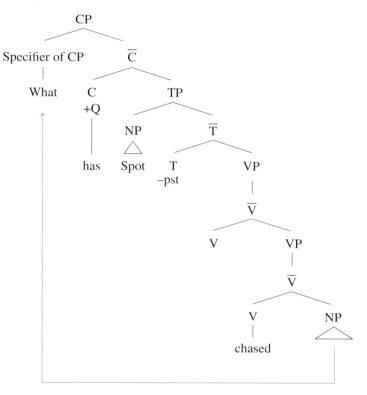

APPENDIX C

This appendix contains the PS rules used in this chapter, but excluding TP and CP X-bar rules, which are applied implicitly by showing their tree structure.

1. S → NP VP
2. NP → Det $\overline{\text{N}}$
3. $\overline{\text{N}}$ → N
4. VP → $\overline{\text{V}}$
5. $\overline{\text{V}}$ → V NP
6. $\overline{\text{V}}$ → V PP
7. $\overline{\text{V}}$ → V AP
8. $\overline{\text{N}}$ → N PP
9. PP → $\overline{\text{P}}$
10. $\overline{\text{P}}$ → P NP
11. AP → $\overline{\text{A}}$
12. $\overline{\text{A}}$ → A
13. $\overline{\text{A}}$ → A PP
14. $\overline{\text{N}}$ → A $\overline{\text{N}}$
15. $\overline{\text{A}}$ → Int $\overline{\text{A}}$

16. $\overline{V} \rightarrow \overline{V}$ PP
17. $\overline{N} \rightarrow \overline{N}$ PP
18. $\overline{V} \rightarrow$ AdvP $\overline{V}$
19. $\overline{V} \rightarrow \overline{V}$ AdvP
20. $\overline{V} \rightarrow$ V VP (in Appendix B)

Summary

Speakers of a language recognize the grammatical sentences of their language and know how the words in a sentence must be ordered and grouped to convey a certain meaning. All speakers are capable of producing and understanding an unlimited number of new sentences that have never before been spoken or heard. They also recognize ambiguities, know when different sentences mean the same thing, and correctly interpret the grammatical relations in a sentence, such as **subject** and **direct object**. This kind of knowledge comes from their knowledge of the **rules of syntax**.

Sentences have structure that can be represented by **phrase structure trees** containing **syntactic categories**. Phrase structure trees reflect the speaker's mental representation of sentences. Ambiguous sentences may have more than one phrase structure tree.

Phrase structure trees reveal the linear order of words and the constituency of each syntactic category. There are different kinds of syntactic categories: **Phrasal categories**, such as NP and VP, are composed of other syntactic categories; **lexical categories**, such as Noun and Verb, and **functional categories**, such as Det and T, often correspond to individual words. The hierarchical structure of the phrasal categories is universal and is specified by the **X-bar schema**, consisting of a **specifier**, a **head**, and its **complements** and **adjuncts**. NPs, VPs, and so on are headed by nouns, verbs, and the like. The sentence (S or TP) is headed by T, which carries such information as tense and modality.

The particular order of elements within the phrase is subject to language-particular variation and can be expressed through the **phrase structure rules** of each language, which conform to the X-bar Schema.

A grammar is a formally stated, explicit description of the mental grammar or the speaker's linguistic competence. The **lexicon** represents the knowledge that a speaker has about the vocabulary of his or her language. This knowledge includes the syntactic categories of words as well as the **subcategorization** or **c-selection** properties of particular lexical items that specify the complements they can take, for example whether a verb is **transitive** or **intransitive**. The lexicon also contains semantic information, including the kinds of NPs that can function as semantically coherent subjects and objects: **s-selection**. Selectional restrictions must be satisfied in the **d-structure** representation of the sentence.

Transformational rules such as Move and *do*-insertion account for relationships between sentences such as declarative and interrogative pairs, including *wh* questions. Transformations such as Move can relocate constituents. The output of the transformational rules is the **s-structure** of a sentence, the structure that most closely determines how the sentence is to be pronounced (or signed). Inflectional information, such as tense, may be represented as abstract features in the phrase structure tree. After the rules of the syntax have applied, these features are sometimes spelled out as affixes such as -*ed* or as function words such as *do*.

The basic design of language is universal. Universal Grammar specifies that syntactic rules are **structure-dependent** and that movement rules may not move phrases out of certain structures such as certain types of clauses, among many other constraints, including a need to not violate the X-bar schema. These constraints exist in all languages—spoken and signed—and need not be learned. UG also contains parameters of variation, such as the order of heads and complements, and the variations on movement rules. A child acquiring a language must fix the parameters of UG for that language.

References for Further Reading

Baker, M. C. 2001. *The atoms of language: The mind's hidden rules of grammar.* New York: Basic Books.
Carney, A. 2007. *Syntax: A generative introduction, 2nd ed.* Cambridge, MA: Blackwell.
Chomsky, N. 1995. *The minimalist program.* Cambridge, MA: MIT Press.
_____. 1972. *Language and mind, rev. ed.* New York: Harcourt Brace Jovanovich.
_____. 1965. *Aspects of the theory of syntax.* Cambridge, MA: MIT Press.
Jackendoff, R. S. 1994. *Patterns in the mind: Language and human nature.* New York: Basic Books.
Pinker, S. 1999. *Words and rules: The ingredients of language.* New York: HarperCollins.
Radford, A. 2009. *Analysing English sentences: A minimalist approach.* Cambridge, UK: Cambridge University Press.
_____. 2004. *English syntax: An introduction.* Cambridge, UK: Cambridge University Press.

Exercises

1. Besides distinguishing grammatical from ungrammatical sentences, the rules of syntax account for other kinds of linguistic knowledge, such as:
   a. when a sentence is structurally ambiguous. (Cf. *The boy saw the man with a telescope.*)
   b. when two sentences with different structures mean the same thing. (Cf. *The father wept silently.* and *The father silently wept.*)
   c. systematic relationships of form and meaning between two sentences, like declarative sentences and their corresponding interrogative forms. (Cf. *The boy can sleep.* and *Can the boy sleep?*)

   Draw on your linguistic knowledge of English to come up with an example illustrating each of these cases. (Use examples that are different from the ones in the chapter.) Explain why your example illustrates the point. If you know a language other than English, provide examples in that language, if possible.

2. Consider the following sentences:
   a. I hate war.
   b. You know that I hate war.
   c. He knows that you know that I hate war.
      i.   Write another sentence that includes sentence (c).
      ii. What does this set of sentences reveal about the nature of language?
      iii. How is this characteristic of human language related to the difference between linguistic competence and performance? (Hint: Review these concepts in chapter 1.)

3. Paraphrase each of the following sentences in two ways to show that you understand the ambiguity involved:

   Example: Smoking grass can be nauseating.

      i. Putting grass in a pipe and smoking it can make you sick.
      ii. Fumes from smoldering grass can make you sick.

   a. Dick finally decided on the boat.
   b. The professor's appointment was shocking.
   c. The design has big squares and circles.
   d. That sheepdog is too hairy to eat.
   e. Could this be the invisible man's hair tonic?
   f. The governor is a dirty street fighter.
   g. I cannot recommend him too highly.
   h. Terry loves his wife and so do I.
   i. They said she would go yesterday.
   j. No smoking section available.
   k. We will dry clean your clothes in 24 hours.
   l. I bought cologne for my boyfriend containing 25% alcohol.

4. i. Consider the following baseball joke (knowledge of baseball required):

      CATCHER TO PITCHER: "Watch out for this guy, he's a great fastball hitter."
      PITCHER TO CATCHER: "No problem. There's no way I've got a great fastball."

      Explain the humor either by paraphrasing, or even better, with a tree structure like the one we used early in the chapter for *old men and women* (without the syntactic categories).
   ii. Do the same for the advertising executive's (honest?) claim that the new magazine "has between one and two billion readers."

5. Draw two phrase structure trees to represent the two meanings of the sentence *The magician touched the child with the wand.* Be sure you indicate which meaning goes with which tree. (Note: Be sure your trees conform to the X-bar schema.) (Hint: *with the wand* is an adjunct, not a complement.)

6. Draw the NP subtrees for the italicized NPs in the following sentences:
   a. *Every mother* hopes for good health.
   b. *A big black dog is* barking.
   c. *Angry men in dark glasses* roamed the streets.
   d. We saw *the destruction of the house.* (Hint: *. . . and the one of the garage)

7. In all languages, sentences can occur within sentences. For example, in exercise 2, sentence (b) contains sentence (a), and sentence (c) contains sentence (b). Put another way, sentence (a) is embedded in sentence (b), and sentence (b) is embedded in sentence (c). Sometimes embedded sentences appear slightly changed from their normal forms, but you should be able to recognize and underline the embedded sentences in the following examples. Underline in the non-English sentences, when given, not in the translations (the first one is done as an example):

   a. Yesterday I noticed <u>my accountant repairing the toilet</u>.
   b. Becky said that Jake would play the piano.
   c. I deplore the fact that bats have wings.
   d. That Guinevere loves Lorian is known to all my friends.
   e. Who promised the teacher that Maxine wouldn't be absent?
   f. It's ridiculous that he washes his own Rolls-Royce.
   g. The woman likes for the waiter to bring water when she sits down.
   h. The person who answers this question will win $100.
   i. The idea of Romeo marrying a 13-year-old is upsetting.
   j. I gave my hat to the nurse who helped me cut my hair.
   k. For your children to spend all your royalty payments on recreational drugs is a shame.
   l. Give this fork to the person I'm getting the pie for.
   m.

khăw	chyâ	waă	khruu	maa. (Thai)
He	believe	that	teacher	come

   He believes that the teacher is coming.

   n.

Je	me	demande	quand	il	partira. (French)
I	me	ask	when	he	will leave

   I wonder when he'll leave.

   o.

Jan	zei	dat	Piet	dit	boek	niet	heeft	gelezen. (Dutch)
Jan	said	that	Piet	this	book	not	has	read

   Jan said that Piet has not read this book.

8. Adhering to the X-bar schema, draw phrase structure trees for the following sentences (TPs): (Hint: place any adverbs directly under AdvP without concern for the internal structure of the adverbial phrase. Also, you may assume possessive terms like *my* and *her* are determiners and that there are no "small clauses.")

   a. The puppy found the child.
   b. A surly passenger insulted the attendant.
   c. The house on the hill collapsed in the earthquake.
   d. The ice melted quickly.
   e. The hot sun melted the ice.
   f. The old tree swayed in the wind.
   g. My guitar gently weeps.

9. Create five phrase structure trees of 6, 7, 8, 9, and 10 words. Use your mental lexicon to fill in the bottoms of the trees. (Note: make sure your trees conform to the X-bar schema and be especially cautious to distinguish adjuncts from complements.)

10. We stated that the rules of syntax specify all and only the grammatical sentences of the language. Why is it important to say *only*? What would be wrong with a grammar that specified as grammatical sentences all of the truly grammatical ones plus a few that were not grammatical?

11. In this chapter we introduced the X-bar schema, according to which each phrasal category without $\overline{\text{X}}$ recursion has three levels of structure. Draw the subtree corresponding to the phrasal category NP (noun phrase) and give an example of the four possibilities: head only; specifier and head only; head and complement only; and specifier, head, and complement only. (Hint: Make sure your complement is not an adjunct using the *one-*replacement test.)

12. Using one or more of the constituency tests (i.e., stand alone, move as a unit, replacement by a pronoun, *one*-replacement) discussed in the chapter, determine which of the boldfaced portions in the sentences are constituents. Provide the grammatical categoryof the constituents.

    a. Martha found **a lovely pillow** for the couch.
    b. The **light in this room** is terrible.
    c. I wonder **whether Bonnie has finished packing her books**.
    d. Melissa slept **in her class**.
    e. **Pete and Max** are fighting over the bone.
    f. I gave a bone to Pete **and to Max** yesterday.
    g. I gave a bone to **Pete and** to Max yesterday.

13. The two sentences below contain a **verbal particle**:

    i. He ran *up* the bill.
    ii. He ran the bill *up*.

    The verbal particle *up* and the verb *run* depend on each other for the unique idiosyncratic meaning of the phrasal verb *run up*. (*Running up a bill* involves neither running nor the location up.) We showed earlier that in such cases the particle and *object* do not form a constituent, hence they cannot move as a unit:

    iii. *Up the bill, John ran.   (Compare this to *Up the hill John ran.*)

    a. Using adverbs such as *completely*, show that the particle forms a constituent with the *verb* in [*run up*] *the bill*, while in *run* [*up the hill*], the preposition and NP object form a constituent.
    b. Now consider the following data:

        i. Michael ran up the hill and over the bridge.
        ii. *Michael ran up the bill and off his mouth.
        iii. Michael ran up the bill and ran off his mouth.

    Use the data to argue that expressions like *up the bill* and *off his mouth* are not constituents.

14. In terms of C-selection restrictions, explain why the following are ungrammatical:

    a. *The man located.
    b. *Jesus wept the apostles.
    c. *Robert is hopeful of his children.
    d. *Robert is fond that his children love animals.
    e. *The children laughed the man.

15. The complement of V may be a single NP direct object as for *find*. English also has **ditransitive verbs**, ones whose complement may be two NPs, such as *give*:

    The emperor gave the vassal a castle.

    Think of three other ditransitive verbs in English and give example sentences. (Note: The analysis of ditransitive verbs in X-bar theory is controversial. See Exercise 27.)

16. Tamil is a language spoken in India by upward of 70 million people. Others, but not you, may find that they talk "funny," as illustrated by word-for-word translations of PPs from Tamil to English:

    Tamil to English Meaning

    the bed on   'on the bed'
    the village from   'from the village'

    i. Based on these data, is Tamil a head initial or a head final language?
    ii. What would the PS tree for a Tamil PP look like? (Note: Make sure your tree conforms to the X-bar schema.)

17. Here are three more word-for-word glosses in Tamil:

    a story tell   'tell a story'
    the boy a cow saw   'the boy saw a cow'
    woman this slept   'this woman slept'

    Do these further data support or detract from your analysis in exercise 16? What would the pertinent VP and NP trees look like in Tamil, based on these data? (Hint: Just give the three levels. You may need to look at Appendix B.)

18. All *wh* phrases can move to the left periphery of the sentence.

    a. Invent three sentences beginning with *what*, *which*, and *where*, in which the *wh* word is not in its d-structure position in the sentence. Give both the s-structure and d-structure versions of your sentences. For example, using *when*:

    When could Marcy catch a flight? from *Marcy could catch a flight when?* (Hint: see Appendix B.)

    b. Draw the phrase structure tree for one of your sentences. (Hint: See the Appendices.) (Note: As always, make sure your trees conform to the X-bar schema.)

19. There are many systematic, structure-dependent relationships among sentences similar to the one discussed in the chapter between declarative and interrogative sentences. Here are some example sentences based on ditransitive verbs (see exercise 15):

    The boy wrote the senator a letter.
    The boy wrote a letter to the senator.
    A philanthropist gave the animal rights movement $1 million.
    A philanthropist gave $1 million to the animal rights movement.

    a. Describe the relationship between the first and second members of each pair of sentences.
    b. State why a Move transformation deriving one of these structures from the other is plausible.

20. State at least three differences between English and the following languages, using just the sentence(s) given. Ignore lexical differences (i.e., the different vocabulary). Here is an example:

Thai:	Dèg	khon	níi	kamlang	kin.
	boy	*classifier*	this	*progressive*	eat

    'This boy is eating.'

	Măa	tua	nán	kin	khâaw.
	dog	*classifier*	that	eat	rice

    'That dog ate rice.'

    Three differences are (1) Thai has "classifiers." They have no English equivalent. (2) The words (determiners, actually) *this* and *that* follow the noun in Thai, but precede the noun in English. (3) The "progressive" is expressed by a single separate word in Thai. The verb does not change form. In English, the progressive is indicated by the presence of the verb *to be* and the adding of *-ing* to the verb.

    a. French

Cet	homme	intelligent	comprendra	la question.
this	man	intelligent	will understand	the question

    'This intelligent man will understand the question.'

Ces	hommes	intelligents	comprendront	les questions.
these	men	intelligent	will understand	the questions

    'These intelligent men will understand the questions.'

    b. Japanese

Watashi	ga	sakana	o	tabete	iru.
I	*subject marker*	fish	*object marker*	eat (*ing*)	am

    'I am eating fish.'

c. Swahili

Mtoto		alivunja			kikombe.	
m-	toto	a-	li-	vunja	ki-	kombe
class	child	he	*past*	break	*class*	cup
marker					*marker*	

'The child broke the cup.'

Watoto		wanavunja			vikombe.	
wa-	toto	wa-	na-	vunja	vi-	kombe
class	child	they	*present*	break	*class*	cup
marker					*marker*	

'The children break the cups.'

d. Korean

Kɨ	sonyɔn-iee		wɨyu-lɨl		masi-ass-ta.		
kɨ	sonyɔn-	iee	wɨyu-	lɨl	masi-	ass-	ta
the	boy	*subject*	milk	*object*	drink	*past*	*assertion*
		marker		*marker*			

'The boy drank milk.'

Kɨ-nɨn		muɔs-ɨl		mɔk-ass-nɨnya.		
kɨ	nɨn	muɔs-	ɨl	mɔk-	ass-	nɨnya
he	*subject*	what	*object*	eat	*past*	*question*
	marker		*marker*			

'What did he eat?'

e. Tagalog

Nakita	ni	Pedro-ng		puno	na	ang	bus.
nakita	ni	Pedro	-ng	puno	na	ang	bus
saw	*article*	Pedro	that	full	already	*topic*	bus
						marker	

'Pedro saw that the bus was already full.'

21. Transformations may delete elements. For example, the s-structure of the ambiguous sentence *George wants the presidency more than Martha* may be derived from two possible d-structures:

a. George wants the presidency more than he wants Martha.
b. George wants the presidency more than Martha wants the presidency.

A deletion transformation either deletes *he wants* from the structure of example (a), or *wants the presidency* from the structure of example (b). This is a case of **transformationally induced ambiguity**: two different d-structures with different semantic interpretations are transformed into a single s-structure.

Explain the role of a deletion transformation similar to the ones just discussed in the following humorous dialogue between "two old married folks."

HE: Do you still love me as much as you used to?

SHE: As much as I used to what?

22. **Challenge exercise**: Compare the following French and English sentences:

French	English
Jean boit toujours du vin.	John always drinks some wine.
Jean drinks always some wine	*John drinks always some wine
(*Jean toujours boit du vin)	
Marie lit jamais le journal.	Mary never reads the newspaper.
Marie reads never the newspaper	*Mary reads never the newspaper.
(*Marie jamais lit le journal)	
Pierre lave souvent ses chiens.	Peter often washes his dogs.
Pierre washes often his dogs	*Peter washes often his dogs.
(*Pierre souvent lave ses chiens.)	

a. Based on the above data, what would you hypothesize concerning the relative positions of adverbs of frequency (e.g., *toujours, jamais, souvent, always, never, often*) and the verbs they modify in French and English?

b. Now suppose that UG specifies that in *all languages* the adverbs of frequency must precede $\overline{V}$, as in the tree below. What transformational rule would you need to hypothesize to derive the correct surface word order for French? (Hint: Think about the auxiliaries *have* and *be* in English and the movements they can make by referring to appendix B.)

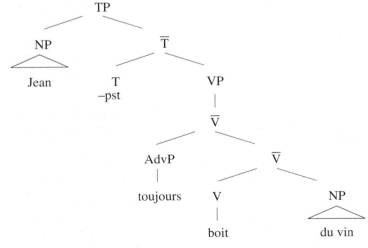

c. How are English and French alike; how are they different?

23. Refer to the tree structures on p. 108.

    a. Give the tree corresponding to the VP *cursed the day I was born the day I was born.*

Which must come first, the AdvP or the NP? (You needn't concern yourself with the internal structure of the AdvP or the NP.)

    b. How would you draw tree structures (i.e., modify the PS rules) to account for NPs that contain multiple adjective phrases with intensifiers such as *the extremely intelligent, happy-about-his-grade boy.*

24. Show that an embedded CP (a CP inside a TP) is a constituent by applying the constituency tests (stand alone, move as a unit, and replace with a pronoun). Consider the following sentences in formulating your answer, and provide further examples if you can. (The boldfaced words are the CPs.)

Sam asked **whether he could play soccer.**

I wonder **whether Michael walked the dog.**

Cher believes **that the students know the answer.**

It is a problem **that Sam broke his arm.**

25. **Challenge exercise** (if you've read Appendices A and B):

    a. Give the d-structure tree for *Which dog does Michael think loves bones?* (Hint: The complementizer *that* must be present.)

    b. Give the d-structure tree for *What does Michael think that his dog loves?*

    c. Consider these data:

    i. *Which dog does Michael think that loves bones?

    ii. What does Michael think his dog loves?

In (ii), a complementizer deletion rule has deleted *that*. The rule is optional because the sentence is grammatical with or without *that*. In (i), however, the complementizer must be deleted to prevent the ungrammatical sentence from being generated. What factor governs the optionality of the rule?

26. Dutch and German are Germanic languages related to English, and as in English, *wh* questions are formed by moving a *wh* phrase to sentence-initial position.

In what way are the rules of question formation in Dutch and German different from those in English? Base your answer on the following data:

German

i.

Was	hat	Karl	gekauft?
what	has	Karl	bought

'What has Karl bought?'

ii.

Was	kauft	Karl?
What	buys	Karl

'What does Karl buy?'

Dutch

i.

Wat	heeft	Wim	gekocht?
what	has	Wim	bought

'What has Wim bought?'

ii.

Wat	koopt	Wim?
what	buys	Wim

'What does Wim buy?'

iii.	Kauft	Karl	das	Buch?	Koopt	Wim	het	boek?
	buys	Karl	the	book	buys	Wim	the	book

'Does Karl buy the book?'   'Does Wim buy the book?'

27. **Challenge research exercise**: X-bar theory demands binary branching and that a head may have one and only one complement. Ditransitive verbs such as *write, give*, etc. (they are numerous) pose problems insofar as fitting into the strict (dare we say "Procrustean") strictures of X-bar. This research project asks you to examine the work that has been done to accommodate the facts of ditransitive verbs with X-bar theory.

28. The *one*-replacement test is an excellent way to determine whether an expression that follows a noun is a complement or an adjunct. Here are four examples of complements and four of adjuncts. Apply the *one*-replacement test to determine which is which:
    a. the man with the golden arm
    b. a voter for proposition eighteen
    c. my cousin's arrival at his home
    d. the construction of a retaining wall
    e. the boat in the river
    f. the ocean white with foam
    g. the desecration of the temple
    h. the betrayal of Julius Caesar

4

The Meaning of Language

Surely all this is not without meaning.

HERMAN MELVILLE, *Moby-Dick*, 1851

For thousands of years philosophers have pondered the **meaning** of *meaning*, yet speakers of a language can easily understand what is said to them and can produce strings of words that are meaningful to other speakers. We use language to convey information to others (*My new bike is pink*), ask questions (*Who left the party early?*), give commands (*Stop lying!*), and express wishes (*May there be peace on Earth*).

What do you know about meaning when you know a language? To begin with, you know when a "word" is meaningful (*flick*) or meaningless (*blick*), and you know when a "sentence" is meaningful (*Jack swims*) or meaningless (*Swims metaphorical every*). You know when a word has two meanings (*bear*) and when a sentence has two meanings (*Jack saw a man with a telescope*). You know when two words have the same meaning (*sofa* and *couch*), and when two sentences have the same meaning (*Jack put off the meeting, Jack put the meeting off*). And you know when words or sentences have opposite meanings (*alive/dead*; *Jack swims/Jack doesn't swim*).

You generally know the real-world objects that words refer to like *the chair in the corner*; and even if the words do not refer to actual objects, such as *the unicorn behind the bush*, you still have a sense of what they mean; and if the particular object happened to exist, you would have the knowledge to identify it.

You know, or have the capacity to discover, when sentences are true or false. That is, if you know the meaning of a sentence, you know its **truth conditions**. In some cases it's obvious, or redundant (*all kings are male* [true], *all bachelors are married* [false]); in other cases you need some further, nonlinguistic knowledge

139

(*Molybdenum conducts electricity*), but by knowing the meaning, you know the kind of world knowledge that is needed. Often, if you know that a sentence is true (*Nina bathed her dogs*), you can infer that another sentence must also be true (*Nina's dogs got wet*): that is, the first sentence **entails** the second sentence.

All of this knowledge about meaning extends to an unlimited set of sentences, just like our syntactic knowledge, and is part of the grammar of the language. One goal of linguistics is to reveal and make explicit this knowledge about meaning that every speaker has.

The study of the linguistic meaning of morphemes, words, phrases, and sentences is called **semantics**. Subfields of semantics are **lexical semantics**, which is concerned with the meanings of words and the meaning relationships among words; and **phrasal** or **sentential semantics**, which is concerned with the meaning of syntactic units larger than the word. The study of how context affects meaning—for example, how the sentence *It's cold in here* comes to be interpreted as 'close the windows' in certain situations—is called **pragmatics**.

What Speakers Know about Sentence Meaning

Language without meaning is meaningless.

ROMAN JAKOBSON

In this section we discuss the linguistic knowledge you have that permits you to determine whether a sentence is true or false, when one sentence implies the truth or falseness of another, and whether a sentence has multiple meanings. One way to account for this knowledge is by formulating semantic rules that build the meaning of a sentence from the meanings of its words and the way the words combine syntactically. This is often called **truth-conditional semantics** because it takes speakers' knowledge of truth conditions as basic. It is also called **compositional semantics** because it calculates the truth value of a sentence by composing, or putting together, the meanings of smaller units. We will limit our discussion to declarative sentences like *Jack swims* and *Jack kissed Laura*, because we can judge these kinds of sentences as either true or false. At least part of their meaning, then, will be their **truth value**.

Truth

. . . Having Occasion to talk of Lying and false Representation, it was with much Difficulty that he comprehended what I meant. . . . For he argued thus: That the Use of Speech was to make us understand one another and to receive Information of Facts; now if any one said the Thing which was not, these Ends were defeated; because I cannot properly be said to understand him. . . . And these were all the Notions he had concerning that Faculty of Lying, so perfectly well understood, and so universally practiced among human Creatures.

JONATHAN SWIFT, *Gulliver's Travels,* 1726

Suppose you are poolside and Jack is swimming in the pool. If you hear the sentence *Jack swims*, and you know the meaning of that sentence, then you will judge the sentence to be true. On the other hand, if you are indoors and you happen to believe that Jack never learned to swim, then when you hear the very same sentence *Jack swims*, you will judge the sentence to be false and you will think the speaker is misinformed or lying. More generally, if you know the meaning of a sentence, then you can determine under what conditions it is true or false.

You do not need to actually <u>know</u> whether a sentence is true or false to know its meaning. Knowing the meaning tells you how to <u>determine</u> the truth value. The sentence *copper conducts electricity* has meaning and is understood because we know how to determine whether it's true or false: for example, by use of a volt meter. We could also comment sensibly on the sentence by noting the use of copper wire in lamps. If the sentence was *Crumple-horned snorkacks incarnadine nargles* you would find it meaningless because you would not have the foggiest idea how to determine whether it is true or false. Reducing the question of meaning to the question of truth conditions has proved to be very fruitful in understanding the semantic properties of language.

For most sentences it does not make sense to say that they are always true or always false. Rather, they are true or false in a given situation, as we previously saw with *Jack swims*. But a restricted number of sentences are indeed always true regardless of the circumstances. They are called **tautologies**. (The term **analytic** is also used for such sentences.) Examples of tautologies are sentences like *Circles are round* and *A person who is single is not married*. Their truth is guaranteed solely by the meaning of their parts and the way they are put together. Similarly, some sentences are always false. These are called **contradictions**. Examples of contradictions are sentences like *Circles are square* or *A bachelor is married*.

Entailment and Related Notions

You mentioned your name as if I should recognize it, but beyond the obvious facts that you are a bachelor, a solicitor, a Freemason, and an asthmatic, I know nothing whatever about you.

SIR ARTHUR CONAN DOYLE, "The Norwood Builder," in *The Memoirs of Sherlock Holmes*, 1894

Much of what we know is deduced from what people say alongside our observations of the world. As we can deduce from the quotation, Sherlock Holmes took deduction to the ultimate degree. Often, deductions can be made based on language alone.

If you know that the sentence *Jack swims beautifully* is true, then you also know that the sentence *Jack swims* is true. This meaning relation is called **entailment**. We say that *Jack swims beautifully* **entails** *Jack swims*. More generally, one sentence entails another if whenever the first sentence is true the second one is also true in all conceivable circumstances.

Generally, entailment goes only in one direction. So while the sentence *Jack swims beautifully* entails *Jack swims*, the reverse is not true. Knowing merely that *Jack swims* is true does not necessitate the truth of *Jack swims beautifully*. Jack could be a poor swimmer. On the other hand, negating both sentences reverses the entailment. *Jack doesn't swim* entails *Jack doesn't swim beautifully*.

The notion of entailment can be used to reveal knowledge that we have about other meaning relations. For example, omitting tautologies and contradictions, two sentences are **synonymous** (or **paraphrases**) if they are both true or both false with respect to the same situations. Sentences like *Jack put off the meeting* and *Jack postponed the meeting* are synonymous, because when one is true the other must be true; and when one is false the other must also be false. We can describe this pattern in a more concise way by using the notion of entailment:

Two sentences are synonymous if they entail each other.

Thus if sentence A entails sentence B and vice versa, then whenever A is true B is true, and vice versa. Although entailment says nothing specifically about false sentences, it's clear that if sentence A entails sentence B, then whenever B is false, A must be false. (If A were true, B would have to be true.) And if B also entails A, then whenever A is false, B would have to be false. Thus mutual entailment guarantees identical truth values in all situations; the sentences are synonymous. Two sentences are **contradictory** if, whenever one is true, the other is false or, equivalently, there is no situation in which they are both true or both false. For example, the sentences *Jack is alive* and *Jack is dead* are contradictory because if the sentence *Jack is alive* is true, then the sentence *Jack is dead* is false, and vice versa. In other words, *Jack is alive* and *Jack is dead* have opposite truth values. Like synonymy, contradiction can be reduced to a special case of entailment.

Two sentences are *contradictory* if one entails the negation of the other.

For instance, *Jack is alive* entails the negation of *Jack is dead*, namely *Jack is not dead*. Similarly, *Jack is dead* entails the negation of *Jack is alive*, namely *Jack is not alive*.

The notions of *contradiction* (always false) and *contradictory* (opposite in truth value) are related in that if two sentences are contradictory, their conjunction with *and* is a contradiction. Thus *Jack is alive and Jack is dead* is a contradiction; it cannot be true under any circumstances.

Ambiguity

Let's pass gas.

SEEN ON A SIGN IN THE LUNCHROOM OF AN ELECTRIC UTILITY COMPANY

Our semantic knowledge tells us when words or phrases (including sentences) have more than one meaning: that is, when they are ambiguous. In chapter 3 we saw that the sentence *The boy saw the man with a telescope* was an instance of structural ambiguity. It is ambiguous because it can mean that the boy saw the man by using a telescope or that the boy saw the man who was holding a telescope. The sentence is structurally ambiguous because it is associated with two different phrase structures, each corresponding to a different meaning. Here are the two structures:

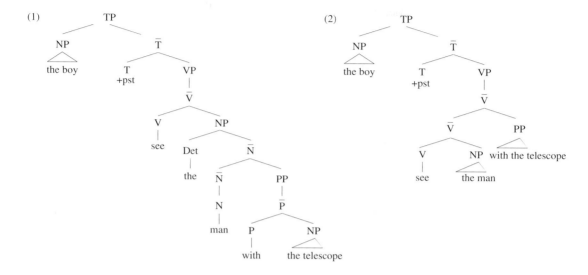

In (1) the PP *with the telescope* modifies the N *man*, so the interpretation is that the man has the telescope. In (2) the PP *with a telescope* modifies $\bar{V}$, the action of seeing the man, so the interpretation is that the boy saw the man by using the telescope.

Lexical ambiguity arises when at least one word in a phrase has more than one meaning. For instance the sentence *This will make you smart* is ambiguous because of the two meanings of the word *smart*: 'clever' and 'feel a burning sensation.'

Our knowledge of lexical and structural ambiguities reveals that the meaning of a linguistic expression is built both on the words it contains and on its syntactic structure. The notion that the meaning of an expression is composed of the meanings of its parts and how they are combined structurally is referred to as the **principle of compositionality**. In the next section we discuss the rules by which the meaning of a phrase or sentence is determined based on its composition.

Compositional Semantics

> To manage a system effectively, you might focus on the interactions of the parts rather than their behavior taken separately.
>
> **RUSSELL L. ACKOFF**

To account for speakers' knowledge of grammaticality, constituent structure, and relations between sentences, as well as for the limitless creativity of our linguistic competence, we concluded (chapter 3) that the grammar must contain syntactic rules.

To account for the knowledge that we have of the truth, reference, entailment, and ambiguity of sentences, as well as for our ability to determine the meaning of a limitless number of expressions, we must suppose that the grammar contains semantic rules that combine the meanings of words into meaningful phrases and sentences.

Semantic Rules

In the sentence *Jack swims*, we know that the word *Jack*, which is a **proper name**, refers to a precise object in the world, which is its **referent**. For instance, in the scenario given earlier, the referential meaning of *Jack* is the guy who is your friend and who is swimming happily in the pool right now. Based on this, we conclude that the meaning of the name *Jack* is the individual it refers to.

What about the meaning of the verb *swim*? At first, it seems as though verbs like *swim* can't pick out a particular thing in the world the way proper names do. But there is a way to think about verbs (and adjectives, and common nouns like *cake*) in terms of what they refer to. Just as the referent of *Jack* relies on what's happening in the world—whether Jack exists, and whether he's swimming in the pool right now—the referent of *swim* depends on what's happening in the world. Based in part on early philosophical work conducted by Gottlob Frege and Bertrand Russell, semanticists think that the best way to define **predicates** (verbs, adjectives and common nouns) is in terms of the individuals that those predicates successfully describe. In particular, the best way to characterize the meaning of *swim*—and a way in which that meaning is reflected in the world—is by having it denote the *set* of individuals (human beings and animals) that swim. You will see in a moment how this way of thinking about the meaning of *swim* helps us understand sentences in a way that accords with our semantic knowledge.

Our semantic rules must be sensitive not only to the meaning of individual words but also to the structure in which they occur. Taking as an example our simple sentence *Jack swims*, let us see how the semantic rules compute its meaning. The meanings of the individual words are summarized as follows:

Word	Meanings
Jack	refers to (or means) the individual Jack
swims	refers to (or means) the set of individuals that swim

The phrase structure tree for our sentence is as follows:

The tree tells us that syntactically the NP *Jack* and the VP *swims* combine to form a sentence (TP). We want to mirror that combination at the semantic level: in other words, we want to combine the meaning of the NP *Jack* (an individual) and the meaning of the VP *swims* (a set of individuals) to obtain the meaning of the sentence *Jack swims*. This is done by means of Semantic Rule I.

Semantic Rule I

The meaning of

is the following truth condition:

> If the meaning of NP (an individual) is a member of the meaning of VP (a set of individuals), then the sentence is TRUE; otherwise it is FALSE.

Rule I states that a sentence composed of a subject NP and a predicate VP is true if the subject NP refers to an individual who is among the members of the set that constitute the meaning of the VP. This rule is entirely general; it does not refer to any particular sentence, individual, or verb. It works equally well for sentences like *Ellen sings* or *Max barks*. Thus the meaning of *Max barks* is the truth condition (i.e., the "if-sentence") that states that the sentence is true if the individual denoted by *Max* is among the set of *barking* individuals.

Let us now try a slightly more complex case: the sentence *Jack kissed Laura*. The main syntactic difference between this example and the previous one is that we now have a transitive verb that requires an extra NP in object position; otherwise our semantic rules derive the meaning using the same mechanical procedure as in the first example. We again start with the word meaning and syntactic structure:

Word	Meanings
Jack	refers to (or means) the individual Jack
Laura	refers to (or means) the individual Laura
kissed	refers to (or means) the set of <u>pairs of individuals</u> X and Y such that X kissed Y.

Here is the phrase structure tree:

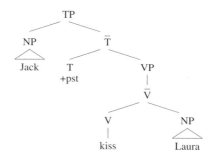

The meaning of the transitive verb *kiss* is still a set, but this time a set of *pairs* of individuals. The meaning of the VP, however, is still a set of single individuals, namely those who kissed Laura. This may be expressed formally in Semantic Rule II.

Semantic Rule II

The meaning of

is the set of individuals X such that X is the first member of any pair in the meaning of V whose second member is the meaning of NP.

The meaning of the sentence is derived by first applying Semantic Rule II, which establishes the meaning of the VP as a certain set of individuals, namely those who kissed Laura. Now Semantic Rule I applies without further ado and gives the meaning of the sentence to be true whenever the meaning of *Jack* is a member of the set that is the meaning of the VP *kissed Laura*. In other words, the sentence is true if Jack kissed Laura and false otherwise. These two semantic rules handle a limitless number of intransitive and transitive sentences.

One last example will illustrate how the semantic knowledge of entailment may be represented in the grammar. Consider *Jack swims beautifully*, and consider further the meaning of the adverb *beautifully*. Its meaning is clearly not an individual or a set of individuals. Rather, the meaning of *beautifully* is an operation that reduces the size of the sets that are the meanings of verb phrases. When applied to the meaning of *swims*, it reduces the set of individuals who swim to the smaller set of those who swim beautifully. We won't express this rule formally, but it is now easy to see one source of entailment. The truth conditions that make *Jack swims beautifully* true are narrower than the truth conditions that make *Jack swims* true by virtue of the fact that among the individuals who swim, fewer of them swim beautifully. Therefore, any truth condition that causes *Jack swims beautifully* to be true necessarily causes *Jack swims* to be true; hence, *Jack swims beautifully* entails *Jack swims*.

These rules, and many more like them, account for our knowledge concerning the truth value of sentences by taking the meanings of words and combining them according to the syntactic structure of the sentence. It is easy to see from these examples how ambiguous meanings arise. Because the meaning of a sentence is computed based on its hierarchical organization, different trees will have different meanings—structural ambiguity—even when the words are the same, as in the example *The boy saw the man with the telescope.*

Similarly, the occurrence of an ambiguous word—lexical ambiguity—when it combines with the other elements of a sentence can make the entire sentence ambiguous, as in *She can't bear children.*

The semantic theory of sentence meaning that we just sketched is not the only possible one, and it is also incomplete, as shown by the paradoxical sentence *This sentence is false.* The sentence cannot be true, else it's false; it cannot be false, else it's true. Therefore it has no truth value, though it certainly has meaning. This notwithstanding, compositional truth-conditional semantics has proven to be an extremely powerful and useful tool for investigating the semantic properties of natural languages.

When Compositionality Goes Awry

A loose sally of the mind; an irregular undigested piece; not a regular and orderly composition.

SAMUEL JOHNSON (1709–1784)

The meaning of an expression is not always obvious, even to a native speaker of the language. Meanings may be obscured in many ways, or at least may require some imagination or special knowledge to be apprehended. Poets, pundits, and yes, even professors can be difficult to understand.

In the previous sections we saw that semantic rules compute sentence meaning compositionally based on the meanings of words and the syntactic structure that contains them. There are, however, interesting cases in which compositionality breaks down, either because there is a problem with words or with the semantic rules. If one or more words in a sentence do not have a meaning, then obviously we will not be able to compute a meaning for the entire sentence. Moreover, even when the individual words have meaning, if they cannot be combined together as required by the syntactic structure and related semantic rules we will also not get to a meaning. We refer to situations of this sort as semantic **anomaly**. Alternatively, it might require a lot of creativity and imagination to derive a meaning. This is what happens in **metaphors**. Finally, some expressions—called **idioms**—have a fixed meaning: that is, a meaning that is not compositional. Applying compositional rules to idioms gives rise to funny or inappropriate meanings.

Anomaly

Don't tell me of a man's being able to talk sense; everyone can talk sense. Can he talk nonsense?

WILLIAM PITT

There is no greater mistake in the world than the looking upon every sort of nonsense as want of sense.

LEIGH HUNT, "On the Talking of Nonsense," 1820

The semantic properties of words determine what other words they can be combined with. A sentence widely used by linguists that we encountered in chapter 3 illustrates this fact:

Colorless green ideas sleep furiously.

The sentence obeys all the syntactic rules of English. The subject is *colorless green ideas* and the predicate is *sleep furiously*. It has the same syntactic structure as the sentence

Dark green leaves rustle furiously.

but there is obviously something semantically wrong with the sentence. The meaning of *colorless* includes the semantic feature 'without color,' but it is combined with the adjective *green*, which has the feature 'green in color.' How can something be both 'without color' and 'green in color'? Other semantic violations occur in the sentence. Such sentences are semantically **anomalous**.

Other English "sentences" make no sense at all because they include "words" that have no meaning; they are **uninterpretable**. They can be interpreted only if some meaning for each nonsense word can be dreamt up. Lewis Carroll's "Jabberwocky" is probably the most famous poem in which most of the content words have no meaning—they do not exist in the lexicon of the language. Still, all the sentences sound as if they should be or could be English sentences:

> 'Twas brillig, and the slithy toves
> Did gyre and gimble in the wabe;
> All mimsy were the borogoves,
> And the mome raths outgrabe.
>
> . . .
>
> He took his vorpal sword in hand:
> Long time the manxome foe he sought—
> So rested he by the Tumtum tree,
> And stood awhile in thought.

Without knowing what *vorpal* means, you nevertheless know that

> He took his vorpal sword in hand

means the same thing as

> He took his sword, which was vorpal, in hand

and

> It was in his hand that he took his vorpal sword.

Knowing the language, and assuming that *vorpal* means the same thing in the three sentences (because the same sounds are used), you can decide that the sense—the truth conditions—of the three sentences are identical. In other words, you are able to decide that two things mean the same thing even though you do not know what either one means. You decide by assuming that the semantic properties of *vorpal* are the same whenever it is used.

We now see why Alice commented, when she had read "Jabberwocky":

> 'It seems very pretty, but it's *rather* hard to understand!' (You see she didn't like to confess, even to herself, that she couldn't make it out at all.) 'Somehow it seems to fill my head with ideas—only I don't exactly know what they are! However, *somebody* killed *something*: that's clear, at any rate—'

Semantic violations in poetry may form strange but interesting aesthetic images, as in Dylan Thomas's phrase *a grief ago. Ago* is ordinarily used with words specified by some temporal semantic feature:

a week ago		*a table ago
an hour ago	but not	*a dream ago
a month ago		*a mother ago
a century ago		

When Thomas used the word *grief* with *ago*, he was adding a durational feature to grief for poetic effect, so while the noun phrase is anomalous, it evokes certain emotions.

In the poetry of E. E. Cummings, there are phrases like

the six subjunctive crumbs twitch
a man . . . wearing a round jeer for a hat
children building this rainman out of snow[1]

Though all of these phrases violate some semantic rules, we can understand them; breaking the rules creates the desired imagery. The fact that we are able to understand, or at least interpret, anomalous expressions, and at the same time recognize their anomalous nature, demonstrates our knowledge of the semantic system and semantic properties of the language.

Metaphor

Our doubts are traitors.

WILLIAM SHAKESPEARE, *Measure for Measure*, c. 1603

Walls have ears.

MIGUEL DE CERVANTES, *Don Quixote*, 1605

The night has a thousand eyes and the day but one.

FRANCES WILLIAM BOURDILLON, "Light," 1873

When what appears to be an anomaly is nevertheless understood in terms of a meaningful concept, the expression becomes a metaphor. There is no strict line between anomalous and metaphorical expressions. Technically, metaphors are anomalous, but the nature of the anomaly creates the salient meanings that metaphors usually have. The anomalous *A grief ago* might come to be interpreted by speakers of English as 'the unhappy time following a sad event' and therefore become a metaphor.

Metaphors may have a literal meaning as well as their metaphorical meaning, so in some sense they are ambiguous. However, when the semantic rules are applied to *Walls have ears*, for example, the literal meaning is so unlikely that listeners use their imagination for another interpretation. The principle of compositionality is very "elastic" and when it fails to produce an acceptable literal meaning, listeners

---

[1]The line from "sonnet entitled how to run the world." Copyright 1935, © 1963, 1991 by the Trustees for the E. E. Cummings Trust. Copyright © 1978 by George James Firmage. The line from "A man who had fallen among thieves." Copyright 1926, 1954, © 1991 by the Trustees for the E. E. Cummings Trust. Copyright © 1985 by George James Firmage. The line from "here is little Effie's head." Copyright 1923, 1925, 1951, 1953, © 1991 by the Trustees for the E. E. Cummings Trust. Copyright © 1976 by George James Firmage. From Complete Poems: 1904–1962 by E. E. Cummings, edited by George J. Firmage. Used by permission of Liveright Publishing Corporation.

try to accommodate and stretch the meaning. This accommodation is based on semantic properties that are inferred or that provide some kind of resemblance or comparison that can end up as a meaningful concept.

This works only up to a certain point, however. It's not clear what the literal meaning of *Our doubts are traitors* might be, though the conceptual meaning that the act of doubting a precious belief is self-betrayal seems plausible. To interpret a metaphor we need to understand the individual words, the literal meaning of the whole expression, and facts about the world. To understand the metaphor

> Time is money

it is necessary to know that in our society we are often paid according to the number of hours or days worked. In fact, "time," which is an abstract concept, is the subject of multiple metaphors. We "save time," "waste time," "manage time," push things "back in time," live on "borrowed time," and suffer the "ravages of time" as the "sands of time" drift away. In effect, the metaphors take the abstract concept of time and treat it as a concrete object of value.

Metaphor has a strong cultural component. Shakespeare uses metaphors that are lost on many of today's playgoers. "I am a man whom Fortune hath cruelly scratched," is most effective as a metaphor in a society like Shakespeare's that commonly depicts "Fortune" as a woman. On the other hand *There's a bug in my program* would make little sense in a culture without computers, even if the idea of having bugs in something indicates a problem.

Many expressions now taken literally may have originated as metaphors, such as "the fall of the dollar," meaning its decline in value on the world market. Many people wouldn't bat an eyelash (another metaphor) at the literal interpretation of saving or wasting time. Metaphorical use of language is language creativity at its highest. Nevertheless, the basis of metaphorical use is very much the ordinary linguistic knowledge that all speakers possess about words, their semantic properties, and their combinatorial possibilities.

Idioms

ARGYLE SWEATER © 2010 Scott Hilburn. Dist. By UNIVERSAL UCLICK. Reprinted with permission. All rights reserved.

Because the words (or morphemes) of a language are arbitrary (not predictable by rule), they must be listed in a mental lexicon. The lexicon is a repository of the words (or morphemes) of a language with their grammatical properties and their meanings. On the other hand, the meanings of morphologically complex words, phrases, and sentences are compositional and are derived by rules. We noted in chapter 2 that the meaning of some words (for example, compounds) is not predictable, so these must also be given in the lexicon. It turns out that languages also contain many phrases whose meanings are not predictable on the basis of the meanings of the individual words. These phrases typically start out as metaphors that "catch on" and are repeated so often that they become fixtures in the language. Such expressions are called *idioms*, or **idiomatic phrases**, as in these English examples:

> sell down the river
> rake over the coals
> drop the ball
> let their hair down
> put his foot in his mouth
> throw her weight around
> snap out of it
> give a piece of your mind

Here is where the usual semantic rules for combining meanings do not apply. The principle of compositionality is superseded by expressions that act very much like individual morphemes in that they are not decomposable, but have a fixed meaning that must be learned. Idioms are similar in structure to ordinary phrases except that they tend to be frozen in form and do not readily undergo rules that change word order or substitution of their parts.

Thus, the sentence in (1) has the same structure as the sentence in (2).

1. She put her foot in her mouth.
2. She put her bracelet in her drawer.

But while the sentences in (3) and (4) are clearly related to (2),

3. The drawer in which she put her bracelet was her own.
4. Her bracelet was put in her drawer.

the sentences in (5) and (6) do not have the idiomatic sense of sentence (1), except, perhaps, humorously.

5. The mouth in which she put her foot was her own.
6. Her foot was put in her mouth.

Also, if we know the meaning of (2) and the meaning of the word *necklace* we will immediately understand (7).

7. She put her necklace in the drawer.

But if we try substituting *hand* for *foot* in sentence (1), we do not maintain the idiomatic meaning, but rather have the literal compositional meaning.

There are, however, some idioms whose parts can be moved without affecting the idiomatic sense:

The FBI kept tabs on radicals.
Tabs were kept on radicals by the FBI.
Radicals were kept tabs on by the FBI.

Like metaphors, idioms can break the rules on combining semantic properties. The object of *eat* must usually be something with the semantic feature "edible," but in

He ate his hat.

and

Eat your heart out.

this restriction is violated.

Idioms often lead to humor:

What did the doctor tell the vegetarian about his surgically implanted
    heart valve from a pig?
That it was okay as long as he didn't "eat his heart out."

Idioms may even show disrespect for syntax, e.g., the expression *deep six*, while containing parts that are never used as verbs, is itself a verb meaning 'to put the kibosh on,' yet another idiom. Where will it ever end!?

With some imagination, idioms may also be used to create what appear to be paradoxes. In many places such as Times Square in New York, a ball is dropped at midnight on New Year's Eve. Now, if the person in charge doesn't drop the ball, then he has "dropped the ball." And if that person does indeed drop the ball, then he has not "dropped the ball." Right?

Idioms, grammatically as well as semantically, have special characteristics. They must be entered into the lexicon or mental dictionary as single items with their meanings specified, and speakers must learn the special restrictions on their use in sentences.

All languages have idioms, but idioms rarely if ever translate word for word from one language to another. Most speakers of American English understand the idiom *to kick the bucket* as meaning 'to die.' The same combination of words in Spanish (*patear el cubo*) has only the literal meaning of striking a specific bucket with a foot. On the other hand, *estirar la pata*, literally 'to stretch the (animal) leg,' has the idiomatic sense of 'to die' in Spanish.

Lexical Semantics (Word Meanings)

"There's glory for you!"
"I don't know what you mean by 'glory,'" Alice said.
Humpty Dumpty smiled contemptuously.
"Of course you don't—till I tell you. I meant 'there's a nice knock-down argument for you!'"
"But 'glory' doesn't mean 'a nice knock-down argument,'" Alice objected.

"When I use a word," Humpty Dumpty said, in rather a scornful tone, "it means just what I choose it to mean—neither more nor less."

"The question is," said Alice, "whether you can make words mean so many different things."

LEWIS CARROLL, *Through the Looking-Glass*, 1871

As just discussed, the meaning of a phrase or sentence is partially a function of the meanings of the words it contains. Similarly, the meaning of a morphologically complex word is a function of its component morphemes, as we saw in chapter 2. However, there is a fundamental difference between word meaning—or *lexical semantics*—and sentence meaning. The meaning of entries in the mental lexicon—be they morphemes, words, or idioms—is conventional; that is, speakers of a language implicitly agree on their meaning, and children acquiring the language must simply learn those meanings outright. On the other hand, the meaning of most sentences must be constructed by the application of semantic rules. Earlier we discussed the rules of semantic composition. In this section we will talk about word meaning and the semantic relationships that exist between words and morphemes.

Although the agreed-upon meaning of a word may shift over time within a language community, we are not free as individuals to change the meanings of words at will; if we did, we would be unable to communicate with each other. Humpty Dumpty seems unwilling to accept this convention, though fortunately for us there are few such bad eggs among speakers. All the speakers of a language share a basic vocabulary—the sounds and meanings of morphemes and words. Each of us knows the meanings of thousands of words. This knowledge permits us to use words to express our thoughts and to understand the thoughts of others. The meaning of words is part of linguistic knowledge. Your mental storehouse of information about words and morphemes is what we have been calling the *lexicon*.

Theories of Word Meaning

It is natural . . . to think of there being connected with a sign . . . besides . . . the reference of the sign, also what I should like to call the sense of the sign. . . .

GOTTLOB FREGE, "On Sense and Reference," 1892

Dictionaries are filled with words and give their meanings using other words rather than in terms of some more basic units of meaning, whatever they might be. In this sense a dictionary really provides *paraphrases* rather than meanings. It relies on our *knowledge* of the language to understand the definitions. The meanings associated with words in our mental lexicon are not like what we find in a conventional dictionary, although it is a challenge to linguists to specify precisely how word meanings are represented in the mind.

If the meaning of a word is not like a dictionary entry, what is it? This question has been debated by philosophers and linguists for centuries. One proposal is that the meaning of a word or expression is its **reference**, its association with the object it refers to. This real-world object is called the *referent*.

Reference

"There's nothing here under 'Superman'—is it possible you made the reservation under another name?"

Michael Maslin / The New Yorker Collection/Cartoonbank.com

We have already determined that the meaning of a proper name like *Jack* is its reference: the link between the word *Jack* and the person named Jack, which is its referent. Proper names are noun phrases (NPs); you can substitute a proper name in any NP position in a sentence and preserve grammaticality. There are other NPs that refer to individuals as well. For instance, NPs like *the happy swimmer, my friend,* and *that guy* can all be used to refer to Jack in the situation in which you've observed Jack swimming. The same is true for pronouns such as *I, you,* and *him,* which also function as NPs. In all these cases, the reference of the NP—which singles out the individual referred to under the circumstances—is part of the meaning of the NP.

On the other hand, not every NP refers to an individual. For instance, the sentence *No baby swims* contains the NP *no baby,* but your linguistic knowledge tells you that this NP does not refer to any specific individual. If *no baby* has no reference, but is not meaningless, then something about meaning beyond reference must be present.

In the fictional world, *Superman* and *Clark Kent* have the same reference— they are one and the same person. But there is more meaning to their names than that. If we substitute *Clark Kent* for *Superman* in the sentence *Lois Lane is in love with Superman* we alter its truth value from true to false. Again, we see that there must be a dimension of meaning beyond mere reference.

Similarly, *Barack Obama* and *the President* have (at this writing) the same reference, but the meaning of the NP *the President* is additionally 'the head of state of the United States of America,' which is an element of meaning separate from reference and more enduring.

Sense

There must be something more to meaning than reference alone. This is also suggested by the fact that speakers know the meanings of many words that have no real-world referents (e.g., *hobbits*, *unicorns*, and *Harry Potter*). Similarly, what real-world entities would function words like *of* and *by*, or modal verbs such as *will* or *may* refer to?

These additional elements of meaning are often termed **sense**. It is the extra something referred to earlier. *Unicorns*, *hobbits*, and *Harry Potter* have sense but no reference (with regard to objects in the real world). Conversely, proper names typically have only reference. A name like *Clem Kadiddlehopper* may point out a certain person, its referent, but has little linguistic meaning beyond that.

Philosophers of language dating back to ancient Greece have suggested that part of the meaning of a word is the mental image it conjures up. This helps with the problem of unicorns, hobbits, and Harry Potter; we may have a clear image of these entities from books, movies, and so on, and that connection might serve as reference for those expressions. However, many meaningful expressions are not associated with any clear, unique image agreed on by most speakers of the language. For example, what image is evoked by the words *very*, *if*, and *every*? It's difficult to say, yet these expressions are certainly meaningful. What is the image of oxygen as distinct from nitrogen—both are colorless, odorless gases, yet they differ in meaning. What mental image would we have of *dog* that is general enough to include Yorkshire Terriers and Great Danes and yet excludes foxes and wolves? And the image of *no man* in *no man is an island* presents a riddle worthy of a Zen koan.

Although the idea that the meaning of a word corresponds to a mental image is intuitive (because many words do provoke imagery), it is clearly inadequate as a general explanation of what people know about word meanings.

Perhaps the best we can do is to note that the reference part of a word's meaning, if it has reference at all, is the association with its referent; and the sense part of a word's meaning contains the information needed to complete the association, and to suggest properties that the referent may have, whether it exists in the real world or in the world of imagination.

Lexical Relations

Does he wear a turban, a fez or a hat?
Does he sleep on a mattress, a bed or a mat, or a Cot,
The Akond of Swat?
Can he write a letter concisely clear,
Without a speck or a smudge or smear or Blot,
The Akond of Swat?

EDWARD LEAR, "The Akond of Swat," in *Laughable Lyrics*, 1877

Although no theory of word meaning is complete, we know that speakers have considerable knowledge about the meaning relationships among different words in their mental lexicons, and any theory must take that knowledge into account.

Words are semantically related to one another in a variety of ways. The words that describe these relations often end in the bound morpheme -*nym*. The best-known lexical relations are synonyms, illustrated in the poem by Edward Lear, and antonyms, or opposites. **Synonyms** are words or expressions that have the same meaning in some or all contexts. There are dictionaries of synonyms that contain many hundreds of entries, such as:

apathetic/phlegmatic/passive/sluggish/indifferent
pedigree/ancestry/genealogy/descent/lineage

A sign in the San Diego Zoo Wild Animal Park states:

Please do not annoy, torment, pester, plague, molest, worry, badger, harry, harass, heckle, persecute, irk, bullyrag, vex, disquiet, grate, beset, bother, tease, nettle, tantalize, or ruffle the animals.

It has been said that there are no perfect synonyms—that is, no two words ever have *exactly* the same meaning. Still, the following two sentences have very similar meanings:

He's sitting on the sofa. / He's sitting on the couch.

During the French Norman occupation of England that began in 1066 CE, many French words of Latin origin were imported into English. As a result, English contains many synonymous pairs consisting of a word with an English (or Germanic) root, and another with a Latin root, such as:

English	**Latin**
manly	virile
heal	recuperate
send	transmit
go down	descend

Words that are opposite in meaning are **antonyms**. There are several kinds of antonymy. There are **complementary pairs**:

alive/dead   present/absent   awake/asleep

They are complementary in that *alive* = *not dead* and *dead* = *not alive*, and so on.
There are **gradable pairs** of antonyms:

big/small   hot/cold   fast/slow   happy/sad

The meaning of adjectives in gradable pairs is related to the objects they modify. The words do not provide an absolute scale. For example, we know that "a small elephant" is much bigger than "a large mouse." *Fast* is faster when applied to an airplane than to a car.

Gradable pairs give rise to implications, so that *An elephant is bigger than a mouse* implies *A mouse is smaller than an elephant*. But beware of idioms! *Blood is thicker than water* as an idiom about family ties does not imply the nonsensical (as an idiom) *water is thinner than blood*.

Another characteristic of certain pairs of gradable antonyms is that one is **marked** and the other **unmarked**. The unmarked member is the one used in questions of degree. We ask, ordinarily, "How *high* is the mountain?" (not "How *low* is it?"). We answer "Ten thousand feet high" but never "Ten thousand feet low," except humorously or ironically. Thus *high* is the *unmarked* member of *high/low*. Similarly, *tall* is the unmarked member of *tall/short*, *fast* the unmarked member of *fast/slow*, and so on.

Another kind of opposition involves pairs like

give/receive   buy/sell   teacher/pupil

They are called **relational opposites**, and they display symmetry in their meanings. If X *gives* Y to Z, then Z *receives* Y from X. If X is Y's *teacher*, then Y is X's *pupil*. Pairs of words ending in *-er* and *-ee* are usually relational opposites. If Mary is Bill's *employer*, then Bill is Mary's *employee*.

In English there are several ways to form antonyms. You can add the prefix *un-*:

likely/unlikely   able/unable   fortunate/unfortunate

or you can add *non-*:

entity/nonentity   conformist/nonconformist

or you can add *in-*:

tolerant/intolerant   discreet/indiscreet   decent/indecent

These strategies occasionally backfire, however. Pairs such as *loosen* and *unloosen*; *flammable* and *inflammable*; *valuable* and *invaluable*; and a few others actually have the same or nearly the same meaning, despite looking like antonyms.

Other lexical relations include homonyms, polysemy, and hyponyms.

Hilary B. Price/King Features Syndicate

Words like *bear* and *bare* are **homonyms** (also called **homophones**). Homonyms are words that have different meanings but are pronounced the same, and may or may not be spelled the same. (They're **homographs** when spelled the same, but when homographs are pronounced differently like *pussy* meaning 'infected' or *pussy* meaning 'kitten,' they are called **heteronyms** rather than homonyms.) Near nonsense sentences like *Entre nous, the new gnu knew nu is a Greek letter* tease us with homonyms. Homonyms easily lead to ambiguity, as the confused canine in the cartoon confirms.

When a word has multiple meanings that are related conceptually or historically, it is said to be **polysemous**. For example, the word *diamond* referring to a jewel and also to a baseball field is polysemous. Many words in English are polysemous and have several separated entries in dictionaries owing to their diverse meanings.

Speakers of English know that the words *red*, *white*, and *blue* are color words. Similarly, *lion*, *tiger*, *leopard*, and *lynx* are all felines. *Hyponymy* is the relationship between the more general term such as *color* and the more specific instances of it, such as *red*. Thus *red* is a hyponym of *color*, and *lion* is a hyponym of *feline*; or equivalently, *color* has the hyponym *red* and *feline* has the hyponym *lion*.

Semantic Features

If it is true that words have meanings, why don't we throw away words and keep just the meanings?

LUDWIG WITTGENSTEIN

In the previous sections we discussed word meaning in relation to objects in the world, and this permitted us to develop a truth-based semantics. We also explored the meaning of words in relation to other words. But it is also possible to look for a more basic set of **semantic features** or properties that are part of word meanings and that reflect our knowledge about what words mean.

Decomposing the meanings of words into semantic features can clarify how certain words relate to other words. For example, the basic property of antonyms is that they share all but one semantic feature. We know that *big* and *red* are not antonyms because they have too few semantic features in common. They are both adjectives, but *big* has a semantic feature "about size," whereas *red* has a semantic feature "about color." On the other hand, *buy/sell* are relational opposites because both contain a semantic feature like "change in possession," and differ only in the direction of the change.

Semantic features are among the conceptual elements that are part of the meanings of words and sentences. Consider, for example, the sentence:

The assassin killed Thwacklehurst.

If the word *assassin* is in your mental dictionary, you know that it was some *person* who murdered some *important person* named Thwacklehurst. Your knowledge of the meaning of *assassin* tells you that an animal did not do the killing, and that Thwacklehurst was not an average citizen. Knowledge of *assassin* includes knowing that the individual to whom that word refers is human, is a murderer, and is a killer of important people. These bits of information are some of the semantic features of the word on which speakers of the language agree. The meaning of all nouns, verbs, adjectives, and adverbs—the content words—and even of some of the function words, such as *with* and *over*, can at least partially be specified by such properties.

Evidence for Semantic Features

Semantic properties are not directly observable. Their existence must be inferred from linguistic evidence. One source of such evidence is the speech errors, or "slips of the tongue," that we all produce. Consider the following unintentional word substitutions that some speakers have actually spoken.

Intended Utterance	Actual Utterance (Error)
bridge of the nose	bridge of the neck
when my gums bled	when my tongues bled
he came too late	he came too early
Mary was young	Mary was early
the lady with the Dachshund	the lady with the Volkswagen
that's a horse of another color	that's a horse of another race
his ancestors were farmers	his descendants were farmers
he has to pay her alimony	he has to pay her rent

These errors, and thousands of others that have been collected and catalogued, reveal that the incorrectly substituted words are not random but share some semantic features with the intended words. *Nose, neck, gums,* and *tongues* are all "body parts" or "parts of the head." *Young, early,* and *late* are related to "time." *Dachshund* and *Volkswagen* are both "German" and "small." The shared semantic features of *color* and *race, ancestor* and *descendant,* and *alimony* and *rent* are apparent.

The semantic properties that describe the linguistic meaning of a word should not be confused with other nonlinguistic properties, such as physical properties. Scientists know that water is composed of hydrogen and oxygen, but such knowledge is not part of a word's meaning. We know that water is an essential ingredient of lemonade and baths. However, we don't need to know any of these things to know what the word *water* means, and to be able to use and understand it in a sentence.

Semantic Features and Grammar

King Features Syndicate

Further evidence that words are composed of smaller bits of meaning is that semantic features interact with different aspects of the grammar such as morphology or syntax. These effects show up in both nouns and verbs.

Semantic Features of Nouns

The same semantic feature may be shared by many words. "Female" is a semantic feature, sometimes indicated by the suffix -ess, that makes up part of the meaning of nouns, such as:

tigress	hen	aunt	maiden
doe	mare	debutante	widow
ewe	vixen	girl	woman

The words in the last two columns are also distinguished by the semantic feature "human," which is also found in:

doctor	dean	professor	teenager
bachelor	parent	baby	child

Another part of the meaning of the words *baby* and *child* is that they are "young." (We will continue to indicate words by using *italics* and semantic features by double quotes.) The word *father* has the properties "male" and "adult," as do *uncle* and *bachelor*.

In some languages, though not English, nouns occur with **classifiers**, grammatical morphemes that indicate the semantic class of the noun. In Swahili a noun that has the semantic feature "human" is prefixed with *m-* if singular and *wa-* if plural, as in *mtoto* (child) and *watoto* (children). A noun that has the feature "human artifact," such as *bed, chair,* or *knife,* is prefixed with the classifiers *ki* if singular and *vi* if plural: for example, *kiti* (chair) and *viti* (chairs).

Semantic properties may have syntactic and semantic effects, too. For example, the kinds of determiners that a noun may occur with are controlled by whether it is a "count" noun or a "mass" noun.

Consider these data:

I have two dogs.	*I have two rice(s).
I have a dog.	*I have a rice.
*I have dog.	I have rice.
He has many dogs.	*He has many rice(s).
*He has much dogs.	He has much rice.

Count nouns can be enumerated and pluralized—*one potato, two potatoes.* They may be preceded by the indefinite determiner *a*, and by the quantifier *many* as in *many potatoes,* but not by *much*: **much potato*. They must also occur with a determiner of some kind. Nouns such as *rice, water,* and *milk,* which cannot be enumerated or pluralized, are **mass nouns**. They cannot be preceded by *a* or *many*, and they can occur with the quantifier *much* or without any determiner at all. The humor of the cartoon is based both on the ambiguity of *toast* and the fact that as a food *French toast* is a mass noun, but as an oration it is a count noun. The count/mass distinction captures the fact that speakers know the properties that govern which determiner types go with different nouns. Without it we could not describe these differences.

Generally, the count/mass distinction corresponds to the difference between discrete objects and homogeneous substances. But it would be incorrect to say that this distinction is grounded in human perception, because different languages may treat the same object differently. For example, in English the words *hair*, *furniture*, and *spaghetti* are mass nouns. We say *Some hair is curly*, *Much furniture is poorly made*, *John loves spaghetti*. In Italian, however, these words are count nouns, as illustrated in the following sentences:

Ivano ha mangiato molti spaghetti ieri sera.
Ivano ate many spaghettis last evening.
Piero ha comprato un mobile nuovo.
Piero bought a new (piece of) furniture.
Luisella ha pettinato i suoi capelli.
Luisella combed her hairs.

We would have to assume a radical form of linguistic determinism (remember the Sapir-Whorf hypothesis from chapter 1) to say that Italian and English speakers have different perceptions of hair, furniture, and spaghetti. It is more reasonable to assume that languages can differ to some extent in the semantic or syntactic features they assign to words with the same referent, somewhat independently of the way their speakers conceptualize that referent. Even within a particular language we can have different words—count and mass—to describe the same object or substance. For example, in English we have *shoes* (count) and *footwear* (mass), *coins* (count) and *change* (mass).

Semantic Features of Verbs

Verbs also have semantic features as part of their meaning. For example, "cause" is a feature of verbs such as *darken*, *kill*, *uglify*, and so on.

darken	cause to become dark
kill	cause to die
uglify	cause to become ugly

"Go" is a feature of verbs that mean a change in location or possession, such as *swim*, *crawl*, *throw*, *fly*, *give*, or *buy*:

Jack swims.
The baby crawled under the table.
The boy threw the ball over the fence.
John gave Mary a beautiful engagement ring.

Words like *swim* have an additional feature like "in liquid," while *crawl* has "close to a surface."

"Become" is a feature expressing the end state of the action of certain verbs. For example, the verb *break* can be broken down into the following components of meaning: "cause" to "become" broken.

Verbal features, like features on nouns, may have syntactic consequences. For example, verbs can either describe **events**, such as *John kissed Mary/John ate oysters*, or **states**, such as *John knows Mary/John likes oysters*. The eventive/stative difference is mirrored in the syntax. Eventive sentences still sound natural when passivized, when expressed progressively, when used as imperatives, and with certain adverbs:

Eventives

Mary was kissed by John.	Oysters were eaten by John.
John is kissing Mary.	John is eating oysters.
Kiss Mary!	Eat oysters!
John deliberately kissed Mary.	John deliberately ate oysters.

The stative sentences seem peculiar, if not ungrammatical or anomalous, when cast in the same form. (The preceding "?" indicates the strangeness.)

Statives

?Mary is known by John.	?Oysters are liked by John.
?John is knowing Mary.	?John is liking oysters.
?Know Mary!	?Like oysters!
?John deliberately knows Mary.	?John deliberately likes oysters.

Negation is a particularly interesting component of the meaning of some verbs. Expressions such as *ever, anymore, have a red cent,* and many more are ungrammatical in certain simple affirmative sentences, but grammatical in corresponding negative ones.

> *Mary will ever smile. (Cf. Mary will not ever smile.)
> *I can visit you anymore. (Cf. I cannot visit you anymore.)
> *It's worth a red cent. (Cf. It's not worth a red cent.)

Such expressions are called **negative polarity items** because they require a negative element such as "not" elsewhere in the sentence. Consider these data:

> *John thinks that he'll ever fly a plane again.
> *John hopes to ever fly a plane again.
> John doubts that he'll ever fly a plane again.
> John refuses to ever fly a plane again.

This suggests that verbs such as *doubt* and *refuse,* but not *think* and *hope,* have "negative" as a component of their meaning. *Doubt* may be analyzed as 'think that not,' and *refuse* as 'intend not to.' The negative feature in the verb allows the negative polarity item *ever* to occur grammatically without the overt presence of *not.*

Argument Structure

Verbs also differ in terms of the number and type of phrases they can take as complements and/or adjuncts. As we noted in chapter 3, transitive verbs such as *find, hit, chase,* and so on take, or c-select, a direct object complement, whereas intransitive verbs like *arrive* or *sleep* do not. Ditransitive verbs such as *give* or *throw* take two objects, as in *John threw Mary a ball.* In addition, most verbs take a subject.

The various NPs that occur with a verb are its **arguments**. Thus intransitive verbs have one argument: the subject; transitive verbs have two arguments: the subject and direct object; ditransitive verbs have three arguments: the subject, direct object, and indirect object. The **argument structure** of a verb is part of its meaning and is included in its lexical entry.

The verb not only determines the number of arguments in a sentence, but it also limits the semantic properties of both its subject and its objects. For example, *find* and *sleep* require (s-select) animate subjects. The well-known *colorless green ideas sleep furiously* is semantically anomalous because ideas (colorless or not) are not animate. Components of a verb's meaning can also be relevant to the choice of arguments it can take. For example, the verbs in (1) and (3) can take two objects—they're ditransitive—while those in (2) and (4) cannot.

1. John threw/tossed/kicked/flung the boy the ball.
2. *John pushed/pulled/lifted/hauled the boy the ball.
3. Mary faxed/radioed/e-mailed/phoned Helen the news.
4. *Mary murmured/mumbled/muttered/shrieked Helen the news.

Although all the verbs in (1) and (2) are verbs of motion, they differ in how the force of the motion is applied: the verbs in (1) involve a single quick motion whereas those in (2) involve a prolonged use of force. Similarly, the verbs in (3) and (4) are all verbs of communication, but their meanings differ in the way the message is communicated; those in (3) involve an external apparatus whereas those in (4) involve the type of voice used. Finally, the ditransitive verbs have "transfer direct object to indirect object" in their meaning. In (1) the ball is transferred to the boy. In (3) the news is transferred, or leastwise transmitted, to Helen. The ditransitive verbs *give*, *write*, *send*, and *throw* all have this property. Even when the transference is not overt, it may be inferred. In *John baked Mary a cake*, there is an implied transfer of the cake from John to Mary. Subtle aspects of meaning are mirrored in the argument structure of the verbs, and indeed, this connection between form and meaning may help children acquire the syntactic and semantic rules of their language, as will be discussed in chapter 9.

Thematic Roles

A feminine boy from Khartoum
Took a masculine girl to his room
They spent the whole night
In one hell of a fight
About who should do what—and to whom?

ANONYMOUS LIMERICK, quoted in *More Limericks*, G. Legman (ed.), 1977

The NP arguments in the VP, which include the subject and any objects, are semantically related in various ways to the verb. The relations depend on the meaning of the particular verb. For example, the NP *the boy* in the sentence:

1. The boy rolled a red ball.
       agent   theme

is the "doer" of the rolling action, also called the **agent**. The NP *a red ball* is the **theme** or the "undergoer" of the rolling action. Relations such as agent and theme are called **thematic roles**. Thematic roles express the kind of relation that holds between the arguments of the verb and the type of situation that the verb describes.

A further example is the sentence:

2. The boy threw the red ball to the girl.
      agent   theme   goal

Here, *the girl* bears the thematic role of **goal**, that is, the endpoint of a change in location or possession. The verb phrase is interpreted to mean that the theme of *throw* ends up in the position of the goal.

Other thematic roles are **source**, where the action originates; **instrument**, the means used to accomplish the action; and **experiencer**, one receiving sensory input:

    Professor Snape awakened Harry Potter with his wand.
       source   experiencer   instrument

The particular thematic roles assigned by a verb can be traced back to components of the verb's meaning. Verbs such as *throw, buy,* and *fly* contain a feature "go" expressing a change in location or possession. The feature "go" is thus linked to the presence of the thematic roles of theme, source, and goal. Verbs like *awaken* or *frighten* have a feature "affects mental state" so that one of its arguments takes on the thematic role of experiencer.

Thematic role assignment, or **theta assignment**, is also connected to syntactic structure. In the sentence in (2) the role of theme is assigned to the direct object *the ball* and the role of goal to the indirect object *the girl*. Verb pairs such as *sell* and *buy* both involve the feature "go." They are therefore linked to a thematic role of theme, which is assigned to the direct object, as in the following sentences:

a. John sold the book to Mary.
      agent   theme   goal

b. Mary bought the book from John.
      agent   theme   source

In addition, *sell* is linked to the presence of a goal (the recipient or endpoint of the transfer), and *buy* to the presence of a source (the initiator of the transfer). Thus, *buy/sell* are relational opposites because both contain the semantic feature "go" (the transfer of goods or services) and they differ only in the direction of transfer, that is, whether the indirect object is a source or goal. Thematic roles are not assigned to arguments randomly. There is a connection between the meaning of a verb and the syntactic structure of sentences containing the verb.

Our knowledge of verbs includes their syntactic category, which arguments they select, and the thematic roles they assign to their arguments.

Thematic roles are the same in sentences that are paraphrases.

1. The dog bit the stick. / The stick was bitten by the dog.
2. The trainer gave the dog a treat. / The trainer gave a treat to the dog.

In both sentences in (1) *the dog* is the agent and *the stick* is the theme. Similarly in (2) *the treat* is the theme and *the dog* is the goal. This is because certain thematic roles must be assigned to the same d-structure position: for example, theme is assigned to the object of *bit/bitten*.

In general, then, an NP receives its thematic role from its position in d-structure, not s-structure. When the s-structure deviates from the d-structure owing to syntactic rules, it is the d-structure that determines the semantic relationships. Thus *the stick* in the passive sentence *the stick was bitten by the dog* must have originated in object position in d-structure and moved to subject position in s-structure by a syntactic rule:

___ was bitten the stick by the dog   →   the stick was bitten ___ by the dog

d-structure   s-structure

Thematic roles may remain the same in sentences that are *not* paraphrases, as in the following instances:

3. The boy opened the door with the key.
4. The key opened the door.
5. The door opened.

In all three of these sentences, *the door* is the theme, the object that is opened. Thus *the door* in (5) originates as the object of *open* in d-structure and undergoes a movement rule, much like in the passive example above.

___ opened the door   →   The door opened ___

Although the sentences in (3)–(5) are not strict paraphrases of one another, they are structurally and semantically related in that they have similar d-structure configurations. Indeed, sentence (3) entails (4) and (5), and (4) alone entails (5).

In the sentences in (3) and (4), *the key*, despite its different positions, has the thematic role of instrument, suggesting greater structural flexibility for some thematic roles. The semantics of the three sentences is determined by the meaning of the verb *open* and the rules that determine how thematic roles are assigned to the verb's NP arguments.

Pragmatics

> We interpret this sketch instantly and effortlessly as a gathering of people before a structure, probably a gateway; the people are listening to a single declaiming figure in the center. . . . But all this is a miracle, for there is little detailed information in the lines or shading (such as there is). Every line is a mere suggestion. . . . So here is the miracle: from a merest, sketchiest squiggle of lines, you and I converge to find adumbration of a coherent scene. . . . The problem of utterance interpretation is not dissimilar to this visual miracle. An utterance is not, as it were, a veridical model or "snapshot" of the scene it describes. . . . Rather, an utterance is just as sketchy as the Rembrandt drawing.
>
> STEPHEN C. LEVINSON, *Presumptive Meanings: The Theory of Generalized Conversational Implicature*, 2000

We've just discussed lexical semantics (the literal meanings of words) and compositional semantics (the literal meaning of sentences). We described the latter in terms of truth-conditions. The idea is that you know what a sentence means if you know what the world would have to look like in order for that sentence to be true.

Literal meaning isn't the only sort of meaning we use when we use language to communicate with others. Some meaning is **extra-truth-conditional**: it comes about as a result of how a speaker uses the literal meaning in conversation, or as a part of a **discourse**. The study of extra-truth-conditional meaning is **pragmatics**.

Just as artists depict scenes with representations that aren't 100% explicit, like the sketch on page 165, language users describe states of affairs with sentences that aren't 100% explicit. And just as there are a number of reasons an artist might choose a sketch or an abstract painting to depict a scene (instead of a photograph), there are a number of reasons a speaker might choose a particular sentence or discourse to describe a state of affairs. In what follows we'll discuss different ways in which speakers can invoke meaning without expressing it literally.

Pronouns and Other Deictic Words

> CHICKEN (shouting to friend across the road): *Hey, how do I get to the other side?*
> FRIEND: *You're on the other side!*
>
> SOURCE OBSCURE

One way in which context can supplement a less-than-explicit sentence meaning is through words that receive part of their meaning via context and the orientation of the speaker. Such words are called **deictic** and include pronouns (*she, it, I*), demonstratives (*this, that*), adverbs (*here, there, now, today*), prepositions (*behind, before*) and complex expressions involving such words (*those towers over there*).

Imagine both sets of sentences in (1) being spoken by Arnold Schwarzenegger in Venice on December 11, 2012.

1. **a.** Arnold Schwarzenegger really likes it in Venice. On December 11, 2012, there was a boat parade in the canals in Venice. On December 12, 2012, an art festival will be held. The art festival on December 12, 2012 will be extremely fun.

   b. I really like it in Venice. Today, there was a boat parade in the canals here. Tomorrow an art festival will be held. It will be extremely fun.

The difference between (1a) and (1b) is that (1a) is extremely explicit, while (1b) relies on deictic terms to determine part of the meaning of the sentences. Because our use of language is relatively inexplicit we're used to interpreting such terms so that (1b) sounds perfectly natural. In fact, it probably will sound more natural to you than (1a), as we are entirely accustomed to using these shortcuts.

And this is despite the fact that we often have to look to context to determine the reference of pronoun. While proper nouns like *December 12, 2012* and *Arnold Schwarzenegger* have context-independent meanings, which means that they'll always pick out the same referents regardless of the context, other words like *here* and *tomorrow* have context-dependent meanings; their reference is determined in part by the context in which they're uttered.

We say "in part" because the particular deictic word itself helps provide restrictions on its own referent. *Here* and *there* have locations as referents; *then* and *now* are temporal referents; *he* and *she* have human referents, and *I* is extremely restrictive: it can only refer to the speaker.

Even though the referent of a pronoun is lexically restricted, we need to look to the context in which the pronoun is uttered to determine the referent. This process is called **reference resolution**. There are two types of context relevant for the resolution of a pronoun: **linguistic** and **situational**. Linguistic context is anything that has been uttered in the discourse prior to or along with the pronoun. Situational context is anything non-linguistic.

Pronouns and Situational Context

Hank Ketcham/North America Syndicate/King Features Syndicate

Situational context often takes the form of a gesture, like pointing or nodding, as in *He went that way!* or *Who IS that masked man?* Similarly, *next week* has a different reference when uttered today than a month from today. If you found an undated notice announcing a "BIG SALE NEXT WEEK," you would not know whether the sale had already taken place.

The "Dennis the Menace" cartoon illustrates the hilarity that may ensue if deictic words are misinterpreted.

Directional terms such as

before/behind left/right front/back

are deictic insofar as you need to know the orientation in space of the conversational participants to know their reference. In Japanese the verb *kuru*, 'come,' can only be used for motion toward the speaker. A Japanese speaker cannot call up a friend and ask

May I *kuru* to your house?

as you might, in English, ask "May I come to your house?" The correct verb is *iku*, 'go,' which indicates motion away from the place of utterance. In Japanese these verbs have a deictic aspect to their meaning. The verbs *come* and *go* have somewhat of the same effect in English. If someone says *A thief came into the house* versus *A thief went into the house*, you would assume the speaker to have been in the house in the first case, and not in the house in the second.

Pronouns and Linguistic Context

King Features Syndicate

There are two different ways in which the reference of a pronoun can be resolved by the linguistic context. The first is sentence-internal; the second is sentence-external. We'll illustrate the first way by discussing reflexive pronouns.

A reflexive pronoun is a sort of pronoun that needs to receive its reference via linguistic context, and more specifically by sentence-internal linguistic context. In other words, it requires that the sentence contain another NP—an **antecedent**—that it can **co-refer** with. In English, reflexive pronouns end with *-self* or *-selves*, like *himself* or *themselves*. (2a) shows that a reflexive pronoun requires an antecedent in the sentence. (2b) shows that a reflexive pronoun must match the person, gender, and number of its antecedent.

2. **a.** *Herself left.

   b. *John wrote herself a letter.

Interestingly, the restriction on reflexive pronouns is even stronger than (2) suggests. It's not enough that they have a matching antecedent in the sentence, but that antecedent must be in the right position with respect to the co-referring reflexive pronoun. (3a) shows that the antecedent must precede the reflexive pronoun. (3b) shows that there can't be another NP in between a reflexive pronoun and its antecedent.

3. **a.** *Himself washed John.

   b. *Jane said the boy bit herself.

Thus one of the things that you know when you know English is that pronouns can receive their reference from their linguistic context. You also know that some pronouns—reflexive pronouns—are particularly picky. Their reference can only be resolved if they have an antecedent which is nearby in the right sort of way.

Non-reflexive pronouns (which we'll refer to simply as *pronouns*) such as *he, she, him, her, it*, etc. also have their reference resolved via linguistic context. These pronouns can have their antecedent in another, preceding sentence. This is demonstrated in (4).

4. Sue likes pizza. She thinks it is the perfect food.

Moreover, the antecedent doesn't even have to be in a sentence spoken by the same speaker. In the discourse in (5), Mary uses a pronoun (*there*) whose antecedent is in Sue's utterance.

5. SUE: I just got back from Rome.

   MARY: I've always wanted to go there!

Depending on the context and the discourse, an antecedent can even be several sentences away from its co-referring pronoun. Indeed, language users are adroit at processing sentences with several different pronouns and their different antecedents. Consider the discourse in (6):

6. JOHN: It seems that the man loves the woman.

   BILL: Many people think he loves her.

A natural interpretation of Bill's utterance is one in which *he* co-refers with *the man* in John's utterance and *she* co-refers with *the woman* in John's utterance. This is a classic case of reference resolution via linguistic context.

But now read Bill's utterance (6) out loud, and put emphasis on *her*. When *her* is emphasized it seems more natural to fix its referent from the situational context. In other words, if Bill were to emphasize *her*, it seems as though *her* would co-refer with some woman in the non-linguistic context different from the woman John had in mind. This utterance—with *her* emphasized—seems natural for a situation in which Bill is pointing at some other woman across the room.

Language users tend to use pronouns to refer to individuals in contexts—linguistic or situational—in which the referent of the pronoun is clear. Exactly which referent the pronoun receives is constrained by a number of different factors, including the gender- and number-marking on the pronoun, whether or not the pronoun is reflexive, and what linguistic and situational contexts the pronoun is uttered in.

Implicature

What does "yet" mean, after all? "I haven't seen *Reservoir Dogs* yet." What does that mean? It means you're going to go, doesn't it?

NICK HORNBY, *High Fidelity*, 1995

Pronouns are an example of how the context in which a sentence is uttered can help fix the meaning of that sentence. There is another way in which context can play a role in meaning: it can supplement the meaning of a sentence. Just as you were able to fill in the gaps in the sketch at the beginning of this chapter with extra details, you as a language user are able to fill in gaps in meaning. And just as there is a right and a wrong way to fill in the gaps in the sketch—Rembrandt probably didn't intend it to depict a sandwich—there is a right and a wrong way to fill in gaps in meaning.

We'll start with an example:

7. DAD: Very nice girl. What do you think, Hon?
   MOM: The turkey sure was moist.

From a semantic standpoint, (7) is very straightforward. With the right semantic theory, we can articulate the literal meanings of the parents' utterances. This semantic theory would summarize (7) literally: Dad asked Mom whether she thinks the girl is nice and Mom asserts that the turkey was moist.

Of course this summary already includes some extra-truth-conditional meaning. It assumes that *girl* gets its reference from the previous remark about Toni, and that the use of the definite article in *the turkey* assures that a turkey is known to the conversational participants. But there is still more meaning to attribute to (7). In many contexts, Dad (and the boy) will infer from Mom's statement that she doesn't particularly like Toni.

If this is right, Mom's answer is more of a sketch than a photograph. The most literal way Mom could have answered the (rhetorical) question is "I do not like Toni." But instead of asserting this, Mom chooses to implicate it. An implicature is a great example of extra-truth-conditional meaning. An implicature is to an assertion what a sketch is to a photograph.

Just as there are a number of reasons to sketch something instead of photographing it, there are a number of reasons to implicate something as opposed to asserting it. Perhaps Mom is an adherent of Miss Manners and, being a good hostess, knows she mustn't disparage a guest. If Dad knows this about Mom then he might infer from the utterance *The turkey sure was moist*—which doesn't seem relevant—that Mom doesn't like Toni but is too polite to say so.

Here are a few other examples of conversational implicatures:

8. SUE: Does Mary have a boyfriend?
   BILL: She's been driving to Santa Barbara every weekend.

9. JOHN: Do you know how to change a tire?
   JANE: I know how to call a tow truck.

10. DANA: Do these slacks make my butt look big?
    JAMIE: You look great in chartreuse.

In (8), Bill asserts that Mary has been driving to Santa Barbara every weekend. But he *implicates* that Mary has a boyfriend (and that the boyfriend lives in Santa Barbara). In (9), Jane asserts that she knows how to call a tow truck. But she *implicates* that she doesn't know how to change a tire. In (10), well, you figure it out.

These discourses should seem fairly natural to you. And it's likely that you calculated the same implicatures we did. That's what's interesting to linguists. Just as morphology, syntax, and semantics is rule-governed, as we have emphasized throughout this book, so is pragmatics (and, by extension, implication).

Maxims of Conversation

POLONIUS: Though this be madness, yet there is method in't.

WILLIAM SHAKESPEARE, *Hamlet*, c. 1600

The most notable effort made to formulate pragmatic rules is found in the work of the British philosopher H. Paul Grice. He attempted to formalize what we know when we know how to perceive implicature in a conversation. He concluded that language users can calculate implicatures because they are all following some implicit principles (and each language user can therefore assume that others are following those principles). Grice called these principles "maxims" of discourse, and used them to serve as the foundation of pragmatics, the study of extra-truth-conditional meaning. We'll list them and then provide examples of each.
Maxim of Quality: Truth

- Do not say what you believe to be false.
- Do not say that for which you lack adequate evidence.

Maxim of Quantity: Information

- Make your contribution as informative as is required for the current purposes of the exchange.
- Do not make your contribution more informative than is required.

Maxim of Relation: Relevance

- Be relevant.

Maxim of Manner: Clarity

- Avoid obscurity of expression.
- Avoid ambiguity.
- Avoid unnecessary wordiness.
- Be orderly.

These are not prescriptive rules but rather part of a strategy used by the community of language users to enable the use of conversational implicature. They tend to be violated only by uncooperative people. (The Maxims are sometimes referred to en masse as Grice's **cooperative principle**.) So if John stops Mary on the street and asks her for directions to the library, and she responds "Walk up three streets and take a left," it's a successful discourse only because Mary is being cooperative (and John assumes Mary is being cooperative). In particular, John assumes that Mary is following the Maxim of Quality.

On the other hand, the following discourse (*Hamlet*, Act II, Scene II), which gave rise to Polonius's famous remark, does not seem quite right—it is not coherent, for reasons that Grice's Maxims can explain.

POLONIUS: What do you read, my lord?
HAMLET: Words, words, words.
POLONIUS: What is the matter, my lord?
HAMLET: Between who?
POLONIUS: I mean, the matter that you read, my lord.
HAMLET: Slanders, sir: for the satirical rogue says here that old men have gray beards, that their faces are wrinkled, their eyes purging thick amber and plum-tree gum, and that they have a plentiful lack of wit, together with most weak hams: all which, sir, though I most powerfully and potently believe, yet I hold it not honesty to have it thus set down; for yourself, sir, should grow old as I am, if like a crab you could go backward.

Hamlet, who is feigning insanity, refuses to answer Polonius's questions "in good faith." He has violated the Maxim of Quantity, which states that a speaker's contribution to the discourse should be as informative as is required—neither more nor less. Hamlet has violated this maxim in both directions. In answering "Words, words, words" to the question of what he is reading, he is providing too little information. His final remark goes to the other extreme in providing too much information (this could also be seen as a violation of the Maxim of Manner). Hamlet also violates the **maxim of relevance** when he "misinterprets" the question about the reading matter as a matter between two individuals.

A maxim is violated when a speaker chooses to be uncooperative for whatever reason. A maxim is obeyed in a literal discourse devoid of implicature, as in (11).

11. DAD: Very nice girl. What do you think, Hon?
    MOM: Not really.

Implicatures can arise when a maxim is flouted. To flout a maxim is to choose not to follow that maxim in order to implicate something. In the Hamlet discourse above, Hamlet is violating the maxim in order to sound insane. But we can easily imagine a slightly different context, one in which Polonius and Hamlet have more or less the same exchange, but one in which Hamlet is not trying to be insane.

POLONIUS: What do you read, my lord?
HAMLET: Words, words, words.

In this context, Hamlet is still not obeying the Maxim of Quantity—he's not saying enough to really answer Polonius' question—but he is instead flouting the maxim to implicate that he doesn't want Polonius to know what he's reading.

The discourse in (7), repeated below, is an example of the Maxim of Relevance being flouted.

7. DAD: Very nice girl. What do you think, Hon?
   MOM: The turkey sure was moist.

Because Mom knows that the quality of the turkey isn't relevant to being a "very nice girl"—and because Dad is assuming that Mom knows it, too—Dad can pick up on the fact that Mom is implicating that she doesn't like the girl.

Bereft of context, if one man says (truthfully) to another "I have never slept with your wife," that would be provocative because the very topic of conversation should be unnecessary, a violation of the maxims of quantity and relevance.

Asking an able-bodied person at the dinner table "Can you pass the salt?"—if answered literally—would force the responder into stating the obvious, also a violation of the maxim of quantity. To avoid this, the person asked seeks a reason for the question, and implicates that the asker would like to have the salt shaker.

The maxim of relevance explains how saying "It's cold in here" to a person standing by an open window might be interpreted as a request to close it: or else why make the remark to that particular person in the first place?

Because implicatures result from violations of one or more maxims, they can be easily cancelled by providing further, clarifying information. For example:

DAD: Very nice girl. What do you think, Hon?
MOM: The turkey sure was moist. *Toni basted it every ten minutes.*

The additional remark cancels, or at least weakens, the implicature that Mom dislikes Toni.

Implicatures are different than entailments. An entailment cannot be cancelled; it is logically necessary. The truth of *Jon killed Jim* entails that Jim is dead and nothing anyone can say will resurrect him. But further world knowledge or verbal clarification may cancel an implicature.

Presupposition

"Take some more tea," the March Hare said to Alice, very earnestly.

"I've had nothing yet," Alice replied in an offended tone, "so I can't take more."

"You mean you can't take less," said the Hatter: "It's very easy to take more than nothing."

LEWIS CARROLL, *Alice's Adventures in Wonderland*

A somewhat different consequence of the maxim of relevance arises for sentences like *I am sorry that the team lost*. To be relevant—to obey the maxim of relevance—it must be true that "the team lost." Else why say it? Situations that must exist for utterances to be appropriate are called **presuppositions**. Questions like *Have you stopped hugging your border collie?* presuppose that you hugged your border collie, and statements like *The river Avon runs through Stratford* presuppose the existence of the river and the town. The presuppositions prevent violations of the maxim of relevance. When presuppositions are ignored, we get the confusion that Alice felt at the tea party. Utterances like *Take some more tea* or *Have another beer* carry the presupposition that one has already had some. The March Hare is oblivious to this aspect of language, of which the exasperated Alice is keenly aware.

Presuppositions hold up under negation. *I am NOT sorry that the team lost* still needs the team to have lost to adhere to the maxim of relevance. If a mad Mad Hatter said *Do not take some more tea* the presupposition of previous tea consumption would still be needed.

Presuppositions are different from implicatures. To cancel a presupposition—oh, the team didn't lose after all—renders the entire utterance *I'm sorry that the team lost* inappropriate and in violation of Grice's Maxims. No such incongruity arises when implicatures are cancelled.

Presuppositions also differ from entailments in that they are taken for granted by speakers adhering to the cooperative principle. Unlike entailments, they remain when the sentence is negated. On the other hand, while *Jon killed Jim* entails *Jim died*, no such entailment follows from *Jon did not kill Jim*.

Speech Acts

ZITS © 1998 ZITS PARTNERSHIP, KING FEATURES SYNDICATE

You can use language to do things. You can use language to make promises, lay bets, issue warnings, christen boats, place names in nomination, offer congratulations, or swear testimony. The theory of **speech acts** describes how this is done.

By saying *I warn you that there is a sheepdog in the closet*, you not only say something, you *warn* someone. Verbs like *bet, promise, warn*, and so on are **performative verbs**. Using them in a sentence (in the first person, present tense) adds something extra over and above the statement.

There are hundreds of performative verbs in every language. The following sentences illustrate their usage:

I *bet* you five dollars the Yankees win.
I *challenge* you to a match.
I *dare* you to step over this line.
I *fine* you $100 for possession of oregano.
I *move* that we adjourn.
I *nominate* Batman for mayor of Gotham City.
I *promise* to improve.
I *resign*!
I *pronounce* you husband and wife.

In all of these sentences, the speaker is the subject (i.e., the sentences are in first person), who by uttering the sentence is accomplishing some additional action, such as daring, nominating, or resigning. In addition, all of these sentences are affirmative, declarative, and in the present tense. They are typical **performative sentences**.

An informal test to see whether a sentence contains a performative verb is to begin it with the words *I hereby*. . . . Only performative sentences sound right when begun this way. Compare *I hereby apologize to you* with the somewhat strange *I hereby know you*. The first is generally taken as an act of apologizing. In all of the examples given, insertion of *hereby* would be acceptable.

In studying speech acts, the importance of context is evident. In some situations *Band practice, my house, 6 to 8* is a reminder, but the same sentence may be a warning in a different context. We call this underlying purpose of the utterance—be it a reminder, a warning, a promise, a threat, or whatever— the **illocutionary force** of a speech act. Illocutionary force may accompany utterances without overt performative verbs, for example *I've got five bucks that says you're wrong* has the illocutionary force of a bet under appropriate circumstances. Because the illocutionary force of a speech act depends on the context of the utterance, speech act theory is a part of pragmatics.

Summary

Knowing a language means knowing how to produce and understand the meaning of infinitely many sentences. The study of linguistic meaning is called **semantics**. **Lexical semantics** is concerned with the meanings of morphemes and words; **compositional semantics** with phrases and sentences. The study of how context affects meaning is called **pragmatics**.

Speakers' knowledge of sentence meaning includes knowing the **truth conditions** of declarative sentences; knowing when one sentence **entails** another sentence; knowing when two sentences are **paraphrases** or **contradictory**; knowing when a sentence is a **tautology**, **contradiction**, or **paradox**; and knowing when sentences are ambiguous, among other things. **Compositional semantics** is the building up of phrasal or sentence meaning from the meaning of smaller units by means of **semantic rules**.

There are cases when the meaning of larger units does not follow from the meaning of its parts. **Anomaly** is when the pieces do not fit sensibly together, as in *colorless green ideas sleep furiously*; **metaphors** are sentences that appear to be anomalous, but to which a meaningful concept can be attached, such as *time is money*; **idioms** are fixed expressions whose meaning is not compositional but rather must be learned as a whole unit, such as *kick the bucket* meaning 'to die.'

Part of the meaning of words may be the association with the objects the words refer to (if any), called **reference**, but often there is additional meaning beyond reference, which is called **sense**. The reference of *the President* is Barack Obama, and the sense of the expression is 'highest executive office.' Some expressions have reference but little sense, such as proper names, and some have sense but no reference, such as *the present king of France*.

Words are related in various ways. They may be **synonyms**, various kinds of **antonyms** such as **gradable pairs** and **relational opposites**, or **homonyms**, words pronounced the same but with different meanings such as *bare* and *bear*.

Part of the meaning of words may be described by **semantic features** such as "female," "young," "cause," or "go." Nouns may have the feature "count," wherein they may be enumerated (one potato, two potatoes), or "mass," in which enumeration may require contextual interpretation (*one milk, *two milks, perhaps meaning 'one glass or quart or portion of milk'). Some verbs have the feature of being "eventive" while others are "stative." The semantic feature of negation is found in many words and is evidenced by the occurrence of **negative polarity** items (e.g., *John doubts that Mary gives a hoot*, but *John thinks that Mary gives a hoot*).

Verbs have various **argument structures**, which describe the NPs that may occur with particular verbs. For example, intransitive verbs take only an NP subject, whereas **ditransitive** verbs take an NP subject, an NP direct object, and an NP indirect object. **Thematic roles** describe the semantic relations between a verb and its NP arguments. Some thematic roles are: **agent**, the doer of an action; **theme**, the recipient of an action; **goal**; **source**; **instrument**; and **experiencer**. The assignment of thematic roles to the NP arguments of verbs occurs in d-structure. However, the positions of the NP arguments may differ in s-structure owing to the application of syntactic rules that move elements.

Some meaning is **extra-truth-conditional**: it comes about as a result of how a speaker uses the literal meaning in conversation, or as a part of a **discourse**. The study of extra-truth-conditional meaning is **pragmatics**.

Language users generally describe states of affairs with sentences that aren't 100% explicit. Context can be used to supplement linguistic meaning in various ways. Context may be *linguistic*—what was previously spoken or written—or *knowledge of the world*, including the speech situation: what we've called **situational context**.

Many pronouns rely on context for their reference to be resolved. Reflexive pronouns such as *himself* and *themselves* require a sentence-internal **antecedent**. Non-reflexive pronouns such as *he, she, him*, and *her* can have an antecedent in another sentence or earlier in the discourse or even determined by context. **Deictic** terms such as *you, there, now*, and *the other side* require knowledge of the situation (person spoken to, place, time, spatial orientation) of the utterance to be interpreted referentially.

Speakers of all languages adhere to various **cooperative principles** for communicating sincerely called **maxims of conversation**. Such maxims as "be relevant" or "say neither more nor less than the discourse requires" permit a person to interpret *It's cold in here* as "Shut the windows" or "Turn up the thermostat." **Implicatures** are the inferences that may be drawn from an utterance in context when one or another of the maxims is violated (either purposefully or naively). When Mary says *It's cold in here*, one of many possible implicatures may be "Mary wants the heat turned up." Implicatures are like entailments in that their truth follows from sentences of the discourse, but unlike entailments, which are necessarily true, implicatures may be cancelled by information added later. Mary might wave you away from the thermostat and ask you to hand her a sweater. **Presuppositions** are situations that must be true for utterances to be appropriate, so that *Take some more tea* has the presupposition "already had some tea."

The theory of **speech acts** tells us that people use language to do things such as lay bets, issue warnings, or nominate candidates. By using the words "I nominate Bill Smith," you may accomplish an act of nomination that allows Bill Smith to run for office. Verbs that "do things" are called **performative verbs**. The speaker's intent in making an utterance is known as **illocutionary force**. In the case of performative verbs, the illocutionary force is mentioned overtly. In other cases it must be determined from context.

References for Further Reading

Austin, J. L. 1962. *How to do things with words.* Cambridge, MA: Harvard University Press.

Chierchia, G., and S. McConnell-Ginet. 2000. *Meaning and grammar, 2nd ed.* Cambridge, MA: MIT Press.

Davidson, D., and G. Harman, eds. 1972. *Semantics of natural languages.* Dordrecht, The Netherlands: Reidel.

Grice, H. P. 1989. Logic and conversation. Reprinted in *Studies in the way of words.* Cambridge, MA: Harvard University Press.

Jackendoff, R. 1993. *Patterns in the mind.* New York: HarperCollins.

____. 1983. *Semantics and cognition.* Cambridge, MA: MIT Press.

Lakoff, G. 1987. *Women, fire, and dangerous things: What categories reveal about the mind.* Chicago: University of Chicago Press.

Lakoff, G., and M. Johnson. 2003. *Metaphors we live by, 2nd ed.* Chicago: University of Chicago Press.

Levinson, S. C. 2000. *Presumptive meanings: The theory of generalized conversational implicature.* Cambridge, MA: The MIT Press.

Lyons, J. 1995. *Linguistic semantics: An introduction.* Cambridge, UK: Cambridge University Press.

Saeed, J. 2009. *Semantics, 3rd ed.* Oxford, UK: Wiley-Blackwell.

Searle, J. R. 1969. *Speech acts: An essay in the philosophy of language.* Cambridge, UK: Cambridge University Press.

Exercises

1. (This exercise requires knowledge of elementary set theory.)

   A. Suppose that the reference (meaning) of *swims* points out the set of individuals consisting of Anna, Lu, Paul, and Benjamin. For which of the following sentences are the truth conditions produced by Semantic Rule I met?

      i. Anna swims.
     ii. Jack swims.
    iii. Benjamin swims.

   B. Suppose the reference (meaning) of *loves* points out the set consisting of the following pairs of individuals: <Anna, Paul>, <Paul, Benjamin>, <Benjamin, Benjamin>, <Paul, Anna>. According to Semantic Rule II, what is the meaning of the verb phrase?

      i. loves Paul
     ii. loves Benjamin
    iii. loves Jack

   C. Given the information in (B), for which of the following sentences are the truth conditions produced by Semantic Rule I met?

      i. Paul loves Anna.
     ii. Benjamin loves Paul.
    iii. Benjamin loves himself.
    iv. Anna loves Jack.

   D. Challenge exercise: Consider the sentence *Jack kissed Laura.* How would the actions of Semantic Rules (I) and (II) determine that the sentence is false if it were true that:

      i. Nobody kissed Laura.

   How about if it were true that:

      ii. Jack did not kiss Laura, although other men did.

2. The following sentences are either tautologies (analytic), contradictions, or situationally true or false. Write T by the tautologies, C by the contradictions, and S by the other sentences.

   a. Queens are monarchs.
   b. Kings are female.
   c. Kings are poor.
   d. Queens are ugly.

  e. Queens are mothers.
  f. Kings are mothers.
  g. Dogs are four-legged.
  h. Cats are felines.
  i. Cats are stupid.
  j. Dogs are carnivores.
  k. George Washington is George Washington.
  l. George Washington is the first president.
  m. George Washington is male.
  n. Uncles are male.
  o. My aunt is a man.
  p. Witches are wicked.
  q. My brother is a witch.
  r. My sister is an only child.
  s. The evening star isn't the evening star.
  t. The evening star isn't Venus.
  u. Babies are adults.
  v. Babies can lift one ton.
  w. Puppies are human.
  x. My bachelor friends are all married.
  y. My bachelor friends are all lonely.
  z. Colorless ideas are green.

3. Here is a passage from *Alice's Adventures in Wonderland*:

"How is bread made?"
"I know *that*!" Alice cried eagerly.
"You take some flour—"
"Where do you pick the flower?" the White Queen asked. "In a garden, or in the hedges?"
"Well, it isn't *picked* at all," Alice explained; "it's ground—"
"How many acres of ground?" said the White Queen.

On what kinds of pairs of words is the humor of this passage based? Identify each pair.

4. Should the semantic component of the grammar account for whatever a speaker means when uttering any meaningful expression? Defend your viewpoint.

5. **Part One**

The following sentences may be lexically or structurally ambiguous, or both. Provide paraphrases showing that you comprehend all the meanings.

Example: I saw him walking by the bank.

Meaning 1: I saw him and he was walking by the bank of the river.

Meaning 2: I saw him and he was walking by the financial institution.

Meaning 3: I was walking by the bank of the river when I saw him.

Meaning 4: I was walking by the financial institution when I saw him.

a. We laughed at the colorful ball.

b. He was knocked over by the punch.

c. The police were urged to stop drinking by the fifth.

d. I said I would file it on Thursday.

e. I cannot recommend visiting professors too highly.

f. The license fee for pets owned by senior citizens who have not been altered is $1.50. (Actual notice)

g. What looks better on a handsome man than a tux? Nothing! (Attributed to Mae West)

h. Wanted: Man to take care of cow that does not smoke or drink. (Actual notice)

i. For Sale: Several old dresses from grandmother in beautiful condition. (Actual notice)

j. Time flies like an arrow. (*Hint*: There are at least four paraphrases, but some of them require imagination.)

Part Two

Do the same thing for the following newspaper headlines:

a. POLICE BEGIN CAMPAIGN TO RUN DOWN JAYWALKERS

b. DRUNK GETS NINE MONTHS IN VIOLIN CASE

c. FARMER BILL DIES IN HOUSE

d. STUD TIRES OUT

e. SQUAD HELPS DOG BITE VICTIM

f. LACK OF BRAINS HINDERS RESEARCH

g. MINERS REFUSE TO WORK AFTER DEATH

h. EYE DROPS OFF SHELF

i. JUVENILE COURT TO TRY SHOOTING DEFENDANT

j. QUEEN MARY HAVING BOTTOM SCRAPED

6. Explain the semantic ambiguity of the following sentences by providing two or more sentences for each that paraphrase the multiple meanings. *Example*: "She can't bear children" can mean either 'She can't give birth to children' or 'She can't tolerate children.'

a. He waited by the bank.

b. Is he really that kind?

c. The proprietor of the fish store was the sole owner.

d. The long drill was boring.

e. When he got the clear title to the land, it was a good deed.

f. It takes a good ruler to make a straight line.

g. He saw that gasoline can explode.

h. You should see her shop.

i. Every man loves a woman.

j. You get half off the cost of your hotel room if you make your own bed.

k. "It's his job to lose" (said the coach about his new player).

l. "We will change your oil in 10 minutes" (sign in front of a garage).

m. **Challenge exercise:** Bill wants to marry a Norwegian woman.

7. Go on an idiom hunt. In the course of some hours in which you converse or overhear conversations, write down all the idioms that are used. If you prefer, watch soap operas or something similar for an hour or two and write down the idioms. Show your parents (or whomever) this book when they find you watching TV and you can claim you're doing your homework.

8. Take a half dozen or so idioms from exercise 7, or elsewhere, and try to find their sources; if you cannot, speculate imaginatively on the source. For example, *sell down the river* meaning 'betray' arose from American slave traders selling slaves from more northern states along the Mississippi River to the harsher southern states. For *snap out of it*, meaning 'pay attention' or 'get in a better mood,' we (truly) speculate that ill-behaving persons were once confined in straitjackets secured by snaps, and to snap out of it meant the person was behaving better.

9. For each group of words given as follows, state what semantic property or properties distinguish between the classes of (a) words and (b) words. If asked, also indicate a semantic property that the (a) words and the (b) words share.

Example: (a) widow, mother, sister, aunt, maid
(b) widower, father, brother, uncle, valet

The (a) and (b) words are "human."
The (a) words are "female" and the (b) words are "male."

a. (a) bachelor, man, son, paperboy, pope, chief
(b) bull, rooster, drake, ram
The (a) and (b) words are:
The (a) words are:
The (b) words are:

b. (a) table, stone, pencil, cup, house, ship, car
(b) milk, alcohol, rice, soup, mud
The (a) words are:
The (b) words are:

c. (a) book, temple, mountain, road, tractor
(b) idea, love, charity, sincerity, bravery, fear
The (a) words are:
The (b) words are:

d. (a) pine, elm, ash, weeping willow, sycamore
(b) rose, dandelion, aster, tulip, daisy
The (a) and (b) words are:
The (a) words are:
The (b) words are:

e. (a) book, letter, encyclopedia, novel, notebook, dictionary
(b) typewriter, pencil, pen, crayon, quill, charcoal, chalk
The (a) words are:
The (b) words are:

    f. (a) walk, run, skip, jump, hop, swim
       (b) fly, skate, ski, ride, cycle, canoe, hang glide
       The (a) and (b) words are:
       The (a) words are:
       The (b) words are:

    g. (a) ask, tell, say, talk, converse
       (b) shout, whisper, mutter, drawl, holler
       The (a) and (b) words are:
       The (a) words are:
       The (b) words are:

    h. (a) absent/present, alive/dead, asleep/awake, married/single
       (b) big/small, cold/hot, sad/happy, slow/fast
       The (a) and (b) word pairs are:
       The (a) words are:
       The (b) words are:

    i. (a) alleged, counterfeit, false, putative, accused
       (b) red, large, cheerful, pretty, stupid
       (*Hint*: Is an alleged murderer always a murderer? Is a pretty girl always a girl?)
       The (a) words are:
       The (b) words are:

10. **Research project:** There are many *-nym/-onym* words that describe classes of words with particular semantic properties. We mentioned a few in this chapter such as synonyms, antonyms, homonyms, and hyponyms. What is the etymology of *-onym*? What common English word is it related to? How many more *-nym* words and their meanings can you come up with? Try for five or ten on your own. With help from the Internet, dozens are possible. (*Hint*: One such *-nym* word was the winning word in the 1997 Scripps National Spelling Bee.)

11. There are several kinds of antonymy. By writing a *c*, *g*, or *r* in column C, indicate whether the pairs in columns A and B are complementary, gradable, or relational opposites.

A	B	C
good	bad	——
expensive	cheap	——
parent	offspring	——
beautiful	ugly	——
false	true	——
lessor	lessee	——
pass	fail	——
hot	cold	——
legal	illegal	——
larger	smaller	——
poor	rich	——
fast	slow	——
asleep	awake	——
husband	wife	——
rude	polite	——

12. For each definition, write in the first blank the word that has that meaning and in the second (and third if present) a differently spelled homonym that has a different meaning. The first letter of each of the words is provided.

Example: "a pair": t(*wo*) t(*oo*) t(*o*)

a. "naked":	b _____	b _____	
b. "base metal":	l _____	l _____	
c. "worships":	p _____	p _____	p _____
d. "eight bits":	b _____	b _____	b _____
e. "one of five senses":	s _____	s _____	c _____
f. "several couples":	p _____	p _____	p _____
g. "not pretty":	p _____	p _____	
h. "purity of gold unit":	k _____	c _____	
i. "a horse's coiffure":	m _____	m _____	m _____
j. "sets loose":	f _____	f _____	f _____

13. Here are some proper names of U.S. restaurants. Can you figure out the basis for each name? (This is for fun—don't let yourself be graded.)

  a. Mustard's Last Stand
  b. Aunt Chilada's
  c. Tony's Toe-Main Café (Hint: silent 'p')
  d. Lion on the Beach
  e. Wiener Take All
  f. Pizza Paul and Mary
  g. Franks for the Memories
  h. Dressed to Grill
  i. Deli Beloved
  j. Gone with the Wings
  k. Aunt Chovy's Pizza
  l. Polly Esther's
  m. Crepevine
  n. Thai Me Up (truly—it's in Edinburgh)
  o. Romancing the Cone
  p. Brew Ha Ha
  q. C U Latte
  r. Fish-cotheque
  s. Franks a lot
  t. Nincomsoup
  u. Via Agra (Indian take-away restaurant in London)

14. The following sentences consist of a verb, its noun phrase subject, and various noun phrases and prepositional phrases. Identify the thematic role of each NP by writing the letter *a*, *t*, *i*, *s*, *g*, or *e* above the noun, standing for *agent*, *theme*, *instrument*, *source*, *goal*, and *experiencer*.

a   t   s   i

Example: The boy took the books from the cupboard with a handcart.

a. Mary found a ball.

b. The children ran from the playground to the wading pool.

c. One of the men unlocked all the doors with a paper clip.

d. John melted the ice with a blowtorch.

e. Helen looked for a cockroach.

f. Helen saw a cockroach.

g. Helen screamed.

h. The ice melted.

i. With a telescope, the boy saw the man.

j. The farmer loaded hay onto the truck.

k. The farmer loaded the hay with a pitchfork.

l. The hay was loaded on the truck by the farmer.

m. Helen heard music coming out of the speaker.

15. Find a complete version of "The Jabberwocky" from *Through the Looking-Glass* by Lewis Carroll. There are some on the Internet. Look up all the nonsense words in a good dictionary (also to be found online) and see how many of them are lexical items in English. Note their meanings.

16. In sports and games, many expressions are "performative." By shouting *You're out*, the first-base umpire performs an act. Think up half a dozen or so similar examples and explain their use.

17. A criterion of a performative utterance is whether you can begin it with "I hereby." Notice that if you say sentence (i) aloud, it sounds like a genuine apology, but to say sentence (ii) aloud sounds funny because you cannot willfully perform an act of noticing:

  i. I hereby apologize to you.

  ii. ?I hereby notice you.

Determine which of the following are performative sentences by inserting "hereby" and seeing whether they sound right.

a. I testify that she met the agent.

b. I know that she met the agent.

c. I suppose the Yankees will win.

d. He bet her $2,500 that Romney would win.

e. I dismiss the class.

f. I teach the class.

g. We promise to leave early.

h. I owe the IRS $1 million.

i. I bequeath $1 million to the IRS.

j. I swore I didn't do it.

k. I swear I didn't do it.

18. **A.** Explain, in terms of Grice's Maxims, the humor or strangeness of the following exchange between mother and child. The child has just finished eating a cookie when the mother comes into the room.

MOTHER: What are these cookie crumbs doing in your bed?

CHILD: Nothing, they're just lying there.

B. Do the same for this "exchange" between an owner and her cat:

OWNER: If cats ruled the world, everyone would sleep on a pile of fresh laundry.

CAT: Cats *don't* rule the world??

19. **A.** Spend an hour or two observing conversations between people, including yourself if you wish. Record five (or more if you're having fun) utterances where the intended meaning is mediated by Grice's Maxims and cite the maxim or maxims involved. For example someone says "I didn't quite catch that," with the possible meaning of "Please say it again," or "Please speak a little louder." In the above example, we would cite the maxims of relevance and quantity.

B. Here is a dialog excerpt from the 1945 motion picture *The Thin Man Goes Home*. The scene is in a shop that sells paintings and Nick Charles is leaving the shop.

NICK CHARLES: Well, thank you very much. Goodbye now.

SHOPKEEPER: I beg your pardon?

NICK CHARLES: I said, goodbye now.

SHOPKEEPER: "Goodbye now?" There's no sense to that! Obviously it's now! I mean, you wouldn't say "goodbye tomorrow" or "goodbye two hours ago!"

NICK CHARLES: You got hold of somethin' there, brother.

SHOPKEEPER: I've got hold of some . . . I haven't got hold of anything . . . And I'm not your brother!

Analyze this dialogue, intended to be humorous (one assumes), in light of Grice's maxims.

20. Consider the following "facts" and then answer the questions.

Part A illustrates your ability to interpret meanings when syntactic rules have deleted parts of the sentence; Part B illustrates your knowledge of semantic features and entailment.

A. Roses are red and bralkions are too.

Booth shot Lincoln and Czolgosz, McKinley.
Casca stabbed Caesar and so did Cinna.
Frodo was exhausted, as was Sam.

a. What color are bralkions?
b. What did Czolgosz do to McKinley?
c. What did Cinna do to Caesar?
d. What did Sam feel?

B. Now consider these facts and answer the questions:
Black Beauty was a stallion.
Mary is a widow.

John pretended to send Martha a birthday card.
Jane didn't remember to send Tom a birthday card.
Tina taught her daughter to swim.
My boss managed to give me a raise last year.
Flipper is walking.
(T = true; F = false)

a. Black Beauty was male.	T ___	F ___
b. Mary was never married.	T ___	F ___
c. John sent Martha a card.	T ___	F ___
d. Jane sent Tom a card.	T ___	F ___
e. Tina's daughter can swim.	T ___	F ___
f. I didn't get a raise last year.	T ___	F ___
g. Flipper has legs.	T ___	F ___

21. The following sentences have certain presuppositions that ensure their appropriateness. What are they?

Example: The minors promised the police to stop drinking.

Presupposition: The minors were drinking.

a. We went to the ballpark again.
b. Valerie regretted not receiving a new T-bird for Labor Day.
c. That her pet turtle ran away made Emily very sad.
d. The administration forgot that the professors support the students.
e. It is an atrocity that the World Trade Center was attacked on September 11, 2001.
f. It isn't tolerable that the World Trade Center was attacked on September 11, 2001.
g. Disa wants more popcorn.
h. Mary drank one more beer before leaving.
i. Jack knows who discovered Pluto in 1930.
j. Mary was horrified to find a cockroach in her bed.

22. Pronouns are so-called because they are nouns; they refer to individuals, just as nouns do. The word 'proform' describes words like 'she' in a way that isn't category-specific. There are words that function as pro-verbs, pro-adjectives, and pro-adverbs, too. Can you come up with an example of each in English (or another language)?

23. Imagine that Alex and Bruce have a plan to throw Colleen a surprise party at work. It is Alex's job meet her for lunch at a local restaurant to get her out of the office, and Bruce's job to decorate as soon as she leaves. Alex phones Bruce and says, "The eagle has landed." What Maxim is Alex flouting? What does his utterance implicate?

24. Each of the following single statements has at least one implicature in the situation described. What is it?

a. Statement: You make a better door than a window.
   Situation: Someone is blocking your view.

    b. Statement: It's getting late.
       Situation: You're at a party and it's 4 A.M.
    c. Statement: The restaurants are open until midnight.
       Situation: It's 10 o'clock and you haven't eaten dinner.
    d. Statement: If you'd diet, this wouldn't hurt so badly.
       Situation: Someone is standing on your toe.
    e. Statement: I thought I saw a fan in the closet.
       Situation: It's sweltering in the room.
    f. Statement: Mr. Smith dresses neatly, is well groomed, and is always on time to class.
       Situation: The summary statement in a letter of recommendation to graduate school.
    g. Statement: Most of the food is gone.
       Situation: You arrived late at a cocktail party.
    h. Statement: John or Mary made a mistake.
       Situation: You're looking over some work done by John and Mary.

25. In each of the following dialogues between Jack and Laura, there is a conversational implicature. What is it?

    a. Jack: Did you make a doctor's appointment?
       Laura: Their line was busy.
    b. Jack: Do you have the play tickets?
       Laura: Didn't I give them to you?
    c. Jack: Does your grandmother have a live-in boyfriend?
       Laura: She's very traditional.
    d. Jack: How did you like the string quartet?
       Laura: I thought the violist was swell.
    e. Laura: What are Boston's chances of winning the World Series?
       Jack: Do bowling balls float?
    f. Laura: Do you own a cat?
       Jack: I'm allergic to everything.
    g. Laura: Did you mow the grass and wash the car like I told you to?
       Jack: I mowed the grass.
    h. Laura: Do you want dessert?
       Jack: Is the Pope Catholic?

26. **A.** Think of ten negative polarity items such as *give a hoot* or *have a red cent*.

    B. **Challenge exercise**: Can you think of other contexts without overt negation that "license" their use? (*Hint*: One answer is discussed in the text, but there are others.)

27. **Challenge exercise**: Suppose that, contrary to what was argued in the text, the noun phrase *no baby* does refer to some individual just like *the baby* does. It needn't be an actual baby but some abstract "empty" object that we'll call Ø. Show that this approach to the semantics of *no baby*, when applying Semantic Rule I and taking the restricting nature of adverbs into account (everyone who swims beautifully also swims), predicts that *No baby sleeps soundly* entails *No baby sleeps*, and explain why this is wrong.

28. Consider: "The meaning of words lies not in the words themselves, but in our attitude toward them," by Antoine de Saint-Exupéry (the author of *The Little Prince*). Do you think this is true, partially true, or false? Defend your point of view, providing examples if needed.

29. The Second Amendment of the Constitution of the United States states:

    A well-regulated Militia, being necessary to the security of a free State, the right of the people to keep and bear Arms, shall not be infringed.

    It has long been argued that the citizens of the United States have an absolute right to own guns, based on this amendment. Apply Grice's Maxims to the Second Amendment and agree or disagree.

30. **Challenge exercise: Research Project**. We observed that ordinarily the antecedent of a reflexive pronoun may not have an intervening NP. Our example was the ungrammatical **Jane said the boy bit herself*. But there appear to be "funny" exceptions and many speakers of English find the following sentences acceptable: *?Yvette said Marcel really loved that sketch of herself that Renoir drew*, or *?Clyde realized that Bonnie had seen a photo of himself on the wall in the post office*. Investigate what's going on here.

5

Phonetics: The Sounds of Language

I gradually came to see that Phonetics had an important bearing on human relations—that when people of different nations pronounce each other's languages really well (even if vocabulary & grammar not perfect), it has an astonishing effect of bringing them together, it puts people on terms of equality, a good understanding between them immediately springs up.

FROM THE JOURNAL OF DANIEL JONES

When you know a language you know the *sounds* of that language, and you know how to combine those sounds into words. When you know English you know the sounds represented by the letters *b*, *s*, and *u*, and you are able to combine them to form the words *bus* and *sub*.

Although languages may contain different sounds, the sounds of all the languages of the world together constitute a class of sounds that the human vocal tract is designed to make. This chapter will discuss these speech sounds, how they are produced, and how they may be classified.

Sound Segments

"Keep out! Keep out! K-E-E-P O-U-T."

LaughingStock Licensing/Ottawa, Canada

The study of speech sounds is called **phonetics**. To describe speech sounds, it is necessary to know what an individual sound is, and how each sound differs from all others. This is not as easy as it may seem, for when we speak, the sounds seem to run together and it isn't at all obvious where one sound ends and the next begins. However, when we know the language we hear the individual sounds in our "mind's ear" and are able to make sense of them, unlike the sign painter in the cartoon.

A speaker of English knows that there are three sounds in the word *bus*. Yet, physically the word is just one continuous sound. You can **segment** that one sound into parts because you know English. And you recognize those parts when they occur elsewhere as *b* does in *bet* or *rob*, as *u* does in *up*, and as *s* does in *sister*.

It is not possible to segment the sound of someone clearing her throat into a sequence of discrete units. This is not because throat-clearing is one continuous sound. It is because such sounds are not speech and are therefore not able to be segmented into the sounds of speech.

Speakers of English can separate *keepout* into the two words *keep* and *out* because they know the language. We do not generally pause between words (except to take a breath), even though we may think we do. Children learning a language reveal this fact. A two-year-old child going down stairs heard his mother say, "hold on." He replied, "I'm holing don, I'm holing don," not knowing where the break between words occurred. In fact, word boundary misperceptions have changed the forms of words historically. At an earlier stage of English, the word *apron* was *napron*. However, the phrase *a napron* was so often misperceived as *an apron* that the word lost its initial *n*.

Some phrases and sentences that are clearly distinct when printed may be ambiguous when spoken. Read the following pairs aloud and see why we might misinterpret what we hear:

grade A	gray day
I scream	ice cream
the sun's rays meet	the sons raise meat

The lack of breaks between spoken words and individual sounds often makes us think that speakers of foreign languages run their words together, unaware that we do too. X-ray motion pictures of someone speaking make the absence of breaks very clear. One can see the tongue, jaw, and lips in continuous motion as the individual sounds are produced.

Yet, if you know a language you have no difficulty segmenting the continuous sounds of speech. It doesn't matter whether there is an alphabet for the language or whether the listener can read and write. Everyone who knows a language knows how to segment sentences into words, and words into sounds. It is not a question of literacy; it is part of being human.

Identity of Speech Sounds

By infinitesimal movements of the tongue countless different vowels can be produced, all of them in use among speakers of English who utter the same vowels no oftener than they make the same fingerprints.

GEORGE BERNARD SHAW, 1950

It is truly amazing, given the continuity of the speech signal, that we are able to understand the individual words in an utterance. This ability is more surprising because no two speakers ever say the same word identically. The speech signal produced when one speaker says *cat* is not the same as that of another speaker's *cat* due to differences in people's size, age, and gender, among other things. Even two utterances of *cat* by the same speaker will differ to some degree.

Our knowledge of a language determines when we judge physically different sounds to be the same. We know which aspects of pronunciation are linguistically important and which are not. For example, if someone coughs in the middle of saying "How (cough) are you?" a listener will ignore the cough and interpret this simply as "How are you?" People speak at different pitch levels, at different rates of speed, and even with their head encased in a helmet, like Darth Vader. However, such personal differences are not linguistically significant.

Our linguistic knowledge makes it possible to ignore nonlinguistic differences in speech. Furthermore, we are capable of making sounds that we know are not speech sounds in our language. Many English speakers can make a clicking sound of disapproval that writers sometimes represent as *tsk*. This sound never occurs as part of an English word. It is even difficult for many English speakers to combine this clicking sound with other sounds. Yet clicks are speech sounds in Xhosa, Zulu, Sosotho, and Khoikhoi—languages spoken in southern Africa—just like the *k* and *t* in English. Speakers of those languages have no difficulty producing them as parts of words. Thus, *tsk* is a speech sound in Xhosa but not in English. The sound represented by the letters *th* in the word *think* is a speech sound in English but not in French. In general, languages differ to a greater or lesser degree in the inventory of speech sounds that words are built from.

The science of phonetics attempts to describe all of the sounds used in all languages of the world. **Acoustic phonetics** focuses on the physical properties of sounds; **auditory phonetics** is concerned with how listeners perceive these sounds; and **articulatory phonetics**—the primary concern of this chapter—is the study of how the vocal tract produces the sounds of language.

The Phonetic Alphabet

The English have no respect for their language, and will not teach their children to speak it. They cannot spell it because they have nothing to spell it with but an old foreign alphabet of which only the consonants—and not all of them—have any agreed speech value.

GEORGE BERNARD SHAW, Preface to *Pygmalion*, 1912

Orthography, a general term for "spelling" in any language, does not necessarily represent the sounds of a language in a consistent way. To be scientific—and phonetics *is* a science—we must devise a way for the same sound to be spelled with the same letter every time, and for any letter to stand for the same sound every time.

To see that ordinary spelling with our Roman alphabet is woefully inadequate for the task, consider sentences such as:

Did h**e** bel**ie**ve that C**ae**sar could s**ee** the p**eo**ple s**ei**ze the s**ea**s?
The sill**y** am**oe**ba stole the k**ey** to the mach**i**ne.

The same sound is represented variously by **e**, **ie**, **ae**, **ee**, **eo**, **ei**, **ea**, **y**, **oe**, **ey**, and **i**. On the other hand, consider:

My f**a**ther w**a**nted m**a**ny **a** vill**a**ge d**a**me b**a**dly.

Here the letter **a** represents the various sounds in *father, wanted, many*, and so on.

Making the spelling waters yet muddier, we find that a combination of letters may represent a single sound:

*sh*oot	*ch*aracter	*Th*omas	*ph*ysics
ei*th*er	dea*l*	rou*gh*	na*ti*on
c*oa*t	gla*ci*al	*th*eater	pl*ai*n

Or, conversely, the single letter **x**, when not pronounced as **z**, usually stands for the *two* sounds **ks** as in sex (you may have to speak aloud to hear that *sex* is pronounced seks).

Some letters have no sound in certain words (so-called *silent* letters):

*m*nemonic	autum*n*	as*th*ma	corp*s*
*h*onest	*ch*thonic	hol*e*	*Ch*ristmas
*p*sychology	s*w*ord	de*b*t	*g*naw
bou*gh*	*ph*thalate	is*l*and	*k*not

Or, conversely, there may be no letter to represent sounds that occur. In many words, the letter *u* represents a *y* sound followed by a *u* sound:

c**u**te	(sounds like k**y**ute; compare: c**oo**t)
f**u**me	(sounds like f**y**ume; compare: f**oo**l)
use	(sounds like **y**use; compare: **u**mlaut)

Throughout several centuries English scholars have advocated spelling reform. George Bernard Shaw complained that spelling was so inconsistent that *fish* could be spelled *ghoti*: *gh* as in *tough*, *o* as in *women*, and *ti* as in *nation*. Nonetheless, spelling reformers failed to change our spelling habits, and it took phoneticians to invent an alphabet that absolutely guaranteed a one-sound-to-one-symbol correspondence. There could be no other way to study the sounds of all human languages scientifically.

In 1888 members of the International Phonetic Association developed a **phonetic alphabet** to symbolize the sounds of all languages. They utilized both ordinary letters and invented symbols. Each character of the alphabet had exactly one value across all of the world's languages. Someone who knew this alphabet would know how to pronounce a word written in it, and upon hearing a word pronounced, would know how to write it using the alphabetic symbols. The inventors of this **International Phonetic Alphabet**, or **IPA**, knew that a phonetic alphabet should include just enough symbols to represent the fundamental sounds of all languages.

Table 5.1 is a list of the IPA symbols that we will use to represent English speech sounds. The symbols do not tell us everything about the sounds, which may vary from person to person and which may depend on their position in

TABLE 5.1 | A Phonetic Alphabet for English Pronunciation

Consonants								Vowels			
p	**p**ill	t	**t**ill	k	**k**ill			i	b**ee**t	ɪ	b**i**t
b	**b**ill	d	**d**ill	g	**g**ill			e	b**ai**t	ɛ	b**e**t
m	**m**ill	n	**n**il	ŋ	ri**ng**			u	b**oo**t	ʊ	f**oo**t
f	**f**eel	s	**s**eal	h	**h**eal			o	b**oa**t	ɔ	b**o**re
v	**v**eal	z	**z**eal	l	**l**eaf			æ	b**a**t	a	p**o**t/b**a**r
θ	**th**igh	tʃ	**ch**ill	r	**r**eef			ʌ	b**u**tt	ə	**so**fa
ð	**th**y	ʤ	**g**in	j	**y**ou			aɪ	b**i**te	aʊ	b**ou**t
ʃ	**sh**ill	ʍ	**wh**ich	w	**w**itch			ɔɪ	b**oy**		
ʒ	mea**s**ure										

a word. They are not all of the phonetic symbols needed for English, but they will suffice for our purposes. When we discuss the sounds in more detail later in the chapter, we will add appropriate symbols. From now on we will enclose phonetic symbols in square brackets [ ] to distinguish them from ordinary letters.

The symbol [ə] in *sofa* toward the bottom right of the chart is called a *schwa*. We use it to represent vowels in syllables that are not emphasized in speaking and whose duration is very short, such as gen*e*ral, *a*bout, read*e*r, etc. All other vowel symbols in the chart occur in syllables that receive at least some emphasis.

Speakers from different parts of the country may pronounce some words differently. For example, some of you may pronounce the words *which* and *witch* identically. If you do, the initial sound of both words is symbolized by [w] in the chart. If you don't, the "breathy" *wh* of *which* is represented by [ʍ].

Some speakers of English pronounce *bought* and *pot* with the same vowel; others pronounce them with the vowel sounds in *bore* and *bar*, respectively. We have therefore listed both words in the chart of symbols. It is difficult to include all the phonetic symbols needed to represent all differences in English. There may be sounds in your speech that are not represented, and vice versa, but that's okay. There are many varieties of English. The versions spoken in England, Australia, Ireland, and India, among others, differ in their pronunciations. And even within American English, phonetic differences exist among the many dialects, as we discuss in chapter 7.

The symbols in Table 5.1 are IPA symbols, with one small exception. The IPA uses an upside-down *r* ([ɹ]) for the English sound *r*. We, and many writers, prefer the right-side-up symbol [r] for clarity when writing for an English-reading audience. Using the IPA symbols, we can now unambiguously represent the pronunciation of words. For example, in the six words below, *ou* represents six distinct vowel sounds; the *gh* is silent in all but *rough*, where it is pronounced [f]; the *th* represents a single sound, either [θ] or [ð], and the *l* in *would* is also silent. However, the phonetic transcription gives us the actual pronunciations.

Spelling	Pronunciation
though	[ðo]
thought	[θɔt]
rough	[rʌf]
bough	[baʊ]
through	[θru]
would	[wʊd]

Articulatory Phonetics

The voice is articulated by the lips and the tongue. . . . Man speaks by means of the air which he inhales into his entire body and particularly into the body cavities. When the air is expelled through the empty space it produces a sound, because of the resonances in the skull. The tongue articulates by its strokes; it gathers the air in the throat and pushes it against the palate and the teeth, thereby giving the sound a definite shape. If the tongue would not articulate each time, by means of its strokes, man would not speak clearly and would only be able to produce a few simple sounds.

HIPPOCRATES (460–377 BCE)

The production of any sound involves the movement of air. Most speech sounds are produced by pushing lung air through the *vocal cords*, up the throat, into the mouth or nose and finally out of the body.

A brief anatomy lesson is in order. The *opening* between the vocal cords is the **glottis** and is located in the voice box or **larynx**, pronounced "lair rinks." The tubular part of the throat above the larynx is the **pharynx** (rhymes with *larynx*). What sensible people call "the mouth," linguists call the **oral cavity** to distinguish it from the **nasal cavity**, which is the nose and the plumbing that connects it to the throat. Finally we have the tongue and the lips, both of which are capable of rapid movement and shape changing. All of these together make up the **vocal tract**. By moving the different parts of the vocal tract we change its shape, which results in the different sounds of language. Figure 5.1 should make these descriptions clearer. (The vocal cords and larynx are not specifically labeled in the figure.)

Consonants

The sounds of all languages fall into two classes: consonants and vowels. Consonants are produced with some restriction or closure in the vocal tract that impedes the flow of air from the lungs. In phonetics, the terms *consonant* and *vowel* refer to types of *sounds*, not to the letters that represent them. In speaking of the alphabet, we may call *a* a vowel and *c* a consonant, but that means only that we use the letter *a* to represent vowel sounds and the letter *c* to represent consonant sounds.

Place of Articulation

Lolita, light of my life, fire of my loins. My sin, my soul. Lo-lee-ta: the tip of the tongue taking a trip of three steps down the palate to tap, at three, on the teeth. Lo. Lee. Ta.

VLADIMIR NABOKOV, *Lolita*, 1955

We classify consonants according to where in the vocal tract the airflow restriction occurs, called the **place of articulation**. Movement of the tongue and lips creates the constriction, reshaping the oral cavity in various ways to produce the various sounds. We are about to discuss the major places of articulation. As you read the description of each sound class, refer to Table 5.1, which provides key words containing the sounds. As you pronounce these words, try to feel which articulators are moving. (Watching yourself in a mirror helps, too.) Look at Figure 5.1 for help with the terminology.

FIGURE 5.1 | The vocal tract. Places of articulation: 1. bilabial; 2. labiodental; 3. interdental; 4. alveolar; 5. (alveo)palatal; 6. velar; 7. uvular; 8. glottal.

Bilabials [p] [b] [m] When we produce a [p], [b], or [m], we articulate by bringing both lips together.

Labiodentals [f] [v] We also use our lips to form [f] and [v]. We articulate these sounds by touching the bottom lip to the upper teeth.

Interdentals [θ] [ð] These sounds, both spelled *th*, are pronounced by inserting the tip of the tongue between the teeth. However, for some speakers the tongue merely touches behind the teeth, making a sound more correctly called **dental**. Watch yourself in a mirror and say *think* or *these* and see where your tongue tip goes.

Alveolars [t] [d] [n] [s] [z] [l] [r] All seven of these sounds are pronounced with the tongue raised in various ways to the **alveolar ridge**.

- For [t], [d], and [n] the tongue tip is raised and touches the ridge, or slightly in front of it.
- For [s] and [z] the sides of the front of the tongue are raised, but the tip is lowered so that air escapes over it.
- For [l] the tongue tip is raised while the rest of the tongue remains down, permitting air to escape over its *sides*. Hence, [l] is called a **lateral** sound. You can feel this in the *l*'s of *Lolita*.
- For [r] (IPA [ɹ]), most English speakers either curl the tip of the tongue back behind the alveolar ridge, or bunch up the top of the tongue behind the ridge. As opposed to the articulation of [l], when [r] is articulated, air escapes through the central part of the mouth. It is a **central** liquid.

Palatals [ʃ] [ʒ] [tʃ] [ʤ] [j] For these sounds, which occur in *mission* [mɪʃən], *measure* [mɛʒər], *cheap* [tʃip], *judge* [ʤʌʤ], and *yoyo* [jojo], the constriction occurs by raising the front part of the tongue to the palate.

Velars [k] [g] [ŋ] Another class of sounds is produced by raising the back of the tongue to the soft palate or **velum**. The initial and final sounds of the words *kick* [kɪk] and *gig* [gɪg] and the final sounds of the words *back* [bæk], *bag* [bæg], and *bang* [bæŋ] are all velar sounds.

Uvulars [ʀ] [q] [ɢ] Uvular sounds are produced by raising the back of the tongue to the **uvula**, the fleshy protuberance that hangs down in the back of our throats. The *r* in French is often a uvular *trill* symbolized by [ʀ]. The uvular sounds [q] and [ɢ] occur in Arabic. These sounds do not ordinarily occur in English.

Glottals [h] [ʔ] The sound of [h] is from the flow of air through the open *glottis* and past the tongue and lips as they prepare to pronounce a vowel sound, which always follows [h].

If the air is stopped completely at the glottis by tightly closed vocal cords, the sound upon release of the cords is a **glottal stop [ʔ]**. The interjection *uh-oh*, which you hope never to hear your dentist utter, has two glottal stops and is spelled phonetically [ʔʌʔo]. The late singer Michael Jackson made free use of glottal stops in many of his most well-known songs.

Table 5.2 summarizes the classification of these English consonants by their place of articulation.

Manner of Articulation

We have described several classes of consonants according to their *places of articulation*, yet we are still unable to distinguish the sounds in each class from one another. What distinguishes [p] from [b] or [b] from [m]? All are bilabial sounds. What is the difference between [t], [d], and [n], which are all alveolar sounds?

Speech sounds also vary in the way the airstream is affected as it flows from the lungs up and out of the mouth and nose. It may be blocked or partially blocked; the vocal cords may vibrate or not vibrate. We refer to this as the **manner of articulation**.

TABLE 5.2 | Places of Articulation of English Consonants

Bilabial	p	b	m				
Labiodental	f	v					
Interdental	θ	ð					
Alveolar	t	d	n	s	z	l	r
Palatal	ʃ	ʒ	ʧ	ʤ			
Velar	k	g	ŋ				
Glottal	h	ʔ					

Voiced and Voiceless Sounds

Sounds are **voiceless** when the vocal cords are apart so that air flows freely through the glottis into the oral cavity. [p] and [s] in *super* [supər] are two of the several voiceless sounds of English.

If the vocal cords are together, the airstream forces its way through and causes them to vibrate. Such sounds are **voiced**. [b] and [z] in *buzz* [bʌz] are two of the many voiced sounds of English. To get a sense of voicing, try putting a finger in each ear and say the voiced "z-z-z-z-z." You can feel the vibrations of the vocal cords. If you now say the voiceless "s-s-s-s-s," you will not sense these vibrations (although you might hear a hissing sound). When you whisper, you are making all the speech sounds voiceless. Try it! Whisper "Sue" and "zoo." No difference, right?

The voiced/voiceless distinction is very important in English. This phonetic property distinguishes the words in pairs like the following:

rope/robe	fate/fade	rack/rag	wreath/wreathe
[rop]/[rob]	[fet]/[fed]	[ræk]/[ræg]	[riθ]/[rið]

The first word of each pair ends with a voiceless sound and the second word with a voiced sound. All other aspects of the sounds in each word pair are identical; the position of the lips and tongue is the same.

The voiced/voiceless distinction also occurs in the following pairs, where in each case the first word begins with a voiceless sound and the second with a voiced sound:

fine/vine	seal/zeal	choke/joke
[faɪn]/[vaɪn]	[sil/zil]	[ʧok]/[ʤok]
peat/beat	tote/dote	kale/gale
[pit]/[bit]	[tot]/[dot]	[kel]/[gel]

In our discussion of [p], we did not distinguish the initial sound in the word *pit* from the second sound in the word *spit*. There is, however, a phonetic difference in these two voiceless stops. During the production of voiceless sounds, the glottis is open and the air flows freely between the vocal cords. When a voiceless sound is followed by a voiced sound such as a vowel, the vocal cords must close so they can vibrate.

Voiceless sounds fall into two classes depending on the timing of the vocal cord closure. When we say *pit*, the vocal cords remain open for a very short time after the lips come apart to release the *p*. We call this *p* **aspirated** because a brief puff of air escapes before the glottis closes.

When we pronounce the *p* in *spit*, however, the vocal cords start vibrating as soon as the lips open. That *p* is **unaspirated**. Hold your palm about two inches in front of your lips and say *pit*. You will feel a puff of air, which you will not feel when you say *spit*. The *t* in *tick* and the *k* in *kin* are also aspirated voiceless stops, while the *t* in *stick* and the *k* in *skin* are unaspirated.

Finally, in the production of the voiced [b] (and [d] and [g]), the vocal cords are vibrating throughout the closure of the lips, and continue to vibrate during the vowel sound that follows after the lips part.

We indicate aspirated sounds by writing the phonetic symbol with a raised *h*, as in the following examples:

pool	[pʰul]	spool	[spul]
tale	[tʰel]	stale	[stel]
kale	[kʰel]	scale	[skel]

Figure 5.2 shows in diagrammatic form the timing of lip closure in relation to the state of the vocal cords.

Nasal and Oral Sounds

The voiced/voiceless distinction differentiates the bilabials [b] and [p]. The sound [m] is also a bilabial, and it is voiced. What distinguishes it from [b]?

Figure 5.1 shows the roof of the mouth divided into the (hard) palate and the soft palate (or velum). The palate is a hard bony structure at the front of

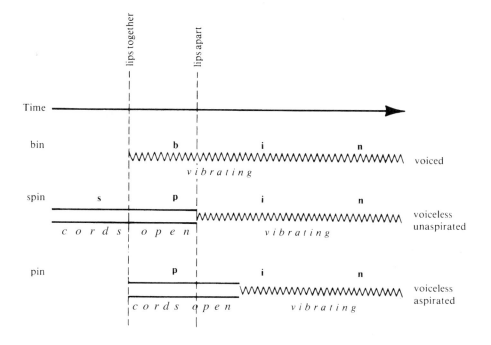

FIGURE 5.2 | Timing of lip closure and vocal-cord vibrations for voiced, voiceless unaspirated, and voiceless aspirated bilabial stops [b], [p], [pʰ].

the mouth. You can feel it with your thumb. First, wash your hands. Now, slide your thumb (nail down) along the hard palate back toward the throat; you will feel the velum, which is where the flesh becomes soft and pliable. The velum terminates in the uvula, which you can see in a mirror if you open your mouth wide and say "aaah." The velum is movable, and when it is raised all the way to touch the back of the throat, the passage through the nose is cut off and air can escape only through the mouth.

Sounds produced with the velum up, blocking the air from escaping through the nose, are **oral sounds**, because the air can escape only through the oral cavity. Most sounds in all languages are oral sounds. When the velum is lowered, air escapes through both the nose and the mouth. Sounds produced this way are **nasal sounds**. The sound [m] is a nasal consonant. Thus [m] is distinguished from [b] because it is a nasal sound, whereas [b] is an oral sound.

The diagrams in Figure 5.3 show the position of the lips and the velum when [m], [b], and [p] are articulated. The sounds [p], [b], and [m] are produced by stopping the airflow at the lips; [m] and [b] differ from [p] by being voiced; [m] differs from [b] by being nasal. (If you ever wondered why people sound "nasally" when they have a cold, it's because excessive mucous prevents the velum from closing properly during speech.)

The same oral/nasal difference occurs in *raid* [red] and *rain* [ren], *rug* [rʌg] and *rung* [rʌŋ]. The velum is raised in the production of [d] and [g], preventing the air from flowing through the nose, whereas for [n] and [ŋ] the velum is down, allowing the air out through both the nose and the mouth when the closure is released. The sounds [m], [n], and [ŋ] are therefore nasal sounds, and [b], [d], and [g] are oral sounds.

The presence or absence of these **phonetic features**—nasal and voiced—permit the division of all speech sounds into four classes: voiced, voiceless, nasal, and oral, as shown in Table 5.3.

We now have three ways of classifying consonants: by voicing, by place of articulation, and by nasalization. For example, [p] is a voiceless, bilabial, oral sound; [n] is a voiced, alveolar, nasal sound, and so on.

m   *b, p*

FIGURE 5.3 | Position of lips and velum for *m* (lips together, velum down) and *b, p* (lips together, velum up).

TABLE 5.3 | Four Classes of Speech Sounds

	Oral	Nasal
Voiced	b d g	m n ŋ
Voiceless	p t k	*

*Nasal consonants in English are usually voiced. Both voiced and voiceless nasal sounds occur in other languages.

Stops [p] [b] [m] [t] [d] [n] [k] [g] [ŋ] [tʃ] [ʤ] [ʔ] We are seeing finer and finer distinctions of speech sounds. However, both [t] and [s] are voiceless, alveolar, oral sounds. What distinguishes them? After all, *tack* and *sack* are different words.

Stops are consonants in which the airstream is completely blocked in the *oral* cavity for a short period (tens of milliseconds). All other sounds are **continuants**. The sound [t] is a stop, but the sound [s] is not, and that is what makes them different speech sounds.

- [p], [b], and [m] are *bilabial stops*, with the airstream stopped at the mouth by the complete closure of the lips.
- [t], [d], and [n] are *alveolar stops*; the airstream is stopped by the tongue, making a complete closure at the alveolar ridge.
- [k], [g], and [ŋ] are *velar stops*, with the complete closure at the velum.
- [tʃ] and [ʤ] are *palatal affricates* with complete stop closures. They will be further classified later.
- [ʔ] is a *glottal stop*; the air is completely stopped at the glottis.

We have been discussing the sounds that occur in English. A variety of stop consonants occur in other languages but not in English. For example, in Quechua, spoken in Bolivia and Peru, uvular stops occur, where the back of the tongue is raised and moved rearward to form a complete closure with the uvula. The phonetic symbol [q] denotes the voiceless version of this stop, which is the initial sound in the name of the language, *Quechua*. The voiced uvular stop [ɢ] also occurs in Quechua.

Fricatives [f] [v] [θ] [ð] [s] [z] [ʃ] [ʒ] [x] [ɣ] [h] In the production of some continuants, the airflow is so severely obstructed that it causes friction, and the sounds are therefore called **fricatives**. The first of each the following pairs of fricatives is voiceless; the second voiced.

- [f] and [v] are *labiodental fricatives*; the friction is created at the lips and teeth, where a narrow passage permits the air to escape.
- [θ] and [ð] are *interdental fricatives*, represented by *th* in *thin* and *then*. The friction occurs at the opening between the tongue and teeth.
- [s] and [z] are *alveolar fricatives*, with the friction created at the alveolar ridge.
- [ʃ] and [ʒ] are *palatal fricatives*, and contrast in such pairs as *mission* [mɪʃən] and *measure* [mɛʒər]. They are produced with friction created as the air passes between the tongue and the part of the palate behind

the alveolar ridge. In English, the voiced palatal fricative never begins words except for foreign words such as *genre*. The voiceless palatal fricative begins the words *shoe* [ʃu] and *sure* [ʃur] and ends the words *rush* [rʌʃ] and *push* [pʊʃ].

- [x] and [ɣ] denote *velar fricatives*. They are produced by raising the back of the tongue toward, but not quite touching, the velum. The friction is created as air passes through that narrow passage, and the sound is not unlike clearing your throat. These sounds do not commonly occur in English, though in some forms of Scottish English the final sound of *loch* meaning 'lake' is [x]. In rapid speech the *g* in *wagon* may be pronounced [ɣ]. The final sound of the composer J. S. Bach's name is also pronounced [x], which is a common sound in German.

- [h] is a glottal fricative. Its relatively weak sound comes from air passing through the open glottis and pharynx.

All fricatives are continuants. Although the airstream is obstructed as it passes through the oral cavity, it is not completely stopped.

Affricates [tʃ] [dʒ] These sounds are produced by a stop closure followed immediately by a gradual release of the closure that produces an effect characteristic of a fricative. The palatal sounds that begin and end the words *church* and *judge* are voiceless and voiced affricates, respectively. Affricates are not continuants because of the initial stop closure.

Liquids [l] [r] In the production of the sounds [l] and [r], there is some obstruction of the airstream in the mouth, but not enough to cause any real constriction or friction. These sounds are **liquids**. They are articulated differently, as described in the earlier alveolar section, but are grouped as a class because they are acoustically similar. Due to that similarity, foreign speakers of English may confuse the two sounds and substitute one for the other.

Glides [j] [w] The sounds [j] and [w], the initial sounds of *you* [ju] and *we* [wi], are produced with little obstruction of the airstream. They are always followed directly by a vowel and do not occur at the ends of words (don't be fooled by spelling; words ending in *y* or *w* like *say* and *saw* end in a vowel sound). After articulating [j] or [w], the tongue glides quickly into place for pronouncing the next vowel, hence the term **glide**.

The glide [j] is a palatal sound; the blade of the tongue (the front part minus the tip) is raised toward the hard palate in a position almost identical to that in producing the vowel sound [i] in the word *beat* [bit]. The glide [w] is produced by both rounding the lips and simultaneously raising the back of the tongue toward the velum. It is thus a **labio-velar** glide. Where speakers of English have different pronunciations for the words *which* and *witch*, the labio-velar glide in the first word is voiceless, symbolized as [ʍ] (an upside-down *w*). The position of the tongue and the lips for [w] is similar to that for producing the vowel sound [u] in *suit* [sut].

Approximants The sounds [w], [j], [r], and [l] may also be called approximants because the articulators approximate a frictional closeness, but no actual friction occurs. The first three are central approximants, whereas [l] is a lateral approximant.

Although in this chapter we focus on the sounds of English, the IPA has symbols and classifications for all the sounds of the world's languages. For example, many languages have sounds that are referred to as trills, and others have clicks. These are described in the following sections.

Trills and flaps The *r*-sound of many languages may be different from the English [r]. A trilled *r* is produced by rapid vibrations of an articulator. An alveolar **trill**, as in the Spanish word for 'dog,' *perro*, is produced by vibrating the tongue tip against the alveolar ridge. Its IPA symbol is [r], strictly speaking, though we have co-opted [r] for the English *r*. Many French speakers articulate the initial sound of *rouge* as a uvular trill, produced by vibrating the uvula. Its IPA symbol is [ʀ].

Another *r*-sound is called a **flap** and is produced by a flick of the tongue against the alveolar ridge. It sounds like a very fast *d*. It occurs in Spanish in words like *pero* meaning 'but.' It may also occur in British English in words such as *very*. Its IPA symbol is [ɾ]. Most American speakers produce a flap instead of a [t] or [d] in words like *writer* and *rider*, which then sound identical and are spelled phonetically as [raɪɾər].

Clicks These "exotic" sounds are made by moving air in the mouth between various articulators. The sound of disapproval often spelled *tsk* is an alveolar **click** that occurs in several languages of southern Africa such as Zulu. A lateral click, which is like the sound one makes to encourage a horse, occurs in Xhosa. In fact, the *X* in *Xhosa* stands for that particular speech sound.

Phonetic Symbols for American English Consonants

We are now capable of distinguishing all of the consonant sounds of English via the properties of voicing, nasality, and place and manner of articulation. For example, [f] is a voiceless, (oral), labiodental fricative; [n] is a (voiced), nasal, alveolar stop. The parenthesized features are usually not mentioned because they are redundant; all sounds are oral unless nasal is specifically mentioned, and all nasals are voiced in English.

Table 5.4 lists the consonants by their phonetic features. The rows stand for manner of articulation and the columns for place of articulation. The entries are sufficient to distinguish all words in English from one another. For example, using [p] for both aspirated and unaspirated voiceless bilabial stops and [b] for the voiced bilabial stop suffices to differentiate the words *pit*, *spit*, and *bit*. If a narrower phonetic transcription of these words is desired, the symbol [pʰ] can be used to indicate aspiration, giving us [pʰɪt], [spɪt], [bɪt]. By "narrow transcription" we mean one that indicates all the phonetic details of a sound, even those that do not affect the words.

Examples of words in which these sounds occur are given in Table 5.5.

TABLE 5.4 | Some Phonetic Symbols for American English Consonants

	Bilabial	Labiodental	Interdental	Alveolar	Palatal	Velar	Glottal
Stop (oral)							
voiceless	p			t		k	ʔ
voiced	b			d		g	
Nasal (voiced)	m			n		ŋ	
Fricative							
voiceless		f	θ	s	ʃ		h
voiced		v	ð	z	ʒ		
Affricate							
voiceless					tʃ		
voiced					ʤ		
Glide							
voiceless	ʍ					ʍ	
voiced	w				j	w	
Liquid (voiced)							
(central)				r			
(lateral)				l			

TABLE 5.5 | Examples of Consonants in English Words

	Bilabial	Labiodental	Interdental	Alveolar	Palatal	Velar	Glottal
Stop (oral)							
voiceless	*p*ie			*t*ie		*k*ite	(ʔ)uh-(ʔ)oh
voiced	*b*uy			*d*ie		*g*uy	
Nasal (voiced)	*m*y			*n*ight		si*ng*	
Fricative							
voiceless		*f*ine	*th*igh	*s*ue	*sh*oe		*h*igh
voiced		*v*ine	*th*y	*z*oo	mea*s*ure		
Affricate							
voiceless					*ch*eese		
voiced					*j*ump		
Glide							
voiceless	*wh*ich					*wh*ich	
voiced	*w*ipe				*y*ou	*w*ipe	
Liquid (voiced)							
(central)				*r*ye			
(lateral)				*l*ye			

Vowels

HIGGINS: Tired of listening to sounds?

PICKERING: Yes. It's a fearful strain. I rather fancied myself because I can pronounce
             twenty-four distinct vowel sounds, but your hundred and thirty beat me. I
             can't hear a bit of difference between most of them.

HIGGINS: Oh, that comes with practice. You hear no difference at first, but
             you keep on listening and presently you find they're all as different
             as A from B.

GEORGE BERNARD SHAW, *Pygmalion*, 1912

Vowels are produced with little restriction of the airflow from the lungs out through the mouth and/or the nose. The quality of a vowel depends on the shape of the vocal tract as the air passes through. Different parts of the tongue may be high or low in the mouth; the lips may be spread or pursed; the velum may be raised or lowered.

Vowel sounds carry pitch and loudness; you can sing vowels or shout vowels. They may be longer or shorter in duration. Vowels can stand alone—they can be produced without consonants before or after them. You can say the vowels of *beat* [bit], *bit* [bɪt], and *boot* [but], for example, without the initial [b] or the final [t], but you cannot say a [b] or a [t] alone without at least a little bit of vowel sound.

Linguists can describe vowels acoustically or electronically. We will discuss that topic in chapter 11. In this chapter we describe vowels by their articulatory features as we did with consonants. Just as we say a [d] is pronounced by raising the tongue tip to the alveolar ridge, we say an [i] is pronounced by raising the body of the tongue toward the palate. With a [b], the lips come together; for an [æ] (the vowel in *cat*) the tongue is low in the mouth with the tongue tip forward, behind the front teeth.

If you watch a side view of an X-ray (that's -*ray*, not -*rated*!) video of someone's tongue moving during speech, you will see various parts of the tongue rise up high and fall down low; at the same time you will see it move forward and backward in the mouth. These are the dimensions over which vowels are produced. We classify vowels according to three questions:

1.   How high or low in the mouth is the tongue?
2.   How forward or backward in the mouth is the tongue?
3.   Are the lips rounded (pursed) or spread?

Tongue Position

(In this section we refer to the vowel symbols of Table 5.1 on page 193.)
The upper two diagrams in Figure 5.4 show that the tongue is high in the mouth in the production of the vowels [i] and [u] in the words *he* [hi] and *who* [hu]. In *he* the front part (but not the tip) of the tongue is raised; in *who* it is the back of the tongue. (Prolong the vowels of these words and try to feel the raised part of your tongue.) These are both *high* vowels, and the [i] is a *high front* vowel while the [u] is a *high back* vowel.

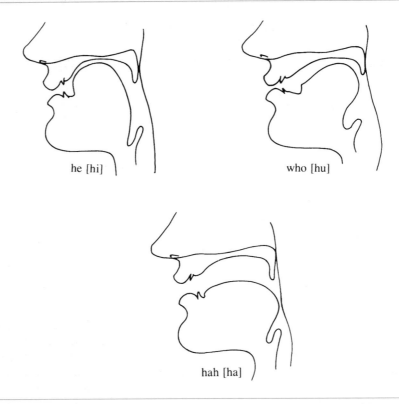

FIGURE 5.4 | Position of the tongue in producing the vowels in *he, who,* and *hah.*

To produce the vowel sound [a] of *hah* [ha], the tongue is low in the mouth, as the third diagram in Figure 5.4 shows. (The reason a doctor examining your throat may ask you to say *ah* is that the tongue is low and easy to see over.)

The vowels [ɪ] and [ʊ] in the words *hit* [hɪt] and *put* [pʰʊt] are similar to those in *heat* [hit] and *hoot* [hut] with slightly lowered tongue positions.

The vowels [e] and [o] in *bait* [bet] and *boat* [bot] are *mid vowels*—they are neither high nor low. [ɛ] in *bet* [bɛt] is also a mid vowel, produced with a slightly lower tongue position than [e]. As well, [e] and [ɛ] are *front* vowels and [o] is a *back* vowel.

The vowel [æ] in *hack* [hæk] or *cat* [kæt] is produced with the front part of the tongue low in the mouth. Thus [æ] is a *low front* vowel. The [ɔ] in *saw* [sɔ] is also a low vowel, but it is pronounced by lowering the *back* of the tongue. It is therefore a *low back* vowel.

The vowel [ʌ] in the word *luck* [lʌk] is a central vowel pronounced with the tongue low in the mouth though not as low as with [a]. Finally the schwa [ə], which occurs as the first sound in *about* [əbaʊt], or the final sound of *sofa* [sofə], is articulated with the tongue in a neutral position between the extremes of high/low, front/back. The schwa is used mostly to represent unstressed vowels. (Figure 5.5 makes this vowel "geography" more apparent.)

Part of the Tongue Involved

| Tongue Height | FRONT ← — CENTRAL — → BACK | | |

FIGURE 5.5 | Classification of American English vowels.

Lip Rounding

Vowels also differ as to whether the lips are rounded or spread. The back vowels [u], [ʊ], [o], and [ɔ] in *boot, put, boat,* and *bawd* are the only **rounded vowels** in (American) English. They are produced with pursed or rounded lips. You can get a feel for the rounding by prolonging the word *who,* as if you were an owl: *whooooooooooo.* Now pose for the camera and say *cheese,* only say it with a prolonged vowel: *cheeeeeeeeeeese.* The high front [i] in *cheese* is unrounded, with the lips in the shape of a smile, and you can feel it or see it in a mirror.

Other languages may differ in whether or not they have rounded vowels. French and Swedish, for example, have *front* rounded vowels, which English lacks. English also lacks a high back *unrounded* vowel, but this sound occurs in Mandarin Chinese, Japanese, and the Cameroonian language Feʔfeʔ, among others. The IPA symbol for this vowel is [ɯ]. The rounding distinction is important, as in Mandarin Chinese the unrounded [sɯ] means 'four' but the round [su] (like *sue*) means 'speed.'

Diphthongs

A **diphthong** is a sequence of two vowel sounds "squashed" together. Diphthongs are present in the phonetic inventory of many languages, including English. The vowels we have studied so far are simple vowels, called **monophthongs.** The vowel sound in the word *bite* [baɪt], however, is the [a] vowel sound of *father* followed rapidly by the [ɪ] sound of *fit,* resulting in the diphthong [aɪ]. Similarly, the vowel in *bout* [baʊt] is [a] followed by the [ʊ] sound of *put,* resulting in [aʊ]. Another diphthong that occurs in English is the vowel sound in *boy* [bɔɪ], which is the vowel [ɔ] of *bore* followed by [ɪ], resulting in [ɔɪ]. The pronunciation of any of these diphthongs may vary from our description because of the diversity of English speakers.

To some extent the midvowels [e] and [o] may be diphthongized, especially in American English, though not in other varieties such as Irish English. Many linguists therefore denote these sounds as [eɪ] and [oʊ] in a narrower transcription. In this book we will stay with [e] and [o] for these vowel sounds.

Nasalization of Vowels

Vowels, like consonants, can be produced with a raised velum that prevents the air from escaping through the nose, or with a lowered velum that permits air to pass through the nasal passage. When the nasal passage is blocked, *oral* vowels result; when the nasal passage is open, *nasal* (or *nasalized*) vowels result. In English, nasal vowels occur for the most part before nasal consonants in the same syllable, and oral vowels occur in all other places.

The words *bean*, *bone*, *bingo*, *boom*, *bam*, and *bang* are examples of words that contain nasalized vowels. To show the nasalization of a vowel in a narrow phonetic transcription, an extra mark called a **diacritic**—the symbol ~ (tilde) in this case—is placed over the vowel, as in *bean* [bĩn] and *bone* [bõn].

In languages like French, Polish, and Portuguese, nasalized vowels occur without nasal consonants. The French word meaning 'sound' is *son* [sõ]. The *n* in the spelling is not pronounced but indicates that the vowel is nasal.

Tense and Lax Vowels

Figure 5.5 shows that the vowel [i] has a slightly higher tongue position than [ɪ]. This is also true for [e] and [ɛ]; and [u] and [ʊ]. The first vowel in each pair is generally produced with greater tension of the tongue muscles than its counterpart, and it is often a little longer in duration. These vowels can be distinguished by the features **tense** and **lax**, as shown in the first three rows of the following:

Tense		Lax	
i	beat	ɪ	bit
e	bait	ɛ	bet
u	boot	ʊ	put
o	boat	ʌ	hut
ɔ	saw	æ	hat
a	pa	ə	about
aɪ	high		
aʊ	how		
ɔɪ	boy		

Tense vowels may occur at the ends of words: [si], [se], [su], [so], [sɔ], [pa], [saɪ], [haʊ], and [sɔɪ] represent the English words *see*, *say*, *sue*, *sew*, *saw*, *pa*, *sigh*, *how*, and *soy*. Lax vowels do not ordinarily occur at the ends of words: [sɪ], [sɛ], [sʊ], [sʌ], [sæ], and [sə] are not possible words in English.

Major Phonetic Classes

Biologists divide life forms into larger and smaller classes. They may distinguish between animals and plants; within animals, between vertebrates and invertebrates; and within vertebrates, between mammals and reptiles; and so on.

Linguists describe speech sounds similarly. All sounds are consonant sounds or vowel sounds, though some play dual roles. Within consonants, all are voiced or unvoiced, and so on. All the classes of sounds described so far in this chapter combine to form larger, more general classes that are important in the patterning of sounds in the world's languages.

Noncontinuants and Continuants

Stops and affricates belong to the class of **noncontinuants**. There is a total obstruction of the airstream in the *oral cavity*. Nasal stops are included, although air does flow continuously out the nose. All other consonants, and all vowels, are continuants, in which the stream of air flows continuously out of the mouth.

Obstruents and Sonorants

The non-nasal stops, the fricatives, and the affricates form a major class of sounds called **obstruents**. The airstream may be fully obstructed, as in non-nasal stops and affricates, or nearly fully obstructed, as in the production of fricatives.

Sounds that are not obstruents are **sonorants**. Vowels, nasal stops [m], [n], and [ŋ], liquids [l] and [r], and glides [j] and [w] are all sonorants. They are produced with much less obstruction to the flow of air than the obstruents, which permits the air to resonate. Nasal stops are sonorants because, although the air is blocked in the mouth, it continues to resonate in the nasal cavity.

Consonantal Sounds

Obstruents, nasal stops, liquids, and glides are all consonants. There is some degree of restriction to the airflow in articulating these sounds. With glides ([j], [w]), however, the restriction is minimal, and they are the most vowel-like, and the least consonant-like, of the consonants. Glides may even be referred to as "semivowels" or "semi-consonants." In recognition of this fact, linguists place the obstruents, nasal stops, and liquids in a subclass of consonants called **consonantal**, from which the glides are excluded.

Here are some other terms used to form subclasses of consonantal sounds. These are not exhaustive, nor are they mutually exclusive (e.g., the interdentals belong to two subclasses). A full course in phonetics would note further classes that we omit.

Labials **[p]** **[b]** **[m]** **[f]** **[v]** **[w]** **[ʍ]** Labial sounds are those articulated with the involvement of the lips. They include the class of *bilabial* sounds [p], [b], and [m], the *labiodentals* [f] and [v], and the *labiovelars* [w] and [ʍ].

Coronals **[θ]** **[ð]** **[t]** **[d]** **[n]** **[s]** **[z]** **[ʃ]** **[ʒ]** **[tʃ]** **[dʒ]** **[l]** **[r]** Coronal sounds are articulated by raising the tongue blade. Coronals include the *interdentals* [θ] and [ð], the *alveolars* [t], [d], [n], [s], and [z], the *palatals* [ʃ] and [ʒ], the *affricates* [tʃ] and [dʒ], and the *liquids* [l] and [r].

Anteriors [p] [b] [m] [f] [v] [θ] [ð] [t] [d] [n] [s] [z] Anterior sounds are consonants produced in the front part of the mouth, that is, from the alveolar area forward. They include the labials, the interdentals, and the alveolars.

Sibilants [s] [z] [ʃ] [ʒ] [tʃ] [dʒ] This class of consonantal sounds is characterized by an acoustic rather than an articulatory property of its members. The friction created by sibilants produces a hissing sound, which is a mixture of high-frequency sounds.

Syllabic Sounds

Sounds that may function as the core of a syllable possess the feature **syllabic**. Clearly vowels are syllabic, but they are not the only sound class that anchors syllables.

Liquids and nasals may also be syllabic, as shown by the words *dazzle* [dæzl̩], *faker* [fekr̩], *rhythm* [rɪðm̩], and *wagon* [wægn̩]. (The diacritic mark under the [l̩], [r̩], [m̩], and [n̩] is the notation for syllabic.) Placing a schwa [ə] before the syllabic liquid or nasal also shows that these are separate syllables. The four words could be written as [dæzəl], [fekər], [rɪðəm], and [wægən]. We will use this transcription. Similarly, the vowel sound in words like *bird* and *verb* are sometimes written as a syllabic *r*: [br̩d] and [vr̩b]. For consistency we shall transcribe these words using the schwa—[bərd] and [vərb]—the only instances where a schwa represents a stressed vowel.

Obstruents and glides are never syllabic sounds because an obstruent or glide is always accompanied by a vowel, and that vowel functions as the syllabic core.

Prosodic Features

ZITS © 2011 ZITS PARTNERSHIP, KING FEATURES SYNDICATE

Length, *pitch*, and *stress* (or "accent") are **prosodic** or **suprasegmental** features. They are features *over and above* the segmental values such as place or manner of articulation, thus the *supra-* in *suprasegmental*. The term *prosodic* comes from poetry, where it refers to the metrical structure of verse. One of the essential characteristics of poetry is the placement of stress on particular syllables, which defines the versification of the poem.

Speech sounds that are identical in their place or manner features may differ in length (duration). Tense vowels are slightly longer than lax vowels, but only by a few milliseconds. However, in some languages when a vowel is prolonged to around twice its normal length, it can make a difference between words. In Japanese the word *biru* [biru] with a regular *i* means 'building,' but with the *i* doubled in length as in *biiru*, spelled phonetically as [bi:ru], the meaning is 'beer.' (The colon-like : is the IPA symbol for segment length or doubling.) In Japanese, vowel length can make the difference between two words.

Japanese, and many other languages such as Finnish and Italian, have long consonants that may contrast words. When a consonant is long, or doubled, either the closure or obstruction is prolonged. Pronounced with a short *k*, the word *saki* [saki] means 'ahead' in Japanese; pronounced with a long *k*—prolonging the velar closure—the word *sakki* [sak:i] means 'before.' In effect, the extended silence of the prolonged closure is meaningful in these languages.

English is not a language in which vowel or consonant length can change a word. You might say "puleeeeeze" to emphasize your request, but the word is still *please*. You may also say in English "Whatttttt a dump!" to express your dismay at a hotel room, prolonging the *t*-closure, but the word *what* is not changed.

When we speak, we also change the **pitch** of our voices. The pitch depends on how fast the vocal cords vibrate: the faster they vibrate, the higher the pitch. If the larynx is small, as in children, the shorter vocal cords vibrate faster and the pitch is higher, all other things being equal. If the larynx is larger, as in adults, the longer vocal cords vibrate more slowly and the pitch is lower. That is why men (being generally larger), women, and children have (to a greater or lesser degree) lower-, medium-, and higher-pitched voices.

In many languages, certain syllables in a word are louder, slightly higher in pitch, and somewhat longer in duration than other syllables in the word. They are **stressed** syllables. For example, the first syllable of *digest*, the noun meaning 'summation of articles,' is stressed, whereas in *digest*, the verb meaning 'to absorb food,' the second syllable receives greater stress. Stress can be marked in several ways: for example, by putting an accent mark over the stressed vowel in the syllable, as in *dígest* versus *digést*.

English is a "stress-timed" language. In general, at least one syllable is stressed in an English word. French is not a stress-timed language. The syllables have approximately the same loudness, length, and pitch. It is a "syllable-timed" language. When native English speakers attempt to speak French, they often stress syllables, so that native French speakers hear French with "an English accent." When French speakers speak English, they often fail to put stress where a native English speaker would, and that contributes to what English speakers call "a French accent."

Tone and Intonation

We have already seen how length and stress can make sounds perceptually different despite having the same segmental properties. In some languages, these differences make different words, such as the two *digests* in English. The pitch with which a word or syllable is spoken can also make a difference in certain languages.

Speakers of all languages vary the pitch of their voice when they speak. The effect of pitch on a syllable differs from language to language. In English, it doesn't matter whether you say *cat* with a high pitch or a low pitch. It will still mean 'cat.' But if you say [ba] with a relatively high pitch in Nupe (a language spoken in Nigeria), it will mean 'to be sour,' whereas if you say it with a relatively low pitch, it will mean 'to count.' Languages that use the pitch of individual vowels or syllables to contrast meanings of words are called **tone languages**. Rather than *pitch* we use the term *tone*.

Over half the world's languages are tone languages. There are more than one thousand tone languages spoken in Africa alone. Many languages of Asia, such as Mandarin Chinese, Burmese, and Thai, are tone languages. In Thai, for example, the same string of segmental sounds represented by [na:] will mean different things if one says the sounds with a low tone, a mid-tone, a high tone, a falling tone from high to low, or a rising tone from low to high. Thai therefore has five linguistic tones, as illustrated as follows:

(Diacritics are used to represent distinctive tones in the phonetic transcriptions.)

[ˋ]	L	low tone	[nà:]	'a nickname'
[ˉ]	M	mid tone	[nā:]	'rice paddy'
[ˊ]	H	high tone	[ná:]	'young maternal uncle or aunt'
[ˆ]	HL	falling tone	[nâ:]	'face'
[ˇ]	LH	rising tone	[nǎ:]	'thick'

There are two kinds of tones. If the pitch is level across the syllable, we have a **register tone**. If the pitch changes across the syllable, whether from high to low or vice versa, we have a **contour tone**. Thai has three level and two contour tones. Commonly, tone languages will have two or three register tones and possibly several contour tones.

In a tone language it is not the absolute pitch of the syllables that is important but the relations among the pitches of different syllables. Thus men, women, and children with differently pitched voices can still communicate in a tone language.

Tones generally have a *lexical* function, that is, they make a difference between words. But in some languages tones may also have a *grammatical* function, as in Edo spoken in midwestern Nigeria. The tone on monosyllabic verbs followed by a direct object indicates the tense and transitivity of the verb. Low tone means present tense, transitive; high tone means past tense, transitive, as illustrated here:

òtà gbề	èbé
Ota write+PRES+TRANS	book
Ota writes a book.	
òtà gbế	èbé
Ota write+PAST+TRANS	book
Ota wrote a book.	

In many tone languages we find a continual lowering of the absolute pitch on the tones throughout an utterance. The *relative* pitches remain the same, however. In the following sentence in Twi, spoken in Ghana, the relative pitch rather than the absolute pitch is important.

'Kofi searches for a little food for his friend's child.'

Kòfí	hwèhwé	áduàŋ	kàkrá mà	ǹ' ádàmfò	bá
| |	| |	| |	| | |	| | | |	|
L H	L H	H L	L H L	L H L L	H

The actual pitches of these syllables would be rather different from each other, as shown in the following musical staff-like figure (the higher the number, the higher the pitch):

7	fí					
6		hwé á				
5	Kò			krá		
4		hwè				á
3			duàŋ kà			bá
2					mà ǹ'	
1						dàmfò

The lowering of the pitch is called **downdrift**. In languages with downdrift, a high tone that occurs after a low tone, or a low tone after a high tone, is lower in pitch than the preceding similarly marked tone. Notice that the first high tone in the sentence is given the pitch value 7. The next high tone (which occurs after an intervening low tone) is 6; that is, it is lower in pitch than the first high tone.

This example shows that in analyzing tones, just as in analyzing segments, not all the physical properties need be considered. Only essential features are important in language—in this case, whether the tone is high or low *in relation to the other pitches*. The absolute pitch is inessential. Speakers of tone languages are able to ignore the linguistically irrelevant absolute pitch differences between individual speakers and attend to the linguistically relevant relative pitch differences, much like speakers of non-tone languages ignore pitch altogether.

Intonation is variation of pitch that is not used to distinguish words. Languages that are not tone languages, such as English or French, are called **intonation** languages. The **pitch contour** of an utterance may affect the meaning of the whole sentence, so that *John is here* spoken with falling pitch at the end is interpreted as a statement, but with rising pitch at the end, a question. We'll have more to say about intonation in the next chapter.

Phonetic Symbols and Spelling Correspondences

I never had any large respect for good spelling.

MARK TWAIN, *Autobiography*

Table 5.6 shows the sound/spelling correspondences for American English consonants and vowels. (We have not given all possible spellings for every sound; however, these examples should help you relate English orthography to the English sound system.) We have included the symbols for the voiceless aspirated stops to illustrate that what speakers usually consider one sound—for example *p*—may occur phonetically as two sounds: [p], [pʰ].

Some of these pronunciations may differ from your own. For example, you may (or may not) pronounce the words *cot* and *caught* identically. In the form of English described here, *cot* and *caught* are pronounced differently, so *cot* is one of the examples of the vowel sound [a] as in *car*. *Caught* illustrates the vowel [ɔ] as in *core*.

There will be other differences, too, because English is a worldwide language and is spoken in many forms in many countries. The English examples

TABLE 5.6 | Phonetic Symbol/English Spelling Correspondences

Consonants	
Symbol	**Examples**
p	s**p**it, ti**p**, La**pp**
pʰ	**p**it, **p**rick, **p**laque, ap**p**ear
b	**b**it, ta**b**, **b**rat, **b**u**bb**le
m	**m**itt, ta**m**, s**m**ack, E**mm**y, co**m**b, Autu**mn**
t	s**t**ick, pi**t**, kiss**ed**, wri**t**e
tʰ	**t**ick, in**t**end, **pt**erodactyl, a**tt**ack
d	**D**ick, ca**d**, **d**rip, love**d**, ri**de**
n	**n**ick, ki**n**, s**n**ow, **mn**emonic, **gn**ome, **pn**eumatic, **kn**ow
k	s**k**in, sti**ck**, s**c**at, criti**qu**e, el**k**
kʰ	**c**url, **k**in, **ch**arisma, **c**ritic, me**ch**anic, **c**lose
g	**g**irl, bur**g**, lon**g**er, Pittsbur**gh**
ŋ	si**ng**, thi**n**k, fi**ng**er
f	**f**at, **ph**ilosophy, **f**lat, **ph**logiston, co**ff**ee, ree**f**, cou**gh**
v	**v**at, do**v**e, gra**v**el
s	**s**ip, **s**kip, p**s**ychology, pa**ss**, pat**s**, democra**c**y, **sc**issors, fa**s**ten, decei**v**e, de**sc**ent
z	**z**ip, ja**zz**, ra**z**or, pad**s**, kisse**s**, **X**erox, de**s**ign, la**z**y, sci**ss**ors, mai**z**e
θ	**th**igh, **th**rough, wra**th**, e**th**er, Ma**tth**ew
ð	**th**y, **th**eir, wea**th**er, la**the**, ei**th**er
ʃ	**sh**oe, mu**sh**, mi**ss**ion, na**ti**on, fi**sh**, gla**ci**al, **s**ure
ʒ	mea**s**ure, vi**s**ion, a**z**ure, ca**s**ual, **g**enre, rou**g**e
tʃ	ma**tch**, ri**ch**, righ**t**eous
tʃʰ	**ch**oke, **T**chaikovsky, dis**ch**arge
ʤ	**j**u**dg**e, mi**dg**et, **G**eorge, ma**g**istrate, resi**d**ual
l	**l**eaf, fee**l**, ca**ll**, sing**l**e
r	**r**eef, fea**r**, Pa**r**is, singe**r**
j	**y**ou, **y**es, feu**d**, **u**se
w	**w**itch, s**w**im, q**u**een
ʍ	**wh**ich, **wh**ere, **wh**ale (for speakers who pronounce *which* differently from *witch*)
h	**h**at, **wh**o, **wh**ole, reha**sh**
ʔ	bo**tt**le, bu**tt**on, glo**tt**al (for some speakers), (**ʔ**)uh-(**ʔ**)oh
ɾ	wri**t**er, ri**d**er, la**tt**er, la**dd**er

TABLE 5.6 | (Continued)

	Vowels
i	b**ee**t, b**ea**t, b**e**, rec**ei**ve, k**ey**, bel**ie**ve, am**oe**ba, p**eo**ple, C**ae**sar, Vas**e**line, ser**e**ne, Ral**eigh**
ɪ	b**i**t, cons**i**st, **i**njury, b**i**n, w**o**men, b**ui**ld
e	g**a**te, b**ai**t, r**ay**, gr**ea**t, **eigh**t, g**au**ge, gr**ey**hound, r**ei**n, f**eig**n
ɛ	b**e**t, ser**e**nity, s**ay**s, g**ue**st, d**ea**d, s**ai**d
æ	p**a**n, **a**ct, l**au**gh, c**o**mrade
u	b**oo**t, l**u**te, wh**o**, s**e**wer, thr**ough**, t**o**, t**oo**, tw**o**, m**o**ve, L**ou**, tr**u**e, s**ui**t
ʊ	p**u**t, f**oo**t, b**u**tcher, c**oul**d
ʌ	c**u**t, t**ou**gh, am**o**ng, **o**ven, d**oe**s, c**o**ver, fl**oo**d
o	c**oa**t, g**o**, b**eau**, gr**ow**, th**ough**, t**oe**, **ow**n, s**ew**
ɔ	c**augh**t, st**a**lk, c**o**re, s**aw**, b**a**ll, **aw**e, **au**to
a	c**o**t, f**a**ther, p**a**lm, s**e**rgeant, **ho**nor, h**o**spital, mel**o**dic
ə	s**o**f**a**, **a**lone, symph**o**ny, s**u**ppose, mel**o**dy, b**i**rd, v**e**rb, th**e**
aɪ	b**i**te, s**igh**t, b**y**, b**uy**, d**ie**, d**ye**, **ai**sle, ch**oi**r, g**ui**de, **i**sland, h**eigh**t, s**ig**n
aʊ	ab**ou**t, br**ow**n, d**ou**bt, c**ow**ard, s**au**erkraut
ɔɪ	b**oy**, **oi**l, R**eu**ters

used in this book are a compromise among several varieties of American English, but this should not deter you. Our purpose is to teach phonetics in general, and to show you how phonetics might describe the speech sounds of any of the world's languages with the proper symbols and diacritics. We merely use American English for illustration, and we provide the major phonetic symbols for American English to show you how such symbols may be used to describe the phonetics of any of the world's languages.

The "Phonetics" of Signed Languages

Earlier we noted that signed languages, like all other human languages, are governed by a grammatical system that includes syntactic and morphological rules. Signed languages are like spoken languages in another respect; signs can be broken down into smaller units analogous to the phonetic features discussed in this chapter. Just as spoken languages distinguish sounds according to place and manner of articulation, so signed languages distinguish signs according to the place and manner in which the signs are articulated by the hands. The signs of ASL, for example, are formed by three major features:

1. The **configuration** of the hand (handshape)
2. The **movement** of the hand and arms in signing space
3. The **location** of the hands in signing space

'Signing space' is the area of space extended approximately forearm-distance from the signer's body, from waist to forehead.

To illustrate how these features define a sign, the ASL sign meaning 'mother' is produced by tapping your chin with the thumb of your hand with all of the fingers extended in a spread five-finger handshape (5-handshape). It has three features: *5-handshape, tapping movement, chin location.*

ASL has over 30 handshapes. But not all signed languages have the same handshapes, just as not all spoken languages share the same places of articulation (French lacks interdental stops; English lacks the uvular trill of French). For example, the T handshape of ASL does not occur in the European signed languages. Similarly, Chinese Sign Language has a handshape formed with an open hand with all fingers extended except the ring finger. ASL does not have this handshape.

Movement can be either straight or in an arc. Secondary movements include wiggling or hooking fingers. Signs can also be unidirectional (moving in one direction) or bidirectional (moving in one direction and then back again). The location of signs is defined relative to the body of the signer. For signs that are produced on or near the body, the location is the part of the body the sign is produced at (e.g. chin). For signs that are not produced on or near the body, the location is instead the relative part of the signing space where the sign is produced (e.g. high/low, ipsilateral/contralateral).

As in spoken language, a change along one of these parameters can result in different words. Just as a difference in voicing or tone can result in different words in a spoken language, a change in location, handshape, or movement can result in different signs with different meanings. For example, the sign meaning 'father' differs from the sign meaning 'fine' only in the place of articulation. Both signs are formed with the 5-handshape, but the thumb touches the signer's forehead in 'father' and it touches his chest in 'fine.'

There are two-handed and one-handed signs. One-handed signs are formed with the speaker's dominant hand, whether left or right. Sign languages never use both hands as if they are autonomous articulators. They always work together, just like the different parts of the vocal tract work together to produce sounds. And just as spoken languages have features that do not distinguish different words (e.g., consonant length in English), in ASL (and probably all signed languages), a difference in handedness does not affect the meaning of the sign.

The parallels that exist in the organization of sounds and signs are not surprising when we consider that similar cognitive systems underlie both spoken and signed languages.

Summary

The science of speech sounds is called **phonetics**. It aims to provide the set of properties necessary to describe and distinguish all the sounds in human languages throughout the world.

When we speak, the physical sounds we produce are continuous stretches of sound, which are the physical representations of strings of discrete linguistic **segments**. Knowledge of a language permits one to separate continuous speech into individual sounds and words.

The discrepancy between spelling and sounds in English and other languages motivated the development of phonetic alphabets in which one letter corresponds to one sound. The major **phonetic alphabet** in use is the **International**

Phonetic Alphabet (**IPA**), which includes modified Roman letters and **diacritics**, by means of which the sounds of all human languages can be represented. To distinguish between **orthography** (spelling) and **phonetic transcriptions**, we write the latter between square brackets, as in [fənɛɹɪk] for *phonetic*.

All English speech sounds come from the movement of lung air through the vocal tract. The air moves through the **glottis** (i.e., between the vocal cords), up the pharynx, through the oral (and possibly the nasal) cavity, and out the mouth or nose.

Human speech sounds fall into classes according to their phonetic properties. All speech sounds are either **consonants** or **vowels**, and all consonants are either **obstruents** or **sonorants**. Consonants have some obstruction of the airstream in the vocal tract, and the location of the obstruction defines their **place of articulation**, some of which are: **bilabial**, **labiodental**, **alveolar**, **palatal**, **velar**, **uvular**, and **glottal**.

Consonants are further classified according to their **manner of articulation**. They may be **voiced** or **voiceless**, **oral** or **nasal**, and long or short. They may be **stops**, **fricatives**, **affricates**, **liquids**, or **glides**. During the production of voiced sounds, the vocal cords are together and vibrating, whereas in voiceless sounds they are apart and not vibrating. Consonants may also be grouped according to certain features to form larger classes such as **labial**, **coronal**, **anterior**, and **sibilant**.

Vowels form the nucleus of syllables. They differ according to the position of the tongue and lips: high, mid, or low tongue; front, central, or back of the tongue; rounded or unrounded lips. The vowels in English may be **tense** or **lax**. Tense vowels are slightly longer in duration and slightly higher than lax vowels. Vowels may also be **stressed** (longer, higher in pitch, and louder) or **unstressed**. Vowels, like consonants, may be nasal or oral, although most vowels in all languages are oral.

Length, pitch, loudness, and stress are **prosodic**, or **suprasegmental**, features. They are imposed over and above the segmental values of the sounds in a syllable. In many languages, the pitch or **tone** of the syllable is linguistically significant. For example, two words with identical segments may contrast in meaning if one has a high tone and the other a low tone. Such languages are **tone languages**. There are also **intonation** languages in which the rise and fall of pitch over an entire phrase may affect meaning.

English and other languages use stress to distinguish different words, such as *cóntent* and *contént*. In some languages, long vowels and long consonants contrast with their shorter counterparts. Thus *biru* [biru] and *biiru* [biːru], *saki* [saki] and *sakki* [sakːi] are different words in Japanese.

Diacritics to specify such properties as nasalization, length, stress, and tone may be combined with the phonetic symbols for more detailed phonetic transcriptions. A phonetic transcription of *men* would use a tilde diacritic to indicate the nasalization of the vowel: [mɛ̃n].

In sign languages there are "phonetic" features analogous to those of spoken languages. In ASL these are handshape, movement, and location. As in spoken languages, changes along one of these parameters can result in a new word. In the following chapter, we discuss this meaning-changing property of features in much greater detail.

References for Further Reading

Catford, J. C. 2001. *A practical introduction to phonetics, 2nd ed.* New York: Oxford University Press.

Crystal, D. 2003. *A dictionary of linguistics and phonetics, 5th ed.* Oxford, UK: Blackwell Publishers.

Emmorey, K. 2002. *Language, cognition and the brain: Insights from sign language research.* London, UK: Routledge.

Fromkin, V. A. (ed.). 1978. *Tone: A linguistic survey.* New York: Academic Press.

International Phonetic Association. 1999. *Handbook of the International Phonetic Association.* Cambridge, UK: Cambridge University Press.

Ladefoged, P. 2005. *Vowels and consonants, 2nd ed.* Oxford, UK: Blackwell Publishers.

Ladefoged, P. and Johnson, K. 2011. *A course in phonetics, 6th ed.* Boston, MA: Wadsworth, Cengage Learning.

Ladefoged, P., and I. Maddieson. 1995. *The sounds of the world's languages.* Oxford, UK: Blackwell Publishers.

Laver, J. 1994. *Principles of phonetics.* Cambridge, UK: Cambridge University Press.

Pullum, G. K., and W. A. Ladusaw. 1995. *Phonetic symbol guide.* Chicago: University of Chicago Press.

Sandler, W. and Lillo-Martin, D.C. 2005. *Sign language and linguistic universals.* Cambridge, UK: Cambridge University Press.

Exercises

1. Write the phonetic symbol for the first sound in each of the following words according to the way you pronounce it.

   Examples: ooze   [u]   psycho   [s]

   a. judge   [   ]   **f.** thought   [   ]
   b. Thomas   [   ]   **g.** contact   [   ]
   c. though   [   ]   **h.** phone   [   ]
   d. easy   [   ]   **i.** civic   [   ]
   e. pneumonia   [   ]   **j.** usual   [   ]

2. Write the phonetic symbol for the *last* sound in each of the following words.

   Example: boy [ɔɪ] (Diphthongs should be treated as one sound.)

   a. fleece   [   ]   **f.** cow   [   ]
   b. neigh   [   ]   **g.** rough   [   ]
   c. long   [   ]   **h.** cheese   [   ]
   d. health   [   ]   **i.** bleached [   ]
   e. watch   [   ]   **j.** rags   [   ]

3. Write the following words in phonetic transcription, according to your pronunciation.

   Examples: knot [nat]; *delightful* [dilaɪtfəl] or [dəlaɪtfəl]. Some of you may pronounce some of these words the same.

   a. physics   **e.** yellow   **i.** tease
   b. merry   **f.** sticky   **j.** weather
   c. marry   **g.** transcriptio **k.** coat
   d. Mary   **h.** Fromkin   **l.** Rodman

m. heath	**p.** cough	**s.** beautiful
n. "your name"	**q.** larynx	**t.** honest
o. touch	**r.** through	**u.** president

4. Following is a phonetic transcription of a verse in the poem "The Walrus and the Carpenter" by Lewis Carroll. The speaker who transcribed it may not have exactly the same pronunciation as you; there are many correct versions. However, there is *one major error* in each line that is an impossible pronunciation for any American English speaker. The error may consist of an extra symbol, a missing symbol, or a wrong symbol in the word. Note that the phonetic transcription that is given is a **narrow** transcription; aspiration is marked, as is the nasalization of vowels. This is to illustrate a detailed transcription. However, none of the errors involve aspiration or nasalization of vowels.

   Write the word in which the error occurs in the correct phonetic transcription.

   Corrected Word

   a. ðə tʰãɪm hæz cʌ̃m   [kʰʌ̃m]
   b. ðə wɔlrəs sed
   c. tʰu tʰɔlk əv mɛ̃ni θɪ̃ŋz
   d. əv ʃuz ãnd ʃɪps
   e. æ̃nd silɪ̃ŋ wæx
   f. əv kʰæbəgəz æ̃nd kʰɪ̃ŋz
   g. æ̃nd waɪ ðə si ɪs bɔɪlɪ̃ŋ hat
   h. æ̃nd wɛθər pʰɪgz hæv wɪ̃ŋz

5. The following are all English words written in a broad phonetic transcription (omitting details such as nasalization and aspiration). Write the words using normal English orthography.

   a. [hit]
   b. [strok]
   c. [fez]
   d. [ton]
   e. [boni]
   f. [skrim]
   g. [frut]
   h. [pritʃər]
   i. [krak]
   j. [baks]
   k. [θæŋks]
   l. [wɛnzde]
   m. [krɔld]
   n. [kantʃiɛntʃəs]
   o. [parləmɛntæriən]
   p. [kwəbɛk]
   q. [pitsə]
   r. [bərak obamə]
   s. [mɪt ramni]
   t. [tu θaʊzənd ænd twɛlv]

6. Write the symbol that corresponds to each of the following phonetic descriptions, then give an English word that contains this sound.

   Example: voiced alveolar stop   [d] *dough*

   a. voiceless bilabial unaspirated stop   [   ]
   b. low front vowel   [   ]
   c. lateral liquid   [   ]
   d. velar nasal   [   ]
   e. voiced interdental fricative   [   ]
   f. voiceless affricate   [   ]
   g. palatal glide   [   ]
   h. mid lax front vowel   [   ]
   i. high back tense vowel   [   ]
   j. voiceless aspirated alveolar stop   [   ]

7. In each of the following pairs of words, the **bold** *italicized* sounds differ by one or more phonetic properties (features). Give the IPA symbol for each italicized sound, state their differences and, in addition, state what properties they have in common.

   Example: clean—cleanse [i]-[ɛ]
               The *ea* in *clean* is high and tense.
               The *ea* in *cleanse* is mid and lax.
               Both are front vowels.

   a. ba*th*—ba*th*e
   b. redu*c*e—redu*c*tion
   c. c*oo*l—c*o*ld
   d. wi*f*e—wi*v*es
   e. cat*s*—dog*s*
   f. i*m*polite—i*n*decent

8. Write a phonetic transcription for each of the italicized words in the following poem entitled "Brush Up Your English" published long ago in a British newspaper.

   I take it you already **know**
   Of **tough** and **bough** and **cough** and **dough**?
   Some may stumble, but not **you**,
   On **hiccough**, **thorough**, **slough** and **through**?
   So now you are ready, perhaps,
   To learn of less familiar traps?
   Beware of **heard**, a dreadful **word**
   That looks like **beard** and sounds like **bird**.
   And **dead**, it's **said** like **bed**, not **bead**;
   For goodness' sake, don't call it **deed**!
   Watch out for **meat** and **great** and **threat**.
   (They rhyme with **suite** and **straight** and **debt**.)
   A **moth** is not a moth in **mother**,
   Nor **both** in **bother**, **broth** in **brother**.[1]

---

[1]T. S. Watt, "Brush Up Your English," *Guardian*, June 21, 1954. Copyright Guardian News & Media Ltd 1954. Reprinted by permission.

9. For each group of sounds listed, state the phonetic feature(s) they all share.

Example: [p] [b] [m] Features: bilabial, stop, consonant

   a. [g] [p] [t] [d] [k] [b]
   b. [u] [ʊ] [o] [ɔ]
   c. [i] [ɪ] [e] [ɛ] [æ]
   d. [t] [s] [ʃ] [p] [k] [ʧ] [f] [h]
   e. [v] [z] [ʒ] [ʤ] [n] [g] [d] [b] [l] [r] [w] [j]
   f. [t] [d] [s] [ʃ] [n] [ʧ] [ʤ]

10. Write the following broad phonetic transcriptions in regular English spelling.

   a. nom ʧamski ɪz e lɪngwɪst hu tiʧəz æt ɛm aɪ ti
   b. fənɛtɪks ɪz ðə stʌdi əv spiʧ saʊndz
   c. ɔl spokən læŋgwɪʤəz juz saʊndz prədust baɪ ðə ʌpər rɛspərətɔri sɪstəm
   d. ɪn wʌn daɪəlɛkt əv ɪŋglɪʃ kat ðə naʊn ænd kɔt ðə vərb ar prənaʊnst ðə sem
   e. sʌm pipəl θɪŋk fənɛtɪks ɪz vɛri ɪntərɛstɪŋ
   f. vɪktɔrijə framkən rabərt radmən ænd ninə haɪəmz ar ðə ɔθərz əv ðɪs bʊk

11. What phonetic property or feature distinguishes the sets of sounds in column A from those in column B?

A	**B**
a. [i] [ɪ]	[u] [ʊ]
b. [p] [t] [k] [s] [f]	[b] [d] [g] [z] [v]
c. [p] [b] [m]	[t] [d] [n] [k] [g] [ŋ]
d. [i] [ɪ] [u] [ʊ]	[e] [ɛ] [o] [ɔ] [æ] [a]
e. [f] [v] [s] [z] [ʃ] [ʒ]	[ʧ] [ʤ]
f. [i] [ɪ] [e] [ə] [ɛ] [æ]	[u] [ʊ] [o] [ɔ]

12. Which of the following sound pairs have the same manner of articulation, and what is that manner of articulation?

   a. [h] [ʔ]   **f.** [f] [ʃ]
   b. [r] [w]   **g.** [k] [θ]
   c. [m] [ŋ]   **h.** [s] [g]
   d. [ð] [v]   **i.** [j] [w]
   e. [r] [t]   **j.** [j] [ʤ]

13. **Part One**

   Which of the following vowels are lax and which are tense?

   a. [i]
   b. [ɪ]
   c. [u]
   d. [ʌ]
   e. [ʊ]
   f. [e]
   g. [ɛ]
   h. [o]
   i. [ɔ]
   j. [æ]

k. [a]

l. [ə]

m. [aɪ]

n. [aʊ]

o. [ɔɪ]

Part Two

Think of ordinary, nonexclamatory one-syllable English words that end in [ʃ] preceded directly by each of the vowels in Part One. Which are possible (or actual) words? Are any such words impossible in English?

Example: *push* [pʊʃ] is an actual word; *nish* [nɪʃ] is a possible word; but words ending in [-aɪʃ] are not possible in English.

Part Three

In terms of tense/lax, which vowel type is found in most such words?

14. Write a made-up sentence in narrow phonetic transcription that contains at least six different monophthongal vowels and two different diphthongs.

15. The front vowels of English, [i], [ɪ], [e], [ɛ], and [æ], are all unrounded. However, many languages have rounded front vowels, such as French. Here are three words in French with rounded front vowels. Transcribe them phonetically by finding out the correct IPA symbols for front rounded vowels: (Hint: Try one of the books given in the references, or Google around.)

 a. *tu*, 'you,' has a high front rounded vowel and is transcribed phonetically as [   ]

 b. *bleu*, 'blue,' has a midfront rounded vowel and is transcribed phonetically as [   ]

 c. *heure*, 'hour,' has a low midfront rounded vowel and is transcribed phonetically as [   ]

16. **Challenge exercise**:

 A. Take all of the vowels from exercise 13, Part One, except the schwa and for each find a monosyllabic word containing that vowel followed directly by [t], and give both the spelling and the phonetic transcription.

  Example: *beat* [bit], *foot* [fʊt]

 B. Now do the same thing for monosyllabic words ending in [r]. Indicate when such a word appears not to occur in your dialect of English.

 C. And do the same thing for monosyllabic words ending in [ŋ]. Indicate when such a word appears not to occur in your dialect of English.

 D. Is there a quantitative difference in the number of examples found as you went from Part One to Part Three in exercise 13?

 E. Are most vowels that "work" in B tense or lax? How about in C?

 F. Write a brief summary of the difficulties you encountered in trying to do this exercise.

17. In the first column are the last names of well-known authors. In the second column are their best-known works (one for each). Match each work to its author and write the author's name and work in conventional spelling.

Example: **a.** [dɪkə̃nz]   **1.** [ɔləvər tʰwɪst]
Answer: a—1 (Dickens, Oliver Twist)

b.	[sɛrvã̃ntɛs]	**2.**	[ə ferwɛl tʰu armz]
c.	[dãnte]	**3.**	[æ̃nə̃məl farm]
d.	[dɪkə̃nz]	**4.**	[dõn kihote]
e.	[ɛliət]	**5.**	[greps ʌv ræθ]
f.	[hɛ̃mĩŋwe]	**6.**	[gret ɛkspɛktʰeʃə̃nz]
g.	[hõmər]	**7.**	[gʌləvərz tʰrævəlz]
h.	[mɛlvɪl]	**8.**	[hæmlət]
i.	[ɔrwɛl]	**9.**	[mobi-dɪk]
j.	[ʃekspir]	**10.**	[saɪləs marnər]
k.	[staĩnbɛk]	**11.**	[ðə dɪvaĩn kʰãmədi]
l.	[swɪft]	**12.**	[ðə ɪliəd]
m.	[tʰɔlstɔɪ]	**13.**	[tʰã̃m sɔɪjər]
n.	[tʰwẽn]	**14.**	[wɔr æ̃nd pʰis]

6

Phonology: The Sound Patterns of Language

> Be a craftsman in speech that thou mayest be strong, for the strength of one is the tongue.
>
> PTAHHOTEP, CA 2400 BCE

> Phonology is the study of telephone etiquette.
>
> A HIGH SCHOOL STUDENT

What do you think is greater: the number of languages in the world, or the number of speech sounds in all those languages? Well, there are thousands of languages, but only hundreds of speech sounds, some of which we examined in the previous chapter. Even more remarkable, only a few dozen features, such as *voicing* and *bilabial*, are needed to describe every speech sound that occurs in every human language.

That being the case, why, you may ask, do languages sound so different? One reason is that the sounds form different patterns in different languages. English has nasalized vowels, but only in syllables with nasal consonants. Portuguese puts nasal vowels anywhere it pleases, with or without nasal consonants. The speech sound that ends the word *song*—the velar nasal [ŋ]—cannot begin a word in English, but it can in Vietnamese. The common Vietnamese name spelled *Nguyen* begins with this sound, and the reason few of us can pronounce this name correctly is that it doesn't follow the English pattern. The ability to pronounce particular sounds depends on the speaker's knowledge of the sound patterns of her own language or languages.

The study of how speech sounds form patterns is **phonology**. These patterns may be as simple as the fact that the velar nasal cannot begin a syllable in English, or as complex as why *g* is silent in *sign* but is pronounced in the related word *signature*. To see that this is a pattern and not a one-time exception, just consider the slippery *n* in *autumn* and *autumnal*, or the illusive *b* in *bomb* and *bombard*.

The word *phonology* refers both to the linguistic knowledge that speakers have about the sound patterns of their language and to the description of that knowledge that linguists try to produce. Thus it is like the way we defined *grammar*: your mental knowledge of your language, or a linguist's description of that knowledge.

Phonology tells you what sounds are in your language and which ones are foreign; it tells you what combinations of sounds comprise a possible word in your language, whether it as an actual word like *black,* or a non-word (in English) like *blick*; and it tells you what combination of sounds is not a possible word in your language like *mbick. It also explains why certain phonetic features are important to identifying a word, for example voicing in English, as in *pat* versus *bat,* while other features such as vowel nasality in English are not crucial to identifying a word—though it is in Portuguese where the word *pão* with a nasalized vowel means 'bread' and *pao* without the nasalization means 'stick.' Finally, it allows us to adjust our pronunciation of morphemes, for example the past and plural morphemes, to suit the different phonological contexts in which they occur.

The Pronunciation of Morphemes

The *t* is silent, as in Harlow.

MARGOT ASQUITH, referring to her name being mispronounced by the actress Jean Harlow

Knowledge of phonology determines how we pronounce words and the parts of words we call morphemes. Often, certain morphemes are pronounced differently depending on their contexts, and we will introduce a way of describing this variation with (usually unconscious) phonological rules. We begin with some examples from English, and then move on to examples from other languages.

The Pronunciation of Plurals

Nearly all English nouns have a plural form: *cat/cats, dog/dogs, fox/foxes*. But have you ever paid attention to how plural forms are *pronounced*? Listen to a native speaker of English (or yourself if you are one) pronounce the plurals of the following nouns.

A	B	C	D
cab	cap	bus	child
cad	cat	bush	ox
bag	back	buzz	mouse
love	cuff	garage	criterion
lathe	faith	match	sheep
cam		badge	
can			
call			
bar			
spa			
boy			

The final sound of the plural nouns from Column A is a [z]—a *voiced* alveolar fricative. For column B the plural ending is an [s]—a *voiceless* alveolar fricative. And for Column C it's [əz]. Here is our first example of a morpheme with different pronunciations. Note also that there is a regularity in columns A, B, and C that does not exist in D. The plural forms in D—*children, oxen, mice, criteria,* and *sheep*—are a hodge-podge of special cases that are memorized individually when you acquire English, whether natively or as a second language. This is because there is no way to predict the plural forms of these words.

How do we know how to pronounce this plural morpheme? The spelling, which adds *s* or *es*, is misleading—not a *z* in sight—yet if you know English, you pronounce it as we indicated. When faced with this type of question, it's useful to make a chart that records the phonological environments in which each variant of the morpheme is known to occur. (The more technical term for a variant of a morpheme is **allomorph**.) Writing the words from the first three columns in broad phonetic transcription, we have our first chart for the plural morpheme. (And also our first example of "phonological analysis.")

Allomorph	Environment
[z]	After [kæb], [kæd], [bæg], [lʌv], [leð], [kæm], [kæn], [bæŋ], [kɔl], [bar], [spa], [bɔɪ], e.g., [kæbz], [kædz] . . . [bɔɪz]
[s]	After [kæp], [kæt], [bæk], [kʌf], [feθ], e.g., [kæps], [kæts] . . . [feθs]
[əz]	After [bʌs], [bʊʃ], [bʌz], [gəraʒ], [mætʃ], [bædʒ], e.g., [bʌsəz], [bʊʃəz] . . . [bædʒəz]

To discover the pattern behind the way plurals are pronounced, we look for some property of the environment associated with each group of allomorphs. For example, what is it about [kæb] or [lʌv] that determines that the plural morpheme will take the form [z] rather than [s] or [əz]?

To guide our search, we look for **minimal pairs** in our list of words. A minimal pair is two words with different meanings that are identical except for one sound segment that occurs in the same place in each word. For example, *cab* [kæb] and *cad* [kæd] are a minimal pair that differ only in their final segments, whereas *cat* [kæt] and *mat* [mæt] are a minimal pair that differ only in their initial segments. Other minimal pairs in our list include *cap/cab*, *bag/ back*, and *bag/badge*.

Minimal pairs whose members take different allomorphs are particularly useful for our search. For example, consider *cab* [kæb] and *cap* [kæp], which respectively take the allomorphs [z] and [s] to form the plural. Clearly, the final segment is responsible, because that is where the two words differ. Similarly for *bag* [bæg] and *badge* [bædʒ]. Their final segments determine the different plural allomorphs [z] and [əz].

Apparently, the distribution of plural allomorphs in English is conditioned by the final segment of the singular form. We can make our chart more concise by considering just the final segment. (We treat diphthongs such as [ɔɪ] as single segments.)

Allomorph	Environment
[z]	After [b], [d], [g], [v], [ð], [m], [n], [ŋ], [l], [r], [a], [ɔɪ]
[s]	After [p], [t], [k], [f], [θ]
[əz]	After [s], [ʃ], [z], [ʒ] , [tʃ], [dʒ]

We now want to understand *why* the English plural follows this pattern. We *always* answer questions of this type by inspecting the *phonetic properties* of the conditioning segments. Such an inspection reveals that the segments that trigger the [əz] plural have in common the property of being *sibilants*. Of the nonsibilants, the *voiceless* segments take the [s] plural, and the *voiced* segments take the [z] plural. Now the rules can be stated in more general terms:

Allomorph	Environment
[z]	After voiced nonsibilant segments
[s]	After voiceless nonsibilant segments
[əz]	After sibilant segments

An even more concise way to express these rules is to assume that the basic or underlying form of the plural morpheme is /z/, with the meaning 'plural.' This is the "default" pronunciation. The rules tell us when the default does *not* apply:

1. Insert a [ə] before the plural morpheme /z/ when a regular noun ends in a sibilant, giving [əz].
2. Change the plural morpheme /z/ to a voiceless [s] when preceded by a voiceless sound. (It's crucial that this rule apply after Rule 1, as we'll see.)

These rules will derive the phonetic forms—that is, the pronunciations—of plurals for all regular nouns. Because the basic form of the plural is /z/, if no rule applies, then the plural morpheme will be realized as [z]. The following chart shows how the plurals of *bus*, *butt*, and *bug* are formed. At the top are the basic forms. The two rules apply or not as appropriate as one moves downward. The output of rule 1 becomes the input of rule 2. At the bottom are the phonetic realizations—the way the words are pronounced.

	bus + pl.	*butt* + pl.	*bug* + pl.
Basic representation	/bʌs + z/	/bʌt + z/	/bʌg + z/
Apply rule (1)	ə	NA*	NA
Apply rule (2)	NA	s	NA
Phonetic representation	[bʌsəz]	[bʌts]	[bʌgz]

*NA means "not applicable."

As we have formulated these rules, (1) must apply before (2). (But see exercise 6 at the end of the chapter.) If we applied the rules in reverse order, we would derive an incorrect phonetic form for the plural of *bus*, as a diagram similar to the previous one illustrates:

Basic representation	/bʌs + z/
Apply rule (2)	s
Apply rule (1)	ə
Phonetic representation	*[bʌsəs]

The particular phonological rules that determine the phonetic form of the plural morpheme and other morphemes of the language are **morphophonemic rules**. Such rules concern the pronunciation of specific morphemes. So the pronunciation of a word like *horse* /hɔrs/ is with a final [s] because there is no morpheme boundary between the /s/ and the voiced /r/ that precedes it.

Additional Examples of Allomorphs

The formation of the regular past tense of English verbs parallels the formation of regular plurals. Like plurals, some irregular past tenses conform to no particular rule and must be learned individually, such as *go/went*, *sing/sang*, and *hit/hit*. And also like plurals, there are three *phonetic* past-tense morphemes for regular verbs: [d], [t], and [əd]. Here are several examples in broad phonetic transcription. Study sets A, B, and C and try to see the regularity before reading further.

Set A: *gloat* [glot], *gloated* [glotəd]; *raid* [red], *raided* [redəd]

Set B: *grab* [græb], *grabbed* [græbd]; *hug* [hʌg], *hugged* [hʌgd]; *faze* [fez], *fazed* [fezd]; *plan* [plæn], *planned* [plænd]

Set C: *reap* [rip], *reaped* [ript]; *poke* [pok], *poked* [pokt]; *kiss* [kɪs], *kissed* [kɪst]; *fish* [fɪʃ], *fished* [fɪʃt]; *patch* [pætʃ], *patched* [pætʃt]

Set A suggests that if the verb ends in a [t] or a [d] (i.e., non-nasal alveolar stops), [əd] is added to form the past tense, similar to the insertion of [əz] to form the plural of nouns that end in sibilants. Set B suggests that if the verb ends in a voiced segment other than [d], you add a voiced [d]. Set C shows us that if the verb ends in a voiceless segment other than [t], you add a voiceless [t].

Just as /z/ was the basic form of the plural morpheme, /d/ is the basic form of the past-tense morpheme, and the rules for past-tense formation of regular verbs are much like the rules for the plural formation of regular nouns. These are also *morphophonemic* rules as they apply specifically to the past-tense morpheme /d/. As with the plural rules, the output of Rule 1, if any, provides the input to Rule 2, and the rules must be applied in order.

1. Insert a [ə] before the past-tense morpheme when a regular verb ends in a non-nasal alveolar stop, giving [əd].
2. Change the past-tense morpheme to a voiceless [t] when a voiceless sound precedes it.

Two further allomorphs in English are the possessive morpheme and the third-person singular morpheme, spelled *s* or *es*. These morphemes take on the same phonetic form as the plural morpheme *according to the same rules*! Add [s] to *ship* to get *ship's*; add [z] to *woman* to get *woman's*; and add [əz] to *judge* to get *judge's*. Similarly for the verbs *eat*, *need*, and *rush*, whose third-person singular forms are *eats* with a final [s], *needs* with a final [z], and *rushes* with a final [əz].

That the rules of phonology are based on properties of segments rather than on individual words is one of the factors that make it possible for young children to learn their native language in a relatively short period. The young child doesn't need to learn each plural, each past tense, each possessive form, and each verb ending, on a noun-by-noun or verb-by-verb basis. Once the rule is learned, thousands of word forms are automatically known. And as we will see when we discuss language development in chapter 9, children give clear evidence of learning morphophonemic rules such as the plural rules by applying the rule too broadly and producing forms such as *mouses*, *mans*, and so on, which are ungrammatical in the adult language.

English is not the only language that has morphemes that are pronounced differently in different phonological environments. Many languages have morpheme variation that can be described by rules similar to the ones we have written for English. For example, the negative morpheme in the West African language Akan has three nasal allomorphs: [m] before *p*, [n] before *t*, and [ŋ] before *k*, as the following examples show ([mɪ] means 'I'):

mɪ pɛ	'I like'	mɪ mpɛ	'I don't like'
mɪ tɪ	'I speak'	mɪ ntɪ	'I don't speak'
mɪ kɔ	'I go'	mɪ ŋkɔ	'I don't go'

The rule that describes the distribution of allomorphs is:

Change the place of articulation of the nasal negative morpheme to agree with the place of articulation of a following consonant.

The rule that changes the pronunciation of nasal consonants as just illustrated is called the **homorganic nasal rule**—*homorganic* means 'same place'—because the place of articulation of the nasal is the same as for the following consonant. The homorganic nasal rule is a common rule in the world's languages.

Phonemes: The Phonological Units of Language

In the physical world the naive speaker and hearer actualize and are sensitive to sounds, but what they feel themselves to be pronouncing and hearing are "phonemes."

EDWARD SAPIR, "The Psychological Reality of Phonemes," 1933

The phonological rules discussed in the preceding section apply only to particular morphemes. However, other phonological rules apply to sounds as they occur in any morpheme in the language. These rules express our knowledge about the sound patterns of the entire language.

This section introduces the notions of **phoneme** and **allophone**. Phonemes are the basic form of a sound as sensed mentally rather than spoken or heard. Each phoneme – a mental abstraction in itself – is manifested aurally by one or more sounds, called allophones, which are the perceivable sounds corresponding to the phoneme in various environments. For example, the phoneme /p/ is pronounced with the aspiration allophone [pʰ] in *pit* but without aspiration [p] in *spit*. Phonological rules operate on phonemes to make explicit which allophones are pronounced in which environments.

Illustration of Allophones

English contains a general phonological rule that determines the contexts in which vowels are nasalized. In chapter 5 we noted that both oral and nasal vowels occur *phonetically* in English. The following examples show this:

bean	[bĩn]	bead	[bid]
roam	[rõm]	robe	[rob]

Taking oral vowels as basic—that is, as the phonemes—we have a phonological rule that states:

Vowels are nasalized before a nasal consonant within the same syllable.

This rule expresses your knowledge of English pronunciation: nasalized vowels occur only before nasal consonants and never elsewhere. The effect of this rule is seen in Table 6.1.

As the table shows, oral vowels in English occur in final position and before non-nasal consonants; nasalized vowels occur only before nasal consonants. The nonwords (starred) show us that nasalized vowels do not occur finally or before non-nasal consonants, nor do oral vowels occur before nasal consonants.

You may be unaware of this variation in your vowel production, but this is natural. Whether you speak or hear the vowel in *bean* with or without nasalization does not change the word's meaning. Without nasalization, it might sound a bit strange, as if you had a foreign accent, but *bean* pronounced [bĩn]

TABLE 6.1 | Nasal and Oral Vowels: Words and Nonwords

Words						Nonwords		
be	[bi]	bead	[bid]	bean	[bĩn]	*[bĩ]	*[bĩd]	*[bin]
lay	[le]	lace	[les]	lame	[lẽm]	*[lẽ]	*[lẽs]	*[lem]

and *bean* pronounced [bin] would convey the same word. Likewise, if you pronounced *bead* as [bĩd], with a nasalized vowel, someone might suspect you had a cold, or that you spoke nasally, but the word would remain *bead*. Because nasalization is an *inessential difference* insofar as what the vowel actually is, we tend to be unaware of it.

Contrast this situation with a change in vowel height. If you intend to say *bead* but say *bed* instead, that makes a difference. The [i] in *bead* and the [ɛ] in *bed* are sounds from *different* phonemes. Substitute one for another and you get a different word (or no word). The [i] in *bead* and the [ĩ] in the nasalized *bead* do not make a difference in meaning. These two sounds, then, belong to the same phoneme, an abstract high front vowel that we denote between slashes as /i/.

Similarly, English also contains a phonological rule that determines the context in which voiceless stops—/p/, /t/, and /k/—are aspirated:

Voiceless stops are aspirated when they occur initially in a stressed syllable

Table 6.2 illustrates the distribution of aspirated stops versus unaspirated stops.

Where the unaspirated stops occur, the aspirated ones do not, and vice versa. If you wanted to, you could say *spit* with an aspirated [pʰ], as [spʰɪt], and it would be understood as *spit*, but listeners would probably think you were spitting out your words. Because aspiration is an *inessential difference* insofar as what the consonant actually is, we do not notice it (unless we're linguists or students of linguistics). Thus there is one phoneme /p/—an abstract voiceless bilabial stop—which may be pronounced [pʰ] or [p] depending on the phonetic context.

TABLE 6.2 | Distribution of Aspirated Voiceless Stops

Syllable-Initial before a Stressed Vowel			After a Syllable-Initial /s/			Nonword*		
[pʰ]	[tʰ]	[kʰ]	[p]	[t]	[k]			
pill	*till*	*kill*	*spill*	*still*	*skill*	[pɪl]*	[tɪl]*	[kɪl]*
[pʰɪl]	[tʰɪl]	[kʰɪl]	[spɪl]	[stɪl]	[skɪl]	[spʰɪl]*	[stʰɪl]*	[skʰɪl]*
par	*tar*	*car*	*spar*	*star*	*scar*	*[par]**	*[tar]**	*[kar]**
[pʰar]	[tʰar]	[kʰar]	[spar]	[star]	[skar]	[spʰar]*	[stʰar]*	[skʰar]*

As a third illustration of allophones, consider the voiceless alveolar stop /t/ along with the following examples:

Spelling	Phonemic representation	Phonetic representation
tick	/tɪk/	[tʰɪk]
stick	/stɪk/	[stɪk]
blitz	/blɪts/	[blɪts]
bitter	/bɪtər/	[bɪɾər]

In *tick* we normally find an aspirated [tʰ], whereas in *stick* and *blitz* we find an unaspirated [t], and in *bitter* we find the flap [ɾ]. Swapping these sounds around will not change word meaning. If we pronounce *bitter* with a [tʰ], it will not change the word; it will simply sound unnatural (to most Americans).

We account for this knowledge of how *t* is pronounced by positing a phoneme /t/ with three allophones [tʰ], [t], and [ɾ]. We also note phonological rules to the effect that the aspirated voiceless stop [tʰ] occurs initially in a stressed syllable, the unaspirated [t] occurs directly before or after /s/, and the flap [ɾ] occurs between a stressed vowel and an unstressed vowel.

Phonemes and How to Find Them

Phonemes are the dark matter of phonology; they are not physical sounds and directly observable. They are abstract mental representations of the phonological units of a language, the units used to represent words in our mental lexicon. The phonological rules of the language apply to phonemes to determine the pronunciation of words.

The process of substituting one sound for another in a word to see if it makes a difference is a good way to identify the phonemes of a language. Here are twelve words differing only in their vowels:

beat	[bit]	[i]	boot	[but]	[u]
bit	[bɪt]	[ɪ]	but	[bʌt]	[ʌ]
bait	[bet]	[e]	boat	[bot]	[o]
bet	[bɛt]	[ɛ]	bought	[bɔt]	[ɔ]
bat	[bæt]	[æ]	bout	[baʊt]	[aʊ]
bite	[baɪt]	[aɪ]	bot	[bat]	[a]

Any two of these words form a *minimal pair*: two *different* words that differ in one sound in the same position. The two sounds that cause the word difference belong to different phonemes. The pair [bid] and [bĭd] are not different words; they are variants of the same word. Therefore, [i] and [ĭ] do *not* belong to different phonemes. They are two actualizations of the same phoneme.

From the minimal set of [b_t] words we can infer that English has at least twelve vowel phonemes. (We consider diphthongs to function as single vowel sounds.) To that total we can add a phoneme corresponding to [ʊ] resulting from minimal pairs such as *book* [bʊk] and *beak* [bik]; and we can add one for [ɔɪ] resulting from minimal pairs such as *boy* [bɔɪ] and *buy* [baɪ].

Our minimal pair analysis has revealed eleven monophthongal and three diphthongal vowel phonemes, namely, /i/, /ɪ/, /e/, /ɛ/, /æ/, /u/, /ʊ/, /o/, /ɔ/, /a/, /ʌ/, and /aɪ/, /aʊ/, and /ɔɪ/. (This set may differ somewhat in other variants of English.) Importantly, each of these vowel phonemes has (at least) two allophones (i.e., two ways of being pronounced: orally as [i], [ɪ], [e], etc., and nasally as [ĩ], [ĩ], [ẽ], etc.), as determined by the phonological rule of nasalization.

A particular realization (pronunciation) of a phoneme is called a **phone**. The aggregate of phones that are the realizations of the same phoneme are called the *allophones* of that phoneme. In English, each vowel phoneme has both an oral and a nasalized allophone. The choice of the allophone is not random or haphazard; it is *rule-governed*.

To distinguish graphically between a phoneme and its allophones, we use slashes / / to enclose phonemes and continue to use square brackets [ ] for allophones or phones. For example, [i] and [ĩ] are allophones of the phoneme /i/; [ɪ] and [ĩ] are allophones of the phoneme /ɪ/, and so on. Thus we will represent *bead* and *bean* phonemically as /bid/ and /bin/. We refer to these as *phonemic* transcriptions of the two words. The rule for the distribution of oral and nasal vowels in English shows that phonetically these words will be pronounced as [bid] and [bĩn]. The pronunciations are indicated by phonetic transcriptions, and written between square brackets.

Complementary Distribution

Minimal pairs illustrate that some speech sounds in a language are contrastive and can be used to make different words such as *big* and *dig*. These contrastive sounds group themselves into the phonemes of that language. Some sounds are non-contrastive and cannot be used to make different words. The sounds [tʰ] and [ɾ] were cited as examples that do not contrast in English, so [raɪtʰər] and [raɪɾər] are not a minimal pair, but rather alternate ways in which *writer* may be pronounced.

Oral and nasal vowels in English are also non-contrastive sounds. What's more, the oral and nasal allophones of each vowel phoneme never occur in the same phonological context, as Table 6.3 illustrates.

Where oral vowels occur, nasal vowels do not occur, and vice versa. In this sense the phones are said to complement each other or to be in **complementary distribution**. Table 6.2 on page 231 also shows that aspirated and unaspirated voiceless stop consonants are in complementary distribution. In general, then, the allophones of a phoneme are in complementary distribution—never occurring in identical environments.

Complementary distribution is a fundamental concept of phonology, and interestingly enough, it shows up in everyday life. Here are a couple of examples that draw on the common experience of reading and writing English.

TABLE 6.3 | Distribution of Oral and Nasal Vowels in English Syllables

	In Final Position	Before Nasal Consonants	Before Oral Consonants
Oral vowels	Yes	No	Yes
Nasal vowels	No	Yes	No

The first example focuses on *printed* letters such as those that appear on the pages of this book. Each printed letter of English has two main variants: lowercase and uppercase (or capital). If we restrict our attention to words that are not proper names or acronyms (such as Ron or UNICEF), we can formulate a simple rule that does a fair job of determining how letters will be printed:

A letter is printed in uppercase if it is the first letter of a sentence; otherwise, it is printed in lowercase.

Even ignoring names and acronyms, this rule is only approximately right, but let's go with it anyway. It helps to explain why written sentences such as the following appear so strange:

phonology is the study of the sound patterns of human languageS.
pHONOLOGY iS tHE sTUDY oF tHE sOUND pATTERNS oF hUMAN lANGUAGES.

These "sentences" violate the rule in funny ways. Despite that, they are comprehensible, just as the pronunciation of *beast* with a nasal [ĩ] as [bĩd] would sound funny but be understood.

To the extent that the rule is correct, the lowercase and uppercase variants of an English letter *are in complementary distribution*. The uppercase variant occurs in one particular context (namely, at the beginning of the sentence), and the lowercase variant occurs in every other context (or elsewhere). Therefore, just as every English vowel phoneme has an oral and a nasalized allophone that occurs in different spoken contexts, every letter of the English alphabet has two variants, or allographs, that occur in different written contexts. In both cases, the two variants of a single mental representation (phoneme or letter) are in *complementary distribution* because they never appear in the same environment. And, substituting one for the other—a nasal vowel in place of an oral one, or an uppercase letter in place of a lowercase one—may sound or look unusual, but it will not change the meaning of what is spoken or written.

Our next example turns to *cursive* handwriting, which you are likely to have learned in elementary school. Writing in cursive is in one sense more similar to the act of speaking than printing is, because in cursive writing each letter of a word (usually) connects to the following letter—just as adjacent sounds connect during speech. The following figure illustrates that the connections between the letters of a word in cursive writing create different variants of a letter in different environments:

Compare how the letter *l* appears after a *g* (as in *glue*) and after a *b* (as in *blue*). In the first case, the *l* begins near the bottom of the line, but in the second case, the *l* begins near the middle of the line (which is indicated by the dashes). In other words, the same letter *l* has two variants. Meaning is unaffected by the position of *l*: wherever the *l* begins, it's still an *l*. Likewise, whether a vowel in English is nasalized or not does not affect meaning, it's still that same vowel. Which variant occurs in a particular word is determined by the immediately preceding letter. The variant that begins near the bottom of the line appears after letters like *g* that end near the bottom of the line. The variant that begins near the middle of the line appears after letters like *b* that end near the middle of the line. The two variants of *l* are therefore in complementary distribution.

This pattern of complementary distribution is not specific to *l* but occurs for other cursive letters in English. By examining the pairs *sat* and *vat*, *mill* and *will*, and *rack* and *rock*, you can see the complementary distribution of the variants of *a*, *i*, and *c*, respectively. In each case, the immediately preceding letter determines which variant occurs, with the consequence that the variants of a given letter are in complementary distribution.

Finally, Superman and Clark Kent, Batman and Bruce Wayne, and Dr. Jekyll and Mr. Hyde—for those of you familiar with these fictional characters—are in complementary distribution *with respect to time*. At a given moment in time, the individual is either one or another of his alter egos.

The Need for Similarity

When sounds are in complementary distribution, they do not contrast with each other. The replacement of one sound for the other will not change the meaning of a word, although it might not sound like typical English pronunciation. Given these facts about the patterning of sounds in a language, a phoneme can be seen as underlying a set of phonetically similar sounds that are in complementary distribution. A set may consist of only one member because a particular phoneme is actualized in all contexts by only one sound; it has one allophone.

Complementary distribution alone is insufficient for determining the allophones when there is more than one allophone in the set. The phones must also be *phonetically similar*, that is, share most phonetic features. In English, the velar nasal [ŋ] and the glottal fricative [h] are in complementary distribution; [ŋ] does not occur word-initially and [h] does not occur word-finally. But they share very few phonetic features; [ŋ] is a voiced velar nasal stop; [h] is a voiceless glottal fricative. Therefore, they are not allophones of the same phoneme; [ŋ] and [h] are allophones of different phonemes.

Speakers of a language generally perceive the different allophones of a single phoneme as the same sound or phone. For example, most speakers of English are unaware that the vowels in *bead* and *bean* are different phones because mentally, speakers produce and hear phonemes, not phones.

Distinctive Features of Phonemes

We are generally not aware of the phonetic properties or features that distinguish the phonemes of our language. *Phonetics* provides the means to describe the phones (sounds) of language, showing how they are produced and how they vary. *Phonology* tells us how various sounds form patterns to create phonemes and their allophones.

For two phones to contrast meaning there must be some phonetic difference between them. The minimal pairs *seal* [sil] and *zeal* [zil] show that [s] and [z] represent two contrasting phonemes in English. They cannot be allophones of one phoneme because one cannot replace the [s] with the [z] without changing the meaning of the word. Furthermore, they are not in complementary distribution as both occur word initially before the vowel [i]. They are therefore allophones of the two different phonemes /s/ and /z/. From the discussion of phonetics in chapter 5 we know that [s] and [z] differ in voicing: [s] is voiceless and [z] is voiced. The phonetic feature of voicing therefore distinguishes the two words. Voicing also distinguishes *feel* and *veal* [f]/[v] and *cap* and *cab* [p]/[b]. When a feature distinguishes one phoneme from another, hence one word from another, it is a **distinctive feature** or, equivalently, a **phonemic feature**.

Feature Values

One can think of voicing and voicelessness as the presence or absence of a single feature, *voiced*. This single feature may have two values: plus (+), which signifies its presence, and minus (–), which signifies its absence. For example, [b] is [+voiced] and [p] is [–voiced].

The presence or absence of nasality can similarly be designated as [+nasal] or [–nasal], with [m] being [+nasal] and [b] and [p] being [–nasal]. A [–nasal] sound is an *oral* sound.

We consider the phonetic and phonemic symbols to be *cover symbols* for sets of distinctive features. They are a shorthand method of specifying the phonetic properties of segments. Phones and phonemes are not indissoluble units; they are composed of phonetic features, similar to the way that molecules are composed of atoms. A more explicit description of the phonemes /p/, /b/, and /m/ may thus be given in a feature matrix of the following sort.

	p	b	m
Labial	+	+	+
Voiced	–	+	+
Nasal	–	–	+

Aspiration is not listed as a phonemic feature in the specification of these units for English (but is for Thai, say, as we shall see), because [p] and [pʰ] do not represent different phonemes in English. In a *phonetic* transcription, however, the aspiration feature would be specified where it occurs.

A phonetic feature is distinctive when the + value of that feature in certain words contrasts with the – value of that feature in other words. At least one feature value difference must distinguish each phoneme from all the other phonemes in a language.

Because the phonemes /b/, /d/, and /g/ contrast in English by virtue of the place of articulation features—*labial, alveolar,* and *velar*—these place features are also distinctive in English. The distinctive features of the voiced stops in English are shown in the following:

	b	m	d	n	g	ŋ
Voiced	+	+	+	+	+	+
Labial	+	+	−	−	−	−
Alveolar	−	−	+	+	−	−
Velar	−	−	−	−	+	+
Nasal	−	+	−	+	−	+

Each phoneme in this chart differs from all the other phonemes by at least one distinctive feature.

Vowels, too, have distinctive features. For example, the feature [±back] distinguishes the vowel in *look* [lʊk] ([+back]) from the vowel in *lick* [lɪk] ([−back]) and is therefore distinctive in English. Similarly, [±tense] distinguishes [i] from [ɪ] (*beat* versus *bit*) and is also a distinctive feature of the English vowel system.

Nondistinctive Features

As we saw, aspiration is not a distinctive feature of English consonants. It is a **nondistinctive** or **redundant** or **predictable feature** (all equivalent terms). Some features may be distinctive for one class of sounds but nondistinctive for another. For example, nasality is a distinctive feature of English consonants but not a distinctive feature for English vowels. There is no way to predict when an /m/ or an /n/ can occur in an English word. You learn this when you learn the words. On the other hand, the nasality feature value of the vowels in *bean*, *mean*, *comb*, and *sing* is predictable because they occur before nasal consonants. Thus the feature nasal is **nondistinctive** *for vowels*.

This is not the case in all languages. As we noted above, nasality on vowels is phonemic in Portuguese. Nasalization is also a distinctive feature for vowels in Akan (spoken in Ghana), as the following examples illustrate:

[ka]	'bite'	[kã]	'speak'
[fi]	'come from'	[fĩ]	'dirty'
[tu]	'pull'	[tũ]	'den'
[nsa]	'hand'	[nsã]	'liquor'
[tʃi]	'hate'	[tʃĩ]	'squeeze'
[pam]	'sew'	[pãm]	'confederate'

Thus, nasalization is not predictable in Akan, as it is in English. There is no nasalization rule in Akan, as shown by the minimal pair [pam] and [pãm], or in Portuguese, as shown by the minimal pair [pão], 'bread,' and [pao], 'stick'. If you substitute an oral vowel for a nasal vowel, or vice versa, you will change the word.

Two languages may have the same phonetic segments (phones) but have two different phonemic systems. Phonetically, both oral and nasalized vowels exist in English, Portuguese, and Akan. However, English does not have nasalized vowel phonemes, but Akan and Portuguese do. The same phonetic segments function differently in English from the way they function in the other two languages. Nasalization of vowels in English is redundant and nondistinctive; nasalization of vowels in Akan and Portuguese is nonredundant and distinctive.

Another nondistinctive feature in English is aspiration for voiceless stops. The voiceless aspirated stops [pʰ], [tʰ], and [kʰ] and the voiceless unaspirated stops [p], [t], and [k] are in complementary distribution. The presence of this feature is predicted by rule and need not be learned by speakers when acquiring words.

Phonemic Patterns May Vary across Languages

The tongue of man is a twisty thing, there are plenty of words there of every kind, the range of words is wide, and their variance.

HOMER, *The Iliad*, c. 900 BCE

We have seen that the same phones may occur in two languages but pattern differently because the phonologies are different. English, Portuguese, and Akan have oral and nasal vowel phones; in English, oral and nasal vowels are allophones of one phoneme, whereas in Portuguese and Akan they represent distinct phonemes.

Aspiration of voiceless stops further illustrates the asymmetry of the phonological systems of different languages. Both aspirated and unaspirated voiceless stops occur in English and Thai, but they function differently in the two languages. Aspiration in English is not a distinctive feature because its presence or absence is predictable. In Thai it is not predictable, as the following examples show:

Voiceless Unaspirated		Voiceless Aspirated	
[paa]	*forest*	[pʰaa]	*to split*
[tam]	*to pound*	[tʰam]	*to do*
[kat]	*to bite*	[kʰat]	*to interrupt*

The voiceless unaspirated and the voiceless aspirated stops in Thai occur in minimal pairs; they contrast and are therefore phonemes. In both English and Thai, the phones [p], [t], [k], [pʰ], [tʰ], and [kʰ] occur. In English they represent the phonemes /p/, /t/, and /k/; in Thai they represent the phonemes /p/, /t/, /k/, /pʰ/, /tʰ/, and /kʰ/. Therefore aspiration is a distinctive feature in Thai; it is a nondistinctive redundant feature in English.

The phonetic facts alone do not reveal what is distinctive or phonemic:

The *phonetic representation* of utterances shows what speakers know about the pronunciation of sounds.

The *phonemic representation* of utterances shows what speakers know about the patterning of sounds.

In English, vowel length and consonant length are nonphonemic. Prolonging a sound in English will not produce a different word. In other languages, long and short vowels that are identical except for length are phonemic. In such languages, length is a nonpredictable distinctive feature. For example, vowel length is phonemic in some dialects of Korean, as shown by the following minimal pairs (recall that the colon-like symbol : indicates length):

il	"day"	i:l	"work"
seda	"to count"	se:da	"strong"
kul	"oyster"	ku:l	"tunnel"

In Italian the word for 'grandfather' is *nonno* /non:o/, which contrasts with the word for 'ninth,' which is *nono* /nono/, so consonant length is phonemic in Italian. In Luganda, an African language, consonant length is also phonemic: /kula/ with a short /k/ means 'grow up,' whereas /k:ula/ with a long /k:/ means 'treasure.' Thus consonant length is unpredictable in Luganda, just as whether a word begins with a /b/ or a /p/ is unpredictable in English.

In ASL, phonology signs can be broken down into smaller units that are in many ways analogous to the phonemes and distinctive features in spoken languages. They can be decomposed into handshape, movement, and location, as discussed in chapter 5. There are minimal pairs that are distinguished by a change in one or another of these features. For example, the signs meaning 'candy,' 'apple,' and 'jealous' are articulated at the same location on the face and involve the same movement, but contrast minimally in hand configuration. 'Summer,' 'ugly,' and 'dry' are a minimal set contrasting only in place of articulation, and 'tape,' 'chair,' and 'train' contrast only in movement. Thus signs can be decomposed into smaller minimal units that contrast meaning. Some features are non-distinctive. Whether a sign is articulated on the right or left hand does not affect its meaning.

Natural Classes of Speech Sounds

It's as large as life, and twice as natural!

LEWIS CARROLL, *Through the Looking-Glass*, 1871

We show what speakers know about the predictable aspects of speech through phonological rules. In English, these rules determine the environments in which vowels are nasalized or voiceless stops aspirated. These rules apply to *all* the words in the language, and even apply to made-up words such as *sint*, *peeg*, and *sparg*, which would be /sɪnt/, /pig/, and /sparg/ phonemically and [sɪ̃nt], [pʰig], and [sparg] phonetically.

The more linguists examine the phonologies of the world's languages, the more they find that similar phonological rules involve the same classes of sounds such as nasals and voiceless stops. For example, many languages besides English have a rule that nasalizes vowels before nasal consonants:

Nasalize a vowel when it precedes a nasal consonant in the same syllable.

The rule will apply to all vowel phonemes when they occur in a context preceding any segment marked [+nasal] in the same syllable, and will add the feature [+nasal] to the feature matrix of the vowel. Our description of vowel nasalization in English needs only this rule. It need not include a list of the individual vowels to which the rule applies or a list of the sounds that result from its application.

Many languages have rules that refer to [+voiced] and [−voiced] sounds. For example, the aspiration rule in English applies to the class of [−voiced] noncontinuant sounds in word-initial position. As in the vowel nasality rule, we do not need to consider individual segments. The rule automatically applies to initial /p/, /t/, /k/, and /tʃ/.

Phonological rules often apply to **natural classes** of sounds. A natural class is a group of sounds described by a small number of distinctive features such as [−voiced], [−continuant], which describe /p/, /t/, /k/, and /tʃ/. Any individual member of a natural class would require more features in its description than the class itself, so /p/ is not only [−voiced], [−continuant], but also [+labial].

The relationships among phonological rules and natural classes illustrate why segments are to be regarded as bundles of features. If segments were not specified as feature matrices, the similarities among /p/, /t/, and /k/ or /m/, /n/, and /ŋ/ would be lost. It would be just as likely for a language to have a rule such as

1. Nasalize vowels before *p*, *i*, or *z*.

as to have a rule such as

2. Nasalize vowels before *m*, *n*, or *ŋ*.

Rule 1 has no phonetic explanation, whereas Rule 2 does: the lowering of the velum in anticipation of a following nasal consonant causes the vowel to be nasalized. In Rule 1, the environment is a motley collection of unrelated sounds that cannot be described with a few features. Rule 2 applies to the natural class of nasal consonants, namely sounds that are [+nasal], [+consonantal].

The various classes of sounds discussed in chapter 5 also define natural classes to which the phonological rules of all languages may refer. They also can be specified by + and − feature values. Table 6.4 illustrates how these feature values combine to define some major classes of phonemes. The presence of +/− indicates that the sound may or may not possess a feature depending on its context. For example, word-initial nasals are [−syllabic] but some word-final nasals can be [+syllabic], as in *wagon* [wægn̩], where the diacritic below the [n̩] indicates its syllabicity.

TABLE 6.4 | Feature Specification of Major Natural Classes of Sounds

Features	Obstruents	Nasals	Liquids	Glides	Vowels
Consonantal	+	+	+	−	−
Sonorant	−	+	+	+	+
Syllabic	−	+/−	+/−	−	+
Nasal	−	+	−	−	+/−

Feature Specifications for American English Consonants and Vowels

Here are feature matrices for vowels and consonants in English. By selecting all segments marked the same for one or more features, you can identify natural classes. For example, the natural class of high vowels /i/, /ɪ/, /u/, /ʊ/ is marked [+high] in the vowel feature chart of Table 6.5; the natural class of voiced stops /b, m, d, n, g, ŋ, ʤ/ are the ones marked [+voice] [−continuant] in the consonant chart of Table 6.6.

TABLE 6.5 | Features of Some American English Vowels

Features	i	ɪ	e	ɛ	æ	u	ʊ	o	ɔ	a	ʌ	ə
High	+	+	−	−	−	+	+	−	−	−	−	−
Low	−	−	−	−	+	−	−	−	+	+	+	−
Back	−	−	−	−	−	+	+	+	+	−	−	−
Central	−	−	−	−	−	−	−	−	−	+	+	+
Round	−	−	−	−	−	+	+	+	+	−	−	−
Tense	+	−	+	−	−	+	−	+	+	+	−	−

The Rules of Phonology

But that to come

Shall all be done by the rule.

WILLIAM SHAKESPEARE, *Antony and Cleopatra*, 1623

Throughout this chapter we have emphasized that the relationship between the *phonemic* representation of a word and its *phonetic* representation, or how it is pronounced, is *rule-governed*. Phonological rules are part of a speaker's knowledge of the language.

The phonemic representations are *minimally specified* because some features or feature values are predictable. For example, in English all nasal consonants are voiced, so we don't need to specify voicing in the phonemic feature matrix for nasals. Similarly, we don't need to specify the feature *round* for back vowels. If Table 6.6 was strictly phonemic, then instead of a + in the *voice* row for *m, n,* and *ŋ,* the cells would be left blank, as would the cells in the *round* row of Table 6.5 for *u, ʊ, o,* and *ɔ.* Such underspecification reflects the redundancy in the phonology, which is also part of a speaker's knowledge of the sound system. The phonemic representation should include only the nonpredictable, distinctive features of the phonemes in a word. The phonetic representation, derived by applying the phonological rules, includes all of the linguistically relevant phonetic aspects of the sounds. It does not include all of the physical properties of the sounds of an utterance, however, because the physical signal may vary in many ways that have little to do with the phonological system.

TABLE 6.6 | Features of Some American English Consonants

Features	p	b	m	t	d	n	k	g	ŋ	f	v	θ	ð	s	z	ʃ	ʒ	tʃ	dʒ	l	r	j	w	h
Consonantal	+	+	+	+	+	+	+	+	+	+	+	+	+	+	+	+	+	+	+	+	+	–	–	–
Sonorant	–	–	+	–	–	+	–	–	+	–	–	–	–	–	–	–	–	–	–	+	+	+	+	+
Syllabic	–	–	–/+	–	–	–/+	–	–	–/+	–	–	–	–	–	–	–	–	–	–	–/+	–/+	–	–	–
Nasal	–	–	+	–	–	+	–	–	+	–	–	–	–	–	–	–	–	–	–	–	–	–	–	–
Voiced	–	+	+	–	+	+	–	+	+	–	+	–	+	–	+	–	+	–	+	+	+	+	+	–
Continuant	–	–	–	–	–	–	–	–	–	+	+	+	+	+	+	+	+	–	–	+	+	+	+	+
Labial	+	+	+	–	–	–	–	–	–	+	+	–	–	–	–	–	–	–	–	–	–	–	+	–
Alveolar	–	–	–	+	+	+	–	–	–	–	–	–	–	+	+	–	–	–	–	+	+	–	–	–
Palatal	–	–	–	–	–	–	–	–	–	–	–	–	–	–	–	+	+	+	+	–	–	+	–	–
Anterior	+	+	+	+	+	+	–	–	–	+	+	+	+	+	+	+	+	–	–	+	+	–	–	–
Velar	–	–	–	–	–	–	+	+	+	–	–	–	–	–	–	–	–	–	–	–	–	–	+	–
Coronal	–	–	–	+	+	+	–	–	–	–	–	+	+	+	+	+	+	+	+	+	+	+	–	–
Sibilant	–	–	–	–	–	–	–	–	–	–	–	–	–	+	+	+	+	+	+	–	–	–	–	–

Note: The phonemes /r/ and /l/ are distinguished by the feature [lateral], not shown here. /l/ is the only phoneme that would be [+lateral].

The absolute pitch of the sound, the rate of speech, or its loudness is not linguistically significant. The phonetic transcription is therefore also an abstraction from the physical signal; it includes the nonvariant phonetic aspects of the utterances, those features that remain relatively constant from speaker to speaker and from one time to another.

Although the specific rules of phonology differ from language to language, the kinds of rules, what they do, and the natural classes they refer to are universal.

Feature-Changing Rules

Many rules change features from one value to its opposite or even add features not present in the phonemic representation. In English, the /z/ plural morpheme has its voicing value changed from plus to minus when it follows a voiceless sound. Similarly, the /n/ in the phonemic negative prefix morpheme /ɪn/ undergoes a change in its place of articulation feature when preceding bilabials or velars.

The rule in English that aspirates voiceless stops at the beginning of a syllable simply adds a nondistinctive feature. Generally, aspiration occurs only if the following vowel is stressed. The /p/ in *pit* and *repeat* is an aspirated [pʰ], but the /p/ in *inspect* or *compass* is an unaspirated [p]. We also note that even with an intervening consonant, the aspiration takes place so that words such as *crib*, *clip*, and *quip* ([kʰrɪb], [kʰlɪp], and [kʰwɪp]) all begin with an aspirated [kʰ]. And finally, the affricate /tʃ/ is subject to the rule, so *chip* is phonetically [tʃʰɪp]. We can now state the rule:

A voiceless noncontinuant has [+aspirated] added to its feature matrix at the beginning of a syllable when followed by a stressed vowel with an optional intervening consonant.

Aspiration is not specified in any phonemic feature matrix of English, as Table 6.6 shows. The aspiration rule adds this feature for reasons having to do with the timing of the closure release.

Assimilation Rules

A particular kind of feature-changing rule is assimilation. We have seen that nasalization of vowels in English is nonphonemic because it is predictable by rule. The vowel nasalization rule is an *assimilation rule* that makes neighboring segments more similar by adding the feature [+nasal] to the vowel.

For the most part assimilation rules stem from articulatory processes. There is a tendency when we speak to increase the ease of articulation. It is easier to lower the velum while a vowel is being pronounced before a nasal stop than to wait for the completion of the vowel and then require the velum to move suddenly.

We now wish to look more closely at the phonological rules we have been discussing. Previously, we stated the vowel nasalization rule:

Vowels are nasalized before a nasal consonant within the same syllable.

This rule specifies the <u>class of sounds</u> affected by the rule:

Vowels

It states what <u>phonetic change</u> will occur by applying the rule:

Change phonemic oral vowels to phonetic nasal vowels.

And it specifies the context or <u>phonological environment</u>.

Before a nasal consonant within the same syllable.

A shorthand notation to write rules, similar to the way scientists and mathematicians use symbols, makes the rule statements more concise. Every physicist knows that $E = mc^2$ means 'Energy equals mass times the square of the velocity of light.' We can use similar notations to state the nasalization rule as:

V → [+nasal] / _ [+nasal] $

Let's look at the rule piece by piece.

V	→	[+nasal]	/	_	[+nasal]	$
Vowels	become	nasalized	in the environment	before	nasal segments	within a syllable

To the left of the arrow is the <u>class of sounds</u> that is affected. To the right of the arrow is the <u>phonetic change</u> that occurs. <u>The phonological environment</u> follows the slash. The underscore _ is the relative position of the sound to be changed within the environment, in this case *before* a nasal segment. The dollar sign denotes a syllable boundary and guarantees that the environment does not cross over to the next syllable.

This rule tells us that the vowels in such words as *den* /dɛn/ will become nasalized to [dɛ̃n], but *deck* /dɛk/ will not be affected and is pronounced [dɛk] because /k/ is not a nasal consonant. As well, a word such as *den$tal* /dɛn$təl/ will be pronounced [dɛ̃n$təl]: we have showed the syllable boundary explicitly. However, the first vowel in *de$note*, /di$not/, will not be nasalized, because the nasal segment does not precede the syllable boundary, so the "within a syllable" condition is not met.

Any rule written in formal notation can be stated in words. The use of formal notation is a shorthand way of presenting the information, and also a way of eliminating ambiguity and making sure the intended meaning of the rule is completely clear. Notation also reveals the *function* of the rule more explicitly than words. It is easy to see in the formal statement of the rule that this is an assimilation rule because the change to [+nasal] occurs before [+nasal] segments. Assimilation rules in languages reflect **coarticulation**—the spreading of phonetic features either in the anticipation or in the perseveration (the "hanging on") of articulatory processes. The auditory effect is that words sound smoother.

The following example illustrates how the English vowel nasalization rule applies. It also shows the assimilatory nature of the rule, that is, the change to [+nasal] before a [+nasal] segment:

	"bob"			"boom"		
Phonemic representation	/b	a	b/	/b	u	m/
Nasality: phonemic feature value	–	0*	–	–	0*	+
Apply nasal rule		NA			↓	
Nasality: phonetic feature value	–	–	–	–	+	+
Phonetic representation	[b	a	b]	[b	ũ	m]

*The ● means not present on the phonemic level.

There are many assimilation rules in English and other languages. Recall that the voiced /z/ of the English regular plural suffix is changed to [s] after a voiceless sound, and that similarly the voiced /d/ of the English regular past-tense suffix is changed to [t] after a voiceless sound. These are instances of voicing assimilation. In these cases the value of the voicing feature goes from [+ voice] to [–voice] because of assimilation to the [–voice] feature of the final consonant of the stem, as in the derivation of *cats*:

/kæt + z/ → [kæts]

We saw a different kind of assimilation rule in Akan, where we observed that the nasal negative morpheme was expressed as [m] before /p/, [n] before /t/, and [ŋ] before /k/. (This is the homorganic nasal rule.) In this case the place of articulation—bilabial, alveolar, velar—of the nasal assimilates to the place of articulation of the following consonant. The same process occurs in English: the negative morpheme prefix spelled *in-* or *im-* agrees in place of articulation with the word to which it is prefixed, so we have *impossible* [ĭmpʰasəbəl], *intolerant* [ĭntʰalərɔ̃nt], and *incongruous* [ĭŋkʰãngruəs]. In effect, the rule makes two consonants that appear next to each other more similar.

ASL and other signed languages also have assimilation rules. One example is handshape assimilation, which takes place in compounds such as the sign for 'blood.' This ASL sign is a compound of the signs for 'red' and 'flow.' The handshape for 'red' alone is formed at the chin by a closed hand with the index finger pointed up. In the compound 'blood' this handshape is replaced by that of the following word 'flow,' which is an open handshape (all fingers extended). In other words, the handshape for 'red' has undergone assimilation. The location of the sign (at the chin) remains the same. Examples such as this tell us that while the features of signed languages are different from those of spoken languages, their phonologies are organized according to principles like those of spoken languages.

Dissimilation Rules

It is understandable that so many languages have assimilation rules; they permit greater ease of articulation. It might seem strange, then, to learn that languages also have feature-changing rules called **dissimilation rules**, in which certain segments becomes less similar to other segments. Ironically, such rules have the same explanation: it is sometimes easier to articulate dissimilar sounds. The difficulty of tongue twisters like "the sixth sheik's sixth sheep is

Dennis the Menace, Hank Ketcham. Reprinted with permission of North America Syndicate.

sick" is based on the repeated similarity of sounds. If one were to make some sounds less similar, as in "the second sheik's tenth sheep is sick," it would be easier to say. The cartoon makes the same point, with *toy boat* being more difficult to articulate repeatedly than *sail boat*, because the [ɔɪ] of *toy* is more similar to the [o] of *boat* than to the [e] of *sail*.

An example of easing pronunciation through dissimilation is found in some varieties of English, in which there is a fricative dissimilation rule. This rule applies to sequences /fθ/ and /sθ/, changing them to [ft] and [st]. Here the fricative /θ/ becomes dissimilar to the preceding fricative by becoming a stop. For example, the words *fifth* and *sixth* come to be pronounced as if they were spelled *fift* and *sikst*.

A classic example of the same kind of dissimilation occurred in Latin, and the results of this process show up in the derivational morpheme /-ar/ in English. In Latin a derivational suffix *-alis* was added to nouns to form adjectives. When the suffix was added to a noun that contained the liquid /l/, the suffix was changed to *-aris*; that is, the liquid /l/ was changed to the dissimilar liquid /r/. These words came into English as adjectives ending in *-al* or in its dissimilated form *-ar*, as shown in the following examples:

-al	-ar
anecdot-al	angul-ar
annu-al	annul-ar
ment-al	column-ar
pen-al	perpendicul-ar
spiritu-al	simil-ar
ven-al	vel-ar

All of the *-ar* adjectives contain /l/, and as *columnar* illustrates, the /l/ need not be the consonant directly preceding the dissimilated segment.

Assimilation rules, dissimilation rules, and other kinds of feature-changing rules are part of Universal Grammar (UG) and are found throughout the world's languages.

Segment Insertion and Deletion Rules

Phonological rules may add or delete entire segments. These are different from the feature-changing rules we have seen so far, which affect only parts of segments. The process of inserting a consonant or vowel is called **epenthesis**.

The rules for forming regular plurals, possessive forms, and third-person singular verb agreement in English all require an epenthesis rule. Here is the first part of that rule that we gave earlier for plural formation:

Insert a [ə] before the plural morpheme /z/ when a regular noun ends in a sibilant, giving [əz].

Letting the symbol Ø stand for 'null,' we can write this *morphophonemic* epenthesis rule more formally as "null becomes schwa between two sibilants," or like this:

Ø → ə / [+sibilant] ___ [+sibilant]

There is a plausible explanation for insertion of a [ə]. If we merely added a [z] to *squeeze* to form its plural, we would get [skwiz:], which would be hard for English speakers to distinguish from [skwiz] because in English we do not contrast long and short consonants. This and other examples suggest that the morphological patterns in a language are closely related to other generalizations about the phonology of that language.

Segment deletion rules are commonly found in many languages and are far more prevalent than segment insertion rules. One such rule occurs in casual or rapid speech. We often delete the unstressed vowels in words like the following:

myst*e*ry gen*e*ral mem*o*ry fun*e*ral vig*o*rous Barb*a*ra

These words in casual speech can sound as if they were written:

mystry genral memry funral vigrous Barbra

The silent *g* that torments spellers in such words as *sign* and *design* is actually the result of a segment deletion rule. Consider the following examples:

A		**B**	
sign	[sãɪn]	signature	[sɪgnətʃər]
design	[dəzãɪn]	designation	[dɛzɪgneʃə̃n]
paradigm	[pʰærədãɪm]	paradigmatic	[pʰærədɪgmærək]

In none of the words in column A is there a phonetic [g], but in each corresponding word in column B a [g] occurs. Our knowledge of English phonology accounts for these phonetic differences. The "[g]—no [g]" alternation is regular and is also seen in pairs like *gnostic* [nastɪk] and *agnostic* [ægnastɪk], and by the silent *g*'s in the cartoon:

Tumbleweeds

"Tumbleweeds". Tom K. Ryan. Reprinted with permission of North America Syndicate.

This rule may be stated as:

Delete a /g/ word-initially before a nasal consonant or before a syllable-final nasal consonant.

Given this rule, the phonemic representations of the stems in *sign/signature*, *design/designation*, *malign/malignant*, *phlegm/phlegmatic*, *paradigm/paradigmatic*, *gnostic/agnostic*, and so on will include a /g/ that will be deleted by the regular rule if a prefix or suffix is not added. By stating the class of sounds that follow the /g/ (nasal consonants) rather than any specific nasal consonant, the rule deletes the /g/ before both /m/ and /n/.

From One to Many and from Many to One

As we've seen, phonological rules that relate phonemic to phonetic representations have several functions, among which are the following:

Function	Example
1. Change feature values	Nasal consonant assimilation rules in Akan and English
2. Add new features	Aspiration in English
3. Delete segments	*g*-deletion before nasals in English
4. Add segments	Schwa insertion in English plural and past tense

The relationship between the phonemes and phones of a language is complex and varied. Rarely is a single phoneme realized as one and only one phone. We often find one phoneme realized as several phones, as in the case with English voiceless stops that may be realized as aspirated or unaspirated, among other possibilities. And we find the same phone may be the realization of several different phonemes. Here is a dramatic example of that many-to-one relationship.

Consider the vowels in the following pairs of words:

	A		**B**	
/i/	comp**e**te	[i]	comp**e**tition	[ə]
/ɪ/	med**i**cinal	[ɪ]	med**i**cine	[ə]
/e/	maint**ai**n	[e]	maint**e**nance	[ə]
/ɛ/	tel**e**graph	[ɛ]	tel**e**graphy	[ə]
/æ/	an**a**lysis	[æ]	an**a**lytic	[ə]
/a/	s**o**lid	[a]	s**o**lidity	[ə]
/o/	ph**o**ne	[o]	ph**o**netic	[ə]

In column A all the boldfaced vowels are stressed vowels with a variety of vowel phones; in column B the boldfaced vowels are without stress, or **reduced,** and are pronounced as schwa [ə]. In these cases the stress pattern of the word varies because of the different suffixes. The vowel that is stressed in one form becomes unstressed in a different form and is therefore pronounced as [ə]. The phonemic representations of all of the root morphemes contain a stressed vowel such as /i/ or /e/ that becomes phonetically [ə] when it is de-stressed. We can conclude, then, that [ə] is an allophone of all English vowel phonemes. The rule to derive the schwa is simple to state:

Change a vowel to a [ə] when the vowel is unstressed.

In the phonological description of a language, it is not always straightforward to determine phonemic representations from phonetic transcriptions. How would we deduce the /o/ in *phonetic* from its pronunciation as [fənɛrɪk] without a complete phonological analysis? However, given the phonemic representation and the phonological rules, we can always derive the correct phonetic representation. In our internal mental grammars this derivation is no problem, because the words occur in their phonemic forms in our mental lexicons and we know the rules of the language.

Similar rules exist in other languages that show that there is no one-to-one relationship between phonemes and phones. For example, in German both voiced and voiceless obstruents occur as phonemes, as is shown by the following minimal pair:

Tier [tiːr] "animal"   *dir* [diːr] "to you"

However, when voiced obstruents occur at the end of a word or syllable, they become voiceless. The words meaning 'bundle,' *Bund* /bʊnd/, and 'colorful,' *bunt* /bʊnt/, are phonetically identical and pronounced [bʊnt] with a final [t]. Obstruent voicing is neutralized in syllable-final position.

The German devoicing rule changes the specifications of features. In German, the phonemic representation of the final stop in *Bund* is /d/, specified as [+voiced]; it is changed by rule to [−voiced] to derive the phonetic [t] in word-final position. Again, this shows there is no simple relationship between phonemes and their allophones. German presents us with this picture:

German Phonemes   /d/   /t/

German Phones   [d]   [t]

The devoicing rule in German provides a further illustration that we cannot discern the phonemic representation of a word given only the phonetic form: [bʊnt] can be derived from either /bʊnd/ or /bʊnt/. The phonemic representations and the phonological rules together determine the phonetic forms.

The Function of Phonological Rules

The function of the phonological rules in a grammar is to provide the phonetic information necessary for the pronunciation of utterances. We may illustrate this point in the following way:

input   *Phonemic (Mental Lexicon) Representation of Words
in a Sentence*

Phonological rules (P-rules)

output   *Phonetic Representation of Words in a Sentence*

The input to the P-rules is the phonemic representation. The P-rules apply to the phonemic strings and produce as output the phonetic representation.

The application of rules in this way is called a **derivation**. We have given examples of derivations that show how plurals are derived, how phonemically oral vowels become nasalized, and how /t/ and /d/ become flaps in certain environments. A derivation is thus an explicit way of showing both the effects and the function of phonological rules in a grammar.

All the examples of derivations we have so far considered show the application of just one phonological rule, except the plural and past-tense rules, which are actually one rule with two parts. In any event, it is common for more than one rule to apply to a word. For example, the word *tempest* is phonemically /tɛmpɛst/ (as shown by the pronunciation of *tempestuous* [tʰɛ̃mpʰɛstʃuəs]) but phonetically [tʰɛ̃mpəst]. Three rules apply to it: the aspiration rule, the vowel nasalization rule, and the schwa rule. We can derive the phonetic form from the phonemic representation as follows:

Underlying phonemic representation	/ t	ɛ	m p	ɛ	s t /
Aspiration rule	tʰ				
Nasalization rule		ɛ̃			
Schwa rule				ə	
Surface phonetic representation	[tʰ	ɛ̃	m p	ə	s t]

Slips of the Tongue: Evidence for Phonological Rules

Slips of the tongue, or **speech errors**, in which we deviate in some way from an intended utterance, show phonological rules in action. We all make speech errors, and they tell us interesting things about language and its use. Consider the following speech errors:

Intended Utterance	Actual Utterance
1. gone to seed	god to seen
[gãn tə sid]	[gad tə sĩn]
2. stick in the mud	smuck in the tid
[stɪk ĩn ðə mʌd]	[smʌk ĩn ðə tʰɪd]
3. speech production	preach seduction
[spitʃ pʰrədʌkʃə̃n]	[pʰritʃ sədʌkʃə̃n]

In the first example, the final consonants of the first and third words were reversed. Notice that the reversal of the consonants also changed the nasality of the vowels. The vowel [ã] in the intended utterance is replaced by [a]. In the actual utterance, the nasalization was lost because [a] no longer occurred before a nasal consonant. The vowel in the third word, which was the non-nasal [i] in the intended utterance, became [ĩ] in the error, because it was followed by /n/. The nasalization rule applied.

In the other two errors, we see the application of the aspiration rule. In the intended *stick*, the /t/ would have been realized as an unaspirated [t] because it follows the syllable initial /s/. When it was switched with the /m/ in *mud*, it was pronounced as the aspirated [tʰ], because it occurred initially. The third example also illustrates the aspiration rule in action. More than being simply amusing, speech errors are linguistically interesting because they provide further evidence for phonological rules and for the decomposition of speech sounds into features.

We will learn more about speech errors in chapter 10, which is about language processing.

Prosodic Phonology

Syllable Structure

Baby Blues. Baby Blues Partnership. King Features Syndicate

Words are composed of one or more syllables. A **syllable** is a phonological unit composed of one or more phonemes. Every syllable has a **nucleus**, which is usually a vowel (but can be a syllabic liquid or nasal). The nucleus may be preceded and/or followed by one or more phonemes called the syllable **onset** and **coda**. From a very early age English-speaking children learn that certain words rhyme. In rhyming words, the nucleus and the coda of the final syllable of both words are identical, as in the following jingle:

> Jack and J**ill**
> Went up the h**ill**
> To fetch a pail of water.
> Jack fell d**own**
> And broke his cr**own**
> And Jill came tumbling after.

For this reason, the nucleus + coda constitute the subsyllabic unit called a **rime** (note the spelling).

A syllable thus has a hierarchical structure. Using the IPA symbol σ (lower-case Greek letter 'sigma') for the phonological syllable, the hierarchical structure of the monosyllabic word *splints* can be shown:

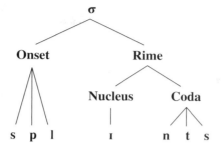

Word Stress

In many languages, including English, one or more of the syllables in every content word are stressed. A stressed syllable, which can be marked by an acute accent (´), is perceived as more prominent than an unstressed syllable, as shown in the following examples:

pérvert	(noun)	as in	"My neighbor is a pervert."
pervért	(verb)	as in	"Don't pervert the idea."
súbject	(noun)	as in	"Let's change the subject."
subjéct	(verb)	as in	"He'll subject us to criticism."

These pairs show that stress can be contrastive in English. In these cases it distinguishes between nouns and verbs. It may also distinguish between words of other categories, such as the adjective inválid (not valid) and the noun ínvalid (a sickly person).

Some words may contain more than one stressed vowel, but exactly one of the stressed vowels is more prominent than the others. The vowel that receives primary stress is marked by an acute accent (´). The other stressed vowels are indicated by grave accents (`) over the vowels (these vowels receive secondary stress).

rèsignátion	lìnguístics	sỳstemátic
fùndaméntal	ìntrodúctory	rèvolútion

Generally, speakers of a stress-timed language like English (as opposed to French, say) know which syllable receives primary stress, which ones receive secondary stress, and which ones are unstressed. It is part of their implicit knowledge of the language. It's usually easy to distinguish between stressed and unstressed syllables because the vowels in unstressed syllables are pronounced as schwa [ə] in English except at the ends of certain words such as *confetti*, *laboratory*, and *motto*. It may be harder to distinguish between primary and secondary stress. If you are unsure of where the primary stress is in a word (and you are a native or near-native speaker of English), try shouting the word as if talking to a person across a busy street. Often, the difference in stress becomes more apparent.

The stress pattern of a word may differ among English-speaking people. For example, in most varieties of American English the word *láboratòry* [lǽbərətʰɔ̀ri] has two stressed syllables, but in most varieties of British English it receives only one stress [ləbɔ̀rətri]. Because English vowels generally reduce to schwa or delete when they are not stressed, the British and American vowels differ in this word. In fact, in the British version the fourth vowel is deleted because it is not stressed.

Stress is a property of the syllable rather than a segment; it is a prosodic or suprasegmental feature. To produce a stressed syllable, one may change the pitch (usually by raising it), make the syllable louder, or make it longer. We often use all three of these phonetic means to stress a syllable.

Sentence and Phrase Stress

"What can *I* do, Tertius?" said Rosamond, turning her eyes on him again. That little speech of four words, like so many others in all languages, is capable by varied vocal inflexions of expressing all states of mind from helpless dimness to exhaustive argumentative perception, from the completest self-devoting fellowship to the most neutral aloofness.

GEORGE ELIOT, *Middlemarch*, 1872

When words are combined into phrases and sentences, one syllable receives greater stress than all others. Just as there is only one primary stress in a word spoken in isolation, only one of the vowels in a phrase (or sentence) receives primary stress or accent. All of the other stressed vowels are demoted to secondary stress. In English we place primary stress on the adjectival part of a compound noun (which may be written as one word, two words separated by a hyphen, or two separate words), but we place the stress on the noun when the words are a noun phrase consisting of an adjective followed by a noun. The differences between the following pairs are therefore predictable:

Compound Noun	Adjective + Noun
tíghtrope ('a rope for acrobatics')	tight rópe ('a rope drawn taut')
Rédcoat ('a British soldier')	red cóat ('a coat that is red')
hótdog ('a frankfurter')	hot dóg ('an overheated dog')
Whíte House ('the President's house')	white hóuse ('a house painted white')

Say these examples out loud, speaking naturally, and at the same time listen or feel the stress pattern. If English is not your native language, listen to a native speaker say them.

These pairs show that stress may be predictable from the morphology and syntax. The phonology interacts with the other components of the grammar. The stress differences between the noun and verb pairs discussed in the previous section (*subject* as noun or verb) are also predictable from the syntactic word category.

Intonation

Depending on inflection, *ah bon* [in French] can express shock, disbelief, indifference, irritation, or joy.

PETER MAYLE, *Toujours Provence*, 1991

In chapter 5 we discussed pitch as a phonetic feature in reference to tone languages and intonation languages and noted its role in determining meaning. We can now see that pitch is also a *phonemic* feature in tone languages such as Chinese, Thai, and Akan. We refer to these relative pitches as **contrasting tones**. In non-tone languages such as English, pitch still plays an important role, but only in the form of the **pitch contour** or **intonation** of the phrase or sentence.

In English, intonation may reflect syntactic or semantic differences. If we ask, "What is your middle name, David?" with falling pitch at the end it is a request to someone named David to reveal his middle name. With rising pitch at the end it is a query as to whether the addressee's middle name is David.

A sentence that is ambiguous in writing may be unambiguous when spoken because of differences in the pitch contour. Written, the following sentence is unclear as to whether Tristram intended for Isolde to read and follow directions, or merely to follow him:

Tristram left directions for Isolde to follow.

Spoken, if Tristram wanted Isolde to follow him, the sentence would be pronounced with a rise in pitch on the first syllable of *follow*, followed by a fall in pitch:

<u>Tristram left directions for Isolde to</u> follow. \

In this pronunciation of the sentence, the primary stress is on the word *follow*.

If the meaning is to read and follow a set of directions, the highest pitch comes on the second syllable of *directions*:

<u>Tristram left di</u> rections for Isolde to follow.

The primary stress in this pronunciation is on the word *directions*.

Pitch plays an important role in both tone and non-tone languages, but in different ways depending on the phonological systems of the respective languages.

Sequential Constraints of Phonemes

If you were to receive the following telegram, you would have no difficulty in correcting the "obvious" mistakes:

BEST WISHES FOR VERY HAPPP BIRTFDAY

because sequences such as BIRTFDAY do not occur in the language.

COLIN CHERRY, *On Human Communication*, 1957

Suppose you were given the following four phonemes and asked to arrange them to form all possible English words:

/b/   /ɪ/   /k/   /l/

You would most likely produce the following:

/blɪk/

/klɪb/

/bɪlk/

/kɪlb/

These are the only permissible arrangements of these phonemes in English. */lbkɪ/, */ɪlbk/, */bkɪl/, and */ɪlkb/ are not possible English words. Although /blɪk/ and /klɪb/ are not now existing words, if you heard someone say:

"I just bought a beautiful new blick."

you might ask: "What's a blick?"

If, on the other hand, you heard someone say:

"I just bought a beautiful new bkli."

you might reply, "You just bought a new *what*?"

Your knowledge of English phonology includes information about what sequences of phonemes are permissible, and what sequences are not. After a consonant like /b/, /g/, /k/, or /p/, another stop consonant in the same syllable is not permitted by the phonology. If a word begins with an /l/ or an /r/, the next segment must be a vowel. That is why */lbɪk/ does not sound like an English word. It violates the restrictions on the sequencing of phonemes. People who like to work crossword puzzles are often more aware of these constraints than the ordinary speaker, whose knowledge, as we have emphasized, may not be conscious.

Other such constraints exist in English. If the initial sounds of *chill* or *Jill* begin a word, the next sound must be a vowel. The words /tʃʌt/ and /tʃon/ and /tʃæk/ are possible in English (*chut, chone, chack*), as are /dʒæl/ and /dʒil/ and /dʒalɪk/ (*jal, jeel, jolick*), but */tʃlɔt/ and */dʒpurz/ are not. No more than three sequential consonants can occur at the beginning of a word, and these three are restricted to /s/ + /p/, /t/, /k/ + /l/, /r/, /w/, /j/. There are even restrictions if this condition is met. For example, /stl/ is not a permitted sequence, so *stlick* is not a possible word in English, but *strick* is, along with *spew* /spju/, *sclaff* /sklæf/ (to strike the ground with a golf club), and *squat* /skwat/.

Other languages have different sequential restrictions. In Polish *zl* and *kt* are permissible syllable-initial combinations, as in /zlev/, 'a sink,' and /kto/, 'who.' Croatian permits words like the name *Mladen*. Japanese has severe constraints on what may begin a syllable; most combinations of consonants (e.g., /br/, /sp/) are impermissible.

The limitations on sequences of segments are called **phonotactic constraints**. Phonotactic constraints have as their basis the syllable, rather than the word. That is, only the clusters that can begin a syllable can begin a word, and only a cluster that can end a syllable can end a word.

In multisyllabic words, clusters that seem illegal may occur, for example the /kspl/ in *explicit* /ɛksplɪsɪt/. However, there is a syllable boundary between the /k/ and /spl/, which we can make explicit using $: /ɛk $ splɪs $ ɪt/. Thus we have a permitted syllable coda /k/ that ends a syllable adjoined to a permitted onset /spl/ that begins a syllable. On the other hand, English speakers know that "condstluct" is not a possible word because the second syllable would have to start with an impermissible onset, either /stl/ or /tl/.

In Twi, a word may end only in a vowel or a nasal consonant. The sequence /pik/ is not a possible Twi word because it breaks the phonotactic rules of the language, whereas /mba/ is not a possible word in English, although it is a word in Twi.

All languages have constraints on the permitted sequences of phonemes, although different languages have different constraints. Just as spoken language has sequences of sounds that are not permitted in the language, so sign languages have forbidden combinations of features. For example, in the ASL compound for 'blood' (red flow) discussed earlier, the total handshape must be assimilated, including the shape of the hand and the orientation of the fingers. Assimilation of just the handshape but not the finger orientation is impossible in ASL. The constraints may differ from one sign language to another, just as the constraints on sounds and sound sequences differ from one spoken language to another. A permissible sign in a Chinese sign language may not be a permissible sign in ASL, and vice versa. Children learn these constraints when they acquire the spoken or signed language, just as they learn what the phonemes are and how they are related to phonetic segments.

Lexical Gaps

> The Mungle pilgriffs far awoy
>
> Religeorge too thee worled.
>
> Sam fells on the waysock-side
>
> And somforbe on a gurled,
>
> With all her faulty bagnose!
>
> JOHN LENNON

The words *bot* [bat] and *crake* [kʰrek] are not known to all speakers of English, but they are words. On the other hand [bʊt] (rhymes with *put*), *creck* [kʰrɛk], *cruke* [kʰruk], *cruk* [kʰrʌk], and *crike* [kʰraɪk] are not words in English now, although they are possible words.

Advertising professionals often use possible but nonoccurring words for the names of new products. Although we would hardly expect a new product or company to come on the market with the name *Zhleet* [ʒlit]—an impossible word in English—we do not bat an eye at *Bic*, *Xerox* /ziraks/, *Kodak*, *Glaxo*, or *Spam* (a meat product, not junk mail), because those once nonoccurring words obey the phonotactic constraints of English.

A *possible word* contains phonemes in sequences that obey the phonotactic constraints of the language. An actual, occurring word is the union of a possible word with a meaning. Possible words without meaning are sometimes called nonsense words and are also referred to as **accidental gaps** in the lexicon, or **lexical gaps**. Thus "words" such as *creck* and *cruck* are nonsense words and represent accidental gaps in the lexicon of English.

Why Do Phonological Rules Exist?

No rule is so general, which admits not some exception.

ROBERT BURTON, *The Anatomy of Melancholy*, 1621

A very important question that we have not addressed thus far is: Why do grammars have phonological rules at all? In other words, why don't underlying or phonemic forms surface intact rather than undergoing various changes?

In the previous section we discussed *phonotactic constraints*, which are part of our knowledge of phonology. As we saw, phonotactic constraints specify which sound sequences are permissible in a particular language, so that in English *blick* is a possible word but **lbick* isn't. Many linguists believe that phonological rules exist to ensure that the surface or phonetic forms of words do not violate phonotactic constraints. If underlying forms remained unmodified, they would often violate the phonotactics of the language.

Consider, for example, the English past-tense rule and recall that it has two subrules. The first inserts a schwa when a regular verb ends in an alveolar stop (/t/ or /d/), as in *mated* [metəd]. The second devoices the past-tense morpheme /d/ when it occurs after a voiceless sound, as in *reaped* [ript] or *peaked* [pʰikt]. Notice that the part of the rule that devoices /d/ reflects the constraint that English words may not end in a sequence consisting of a voiceless stop -*d*. Words such as [lɪpd] and [mɪkd] do not exist, nor could they exist. They are impossible words of English, just as [bkɪl] is.

More generally, there are no words that end in a sequence of obstruents whose voicing features do not match. Thus words such as [kasb], where the final two obstruents are [–voice] [+voice] are not possible, nor are words such as [kabs] whose final two obstruents are [+voice] [–voice]. On the other hand, [kasp] and [kɛbz] are judged to be possible words because the final two segments agree in voicing. Thus, there appears to be a phonotactic constraint in English, stated as follows:

(A) Obstruent sequences may not differ with respect to their voice feature at the end of a word.

We can see then that the devoicing part of the past-tense rule changes the underlying form of the past-tense morpheme to create a surface form that conforms to this general constraint.

Similarly, the schwa insertion part of the past-tense rule creates possible sound sequences from impossible ones. English does not generally permit sequences of sounds within a single syllable that are very similar to each other, such as [kk], [kg], [gk], [gg], [pp], [sz], [zs], and so on. (The words spelled *egg* and *puppy* are phonetically [ɛg] and [pʌpɪ].) Thus the schwa insertion rule separates sequences of sounds that are otherwise not permitted in the language because they are too similar to each other: for example, the sequence of /d/ and /d/ in /mɛnd + d/, which becomes [mɛ̃ndəd] *mended*, and /t/ and /d/ in /vent + d/, which becomes [vɛntəd] *vented*. The relevant constraint is stated as follows:

(B) Sequences of obstruents that differ at most with respect to voicing are not permitted within English words.

Constraints such as (A) and (B) are far more general than any particular rule like the past-tense rule. For example, constraint B might also explain why an adjective such as *smooth* turns into the abstract noun *smoothness*, rather than taking the affix *-th* [θ], as in *wide/width*, *broad/breadth*, and *deep/depth*. Suffixing *smooth* with *-th* would result in a sequence of too-similar obstruents, smoo[ðθ], which differ only in their voicing feature. This suggests that languages may satisfy constraints in various grammatical situations.

Thus phonological rules exist because languages have general principles that constrain possible sequences of sounds. The rules specify minimal modifications of the underlying forms that bring them in line with the surface constraints. Therefore, we find different variants of a particular underlying form depending on the phonological context.

Optimality Theory

Out of clutter, find simplicity.

From discord, find harmony.

ALBERT EINSTEIN (1879–1955)

It has also been proposed that a universal set of phonological constraints exists, and that this set is ordered, with some constraints being more highly ranked than others. The higher the constraint is ranked, the more influence it exerts on the language. This proposal, known as **Optimality Theory**, also holds that the particular constraint rankings can differ from language to language, and that the different rankings generate the different sound patterns shown across languages.

For example, constraint B discussed above is highly ranked in English; and so we have the English past-tense rule, as well as many other rules, including the plural rule (with some modification), that modify sequences of sounds that are too similar. Constraint B is also highly ranked in other languages such as Modern Hebrew, in which suffixes that begin with /t/ are always separated from stems ending in /t/ or /d/ by inserting [e], as in /kiʃat + ti/ → [kiʃatetɪ] meaning 'I decorated.'

On the other hand, in Berber similar consonants such as [tt], [dd], and [ss] can surface at the end of words from underlying /tt/, /dd/, and /ss/. In this language constraint B is not highly ranked; other constraints outrank it and therefore exert a stronger effect on the language. These constraints, known as *faithfulness constraints*, require that surface forms not deviate from corresponding underlying forms. They compete in the rankings with constraints that modify the underlying forms. Faithfulness constraints reflect the drive among languages for morphemes to have single identifiable forms, a drive that competes with constraints such as A and B. In the case of the English past-tense morpheme, the drive toward a single morpheme shows up in the spelling, which is always *-ed*.

In our discussion of syntactic rules in chapter 3 we noted that there are principles of Universal Grammar (UG) operating in the syntax. Two examples of this are the principle that transformational rules are structure-dependent and the constraint that movement rules may not move phrases out of coordinate structures. If Optimality Theory is correct, and universal phonological constraints exist that differ among languages only in their rankings, then phonological rules, like syntactic rules, are constrained by universal principles. The differences in constraint rankings across languages are in some ways parallel to the different parameter settings that exist in the syntaxes of different languages, also discussed in chapter 3. We noted that in acquiring the syntax of her language, the young child must set the parameters of UG at the values that are correct for the language of the environment. Similarly, in acquiring the phonology of her language, the child must determine the correct constraint rankings as evidenced in the input language. We will have more to say about language acquisition in chapter 9.

Phonological Analysis

> Everything it is possible to analyze depends on a clear method of distinguishing the similar from the dissimilar.
>
> CARL LINNAEUS

Children recognize phonemes at an early age without being taught, as we shall see in chapter 9. Before reading this book, or learning anything about phonology, you knew a *p* sound was a phoneme in English because it contrasts words like *pat* and *cat*, *pat* and *sat*, *pat* and *mat*. But you probably did not know that the *p* in *pat* and the *p* in *spit* are different sounds. There is only one /p/ phoneme in English, but that phoneme has more than one allophone (pronunciation), including an aspirated one and an unaspirated one.

If a non-English-speaking linguist analyzed English, how could this fact about the sound *p* be discovered? More generally, how do linguists discover the phonological system of a language?

To do a phonological analysis, the words to be analyzed must be transcribed in great phonetic detail, because we do not know in advance which phonetic features are distinctive and which are not.

Consider the following Finnish words:

1. [kudot] 'failures'
2. [kate] 'cover'
3. [katot] 'roofs'
4. [kade] 'envious'

5. [madon] 'of a worm'
6. [maton] 'of a rug'
7. [ratas] 'wheel'
8. [radon] 'of a track'

Given these words, do the voiceless/voiced alveolar stops [t] and [d] represent different phonemes, or are they allophones of the same phone?

Here are a few hints as to how a phonologist might proceed:

1. Check to see whether there are any minimal pairs.
2. Items (2) and (4) are minimal pairs: [kate] 'cover' and [kade] 'envious.'
   Items (5) and (6) are minimal pairs: [madon] 'of a worm' and [maton] 'of a rug.'
3. Conclude that [t] and [d] in Finnish represent the distinct phonemes /t/ and /d/.

That was an easy problem. Now consider the following data from English, again focusing on [t] and [d] together with the alveolar flap [ɾ] and primary stress ´:

[ráɪt]	'write'	[ráɪɾər]	'writer'
[déɾə]	'data'	[dét]	'date'
[mǽd]	'mad'	[mǽt]	'mat'
[bətróð]	'betroth'	[lǽɾər]	'ladder'
[lǽɾər]	'latter'	[dístə̃ns]	'distance'
[ráɪɾər]	'rider'	[ráɪd]	'ride'
[déɾĩŋ]	'dating'	[bédsaɪd]	'bedside'
[mʌ́ɾər]	'mutter'	[túɾər]	'tutor'
[mǽɾər]	'madder'	[mǽdnɪs]	'madness'

A broad examination of the data reveals minimal pairs involving [t] and [d], so clearly /t/ and /d/ are phonemes. We also see some interesting homophones, such as *ladder* and *latter*, and *writer* and *rider*. And the flap [ɾ]? Is it a phoneme? Or is it predictable somehow? At this point the linguist undertakes the tedious task of identifying *all* of the immediate environments for [t], [d], and [ɾ], using # for a word boundary:

[t]: áɪ_#, é_#, ǽ_#, ə_r, s_ə, #_ú

[d]: #_é (3 times), ǽ_#, #_í, áɪ_#, ɛ́_s, ǽ_n

[ɾ]: áɪ_ə (2 times), é_ə, ǽ_ə (3 times), é_ɪ, ú_ə, ʌ́_ə

It does not appear at this point that anything systematic is going on with vowel or consonant quality, so we abstract the data a little, using v for an unstressed vowel, v́ for a stressed vowel, C for a consonant, and # for a word boundary:

[t]: v́_#, #_v́, C_v, v_C
[d]: #_v́, v́_#, v́_C
[ɾ]: v́_v

Now we see clearly that [ɾ] is in complementary distribution with both [t] and [d]. It occurs only when preceded by a stressed vowel and followed by an unstressed vowel, and neither [t] nor [d] ever do. We may conclude, based on these data, that [ɾ] is an allophone of both /t/ and /d/. We tentatively propose the "alveolar flap rule":

An alveolar stop becomes a flap in the environment between a stressed and unstressed vowel.

The phonemic forms lack a flap, so that *writer* is phonemically /raɪtər/ and *rider* is /raɪdər/, based on [raɪt] and [raɪd]. Similarly, we can propose /mædər/ for *madder* based on [mæd] and [mædnɪs], and /detɪŋ/ for *dating* based on [det]. But we don't have enough information to determine phonemic forms of *data*, *latter*, and *tutor*. This is typically the case in actual analyses. Rarely is there sufficient evidence to provide all the answers.

Finally, consider these data from Greek, focusing on the following sounds:

[x]   voiceless velar fricative
[k]   voiceless velar stop
[c]   voiceless palatal stop
[ç]   voiceless palatal fricative

1.	[kano]	'do'	9.	[çeri]	'hand'
2.	[xano]	'lose'	10.	[kori]	'daughter'
3.	[çino]	'pour'	11.	[xori]	'dances'
4.	[cino]	'move'	12.	[xrima]	'money'
5.	[kali]	'charms'	13.	[krima]	'shame'
6.	[xali]	'plight'	14.	[xufta]	'handful'
7.	[çeli]	'eel'	15.	[kufeta]	'bonbons'
8.	[ceri]	'candle'	16.	[oçi]	'no'

To determine the status of [x], [k], [c], and [ç], you should answer the following questions.

1. Are there are any minimal pairs in which these sounds contrast?
2. Are any noncontrastive sounds in complementary distribution?
3. If noncontrasting phones are found, what are the phonemes and their allophones?
4. What are the phonological rules by which the allophones can be derived?

1. By analyzing the data, we find that [k] and [x] contrast in a number of minimal pairs, for example, in [kano] and [xano]. [k] and [x] are therefore distinctive. [c] and [ç] also contrast in [çino] and [cino] and are therefore distinctive. But what about the velar fricative [x] and the palatal fricative [ç]?

And the velar stop [k] and the palatal stop [c]? We can find no minimal pairs that would conclusively show that these represent separate phonemes.

2. We now proceed to answer the second question: Are these noncontrasting phones, namely [x]/[ç] and [k]/[c], in complementary distribution? One way to see whether sounds are in complementary distribution is to list each phone with the environment in which it is found, as follows:

Phone	Environment
[k]	before [a], [o], [u], [r]
[x]	before [a], [o], [u], [r]
[c]	before [i], [e]
[ç]	before [i], [e]

We see that [k] and [x] are not in complementary distribution; they both occur before non-front vowels. Nor are [c] and [ç] in complementary distribution. They both occur before front vowels. But the stops [k] and [c] are in complementary distribution; [k] occurs before non-front vowels and [r], and never occurs before front vowels. Similarly, [c] occurs only before front vowels and never before non-front vowels or [r]. Finally, [x] and [ç] are in complementary distribution for the same reason. We therefore conclude that [k] and [c] are allophones of one phoneme, and the fricatives [x] and [ç] are also allophones of one phoneme. The pairs of allophones also fulfill the criterion of phonetic similarity. The first two are [–anterior] stops; the second are [–anterior] fricatives. (This similarity discourages us from pairing [k] with [ç], and [c] with [x], which are less similar to each other.)

3. Which of the phone pairs are more basic, and hence the ones whose features would define the phoneme? When two allophones can be derived from one phoneme, one selects as the underlying segment the allophone that makes the rules and the phonemic feature matrix as simple as possible, as we illustrated with the English unaspirated and aspirated voiceless stops.

In the case of the velar and palatal stops and fricatives in Greek, the rules appear to be equally simple. However, in addition to the simplicity criterion, we wish to state rules that have natural phonetic explanations. Often these turn out to be the simplest solutions. In many languages, velar sounds become palatal before front vowels. This is an assimilation rule; palatal sounds are produced toward the front of the mouth, as are front vowels. Thus we select /k/ as a phoneme with the allophones [k] and [c], and /x/ as a phoneme with the allophones [x] and [ç].

4. We can now state the rule by which the palatals can be derived from the velars.

Palatalize velar consonants before front vowels.

Using feature notation we can state the rule as:

[+velar] → [+palatal] / __ [–back]

Because only consonants are marked for the feature [velar], and only vowels for the feature [back], it is not necessary to include the features [consonantal] or [syllabic] in the rule. We also do not need to include any other features that are redundant in defining the segments to which the rule applies or the environment in which the rule applies. Thus [+palatal] in the change part of the rule is sufficient, and the feature [–back] also suffices to specify the front vowels. The simplicity criterion constrains us to state the rule as simply as we can. Finally, it is important to note that this analysis describes the data at hand, and further data may oblige us to re-analyze the situation. In "real life" this is more often the case than not.

Summary

Part of one's knowledge of a language is knowledge of the **phonology** or sound system of that language. It includes the inventory of **phones**—which are the phonetic sounds that occur in the language—and the ways in which they pattern. This patterning determines the inventory of **phonemes**—the abstract basic units that differentiate words.

When similar phones occur in **complementary distribution**, they are **allophones**—predictable phonetic variants—of one phoneme. Thus the aspirated [pʰ] and the unaspirated [p] are allophones of the phoneme /p/ because they occur in different phonetic environments.

Some phones may be allophones of more than one phoneme. There is no one-to-one correspondence between the phonemes of a language and their allophones. In English, for example, stressed vowels become unstressed according to regular rules, and ultimately reduce to schwa [ə], which is an allophone of each English vowel.

Phonological segments—phonemes and phones—are composed of **phonetic features** such as *voiced, nasal, labial,* and *continuant,* whose presence or absence is indicated by + or – signs. The set of features is universal but languages can differ with respect to which of the features are distinctive (or phonemic) and which are non-distinctive (redundant, predictable). *Voiced, continuant,* and many others are **distinctive features** in English—they can contrast phonemes. Other features like *aspiration* are **nondistinctive** in English and are predictable from phonetic context. Some features like *nasal* may be distinctive for one class of sounds (e.g., English consonants) but nondistinctive for a different class of sounds (e.g., English vowels). Phonetic features that are nondistinctive in one language may be distinctive in another. Aspiration is distinctive in Thai and nondistinctive in English.

When two distinct words are distinguished by a single phone occurring in the same position, they constitute a **minimal pair** (e.g., *fine* /faɪn/ and *vine* /vaɪn/). Minimal pairs also occur in sign languages. Signs may contrast by handshape, location, and movement.

Words in some languages may also be phonemically distinguished by **prosodic** or **suprasegmental** features, such as pitch, stress, and segment length. Languages in which syllables or words are contrasted by pitch are called **tone languages**. Non-tone languages may still use pitch variations to distinguish meanings of phrases and sentences.

The relationship between phonemic representation and phonetic representation (pronunciation) is determined by phonological rules. Phonological rules

apply to phonemic strings and alter them in various ways to derive their phonetic pronunciation, or in the case of signed languages, their hand configuration. They may be **assimilation rules**, **dissimilation rules**, rules that *add*
nondistinctive features, **epenthetic** rules that insert segments and **deletion**
rules that delete segments.

Phonological rules generally refer to entire classes of sound. These are **natural classes**, characterized by a small set of phonetic features shared by all
the members of the class, e.g., [–continuant], [–voiced], to designate the natural class of voiceless stops.

Linguists may use a mathematical-like formulation to express phonological
rules in a concise way. For example, the rule that nasalizes vowels when they
occur before a nasal consonant may be written V → [+nasal] / _ [+nasal].

Morphophonemic rules apply to specific morphemes such as the past
tense morpheme /d/, which is phonetically [d], [t], or [əd] depending on the
final phoneme of the verb to which it is attached.

The phonology of a language also includes sequential constraints (**phonotactics**) that determine which sounds may be adjacent within the syllable.
These determine what words are possible in a language, and what phonetic
strings are impermissible. Possible but nonoccurring words constitute **accidental gaps** and are **nonsense words**, e.g., *blick* [blɪk].

Phonological rules exist in part to enforce phonotactic constraints. **Optimality Theory** hypothesizes a set of ranked constraints that govern the phonological rules.

To discover the phonemes of a language, linguists (or students of linguistics) can use a methodology such as looking for minimal pairs of words, or for
sounds that are in complementary distribution.

The phonological rules in a language show that the phonemic shape of
words is not identical with their phonetic form. The phonemes are not the
actual phonetic sounds, but are abstract mental constructs that are realized
as sounds by the operation of rules such as those described in this chapter. No
one is taught these rules, yet everyone knows them subconsciously.

References for Further Reading

Anderson, S. R. 1985. *Phonology in the twentieth century: Theories of rules and theories
of representations.* Chicago: University of Chicago Press.

Bybee, J. 2002. *Phonology and language use.* Cambridge, UK: Cambridge University Press.

Chomsky, N., and M. Halle. 1968. *The sound pattern of English.* New York: Harper & Row.

Clements, G. N., and S. J. Keyser. 1983. *CV phonology: A generative theory of the syllable.* Cambridge, MA: MIT Press.

Goldsmith, J. A. (ed.). 1995. *The handbook of phonological theory.* Cambridge, MA:
Blackwell.

Gussman, E., S. R. Anderson, J. Bresnan, B. Comrie, W. Dressler, and C. J. Ewan.
2002. *Phonology: Analysis and theory.* Cambridge, UK: Cambridge University Press.

Hayes, B. 2009. *Introductory phonology.* Oxford, UK. Wiley-Blackwell

Hyman, L. M. 1975. *Phonology: Theory and analysis.* New York: Holt, Rinehart & Winston.

Kaye, Jonathan. 1989. *Phonology: A cognitive view.* Hillsdale, NJ: Erlbaum.

Kenstowicz, M. J. 1994. *Phonology in generative grammar.* Oxford, UK: Blackwell
Publications.

Exercises

Data in languages other than English are given in phonetic transcription without square brackets unless otherwise stated. The phonetic transcriptions of English words are given within square brackets.

1. The following sets of minimal pairs show that English /p/ and /b/ contrast in initial, medial, and final positions.

Initial	Medial	Final
pit/**b**it	ra**p**id/ra**b**id	ca**p**/ca**b**

   Find similar sets of minimal pairs for each pair of consonants given:

   a. /k/—/g/   **d.** /b/—/v/   **g.** /s/—/ʃ/
   b. /m/—/n/   **e.** /b/—/m/   **h.** /tʃ/—/ʤ/
   c. /l/—/r/   **f.** /p/—/f/   **i.** /s/—/z/

2. A young patient at the Radcliffe Infirmary in Oxford, England, following a head injury, appears to have lost the spelling-to-pronunciation and pronunciation-to-spelling rules that most of us can use to read and write new words or nonsense strings. He also is unable to get to the phonemic representation of words in his lexicon. Consider the following examples of his reading pronunciation and his writing from dictation:

Stimulus	Reading Pronunciation	Writing from Dictation
fame	/fæmi/	FAM
café	/sæfi/	KAFA
time	/taɪmi/	TIM
note	/noti/ or /nɔti/	NOT
praise	/pra-aɪ-si/	PRAZ
treat	/tri-æt/	TRET
goes	/go-ɛs/	GOZ
float	/flɔ-æt/	FLOT

   What rules or patterns relate his reading pronunciation to the written stimulus? What rules or patterns relate his spelling to the dictated stimulus? For example, in reading, *a* corresponds to /a/ or /æ/; in writing from dictation /e/ and /æ/ correspond to written A.

3. Read "A Case of Identity," the third story in *The Adventures of Sherlock Holmes* by Sir Arthur Conan Doyle (and no fair reading summaries, synopses, or anything other than the original—it's online). Now all you have to do is explain what *complementary distribution* has to do with this mystery.

4. **Part One**

   Consider the distribution of [r] and [l] in Korean in the following words. (Some simplifying changes have been made in these transcriptions, which have no bearing on the problem.)

rubi	'ruby'	mul	'water'
kir-i	'road (nom.)'	pal	'arm'

saram   'person'   səul   'Seoul'
irum-i   'name (nom.)'   ilgop   'seven'
ratio   'radio'   ibalsa   'barber'

    a. Are [r] and [l] allophones of one or two phonemes?
    b. Do they occur in any minimal pairs?
    c. Are they in complementary distribution?
    d. In what environments does each occur?
    e. If you conclude that they are allophones of one phoneme, state the rule that can derive the phonetic allophonic forms.

Part Two

Here are some additional data from Korean:

son   'hand'   ʃihap   'game'
som   'cotton'   ʃilsu   'mistake'
sosəl   'novel'   ʃipsam   'thirteen'
sɛk   'color'   ʃinho   'signal'
isa   'moving'   maʃita   'is delicious'
sal   'flesh'   oʃip   'fifty'
kasu   'singer'   miʃin   'superstition'
miso   'grin'   kaʃi   'thorn'

    a. Are [s] and [ʃ] allophones of the same phoneme, or is each an allophone of a separate phoneme? Give your reasons.
    b. If you conclude that they are allophones of one phoneme, state the rule that can derive the phonetic allophones.

5. Consider these data from a common German dialect ([x] is a velar fricative; [ç] is a palatal fricative; : indicates a long vowel).

nɪçt   'not'   baːx   'Bach'
reːçə̃n   'rake'   laːxə̃n   'to laugh'
ʃlɛçt   'bad'   kɔxt   'cooks'
riːçə̃n   'to smell'   fɛrsuːxə̃n 'to try'
hãɪmlɪç   'sly'   hoːx   'high'
rɛçts   'rightward'   ʃlʊxt   'canyon'
kriːçə̃n   'to crawl'   fɛrflʊxt   'accursed'

    a. Are [x] and [ç] allophones of the same phoneme, or is each an allophone of a separate phoneme? Give your reasons.
    b. If you conclude that they are allophones of one phoneme, state the rule that can derive the phonetic allophones.

6. Reconsider the two rules for the plural morpheme /z/:

    a. Insert a [ə] before the plural morpheme /z/ when a regular noun ends in a sibilant, giving [əz].
    b. Change the plural morpheme /z/ to a voiceless [s] when preceded by a voiceless sound.

Reformulate these two rules so that their order of application doesn't matter. (This shows that the necessity for rule ordering depends on how the rules are formulated, but that if we make the rules very specific to avoid rule ordering, we may sacrifice a degree of simplicity.) How is your reformulation somehow less simple than the one that requires rule ordering?

7. In Southern Kongo, a Bantu language spoken in Angola, the nonpalatal segments [t], [s], and [z] are in complementary distribution with their palatal counterparts [tʃ], [ʃ], and [ʒ], as shown in the following words:

tobola	'to bore a hole'	tʃina	'to cut'
tanu	'five'	tʃiba	'banana'
kesoka	'to be cut'	ŋkoʃi	'lion'
kasu	'emaciation'	nselele	'termite'
kunezulu	'heaven'	aʒimola	'alms'
nzwetu	'our'	lolonʒi	'to wash house'
zevo	'then'	zeŋga	'to cut'
ʒima	'to stretch'	tenisu	'tennis'

a. State the distribution of each pair of segments.

Example: [t]—[tʃ]: [t] occurs before [o], [a], [e], and [u]; [tʃ] occurs before [i].
[s]—[ʃ]:
[z]—[ʒ]:

b. Using considerations of simplicity, which phone should be used as the underlying phoneme for each pair of nonpalatal and palatal segments in Southern Kongo?

c. State in your own words the *one* phonological rule that will derive all the phonetic segments from the phonemes. Do not state a separate rule for each phoneme; a general rule can be stated that will apply to all three phonemes you listed in (b). Try to give a formal statement of your rule.

d. Which of the following are possible words in Southern Kongo, and which are not?

i. tenesi   ii. lotʃunuta   iii. zevoʒiʒi   iv. ʃiʃi   v. ŋkasa
vi. iʒiloʒa

8. In some dialects of English, the following words have different vowels, as is shown by the phonetic transcriptions:

A		**B**		**C**	
bite	[bʌɪt]	bide	[baɪd]	die	[daɪ]
rice	[rʌɪs]	rise	[raɪz]	by	[baɪ]
ripe	[rʌɪp]	bribe	[braɪb]	sigh	[saɪ]
wife	[wʌɪf]	wives	[waɪvz]	rye	[raɪ]
dike	[dʌɪk]	dime	[dãɪm]	guy	[gaɪ]
		nine	[nãɪn]		
		rile	[raɪl]		
		dire	[daɪr]		
		writhe	[raɪð]		

a. How may the classes of sounds that end the words in columns A and B be characterized? That is, what feature specifies all the final segments in A and all the final segments in B?

b. How do the words in column C differ from those in columns A and B?

c. Are [ʌɪ] and [aɪ] in complementary distribution? Give your reasons.

d. If [ʌɪ] and [aɪ] are allophones of one phoneme, should they be derived from /ʌɪ/ or /aɪ/? Why?

e. Give the phonetic representations of the following words as they would be spoken in the dialect described here:

life _____   lives _____   lie _____
file _____   bike _____   lice _____

f. Formulate a rule that will relate the phonemic representations to the phonetic representations of the words given above.

9. Pairs like *top* and *chop*, *dunk* and *junk*, *so* and *show*, and *Caesar* and *seizure* reveal that /t/ and /tʃ/, /d/ and /ʤ/, /s/ and /ʃ/, and /z/ and /ʒ/ are distinct phonemes in English. Consider these same pairs of nonpalatalized and palatalized consonants in the following data. (The palatal forms are optional forms that often occur in casual speech.)

Nonpalatalized   **Palatalized**

[hɪt mi]   'hit me'   [hɪtʃ ju]   'hit you'
[lid hĩm]   'lead him'   [liʤ ju]   'lead you'
[pʰæs ʌs]   'pass us'   [pʰæʃ ju]   'pass you'
[luz ðem]   'lose them'   [luʒ ju]   'lose you'

Formulate the rule that specifies when /t/, /d/, /s/, and /z/ become palatalized as [tʃ], [ʤ], [ʃ], and [ʒ]. Restate the rule using feature notations. Does the formal statement reveal the generalizations?

10. Here are some Japanese words in broad phonetic transcription. Note that [ts] is an alveolar affricate (cf. the palatal affricate [tʃ]) and should be taken as a *single* symbol. It is pronounced as the initial sound in *tsunami*. Japanese words (except certain loan words) never contain the phonetic sequences *[ti] or *[tu].

tatami	'mat'	tomodatʃi	'friend'	utʃi	'house'
tegami	'letter'	totemo	'very'	otoko	'male'
tʃitʃi	'father'	tsukue	'desk'	tetsudau	'help'
ʃita	'under'	ato	'later'	matsu	'wait'
natsu	'summer'	tsutsumu	'wrap'	tʃizu	'map'
kata	'person'	tatemono	'building'	te	'hand'

a. Based on these data, are [t], [tʃ], and [ts] in complementary distribution?

b. State the distribution—first in words, then using features—of these phones.

c. Give a phonemic analysis of these data insofar as [t], [tʃ], and [ts] are concerned. That is, identify the phonemes and the allophones.

d. Give the *phonemic* representation of the phonetically transcribed Japanese words shown as follows. Assume phonemic and phonetic representations are the same except for [t], [tʃ], and [ts].

tatami	ʦukue	ʦuʦumu
tomodaʧi	tetsudau	ʧizu
uʧi	ʃita	kata
tegami	ato	koto
totemo	matsu	tatemono
otoko	deguʧi	te
ʧiʧi	natsu	tsuri

11. The following words are Paku, a language created by V. Fromkin and spoken by the Pakuni in the cult classic *Land of the Lost*, originally an NBC television series and recently a major motion picture. The acute accent indicates a stressed vowel.

   a. ótu   'evil' (N)
   b. túsa   'evil' (Adj)
   c. etógo   'cactus' (sg)
   d. etogni   'cactus' (pl)
   e. páku   'Paku' (sg)
   f. pakűni   'Paku' (pl)
   g. épo   'hair'

   h. mpósa   'hairless'
   i. ã́mpo   'hairless one'
   j. ãmpőni   'hairless ones'
   k. ã́mi   'mother'
   l. ãmíni   'mothers'
   m. áda   'father'
   n. adã́ni   'fathers'

   i. Is stress predictable? If so, what is the rule?
   ii. Is nasalization a distinctive feature for vowels? Give the reasons for your answer.
   iii. How are plurals formed in Paku?

12. Consider the following English verbs. Those in column A have stress on the penultimate (next-to-last) syllable, whereas the verbs in column B and C have their last syllables stressed.

A	B	C
astónish	collápse	amáze
éxit	exíst	impróve
imágine	resént	surpríse
cáncel	revólt	combíne
elícit	adópt	belíeve
práctice	insíst	atóne

   a. Transcribe the words under columns A, B, and C phonemically. (Use a schwa for the unstressed vowels even if they can be derived from different phonemic vowels. This should make it easier for you.)

   Examples: *astonish* /əstanɪʃ/, *collapse* /kəlæps/, *amaze* /əmez/

   b. Consider the phonemic structure of the stressed syllables in these verbs. What is the difference between the final syllables of the verbs in columns A and B? Formulate a rule that predicts where stress occurs in the verbs in columns A and B.

   c. In the verbs in column C, stress also occurs on the final syllable. What must you add to the rule to account for this fact? (*Hint:* For the forms in columns A and B, the final consonants had to be considered; for the forms in column C, consider the vowels.)

13. Following are listed the phonetic transcriptions of ten "words." Some are English words, some are not words now but are possible words or nonsense words, and others are not possible because they violate English sequential constraints.

Write the English words in regular spelling. Mark the other words as *possible* or *not possible*. For each word you mark as "not possible," state your reason.

	Word	Possible	Not Possible	Reason
Example:				
[θrot]	throat			
[slig]		X		
[lsig]			X	No English word can begin with a liquid followed by an obstruent.

	Word	Possible	Not Possible	Reason
a.	[pʰril]			
b.	[skrɪtʃ]			
c.	[kʰno]			
d.	[maɪ]			
e.	[gnostɪk]			
f.	[jūnəkʰɔrn]			
g.	[fruit]			
h.	[blaft]			
i.	[ŋar]			
j.	[æpəpʰlɛksi]			

14. Consider these phonetic forms of Hebrew words:

[v]—[b]		**[f]—[p]**	
bika	'lamented'	litef	'stroked'
mugbal	'limited'	sefer	'book'
ʃavar	'broke' (masc.)	sataf	'washed'
ʃavra	'broke' (fem.)	para	'cow'
ʔikev	'delayed'	mitpaxat	'handkerchief'
bara	'created'	haʔalpim	'the Alps'

Assume that these words and their phonetic sequences are representative of what may occur in Hebrew. In your answers, consider classes of sounds rather than individual sounds.

a. Are [b] and [v] allophones of one phoneme? Are they in complementary distribution? In what phonetic environments do they occur? Can you formulate a phonological rule stating their distribution?

b. Does the same rule, or lack of a rule, that describes the distribution of [b] and [v] apply to [p] and [f]? If not, why not?

c. Here is a word with one phone missing. A blank appears in place of the missing sound: hid__ik.

Check the one correct statement.

    i. [b] but not [v] could occur in the empty slot.
    ii. [v] but not [b] could occur in the empty slot.
    iii. Either [b] or [v] could occur in the empty slot.
    iv. Neither [b] nor [v] could occur in the empty slot.

d. Which of the following statements is correct about the incomplete word__ana?

    i. [f] but not [p] could occur in the empty slot.
    ii. [p] but not [f] could occur in the empty slot.
    iii. Either [p] or [f] could fill the blank.
    iv. Neither [p] nor [f] could fill the blank.

e. Now consider the following possible words (in phonetic transcription):

laval   surva   labal   palar   falu   razif

If these words actually occurred in Hebrew, would they:

    i. Force you to revise the conclusions about the distribution of labial stops and fricatives you reached on the basis of the first group of words given above?
    ii. Support your original conclusions?
    iii. Neither support nor disprove your original conclusions?

15. Consider these data from the African language Maninka.

bugo	'hit'	bugoli	'hitting'
dila	'repair'	dilali	'repairing'
don	'come in'	donni	'coming in'
dumu	'eat'	dumuni	'eating'
gwen	'chase'	gwenni	'chasing'

a. What are the two forms of the morpheme meaning *-ing*?
b. Can you predict which phonetic form will occur? If so, state the rule.
c. What are the "-ing" forms for the following verbs?

    da   'lie down'
    men   'hear'
    famu   'understand'

d. What does the rule that *you* formulated predict for the "-ing" form of sunogo 'sleep'?
e. If your rule predicts *sunogoli*, modify it to predict *sunogoni* without affecting the other occurrences of *-li*. Conversely, if your rule predicts *sunogoni*, modify it to predict *sunogoli* without affecting the other occurrences of *-ni*.

16. Consider the following phonetic data from the Bantu language Luganda. (The data have been somewhat altered to make the problem easier.) In each line except the last, the same root occurs in both columns A and B, but it has one prefix in column A, meaning 'a' or 'an,' and another prefix in column B, meaning 'little.'

A		B	
ẽnato	'a canoe'	aka:to	'little canoe'
ẽnapo	'a house'	aka:po	'little house'
ẽnobi	'an animal'	akaobi	'little animal'
ẽmpipi	'a kidney'	akapipi	'little kidney'
ẽŋko:sa	'a feather'	akako:sa	'little feather'
ẽm:ã:m:o	'a peg'	akabã:m:o	'little peg'
ẽŋ:õ:m:e	'a horn'	akagõ:m:e	'little horn'
ẽn:ĩmiro	'a garden'	akadĩmiro	'little garden'
ẽnugẽni	'a stranger'	akatabi	'little branch'

Base your answers to the following questions on only these forms. Assume that all the words in the language follow the regularities shown here. (*Hint:* You may write long segments such as /m:/ (: means long) as /mm/ to help you visualize more clearly the phonological processes taking place.)

a. Are nasal vowels in Luganda phonemic? Are they predictable?
b. Is the phonemic representation of the morpheme meaning 'garden,' /dimiro/?
c. What is the phonemic representation of the morpheme meaning 'canoe'?
d. Are [p] and [b] allophones of one phoneme?
e. If /am/ represents a bound prefix morpheme in Luganda, can you conclude that [ãmdãno] is a possible phonetic form for a word in this language starting with this prefix?
f. Is there a homorganic nasal rule in Luganda?
g. If the phonetic representation of the word meaning 'little boy' is [akapo:be], give the phonemic and phonetic representations for 'a boy.'

   Phonemic _____ Phonetic _____

h. Which of the following forms is the phonemic representation for the prefix meaning 'a' or 'an'?

   i. /en/   **ii.** /ẽn/   **iii.** /ẽm/   **iv.** /em/   **v.** /e:/

i. What is the *phonetic* representation of the word meaning 'a branch'?
j. What is the *phonemic* representation of the word meaning 'little stranger'?
k. State the three phonological rules revealed by the Luganda data.

17. Here are some Japanese verb forms given in broad phonetic transcription. They represent two styles (informal and formal) of present-tense verbs. Morphemes are separated by +.

Gloss	Informal	Formal
call	yob + u	yob + imasu
write	kak + u	kak + imasu

Gloss	Informal	Formal
eat	tabe + ru	tabe + masu
see	mi + ru	mi + masu
leave	de + ru	de + masu
go out	dekake + ru	dekake + masu
die	ʃin + u	ʃin + imasu
close	ʃime + ru	ʃime + masu
swindle	katar + u	katar + imasu
wear	ki + ru	ki + masu
read	yom + u	yom + imasu
lend	kas + u	kaʃ + imasu
wait	mats + u	matʃ + imasu
press	os + u	oʃ + imasu
apply	ate + ru	ate + masu
drop	otos + u	otoʃ + imasu
have	mots + u	motʃ + imasu
win	kats + u	katʃ + imasu
steal a lover	netor + u	netor + imasu

a. List each of the Japanese verb roots in its phonemic representation.
b. Formulate the rule that accounts for the different phonetic forms of these verb roots.
c. There is more than one allomorph for the suffix designating formality and more than one for the suffix designating informality. List the allomorphs of each. Formulate the rule or rules for their distribution.

18. Consider these data from the Native American language Ojibwa.[1] (The data have been somewhat altered for the sake of simplicity; /c/ is a palatal stop.)

anokːiː	'she works'	nitanokːiː	'I work'
aːkːosi	'she is sick'	nitaːkːosi	'I am sick'
ayeːkːosi	'she is tired'	kiʃayeːkːosi	'you are tired'
ineːntam	'she thinks'	kiʃineːntam	'you think'
maːcaː	'she leaves'	nimaːcaː	'I leave'
takoʃːin	'she arrives'	nitakoʃːin	'I arrive'
pakiso	'she swims'	kipakiso	'you swim'
wiːsini	'she eats'	kiwiːsini	'you eat'

a. What forms do the morphemes meaning 'I' and 'you' take; that is, what are the allomorphs?
b. Are the allomorphs for 'I' in complementary distribution? How about for 'you'?
c. Assuming that we want one phonemic form to underlie each allomorph, what should it be?

---

[1]From Baker, C. L. & John McCarthy, *The Logical Problem of Language Acquisition*, Table: Example of Ojibwa Allomorphy. © 1981 Massachusetts Institute of Technology, by permission of The MIT Press.

    d. State a rule that derives the phonetic forms of the allomorphs. Make it as general as possible; that is, refer to a broad natural class in the environment of the rule. You may state the rule formally, in words, or partially in words with some formal abbreviations.

    e. Is the rule a morphophonemic rule? That is, does it (most likely) apply to specific morphemes but not in general? What evidence do you see in the data to suggest your answer?

19. Consider these data from the Burmese language, spoken in Myanmar. The small ring under the nasal consonants indicates a voiceless nasal. Tones have been omitted, as they play no role in this problem.

ma	'health'	n̥eɪ	'unhurried'
na	'pain'	m̥i	'flame'
mjiʔ	'river'	m̥on	'flour'
nwe	'to flex'	m̥a	'order'
nwa	'cow'	n̥weɪ	'heat' (verb)
mi	'flame'	n̥a	'nostril'

Are [m] and [m̥], and [n] and [n̥], allophones or phonemic? Present evidence to support your conclusion.

What do the words mi and m̥i, both meaning 'flame' show? Do they contradict your conclusion? (*Hint:* Think of the two American English pronunciations of 'economics,' namely [ɛkənamɪks] and [ikənamɪks], which are the same word although [ɛ] and [i] are different phonemes. This phenomenon is sometimes called free variation.

20. Here are some short sentences in a made-up language called Wakanti. (Long consonants are written as doubled letters to make the analysis easier.)

aba	'I eat'	amma	'I don't eat'
ideɪ	'You sleep'	inneɪ	'You don't sleep'
aguʊ	'I go'	aŋŋuʊ	'I don't go'
upi	'We come'	umpi	'We don't come'
atu	'I walk'	antu	'I don't walk'
ika	'You see'	iŋka	'You don't see'
ijama	'You found out'	injama	'You didn't find out'
aweli	'I climbed up'	amweli	'I didn't climb up'
ioa	'You fell'	inoa	'You didn't fall'
aie	'I hunt'	anie	'I don't hunt'
ulamaba	'We put on top'	unlamaba	'We don't put on top'

    a. What is the phonemic form of the negative morpheme based on these data?

    b. What are its allomorphs?

    c. State a rule that derives the phonetic forms of the allomorphs from the underlying, phonemic form.

    d. Another phonological rule applies to these data. State explicitly what the rule does and to what natural class of consonants it applies.

    e. Give the phonemic forms for all the negative sentences.

21. Here are some data from French:

Phonetic	Gloss
pəti tablo	'small picture'
no tablo	'our pictures'
pəti livr	'small book'
no livr	'our books'
pəti navɛ	'small turnip'
no navɛ	'our turnips'
pətit ami	'small friend'
noz ami	'our friends'
pətit wazo	'small bird'
noz wazo	'our birds'

a. What are the two forms for the words 'small' and 'our'?
b. What are the phonetic environments that determine the occurrence of each form?
c. Can you express the environments by referring to word boundaries and using exactly one phonetic feature, which will refer to a certain natural class? (*Hint:* A more detailed phonetic transcription would show the word boundaries (#), e.g., [#no##livr#].)
d. What are the basic or phonemic forms?
e. State a rule in words that derives the nonbasic forms from the basic ones.
f. **Challenge exercise:** State the rule formally, using Ø to represent 'null' and # to represent a word boundary.

22. Consider these pairs of semantically related phonetic forms and glosses in a commonly known language (the + indicates a morpheme boundary):

Phonetic	Gloss	Phonetic	Gloss
[bãm]	explosive device	[bãmb + ard]	to attack with explosive devices
[kʰrʌ̃m]	a morsel or bit	[kʰrʌ̃mb + əl]	to break into bits
[aɪæ̃m]	a metrical foot	[aɪæ̃mb + ɪc]	consisting of metrical feet
[θʌ̃m]	an opposable digit	[θʌ̃mb + əlĩnə]	a tiny woman of fairy tales
[rãm]	a rhombus	[rãmb + ɔɪd]	having a shape similar to a rhombus
[tũm]	a mausoleum	[tũmb + əl]	like a mausoleum

a. What are the two allomorphs of the root morpheme in each line of data?
b. What is the phonemic form of the underlying root morpheme? (*Hint:* Consider pairs such as *atom/atomic* and *form/formal* before you decide.)
c. State a rule that derives the allomorphs.
d. Spell these words using the English alphabet.

23. Consider these data from Hebrew. (*Note: ts* is an alveolar affricate and is a single [+sibilant] sound). The word *lehit* is a reflexive pronoun.)

Nonsibilant–Initial Verbs		Sibilant–Initial Verbs	
kabel	'to accept'	*tsadek*	'to justify'
lehit-kabel	'to be accepted'	*lehits-tadek*	'to apologize'
		(not *lehit-tsadek*)	
pater	'to fire'	*shamesh*	'to use for'
lehit-pater	'to resign'	*lehish-tamesh*	'to use'
		(not *lehit-shamesh*)	
bayesh	'to shame'	*sader*	'to arrange'
lehit-bayesh	'to be ashamed'	*lehis-tader*	'to arrange
		(not *lehit-sader*)	oneself'

   a. Describe the phonological change taking place in the second column of Hebrew data.
   b. Describe in words as specifically as possible a phonological rule that accounts for the change. Make sure your rule doesn't affect the data in the first column of Hebrew.

24. Here are some Japanese data, many of them from exercise 10, in a fine enough phonetic transcription to show voiceless vowels (the ones with the little rings under them).

Word	Gloss	Word	Gloss	Word	Gloss
tatami	mat	tomodatʃi	friend	utʃi	house
tegami	letter	totemo	very	otoko	male
su̥kiyaki	sukiyaki	ki̥setsu	a season	busata	silence
tʃi̥tʃi	father	tsu̥kue	desk	tetsudau	help
ʃi̥ta	under	ki̥ta	north	matsu	wait
degutʃi	exit	tsuri	fishing	ki̥setsu	existing
natsu	summer	tsu̥tsumu	wrap	tʃizu	map
kata	person	fu̥ton	futon	fugi	discuss
matsu̥ʃita	(a proper name)	etsu̥ko	(a girl's name)	fu̥kuan	a plan

   a. Which vowels may occur voiceless?
   b. Are they in complementary distribution with their voiced counterparts? If so, state the distribution.
   c. Are the voiced/voiceless pairs allophones of the same phonemes?
   d. State in words, or write in formal notation if you can, the rule for determining the allophones of those vowels that have voiceless allophones.

25. With regard to English plural and past-tense rules, we observed that the two parts of the rules must be carried out in the proper order. If we reverse the order, we would get *[bʌsəs] instead of [bʌsəz] for the plural of *bus* (as illustrated in the text), and *[stetət] instead of [stetəd] for the past tense of *state*. Although constraints A and B (given below) are the motivation for the plural and past-tense rules, both the correct

and incorrect plural and past-tense forms are consistent with those constraints. What additional constraint is needed to prevent [bʌsəs] and [stetət] from being generated?

(A) Obstruent sequences may not differ with respect to their voice features at the end of a word.

(B) Sequences of obstruents that differ at most with respect to voicing are not permitted within English words.

26. There is a rule of word-final obstruent devoicing in German (e.g., German /bund/ is pronounced [bũnt]). This rule is actually a manifestation of the constraint:

Voiced obstruents are not permitted at the end of a word.

Given that this constraint is universal, explain why English *band* /bænd/ is nevertheless pronounced [bæ̃nd], not [bæ̃nt], in terms of Optimality Theory (OT).

27. For many English speakers, word-final /z/ is devoiced when the /z/ represents a separate morpheme. These speakers pronounce plurals such as *dogs*, *days*, and *dishes* as [dɔgs], [des], and [dɪʃəs] instead of [dɔgz], [dez], and [dɪʃəz]. Furthermore, they pronounce possessives such as *Dan's*, *Jay's*, and *Liz's* as [dæ̃ns], [ʤes], and [lɪzəs] instead of [dæ̃nz], [ʤez], and [lɪzez]. Finally, they pronounce third-person singular verb forms such as *reads*, *goes*, and *fusses* as [rids], [gos], and [fʌsəs] instead of [ridz], [goz], and [fʌsəz].

(However, words such as *daze* and *Franz* are still pronounced [dez] and [frænz], because the /z/ is not a separate morpheme. Interestingly, in this dialect *Franz* and *Fran's* are not homophones, nor are *daze* and *day's*.) How might OT explain this phenomenon?

28. In German the third-person singular suffix is *-t*. Following are three German verb stems (underlying forms) and the third-person forms of these verbs:

Stem	Third person	
/loːb/	[loːpt]	he praises
/zag/	[zakt]	he says
/raɪz/	[raɪst]	he travels

The final consonant of the verb *stem* undergoes devoicing in the third-person form, even though it is not at the end of the word. What constraint is operating to devoice the final stem consonant? How is this similar to or different from the constraint that operates in the English plural and past tense?

7

Language in Society

Language is a city to the building of which every human being brought a stone.

RALPH WALDO EMERSON, *Letters and Social Aims*, **1876**

Dialects

A language is a dialect that has an army and a navy.

MAX WEINREICH (1894–1969)

All speakers of English can talk to each other and pretty much understand each other. Yet, no two of us speak exactly alike. Some differences are the result of age, sex, social situation, and where and when the language was learned. These differences are reflected in word choices, the pronunciation of words, and grammatical rules. The language of an individual speaker with its unique characteristics is referred to as the speaker's **idiolect**. English may then be said to consist of anywhere from 450 million to 850 million idiolects, or the number of speakers of English (which seems to be growing every day and is difficult to estimate).

Like individuals, different groups of people who speak the same language speak it differently. Bostonians, New Yorkers, Texans, blacks in Chicago, whites in Denver, and Hispanics in Albuquerque all exhibit variation in the way they speak English. When there are systematic differences in the way groups speak a language, we say that each group speaks a **dialect** of that language. Dialects are *mutually intelligible* forms of a language that *differ in systematic ways*. *Every* speaker, whether rich or poor, regardless of region or racial origin, speaks at least one dialect, just as each individual speaks an idiolect. A dialect is *not* an inferior or degraded form of a language, and logically could not be so because a language is a collection of dialects.

It is not always easy to decide whether the differences between two speech communities reflect two dialects or two languages. Sometimes this rule-of-thumb definition is used: When dialects become mutually *un*intelligible— when the speakers of one dialect group can no longer understand the speakers of another dialect group—these dialects become different languages.

However, this rule of thumb does not always jibe with how languages are officially recognized, which is determined by political and social considerations. For example, Danes speaking Danish and Norwegians speaking Norwegian and Swedes speaking Swedish can converse with each other. Nevertheless, Danish and Norwegian and Swedish are considered separate languages because they are spoken in separate countries in addition to the regular differences in their grammars. Similarly, Hindi and Urdu are mutually intelligible "languages" spoken in Pakistan and India, although the differences between them are not much greater than those between the English spoken in America and the English spoken in Australia. The fact that they use different writing systems contributes to the impression of utterly different languages.

The recent history of Serbo-Croatian, the language of most of the former nation of Yugoslavia, illustrates the factors that can determine whether a particular way of speaking is considered to be a dialect or a language. From a linguistic point of view, Serbo-Croatian is a single Slavic language: Even though Croats use Roman script (as do English speakers) while Serbs use Cyrillic script (as do Russian speakers), in speech the varieties are mutually intelligible, differing slightly in vocabulary just as the British and American English dialects do. But from a sociopolitical point of view, following the breakup of Yugoslavia in the 1990s, the Serbo-Croatian language "broke up" as well. After years of conflict, the two now-independent nations declare that they speak not just different dialects but different languages.

On the other hand, linguistically distinct languages in China, such as Mandarin and Cantonese, although mutually unintelligible when spoken, are nevertheless referred to as dialects of Chinese in the media and elsewhere because they have a common writing system that can be read by all speakers (because it's ideographic—see chapter 12), and because they are spoken in a single country.

It is also not easy to draw a distinction between dialects and languages on strictly linguistic grounds. Dialects and languages reflect the underlying grammars and lexicons of their speakers. It would be completely arbitrary to say, for example, that grammars that differ from one another by, say, twenty rules represent different languages whereas grammars that differ by fewer than twenty rules are dialects. Why not ten rules or thirty rules? In reality, what one finds is that there is no sudden major break between dialects. Rather, dialects merge into each other, forming a **dialect continuum**.

Imagine, for example, a traveler journeying from Vienna to Amsterdam by bicycle. She would notice small changes in the German spoken as she bicycled from village to village, and the people in adjacent villages would have no trouble communicating with one another. Yet by the time our traveler reached Dutch-speaking Amsterdam, she would realize that the accumulated differences made the German of Vienna and the Dutch of Amsterdam nearly mutually unintelligible.

Because neither mutual intelligibility, nor degree of grammatical difference, nor the existence of political or social boundaries is decisive, it is not possible to precisely define the difference between a language and a dialect. We shall, however, use the rule-of-thumb definition and refer to dialects of one language as mutually intelligible linguistic systems, with systematic differences among them.

As we will discuss in the next chapter, languages change continually but these changes occur gradually. They may originate in one geographic region or in one social group and spread slowly to others, and often over the life spans of several generations of speakers. Dialect diversity develops when the changes that occur in one region or group do not spread. When speakers are in regular contact with one another, linguistic properties spread and are acquired by children. However, when some communication barrier separates groups of speakers—be it a physical barrier such as an ocean or a mountain range, or social barriers of a political, racial, class, educational, or religious kind—linguistic changes do not spread so readily, and the differences between groups are reinforced and grow in number.

Dialect leveling is movement toward greater uniformity and less variation among dialects. Though one might expect dialect leveling to occur as a result of the ease of travel and mass media, this is not generally the case. Dialect variation in the United Kingdom is maintained although only a few major dialects are spoken on national radio and television. There may actually be an increase in dialects in urban areas, where different groups attempt to maintain their distinctness and group identity.

Regional Dialects

Phonetics . . . the science of speech. That's my profession. . . . (I) can spot an Irishman or a Yorkshireman by his brogue. I can place any man within six miles. I can place him within two miles in London. Sometimes within two streets.

GEORGE BERNARD SHAW, *Pygmalion*, 1912

The educated Southerner has no use for an r except at the beginning of a word.

MARK TWAIN, *Life on the Mississippi*, 1883

When various linguistic differences accumulate in a particular geographic region (e.g., the city of Boston or the southern area of the United States), the language spoken has its own character. Each version of the language is referred to as a **regional dialect**. The hypothetical journey from Vienna to Amsterdam discussed previously crossed regional dialects. In the United States, most dialectal differences are based on geographic region.

The origins of many regional dialects of American English can be traced to the people who settled in North America in the seventeenth and eighteenth centuries. Because they came from different parts of England, these early settlers already spoke different dialects of English, and these differences were carried to the original thirteen American colonies. By the time of the American Revolution, there were three major dialect regions in the British colonies: the Northern dialect spoken in New England and around the Hudson River, the Midland dialect spoken in Pennsylvania, and the Southern dialect. (There were, of course, a number of minor dialect areas as well.) These dialects differed from one another and from the English spoken in England in systematic ways. Some of the changes that occurred in British English spread to the colonies; others did not.

How dialects develop is illustrated by the pronunciation of words with an *r* in different parts of United States. As early as the eighteenth century, the British in southern England were dropping their *r*'s before consonants and at the ends of words. Words such as *farm*, *farther*, and *father* were pronounced as [faːm], [faːðə], and [faːðə], respectively. By the end of the eighteenth century, *r*-drop was a general rule among many of the early settlers in New England and the southern Atlantic seaboard. Close commercial ties were maintained between the New England colonies and London, and Southerners sent their children to England to be educated, which reinforced the *r*-drop rule. The *r*-less dialect still spoken today in Boston, New York, and Savannah maintains this characteristic. Later settlers, however, came from northern England, where the *r* had been retained; as the frontier moved westward, so did the *r*. Pioneers from all three dialect areas spread westward. The mingling of their dialects leveled many of their dialect differences, which is why the English used in large sections of the Midwest and the West is similar.

Regional phonological or phonetic distinctions are often referred to as different **accents**. A person is said to have a Boston or Brooklyn or Midwestern accent, a Southern drawl, an Irish brogue, and so on. Thus, *accent* refers to the characteristics of speech that convey information about the speaker's dialect, which may reveal in what country or in what part of the country the speaker grew up, or to which sociolinguistic group the speaker belongs. People in the United States often refer to someone as having a British accent or an Australian accent; in Britain they refer to an American accent.

The term *accent* is also used to refer to the speech of non-native speakers, who have learned a language as a second language. For example, a native French speaker's English is described as having a French accent. In this sense, *accent* refers to phonological differences caused by one's native language. Unlike regional dialect accents, such foreign accents do not reflect differences in the speech of the community where the language was learned.

Regional dialects may differ not only in their pronunciation but also in their lexical choices and grammatical rules. A comedian once remarked that "the Mason-Dixon line is the dividing line between *you-all* and *youse-guys*." In the following sections we discuss the different linguistic levels at which dialects may vary.

Phonological Differences

I have noticed in traveling about the country a good many differences in the pronunciation of common words. . . . Now what I want to know is whether there is any right or wrong about this matter. . . . If one way is right, why don't we all pronounce that way and compel the other fellow to do the same? If there isn't any right or wrong, why do some persons make so much fuss about it?

LETTER QUOTED IN "THE STANDARD AMERICAN," in J. V. Williamson and V. M. Burke, eds., *A Various Language*, 1971

A comparison of the *r*-drop and other dialects illustrates the many phonological differences among dialects of American English. These variations created difficulties for us in writing chapter 5 (phonetics), where we wished to illustrate the different sounds of English by using key words in which the sounds occur. As mentioned, some people pronounce *caught* [kɔt] with the vowel [ɔ] and *cot* [kat] with [a], whereas others pronounce them both [kat]. Some pronounce *Mary*, *merry*, and *marry* the same; others pronounce the three words differently as [meri], [mɛri], and [mæri]; and still others pronounce just two of them the same. In the south and northeast *pajamas* is pronounced [pədʒãməz] with tense [a] but as [pədʒæ̃məz] with a lax [æ] in the Midlands. Many speakers of American English pronounce *pin* and *pen* identically, whereas others pronounce the first [pĭn] and the second [pɛ̃n].

The pronunciation of British English (or many dialects of it) differs in systematic ways from pronunciations in many dialects of American English. In a survey of hundreds of American and British speakers conducted via the Internet, 48 percent of the Americans pronounced the mid consonants in *luxury* as voiceless [lʌkʃəri], whereas 96 percent of the British pronounced them as voiced [lʌgʒəri]. Sixty-four percent of the Americans pronounced the first vowel in *data* as [e] and 35 percent as [æ], as opposed to 92 percent of the British pronouncing it with an [e] and only 2 percent with [æ]. The most consistent difference occurred in the placement of primary stress, with most Americans putting stress on the first syllable and most British on the second or third in polysyllabic words like *cigarette*, *applicable*, *formidable*, and *laboratory*.

The United Kingdom also has many regional dialects. The British vowels described in the phonetics chapter are used by speakers of the dialect called RP for "received pronunciation" because it is "received" (accepted) in the court of the monarch. In this dialect, *h* is pronounced at the beginning of both *head* and *herb*, whereas in most American English dialects *h* is not pronounced in *herb*. In some British English dialects the *h* is regularly dropped from most words in which it is pronounced in American, such as *house*, pronounced [aʊs], and *hero*, pronounced [iro]. As is true of the origin of certain American dialects, many of the regional dialects of British English, such as the West Country dialect, the East Anglia dialect, and the Yorkshire dialect, are not deviations from the "standard" dialect spoken in London, but are direct descendants of earlier varieties that existed alongside London English as far back as the eleventh century. (Watch old Harry Potter movies to hear some of what we've been discussing vis-à-vis British English.)

English is the most widely spoken language in the world (as a first or second language). It is the national language of several countries, including the United States, large parts of Canada, the British Isles, Australia, and New Zealand. For many years it was the official language in countries that were once colonies of Britain, including India, Nigeria, Ghana, Kenya, and the other "anglophone" countries of Africa. There are many other phonological differences in the various dialects of English used around the globe.

Lexical Differences

BY FRANK "CAFFEINE FREE" CHO

Frank Cho/Creators Syndicate

Regional dialects may differ in the words people use for the same object, as well as in phonology. Hans Kurath, an eminent dialectologist, in his paper "What Do You Call It?" asked:

> Do you call it a *pail* or a *bucket*? Do you draw water from a *faucet* or from a *spigot*? Do you pull down the *blinds*, the *shades*, or the *curtains* when it gets dark? Do you *wheel* the baby, or do you *ride* it or *roll* it? In a *baby carriage*, a *buggy*, a *coach*, or a *cab*?

People take a *lift* to the *first floor* (our *second floor*) in England, but an *elevator* in the United States; they fill up with *petrol* (not *gas*) in London; in Britain a *public school* is 'private' (you have to pay), and if a student showed up there wearing *pants* ('underpants') instead of *trousers* ('pants'), he would be sent home to get dressed.

If you ask for a *tonic* in Boston, you will get a drink called *soda* or *soda-pop* in Los Angeles; ice cream cones can be covered in *jimmies* in Boston and *sprinkles* in New York; and a *freeway* in Los Angeles is a *thruway* in New York, a *parkway* in New Jersey, a *motorway* in England, and an *expressway* or *turnpike* in other dialect areas.

Syntactic Differences

Dialects can also be distinguished by systematic syntactic differences. In most American dialects, sentences may be conjoined as follows:

1. John will eat and Mary will eat. → John and Mary will eat.

In the Ozark dialect of southern Missouri, the following conjoining is also possible:

2.   John will eat and Mary will eat. → John will eat and Mary.

In (1) the VP *will eat* in the first conjunct is deleted, while in (2) the VP in the second conjunct is deleted. Most dialects of English allow deletion of only the first conjunct and in those dialects *John will eat and Mary* is ungrammatical. The Ozark dialect differs in allowing the second VP to delete.

Speakers of some American dialects say *Have them come early!* where others would say *Have them **to** come early!* Many speakers of the latter dialect also exhibit double modal auxiliary verbs, so that expressions like *He **might could** do it* or *You **might should** go home* are grammatical. Most dialects of English may contain no more than one modal.

Some of the dialects that permit double modals (e.g., Appalachian English) also exhibit double objects (e.g., *I caught me a fish*); and *a*-prefixing with progressives (*He came a-runnin'*). Several distinguishing syntactic characteristics contribute to a *bundle* of syntactic isoglosses that separate these regional dialects.

In some American English dialects, the pronoun *I* occurs when *me* would be used in other dialects. This difference is a syntactically conditioned morphological difference.

Dialect 1	**Dialect 2**
between you and I	between you and me
Won't he let you and I swim?	Won't he let you and me swim?
*Won't he let I swim?	

The use of *I* in these structures is only permitted in a conjoined NP, as the starred (ungrammatical) sentence shows. *Won't he let me swim?*, however, is grammatical in both dialects. Dialect 1 is growing, and these forms are becoming Standard English, spoken by TV announcers, political leaders, and university professors, although language purists still frown on this usage.

In British English the pronoun *it* in the sentence *I could have done it* can be deleted. British speakers say *I could have done*, which is not in accordance with the syntactic rules of American English. American English, however, permits the deletion of *done it*, and Americans say *I could have*, which does not accord with the British syntactic rules.

About one third of the students reading this textbook will not accept the sentence *John promised Mary to leave* as grammatical while two thirds will, with the meaning 'John promised Mary that he, John, would leave.'

Despite such differences, we are still able to understand speakers of other English dialects. Although regional dialects differ in pronunciation, vocabulary, and syntactic rules, the differences are minor when compared with the totality of the grammar. Dialects typically share most rules and vocabulary, which explains why the dialects of a language are mutually intelligible.

Dialect Atlases

Linguist Hans Kurath published **dialect maps** and **dialect atlases** of a region on which dialect differences are geographically plotted (see Figure 7.1). The

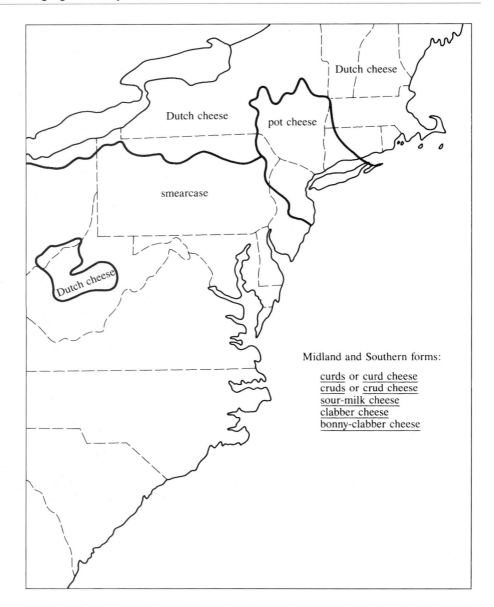

FIGURE 7.1 | A dialect map showing the isoglosses separating the use of different words that refer to the same cheese.

Kurath, Hans. "A Word Geography of the Eastern United States." Ann Arbor, MI: University of Michigan Press, copyright © 1949. Reprinted with permission of University of Michigan Press.

dialectologists who created the map noted the places where speakers use one word or another word for the same item. For example, the area where the term *Dutch cheese* is used is not contiguous; there is a small pocket mostly in West Virginia where speakers use that term for what other speakers call *smearcase*.

In similar maps, areas were differentiated based on the variation in pronunciation of the same word, such as [krik] and [krɪk] for *creek*. The concentrations defined by different word usages and varying pronunciations, among other linguistic differences, form **dialect areas**.

A line drawn on the map to separate the areas is called an **isogloss**. When you cross an isogloss, you are passing from one dialect area to another. Sometimes several isoglosses coincide, often at a political boundary or at a natural barrier such as a river or mountain range. Linguists call these groupings a *bundle* of isoglosses. Such a bundle can define a regional dialect.

DARE is the acronym for the *Dictionary of American Regional English*, whose chief editor was the distinguished American dialectologist Frederick G. Cassidy (1907–2000). This work represents decades of research and scholarship by Cassidy and other American dialectologists and is a major resource for those interested in American English dialects. Its five volumes are now published—the fifth volume as recently as March 2012—covering *A* through *Z*. Its purpose has been described as follows:

> The *Dictionary of American Regional English* (*DARE*) is a reference tool unlike any other. Its aim is not to prescribe how Americans should speak, or even to describe the language we use generally, the "standard" language. Instead, it seeks to document the varieties of English that are **not** found everywhere in the United States—those words, pronunciations, and phrases that vary from one region to another, that we learn at home rather than at school, or that are part of our oral rather than our written culture. Although American English is remarkably homogeneous considering the tremendous size of the country, there are still many thousands of differences that characterize the various dialect regions of the United States. It is these differences that *DARE* records.

While Professor Cassidy did not live to see the completion of DARE, he took his life's work with him to the grave, where on his tombstone is inscribed "On to Z!" (The volumes were completed through *Sk* when he died.) The capstone entry into *DARE* is *zydeco*, a form of Cajun music.

Social Dialects

> Why do these people speak in such a high pitch? Why do their jaws barely open when they talk? Why do the ends of their sentences go up as if they're asking a question? Odd vowels, clipped words, and always a hiss on the letter *s* . . . no wonder it's impossible not to mimic them.
>
> SUZANNE COLLINS, *The Hunger Games*, 2008

In many respects, social boundaries and class differences are as confining as the physical barriers that often define regional dialects. It is therefore not surprising that different dialects of a language evolve within social groups.

The social boundaries that give rise to dialect variation are numerous. They may be based on socioeconomic status, religious, ethnic, and racial differences, country of origin, and even gender. Middle-class American and British speakers are often distinguishable from working-class speakers; in Baghdad the Christian, Muslim, and Jewish groups all speak different varieties of Arabic; in India people often use different dialects of a standard regional language such as Hindi, Gujarati, or Bengali depending on the social *caste* they belong to; in America, many speakers of African descent speak a different dialect than those of European, Asian, or Hispanic descent; and, as we shall see, women and men each have their own distinguishing speech characteristics.

Dialect differences that seem to come about because of social factors are called **social dialects**, as opposed to *regional dialects*, which are spawned by geographical factors. However, there are regional aspects to social dialects and, clearly, social aspects to regional dialects, so the distinction is not entirely cut and dried.

The "Standard"

> We don't talk fancy grammar and eat anchovy toast. But to live under the kitchen doesn't say we aren't educated.
>
> MARY NORTON, *The Borrowers*, 1952

Even though every language is a composite of dialects, many people talk and think about a language as if it were a well-defined fixed system with various dialects diverging from this norm. This is false, although it is a falsehood that is widespread. One writer of books on language accused the editors of *Webster's Third New International Dictionary*, published in 1961, of confusing "to the point of obliteration the older distinction between standard, substandard, colloquial, vulgar, and slang," attributing to them the view that "good and bad, right and wrong, correct and incorrect no longer exist." In the next section we argue that such criticisms are ill-founded.

Language Purists

> A woman who utters such depressing and disgusting sounds has no right to be anywhere—no right to live. Remember that you are a human being with a soul and the divine gift of articulate speech: that your native language is the language of Shakespeare and Milton and the Bible; and don't sit there crooning like a bilious pigeon.
>
> GEORGE BERNARD SHAW, *Pygmalion*, 1912

Prescriptive grammarians, or language purists, usually consider the dialect used by political leaders and national newscasters as the correct form of the language. (See chapter 1 for a discussion of prescriptive grammars.) This is the dialect taught in "English" or "grammar" classes in school, and it is closer to the written form of the language than many other dialects, which also lends it an air of superiority.

Otto Jespersen, the great Danish linguist, ridiculed the view that a particular dialect is better than any other when he wrote: "We set up as the best language that which is found in the best writers, and count as the best writers those that best write the language. We are therefore no further advanced than before."

The dominant, or **prestige**, dialect is often called the standard dialect. **Standard American English** (SAE) is a dialect of English that many Americans *nearly* speak; divergences from this "norm" are labeled "Philadelphia dialect," "Chicago dialect," "African American English," and so on.

SAE is an idealization. Nobody speaks this dialect; and if somebody did, we would not know it, because SAE is not defined precisely (like most dialects, none of which are easy to clarify). Teachers and linguists held a conference in the 1990s that attempted to come up with a precise definition of SAE. This meeting did not succeed in satisfying everyone's view of SAE. SAE was once represented by the language used by national news broadcasters, but today many of them speak a regional dialect or a style of English that is not universally accepted as "standard." For example, the British Broadcasting Corporation (BBC) once used mostly speakers of RP English, but today speakers of Irish, Welsh, Scottish, and other regional dialects of English are commonly heard on BBC programs. The BBC describes its English as "the speech of educated professionals."

A standard dialect (or prestige dialect) of a particular language may have social functions. Its use in a group may bind people together or provide a common written form for multidialectal speakers. If it is the dialect of the wealthy, influential, and powerful members of society, this may have important implications for the entire society. All speakers who aspire to become successful may be required to speak that dialect even if it isn't their own.

In 1954 the British scholar Alan Ross published *Linguistic Class-Indicators in Present-Day English*, in which he compared the speech habits of the English upper class, whom he labeled "U," with the speech habits of "non-U" speakers. Ross concluded that although the upper class had words and pronunciations peculiar to it, the main characteristic of U speech is the avoidance of non-U speech; and the main characteristic of non-U speech is, ironically, the effort to sound U. "They've a lovely home," for example, is pure non-U, because it is an attempt to be refined. Non-U speakers say "wealthy" and "ever so"; U speakers say "rich" and "very." Non-U speakers "recall"; U-speakers simply "remember."

Non-U speech habits often include **hypercorrections**, deviations from the norm *thought* to be "proper English," such as pronouncing *often* with a [t], or saying *between you and I*, while U speakers, who are generally more secure about their dialect, say [ɔfən] and *between you and me*. Ironically, in some cases non-U speech is so pervasive it eventually becomes part of the prestige dialect, as we are seeing today with *often* and *between you and I/me*.

No dialect, however, is more expressive, less corrupt, more logical, more complex, or more regular than any other dialect or language. They are simply different. More precisely, dialects reflect a different set of rules or lexical items represented in the minds of their speakers. Any judgments, therefore, as to the superiority or inferiority of a particular dialect or language are social judgments, which have no linguistic or scientific basis.

To illustrate the arbitrariness of "standard usage," consider the English *r*-drop rule discussed earlier. Britain's prestigious RP accent omits the *r* in words such as *car*, *far*, and *barn*. Thus an *r*-less pronunciation is thought to be better than the less prestigious rural dialects that maintain the *r*. However, *r*-drop in the northeast United States is generally considered substandard, and the more prestigious dialects preserve the *r*, though this was not true in the past when *r*-drop was considered more prestigious. This shows that there is nothing inherently better or worse about one pronunciation over another, but simply that one variant is perceived as better or worse depending on a variety of social factors.

Banned Languages

> A Wisconsin seventh-grader was suspended from a school's basketball team for speaking a Native American language. [The school] is 60 percent Native American, yet when a teacher heard [a female student], 12, telling a friend how to say "I love you" in the Menominee tongue, the teacher angrily objected, saying, "how do I know you're not saying something bad?"
>
> THE WEEK, 2/24/12, P. 6

Language purists wish to prevent language or dialect differentiation because of their false belief that some languages are better than others, or that change leads to corruption. Languages and dialects have also been banned as a means of political control. Russian was the only legal language permitted by the Russian tsars, who banned the use of Ukrainian, Lithuanian, Georgian, Armenian, Azeri, and all the other languages spoken by national groups under the rule of Russia.

Cajun English and French were once banned in southern Louisiana by practice if not by law. Even as recently as August 8, 2006, Mary Tutwiler writes in a blog entitled "The French Connection," "Many local French speakers were so traumatized by the experience of being punished for speaking their mother tongue in school that they suppress their linguistic knowledge in public."

For many years, American Indian languages were banned in federal and state schools on reservations. Speaking Faroese was formerly forbidden in the Faroe Islands. A proscription against speaking Korean was imposed by the Japanese during their occupation of Korea between 1910 and 1945. Throughout history many languages and dialects have been banned to various degrees.

In France, a notion of the "standard" (the dialect spoken in Paris) as the only correct form of the language is promoted by the French Academy, an official panel of "scholars" who determine what usage constitutes the "official

French language." Some years ago, the Academy enacted a law forbidding the use of "Franglais," which are words of English origin like *le parking, le week-end*, and *le hotdog*. The French, of course, continue to use them, and because such words are notorious, they are widely used in advertising, where being noticed is more important than being correct. Only in government documents can these proscriptions be enforced.

In the past (and to some extent in the present), a French citizen from the provinces who wished to succeed in French society nearly always had to learn the prestigious Parisian French dialect. Then, several decades ago, members of regional autonomy movements demanded the right to use their own languages in their schools and for official business. In the section of France known as l'Occitanie, the popular singers sing in Langue d'oc, a Romance language of the region, both as a protest against the official language policy and as part of the cultural revival movement.

In many places in the world (including the United States), the use of sign languages of the deaf was once banned. Children in schools for the deaf were often punished if they used any gestures at all. The aim of these schools was to teach deaf children to read lips and to communicate through sound. This view prevented early exposure to language. It was mistakenly thought that children, if exposed to sign, would not learn to read lips or produce sounds. Individuals who become deaf after learning a spoken language are often able to use their knowledge to learn to read lips and continue to speak. This is, however, very difficult if one has never heard speech sounds. Furthermore, even the best lip readers can comprehend only about one-third of the sounds of spoken language. Imagine trying to decide whether *lid* or *led* was said by reading the speaker's lips. Mute the sound on a TV set and see what percentage of a news broadcast you can understand, even if recorded and played back in slow motion, and even if you know the subject matter.

In recent years in the United States, a movement has arisen to establish English as an official language by amending the Constitution. An "Official English" initiative was passed by the electorate in California in 1986; in Colorado, Florida, and Arizona in 1988; and in Alabama in 1990. Such measures have also been adopted by seventeen state legislatures. This kind of linguistic chauvinism is opposed by civil rights minority-group advocates, who point out that such a measure could be used to prevent large numbers of non-English-speaking citizens from participating in civil activities such as voting, and from receiving the benefits of a public education, for which they pay through taxes. Fortunately, as of this writing, the movement appears to have lost momentum.

African American English

The language, only the language. . . . It is the thing that black people love so much—the saying of words, holding them on the tongue, experimenting with them, playing with them. It's a love, a passion. Its function is like a preacher's: to make you stand up out of your seat, make you lose yourself and hear yourself. The worst of all possible things that could happen would be to lose that language.

TONI MORRISON, interviewed in *The New Republic*, March 21, 1981

Most regional dialects of the United States are largely free from stigma. Some regional dialects, like the *r*-less NewYorkese, are the victims of so-called humor, and speakers of one dialect may ridicule the "drawl" (vowel diphthongization) of southerners or the "twang" (excessive nasality) of Texans, even though not all speakers of southern dialects drawl, nor do all Texans twang.

There is, however, a *social* dialect of North American English that has been a victim of prejudicial ignorance. This dialect, **African American English (AAE)**,[1] is spoken by a large population of Americans of African descent. The distinguishing features of this English dialect persist for social, educational, and economic reasons. The historical discrimination against African Americans has created the social boundaries that permit this dialect to thrive. In addition, particularly in recent years, many blacks have embraced their dialect as a means of positive group identification. AAE is generally used in casual and informal situations, and is much more common among working-class people. African Americans from middle- or upper-class backgrounds and with higher levels of education are now more likely to be speakers of SAE. U.S. President Barack Obama and First Lady Michelle Obama are cases in point.

Since the onset of the civil rights movement in the 1960s, AAE has been the focus of national attention. Some critics attempt to equate its use with inferior genetic intelligence and cultural deprivation, justifying these incorrect notions by stating that AAE is a "deficient, illogical, and incomplete" language. Such epithets cannot be applied to any language, and they are as unscientific in reference to AAE as to Russian, Chinese, or Standard American English. The cultural-deprivation myth is as false as the idea that some dialects or languages are inferior. A person may be "deprived" of one cultural background, but be rich in another.

Some people, white and black, think they can identify the race of a person by speech alone, believing that different races inherently speak differently. This belief is patently false. A black child raised in Britain will speak the British dialect of the household. A white child raised in an environment where AAE is spoken will speak AAE. Children learn the language they hear around them.

AAE is discussed here more extensively than other American dialects because it provides an informative illustration of the morphological and syntactic regularities of a dialect of a major language, and the systematic differences from the so-called standard dialects of that language. A vast body of research shows that there are the same kinds of linguistic differences between AAE and SAE as occur between many of the world's major dialects.

Phonological Differences between African American English and SAE

Because AAE is not a single, monolithic dialect, but rather refers to a collection of tightly related dialects, not everything discussed in this section applies to all speakers of AAE.

---

[1]AAE is actually a group of closely related dialects also variously called African American Vernacular English (AAVE), Black English (BE), Inner City English (ICE), and Ebonics.

r-Deletion

Similar to several dialects of both British and American English, some speakers of AAE have a rule of *r-deletion* that deletes /r/ everywhere except before a vowel. Pairs of words like *guard* and *god*, *nor* and *gnaw*, *sore* and *saw*, *poor* and *Poe*, *fort* and *fought*, and *court* and *caught* may be pronounced identically by those speakers of AAE because of this phonological rule. There is also an *l-deletion* rule for some speakers of AAE, creating identically pronounced pairs like *toll* and *toe*, *all* and *awe*, *help* and *hep*.

A *consonant cluster reduction* rule in AAE simplifies consonant clusters, particularly at the ends of words and when one of the two consonants is an alveolar (/t/, /d/, /s/, or /z/). The application of this rule may delete the past-tense morpheme so that *meant* and *mend* are both pronounced as *men*, and *past* and *passed* (*pass + ed*) may both be pronounced like *pass*. When speakers of this dialect say *I pass the test yesterday*, they are not showing an ignorance of past and present-tense forms of the verb, but are pronouncing the past tense according to this rule in their grammar.

The deletion rule is optional; it does not always apply, and studies have shown that it is more likely to apply when the final [t] or [d] does not represent the past-tense morpheme, as in nouns like *paste* [pest] as opposed to verbs like *chased* [tʃest], where the final past tense [t] will not always be deleted. This has also been observed with final [s] and [z], which will be retained more often by speakers of AAE in words like *seats* /sit + s/, where the /s/ represents plural, than in words like *Keats* /kits/, where it is more likely to be deleted to yield the surface form [kit].

Consonant cluster reduction is not unique to AAE. It exists optionally for many speakers of other dialects including SAE. For example, in SAE the medial [d] in *didn't* is often deleted, producing [dĩnt]. Furthermore, nasals are commonly deleted before final voiceless stops, to result in [hĩt] versus [hĩnt].

Neutralization of [ɪ] and [ɛ] before Nasal Consonants

AAE shares with many regional dialects a lack of distinction between /ɪ/ and /ɛ/ before nasal consonants, producing identical pronunciations of *pin* and *pen*, *bin* and *Ben*, *tin* and *ten*, *him* and *hem* and so on. The vowel sound in these words is roughly between the [ɪ] of *pit* and the [ɛ] of *pet*.

Diphthong Reduction

AAE has a rule that reduces the diphthong /ɔɪ/ before /l/ to the simple vowel [ɔ] without the glide, so that *boil* and *boy* are pronounced [bɔ].

$$/ɔɪ/ \rightarrow /ɔ/$$

This rule is common throughout the regional dialects of the South irrespective of race and social class.

Loss of Interdental Fricatives

A regular feature is the change of /θ/ to /f/ and /ð/ to /v/ at the ends of syllables so that *Ruth* is pronounced [ruf] and *brother* is pronounced [brʌvər]. This [θ]-[f] correspondence also holds in some dialects of British English, in which /θ/ is not even a phoneme. *Think* is regularly [fĩnk] in Cockney English.

Initial /ð/ in such words as *this*, *that*, *these*, and *those* are pronounced as [d]. This is again not unique to AAE, but a common characteristic of certain regional, nonethnic dialects of English, many of which are found in the state of New Jersey as well as in New York City and Boston.

Another regular feature found in many varieties of AAE (and non-AAE) is the substitution of a glottal stop for /d/ at the end of non-word-final syllables; thus the name *Rodman* is pronounced [raʔmə̃n], but the word *rod* is pronounced [rad]. In fact, we observed in chapter 5 on phonetics that the glottal stop [ʔ] is a common allophone of /t/ in many dialects of English.

All of these differences are rule-governed and similar to the kinds of phonological variations that are found in languages all over the world, including Standard American English.

Syntactic Differences between AAE and SAE

And of his port as meeke as is a mayde
He nevere yet no vileynye ne sayde

GEOFFREY CHAUCER, Prologue to *The Canterbury Tales*, 14th century

Syntactic differences also exist between dialects. They have often been used to illustrate the illogic of AAE, and yet these differences are evidence that AAE is as syntactically complex and as logical as SAE.

Multiple Negatives

Constructions with multiple negatives akin to AAE *He don't know nothing* are commonly found in languages of the world, including French, Italian, and the English of Chaucer, as illustrated in the epigraph from *The Canterbury Tales*. The multiple negatives of AAE are governed by rules of syntax and are not illogical.

Deletion of the Verb Be

In most cases, if in Standard American English the verb can be contracted, in African American English sentences it is deleted; where it can't be contracted in SAE, it can't be deleted in AAE, as shown in the following sentences:

SAE	AAE
He is nice/He's nice.	He nice.
They are mine/They're mine.	They mine.
She is going to do it/She's gonna do it.	She gonna do it.
He is/he's as nice as he says he is.	He as nice as he say he is.
*He's as nice as he says he's	*He as nice as he say he.
How beautiful you are.	How beautiful you are.
*How beautiful you're.	*How beautiful you.
Here I am.	Here I am.
*Here I'm.	*Here I.

These examples show that syntactic reduction rules operate in both dialects although they show small systematic differences.

Habitual **Be**

In SAE, the sentence *John is happy* can be interpreted to mean *John is happy now* or *John is generally happy*. One can make the distinction clear in SAE only by lexical means, that is, the addition of words. One would have to say *John is generally happy* or *John is a happy person* to disambiguate the meaning from *John is presently happy*.

In AAE, this distinction is made syntactically; an uninflected form of *be* is used if the speaker is referring to *habitual* state.

John be happy.	"John is always happy."
John happy.	"John is happy now."
*John be happy at the moment.	
He be late.	"He is habitually late."
He late.	"He is late this time."
*He be late this time.	
Do you be tired?	"Are you generally tired?"
You tired?	"Are you tired now?"
*Do you be tired today?	

The ungrammatical sentences are caused by a conflict of the habitual meaning with the momentary meaning conveyed by *at the moment, this time,* and *today*. The syntactic distinction between habitual and nonhabitual aspect also occurs in SAE, but with verbs other than *be*. In SAE eventive verbs (see chapter 4) such as *walk*, when marked with the present-tense *-s* morpheme, have only a habitual meaning and cannot refer to an ongoing situation: *Susan walks to school* is habitual, and *Susan walks to school* is ungrammatical if the intended meaning is *Susan is walking to school* as a description of a presently observed event. On the other hand, with a stative verb such as *love, John loves Mary* refers to an ongoing or habitual situation and *John is loving Mary* is ungrammatical with that meaning though it may be interpretable as something like 'John is presently *making* love to Mary.'

There Replacement

Some AAE dialects replace SAE *there* with *it's* in positive sentences, and *don't* or *ain't* in negative sentences.

It's a fly messing with me.	"There's a fly messing with me."
Ain't no one going to help you.	
Don't no one going to help you.	"There's no one going to help you."

Combined with multiple negatives, consonant cluster simplification, and complement deletion, speakers produce highly condemned, but clear, logically sound, even colorful sentences like *Ain't no hard worker never get no good payin' job*: 'There isn't a hard worker who never gets a good paying job.'

Latino (Hispanic) English

A major group of American English dialects is spoken by native Spanish speakers or their descendants. For more than a century large numbers of immigrants from Spanish-speaking countries of South and Central America, Mexico, and the Caribbean islands have been enriching the United States with their language and culture. Among these groups are native speakers of Spanish who have learned or are learning English as a second language. There are also those born in Spanish-speaking homes whose native language is English, some of whom are monolingual, and others who speak Spanish as a second language.

One cannot speak of a homogeneous Latino dialect. In addition to the differences between bilingual and monolingual speakers, the dialects spoken by Puerto Rican, Cuban, Guatemalan, and El Salvadoran immigrants or their children are somewhat different from one another and also from those spoken by many Mexican Americans in the Southwest and California, called **Chicano English (ChE)**. Although ChE is not homogeneous, we can still recognize it as a distinct dialect of American English with systematic differences from other dialects of English.

Chicano English

Chicano English (ChE) is acquired as a first language by many children, making it the native language of hundreds of thousands, if not millions, of Americans. It is not English with a Spanish accent but, like African American English, a mutually intelligible dialect that differs systematically from SAE. Many of the differences, however, depend on the social context of the speaker. (This is also true of AAE and most "minority" dialects.) Linguistic differences of this sort that vary with the social situation of the speaker are termed **sociolinguistic variables**. For example, the use of nonstandard forms like double negation is often associated with pride of ethnicity, which is part of the social context. Many Chicano speakers (and speakers of AAE) are **bidialectal**; they can use either ChE (or AAE) or SAE, depending on the social situation.

Phonological Variables of ChE

Phonological differences between ChE and SAE reveal the influence of Spanish on ChE. For example, as discussed in chapters 5 and 6, English has eleven vowel phonemes (not counting the diphthongs): /i, ɪ, e, ɛ, æ, u, ʊ, o, ɔ, a, ʌ/. Spanish, however, has only five: /i, e, u, o, a/. Chicano speakers whose native language is Spanish may substitute the Spanish vowel system for the English. When this is done, several homonyms result that have distinct pronunciations in SAE. Thus *ship* and *sheep* are both pronounced like *sheep*; *rid* is pronounced like *read*, and so on. Chicano speakers whose native language is English may choose to speak the ChE dialect despite having knowledge of the full set of American English vowels.

Other differences involve consonants. The affricate /tʃ/ and the fricative /ʃ/ are interchanged, so that *shook* is pronounced as if spelled with a *ch* and *check* as if spelled with an *sh*. Also, some consonants are devoiced; for example, /z/ is pronounced [s] in words like *easy* [isi] and *guys* [gaɪs]. Another difference is the substitution of /t/ for /θ/, and /d/ for /ð/ word initially, so *thin* is pronounced like *tin* or *teen* and *they* is pronounced *day*.

ChE has word-final consonant cluster reduction. *War* and *ward* are both pronounced like *war*; *star* and *start* like *star*. This process may also delete past-tense suffixes (*poked* is pronounced like *poke*) and third-person singular agreement suffixes (*He loves her* becomes *he love her*). Word-final alveolar-cluster reduction (e.g., pronouncing *fast* as if it were spelled *fass*) has become widespread among all dialects of English, including SAE. Although this process is often singled out for speakers of ChE and AAE, it is actually no longer dialect-specific.

Prosodic aspects of speech in ChE such as vowel length and intonation patterns may also differ from SAE and give ChE a distinctive flavor. The Spanish sequential constraint, which does not permit a word to begin with an /s/ cluster, is sometimes carried over to ChE in speakers who acquire English after early childhood. Thus *scare* may be pronounced as if it were spelled *escare*, and *school* as if it were spelled *eschool*.

Syntactic Variables in ChE

There are also regular syntactic differences between ChE and SAE. In Spanish, a negative sentence uses a negative morpheme before the verb even if another negative appears; thus negative concord (the multiple negatives mentioned earlier) is a regular rule of ChE syntax:

SAE	ChE
I don't have any money.	I don have no money.
I don't want anything.	I no want nothin.

Lexical differences also occur, such as the use of *borrow* in ChE for *lend* in SAE (*Borrow me a pencil*), or *barely* in ChE for *just* in SAE (*The new Prius had barely come out when I bought one*), as well as many other often subtle differences.

Genderlects

2006 Berkeley Breathed/Washington Post Writer's Group/Cartoonist Group

Dialects are defined in terms of groups of speakers, and speakers are most readily grouped by geography. Thus, regional dialects are the most apparent and generally are what people mean when they use the word *dialect*. Social groups are more amorphous, and social dialects correspondingly less well delineated and, until recently, less well studied. Surprisingly, the most obvious division of humankind into groups—women and men—has not engendered (if you'll pardon the expression) as much dialectal attention as regional and social divisions.

In the earliest work on women and language a number of features were identified that occurred more frequently in women's speech than in men's. For example, women "hedge" their speech more often than men do, with expressions like *I suppose, I would imagine, This is probably wrong, sort of, but . . .* , and so on. Women also use tag questions more frequently to qualify their statements (*He's not a very good actor, is he?*), as well as words of politeness (e.g., *please, thank you*) and intensifying adjectives such as *really* and *so* (*It's a really good film, It's so nice of you*). It was claimed that the use of these devices was due to uncertainty and a lack of confidence on the part of women.

Since this early work, an increasing number of scholars have been conducting research on language, gender, and sexism, investigating the differences between male and female speech and their underlying causes. Many sociolinguists studying gender differences in speech now believe that women use hedges and other, similar devices not because they lack confidence but in order to express friendliness and solidarity, a sharing of attitudes and values, with their listeners.

There is a widespread belief that when men and women converse, women talk more and also that they tend to interrupt more than men in conversation. This is a frequent theme in sitcoms and the subject of jokes and sayings in various cultures, such as the Irish proverb: "Where there are women there is talk, and where there are geese there is cackling," or the Native American "A squaw's tongue runs faster than the wind's legs." However, serious studies of mixed-sex conversations show that in a number of different contexts men dominate the talking, particularly in non-private conversation such as television interviews, business meetings, and conference discussion where talking can increase one's status.

This dominance of males in mixed speech situations seems to develop at an early age. It occurs in classroom situations in which boys dominate talk time with the teachers. One study found that boys were eight times more likely to call out answers than girls. There is also evidence that teachers encourage this dominant behavior, reprimanding girls more often than boys when they call out.

It has also been observed that women typically have a more standard speech style. For example, they are less likely to use vernacular forms such as the reduction of *-ing* to *-in'* or *him* to *'im* as in *I was walkin' down the street when I saw 'im*. Some dialects of British English drop word-initial [h] in casual speech as in *'arf an hour* (half an hour), *'enry* (Henry), *'appy* (happy). This *h*-less pronunciation happens more frequently in the speech of men than women. The tendency for women to speak more "properly" than men has been confirmed in many studies and appears to develop at an early age. Children as young as six show this pattern, with girls avoiding the vernacular forms used more commonly by boys from the same background.

The general view among sociolinguists is that women speak more "proper" English than men because of an insecurity caused by sexism in society. Among the more specific reasons that have been suggested are that women use more standard language to gain access to senior-level jobs that are often less available to them, that society tends to expect "better" behavior in general from women than men, that people who find themselves in subordinate roles (as women do in many societies) must be more polite, and that men prefer to use more vernacular forms because it helps to identify them as tough and strong. However, elsewhere it has been suggested that most sociolinguistic experiments are conducted by middle-class, well-educated academics and it is possible that the women who are interviewed "accommodate" to the interviewer, changing their speech to be more like the interviewer's or simply in response to the more formal nature of the interview situation. Men, on the other hand, may be less responsive to these perceived pressures.

The different variants of English used by men and women are sometimes called "genderlects" (a blend of *gender* and *dialect*). Variations in the language of men and women occur in many, if not all, languages. In Japanese, women may choose to speak a distinct female dialect, although they know the standard dialect used by both men and women. The Japanese language has many *honorific* words—words intended to convey politeness, respect, humility, and lesser social status in addition to their regular meaning. As noted earlier, women tend to use polite forms more often than men. Japanese has formal and informal verbal inflections (see exercise 17, chapter 6), and again, women use the formal forms more frequently. There are also different words in Japanese used in male and female speech: for example,

	Women's Word	Men's Word
stomach	onaka	hara
delicious	oishii	umai
I/me	watashi	boku

and phrases such as:

eat a meal	gohan-o taberu	meshi-o kuu
be hungry	onaka-ga suita	hara-ga hetta
	'stomach become empty'	'stomach decrease'

One effect of the different genderlects of Japanese shows up in the training of guide and helper dogs. The animals learn their commands in English because the sex of the owner is not known in advance, and it is easier for an impaired person to use English commands than it is for trainers to train the dog in both language styles.

The differences discussed thus far have more to do with language use—lexical choices and conversational style—than with grammatical rules. There are, however, cases in which the language spoken by men and women differs in its grammar. In the Muskogean language Koasati, spoken in Louisiana, words that end in /s/ when spoken by men end in /l/ or /n/ when used by women;

for example, the word meaning 'lift it' is *lakawhol* for women and *lakawhos* for men. Similarly, in Bengali women often use [l] at the beginning of words where men use [n]. In Yana, women's words are sometimes shorter than men's because of a suffix that men use. For example, the women's form for 'deer' is *ba*, the men's *ba-na*; for 'person' we find *yaa* versus *yaa-na*; and so on. Early explorers reported that the men and women of the Carib Indians used different dialects. The putative historical reason for this is that long ago a group of Carib-speaking men invaded an area inhabited by Arawak-speaking people and killed all the men. The women who remained then continued to use Arawak while their new husbands spoke Carib.

In Chiquitano, a Bolivian language, the grammar of male language includes a noun-class gender distinction, with names for males and supernatural beings morphologically marked in one way, and nouns referring to females marked in another. In Thai, utterances may end with "politeness particles," *kʰrap* for men and *kʰa* for women (tones omitted). Thai also has different pronouns and fixed expressions like *please* and *thank you* that give each genderlect a distinctive character.

One obvious phonetic characteristic of female speech is its relatively higher pitch, caused mainly by shorter vocal tracts. Nevertheless, studies have shown that the difference in pitch between male and female voices is generally greater than could be accounted for by physiology alone, suggesting that some social factors may be at work, possibly beginning during language acquisition.

Margaret Thatcher, the former prime minister of England, is a well-known example of a woman altering her vocal pitch, in this case for political reasons. Thatcher's regular speaking voice was quite high and a little shrill. She was counseled by her advisors to lower her voice and to speak more slowly and monotonously in order to sound more like an authoritative man. This artificial speaking style became a strong characteristic of her public addresses.

Sociolinguistic Analysis

Speakers from different socioeconomic classes often display systematic speech differences, even when region and ethnicity are not factors. These social-class dialects differ from other dialects in that their sociolinguistic variables are often statistical in nature. With regional and social dialects, a differing factor is either present or absent (for the most part), so regional groups who say *frying pan* say it pretty much all the time, as do the regional groups who say *skillet*. Speakers of AAE dialects will say *she pretty* meaning 'she is pretty' with great regularity, other factors being equal. But social-class dialects differentiate themselves in a more quantitative way; for example, one class of speakers may apply a certain rule 80 percent of the time to distinguish it from another that applies the same rule 40 percent of the time.

The linguist William Labov carried out a sociolinguistic analysis in New York City that focused on the rule of *r*-dropping that we discussed earlier, and its use by upper-, middle-, and lower-class speakers.[2] In this classic study, a model for subsequent sociolinguistic analyses, Labov first identified three department stores that catered primarily to the three classes: Saks Fifth Avenue, Macy's, and S. Klein—upper, middle, and lower, respectively. To elicit data,

---

[2]Labov, W. 1966. *The social stratification of English in New York City.* Washington, DC: Center for Applied Linguistics.

he would go to the three stores and ask questions that he knew would evoke the words *fourth* and *floor*. People who applied the *r*-dropping rule would pronounce these words [fɔθ] and [flɔ], whereas ones who did not apply the rule would say [fɔrθ] and [flɔr].

The methodology behind much of this research is important to note. Labov interacted with all manner of people in their own environment where they were comfortable, although he took care when analyzing the data to take into account ethnic and gender differences. In gathering data he was careful to elicit naturally spoken language through his casual, unassuming manner. Finally, he would evoke the same answer twice by pretending not to hear or understand, and in that way was able to collect both informal, casual utterances, and utterances spoken (the second time) with more care.

In Saks, the high-end department store, 62 percent of respondents pronounced the *r* at least some of the time; in Macy's, the less expensive store, it was 52 percent, and in Klein's, the lower-end retailer, a mere 21 percent. The *r*-dropping rule, then, is socially "stratified," to use Labov's terminology, with the lower socio-class dialects applying the rule most often. What makes Labov's work so distinctive is his methodology and his discovery that the differences among dialects can be usefully defined on a quantitative basis of rule applications rather than as the strict presence or absence of a rule. He also showed that social context and the sociolinguistic variables that it governs play an important role in language change (discussed in the following chapter).

Languages in Contact

Even a dog we do know is better company than a man whose language we know not.

ST. AUGUSTINE, *City of God*, 5th century

Human beings are great travelers and traders and colonizers. The mythical tales of nearly all cultures tell of the trials and tribulations of travel and exploration, such as those of Odysseus (Ulysses) in Homer's *Odyssey*. Surely one of the tribulations of ranging outward from your home is that sooner or later you will encounter people who do not speak your language, nor you theirs. In some parts of the world, for example in bilingual communities, you may not have to travel very far at all to find the language disconnect, and in other parts you may have to cross an ocean. Because this situation is so common in human history and society, several solutions for bridging this communication gap have arisen.

Lingua Francas

Language is a steed that carries one into a far country.

ARAB PROVERB

Many areas of the world are populated by people who speak diverse languages. In such areas, where groups desire social or commercial communication, one language is often used by common agreement. Such a language is called a **lingua franca**.

In medieval times, a trade language based largely on the languages that became modern Italian and Provençal came into use in the Mediterranean ports. That language was called Lingua Franca, 'Frankish language.' The term *lingua franca* was generalized to other languages similarly used. Thus, any language can be a lingua franca.

English has been called "the lingua franca of the whole world" and is standardly used at international business meetings and academic conferences. French, at one time, was "the lingua franca of diplomacy." Russian serves as the lingua franca in the countries of the former Soviet Union, where many different local languages are spoken. Latin was a lingua franca of the Roman Empire and of western Christendom for a millennium, just as Greek served eastern Christendom as its lingua franca. Yiddish has long served as a lingua franca among Jewish people, permitting Jews of different nationalities to communicate with one another.

More frequently, lingua francas serve as trade languages. East Africa is populated by hundreds of villages, each speaking its own language, but most Africans of this area learn at least some Swahili as a second language, and this lingua franca is used and understood in nearly every marketplace. A similar situation exists in Nigeria, where Hausa is the lingua franca.

Hindi and Urdu are the lingua francas of India and Pakistan. The linguistic situation of this area of the world is so complex that there are often regional lingua francas—usually local languages surrounding commercial centers. Thus the Dravidian language Kannada is a lingua franca for the area surrounding the southwestern Indian city of Mysore. A similar situation existed in Imperial China.

In modern China, 94 percent of the people speak Han languages, which can be divided into eight major language groups that for the most part are mutually unintelligible. Within each language group there are hundreds of dialects. In addition to the Han languages, there are more than fifty "national minority" languages, including the five principal ones: Mongolian, Uighur, Tibetan, Zhuang, and Korean.

The situation is complex, and therefore the government inaugurated an extensive language reform policy to establish as a lingua franca the Beijing dialect of Mandarin, with elements of grammar from northern Chinese dialects, and enriched with the vocabulary of modern colloquial Chinese. They called this dialect *Putonghua*, meaning 'common speech.' The native languages and dialects are not considered inferior. Rather, the approach is to spread the "common speech" so that all may communicate with one another in this lingua franca.

Certain lingua francas arise naturally; others are instituted by government policy and intervention. In many parts of the world, however, people still cannot speak with their neighbors only a few miles away.

Contact Languages: Pidgins and Creoles

The charmer's name was Gaff. I'd seen him around. Bryant must have upped him to the Blade Runner unit. That gibberish he talked was city speak—gutter talk—a mishmash of Japanese, Spanish, German, what have you. I didn't really need a translator. I knew the lingo. Every good cop did. But I wasn't gonna make it easier for him.

DECKARD, from the motion picture *Bladerunner*, 1981

A lingua franca is typically a language with a broad base of native speakers, likely to be used and learned by persons with different native languages (usually in the same language family). Often in history, however, speakers of mutually unintelligible languages have been brought into contact under specific socioeconomic and political conditions and have developed a language to communicate with one another that is not native to anyone. Such a language is called a **pidgin**.

Many pidgins developed during the seventeenth, eighteenth, and nineteenth centuries, in trade colonies along the coasts of China, Africa, and the New World. These pidgins arose through contact between speakers of colonial European languages such as English, French, Portuguese, and Dutch, and the indigenous, non-European languages. Some pidgins arose among extended groups of slaves and slave owners in the United States and the Caribbean in the nineteenth century. Other cases include Hawaiian Pidgin English, which was established on the pineapple plantations of Hawaii among immigrant workers from Japan, China, Portugal, and the Philippines; Chinook Jargon, which evolved among the Indian tribes of the Pacific Northwest as a lingua franca among the tribes themselves as well as between the tribes and European traders; and various pidgins that arose during the Korean and Vietnam Wars for use between foreign soldiers and local civilians.

In all these cases the contact is too specialized and the cultures too widely separated for the native language of any one group to function effectively as a lingua franca. Instead, the two or more groups use their native languages as a basis for developing a rudimentary lingua franca with reduced grammatical structures and small lexicons. Also in these situations, it is generally the case that one linguistic group is in a more powerful position, economically or otherwise, such as the relationship of plantation owner to worker or slave owner to slave. Most of the lexical items of the pidgin come from the language of the dominant group. This language is called the **superstrate** or **lexifier language**. For example, English (the language of the plantation owners) is the superstrate language for Hawaiian Pidgin English, Swahili for the various forms of Pidgin Swahili spoken in East and Central Africa, and Bazaar Malay for pidgins spoken in Malaysia, Singapore, and Indonesia. The other language or languages also contribute to the lexicon and grammar, but in a less obvious way. These are called **substrate languages**. Japanese, Chinese, Tagalog, and Portuguese were the substrate languages of Hawaiian Pidgin English and all contributed to its grammar. Chinook Jargon had features both from indigenous languages of the area such as Chinook and Nootka and from French and English.

Many linguists believe that pidgins form part of a linguistic "life cycle." In the very early stage of development the pidgin has no native speakers and is strictly a contact language. Its use is reserved for specialized functions, such as trading or work-oriented tasks, and its speakers speak their (respective) native languages in all other social contexts. In this early stage the pidgin has little in the way of clear grammatical rules and few (usually specialized) words. Later, however, if the language continues to exist and be necessary, a much more regular and complex form of pidgin evolves—what is sometimes called a "stabilized pidgin"—and this allows it to be used more effectively in a variety of situations. Further development leads to the creation of a **creole**, which most linguists believe has all the grammatical complexity of an ordinary language. **Pidginization** (the creation of a pidgin) thus involves a *simplification* of languages and a reduction in the number of domains of use. **Creolization**, in contrast, involves the linguistic *expansion* in the lexicon and grammar of existing pidgins, and an increase in the contexts of use. We discuss creoles and creolization further in the next section.

Although pidgins are in some sense rudimentary, they are not devoid of rules. The phonology is rule-governed, as in any human language. The inventory of phonemes is generally small; for example, whereas Standard English has fourteen distinct vowel sounds, pidgins commonly have only five to seven, and each phoneme may have many allophonic pronunciations. In one English-based pidgin, for example, [s], [ʃ], and [tʃ] are all possible pronunciations of the phoneme /s/; [masin], [maʃin], and [matʃin] all mean 'machine.' Sounds that occur in both the superstrate and substrate languages will generally be maintained, but if a sound occurs in the superstrate but not in the substrates, it will tend to be eliminated. For example, the English sounds [ð] and [θ] as in *this* and *thing* are quite uncommon across languages. Many speakers of English pidgins convert these *th* sounds to more common ones, pronouncing "this thing" as *dis ting*.

Typically, pidgins have fewer grammatical words such as auxiliary verbs, prepositions, and articles, and inflectional morphology, including tense and case endings, as in:

He bad man.   "He is a bad man."
I no go bazaar.   "I'm not going to the market."

Affixal morphology is largely absent. For example, some English pidgins have the word *sus* from the English *shoes*, but *sus* does not include a plural morpheme as it is used to refer to both a single shoe and multiple shoes. Note that this has happened in the development of English, too. Originally, the ending *–a* was a plural marker for Latinate words such as *agenda* but has come to have a singular meaning and the plural of agenda is now *agendas*.

Verbs and nouns usually have a single shape and are not altered to mark tense, number, gender, or case. The set of pronouns is often simpler in pidgins. In Kamtok, an English-based pidgin spoken in Cameroon, the pronoun system does not show gender or all the case differences that exist in Standard English (SE).

Kamtok			**SE**		
a	mi	ma	I	me	my
yu	yu	yu	you	you	your
i	i/am	i	he	him	his
i	i/am	i	she	her	her
wi	wi	wi	we	us	our
wuna	wuna	wuna	you	you	your
dem	dem/am	dem	they	them	their

Pidgins also may have fewer prepositions than the languages on which they are based. In Kamtok, for example, *fɔ* means 'to,' 'at,' 'in,' 'for,' and 'from,' as shown in the following examples:

Gif di buk fɔ mi.	"Give the book to me."
I dei fɔ fam.	"She is at the farm."
Dɛm dei fɔ chɔs.	"They are in the church."
Du dis wan fɔ mi, a bɛg.	"Do this for me, please."
Di mɔni dei fɔ tebul.	"The money is on the table."
You fit muf tɛn frank fɔ ma kwa.	"You can take ten francs from my bag."

Other morphological processes are more productive in pidgins. Reduplication is common, often to indicate emphasis. For example, in Kamtok, *big* means 'big' and *big-big* means 'enormous'; *luk* means 'look' and *luk-luk* means 'stare at.' Compounding is also productive and serves to increase the otherwise small lexicons.

big ai	greedy
drai ai	brave
gras bilong fes	beard
gras antap long ai	eyebrow
gras bilong head	hair
han bilong pisin	wing (of a bird)
fella bilong Mrs. Queen	husband of the queen

Most words in pidgin languages also function as if they belong to several syntactic categories. For example, the Kamtok word *bad* can function as an adjective, noun, or adverb:

Adjective	tu bad pikin	two bad children
Noun	We no laik dis kain bad.	We don't like this kind of badness.
Adverb	A liakam bad.	I liked it very much.

In terms of syntax, early pidgins have a simple clausal structure, lacking embedded sentences and other complex complements. And word order may be variable so that speakers from different linguistic backgrounds can adopt the word order of their native language and still be understood. For example, Japanese is an SOV (verb final) language, and a Japanese speaker of an English-based pidgin may put the verb last, as in *The poor people all potato eat*. On the other hand, a Filipino speaker of Tagalog, a VSO language, may put the verb first, as in *Work hard these people*. Word order eventually becomes more established in pidgins and creoles, which over time become more like other languages with respect to the range of clause types.

Pidgin has come to have negative connotations, perhaps because many pidgins were associated with European colonial empires. The *Encyclopedia Britannica* once described a pidgin as "an unruly bastard jargon, filled with nursery imbecilities, vulgarisms and corruptions." It no longer uses such a definition. In recent times there is greater recognition that pidgins reflect human creative linguistic ability and show many of the same design properties as other languages.

Pidgins also serve a useful function. For example, it is possible to learn an English-based pidgin well enough in six months to begin many kinds of semi-professional training. Learning English for the same purpose might take ten times as long. In areas with many mutually unintelligible languages, a pidgin can play a vital role in unifying people of different cultures and ethnicities.

In general, pidgins are short-lived, perhaps spanning several human generations, though a few have lasted much longer. Pidgins may die out because the speakers all come to share a common language. This was the fate of Chinook Jargon, whose speakers all learned English. Also, because pidgins are often disdained, there is social pressure for speakers to learn a "standard" language, usually the one on which the pidgin is based. For example, through massive education, English replaced a pidgin spoken on New Zealand by the Maoris. Though it failed to succumb to years of government interdiction, Chinese Pidgin English could not resist the onslaught of English that fueled its demise by the close of the nineteenth century. Finally, and ironically, the death of a pidgin language may come about because of its success in uniting diverse communities; the pidgin proves so useful and becomes so widespread that successive generations in the communities in which it is spoken adopt it as their native tongue, elaborating its lexicon and grammar to become a creole.

Creoles and Creolization

Padi dɛm; kɔntri; una ɔl we de na Rom.
Mɛk una ɔl kak una yes. A kam bɛr Siza,
a nɔ kam prez am.

WILLIAM SHAKESPEARE, *Julius Caesar*, translated to Krio by Thomas Decker

Creoles are particularly interesting because they represent an extreme of language change, but it is the mechanisms of language change, which are ubiquitous in the history of every language and every language family, that have made creoles what they are.

IAN ROBERTS, "Verb Movement and Markedness," in Michel DeGraff, ed., *Language Creation and Language Change*, 1999

A creole is defined as a language that has evolved in a contact situation to become the native language of a generation of speakers. The traditional view is that creoles are the creation of children who, exposed to an impoverished and unstable pidgin, develop a far richer and more complex language that shares the fundamental characteristics of a "regular" human language and allows speakers to use the language in all domains of daily life.

In contrast to pidgins, creoles may have inflectional morphology for tense, plurality, and so on. For example, in creoles spoken in the South Pacific the affix *-im* is added to transitive verbs, but when the verb has no object the *-im* ending does not occur:

man i pairip**im** masket.
man be fired-him musket
'The man fired the musket.'

masket i pairip.
musket be fired
'The gun was fired.'

The same affix *-im* is used derivationally to convert adjectives into verbs like English *-en* in *redden*:

bik	big	bikim	to enlarge; to make something bigger
daun	down	daunim	to lower; to make something go down
nogut	no good	nogutim	to spoil, damage; to make something no good

Creoles typically develop more complex pronoun systems. For example, in the creoles of the South Pacific there are two forms of the pronoun *we*: inclusive *we* referring to speaker and listener, and exclusive *we* referring to the speaker and other people but not the listener. The Portuguese-based Cape Verdean Creole has three classes of pronouns: strong, weak, and clitic (meaning affixed to another word, like the possessive *'s* of English), as illustrated in Table 7.1.

The compounds of pidgins often reduce in creoles: for example, *wara bilong skin* (water belong skin) meaning 'sweat' becomes *skinwara*. The compound *baimbai* (by and by), used to indicate future time, becomes a tense inflection *ba* in the creole. Thus, the sentence *baimbai yu go* ('you will go') becomes *yu bago*. The phrasal structure of creoles is also vastly enriched, including embedded and relative clauses, among many other features of "regular" languages.

How are children able to construct a creole based on the rudimentary input of the pidgin? One answer is that they used their innate linguistic capacities to rapidly transform the pidgin into a full-fledged language. This would account for the many grammatical properties that creoles have in common: for example, SVO word order and tense and aspect distinctions.

It should be noted that defining pidgins and creoles in terms of whether they are native (creoles) versus non-native second languages (pidgins) is not without problems. There are languages such as Tok Pisin, widely spoken in New Guinea, which are first languages to many speakers, but also used as second contact languages by other speakers. Some linguists have also rejected the

TABLE 7.1 | Cape Verdean Creole Pronouns

	Emphatic (Strong) Forms	Free (Weak) Forms	Subject Clitics	Object Clitics
1sg	ami	mi	N-	-m
2sg (informal)	abo	bo	bu-	-bu/-u
2sg (formal, masc.)	anho	nho	nhu-	
2sg (formal, fem.)	anha	nha		
3sg	ael	el	e-	-l
1pl	anos	nos	nu-	-nu
2pl	anhos	nhos		
3pl	aes	es	-s	

idea that creoles derive from pidgins, claiming that the geographic areas and social conditions under which they develop are different.

Moreover, the view that children are the creators of creoles is not universally accepted. Various linguists believe that creoles are the result of imperfect second language learning of the lexifier or dominant language by adults and the "transfer" of grammatical properties from their native non-European languages. This hypothesis would account for some of the characteristics that creoles share with L2 "interlanguages" (see chapter 9 on language acquisition): for example, invariant verb forms, lack of determiners, and the use of adverbs rather than verbs and auxiliaries to express tense and modality.

Although some linguists believe that creoles are simpler systems than "regular" languages, most researchers who have closely examined the grammatical properties of various creoles argue that they are not structurally different from non-creole languages and that the only exceptional property of creoles is the sociohistorical conditions under which they evolve.

Creoles often arose on slave plantations where Africans of many different tribes spoke mutually incomprehensible African languages. Haitian Creole, based on French, developed in this way, as did the "English" spoken in parts of Jamaica. Gullah is an English-based creole spoken by the descendants of African slaves on islands off the coast of Georgia and South Carolina. Louisiana Creole, related to Haitian Creole, is spoken by large numbers of blacks and whites in Louisiana. Krio, the language spoken by as many as a million Sierra Leoneans, and illustrated in the epigraph to this section, developed at least in part from an English-based pidgin.

One of the theories concerning the origins of African American English is that it derives from an earlier English-based creole that developed when Africans slaves had no common language other than the English spoken by their colonial masters. Proponents of this hypothesis point out that at least some of the unique features of AAE are traceable to influences of the West African languages once spoken by the slaves, or their parents/grandparents in any case. Also, several of the features of AAE, such as aspect marking (distinct from that which occurs in Standard English), are typical of creole languages.

The alternative view is that AAE formed directly from English without any pidgin/creole stage. It is apparent that AAE is closer to Southern dialects of American English than to other dialects. It is possible that the African slaves learned the English of white Southerners as a second language. It is also possible that many of the distinguishing features of Southern dialects were acquired from AAE during the many decades in which a large number of Southern white children were raised by black women and played with black children.

Tok Pisin, originally a pidgin, was gradually creolized throughout the twentieth century. It evolved from Melanesian Pidgin English, once a widely spoken lingua franca of Papua New Guinea used by English-speaking traders and the native population. Because New Guinea is so linguistically diverse—more than eight hundred different languages were once spoken on the island—the pidgin came to be used as a lingua franca among the indigenous population as well.

Tok Pisin has its own writing system, its own literature, and its own newspapers and radio programs; it has even been used to address a United Nations meeting. Papers in (not *on*!) Tok Pisin have been presented at linguistics conferences in Papua New Guinea, and it is commonly used for debates in the parliament of the country. Today, Tok Pisin is one of the three recognized national languages of The Independent State of Papua New Guinea, alongside English and Kiri Motu, another creole.

Sign languages may also be pidgins. In Nicaragua in the 1980s, adult deaf people came together and constructed a crude system of "home" signs and gestures in order to communicate. It had the characteristics of a pidgin in that different people used it differently and the grammatical rules were few and varied. However, when young deaf children joined the community, an amazing event took place. The crude sign language of the adults was tremendously enhanced by the children learning it, so much so that it emerged as a rich and complex sign language called Idioma de Signos Nicaragüense (ISN), or Nicaraguan Sign Language. ISN provides an impressive demonstration of the development of a grammatically complex language from impoverished input and the power of human linguistic creativity.

The study of pidgins and creoles has contributed a great deal to our understanding of the nature of human language and the processes involved in language creation and language change, and of the sociohistorical conditions under which these instances of language contact occurred.

Bilingualism

He who has two languages has two souls.

ANONYMOUS

The term **bilingualism** refers to the ability to speak two (or more) languages, either by an individual speaker, **individual bilingualism**, or within a society, **societal bilingualism**. In chapter 9, on language acquisition, we discuss how bilingual children may simultaneously acquire their two languages, and how second languages are acquired by children and adults. There are various degrees of individual bilingualism. Some people have native-like control of two languages, whereas others make regular use of two languages with a high degree of proficiency but lack the linguistic competence of a native or near-native speaker in one or the other language. Also, some bilinguals may have oral competence but cannot read or write one or more of their languages.

The situations under which people become bilingual may vary. Some people grow up in a household in which more than one language is spoken; others move to a new country where they acquire the local language, usually from people outside the home. Still others learn second languages in school. In communities with rich linguistic diversity, contact between speakers of different languages may also lead to bilingualism.

Bilingualism (or multilingualism) also refers to the situation in nations in which two (or more) languages are spoken and recognized as official or national languages. Societal bilingualism exists in many countries, including Canada, where English and French are both official languages, and Switzerland, where French, German, Italian, and Romansch all have official status.

Interestingly, research shows that there are fewer bilingual individuals in bilingual countries than in so-called "unilingual" countries. This makes sense when you consider that in unilingual countries such as the United States, Italy, and France, people who do not speak the dominant language must learn some amount of it to function. Also, the main concern of multilingual states has been the maintenance and use of two or more languages, rather than the promotion of individual bilingualism among its citizens.

The United States is broadly perceived as a monolingual English-speaking society even though there is no reference to a national language in the Constitution. However, there are numerous bilingual communities with long histories throughout the country. English-Spanish bilinguals are measurably more numerous than any other combination according to the 2010 census, but the variety of languages found among bilingual and multilingual people living in the U.S. is far too numerous to mention and perhaps not even known to its fullest extent.

Recent studies reveal that a shift to monolingual English is growing rapidly and that knowledge of Spanish and other common bilingual partners of English (e.g., Tagalog, Vietnamese, and various languages of China) is being lost faster in the twenty-first century than at any other period of history.

Codeswitching

When they first met, she'd never seemed to stop talking, bubbling over, switching from German to English as if one language couldn't contain it, everything she had to say.

JOSEPH KANON, *Istanbul Passage*, 2012

Codeswitching is a speech style unique to bilinguals, in which fluent speakers switch languages between or within sentences, as illustrated by the following sentence:

Sometimes I'll start a sentence in English and termino en español.
Sometimes I'll start a sentence in English and finish it in Spanish.

Codeswitching is a universal language-contact phenomenon that reflects the grammars of both languages working simultaneously. Bilingual Spanish-English speakers may switch between English and Spanish as in the above example, whereas Quebecois in Canada switch between French and English:

I mean, c'est un idiot, ce mec-là.
I mean he's an idiot, that guy.

The following examples are from German-English, Korean-English, and Mandarin-English bilinguals:

Johan hat mir gesagt that you were going to leave.
Johan told me you were going to leave.

Chigum ton-uls ops-nunde, I can't buy it.
As I don't have money now, I can't buy it.

Women zuotian qu kan de movie was really amazing.
The movie we went to see yesterday was really amazing.

Codeswitching occurs wherever groups of bilinguals speak the same two languages. Furthermore, codeswitching occurs in specific social situations, enriching the repertoire of the speakers.

A common misconception is that codeswitching is indicative of a language disability of some kind, for example, that bilinguals use codeswitching as a coping strategy for incomplete mastery of both languages, or that they are speaking "broken" English. These characterizations are completely inaccurate. Recent studies of the social and linguistic properties of codeswitching indicate that it is a marker of bilingual identity, and has its own internal grammatical structure. For example, bilinguals will commonly codeswitch between a subject and a verb, as in:

Mis amigos finished first.   My friends finished first.

but would judge ungrammatical a switch between a subject pronoun and a verb as in:

*Ellos finished first.   They finished first.

Codeswitchers also follow the word order rules of the languages. For example, in a Spanish noun phrase, the adjective usually follows the noun, as opposed to the English NP in which it precedes, as shown by the following:

English: My mom fixes **green tamales**.   (Adj N)
Spanish: Mi mamá hace **tamales verdes**.   (N Adj)

A speaker might codeswitch as follows:

My mom fixes **tamales verdes**.
or   Mi mamá hace **green tamales**.

but would not accept or produce such utterances as

*My mom fixes **verdes tamales**.
or   *Mi mamá hace **tamales green**.

because the word order within the NPs violates the rules of the language.

Codeswitching is to be distinguished from (bilingual) **borrowing**, which occurs when a word or short expression from one language occurs embedded among the words of a second language and adapts to the regular phonology, morphology, and syntax of the second language. In codeswitching, in contrast, the two languages that are interwoven preserve their own phonological and other grammatical properties. Borrowing can be easily distinguished from codeswitching by the pronunciation of an element. Sentence (1) involves borrowing, and (2) codeswitching.

(1) I love biscottis [bɪskaɾiz] with my coffee.
(2) I love biscotti [biskɔt:i] with my coffee.

In sentence (1) *biscotti* takes on an (American) English pronunciation and plural *-s* morphology, while in (2) it preserves the Italian pronunciation and plural morpheme *-i* (plural for *biscotto*, 'cookie').

What needs to be emphasized is that people who codeswitch have knowledge not of one but of two (or more) languages and that codeswitching, like linguistic knowledge in general, is highly structured and rule-governed.

Language and Education

> Outside of a dog, a book is a man's best friend; inside of a dog, it's too dark to read.
>
> GROUCHO MARX (1890–1977)

The study of language has important implications in various educational arenas. An understanding of the structure, acquisition, and use of language is essential to the teaching of foreign and second languages, as well as to reading instruction. It can also promote a fuller understanding of language variation and use in the classroom and inform the often heated debates surrounding issues such as how to teach reading to children, bilingual education, and Ebonics.

Second-Language Teaching Methods

> He can learn a language in a fortnight. Knows dozens of them: the sure mark of a fool.
>
> HENRY HIGGINS, From the script of the motion picture *Pygmalion*, 1938.

We may disagree with Professor Higgins on two counts: first, despite claims on the Internet to the contrary, one cannot learn a language in two weeks, certainly not with a useful degree of fluency. And secondly, a person who *does* know "dozens of them" is surely not a fool.

Many approaches to second or foreign language teaching have been developed over the years. Though these methods can differ significantly from one another, many experts believe that there is no single best method for teaching a second language. All methods have something to offer, and virtually any method can succeed with a gifted teacher who is a native or near-native speaker, motivated students, and appropriate teaching materials. All methods are most effective when they fit a given educational setting and when they are understood and embraced by the teacher.

Second-language teaching methods fall into two broad categories: the *synthetic approach* and the *analytic approach*. As the name implies, the synthetic approach stresses the teaching of the grammatical, lexical, phonological, and functional units of the language step by step. This is a bottom-up method. The task of the learner is to put together—or synthesize—the discrete elements that make up the language. The more traditional language teaching methods, which stress grammar instruction, fall into this category.

An extreme example of the synthetic approach is the **grammar translation** method favored up until the mid-1960s, in which students learned lists of vocabulary, verb paradigms, and grammatical rules. Learners translated passages from the target language into their native language. The teacher typically conducted class in the students' native language, focusing on the grammatical parsing of texts, and there was little or no contextualization of the language being taught. Reading passages were carefully constructed to contain only vocabulary and structures to which learners had already been exposed, and errors in translation were corrected on the spot. Learners were tested on their mastery of rules, verb paradigms, and vocabulary. The students did not use the target language very much except in reading translated passages aloud.

Analytic approaches are more top-down. The goal is not to explicitly teach the component parts or rules of the target language. Rather, the instructor selects topics, texts, or tasks that are relevant to the needs and interests of the learner, whose job then is to discover the constituent parts of the language. This approach assumes that adults can extract the rules of the language from unstructured input, more or less like a child does when acquiring his first language.

Currently, one of the most widely practiced analytic approaches is *content-based instruction*, in which the focus is on making the language meaningful and on getting the student to communicate in the target language. Learners are encouraged to discuss issues and express opinions on various topics of interest to them in the target language. Topics for discussion might include "Online Dating" or "Taking Responsibility for Our Environment." Grammar rules are taught on an as-needed basis, and fluency takes precedence over grammatical accuracy. Classroom texts (both written and aural) are generally taken from sources that were not created specifically for language learners, on the assumption that these will be more interesting and relevant to the student. Assessment is based on the learner's comprehension of the target language.

Not all second-language teaching methods fall clearly into one or the other category. The synthetic and analytic approaches should be viewed as the opposite ends of a continuum along which various second-language methods may fall. Also, teachers practicing a given method may not strictly follow all the principles of the method. Actual classroom practices tend to be more eclectic, with teachers using techniques that work well for them and to which they are accustomed—even if these techniques are not in complete accordance with the method they are practicing.

Teaching Reading

"Baby Blues" © Baby Blues Partnership. Reprinted with permission of King Features Syndicate.

As we shall discuss in chapter 9, language development (whether of a spoken or sign language) is a biologically driven process with a substantial innate component. Parents do not teach their children the grammatical rules of their language. Indeed, they are typically not even aware of the rules themselves. Rather, the young child is naturally predisposed to uncover these rules from the language he hears around him. The way we learn to read and write, however, is quite different from the way we acquire the spoken/signed language.

First, and most obviously, children learn to talk (or sign) at a very young age, while reading typically begins when the child is school-age (around five or six years old in most cases, although some children are not reading-ready until even later). A second important difference is that across cultures and languages, given appropriate language input from the environment all children acquire a spoken/signed language while many children never learn to read or write. This may be because they are born into cultures for which there is no written form of the language. It is also unfortunately the case that even some children born into literate societies do not learn to read, either because they suffer from a specific reading disability, **dyslexia**; because of other yet-to-be-diagnosed learning disabilities; or simply because they have not been properly taught. It is important to recognize, however, that even an illiterate child or adult has a mental grammar of his or her language and is able to speak/sign and understand perfectly well.

The most important respect in which spoken/signed language development differs from learning to read is that reading requires specific instruction and conscious effort, whereas under normal circumstances language acquisition does not. Which kind of instruction works best for teaching reading has been a topic of considerable debate for many decades. Three main approaches have been tried.

The first—the *whole-word approach*—teaches children to recognize a vocabulary of some fifty to one hundred words by rote learning, often by seeing the words used repeatedly in a story: for example, *Run, Spot, Run* from the Dick and Jane series well-known to people who learned to read in the 1950s. Other words are acquired gradually. This approach does not teach children to "sound out" words according to the individual sounds that make up the words. Rather, it treats the written language as though it were a logographic system, like that of Chinese, in which a single written character corresponds to a whole word or word root. In other words, the whole-word approach fails to take advantage of the fact that English (and the writing systems of most literate societies) is based on an alphabet, in which the symbols correspond to the individual sounds (roughly phonemes) of the language. This is ironic because alphabetic writing systems are the easiest to learn and are maximally efficient for transcribing any human language.

A second approach—*phonics*—emphasizes the correspondence between letters and the sounds associated with them. Phonics instruction begins by teaching children the letters of the alphabet and then encourages them to sound out words based on their knowledge of the sound-letter correspondences. So, if you have learned to read the word *gave* (understanding that the *e* is silent), then it is easy to read *save* and *pave*.

However, English and many other languages do not show a perfect correspondence between sounds and letters. For example, the rule for *gave*, *save*, and *pave* does not extend to *have*. The existence of many such exceptions has encouraged some schools to adopt a third approach to reading, the *whole-language approach* (also called "literature-based" or "guided reading"), which was most popular in the 1990s. The key principle is that phonics should not be taught directly. Rather, the child is supposed to make the connections between sounds and letters herself based on exposure to text. For example, she would be encouraged to figure out an unfamiliar word based on the context of the sentence or by looking for clues in the story line or the pictures rather than by sounding it out, as illustrated in the cartoon.

The philosophy behind the whole-language approach is that learning to read, like learning to speak, is a natural act that children can basically do on their own—an assumption that, as we noted earlier, is questionable at best. With the whole-language approach, the main job of the teacher is to make the reading experience an enjoyable one. To this end, children are presented with engaging books and are encouraged to write stories of their own as a way of instilling a love of reading and words.

Despite the intuitive appeal of the whole-language approach—after all, who would deny the educational value of good literature and creative expression in learning?—research has clearly shown that under most circumstances understanding the relationship between letters and sounds is critically important in reading. One of the assumptions of the whole-language approach is that skilled adult readers do not sound out words when reading, so proponents question the value of focusing on sounding out in reading instruction. However, research shows that the opposite is true: skilled adult readers *do* sound out words mentally, and they do so very rapidly. Another study compared groups of college students who were taught to read unfamiliar symbols such as Arabic letters, one group by a phonics approach and the other with a whole-word approach. Those trained with phonics could read many more new words. Similar results have been obtained through computer modeling of how children learn to read. Classroom studies have also compared phonics with whole-word or whole-language approaches and have shown that phonics instruction produces better results for beginning readers.

At this point, the consensus among psychologists and linguists who do research on reading—and a view shared by many teachers—is that reading instruction must be grounded in a firm understanding of the connections between letters and sounds, and that whole-language activities that make reading fun and meaningful for children should be used to supplement phonics instruction. Based on such research, the federal government now promotes the inclusion of phonics in reading programs across the United States.

Literacy in the Deaf Community

Hearing children use their knowledge of the sound-letter correspondences to learn to read, but deaf children do not have access to this phonological base. Learning to read poses a particular challenge for deaf children and literacy rates in the deaf community are very low. On average deaf high school graduates in the Unites States read at a fourth grade level, barely enough to read the newspaper. However, some deaf students learn to read very well, at levels equal to hearing students. How do they do this without being able to rely on a phonological code?

Prior to 1960 deaf children in the United States were educated exclusively through oral instruction, using lip reading and amplification via hearing aids to increase awareness of sound. Nowadays a widespread method of reading instruction is to first teach deaf children one of a number of signing systems referred to as Manually Coded English (MCE), essentially English on the hands. Unlike ASL, MCE systems are synthesized, consisting essentially in the replacement of each spoken English word (and grammatical elements such as the -*s* ending for plurals and the -*ed* ending for past tense) by a sign. So the syntax and morphology of MCE is approximately the same as those of spoken English. As a communication system MCE is unnatural—similar to trying to speak French by translating every English word or ending into its French counterpart. Difficulties also arise because there are not always corresponding forms in the two languages. The problem is amplified with sign languages because they use multidimensional space while spoken languages are sequential. Consequently, deaf children frequently distort aspects of MCE so that it more closely resembles a natural sign language, for example by making creative use of signing space. However, many teachers of the deaf believe that learning *to sign* English can facilitate learning *to read* English.

Surprisingly perhaps, the most successful deaf readers are not those with the most intensive oral training in English. Rather, various studies show that deaf children born to deaf parents—children who are fluent, early learners of ASL—tend to be better readers than deaf children born to hearing parents who are generally not exposed to ASL, or exposed later in life. Many researchers therefore believe that the most important factor contributing to reading success in deaf children is deep knowledge of a language. ASL and other signed languages are the most accessible to deaf people and therefore facilitate reading, even despite the fact that ASL and English are structured quite differently. Additionally, some deaf children of hearing parents who receive sustained MCE input from parents and who are fluent users of MCE also achieve reading levels comparable to deaf children of deaf parents. According to Rachel Mayberry, a leading researcher of sign language and deaf education, this "confirms the suspicion that robust language is the key to learning to read."

In line with many bilingual educators, as discussed in the next section, the most current thinking in deaf education (though not the most widespread at this point) is that knowing one language (ASL) makes it easier to learn another language (English). Under this view the goal of the deaf school should be to provide deaf bilingual education, promoting, or when necessary teaching ASL as a first language, and then English as a second language, through the use of print, sound, or sign.

Bilingual Education

> The United States of America has more monolingual experts on bilingual education than any other country in the world.
>
> ROBERTO BAHRUTH, Perspective on Teaching English Language Learners, 2004

As discussed earlier, there are many bilingual communities in the United States and members of these communities typically have varying levels of English proficiency. People who have recently arrived in the United States may have virtually no knowledge of English, other individuals may have only limited knowledge, and others may be fully bilingual. Native language development is untutored and happens before children begin school, but many children find themselves in classroom situations in which their native language is not the language of instruction. There has been a great deal of debate among researchers, teachers, parents, and the general public over the best methods for teaching English to school-age children as well as over the value of maintaining and promoting their native language abilities.

There are several kinds of bilingual programs in American schools for immigrant children. In **Transitional Bilingual Education** (TBE) programs, students receive instruction in both English and their native language, and the native language support is gradually phased out over two or three years. In **Bilingual Maintenance** (BM) programs, students remain in bilingual classes for their entire educational experience. Another program, **Dual Language Immersion**, enrolls English-speaking children and students who are native in another language in roughly equal numbers. The goal here is for all the students to become bilingual. This kind of program serves as a BM program for non-English speakers and a foreign language immersion program for the English-speaking children.

Many studies have shown that immigrant children benefit from instruction in their native language. Bilingual classes allow the children to first acquire in their native language school-related vocabulary, speech styles, and other aspects of language that are specific to a school environment while they are learning English. It also allows them to learn content material and keep up with other children during the time it takes them to master English. Recent studies that compared the effectiveness of different types of programs have found that children enrolled in bilingual programs outperformed children in English-only programs, and that children enrolled in BM programs did better than TBE students.

Despite the benefits that a bilingual education affords immigrant students, these programs have been under increasing attack since the 1970s. In the past few years measures against bilingual education have been passed in several states, including California, Arizona, and Massachusetts. These measures mandate that immigrant students "be taught English by being taught in English" in an English-only approach known as Sheltered English Immersion (SEI). Proponents claim that one year of SEI is sufficient for children, especially young children, to learn English well enough to be transferred to a mainstream classroom. Research does not bear out these claims, however. Studies show that only a small minority of children, around 3 percent to 4 percent of children in SEI programs and 13 percent to 14 percent in bilingual programs, acquire English within a year. A considerable body of research shows that for the vast majority of children it takes from two to five years to develop oral proficiency in English and four to seven years to develop proficiency in academic English.

There are several possible causes for the chasm between research results and public policy regarding bilingual education. Bilingual programs can be poorly implemented and so not achieve the desired results. There may also be a public perception that it is too costly to implement bilingual programs. It is likely that some of the backlash against bilingual education is due to anti-immigrant sentiment, but there are also many well-intentioned people who mistakenly believe that bilingualism is a handicap and that children will be more successful academically and socially if they are quickly and totally immersed in the more prestigious majority language.

Minority Dialects

Children who speak a dialect of English that differs from the language of instruction—usually close to Standard English—may also be disadvantaged in a school setting. Literacy instruction is generally based on SAE. It has been argued that the phonological and grammatical differences between African American English (AAE) and SAE make it harder for AAE-speaking children to learn to read and write.

One approach to this problem has been to discourage children from speaking AAE and to correct each departure from SAE that the children produce. SAE is presented as the "correct" way to speak and AAE as substandard or incorrect. This approach has been criticized as being psychologically damaging to the child as well as impractical. Attempts to consciously correct children's nonstandard dialect speech are routinely met with failure. Moreover, one's language/ dialect expresses group identity and solidarity with friends and family. A child may take a rejection of his language as a rejection of him and his culture.

A more positive approach to teaching literacy to speakers of nonstandard dialects is to encourage **bidialectalism**. This approach teaches children to take pride in their language, encouraging them to use it in informal circumstances, with family and friends, while also teaching them a second dialect—SAE—that is necessary for reading, writing, and classroom discussion. As a point of comparison, in many countries, including Switzerland, Germany, and Italy, children grow up speaking a nonstandard dialect at home but learn the standard language once they enter school. This underscores that bidialectalism that combines a home dialect and a school/national language is entirely feasible. Educational programs that respect the home language may better facilitate the acquisition of a standard dialect. Ideally, the bidialectal method would also include class discussion of the phonological and grammatical differences between the two dialects, which would require that teachers understand the linguistic properties of AAE, or whatever the minority dialect happens to be, as well as some linguistics in general.

Language in Use

Language is not an abstract construction of the learned, or of dictionary-makers, but is something arising out of the work, needs, ties, joys, affections, tastes, of long generations of humanity, and has its bases broad and low, close to the ground.

WALT WHITMAN, "*Slang in America*," 1885

One of the themes of this book is that you have a lot of linguistic knowledge that you may not be aware of, but that can be made explicit through the rules of phonology, morphology, syntax, and semantics. You also have a deep social knowledge of your language. You know the appropriate way to talk to your parents, your friends, your clergy, and your teachers. You know about "politically correct" (PC) language: to say "mail *carrier*," "fire*fighter*," and "police *officer*," and not to say "nigger," "wop," and "bitch." In short, you know how to *use* your language appropriately, even if you sometimes choose not to. This section discusses some of the many ways in which the use of language varies in society.

Styles

Most speakers of a language speak one way with friends, another on a job interview or presenting a report in class, another talking to small children, another with their parents, and so on. These "situation dialects" are called **styles**, or **registers**.

Nearly everybody has at least an informal and a formal style. In an informal style, the rules of contraction are used more often, the syntactic rules of negation and agreement may be altered, and many words are used that do not occur in the formal style.

Informal styles, although permitting certain abbreviations and deletions not permitted in formal speech, are also rule-governed. For example, questions are often shortened with the subject *you* and the auxiliary verb deleted. You can ask *Running the marathon?* or *You running the marathon?* instead of the more formal *Are you running the marathon?* but you cannot shorten the question to **Are running the marathon?* Informal talk is not anarchy. It is rule-governed, but the rules of deletion, contraction, and word choice are different from those of the formal language.

It is common for speakers to have competence in several styles, ranging between the two extremes of formal and informal. The use of styles is often a means of identification with a particular group (e.g., family, gang, church, team), or a means of excluding groups believed to be hostile or undesirable (cops, teachers, parents).

Many cultures have rules of social behavior that govern style. Some Indo-European languages distinguish between *you* (familiar) and *you* (polite). German *du* and French *tu* are to be used only with "intimates"; *Sie* and *vous* are more formal and used with nonintimates. Thai has three words meaning 'eat' depending on the social status of who is speaking with whom.

Social situations affect the details of language usage, but the core grammar remains intact, with a few superficial variations that lend a particular flavor to the speech.

Slang

Slang is a language that rolls up its sleeves, spits on its hands, and goes to work.

CARL SANDBURG, quoted in "Minstrel of America: Carl Sandburg," *New York Times*, February 13, 1959

One mark of an informal style is the frequent occurrence of **slang**. Slang is something that nearly everyone uses and recognizes, but nobody can define precisely. It is more metaphorical, playful, elliptical, vivid, and shorter-lived than ordinary language.

The use of slang has introduced many new words into the language by recombining old words into new meanings. *Spaced out, right on, hang-up, drill down,* and *rip-off* have all gained a degree of acceptance. Slang also introduces entirely new words such as *barf, flub, hoodie,* and *dis.* Finally, slang often consists of ascribing entirely new meanings to old words. *Rave* has broadened its meaning to 'an all-night dance party,' where *ecstasy* (slang for a kind of drug) is taken to provoke wakefulness; *crib* refers to one's home and *posse* to one's cohorts. *Weed* and *pot* widened their meaning to 'marijuana'; *pig* and *fuzz* are derogatory terms for 'police officer'; *rap, cool, dig, stoned, split,* and *suck* have all extended their semantic domains.

The words we have cited may sound slangy because they have not gained total acceptability. Words such as *dwindle, freshman, glib,* and *mob* are former slang words that in time overcame their "unsavory" origin. It is not always easy to know where to draw the line between slang words and regular words. The borderland between slang and formal language is ill-defined and is more of a continuum than a strict boundary.

There are scads (another slang word) of sources of slang. It comes from the underworld: *crack, payola, to hang paper.* It comes from college campuses: *crash, wicked, peace.* It even comes from the White House: *pencil* (writer), *still* (photographer), *football* (black box of security secrets).

Slang is universal. It is found in all languages and all time periods. It varies from region to region, and from past to present. Slang meets a variety of social needs and rather than a corruption of the language, it is yet further evidence of the creativity of the human language user. If you are a lover of "crazy" words, you need to know about the online Urban Dictionary at http://www.urbandictionary.com/

Jargon and Argot

Practically every conceivable science, profession, trade, and occupation uses specific slang terms called **jargon**, or **argot**. Linguistic jargon, some of which is used in this book, consists of terms such as *phoneme, morpheme, case, lexicon, phrase structure rule, X-bar schema,* and so on. Part of the reason for specialized terminology is for clarity of communication, but part is also for speakers to identify themselves with persons with whom they share interests.

Because the jargon used by different professional and social groups is so extensive (and so obscure in meaning), court reporters in the Los Angeles Criminal Courts Building have a library that includes books on medical terms, guns, trade names, and computer jargon, as well as street slang.

The computer age not only ushered in a technological revolution, it also introduced a slew of jargon, called, slangily, *computerese,* used by computer "hackers" and others. So vast is this specialized vocabulary that *Webster's New World Computer Dictionary* has four hundred pages and contains thousands of computer terms as entries. A few such words that are familiar to most people are *modem* (from **mod**ulator-**dem**odulator), *bit* (from **b**inary dig**it**), and *byte* ('eight *bits*'). Acronyms and alphabetic abbreviations abound in computer jargon. *ROM* ('read-only memory'), *RAM* ('random-access memory'), *CPU* ('central processing unit'), and *DVD* ('digital video disk') are a small fraction of what's out there.

Some jargon may over time pass into the standard language. Jargon, like all types of slang, spreads from a narrow group that originally embraced it until it is used and understood by a large segment of the population.

Taboo or Not Taboo?

Sex is a four-letter word.

BUMPER STICKER SLOGAN

An item in a newspaper once included the following paragraph:

"This is not a Sunday school, but it is a school of law," the judge said in warning the defendants he would not tolerate the "use of expletives during jury selection." "I'm not going to have my fellow citizens and prospective jurors subjected to filthy language," the judge added.

How can language be filthy? In fact, how can it be clean? The filth or beauty of language must be in the ear of the listener, or in the collective ear of society. The writer Paul Theroux points this out:

A foreign swear-word is practically inoffensive except to the person who has learned it early in life and knows its social limits.

Nothing about a particular string of sounds makes it intrinsically clean or dirty, ugly or beautiful. If you say that you *pricked* your finger when sewing, no one would raise an eyebrow, but if you refer to your professor as a *prick*, the judge quoted previously would undoubtedly censure this "dirty" word.

You know the obscene words of your language, and you know the social situations in which they are desirable, acceptable, forbidden, and downright dangerous to utter. This is true of all speakers of all languages. All societies have their taboo words. (*Taboo* is a Tongan word meaning 'forbidden.') People everywhere seem to have a need for undeleted expletives to express their emotions or attitudes.

Forbidden acts or words reflect the particular customs and views of the society. Among the Zuni Indians, it is improper to use the word *takka*, meaning 'frogs,' during a religious ceremony. In the world of Harry Potter, the evil Voldemort is not to be named but is referred to as "You-Know-Who." In some religions, believers are forbidden to "take the Lord's name in vain," and this prohibition often extends to other religious jargon. Thus the taboo words *hell* and *damn* are changed to *heck* and *darn*, though the results are sometimes not euphonious. Imagine the last two lines of Act II, Scene 1, of *Macbeth* if they were "cleaned up":

Hear it not, Duncan; for it is a knell
That summons thee to heaven, or to heck

Words relating to sex, sex organs, and natural bodily functions make up a large part of the set of taboo words of many cultures. Often, two or more words or expressions can have the same linguistic meaning, with one acceptable and the other taboo. In English, words borrowed from Latin sound "scientific" and therefore appear to be technical and "clean," whereas native Anglo-Saxon counterparts are taboo. Such pairs of words are illustrated as follows:

Anglo-Saxon Taboo Words	Latinate Acceptable Words
cunt	vagina
cock	penis
prick	penis
tits	mammaries
shit	feces, defecate

There is no grammatical reason why the word *vagina* is "clean" whereas *cunt* is "dirty," or why *balls* is taboo but *testicles* acceptable. Although there is no grammatical basis for such preferences, there certainly are sociolinguistic reasons to embrace or eschew such usages, just as there are sociolinguistic reasons for speaking formally, respectfully, disrespectfully, informally, in jargon-, and so on.

Euphemisms

Banish the use of the four-letter words
Whose meaning is never obscure.
The Anglos, the Saxons, those bawdy old birds
Were vulgar, obscene, and impure.
But cherish the use of the weaseling phrase
That never quite says what it means;
You'd better be known for your hypocrite ways
Than vulgar, impure, and obscene.

FOLK SONG ATTRIBUTED TO WARTIME ROYAL AIR FORCE OF GREAT BRITAIN

The existence of taboo words and ideas motivates the creation of **euphemisms**. A euphemism is a word or phrase that replaces a taboo word or serves to avoid frightening or unpleasant subjects. In many societies, because death is feared, there are many euphemisms related to this subject. People are less apt to *die* and more apt to *pass on* or *pass away*. Those who take care of your loved ones who have passed away are more likely to be *funeral directors* than *morticians* or *undertakers*. And then there's *feminine protection*. . . .

The use of euphemisms is not new. It is reported that the Greek historian Plutarch in the first century CE wrote that "the ancient Athenians . . . used to cover up the ugliness of things with auspicious and kindly terms, giving them polite and endearing names. Thus they called harlots *companions*, taxes *contributions*, and prison a *chamber*."

Just as surely as all languages and societies have taboo words, they have euphemisms. The aforementioned taboo word *takka*, meaning 'frogs,' is replaced during a Zuni religious ceremony by a complex compound word that literally translates as 'several-are-sitting-in-a-shallow-basin-where-they-are-in-liquid.' The euphemisms for bodily excretions and sexual activity are legion, and lists of them may be found in online dictionaries of slang. There you will find such gems for urination as *siphon the python* and *point Percy at the porcelain*, and for intercourse *shag*, *hide the ferret* (*salami*, *sausage*), and *toss a little leg*, among a gazillion others.

These euphemisms, as well as the difference between the accepted Latinate "genteel" terms and the "dirty" Anglo-Saxon terms, show that a word or phrase has not only a linguistic **denotative meaning** but also a **connotative meaning** that reflects attitudes, emotions, value judgments, and so on. In learning a language, children learn which words are taboo, and these taboo words differ from one child to another, depending on the value system accepted in the family or group in which the child grows up.

Racial and National Epithets

The use of epithets for people of different religions, nationalities, or races tells us something about the speakers. Words like *kike* (for Jew), *wop* (for Italian), *nigger* or *coon* (for African American), *slant* (for Asian), *towelhead* (for Middle Eastern Arab), and so forth reflect racist and chauvinist views of society.

Even words that sound like epithets are perhaps to be avoided (see exercise 13). An administrator in Washington, D.C. described a fund he administers as "niggardly," meaning stingy. He resigned his position under fire for using a word "so close to a degrading word."

Language, however, is creative, malleable, and ever-changing. The epithets used by a majority to demean a minority may be reclaimed as terms of bonding and friendship among members of the minority. Thus, for some—we emphasize *some*—African Americans, the word *nigger* is used to show affection. Similarly, the ordinarily degrading word *queer* is used among *some* gay people as a term of endearment, as is *cripple* or *crip* among *some* individuals who share a disability.

Language and Sexism

doctor, n. . . . a man of great learning.

THE AMERICAN COLLEGE DICTIONARY, 1947

A businessman is aggressive; a businesswoman is pushy. A businessman is good on details; she's picky. . . . He follows through; she doesn't know when to quit. He stands firm; she's hard. . . . He isn't afraid to say what is on his mind; she's mouthy. He exercises authority diligently; she's power mad. He's closemouthed; she's secretive. He climbed the ladder of success; she slept her way to the top.

FROM "HOW TO TELL A BUSINESSMAN FROM A BUSINESSWOMAN," *The Balloon*, Graduate School of Management, UCLA, 1976

The discussion of obscenities, blasphemies, taboo words, and euphemisms showed that words of a language are not intrinsically good or bad but reflect individual or societal values. This is also seen in references to a woman as a *castrating female, ballsy women's libber*, or *courageous feminist advocate*, depending on who is talking.

Early dictionaries often gave clues to the social attitudes of that time. In some twentieth-century dictionaries, examples used to illustrate the meaning of words include "manly courage" and "masculine charm," as opposed to "womanish tears" and "feminine wiles." Contemporary dictionaries are far more enlightened and try to be scrupulous in avoiding sexist language.

Until recently, most people who heard "My cousin is a professor (or a doctor, or the chancellor of the university, or a steelworker)" would assume that the cousin is a man; if they heard "My cousin is a nurse (or elementary school teacher, or clerk-typist, or house worker)," they would conclude that the cousin is a woman. This is changing because society is changing and people of either sex commonly hold jobs once held primarily by one sex.

Despite flashes of enlightenment, words for women with abusive or sexual overtones abound: *dish, piece, piece of ass, piece of tail, bunny, chick, pussy, bitch, doll, slut, cow*—to name just a few. Far fewer such sexual terms exist for men, and those that do, such as *boy toy, stud muffin, hunk,* and *jock,* are not pejorative in the same way.

It's clear that language reflects sexism. It reflects any societal attitude, positive or negative; languages are infinitely flexible and expressive. But is language itself amoral and neutral? Or is there something about language, or a particular language, that abets sexism? Before we attempt to answer that question, let's look more deeply into the subject, using English as the illustrative language.

Marked and Unmarked Forms

> If the English language had been properly organized . . . then there would be a word which meant both "he" and "she," and I could write, "If John or Mary comes, heesh will want to play tennis," which would save a lot of trouble.
>
> **A. A. MILNE**, *The Christopher Robin Birthday Book*, 1930

In chapter 4 we saw that with gradable antonyms such as *high/low*, one is marked (*low*) and the other unmarked. Ordinarily, the unmarked member of the pair is the one used in questions (*How <u>high</u> is the building?*), measurements (*The building is twenty stories <u>high</u>*), and so on.

Similar to this is an asymmetry between male and female terms in many languages in which there are male/female pairs of words. The male form is generally unmarked and the female term is created by adding a bound morpheme. We have many such examples in English:

Male	Female
heir	heir**ess**
major	major**ette**
hero	hero**ine**
Robert	Robert**a**
equestrian	equestri**enne**
aviator	aviat**rix**

When referring in general to the profession of acting, or flying, or riding horseback, the unmarked terms *actor, aviator,* and *equestrian* are used. The marked terms are used to emphasize the female gender. (A rare exception to this is the unmarked word *widow* for a woman with a deceased husband but *widow**er*** for a man with a deceased wife.)

Moreover, the unmarked third person pronoun in English is male (*he, him, his*). *Everybody had better pay **his** fee next time* allows for the clients to be male or female, but *Everybody had better pay **her** fee next time* presupposes a female client. While there has been some attempt to neutralize the pronoun by using *they,* as in *Every teenager loves their first car,* most teachers find this objectionable and it is unlikely to become the standard. Other attempts to find a suitable genderless third person pronoun have produced such attempts as *e, hesh, po, tey, co, jhe, ve, xe, he'er, thon,* and *na,* none of which speakers have the least inclination to adopt, and it appears likely that *he* and *she* are going to be with us for a while.

With women occupying more and varied roles in society (from combat military to "Wichita Linemen"), many of the marked female forms have been replaced by the male forms, which are used to refer to either sex. Thus women, as well as men, are authors, actors, poets, heroes, heirs, postal carriers, firefighters, and police officers. Women, however, remain countesses, duchesses, and princesses, if they are among this small group of female aristocrats.

The Sapir-Whorf hypothesis, discussed in chapter 1, proposes that the way a language encodes—puts into words—different categories like male and female subtly affects the way speakers of the language think about those categories. Thus, it may be argued that because English speakers are often taught to choose *he* as the unmarked pronoun (*Everyone should respect **him**self*), and to choose *she* only when the referent is overtly female, they tend to think of the male sex as predominant. Likewise, the fact that nouns require special affixes to make them feminine forces people to think in terms of male and female, with the female somehow more derivative because of affixing. The different titles, Mr., Mrs., Miss, and Ms., also emphasize the male/female distinction. Finally, the preponderance of words denigrating females in English and in many other languages may create a climate that is more tolerant of sexist behavior.

Nevertheless, although people can undoubtedly be sexist and even cultures can be sexist, can language be sexist? That is, can we be molded by our language to be something we may not want to be? Or does language merely facilitate any natural inclinations we may have? Or is it simply a reflection of societal values? These questions are still being debated by linguists, anthropologists, psychologists, and philosophers, and no definitive answer has yet emerged.

Secret Languages and Language Games

Throughout the world and throughout history, people have invented secret languages and language games. They have used these special languages as a means of identifying with their group and/or to prevent outsiders from knowing what is being said. One such case is *Nushu*, the women's secret writing of Chinese, which originated in the third century as a means for women to communicate with one another in the sexually repressive societies of imperial China (see exercise 17, chapter 12). American slaves developed an elaborate code that could not be understood by the slave owners. References to "the promised land" or the "flight of the Israelites from Egypt" sung in spirituals were codes for the North and the Underground Railroad.

Language games such as Pig Latin[3] and Ubbi Dubbi (see exercise 7) are used for amusement by children and adults. They exist in all the world's languages and take a wide variety of forms. In some, a suffix is added to each word; in others a syllable is inserted after each vowel. There are rhyming games and

---

[3]Dog is pronounced *og-day*, parrot as *arrot-pay*, and elephant as *elephant-may*, etc., but see exercise 6.

games in which phonemes are reversed. A game in Brazil substitutes an /i/ for all the vowels.

The Walbiri, natives of central Australia, play a language game in which the meanings of words are distorted. In this play language, all nouns, verbs, pronouns, and adjectives are replaced by semantically contrastive words. Thus, the sentence *Those men are small* means *This woman is big*.

These language games provide evidence for the phonemes, words, morphemes, semantic features, and so on that are posited by linguists for descriptive grammars. They also illustrate the boundless creativity of human language and human speakers.

Summary

Every person has a unique way of speaking, called an **idiolect**. The language used by a group of speakers is a **dialect**. The dialects of a language are the mutually intelligible forms of that language that differ in systematic ways from each other. Dialects develop because languages change, and the changes that occur in one group or area may differ from those that occur in another. **Regional dialects** and **social dialects** develop for this reason. Some differences in U.S. regional dialects may be traced to the dialects spoken by colonial settlers from England. Those from southern England spoke one dialect and those from the north spoke another. In addition, the colonists who maintained close contact with England reflected the changes occurring in British English, while earlier forms were preserved among Americans who spread westward and broke communication with the Atlantic coast. The study of regional dialects has produced **dialect atlases**, with **dialect maps** showing the areas where specific dialect characteristics occur in the speech of the region. A boundary line called an **isogloss** delineates each area.

Social dialects arise when groups are isolated socially, such as Americans of African descent in the United States, many of whom speak dialects collectively called African American (Vernacular) English, which are distinct from the dialects spoken by non-Africans.

Dialect differences include phonological or pronunciation differences (often called **accents**), vocabulary distinctions, and syntactic rule differences. The grammar differences among dialects are not as great as the similarities, thus permitting speakers of different dialects to communicate.

In many countries, one dialect or dialect group is viewed as the **standard**, such as **Standard American English** (**SAE**). Although this particular dialect is not linguistically superior, some language purists consider it the only correct form of the language. Such a view has led to the idea that some nonstandard dialects are deficient, as is erroneously suggested regarding **African American English**. A study of African American English shows it to be as logical, complete, rule-governed, and expressive as any other dialect. This is also true of the dialects spoken by Latino Americans whose native language or those of their parents is Spanish. There are bilingual and monolingual Latino speakers of English. One Latino dialect spoken in the Southwest, referred to as **Chicano English** (**ChE**), shows systematic phonological and syntactic differences from SAE that stem from the influence of Spanish. Other differences are shared with many nonstandard ethnic and nonethnic dialects. **Codeswitching** is shifting between languages within a single sentence or discourse by a bilingual speaker. It reflects both grammars working simultaneously and does not represent a form of "broken" English or Spanish or whatever language.

Attempts to legislate the use of a particular dialect or language have been made throughout history and exist today, even extending to banning the use of languages other than the preferred one.

In areas where many languages are spoken, one language may become a **lingua franca** to ease communication among people. In other cases, where traders, missionaries, or travelers need to communicate with people who speak a language unknown to them, a **pidgin** may develop. A pidgin is a simplified system with properties of both the **superstrate** (**lexifier**) and **substrate** languages. When a pidgin is widely used, and constitutes the primary linguistic input to children, it is *creolized*. The grammars of **creole** languages are similar to those of other languages, and languages of creole origin now exist in many parts of the world and include sign languages of the deaf.

The study of language has important implications for education especially as regards reading instruction and the teaching of second language learners, language-minority students, and speakers of nonstandard dialects. Several second-language teaching methods have been proposed for adult second language learners. Some of them focus more on the grammatical aspects of the target language, and others focus more on getting students to communicate in the target language, with less regard for grammatical accuracy.

Writing and reading, unlike speaking and understanding, must be taught. Three methods of teaching reading have been used in the United States: *whole-word*, *whole-language*, and *phonics*. In the whole-word and whole-language approaches, children are taught to recognize entire words without regard to individual letters and sounds. The phonics approach emphasizes the spelling-sound correspondences of the language, and thus draws on the child's innate phonological knowledge.

Immigrant children must acquire English (or whatever the majority language is in a particular country). Younger students must at the same time acquire literacy skills (reading and writing), and students of all ages must learn content material such as math, science, and so on. This is a formidable task. **Bilingual education** programs are designed to help achieve these multiple aims by teaching children literacy and content material in their native language while they are acquiring English. Research has shown that immigrant children benefit from instruction in their native language, but many people oppose these programs.

Children who speak a nonstandard dialect of English that differs from the language of instruction may also be at a disadvantage in a school setting, especially in learning reading and writing. There have been contentious debates over the use of **AAE** in the classroom as a method for helping speakers of that dialect learn Standard English.

Besides regional and social dialects, speakers may use different **styles**, or **registers**, depending on the context. **Slang** is not often used in formal situations or writing but is widely used in speech; **argot** and **jargon** refer to the unique vocabularies used by particular groups of people to facilitate communication, provide a means of bonding, and exclude outsiders.

In all societies, certain acts or behaviors are frowned on, forbidden, or considered **taboo**. The words or expressions referring to these taboo acts are then also avoided or considered "dirty." Language cannot be obscene or clean; attitudes toward specific words or linguistic expressions reflect the views of a culture or society toward the behaviors and actions of the language users. At times, slang words may be taboo while scientific or standard terms with the same meaning are acceptable in "polite society." Taboo words and acts give rise to **euphemisms**, which are words or phrases that replace the expressions to be avoided. Thus, *powder room* is a euphemism for *toilet*, which started as a euphemism for *lavatory*, which is now more acceptable than its replacement.

Just as the use of some words may indicate society's views toward sex, natural bodily functions, or religious beliefs, some words may also indicate racist, chauvinist, or sexist attitudes. Language is not intrinsically racist or sexist but reflects the views of various sectors of a society. However, the availability of offensive terms, and particular grammatical peculiarities such as the lack of a genderless third-person singular pronoun, may perpetuate and reinforce biased views and be demeaning and insulting to those addressed. Thus culture influences language, and, arguably, language may have an influence on the culture in which it is spoken.

The invention or construction of secret languages and language games like Pig Latin attest to human creativity with language and the unconscious knowledge that speakers have of the phonological, morphological, and semantic rules of their language.

References for Further Reading

Carver, C. M. 1987. *American regional dialects: A word geography.* Ann Arbor, MI: University of Michigan Press.

Cassidy, F. G. (chief ed.). 1985, 1991, 1996, 2002, 2012. *Dictionary of American regional English,* Volumes 1, 2, 3, 4, 5. Cambridge, MA: Harvard University Press.

Chambers, J., and P. Trudgill. 1998. *Dialectology, 2nd ed.* Cambridge, UK: Cambridge University Press.

Chambers, J.K. (ed.), P. Trudgill (ed.), and N. Schilling-Estes (ed.). 2004. *The handbook of language variation and change.* Hoboken, NJ: Wiley-Blackwell.

Finegan, E., and J. Rickford (eds.). 2004. *Language in the USA.* Cambridge, UK: Cambridge University Press.

Holm, J. 2000. *An introduction to pidgins and creoles.* Cambridge, UK: Cambridge University Press.

Labov, W. 1972. *Sociolinguistic patterns.* Philadelphia: University of Pennsylvania Press.

————. 1969. The logic of nonstandard English. *Georgetown University 20th Annual Round Table, Monograph Series on Languages and Linguistics,* No. 22.

————. 1966. *The social stratification of English in New York City.* Washington, DC: Center for Applied Linguistics.

Lakoff, R. 1990. *Talking power: The politics of language.* New York: Basic Books.

Roberts, I. 1999. Verb movement and markedness. In Michel DeGraff (ed.), *Language creation and language change, creolization, diachrony and development.* Cambridge, MA: MIT Press, 287–327.

Tannen, D. 1994. *Gender and discourse.* New York: Oxford University Press.

_____. 1990. *You just don't understand: Women and men in conversation.* New York: Ballantine.

Trudgill, P. 2001. *Sociolinguistics: An introduction to language and society, 4th ed.* London: Penguin Books.

Wardhaugh, R. 2006. *An introduction to sociolinguistics, 5th ed.* Oxford: Blackwell.

Wolfram, W., and N. Schilling-Estes. 2006. *American English dialects and variation, 2nd ed.* London: Wiley-Blackwell Publishers.

Exercises

1. Each pair of words is pronounced as shown phonetically in at least one American English dialect. Write in phonetic transcription your pronunciation of each word that you pronounce differently.

    a. horse   [hɔrs]   hoarse   [hors]
    b. morning   [mɔrnɪ̃ŋ]   mourning   [mornɪ̃ŋ]
    c. for   [fɔr]   four   [for]
    d. ice   [ʌɪs]   eyes   [aɪz]
    e. knife   [nʌɪf]   knives   [naɪvz]
    f. mute   [mjut]   nude   [njud]
    g. din   [dĭn]   den   [dẽn]
    h. hog   [hɔg]   hot   [hat]
    i. marry   [mæri]   Mary   [meri]
    j. merry   [mɛri]   marry   [mæri]
    k. rot   [rat]   wrought   [rɔt]
    l. lease   [lis]   grease (v.) [griz]
    m. what   [ʌmat]   watt   [wat]
    n. ant   [ænt]   aunt   [ãnt]
    o. creek   [kʰrɪk]   creak   [kʰrik]

2. **A.** Below is a passage from the Gospel according to St. Mark in Cameroon English Pidgin. See how much you can understand before consulting the English translation given below. State some of the similarities and differences between CEP and SAE.

    a. Di fos tok fo di gud nuus fo Jesus Christ God yi Pikin.
    b. I bi sem as i di tok fo di buk fo Isaiah, God yi nchinda (Prophet), "Lukam, mi a di sen man nchinda fo bifo yoa fes weh yi go fix yoa rud fan."
    c. Di vos fo som man di krai fo bush: "Fix di ples weh Papa God di go, mek yi rud tret."

    Translation:

    a. The beginning of the gospel of Jesus Christ, the Son of God.
    b. As it is written in the book of Isaiah the prophet, "Behold, I send my messenger before thy face, which shall prepare thy way before thee."
    c. The voice of one crying in the wilderness, "Prepare ye the way of the Lord, make his paths straight."

    B. Here are some words from Tok Pisin. What are the English words from which they are derived? The answer is shown for the first entry.

Tok Pisin	Gloss	Answer
taim bilong kol	winter	time belong cold
pinga bilong fut	toe	
hamas krismas yu gat?	how old are you?	
kukim long paia	barbecue	
sapos	if	
haus moni	bank	
kamup	arrive	
tasol	only	
olgeta	all	
solwara	sea	
haus sik	hospital	
handet yia	century	

3. In the period from 1890 to 1904, *Slang and Its Analogues,* by J. S. Farmer and W. E. Henley, was published in seven volumes. The following entries are included in this dictionary. For each item (1) state whether the word or phrase still exists; (2) if not, state what the modern slang term would be; and (3) if the word remains but its meaning has changed, provide the modern meaning.

all out: completely, as in "All out the best." (The expression goes back to as early as 1300.)

to have apartments to let: be an idiot; one who is empty-headed.

been there: in "Oh, yes, I've been there." (Applied to a man who is shrewd and who has had many experiences.)

belly-button: the navel.

berkeleys: a woman's breasts.

bitch: most offensive appellation that can be given to a woman, even more provoking than *whore*.

once in a blue moon: seldom.

boss: master; one who directs.

bread: employment. (1785—"out of bread" = "out of work.")

claim: to steal.

cut dirt: to escape.

dog cheap: of little worth. (Used in 1616 by Dekker: "Three things there are dog-cheap, learning, poorman's sweat, and oathes.")

funeral: as in "It's not my funeral." "It's no business of mine."

to get over: to seduce, to fascinate.

groovy: settled in habit; limited in mind.

grub: food.

head: toilet (nautical use only).

hook: to marry.

hump: to spoil.

hush money: money paid for silence; blackmail.

itch: to be sexually excited.

jam: a sweetheart or a mistress.

leg bags: stockings.

to lie low: to keep quiet; to bide one's time.

to lift a leg on: to have sexual intercourse.

looby: a fool.
malady of France: syphilis. (Used by Shakespeare in 1599.)
nix: nothing.
noddle: the head.
old: money. (1900—"Perhaps it's somebody you owe a bit of the old to, Jack.")
to pill: talk platitudes.
pipe layer: a political intriguer; a schemer.
poky: cramped, stuffy, stupid.
pot: a quart; a large sum; a prize; a urinal; to excel.
puny: a freshman.
puss-gentleman: an effeminate.

4. Suppose someone asked you to help compile items for a new dictionary of slang. List ten slang words, and provide a short definition for each.

5. Below are some words used in British English for which different words are usually used in American English. See whether you can match the British and American equivalents.

British	American
a. clothes peg	candy
b. braces	truck
c. lift	line
d. pram	main street
e. waistcoat	crackers
f. shop assistant	suspenders
g. sweets	wrench
h. boot (of car)	flashlight
i. bobby	potato chips
j. spanner	vacation
k. biscuits	baby buggy
l. queue	elevator
m. torch	can
n. underground	cop
o. high street	wake up
p. crisps	trunk
q. lorry	vest
r. holiday	subway
s. tin	clothes pin
t. knock up	clerk

6. Pig Latin is a common language game of English; but even Pig Latin has dialects, forms of the "language game" with different rules.

   A. Consider the following data from three dialects of Pig Latin, each with its own rule applied to words beginning with vowels:

	Dialect 1	Dialect 2	Dialect 3
"eat"	[itme]	[ithe]	[ite]
"arc"	[arkme]	[arkhe]	[arke]
"expose"	[ɛkspozme]	[ɛkspozhe]	[ɛkspoze]

    i. State the rule that accounts for the Pig Latin forms in each dialect.

    ii. How would you say *honest, admire,* and *illegal* in each dialect? Give the phonetic transcription of the Pig Latin forms.

B. In one dialect of Pig Latin, the word *strike* is pronounced [aɪkstre], and in another dialect it is pronounced [traɪkse]. In the first dialect *slot* is pronounced [atsle] and in the second dialect, it is pronounced [latse].

    i. State the rules for each of these dialects that account for these different Pig Latin forms of the same words.

    ii. Give the phonetic transcriptions for *spot, crisis,* and *scratch* in both dialects.

7. Below are some sentences representing different English language games. Write each sentence in its undistorted form; state the language-game rule.

    a. /aɪ-o tʊk-o maɪ-o dag-o aʊt-o saɪd-o/

    b. /hirli ɪzli əli mɔrli kamliplɪlikelitədli gemli/

    c. Mary-shmary can-shman talk-shmalk in-shmin rhyme-shmyme.

    d. Betpeterer latepate thanpan nevpeverer.

    e. thop-e fop-oot bop-all stop-a dop-i op-um blop-ew dop-own/ðapə fapʊt bapɔl stape dapi apəm blapu dapaʊn/

    f. /kʌbæn jʌbu spʌbik ðʌbɪs kʌbaɪnd ʌbəv ʌbɪŋglʌbɪʃ/ (This sentence is in "Ubby Dubby" from a children's television program popular in the 1970s.)

8. Below are sentences that might be spoken between two friends chatting informally. For each, state what the nonabbreviated full sentence in SAE would be. In addition, state in your own words (or formally if you wish) the rule or rules that derived the informal sentences from the formal ones.

    a. Where've ya been today?

    b. Watcha gonna do for fun?

    c. Him go to church?

    d. There's four books there.

    e. Who ya wanna go with?

9. Compile a list of argot (or jargon) terms from some profession or trade (e.g., lawyer, musician, doctor, longshoreman). Give a definition for each term in nonjargon terms.

10. "Translate" the first paragraph of any well-known document or speech—such as the Declaration of Independence, the Gettysburg Address, or the Preamble to the U.S. Constitution—into informal, colloquial language.

11. Cockney rhyming slang, which arose in the East End of London in the nineteenth century, is a language game played by creating a rhyme as a substitute for a specific word. Thus, for *table* the rhymed slang may be *Cain and Abel*; *missus* is *cows and kisses*; *stairs* are *apples and pears*; *head* is

loaf of bread, and so on. Column A contains some Cockney rhyming slang expressions. Match these to the items in Column B to which they refer.

A	B
a. drip dry	balls (testicles)
b. in the mood	bread
c. insects and ants	ale
d. orchestra stalls	cry
e. Oxford scholar	food
f. strike me dead	dollar
g. ship in full sail	pants

Now construct your own version of Cockney rhyming slang for the following words:

h. chair
i. house
j. coat
k. eggs
l. pencil

12. Column A lists euphemisms for words in Column B. Match each item in A with its appropriate B word.

A	B
a. Montezuma's revenge	condom
b. joy stick	genocide
c. friggin'	fire
d. ethnic cleansing	diarrhea
e. French letter (old)	masturbate
f. diddle oneself	kill
g. holy of holies	urinate
h. spend a penny (British)	penis
i. ladies' cloak room	die
j. knock off (from 1919)	waging war
k. vertically challenged	vagina
l. hand in one's dinner pail	women's toilet
m. sanitation engineer	short
n. downsize	fuckin'
o. peace keeping	garbage collector

13. Defend or criticize the following statement in a short essay:

    A person who uses the word *niggardly* in a public hearing should be censured for being insensitive and using a word that resembles a degrading, racist word.

14. The words *waitron* and *waitperson* are currently fighting it out to see which, if either, will replace *waitress* as a gender-neutral term. Using dictionaries, the Internet, and whatever other resources you can think

of, predict the winner or the failure of both candidates. Give reasons for your answers. If you count hits on Google, analyze the sources to support your conclusions.

15. Search for Tok Pisin on the Internet. You will quickly find Web sites where it is possible to hear Tok Pisin spoken. Listen to a passage several times. How much of it can you understand without looking at the text or the translation? Then follow along with the text (generally provided) until you can hear the individual words. Now try a new passage. Does your comprehension improve? How much practice do you think you would need before you could understand roughly half of what is being said the first time you heard it?

16. A popular language game is to take a word or (well-known) expression and alter it by adding, subtracting, or changing one letter, and supplying a new (clever) definition. Read the following examples, try to figure out the expressions from which they are derived, and then try to produce ten on your own. (Hint: Lots of Latin.)

Cogito eggo sum	I think, therefore I am a waffle.
Foreploy	A misrepresentation about yourself for the purpose of getting laid
Veni, vipi, vici	I came, I am important, I conquered.
Giraffiti	Dirty words sprayed very, very high
Ignoranus	A person who is both stupid and an asshole
Rigor Morris	The cat is dead (maybe for older students)
Felix navidad	Our cat has a boat.
Veni, vidi, vice	I came, I saw, I sold my sister.
Glibido	All talk, no action
Haste cuisine	Fast French food
L'état, c'est moo	I'm bossy around here.
Intaxication	The euphoria that accompanies a tax refund
Ex post fucto	Lost in the mail
Aporcalypse	A disasterous shortage of bacon

17. In his original, highly influential novel *1984*, George Orwell introduces Newspeak, a government-enforced language designed to keep the masses subjugated. He writes:

Its vocabulary was so constructed as to give exact and often very subtle expression to every meaning that a Party member could properly wish to express, while excluding all other meanings and also the possibility of arriving at them by indirect methods. This was done partly by the invention of new words, but chiefly by eliminating undesirable words and by stripping such words as remained of unorthodox meanings, and so far as possible of all secondary meanings whatever. To give a single example, the word *free* still existed in Newspeak, but it could only be used in such statements as "This dog is free from lice" or "This field is free from weeds." It could not be used in its old sense of "politically free" or "intellectually free," since political and intellectual freedom no longer existed even as concepts, and were therefore of necessity nameless.

Critique Newspeak. Will it achieve its goal? Why or why not? (Hint: You may want to review concepts such as language creativity and arbitrariness as discussed in the first few pages of chapter 1.)

18. In *1984* Orwell proposed that if a concept does not exist, it is nameless. In the passage quoted below, he suggests that if a crime were nameless, it would be unimaginable, hence impossible to commit:

    A person growing up with Newspeak as his sole language would no more know that . . . *free* had once meant "intellectually free," than, for instance, a person who had never heard of chess would be aware of the secondary meanings attaching to *queen* and *rook* and *checkmate*. There would be many crimes and errors which it would be beyond his power to commit, simply because they were nameless and therefore unimaginable.

    Critique this notion.

19. One aspect of different English genderlects is lexical choice. For example, women say *darling* and *lovely* more frequently than men; men use sports metaphors such as *home run* and *slam dunk* more than women. Think of other lexical usages that appear to be asymmetric between the sexes.

20. **Research project**: Throughout history many regimes have banned languages. Write a report in which you mention several such regimes, the languages they banned, and possible reasons for banning them (e.g., you might have discovered that the Basque language was banned in Spain under the regime of Francisco Franco (1936–1975) owing in part to the separatist desires of the Basque people and because the Basques opposed his dictatorship).

21. Abbreviated English (AE) is a register of written English used in newspaper headlines and elsewhere. Some examples follow:

    CLINTON IN BULGARIA THIS WEEK
    OLD MAN FINDS RARE COIN
    BUSH HIRES WIFE AS SECRETARY
    POPE DIES IN VATICAN

    AE does not involve an arbitrary omission of parts of the sentence but is regulated by grammatical rules.

    A. Translate each of these headlines into Standard American English (SAE).
    B. What features or rules distinguish AE from SAE?
    C. Are there other contexts (besides headlines) in which we find AE? If so, provide examples.
    D. **Challenge exercise**: What is the time reference of the above headlines (e.g., present, recent past, remote past, future)?
    E. **Challenge exercise**: Is there a difference in possible tense interpretations when the predicate is eventive (e.g., *dies*) and when it is stative (e.g., *in Bulgaria*)? (You may have to review these terms in chapter 4.)

22. Watch several hours of daytime soap operas on television. Write down any euphemisms you think you hear and the taboo subjects they conceal. And yes, if anybody rags on you for wasting your life on daytime TV, show them this homework assignment.

23. You overhear somebody say, "That's not a language, it's a dialect." Compose a brief retort.

24. Recommend three ways in which society can act to preserve linguistic diversity. Be realistic and concrete.

25. Research the history and controversy surrounding the use of "Ebonics" in the classroom. The Internet is a good place to start. Consider both sides of the argument and discuss whether you think this is a good idea and why or why not.

26. The Karen-speaking people of Myanmar claim that their languages (dialects?)—thought to be a Tibeto-Burman group of the Sino-Tibetan family of languages—are banned by the government of Myanmar (as of the year 2012). Research the assertion of this ethnic minority that their language is outlawed and offer evidence regarding the validity of this claim or its falsehood.

27. Quoting again from the script of the movie *Pygmalion*, critique the following lines spoken by Professor Henry Higgins:

   "The English do not know how to speak their own language. Only foreigners who have been taught to speak it speak it well."

8

Language Change: The Syllables of Time

> No language as depending on arbitrary use and custom can ever be permanently the same, but will always be in a mutable and fluctuating state; and what is deem'd polite and elegant in one age, may be accounted uncouth and barbarous in another.

BENJAMIN MARTIN (1704–1782)

All living languages change with time. It is fortunate that they do so rather slowly compared to the human life span. It would be inconvenient to have to relearn our native language every twenty years. As years pass we hardly notice any change. Yet if we were to turn on a radio and miraculously receive a broadcast in our "native language" from the year 1000, we would probably think we had tuned into a foreign language station.

Bereft of spoken recordings, we must consult written records to achieve a sense of language change. We know a great deal of the history of English because it has been a written language for more than 1,300 years. Old English, spoken in England during the first millennium, is scarcely recognizable as English. (Of course, our linguistic ancestors did not call their language Old English!) A speaker of Modern English would find the language unintelligible. There are college courses in which Old English is studied as a foreign language.

A line from *Beowulf* illustrates why Old English must be translated:[1]

Wolde guman findan þone þe him on sweofote sare geteode.
'He wanted to find the man who harmed him while he slept.'

Approximately five hundred years after *Beowulf*, Chaucer wrote *The Canterbury Tales* in what is now called Middle English, spoken from around

---

[1]The letter þ is called *thorn* and is pronounced [θ] in this example.

1100 to 1500. It is more easily understood by present-day readers, as seen by reading the opening of the *Tales*:

> Whan that Aprille with his shoures soote
> The droght of March hath perced to the roote . . .
> 'When April with its sweet showers
> The drought of March has pierced to the root . . .'

Two hundred years after Chaucer, in a language that is considered an early form of Modern English, Shakespeare's *Hamlet* says:

> A man may fish with the worm that hath eat of a king, and eat of the fish that hath fed of that worm.

The stages of English are Old English (449–1100 CE), Middle English (1100–1500), and Modern English (1500–present). This division is somewhat arbitrary, being marked by important dates in English history, such as the Norman Conquest of 1066, the results of which profoundly influenced the English language.

The branch of linguistics that deals with how languages change, what kinds of changes occur, and why they occurred is called **historical and comparative linguistics**. It is "historical" because it deals with the history of particular languages; it is "comparative" because it deals with relations among languages.

Changes in a language are changes in the grammars and the lexicon of people who speak the language and are perpetuated as new generations of children acquire the altered grammars and perhaps make further changes to be passed on to their children. All parts of the grammar are subject to change over the course of time—the phonological, morphological, syntactic, and semantic components may be affected. Although most of the examples in this chapter are from English, the histories of all languages show similar effects. This is true of sign languages as well as spoken languages. Like all living languages, American Sign Language continues to change. Not only have new signs entered the language over the past two hundred years, but also the forms of the signs have changed in ways similar to the ways spoken languages change.

The Regularity of Sound Change

> That's not a regular rule: you invented it just now.
>
> **LEWIS CARROLL**, *Alice's Adventures in Wonderland*, 1865

The southern United States represents a major dialect area of American English. For example, words pronounced with the diphthong [aɪ] in non-Southern English will usually be pronounced with the monophthong [aː] in the South. Local radio and TV announcers at the 1996 Olympics in Atlanta called athletes to the [haː] "high" jump, and local natives invited visitors to try Georgia's famous pecan [paː] "pie." The [aɪ]-[aː] correspondence of these two dialects is an example of a **regular sound correspondence**. When [aɪ] occurs in a word in non-Southern dialects, [aː] occurs in the Southern dialect, and *this is true for all such words.*

The different pronunciations of *I*, *my*, *high*, *pie*, and so on did not always exist in English. In this chapter we will discuss how such dialect differences arose and why the sound differences are usually regular and not confined to just a few words. We will also consider changes that occur in other parts of the grammar and in the lexicon.

Sound Correspondences

In Middle English a *mouse* [maʊs] was called a *mūs* [muːs], and this *mūs* may have lived in someone's *hūs* [huːs], as *house* was pronounced at that time. In general, Middle English speakers pronounced [uː] where we now pronounce [aʊ]. This is a regular correspondence like the one between [aɪ] and [aː]. Thus *out* [aʊt] was pronounced [uːt], *south* [saʊθ] was pronounced [suːθ], and so on. Many such regular correspondences show the relation of older and newer forms of English, just as they show the relation of differing regional pronunciations of current forms of English.

The regular sound correspondences we observe are the result of phonological changes that affect certain sounds, or classes of sounds, rather than individual words. Centuries ago English underwent a phonological change called a **sound shift** in which [uː] became [aʊ].

Phonological changes can also account for dialect or regional differences. At an earlier stage of American English a sound shift of [aɪ] to [aː] took place among certain speakers in the southern region of the United States. The change did not spread beyond the South because the region was somewhat isolated. Many dialect differences in pronunciation result from sound shifts whose spread is limited.

Regional dialect differences may also arise when innovative changes occur everywhere but in a particular region. The regional dialect may be conservative relative to other dialects. The pronunciation of *it* as *hit*, found in the Appalachian region of the United States, was standard in older forms of English. The dropping of the [h] was the innovation.

Ancestral Protolanguages

The living languages, as they were called by the Harvard fellows, were little more than cheap imitations, low distortions. Italian, like Spanish and German, particularly represented the loose political passions, bodily appetites, and absent morals of decadent Europe.

MATTHEW PEARL, *The Dante Club*, 2003

Many modern languages developed from regional dialects that became widely spoken and highly differentiated, finally becoming separate languages. The Romance languages—French, Spanish, Italian, and so on—were once dialects of Latin spoken in the Roman Empire. There is nothing degenerate about regional pronunciations. They are the result of natural sound changes that occur wherever human language is spoken.

In a sense, the Romance languages are the offspring of Latin, their metaphorical parent. Because of their common ancestry, the Romance languages are

genetically related. Early forms of English and German, too, were once dialects of a common ancestor called **Proto-Germanic**. A **protolanguage** is the ancestral language from which related languages have developed. Both Latin and Proto-Germanic were descendants of an older language called **Indo-European** or **Proto-Indo-European**. Protolanguages are not actually attested languages, but are hypothesized by linguists to explain the relationships between existing languages. We will discuss protolanguages further below. Thus, Germanic languages such as English and German are genetically related to the Romance languages such as French and Spanish. All these national languages were once regional dialects. Proto-Indo-European explains these genetic relationships.

How do we know that the Germanic and Romance languages have a common ancestor? One clue is the large number of sound correspondences. If you have studied a Romance language such as French or Spanish, you may have noticed that where an English word begins with *f*, the corresponding word in a Romance language often begins with *p*, as shown in the following examples:

English /f/	French /p/	Spanish /p/	Italian /p/
father	père	padre	padre
fish	poisson	pescado	pesce

This /f/-/p/ correspondence is another example of a regular sound correspondence. There are many such correspondences between the Germanic and Romance languages, and their prevalence cannot be explained by chance. What then accounts for them? A reasonable guess is that a common ancestor language used a *p* in words for *fish*, *father*, and so on. We posit a /p/ rather than an /f/ because more languages show a /p/ in these words. At some point speakers of this language separated into two groups that lost contact with each other. In one of the groups a sound change of *p* → *f* took place. The language spoken by this group eventually became the ancestor of the Germanic languages. This ancient sound change left its trace in the *f-p* sound correspondence that we observe today, as illustrated in the diagram.

Phonological Change

Etymologists . . . for whom vowels did not matter and who cared not a jot for consonants.

VOLTAIRE (1694–1778)

Regular sound correspondences illustrate changes in the phonological system of a language. In earlier chapters we discussed speakers' knowledge of phonology, including knowledge of the phonemes and phonological rules of the language. Both of these aspects of the phonology are subject to change.

The velar fricative /x/ is no longer part of the phonemic inventory of most Modern English dialects. Night used to be pronounced [nɪxt] and drought was pronounced [druxt]. This phonological change—the loss of /x/—took place between the times of Chaucer and Shakespeare. All words that were once pronounced with an /x/ no longer include this sound. In some cases it disappeared altogether, as in *night* and *light*. In other cases the /x/ became a /k/, as in *elk* (Old English *eolh* [ɛɔlx]). In yet other cases it disappeared to be replaced by a vowel, as in *hollow* (Old English *holh* [hɔlx]). Dialects of Modern English spoken in Scotland have retained the /x/ sound in some words, such as *loch* [lɔx] meaning 'lake.'

These examples show that changes in the inventory of sounds in a language can occur through the loss of phonemes. The inventory can also change through the addition of phonemes. Old English did not have the phoneme /ʒ/ of *leisure* [liʒər]. Through a process of palatalization—a change in place of articulation to the palatal region—certain occurrences of /z/ were pronounced [ʒ]. Eventually the [ʒ] sound became a phoneme in its own right, reinforced by the fact that it occurs in French words familiar to many English speakers such as *azure* [æʒər].

An allophone of a phoneme may, through sound change, become a separate phoneme, thus adding to the phonemic inventory. Old English lacked a /v/ phoneme. The phoneme /f/, however, had the allophone [v] when it occurred between vowels. Thus *ofer* /ofer/ meaning 'over' was pronounced [ɔvər]. Old English also had a long consonant phoneme /f:/ that contrasted with /f/ between vowels. The name *Offa* /of:a/ was pronounced [ɔf:a]. A sound change occurred in which the pronunciation of /f:/ was simplified to [f]. Now /f:/ was pronounced [f] between vowels so it contrasted with [v]. This made it possible for English to have minimal pairs involving [f] and [v] such as *shuffle* [ʃʌfəl] and *shovel* [ʃʌvəl]. Speakers therefore perceived the two sounds as separate phonemes, in effect creating a new phoneme /v/.

Similar changes occur in the history of all languages. Neither /tʃ/ nor /ʃ/ were phonemes of Latin, but /tʃ/ is a phoneme of modern Italian and /ʃ/ a phoneme of modern French, both of which descended from Latin. In American Sign Language many signs that were originally formed at the waist or chest level are now produced at a higher level near the neck or upper chest, a reflection of changes in the "phonology."

Phonological Rules

> It's a good idea to obey all the rules when you're young just so you'll have the strength to break them when you're old.
>
> **MARK TWAIN** (1835–1910)

An interaction of phonological rules may result in changes in the lexicon. The nouns *house* and *bath* were once differentiated from the verbs *house* and *bathe* by the fact that the verbs ended with a short vowel sound. Furthermore, the same rule that realized /f/ as [v] between vowels also realized /s/ and /θ/ as the allophones [z] and [ð] between vowels. This general rule added voicing to intervocalic fricatives. Thus the /s/ in the verb *house* was pronounced [z], and the /θ/ in the verb *bathe* was pronounced [ð].

Later, a rule was added to the grammar of English deleting unstressed short vowels at the end of words (even though the final vowel still appears in the written words). A contrast between the voiced and voiceless fricatives resulted, and the new phonemes /z/ and /ð/ were added to the phonemic inventory. The verbs *house* [haʊz] and *bathe* [beð] were now represented in the mental lexicon with final voiced consonants.

Eventually, both the unstressed vowel deletion rule and the intervocalic-voicing rule were lost from the grammar of English. The set of phonological rules can change both by addition and by loss of rules.

Changes in phonological rules can, and often do, result in dialect differences. In the previous chapter we discussed the addition of an *r*-dropping rule in English (/r/ is not pronounced unless followed by a vowel) that did not spread throughout the language. Today, we see the effect of that rule in the *r*-less pronunciation of British English and of American English dialects spoken in the northeastern and the southern United States.

From the standpoint of the language as a whole, phonological changes occur gradually over the course of many generations of speakers, although any given speaker's grammar may or may not reflect the change. The changes are not planned any more than we are presently planning what changes will take place in English by the year 2300. In a single generation changes are evident only through dialect differences.

The Great Vowel Shift

Between 1400 and 1600 a major change took place in English that resulted in new phonemic representations of words and morphemes. This phonological restructuring is known as the **Great Vowel Shift**. The seven long, or tense, vowels of Middle English underwent the following change:

Shift		Example		
Middle English	**Modern English**	**Middle English**	**Modern English**	
[iː] →	[aɪ]	[miːs] →	[maɪs]	mice
[uː] →	[aʊ]	[muːs] →	[maʊs]	mouse
[eː] →	[iː]	[geːs] →	[giːs]	geese
[oː] →	[uː]	[goːs] →	[guːs]	goose
[ɛː] →	[eː]	[brɛːken] →	[breːk]	break
[ɔː] →	[oː]	[brɔːken] →	[broːk]	broke
[aː] →	[eː]	[naːmə] →	[neːm]	name

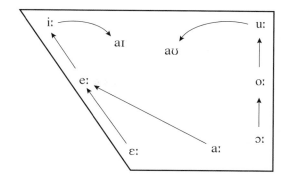

FIGURE 8.1 | The Great Vowel Shift.

By diagramming the Great Vowel Shift on a vowel chart (Figure 8.1), we can see that the high vowels [iː] and [uː] became the diphthongs [aɪ] and [aʊ], while the long vowels underwent an increase in tongue height, as if to fill in the space vacated by the high vowels. In addition, [aː] was fronted to become [eː].

These changes are among the most dramatic examples of regular sound shift. The phonemic representation of many thousands of words changed. Today, some reflection of this vowel shift is seen in the alternating forms of morphemes in English: *please—pleasant*; *serene—serenity*; *sane—sanity*; *crime—criminal*; *sign—signal*; and so on. Before the Great Vowel Shift, the vowels in each pair were pronounced the same. Then the vowels in the second word of each pair were shortened by the **Early Middle English Vowel Shortening** rule. As a result, the Great Vowel Shift, which occurred later and applied only to long vowels, affected only the first word in each pair. This is why the vowels in the morphologically related words are pronounced differently today, as shown in Table 8.1.

The Great Vowel Shift is a primary source of many spelling inconsistencies of English because our spelling system still reflects the way words were pronounced before it occurred. In general, the written language is more conservative, that is, slower to change, than the spoken language.

TABLE 8.1 | Effect of Vowel Shift on Modern English

Middle English Vowel	Shifted Vowel	Short Vowel	Word with Shifted Vowel	Word with Short Vowel
ī	aɪ	ɪ	divine	divinity
ū	aʊ	ʌ	abound	abundant
ē	i	ɛ	serene	serenity
ō	u	a	fool	folly
ā	e	æ	sane	sanity

Morphological Change

And is he well content his son should find

No nourishment to feed his growing mind,

But conjugated verbs and nouns declin'd?

WILLIAM COWPER, "Tirocinium," 1785

Like phonological rules, rules of morphology may be lost, added, or changed. We can observe some of these changes by comparing older and newer forms of the language and by looking at different dialects.

Extensive changes in morphology have occurred in the history of the Indo-European languages. Latin had **case endings**, suffixes on nouns based on their thematic role or grammatical relationship to the verb. These are no longer found in the Romance languages. (See chapter 4 for a more extensive discussion of thematic roles; the terms used by historical linguists are somewhat different than those used by modern semanticists.) The following is a **declension**, or list of cases, for the Latin noun *lupus,* 'wolf':

Noun	Noun Stem		Case Ending	Case	Example
lupus	lup	+	us	nominative	The *wolf* runs.
lupī	lup	+	ī	genitive	A sheep in *wolf's* clothing.
lupō	lup	+	ō	dative	Give food to *the wolf.*
lupum	lup	+	um	accusative	I love *the wolf.*
lupō	lup	+	ō	ablative	She walked with *the wolf.*
lupe	lup	+	e	vocative	*Wolf,* come here!

In *Alice's Adventures in Wonderland,* Lewis Carroll has Alice give us a brief lesson in grammatical case. Alice has become very small and is swimming around in a pool of her own tears with a mouse that she wishes to befriend:

"Would it be of any use, now," thought Alice, "to speak to this mouse? Everything is so out-of-the-way down here, that I should think very likely it can talk: at any rate, there's no harm in trying." So she began: "O Mouse, do you know the way out of this pool? I am very tired of swimming about here, O Mouse!" (Alice thought this must be the right way of speaking to a mouse: she had never done such a thing before, but she remembered having seen in her brother's Latin Grammar, "A mouse–of a mouse–to a mouse–a mouse–O mouse!")

Alice gives the English corresponding to the nominative, genitive, dative, accusative, and vocative cases, which existed in Latin and in Old English but not in Modern English, where word order and prepositions convey the same information.

Ancient Greek and Sanskrit also had extensive case systems expressed through noun suffixing, as did Old English, as illustrated by the following noun forms:

Case	OE Singular		OE Plural	
nominative	stān	"stone"	stānas	"stones"
genitive	stānes	"stone's"	stāna	"stones'"
dative	stāne	"stone"	stānum	"stones"
accusative	stān	"stone"	stānas	"stones"

Lithuanian and Russian retain much of the early Indo-European case system, but it is nearly obliterated in most modern Indo-European languages.

English retains traces of the genitive case, which is written with an apostrophe *s*, as in *Robert's dog*, but that's all that remains as far as possessives are concerned. (The use of the genitive case on nouns following certain prepositions is gone.) Pronouns retain a few more case distinctions: *he/she* are nominative, *him/her* accusative and dative, and *his/hers* genitive. And of course English (barely) retains the *who/whom* distinction, much beloved by English teachers, reflecting nominative and accusative cases. English has replaced its depleted case system with an equally expressive system of prepositions. For example, what would be the dative case is often indicated by the preposition *to*, the genitive case by the preposition *of*, and the accusative case by no preposition together with the word order V NP in d-structure.

Syntactic Change

Understanding changes in grammar is a key component in understanding changes in language.

DAVID LIGHTFOOT, *The Development of Language*, 1999

When we see a word-for-word translation of older forms of English, we are most struck by the differences in word order. Consider again the opening lines of *The Canterbury Tales*, this time translated word-for-word:

Whan that Aprille with his shoures soote
'When that April with its showers sweet'
The droght of March hath perced to the roote . . .
'The drought of March has pierced to the root . . .'

In Modern English, adjectives generally precede the nouns they modify: thus we would say *sweet showers* in place of *showers sweet*. Moreover, a direct object now generally follows its verb, so *has pierced the drought of March to the root* would be a modern rendering of the second line. Thus the rules of syntax that govern these word orders, even taking "poetic license" into account, appear to have changed. It is safe to say that syntactic change in English and other languages is most evident in the changes of permitted word orders.

Syntactic change in English is a good illustration of the interrelationship of the various modules of the grammar. Changes in syntax were often influenced by changes in morphology, and these in turn by changes in the phonology of the language. And contrariwise, there is evidence that changes in syntax may very well have precipitated changes in the other two systems. These interrelations between the different components of grammar are complex. It is not always easy for historical linguists to determine which part of the grammar affected which other part and when. As in nearly all subfields of linguistics, much more research is needed to solve the many outstanding questions.

When the rich system of case endings of Old English became simplified in part because of phonological changes, and in part because syntactic changes were underway, speakers of English were forced to rely more heavily on word order to convey the function of noun phrases. A sentence such as

sē	man	þone	kyning	sloh
the (nominative)	man	the (accusative)	king	slew

was understood to mean 'the man slew the king' because of the case markings (given in parentheses). There would have been no confusion on the listeners' part as to who did what to whom. Also, in earlier stages of English the verb had a richer system of subject-verb agreement. For example, the verb *to sing* had the following forms: *singe* (I sing), *singest* (you sing), *singeth* (he sings), and *singen* (we, plural you, they sing). It was therefore also possible in many instances to identify the subject on the basis of verb inflection even if it was not apparent from word order, which was already evolving from the subject-object-verb (SOV) word order of the example to the now more usual subject-verb-object (SVO).

In Modern English *the man the king slew* is only grammatical as a relative clause meaning 'the man that the king slew,' with the subject and object of *slew* reversed. To convey the meaning 'the man slew the king,' Modern English speakers *must* rely on word order—subject-verb-object—or other syntactic devices such as the ones that generate sentences like *It was the king that the man slew*.

The change in English word order reflects a change in the structures of grammar. In Old English the VP was head-final, as indicated by the following structure:

The Old English phrase structure was like the phrase structure of Dutch and German, closely related languages. The English VP (but not the German and the Dutch) underwent a change in parameter setting and became head-initial as follows:

As a result Modern English has a basic SVO word order whereas Old English (and modern Dutch and German) have a basic SOV word order. However, Modern English still has remnants of the original SOV word order in "old-fashioned" kinds of expressions such as *I thee wed*. Word order and morphological distinctions, dancing as partners through time, affected each other: word order became more rigid at the same time that morphological distinctions were vanishing.

As discussed in chapter 3, in Modern English we form questions by moving an auxiliary verb, if there is one, before the NP subject:

Can the girl kiss the boy?
Will the girl kiss the boy?
Has the girl kissed the boy yet?
Was the girl kissing the boy when you arrived?

However, if an auxiliary verb is absent, Modern English requires the word *do* to spell out the tense of the sentence:

Does the girl kiss the boy often?
*Kisses the girl the boy often?

Older forms of English had a more general rule that moved the first verbal element, which meant that if no auxiliary occurred in the sentence, then the main verb moved. The question

Kisses the girl the boy often?

was grammatical in English through the time of Shakespeare (e.g., *Goes Fleance with you?*, Macbeth, III, 1). This more general verb movement rule still exists in languages like Dutch and German. In English, however, the rule of question formation changed, as indicated above: now only auxiliary verbs move and if no auxiliary verb is present, a *do* fills its role. This rule change interacted with the English case system. In Old English, *the girl* and *the boy* would have been marked for case, so there was no confusion over who was kissing whom. In effect, the sentence would be:

Kisses the (nominative) girl the (accusative) boy often?

With the new question rule in place the need for case distinctions was less vital and it could die out without creating an excess of ambiguity; and at the same time as the morphological distinctions were dying out their absence reinforced the strength of the rule change.

Another example of how syntax influences morphology is with Old English case endings on nouns that follow prepositions. Certain prepositions "governed" certain cases:

Old English	Modern English
in þæt hūs (accusative, singular)	'into that house'
fram þæm hūse (dative, singular)	'from that house'
til þæs hūses (genitive, singular)	'up to/as far as that house'

Since the word order of prepositional phrases was already fixed in Old English, and the meaning conveyed by the preposition, the case endings were redundant and therefore omissible, which in turn "allowed" the sound changes to take place that doomed those endings to the dustbin of history.

Modern English, with its rudimentary case system, specifies grammatical relations structurally: the direct object is the NP that is sister to the verb. If the main verb were to move, this sisterhood configuration would be violated. The introduction of *do* allows the verb to remain in its base position, and the sentence thus retains the SVO word order that most plainly indicates the subject and object of the sentence.

Another syntactic change in English affected the rules of comparative and superlative constructions. Today we form the comparative by adding *-er* to the adjective or by inserting *more* before it; the superlative is formed by adding *-est* or by inserting *most*. In Malory's *Tales of King Arthur*, written in 1470, double comparatives and double superlatives occur, which today are ungrammatical: *more gladder, more lower, moost royallest, moost shamefullest.*

Both Old English and Middle English permitted split genitives, that is, possessive constructs in which the words that describe the possessor occur on both sides of the head noun:

Inwæres   broþur   ond   Healfdenes (Old English)
Inwær's   brother   and   Healfden's
'Inwær's and Healfden's brother'

The Wife's tale of Bath (Middle English)
'The Wife of Bath's tale'

Modern English does not allow such structures—only possessor-possessed-head noun is allowed, but English does permit rather complex genitive expressions to precede the head noun:

The man with the two small children's hat
The girl whose sister I'm dating's roommate
When does you guys's party begin? (Cf. When does your (pl.) party begin?)

Owing to non-occurrence in written records, we can infer that expressions like *the Queen of England's crown* were ungrammatical in earlier periods of English. The title *The Wife's Tale of Bath* (rather than *The Wife of Bath's Tale*) in *The Canterbury Tales* supports this inference.

Interestingly enough, the fixing of the possessor-possessed-head noun word order, and the generalization of the *-s* genitive, came several generations later than the restrictive use of the genitive case, indicating again how changes in syntactic rules "grease the skids" for changes in other grammatical venues. And conversely, as the case system weakened, there was insufficient noun morphology to carry the semantic burden of expressing possession in multiple structures, reinforcing the generalization of *'s* to syntactic units larger than the noun. Thus the word order permitted in possessive constructions became more fixed and split genitives are now ungrammatical.

The big picture is that the loss of information that accompanies morphological simplification, and the increase of information that accompanies more rigid rules of word order, interact to reinforce or weaken each other, much like the peaks and troughs of two ocean waves that interfere with each other as they approach the shore. Such grammatical changes may take centuries to be completed and there are often intermediate stages.

Modern Brazilian Portuguese (BP) may illustrate one such intermediate stage of language change. Until the middle of the nineteenth century, speakers of BP didn't need to explicitly mention a subject pronoun because that information came from the person and number agreement on the verb, as illustrated for the verb *cozinhar* meaning 'to cook.'

cozinh<u>o</u>	I cook	cozinh<u>amos</u>	we cook
cozinh<u>as</u>	you cook		
cozinh<u>a</u>	he/she cooks	cozinh<u>am</u>	they/you (pl.) cook

At that time speakers dropped subjects in about 80 percent of their sentences, as in the second sentence of the following example:

A	Clara	sabe		fazer	tudo	muito	bem.
the	Clara	knows how		to do	everything	very	well

Cozinha		que	é	uma	maravilha.
cooks (3rd per.)		that	is	a	marvel

'Clara knows how to do everything well. She cooks wonderfully.'

By the end of the twentieth century, subject-drop was reduced to 20 percent and the agreement endings were also reduced. In certain dialects only a two-way distinction is maintained: first-person singular is marked with *-o*, as in *cozinho*, and all other grammatical persons are marked with *-a*. While sentences without subjects are still grammatical in European Portuguese (spoken in Portugal), they are ungrammatical for most speakers of Modern BP, which requires the expression of an overt subject, for example *ela*, 'she,' as follows:

A Clara sabe fazer tudo muito bem. Ela cozinha que é uma maravilha.

Many of the other Romance languages, including Italian, Spanish, Catalan, and European Portuguese, are still null-subject languages and maintain a rich verb morphology as illustrated for Italian in chapter 2. In the future null subjects may become ungrammatical for all speakers in BP. If so, BP will follow the route of another Romance language, French, which evolved from a richly inflected null-subject language in the thirteenth century to a language that now requires subject pronouns and that in its spoken form also has a very impoverished verb morphology.

Just as the loss of Old English noun and verb morphology both resulted in and was influenced by stricter word order, so the loss of agreement morphology in Brazilian Portuguese, and earlier in French, interacted with a syntactic change from a null-subject grammar to one that requires subjects. In this respect Brazilian Portuguese is diverging from the other Romance languages, as French did in earlier times.

Lexical Change

appletini

chocotini

crantini

flirtini

frostini

mintatini

mochatini

peachatini

peartini

VeeV treetini

A SELECTION OF MARTINI VARIANTS FROM THE MENU OF A "MARTINI BAR"

Changes in the lexicon also occur, among which are changes in the lexical categories of words (i.e., their "parts of speech"), addition of new words, the "borrowing" of words from other languages, the loss of words, the shift in the meanings of words over time, and even the faux back formations (see chapter 2) that create new <u>bound</u> morphemes such as *–tini* noted above (and yes, your authors are still working their way through the list).

Change in Category

Darby Conley/United Feature Syndicate

The words *food* and *verb* are ordinarily used as nouns, but Bucky the cat refuses to be so restricted and "wordifies" them into verbs. If we speakers of English adopt Bucky's usage, then *food* and *verb* will become verbs in addition to nouns. Recently, a radio announcer said that Congress was *to-ing and fro-ing* on a certain issue, to mean 'wavering.' This strange compound verb is derived from the adverb *to and fro*. In British English, *hoover* is a verb meaning 'to vacuum up,' derived from the proper noun *Hoover*, the name of a vacuum cleaner manufacturer. American police *Mirandize* arrested persons, meaning 'read them their rights according to the Miranda rule.' The judicial ruling was made in 1966, so we have a complete history of how a proper name became a verb. More recently the noun *text* has been "verbed" and means 'to communicate by text message,' and even more recent is the hijacking of the verb *twitter* and "Proper Noun-ing" it as the name of a social networking and microblogging service.

Addition of New Words

And to bring in a new word by the head and shoulders, they leave out the old one.

MONTAIGNE (1533–1592)

"Pickles" used with the permission of Brian Crane, the Washington Post Writers Group and the Cartoonist Group. All rights reserved.

One of the most obvious ways a language changes is through the addition of new words. Unlike grammatical change, which may take generations to notice, new words are readily apparent. Societies often require new words to describe changes in technology, sports, entertainment, and so on. Languages are accommodating and inventive in meeting these needs.

In chapter 2 we discussed some ways in which new words are born, such as through derivational processes, back-formations, and compounding. There are other ways that words may enter the vocabulary of a language, thus adding to the inventory of lexical items. These include out-and-out word coinage, deriving words from names, blending words to form new words, shortening old words to form new ones, forming acronyms, and borrowing words from other languages.

Word Coinage

Words may be created outright to fit some purpose. The advertising industry has added many words to English, such *as Kodak, nylon, Orlon,* and *Dacron.* Specific brand names such as *Xerox, Band-Aid, Kleenex, Jell-O, Brillo,* and *Vaseline* are now sometimes used as the generic names for different brands of these types of products. Some of these words were actually created from existing words (e.g., *Kleenex* from the word *clean* and *Jell-O* from *gel*).

The sciences have given us a raft of newly coined words over the ages. Words like *asteroid, neutron, genome, krypton, brontosaurus*, and *vaccine* were created to describe the objects or processes arising from scientific investigation.

A word so new that its spelling is still in doubt is *dot-com*, also seen in magazines as *.com, dot.com*, and even *dot com* without the hyphen. It means 'a company whose primary business centers on the Internet.' *Bling* (or *bling-bling*), meaning 'gaudy jewelry,' was a possible but nonexistent word like *blick* until a few years ago, and unless you have a recently published dictionary or use an online dictionary, you won't find an entry for *bling*. Also new to this millennium are *Bollywood*, 'the film industry of India,' and *sudoku*, 'a puzzle printed on a square grid of nine large squares each subdivided into nine smaller squares, the object of which is to fill in each of the 81 squares so that each column, row, and large square contains every number from 1 to 9. Sometimes words originally coined for one purpose, such as the company name *Google*, are put to work to serve a related purpose, such as *google*, meaning 'to search on the Internet.'

Greek roots borrowed into English have also provided a means for coining new words. *Thermos*, 'hot,' plus *metron*, 'measure,' gave us *thermometer*. From *akros*, 'topmost,' and *phobia*, 'fear,' we get *acrophobia*, 'dread of heights.' To avoid going out on Friday the thirteenth, you may say that you have *triskaidekaphobia*, a profound fear of the number 13. An ingenious cartoonist, Robert Osborn, has "invented" some phobias, to each of which he gives an appropriate name:[2]

logizomechanophobia	'fear of reckoning machines' from Greek *logizomai,* 'to reckon or compute,' + *mekhane,* 'device,' + *phobia*
ellipsosyllabophobia	'fear of words with missing syllables' from Greek *elleipsis,* 'a falling short,' + *syllabē,* 'syllable,' + *phobia*
pornophobia	'fear of prostitutes' from Greek *porne* 'harlot,' + *phobia*

Latin, like Greek, has also provided prefixes and suffixes that are used productively with both native and nonnative roots. The prefix *ex-* comes from Latin:

ex-husband ex-wife ex-sister-in-law ex-teacher

The suffix *-able/-ible* is also Latin and can be attached to almost any English verb:

writable readable answerable movable learnable

Even new bound morphemes may enter the language. The prefix *e-*, as in *e-commerce, e-mail*, and *e-trade*, meaning 'electronic,' is barely two decades old,

---

[2]From *An Osborn Festival of Phobias* by Robert Osborn and Eve Wengler. Copyright © 1971 Robert Osborn. Text copyright © 1971 Eve Wengler. Used by permission of Liveright Publishing Corporation.

and most interestingly has given rise to the prefix *s-* as in *s-mail* to contrast with *e-mail*. The suffix *-gate*, meaning 'scandal,' which was derived from the Watergate scandal of the 1970s, may now be suffixed to a word to convey that meaning. Thus *Irangate* means a scandal involving Iran, and *Dianagate*, a British usage, refers to a scandal involving wiretapped conversations of the late Princess of Wales, Diana. A change currently under way is the use of *-peat* to mean 'win a championship so many years in succession,' as in *threepeat* and *fourpeat*, which we have observed in the newspaper. And of course nowadays we can take anything soluble and edible, mix it with gin, and voila we have, um, a pomegranatini.

Also so new that they haven't made the dictionaries are words that take *-zilla* as a bound suffix with the meaning 'huge or extreme,' as in *shopzilla*, *bridezilla*, *FDAzilla* (from the American Federal Drug Administration website) and the British band *Dogzilla*: the source for this suffix is the world-famous Japanese movie monster *Godzilla*. The bound prefix *uber-* of German origin meaning 'the best' or 'the most' allows myriad new words to be formed by "supersizing" old ones, as in *linguistics is uber-cool*, or *the jokes in this book are uberlame*.

FLASH! Hold the presses. As we go to print the New York Times has sanctified the new word *99%* ("ninety-nine percent"), spun off from the "Occupy" movement with roots in the year 2011, and meaning 'people who are not among the richest one percent.' Also just coined, and not in our online dictionary, is *bracketology*: 'the ranking and matching up of sports teams for a winner-take-all elimination sports tournament.' Language is little else if not creative and infinitely flexible.

And finally there are occasions when signers need to represent a word or concept for which there is no sign. New coinages, foreign words, acronyms, certain proper nouns, technical vocabulary, or obsolete words as might be found in a signed interpretation of a play by Shakespeare, or a technical oral presentation, are among some of these. For such cases ASL may conceive a series of new hand shapes and movements that represent the word or concept, but absent this possibility, letters of the English alphabet may be expressed through finger spelling, conveying any meaning that might be written.

Words from Names

Eponyms are words that are coined from proper names and are another of the many creative ways that the vocabulary of a language expands. Here are some examples:

sandwich	Named for the fourth Earl of Sandwich, who put his food between two slices of bread so that he could eat while he gambled.
robot	After the mechanical creatures in the Czech writer Karel Capek's play *R.U.R.*, the initials standing for 'Rossum's Universal Robots.'
gargantuan	Named for Gargantua, the creature with a huge appetite created by Rabelais.

jumbo   After an elephant brought to the United States by P. T. Barnum. ("Jumbo olives" need not be as big as an elephant, however.)

We admit to ignorance of the Susan, an unknown servant from whom the compound *lazy susan* is derived; or the Betty or Charlotte or Chuck from whom we got *brown betty*, *charlotte russe*, or *chuck wagon*. We can point out, however, that *denim* was named for the material used for overalls and carpeting, which originally was imported *de Nîmes* ('from Nîmes') in France, and *argyle* from the kind of socks worn by the chiefs of Argyll of the Campbell clan in Scotland.

The word *paparazzo*, 'a freelance photographer who doggedly pursues celebrities,' was a little-known word until the death of Princess Diana in 1997, who was hounded by paparazzi (plural) before her fatal automobile accident. This eponym comes from the character of Signor Paparazzo, the news photgrapher in the motion picture *La Dolce Vita*.

Blends

Blends are similar to compounds in that they are produced by combining two words, but in blends parts of the words that are combined are deleted. *Smog*, from *smoke* + *fog*; *brunch*, from *breakfast* and *lunch*; *motel*, from *motor* + *hotel*; *infomercial*, from *info* + *commercial*; and *urinalysis*, from *urine* + *analysis* are examples of blends that have attained full lexical status in English. *Podcast* (*podcasting*, *podcaster*) is a relatively new word meaning 'Internet audio broadcast' and recently joined the English language as a blend of *iPod* and *broadcast*. *Debtpocalypse* is a recent blend used to describe nations whose national debt has reached, well, apocalyptic proportions, such as Greece and Spain in 2012. And in Los Angeles, California, the temporary closure of a major freeway for repairs led to dire predictions of *Carmegeddon*.

Lewis Carroll's *chortle*, from *chuckle* + *snort*, has achieved limited acceptance in English. Carroll is famous for both coining and blending words. In *Through the Looking-Glass*, he describes the "meanings" of the made-up words in "Jabberwocky" as follows:

> "Brillig" means four o' clock in the afternoon—the time when you begin broiling things for dinner . . . "Slithy" means "lithe and slimy" . . . You see it's like a portmanteau—there are two meanings packed up into one word. . . . "Toves" are something like badgers—they're something like lizards—and they're something like corkscrews . . . also they make their nests under sun-dials—also they live on cheese. . . . To "gyre" is to go round and round like a gyroscope. To "gimble" is to make holes like a gimlet. And "the wabe" is the grass-plot round a sun-dial . . . It's called "wabe" . . . because it goes a long way before it and a long way behind it. . . . "Mimsy" is "flimsy and miserable" (there's another portmanteau . . . for you).

Carroll's "portmanteaus" are what we have called blends, and such words can become part of the regular lexicon.

Blending is even done by children. The blend *crocogator* from crocodile + alligator is attributed to three-year-old Elijah Peregrine. Grandmothers are not to be left out, and a Jewish one of African descent that we know came up with *shugeleh*, 'darling,' which we think is a blend of *sugar + bubeleh*, and which we confess we don't know how to spell. (*Bubeleh* is a Yiddish term of endearment.) And we recently heard the expression *the yood* [jʊd] (compare *the 'hood*) applied to a neighborhood with many speakers of Yiddish, perhaps a blend of *Yiddish* and *neighborhood*. Finally, a concern nowadays in food and weight has led *Merriam-Webster's Collegiate Dictionary* to add *flexitarian, locavore,* and *obesogenic*. You may look up their meanings yourself now that they have become "sanctioned."

Reduced Words

> This perpetual Disposition to shorten our Words, by retrenching the Vowels, is nothing else but a tendency to lapse into the Barbarity of those Northern Nations from whom we are descended, and whose Languages labour all under the same Defect.
>
> **JONATHAN SWIFT**, *A Proposal for Correcting, Improving and Ascertaining the English Tongue*, 1712

Speakers tend to abbreviate words in various ways to shorten the messages they convey. We used to find this in telegrams and telexes. Now it is seen in the texts of short message services (SMSs) so prolific in today's electronic world. However, we will concern ourselves with *spoken* language and observe three reduction phenomena: *clipping, acronyms,* and *alphabetic abbreviations*.

Clipping is the abbreviation of longer words into shorter ones by leaving out one or more syllables such as *fax* for *facsimile*, the British word *telly* for *television*, *flu* for *influenza*, *porn* for *pornography*, and *droid* for *android*. Once marginalized as slang, and despite Jonathan Swift's contempt, many of these words have over time become lexicalized, that is, bona fide members of the English vocabulary. Clippings may clip the beginning of a word (*phone* for *telephone*), most commonly the end of a word (*prof* for *professor),* or both ends (*fridge* for *refrigerator).*

There are two possible semantic outcomes of clipping. The most common by far is that the clipped word has the same meaning as its source. All of the examples in the previous paragraph are of that ilk. In a minority of instances, the clipped word takes on a different meaning. *Fan, van, rad*, and *mutt* are clipped from *fanatic, caravan, radical,* and *muttonhead*, but fans are not (generally) fanatics, a van is a single vehicle, not a cavalcade, something that is rad is marvelous and not necessarily radical, and a mutt is a mongrel dog with little to do with a muttonhead, which is a foolish person. The use of *droid* to mean a certain kind of smartphone (itself a recent word) has a different meaning than *android*, though the use of the word is intended to convey the impression of robotic intelligence.

Clippings continue to come into existence. *Dis,* once rapper slang for *disrespect,* is gaining acceptance with the meaning 'show contempt for.' *Blog* (from *weblog,* another new word!) is perhaps the most successful clip of the current millennium, being today both a noun and a verb with all the related morphology (*blogs, blogging, blogged, blogger,* and so on; see exercise 4f.)

Acronyms are words derived from the initials of several words. Such words are pronounced as the spelling indicates: *NASA* [næsə] from *National Aeronautics and Space Administration, UNESCO* [junɛsko] from *United Nations Educational,*

Scientific, and Cultural Organization, and *UNICEF* [junəsɛf] from *United Nations International Children's Emergency Fund*. *Radar* from *radio detecting and ranging, laser* from *light amplification by stimulated emission of radiation, scuba* from *self-contained underwater breathing apparatus*, and *RAM* from *random access memory* show the creative efforts of word coiners, as does *snafu*, which was coined by soldiers in World War II and is rendered in polite circles as *situation normal, all fouled up*. Recently coined additions are *AIDS* (1980s), from the initials of *acquired immune deficiency syndrome*, and *SARS* (2000s), from *severe acute respiratory syndrome*.

When the string of letters is not easily pronounced as a word, the "acronym" is produced by sounding out each letter, as in *NFL* [ɛ̃nɛfɛl] for *National Football League, UCLA* [jusiɛle] for *University of California, Los Angeles*, and *MRI* [ɛ̃maraɪ] for *magnetic resonance imaging*. These special kinds of acronyms are sometimes called **alphabetic abbreviations**.

Acronyms and alphabetic abbreviations are being added to the vocabulary daily with the proliferation of computers and widespread use of the Internet, including *jpeg* (*joint photographics expert group*), *GUI*, pronounced "gooey," for *graphical user interface, PDA* (*personal digital assistant*), and *MP3* for *MPEG layer 3*, where *MPEG* itself is the acronym for *moving picture experts group*.

Unbelievable though it may seem, acronyms in use somewhere in the English-speaking world number more than one million according to the online Acronym Finder, about the same number as English words if we look back four centuries, a dramatic nod to the creativity and changeability of human language.

Borrowings or Loan Words

> Neither a borrower, nor a lender be.
>
> **WILLIAM SHAKESPEARE**, *Hamlet*, c. 1600

Languages pay little attention to Polonius's admonition quoted above, and many are avid borrowers and lenders, and poor ones at that, for the borrowers rarely return the borrowed items, and the lenders nearly never demand the return of the loans.

Borrowing words from other languages is an important source of new words, which are called **loan words**. Borrowing occurs when one language adds a word or morpheme from another language to its own lexicon. This often happens in situations of language contact, when speakers of different languages regularly interact with one another, and especially where there are many bilingual or multilingual speakers.

The pronunciation of loan words is often (but not always) altered to fit the phonological rules of the borrowing language. For example, English borrowed *ensemble* [ɑ̃sɑbəl] from French but pronounce it [ɑ̃nsɑ̃mbəl], with [n] and [m] inserted, because English doesn't ordinarily have syllables centered on nasal vowels alone. Other borrowed words such as the composer's name *Bach* will often be pronounced as the original German [bax], with a final velar fricative, even though such a pronunciation does not conform to the rules of English.

Larger units than words may be borrowed. French provides us with *ménage à trois* [mẽnaʒ a tRa], where [R] is a uvular trill, meaning a 'three-way romance,' and which is pronounced in the French way by those who know French, but is also anglicized in various ways such as [mẽnadʒ a twa].

When an expression is borrowed and then translated into the borrowing language, such as *worldview* from German *Weltanschauung*, it is called a **loan translation**. *It goes without saying* from French *il va sans dire* is a loan translation from French. On the other hand, Spanish speakers eat *perros calientes*, a loan translation of *hot dogs* with an adjustment reversing the order of the adjective and noun, as required by the rules of Spanish syntax.

The lexicons of most languages can be divided into native words and loan words. A native word is one whose history or **etymology** can be traced back to the earliest known stages of the language.

A language may borrow a word directly or indirectly. A direct borrowing means that the borrowed item is a native word in the language from which it is borrowed. For example, *feast* was borrowed directly from French, along with a host of terms, as a result of the Norman Conquest. By contrast, the word *algebra* was borrowed from Spanish, which in turn had borrowed it from Arabic. Thus *algebra* was indirectly borrowed from Arabic, with Spanish as an intermediary. Some languages are heavy borrowers. Albanian has borrowed so heavily that few native words are retained. On the other hand, most Native American languages borrowed little from their neighbors.

English has borrowed extensively. Of the 20,000 or so words in common use, about three-fifths are borrowed. But of the 500 most frequently used words, only two-sevenths are borrowed, and because these words are used repeatedly in sentences—they are mostly function words—the actual frequency of appearance of native words is about 80 percent. The frequently used function words *and, be, have, it, of, the, to, will, you, on, that,* and *is* are all native to English.

Language may borrow not only words and phrases but other linguistic units as well. We saw earlier how English in effect borrowed the phonemes /v/ and /ʒ/ from French. The bound morpheme suffixes *ible/able* were also borrowed from French, arriving in English by hitchhiking on French words such as *incredible* but soon attaching themselves to native words such as *drinkable*.

History through Loan Words

A morsel of genuine history is a thing so rare as to be always valuable.

THOMAS JEFFERSON, in a letter to John Adams, 1817

We may trace the history of the English-speaking peoples by studying the kinds of loan words in their language, their source, and when they were borrowed. Until the Norman Conquest in 1066, the Angles, the Saxons, and the Jutes inhabited England. They were of Germanic origin when they came to Britain in the fifth century to eventually become the English. Originally, they spoke Germanic dialects, from which Old English developed. These dialects contained some Latin borrowings but few foreign elements beyond that. These

Germanic tribes had displaced the earlier Celtic inhabitants, whose influence on Old English was confined mostly to a few Celtic place names. (The modern languages Welsh, Irish, and Scots Gaelic are descended from the Celtic dialects.)

The Normans spoke French, and for three centuries after the Conquest, French was used for all affairs of state and for most commercial, social, and cultural matters. The West Saxon literary language was abandoned, but regional varieties of English continued to be used in homes, churches, and the marketplace. This was a situation of language contact between French, the culturally dominant language at the time, and English. During these three centuries vast numbers of French words entered English, of which the following are representative:

government	crown	prince	estate	parliament
nation	jury	judge	crime	sue
attorney	saint	miracle	charity	court
lechery	virgin	value	pray	mercy
religion	chapel	royal	money	society

Until the Normans came, when an Englishman slaughtered an ox for food, he ate *ox*. If it was a pig, he ate *pig*. If it was a sheep, he ate *sheep*. However, 'ox' served at the Norman tables was *beef* (*boeuf*), 'pig' was *pork* (*porc*), and 'sheep' was *mutton* (*mouton*). These words were borrowed from French into English, as were the food-preparation words *boil*, *fry*, *stew*, and *roast*. Over the years French foods have given English a flood of borrowed words for menu preparers:

aspic	bisque	bouillon	brie	brioche
canapé	caviar	consommé	coq au vin	coupe
crêpe	croissant	croquette	crouton	escargot
fondue	mousse	pâté	quiche	ragout

English borrowed many "learned" words from foreign sources during the Renaissance. In 1475 William Caxton introduced the printing press in England. By 1640, 55,000 books had been printed in English. The authors of these books used many Greek and Latin words, which consequently entered the language.

From Greek came *drama*, *comedy*, *tragedy*, *scene*, *botany*, *physics*, *zoology*, and *atomic*. Latin loan words in English are numerous. They include:

bonus   scientific   exit   alumnus   quorum   describe

During the ninth and tenth centuries, Scandinavian raiders, who eventually settled in the British Isles, left their traces in the English language. The pronouns *they*, *their*, and *them* are loan words from Old Norse, the predecessor of modern Danish, Norwegian, and Swedish. This period is the only time that English ever borrowed pronouns.

Bin, *flannel*, *clan*, *slogan*, and *whisky* are all words of Celtic origin, borrowed at various times from Welsh, Scots Gaelic, or Irish. Dutch was a source of borrowed words, too, many of which are related to shipping: *buoy*, *freight*, *leak*, *pump*, *yacht*. From German came *quartz*, *cobalt*, and—as we might guess—*sauerkraut*. From Italian, many musical terms, including words describing opera houses, have been borrowed: *opera*, *piano*, *virtuoso*, *balcony*, and *mezzanine*. Italian also gave us *influenza*, which was derived from the Italian word for 'influence' because the Italians were convinced that the disease was *influenced* by the stars.

Many scientific words were borrowed indirectly from Arabic, because early Arab scholarship in these fields was quite advanced. *Alcohol*, *algebra*, *cipher*, and *zero* are a small sample. Spanish has loaned us (directly) *barbecue*, *cockroach*, and *ranch*, as well as *California*, literally 'hot furnace.' In America, the English-speaking colonists borrowed from Native American languages, another situation of language contact, but in which English is the culturally dominant language. Native American languages provided us with *hickory*, *chipmunk*, *opossum*, and *squash*, to mention only a few. Nearly half the names of U.S. states are borrowed from one American Indian language or another.

English has borrowed from Yiddish. Many non-Jews as well as non-Yiddish-speaking Jews use Yiddish words. There was once even a bumper sticker proclaiming: "Marcel Proust is a yenta." *Yenta* is a Yiddish word meaning 'gossipy woman.' *Lox*, meaning 'smoked salmon,' and *bagel*, 'a doughnut dipped in cement,' now belong to English, as well as Yiddish expressions like *chutzpah*, *schmaltz*, *schlemiel*, *schmuck*, *schmo*, *schlep*, and *kibitz*.

English is a lender of many words to other languages, especially in the areas of technology, sports, and entertainment. Words and expressions such as *jazz*, *whisky*, *blue jeans*, *rock music*, *supermarket*, *baseball*, *picnic*, and *computer* have been borrowed from English into languages as diverse as Twi, Hungarian, Russian, and Japanese.

Loss of Words

RED ROVER © 2012 Brian Basset Dist. By UNIVERSAL UCLICK. Reprinted with permission. All rights reserved.

Languages may be said to lose words in the sense that the frequency of usage falls below a certain threshold. Such words may still be counted when tallying up the size of the lexicon (see *The Culturomic Revolution* section in chapter 11), but they are lost to the general population. The departure of an old word is never as striking as the arrival of a new one. When a new word comes into vogue, its unusual presence draws attention, but a word is lost through inattention—nobody thinks of it, nobody uses it, and its usage fades away to nothing.

A reading of Shakespeare's works shows that English has lost many words, such as these taken from *Romeo and Juliet*: *beseem*, 'to be suitable,' *mammet*, 'a doll or puppet,' *wot*, 'to know,' *gyve*, 'a fetter,' *fain*, 'gladly,' and *wherefore*, 'why,' as in Juliet's plaintive cry: "O Romeo, Romeo! wherefore art thou Romeo," in which she is questioning why he is so named, not his current whereabouts.

More recently, there are expressions used by your grandparents that have already been lost. For example, *two bits*, meaning 'twenty-five cents,' is now rarely used and the same for *lickety-split* and *pell-mell*, meaning 'very fast' and 'recklessly hurried.' Even words used by your parents (and us) sound dated, for example, *groovy* ('excellent'), *davenport* ('sofa'), and *grass* and *Mary Jane*, now called *weed*, referring to 'marijuana.' The word *stile*, meaning 'steps crossing a fence or gate,' is no longer widely understood. Other similar words for describing rural objects are fading out of the language as a result of urbanization. *Pease*, from which *pea* is a back-formation, is rare, and *porridge*, meaning 'boiled cereal grain,' is falling out of usage, although it is sustained by a discussion of its ideal serving temperature in the children's story *Goldilocks and the Three Bears* and its appearance on Harry Potter's breakfast table.

Technological change may also be the cause for the loss of words. *Acutiator* once meant 'sharpener of weapons,' and *tormentum* once meant 'siege engine.' Advances in warfare have put these terms out of business but given us *cruise missile* and an extension of the word *drone*. *Whiteboard* is in and *blackboard* is out insofar as classroom teaching is concerned. Although one still finds the words *buckboard*, *buggy*, *dogcart*, *hansom*, *surrey*, and *tumbrel* in the dictionary—all of them referring to subtly different kinds of horse-drawn carriages—progress in transportation is likely to render these terms obsolete and eventually they will be lost.

Semantic Change

> The language of this country being always upon the flux, the Struldbruggs of one age do not understand those of another, neither are they able after two hundred years to hold any conversation (farther than by a few general words) with their neighbors the mortals, and thus they lie under the disadvantage of living like foreigners in their own country.
>
> **JONATHAN SWIFT**, *Gulliver's Travels*, 1726

We have seen that a language may gain or lose lexical items. Additionally, the meaning or semantic representation of words may change, by becoming broader or narrower, or by shifting.

Broadening

When the meaning of a word becomes broader, it means everything it used to mean and more. The Middle English word *dogge* referred to a specific breed of dog, but was eventually **broadened** to encompass all members of the species *canis familiaris.* The word *holiday* originally meant a day of religious significance, from 'holy day.' Today the word refers to any day that we do not have to work. *Picture* used to mean 'painted representation,' but now you can take a picture with a camera, not to mention a host of other electronic "toys." *Quarantine* once had the restricted meaning of 'forty days' isolation,' and *manage* once meant simply 'to handle a horse.'

More recent broadenings, spurred by the computer age, are *computer, mouse, cookie, cache, virus,* and *bundle. Footage* used to refer to a certain length of film or videotape, but nowadays it means any excerpt from the electronic video media, such as DVDs, irrespective of whether its length can be measured in feet. *Google* was broadened first from the name of a company to a verb meaning 'to use that company's search engine on the Internet,' and from there further broadened to simply 'search the Internet.' *Twitter* and *tweet* were once words confined to the aviary—need we say more?

Narrowing

In the King James Version of the Bible (1611 CE), God says of the herbs and trees, "to you they shall be for meat" (Genesis 1:29). To a speaker of seventeenth-century English, *meat* meant 'food,' and *flesh* meant 'meat.' Since that time, semantic change has narrowed the meaning of *meat* to what it is in Modern English. The word *deer* once meant 'beast' or 'animal,' as its German cognate *Tier* still does. The meaning of *deer* has been narrowed to a particular kind of animal. Similarly, the word *hound* used to be the general term for 'dog,' like German *Hund.* Today *hound* refers to a certain class of dog breeds. *Skyline* once meant 'horizon' but has been narrowed to mean 'the outline of a city at the horizon.'

Meaning Shifts

The third kind of semantic change that a lexical item may undergo is a shift in meaning. The word *knight* once meant 'youth' but shifted to 'mounted man-at-arms.' *Lust* used to mean simply 'pleasure,' with no negative or sexual overtones. *Lewd* was merely 'ignorant,' and *immoral* meant 'not customary.' *Silly* used to mean 'happy' in Old English. By the Middle English period it had come to mean 'naive,' and only in Modern English does it mean 'foolish.' The overworked Modern English word *nice* meant 'ignorant' a thousand years ago. When Juliet tells Romeo, "I am too *fond*," she is not claiming she likes Romeo too much. She means 'I am too *foolish*.' And if a drone has you in its sights, look forward to something rather worse than a bee sting.

Reconstructing "Dead" Languages

None of your living languages for Miss Blimber. They must be dead—stone dead—and then Miss Blimber dug them up like a Ghoul.

CHARLES DICKENS, *Dombey and Son,* 1848

"Shoe," 1989, Macnelly/King Features Syndicate

Despite the disdain for the modern languages expressed by Miss Blimber, and the lament of Skyler, the hapless Latin pupil, it is through the comparative study of the living languages that linguists are able to learn about older languages and the changes that occurred over time.

The Nineteenth-Century Comparativists

> When agreement is found in words in two languages, and so frequently that rules may be drawn up for the shift in letters from one to the other, then there is a fundamental relationship between the two languages.
>
> **RASMUS RASK** (1787–1832)

The chief goal of the nineteenth-century historical and comparative linguists was to develop and elucidate the genetic relationships that exist among the world's languages. They aimed to establish the major language families of the world and to define principles for the classification of languages. They based their theories on observations of regular sound correspondences among certain languages. They proposed that languages displaying systematic similarities and differences must have descended from a common source language—that is, were genetically related.

As a child, Sir William Jones had an astounding propensity for learning languages, including so-called dead ones such as Ancient Greek and Latin. While residing in India he added Sanskrit to his studies and observed that Sanskrit bore to Greek and Latin "a stronger affinity . . . than could possibly have been produced by accident." Jones suggested that these three languages had "sprung from a common source" and that probably Germanic and Celtic had the same origin.

Following up on Jones's research, the German linguist Franz Bopp pointed out relationships among Sanskrit, Latin, Greek, Persian, and Germanic. At the same time, a young Danish scholar named Rasmus Rask corroborated these results, and brought Lithuanian and Armenian into the relationship as well. Rask was the first scholar to formally describe the regularity of certain phonological differences between related languages.

Earlier stage:[a]	bh	dh	gh	b	d	g	p	t	k
	↓	↓	↓	↓	↓	↓	↓	↓	↓
Later stage:	b	d	g	p	t	k	f	θ	x (or h)

FIGURE 8.2 | Grimm's Law, an early Germanic sound shift. Grimm's Law can be expressed in terms of natural classes of speech sounds: Voiced aspirates become unaspirated; voiced stops become voiceless; voiceless stops become fricatives.

[a]This "earlier stage" is Indo-European. The symbols bh, dh, and gh are breathy voiced stop consonants. These phonemes are often called "voiced aspirates."

Rask's work inspired the German linguist Jakob Grimm (of fairy-tale fame), who published a four-volume treatise (1819–1822) that specified the regular sound correspondences among Sanskrit, Greek, Latin, and the Germanic languages. Not only did the *similarities* intrigue Grimm, but so did the *systematic nature of the differences.* Where Latin has a [p], English often has an [f]; where Latin has a [t], English often has a [θ]; where Latin has a [k], English often has an [h].

Grimm posited a far earlier language (which we now refer to as Indo-European) from which all these languages evolved. He explained the sound correspondences by means of rules of phonological change (which historical linguists called **sound shift**, or **sound change**). Grimm's major discovery was that certain rules of sound change that applied to the Germanic family of languages, including the ancestors of English, did not apply to Sanskrit, Greek, and Latin. This accounted very nicely for many of the regular differences between the Germanic languages and the others. Because the sound changes discovered by Grimm were so strikingly regular, they became known as **Grimm's Law**, illustrated in Figure 8.2.

Cognates

The Family Circus

12-10
©1992 Bil Keane, Inc.
Dist. by Cowles Synd., Inc.

"Shouldn't a unicorn be called a uniHORN?"

Indo-European	Sanskrit	Latin	English
*p	p	p	f
	pitar-	pater	father
	pad-	ped-	foot
	No cognate	piscis	fish
	paśu[a]	pecu	fee

FIGURE 8.3 | Cognates of Indo-European *p.

[a] ś is a sibilant pronounced differently from s.

Cognates are words in related languages that developed from the same ancestral root, such as English *horn* and Latin *cornū*. Cognates often, but not always, have the same meaning in the different languages. From cognates we can observe sound correspondences and from them deduce sound changes. In Figure 8.3 the regular correspondence *p-p-f* of cognates from Sanskrit, Latin, and Germanic (represented by English) indicates that the languages are genetically related. Indo-European *p* is posited as the origin of the *p-p-f* correspondence.[3]

Figure 8.4 is a more detailed chart of correspondences, showing an example of each regular correspondence. For each line in the chart linguists can identify many further correspondences such as Sanskrit *pād-*, Latin *ped-*, and English *foot* for p-p-f, thereby showing the consistent and systematic relationships that lead to the reconstruction of the Indo-European sound shown in the first column.

Sanskrit underwent the fewest consonant changes (has more sounds in common with Indo-European), Latin somewhat more, and Germanic (under Grimm's Law) underwent almost a complete restructuring. The changes we observe are changes to the phonemes and phonological rules, and all words with those phonemes will reflect those changes (but see the "caveat" in the following paragraph). If we imagine that the changes happened independently to individual words, rather than individual sounds, we could not explain why so many words beginning with /p/ in Sanskrit and Latin just happen to begin with /f/ in Germanic, and so on. It would far exceed the possibilities of coincidence. It is the fact that the changes are in the phonology of the languages that has resulted in the remarkably regular, pervasive correspondences that allow us to reconstruct much of the Indo-European sound system.

Grimm noted that there were exceptions to the regular correspondences he observed. He stated: "The sound shift is a general tendency; it is not followed in every case." Several decades later, in 1875, Karl Verner explained some of

---

[3]The asterisk before a letter indicates a reconstructed sound, not an unacceptable form. This use of the asterisk occurs only in this chapter.

Indo-European	Sanskrit		Latin		English	
*p	p	pitar-	p	pater	f	father
*t	t	trayas	t	trēs	θ	three
*k	ś	śun	k	canis	h	hound
*b	b	No cognate	b	labium	p	lip
*d	d	dva-	d	duo	t	two
*g	j	ajras	g	ager	k	acre
*bh	bh	bhrātar-	f	frāter	b	brother
*dh	dh	dhā	f	fē-ci	d	do
*gh	h	vah-	h	veh-ō	g	wagon

FIGURE 8.4 | Some Indo-European sound correspondences.

the exceptions to Grimm's Law. He formulated **Verner's Law** to show why Indo-European *p, t,* and *k* failed to correspond to *f, θ,* and *x* in certain cases:

> *Verner's Law:* When the preceding vowel was unstressed *f, θ,* and *x* underwent a further change to *b, d,* and *g.*

Encouraged by the regularity of sound change, a group of young nineteenth-century linguists proposed the **Neo-Grammarian hypothesis**, which says that sound shifts are not merely tendencies (as Grimm claimed), but apply in *all* words that meet their environment. If exceptions were nevertheless observed, it was trusted that further laws would be discovered to explain them, just as Verner's Law explained the exceptions to Grimm's Law. The **Neogrammarians** viewed linguistics as a natural science and therefore believed that laws of sound change were unexceptionable natural laws. The "laws" they put forth often did have exceptions, however, which could not always be explained as dramatically as Verner's Law explained the exceptions to Grimm's Law. Still, the work of these linguists provides important data and insights into language change and why such changes occur.

The linguistic work that we have been discussing had some influence on Charles Darwin, and in turn, Darwin's theory of evolution had a profound influence on linguistics and on all science. Some linguists thought that languages had a "life cycle" and developed according to evolutionary laws. In addition, it was believed that every language could be traced to a common ancestor. This theory of biological naturalism has an element of truth to it, but it is an oversimplification of how languages change and evolve into other languages.

Comparative Reconstruction

. . . Philologists who chase

A panting syllable through time and space

Start it at home, and hunt it in the dark,

To Gaul, to Greece, and into Noah's Ark.

WILLIAM COWPER, "Retirement," 1782

When languages resemble one another in ways not attributable to chance or borrowing, or to general principles of Universal Grammar, we may conclude they are descended from a common source. That is, they evolved via linguistic change from an ancestral protolanguage.

The similarity of the basic vocabulary of languages such as English, German, Danish, Dutch, Norwegian, and Swedish is too pervasive for chance or borrowing. We therefore conclude that these languages have a common parent, Proto-Germanic. There are no written records of Proto-Germanic and certainly no native speakers alive today. Proto-Germanic is a partially reconstructed language whose properties have been deduced based on its descendants. In addition to related vocabulary, the Germanic languages share grammatical properties such as similar sets of irregular verbs, particularly the verb *to be*, and syntactic rules such as the verb (or auxiliary) movement rule discussed earlier in this chapter, further supporting their relatedness.

Once we know or suspect that several languages are related, their protolanguage may be partially determined by **comparative reconstruction**. This is done by applying the **comparative method**, which we illustrate with the following brief example.

Restricting ourselves to English, German, and Swedish, we find the word for 'man' is *man* /mæn/, *Mann* /man/, and *man* /man/, respectively. This is one of many word sets in which we can observe the regular sound correspondence m-m-m and n-n-n in the three languages. Based on this evidence, the comparative method has us reconstruct **mVn* as the word for 'man' in Proto-Germanic. The *V* indicates a vowel whose quality we are unsure of because, despite the similar spelling, the vowel is phonetically different in the various Germanic languages, and it is unclear how to reconstruct it without further evidence.

Although we are confident that we can reconstruct much of Proto-Germanic with relative accuracy, our reconstructions are hypotheses that we can never be sure about, and many details remain obscure. To build confidence in the comparative method, we can apply it to Romance languages such as French, Italian, Spanish, and Portuguese. Their parent language is the well-known Latin, so we can verify the method by testing it against written records of Latin. Consider the following data, focusing on the initial consonant of each word. In these data, *ch* in French is [ʃ], and *c* in the other languages is [k].

French	Italian	Spanish	Portuguese	English
cher	**c**aro	**c**aro	**c**aro	'dear'
champ	**c**ampo	**c**ampo	**c**ampo	'field'
chandelle	**c**andela	**c**andela	**c**andeia	'candle'

The French [ʃ] corresponds to [k] in the three other languages. This regular sound correspondence, [ʃ]-[k]-[k]-[k], supports the view that French, Italian, Spanish, and Portuguese descended from a common language. The comparative method leads to the reconstruction of [k] in 'dear,' 'field,' and 'candle' of the parent language, and shows that [k] underwent a change to [ʃ] in French, but not in Italian, Spanish, or Portuguese, which retained the original [k] of the parent language, Latin.

To use the comparative method, analysts identify regular sound correspondences in the cognates of potentially related languages. For each correspondence, they deduce the most likely sound in the parent language. In this way, much of the sound system of the parent may be reconstructed. The various phonological changes in the development of each daughter language as it descended and changed from the parent are then identified. Sometimes the sound that analysts choose in their reconstruction of the parent language is the one that appears most frequently in the correspondence. This is the "majority rule" principle, which we illustrated with the four Romance languages.

Other considerations may outweigh the majority rule principle. The likelihood of certain phonological changes may persuade the analyst to reconstruct a less frequently occurring sound, or even a sound that does not occur in the correspondence. Consider the data in these four hypothetical languages:

Language A	Language B	Language C	Language D
hono	hono	fono	vono
hari	hari	fari	veli
rahima	rahima	rafima	levima
hor	hor	for	vol

Wherever Languages A and B have an *h*, Language C has an *f* and Language D has a *v*. Therefore, we have the sound correspondence *h-h-f-v*. Using the majority rule principle, we might first consider reconstructing the sound *h* in the parent language, but from other data on historical change, and from phonetic research, we know that *h* seldom becomes *v*. The reverse, /f/ and /v/ becoming [h], occurs both historically and as a phonological rule and has an acoustic explanation. Therefore, linguists reconstruct an **f* in the parent, and posit the sound change "*f* becomes *h*" in Languages A and B, and "*f* becomes *v*" in Language D. This is the "naturalness principle" and one obviously needs experience and knowledge to apply it.

The other correspondences are not problematic as far as these data are concerned:

o-o-o-o   n-n-n-n   a-a-a-e   r-r-r-l   m-m-m-m

They lead to the reconstructed forms **o, *n, *a, *r,* and **m* for the parent language, and the sound changes "*a* becomes *e*" and "*r* becomes *l*" in Language D. These are natural sound changes found in many of the world's languages.

It is now possible to reconstruct the words of the protolanguage. They are **fono, *fari, *rafima,* and **for*. In this example, Language D is the most innovative of the three languages, because it has undergone three sound changes.

Language C is the most conservative in that it is identical to the protolanguage insofar as these data are concerned.

The sound changes seen in the previous illustrations are examples of **unconditioned sound change**. The changes occurred irrespective of phonetic context. Following is an example of **conditioned sound change**, taken from three dialects of Italian:

Standard	Northern	Lombard	
fisːo	fiso	fis	'fixed'
kasːa	kasa	kasə	'cabinet'

The correspondence sets are:

f-f-f   i-i-i   sː-s-s   o-o-<>[4]   k-k-k   a-a-a   a-a-ə

It is straightforward to reconstruct *f, *i, and *k. Knowing that a long consonant like sː commonly becomes s (recall Old English fː became f), we reconstruct *sː for the sː-s-s correspondence. A shortening change took place in the Northern and Lombard dialects.

There is evidence in these (very limited) data for a weakening of word-final vowels, again a change we discussed earlier for English. We reconstruct *o for o-o-<> and *a for a-a-ə. In Lombard, a conditioned sound change took place. The sound o was deleted in word-final position, but remained o elsewhere. The sound a became ə in word-final position and remained a elsewhere. As far as we can tell from the data presented, the conditioning factor is word-final position. Vowels in other positions do not undergo change.

We reconstruct the parent dialect as having had the words *fisːo meaning 'fixed' and *kasːa meaning 'cabinet.'

As our last example consider these data from an earlier and later form of a Slavic language. The question is, which came first? (When the comparative method is applied to earlier and later forms of a language the process is called **internal reconstruction**.)

L1	L2	
lovuka	lofkə	'clever'
gladuka	glatkə	'smooth'
ʒeʒika	ʒeʃkə	'burning hot'
kratuka	kratkə	'short'
blizuka	bliskə	'near'

The sound correspondences reading down through the data are: l-l, o-o, v-f, u-<>, k-k, a-ə, g-g, a-a, d-t, ʒ-ʒ, e-e, ʒ-ʃ, i-<>, r-r, t-t, b-b, i-i, z-s. These we reorganize into *nonproblematic*, where no change took place between older and newer forms, and *problematic*, where some kind of changes must have occurred:

Nonproblematic: l-l, o-o, k-k, g-g, e-e, r-r, b-b
Problematic: v-f, u-<>, a-ə, a-a, d-t, ʒ-ʒ, ʒ-ʃ, i-<>, t-t, i-i, z-s

To further understand the problematic correspondences we further reorganize by grouping vowels and consonants:

---

[4] The empty angled brackets indicate a loss of the sound.

Vowel correspondences: a-a, a-ə; i-i, i-<>; u-<>
Consonant correspondences: d-t, t-t; v-f; ʒ-ʒ, ʒ-ʃ; z-s

We now see that as far as vowels are concerned, L1 is an earlier form because there is evidence of a vowel weakening change, with vowels either deleted or reduced to schwa. The opposite change, of vowel insertion or strengthening, is unlikely. This is clearly a conditioned change because it doesn't occur in all phonetic contexts. There appear to be two such changes:

Change A: *a* becomes schwa in word-final position
Change: B: *i* and *u* are deleted in penultimate syllables

This is the best we can do with the data at hand. Further research may reveal that Change A applies to all vowels in word-final position, and that Change B applies to high vowels only, or perhaps to all vowels. We can't say anything more about the vowel *o*, either, given this restricted data. The matter is under-determined.

As for consonants, there is a change in voicing and while changes go both ways historically, from voiced to unvoiced or vice-versa, once persuaded by the vowel changes that L1 is earlier, a devoicing rule is seen as plausible. The d-d and d-t correspondence suggests a conditioned change, and a closer look at the data suggests a voicing assimilation rule.

Change C: Obstruents are devoiced when followed by a voiceless obstruent.

This is a commonly observed change and it supports the hypothesis that L1 is the earlier form.

There is one catch, however. In order for Change C to take place, Change B must have taken place first to bring the obstruents together. This, then, is an instance of historical rule ordering, not unlike the ordering of phonological rules that we observed in chapter 6.

It is by means of the comparative method that nineteenth-century linguists were able to initiate the reconstruction of Indo-European, the long-lost ancestral language so aptly conceived by Jones, Bopp, Rask, and Grimm: a language that flourished about 6,000 years ago.

Historical Evidence

You know my method. It is founded upon the observance of trifles.

SIR ARTHUR CONAN DOYLE, "The Boscombe Valley Mystery," in *The Memoirs of Sherlock Holmes*, 1891

The comparative method is not the only way to explore the history of a language or language family, and it may prove unable to answer certain questions because data are lacking or because reconstructions are untenable. For example, how do we know positively how Shakespeare or Chaucer or the author of *Beowulf* pronounced their versions of English? The comparative method leaves many details in doubt, and we have no recordings that give us direct knowledge.

Various documents from the past can be examined for evidence. Private letters are an excellent source of data. Linguists prefer letters written by naive spellers, who misspell words according to the way they pronounce them. For instance, at one point in English history, all words spelled with *er* in their stems were pronounced as if they were spelled with *ar*, just as in modern British English *clerk* and *derby* are pronounced "clark" and "darby." Some poor speller kept writing *parfet* for *perfect*, which helped linguists discover the older pronunciation.

Clues are also provided by the writings of the prescriptive grammarians of the period. Between 1550 and 1750 scholars known as orthoepists attempted to preserve the "purity" of English. In prescribing how people should speak, they told us how people actually spoke. An orthoepist alive in the United States today might write in a manual: "It is incorrect to pronounce *Cuba* with a final *r*." Future scholars would know that some speakers of English pronounced it that way.

Some of the best clues to earlier pronunciation are provided by puns and rhymes in literature. Two words rhyme if the vowels and final consonants are the same. When a poet rhymes the verb *found* with the noun *wound*, as in Shakespeare's *Romeo and Juliet*, it strongly suggests that the vowels of these two words were identical:

BENVOLIO: . . . 'tis in vain to seek him here that means not to be found.
ROMEO: He jests at scars that never felt a wound.

Shakespeare's rhymes are helpful in reconstructing the sound system of Elizabethan English. The rhyming of *convert* with *depart* in Sonnet XI strengthens the conclusion that *er* was pronounced as *ar*.

For many languages, written records go back more than a thousand years. With the invention of the printing press in the fifteenth century, written matter became increasingly prolific. Today an effort is underway to digitize everything ever printed so as to make it computer analyzable (see the section *The Culturomic Revolution* in chapter 11). With just four percent of the task accomplished the resulting corpus contains over 500 billion words of which 361 billion are in English, 45 billion in French, another 45 billion in Spanish, and so on down to Hebrew at two billion.

Using computers, linguists study these records to find out how languages were once pronounced. The spelling in early manuscripts tells us a great deal about the sound systems of older forms of modern languages. Two words spelled differently were probably pronounced differently. Once several orthographic contrasts are identified, good guesses can be made as to actual pronunciation. For example, because we spell *Mary*, *merry*, and *marry* differently, we may conclude that at one time most speakers pronounced them differently, probably [meri], [mɛri], and [mæri]. For at least one modern American dialect, only /ɛ/ can occur before /r/, so the three words are all pronounced [mɛri]. That is the result of a sound shift in which both /e/ and /æ/ shifted to /ɛ/ when followed immediately by /r/. This is another instance of a conditioned sound change.

As we will see in chapter 11, "culturomic analysis" reveals the change in usage of irregular versus regular morphological forms over the past two hundred years. Taking the observed rate of change as a measuring rod, historical linguists may be able to apply it to earlier periods that lack dated, written records to determine the span of time between earlier, reconstructed forms and their later counterparts.

Computer analysis of printed texts may be combined with the comparative method to deepen knowledge of language change and of earlier forms of a language. Dialect differences discovered through written records may permit comparison of the pronunciation of various words in several dialects. On that basis we can draw conclusions about earlier forms and see what changes took place in the inventory of sounds and in the phonological rules. We illustrated one such case with three Italian dialects on page 368. With the vast amounts of data now available, analyses of this kind should reveal more and more details about earlier forms of a language and how current forms evolved. (Much of this is discussed in chapter 11, which is about computational linguistics.)

The historical comparativists working on languages with written records have a challenging job, but not nearly as challenging as that of scholars who are attempting to discover genetic relationships among languages with no written history. Linguists must first transcribe large amounts of language data from all the languages; analyze them phonologically, morphologically, and syntactically; and establish a basis for relatedness such as similarities in basic vocabulary and regular sound correspondences not resulting from chance or borrowing. Only then can the comparative method be applied to reconstruct some extinct protolanguage.

Proceeding in this manner, linguists have discovered many relationships among Native American languages and have successfully reconstructed Amerindian protolanguages. Similar achievements have been made with the numerous languages spoken in Africa, which have been grouped into four overarching families: Afroasiatic, Nilo-Saharan, Niger-Congo, and Khoisan, spanning the continent more or less from the north to the south. For example, Somali is in the Afroasiatic family; Zulu is in the Niger-Congo family; and Hottentot, spoken in South Africa, is in the Khoisan family. These familial divisions are subject to revision if new discoveries or analyses deem it necessary.

Extinct and Endangered Languages

Any language is the supreme achievement of a uniquely human collective genius, as divine and unfathomable a mystery as a living organism.

MICHAEL KRAUSS, in a speech to the Linguistic Society of America, 1991

I am always sorry when any language is lost, because languages are the pedigree of nations.

SAMUEL JOHNSON (1709–1784)

A language dies and becomes extinct when no children learn it. Linguists have identified several ways in which a language might cease to exist, at least in its spoken form.

A language may die out more or less suddenly when all of the speakers of the language themselves die or are killed. Such was the case with Tasmanian languages, once spoken on the island of Tasmania, and Nicoleño, a Native American Indian language once spoken in California.

Similarly, a language may cease to exist relatively abruptly when its speakers all stop speaking the language. This may happen under the threat of political repression or even genocide. Indigenous languages embedded in other cultures suffer death this way. In order to avoid being identified as "natives," speakers simply stop speaking their native language. Children are unable to learn a language that is not spoken to them, so when the last speaker dies, the language dies.

Most commonly, languages that become extinct do so gradually, often over several generations. This happens to minority languages that are in contact with a dominant language, much as American Indian languages are in contact with English. In each generation, fewer and fewer children learn the language until there are no new learners. The language is said to be dead when the last generation of speakers dies out. Cornish suffered this fate in Britain in the eighteenth century (though recent attempts at revival have resulted in about three hundred nonnative speakers of the language), as have many Native American languages in both North and South America.

While this phenomenon is not common, some languages suffer "partial death" in that they survive only in specific contexts, such as a liturgical language. Latin and (at one time) Hebrew are such languages. Latin evolved into the Romance languages and by the ninth century there were few if any peoples speaking Latin in daily situations. Today its use is confined to scholarly and religious contexts.

Many Native American languages are experiencing a reduction in the number of native speakers over time. Only 20 percent of the remaining indigenous languages in the United States are being acquired by children. Hundreds have already ceased to be written or spoken. In the 1500s, at the time of the first European contact, there were over 1,000 indigenous languages spoken throughout the Americas. Once widely spoken American Indian languages such as Comanche, Apache, and Cherokee have fewer native speakers every generation.

Doomed languages have existed throughout time. The Indo-European languages Hittite and Tocharian no longer exist. Hittite disappeared 3,200 years ago, and both dialects of Tocharian gave up the ghost around 1000 CE.

Dialects, too, may become extinct. Here is an excerpt from the first paragraph of an AP press release, 10/4/2012:

> LONDON—In a remote fishing town on the tip of Scotland's Black Isle, the last native speaker of the Cromarty dialect has passed away, taking with him a little fragment of the English linguistic mosaic.

Many dialects spoken in the United States are considered endangered by linguists. For example, the sociolinguist Walt Wolfram is studying the dialect spoken on Ocracoke Island off the coast of North Carolina. One reason for the study is to preserve the dialect, which is in danger of extinction because so many young Ocracokers leave the island and raise their children elsewhere, a case of *gradual dialect death*. Vacationers and retirees are diluting the dialect-speaking population, because they are attracted to the island by its unique character, including, ironically, the quaint speech of the islanders.

Linguists have placed many languages on an endangered list. They attempt to preserve these languages by studying and documenting their grammars—the phonetics, phonology, and so on—and by recording for posterity the speech of the last few speakers. Each language provides new evidence on the nature of human cognition through its grammar. In its literature, poetry, ritual speech, and word structure, each language stores the collective intellectual achievements of a culture, offering unique perspectives on the human condition. The disappearance of a language is tragic; not only are these insights lost, but the major medium through which a culture maintains and renews itself is gone as well.

Linguists are not alone in their preservation efforts. Under the sponsorship of language clubs, and occasionally even governments, adults and children learn an endangered language as a symbol of the culture. Gael Linn is a private organization in Ireland that runs language classes in Irish (Gaelic) for adults. Hundreds of public schools in Ireland and Northern Ireland are conducted entirely in Gaelic. In the U.S. state of Hawaii, a movement is under way to preserve and teach Hawaiian, the native language of the islands.

This attempt to slow down or reverse the dying out of a language is also illustrated by the French in Quebec. In 1961, the Quebec Office of the French Language was formed to standardize the dialect of French spoken in Quebec, but ironically refuses to do so for fear of reducing the interintelligibility with other French-speaking communities. It is believed that standardization would linguistically isolate Quebecers and lead to the extinction of French in Canada. Instead, the office uses its powers to promote the use of French, irrespective of dialect.

An astonishing example of the revival of a dormant language occurred in Israel. For centuries, classical Hebrew was used only in religious ceremonies, but today, with some modernization, it has become the national language of Israel. The Academy of the Hebrew Language in Israel undertook a task that had never been done in the history of humanity—to awaken an ancient written language to serve the daily colloquial needs of the people. Twenty-three lexicologists worked with the Bible and the Talmud to add new words to the language. While there is some attempt to keep the language "pure," the academy has given way to popular pressure. Thus, a bank check is called a *check* [tʃɛk] in the singular and pluralized by adding the Hebrew plural suffix *-im* to form *check-im*, although the Hebrew word *hamcha'ah* was proposed. Similarly, *lipstick* has triumphed over *s'faton* and *pajama* over *chalifat-sheinah* (lit., sleeping suit).

The United Nations, too, is concerned about endangered languages. In 1991, the United Nations Educational, Scientific, and Cultural Organization (UNESCO) passed a resolution that states:

> As the disappearance of any one language constitutes an irretrievable loss to mankind, it is for UNESCO a task of great urgency to respond to this situation by promoting . . . the description—in the form of grammars, dictionaries, and texts—of endangered and dying languages.

The documentation and preservation of dying languages is not only important for social and cultural reasons. There is also a scientific reason for studying these languages. Through examining a wide array of different types of languages, linguists can develop a comprehensive theory of language that accounts for both its universal and language-specific properties.

The Genetic Classification of Languages

The Sanskrit language, whatever be its antiquity, is of a wonderful structure, more perfect than the Greek, more copious than the Latin, and more exquisitely refined than either, yet bearing to both of them a stronger affinity, both in the roots of verbs and in the forms of grammar, than could possibly have been produced by accident; so strong, indeed, that no philologer could examine all three, without believing that they have sprung from some common source, which, perhaps, no longer exists. . . .

SIR WILLIAM JONES (1746–1794)

We have discussed how different languages evolve from one language and how historical and comparative linguists classify languages into families such as Germanic or Romance and reconstruct earlier forms of the ancestral language. When we examine the languages of the world, we perceive similarities and differences among them that provide evidence for degrees of relatedness or for nonrelatedness.

Counting to five in English, German, and Vietnamese shows similarities between English and German not shared by Vietnamese (shown with tones omitted):

English	German	Vietnamese
one	eins	mot
two	zwei	hai
three	drei	ba
four	vier	bon
five	fünf	nam

The similarity between English and German is pervasive. Sometimes it is extremely obvious (*man/Mann*), but at other times a little less obvious (*child/Kind*). No regular similarities or differences apart from those resulting from chance are found between them and Vietnamese.

Pursuing the metaphor of human genealogy, we say that English, German, Norwegian, Danish, Swedish, Icelandic, and so on are sister languages in that they descended from one parent and are more closely related to one another than any of them are to non-Germanic languages such as French or Russian.

The Romance languages are also sister languages whose parent is Latin. If we carry the family metaphor to an extreme, we might describe the Germanic languages and the Romance languages as cousins, because their respective parents, Proto-Germanic and early forms of Latin, were siblings.

As anyone from a large family knows, there are cousins, and then there are distant cousins, encompassing nearly anyone with a claim to family bloodlines. This is true of the Indo-European family of languages. If the Germanic and Romance languages are truly cousins, then languages such as Greek, Armenian, Albanian, and even the extinct Hittite and Tocharian are distant cousins. So are Irish, Scots Gaelic, Welsh, and Breton, whose protolanguage, Celtic, was once spoken widely throughout Europe and the British Isles. Breton is spoken in Brittany in the northwest coastal regions of France. It was brought there by Celts fleeing from Britain in the seventh century.

Russian is also a distant cousin, as are its sisters, Bulgarian, Serbo-Croatian, Polish, Czech, and Slovak. The Baltic language Lithuanian is related to English, as is its sister language, Latvian. A neighboring language, Estonian, however, is not a relative. Sanskrit, although far removed geographically, is nonetheless a relative, as pointed out by Sir William Jones. Its offspring, Hindi and Bengali, spoken primarily in South Asia, are distantly related to English. Persian (called Farsi in Iran, Dari in Afghanistan) is a distant cousin of English, as is Kurdish, which is spoken in Iran, Iraq, and Turkey; and Pashto, which is spoken in Afghanistan and Pakistan. All these languages, except for Estonian, are related, more or less distantly, to one another because they all descended from Indo-European.

Figure 8.5 on page 376 is an abbreviated family tree of the Indo-European languages that gives a genealogical and historical classification of the languages shown. This diagram is somewhat simplified. For example, it appears that all the Slavic languages are sisters. In fact, the nine languages shown can be organized hierarchically, showing some more closely related than others. In other words, the various separations that resulted in the nine Slavic languages we see today occurred several times over a long stretch of time. Similar remarks apply to the other families, including Indo-European.

Another simplification is that the "dead ends"—languages that evolved and died leaving no offspring—are not included. We have already mentioned Hittite and Tocharian as two such Indo-European languages. The family tree also fails to show several intermediate stages that must have existed in the evolution of modern languages. Languages do not evolve abruptly, which is why comparisons with the genealogical trees of biology have limited usefulness. Finally, the diagram fails to show some Indo-European languages because of lack of space.

Languages of the World

And the whole earth was of one language, and of one speech.

GENESIS 11:1, *The Bible*, King James Version

Let us go down, and there confound their language, that they may not understand one another's speech.

GENESIS 11:7, *The Bible*, King James Version

Most of the world's languages do not belong to the Indo-European family. Linguists have also attempted to classify the non-Indo-European languages according to their genetic relationships. The task is to identify the languages that constitute a family and the relationships that exist among them.

The two most common questions asked of linguists are: "How many languages do you speak?" and "How many languages are there in the world?" Both questions are difficult to answer precisely. Most linguists have varying degrees of familiarity with several languages, and many are **polyglots**, persons who speak and understand several languages. Charles V, the Holy Roman

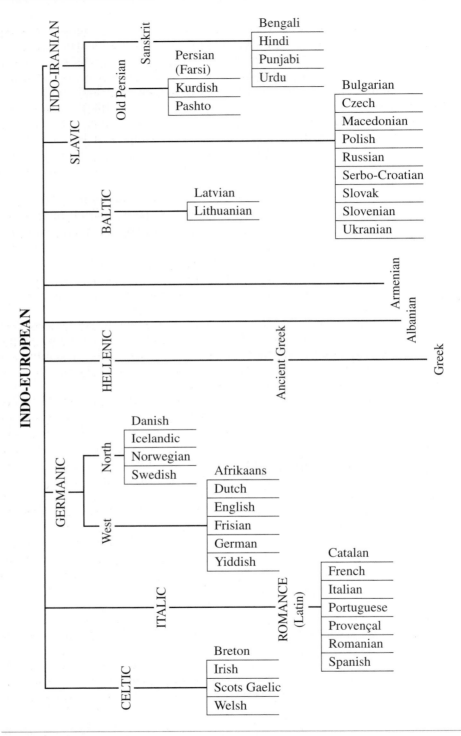

FIGURE 8.5 | The Indo-European family of languages.

Emperor from 1519 to 1558, was a polyglot, for he proclaimed: "I speak Spanish to God, Italian to women, French to men, and German to my horse."

As to the second question, it's difficult to ascertain the precise number of languages in the world because there are no clear criteria to decide what is a language and what is a dialect, as discussed in the previous chapter.

With this caveat in mind, recent estimates place the number of spoken languages in the world today (2013) at somewhat less than 7,000, according to the encyclopedia Ethnologue: Languages of the World (see http://www.ethnologue .com/web.asp for more detail). The Ethnologue lists 130 sign languages, from every continent where languages are spoken, though this number is in dispute and may be very much larger. In the city of Los Angeles alone, more than 80 languages are spoken. Students at Hollywood High School go home to hear their parents speak Amharic, Armenian, Arabic, Marshallese, Urdu, Sinhalese, Ibo, Gujarati, Hmong, Afrikaans, Khmer, Ukrainian, Cambodian, Spanish, Tagalog, and Russian, among others.

It is often surprising to discover which languages are genetically related and which ones are not. Nepali, the language of remote Nepal, is an Indo-European language, whereas Hungarian, surrounded on all sides by Indo-European languages, is not.

Some languages have no demonstrable genealogical relationship with other living languages. They are called **language isolates**. Ainu, spoken on the island of Hokkaido, Japan, and Zuni spoken in the southwestern United States are among the fifty or so isolates mentioned in the Ethnologue. Many sign languages, insofar as it can be determined, are isolates.

It is not possible in an introductory text to give an exhaustive table of families, subfamilies, and individual languages. Besides, some genetic relationships have not yet been firmly established. For example, linguists are divided as to whether Japanese and Turkish are related. We simply mention several language families in the following paragraphs with a few of their members. These language families do not appear to be related to one another or to Indo-European. This, however, may be an artifact of being unable to delve into the past far enough to see common features that time has erased. We cannot eliminate the possibility that the entire world's languages spring ultimately from a single source, an "ur-language" that some have termed **Nostratic**, which is buried, if not concealed, in the depths of the past. Readers interested in this fascinating topic may wish to read the writings of Professor Johanna Nichols of the University of California at Berkeley. And of course more can be found by googling *nostratic*.

Uralic is the other major family of languages, besides Indo-European, that is spoken on the European continent. Hungarian, Finnish, and Estonian are the major representatives of this group.

Afro-Asiatic is a large family of languages spoken in northern Africa and the Middle East. It includes the modern *Semitic* languages of Hebrew and Arabic, as well as languages spoken in biblical times such as Aramaic, Babylonian, Canaanite, and Moabite.

The *Sino-Tibetan* family includes Mandarin, the most populous language in the world, spoken by more than one billion Chinese. This family also includes all of the other Chinese languages, as well as Burmese and Tibetan.

Most of the languages of Africa belong to the *Niger-Congo* family, a huge family comprising more than one-fifth of the world's languages (about fifteen hundred). These include more than nine hundred languages grouped into sub-families such as Kordofanian and Atlantic-Congo. The latter includes individual languages such as Swahili and Zulu.

Nearly as numerous, the *Austronesian* family contains about thirteen hundred languages, spoken over a wide expanse of the globe, from Madagascar, off the coast of Africa, to Hawaii. Hawaiian is an Austronesian language, as are Maori, spoken in New Zealand; Tagalog, spoken in the Philippine Islands; and Malay, spoken in Malaysia and Singapore, to mention just a few.

Surprisingly, the next most numerous family, called *Trans-New Guinea*, is crowded into the relatively small geographic area of New Guinea and neighboring islands, and contains nearly five hundred languages, most of them being Papuan languages. Thus three language families alone make up half of the languages spoken in the world.

Dozens of families and hundreds of languages are, or were, spoken in North and South America. Knowledge of the genetic relationships among these families of languages is often tenuous, and because so many of the languages are approaching extinction, there may be little hope for as thorough an understanding of the Amerindian language families as linguists have achieved for Indo-European.

For those readers interested in far more information regarding endangered languages, we encourage you to examine the website http://www.endangeredlanguages.com created in 2012 by the Alliance for Linguistic Diversity.

Types of Languages

All the Oriental nations jam tongue and words together in the throat, like the Hebrews and Syrians. All the Mediterranean peoples push their enunciation forward to the palate, like the Greeks and the Asians. All the Occidentals break their words on the teeth, like the Italians and Spaniards. . . .

ISIDORE OF SEVILLE, 7th century CE

There are many ways to classify languages. One way already discussed in this chapter is according to the language family—the genetic classification. This method is like classifying people according to whether they were related by blood. Another way of classifying languages is by certain linguistic traits, regardless of family. With people, this method would be like classifying them according to height and weight, political preference, religion, degree of wealth, and so on.

So far in this book we have hinted at the different ways that languages might be classified. From a phonological point of view, we have tone languages versus non-tone languages—Thai versus English. We have languages with varying numbers of vowel phonemes, from as few as three to as high as a dozen or more. Languages may be classified according the number and kinds of consonants they have and also in terms of what combinations of consonants and vowels may form syllables. Japanese and Hawaiian allow few syllable types (CV and V, mostly), whereas English and most Indo-European languages allow a much wider variety. Languages may use stress phonemically (English), or not (French).

From a morphological standpoint, languages may be classified according to the richness of verb and noun morphology. For example, Vietnamese has little if any word morphology, so its words are monomorphemic; there are no plural affixes on nouns or agreement affixes on verbs. Such languages are referred to as **isolating** or **analytic**. Languages like English have a middling amount of morphology, much less than Old English or Latin once had, or than Russian has today. Languages with more than one morpheme per word are called **synthetic**. Yet other languages—termed **polysynthetic** by linguists—have extraordinarily rich morphologies in which a single word may have ten or more affixes and carry the semantic load of an entire English sentence. Many native languages of North America are polysynthetic, including Mohawk, Cherokee, and Menominee. For example, the Menominee word *paehtāwāēwesew* means 'He is heard by higher powers.'

Some synthetic languages are **agglutinative**: words may be formed by a root and multiple affixes where the affixes are easily separated and always retain the same meaning. Swahili is such a language (see exercise 9, chapter 2). The word *ninafika* is *ni* + *na* + *fika*, meaning 'I-present-arrive'; *ni* + *ta* + *fika* means 'I-will-arrive'; *wa* + *li* + *fika* means 'we-past-arrive'; and so on. Each morpheme is unchanging in form and meaning from one word to the next. Turkish is also an agglutinative language, as illustrated in exercise 17 in chapter 2.

In a **fusional** synthetic language the morphemes are, well, fused together, so it is hard to identify their basic shape. Many Indo-European languages are of this type, such as Spanish. In *hablo, hablan, hablé*, meaning 'I speak', 'they speak', 'I spoke,' the affixes carry a fusion of the meanings 'person' and 'number' and 'tense' so that *-o* means 'first person, singular, present,' *-an* means 'third person, plural, present' and *-e* means 'first person, singular, past.' The affixes themselves cannot be decomposed into the individual meanings that they bear.

From a lexical standpoint, languages are classifiable as to whether they have articles like *the* and *a* in English; as to their system of pronouns and what distinctions are made regarding person, number, and gender; as to their vocabulary for describing family members; as to whether they have noun classes such as the masculine, feminine, and neuter nouns of German, or the multiple noun classes present in Swahili that we observed in chapter 2, and so on.

Every language has sentences that include a subject (S), an object (O), and a verb (V), although individual sentences may not contain all three elements. From the point of view of syntax, languages have been classified according to the dominant order in which these elements occur in sentences. There are six possible orders—SVO (subject, verb, object), SOV, VSO, VOS, OVS, and OSV—permitting, in theory, six possible language types. Of these, SVO and SOV languages make up nearly 90 percent of investigated languages in roughly equal proportions. English, Spanish, and Thai are SVO; German, Dutch, and Japanese illustrate SOV languages.

In SVO languages, auxiliary verbs precede main verbs, adverbs follow main verbs, and prepositions precede the noun in PPs. Here are English examples:

They are eating. (Aux-V)
They sing beautifully. (V-Adv) (Cf. *They beautifully sing.)
They are from Tokyo. (Prep-N)

In SOV languages, the opposite tendencies are true. Auxiliary verbs follow the main verb, adverbs precede main verbs, and "prepositions," now called *postpositions*, follow the noun in PPs. Here are Japanese examples:

Akiko	wa	sakana	o		tabete	iru. (V-Aux)
Akiko	*topic marker*	fish	*object marker*		eating	is

'Akiko is eating fish.'

Akiko	wa	hayaku	tabemasu.	(Adv-V)
Akiko	*topic marker*	quickly	eats	

'Akiko eats quickly.'

Akiko	wa	Tokyo	kara		desu.	(N-PostP)
Akiko	*topic marker*	Tokyo	from		is	

'Akiko is from Tokyo.'

These differences, and many more like them, stem from a single underlying parameter choice: the placement of the head of phrase. SVO languages are head-initial; SOV languages are head-final.

The question of why SVO and SOV languages are dominant is not completely understood, but linguists have observed that two principles or constraints are favored:

(1) Subjects precede objects.
(2) The verb V is adjacent to the object O.

SVO and SOV are the only two types that obey both principles. The next most common type in appearance is VSO, here illustrated by Tagalog, which is widely spoken in the Philippine Islands:

Sumagot	siya	sa	propesor.
answered	he	the	professor

'He answered the professor.'

VSO languages account for nearly 10 percent of languages investigated—the lion's share of what's left over after SVO and SOV languages. It is possible, however, that the VSO order is derived from an underlying order in which the verb and object are adjacent, so there is no violation of principle (2).

Malagasy, spoken on the island of Madagascar, has sentences that on the surface translate literally as the VOS sentence *put—the book on the table—the woman*, meaning 'The woman put the book on the table.' This would violate principle (1). However, linguists have shown that such sentences are derived from a deeper SVO order that is then transformed by rules that move constituents. Apparent OVS and OSV languages may also be derived from underlying orders that are either SVO or SOV and conform to the two principles, though this remains a subject for linguistic research.

That a language is SVO does not mean that SVO is the only possible word order in surface structure. The correlations between language type and the word order of syntactic categories in sentences are *preferred* word orders, and for the most part are violable tendencies. Different languages follow them to a greater or lesser degree. Thus, when a famous comedian said "Believe you me" on network TV, he was understood and imitated despite the VSO word order. Yoda, the Jedi Master of *Star Wars* fame, speaks a strange but perfectly understandable style of English that achieves its eccentricity by being OSV. (Objects may be categories other than Noun Phrases.) Some of Yoda's utterances are:

Sick I've become.
Around the survivors a perimeter create.
Strong with The Force you are.
Impossible to see the future is.
When nine hundred years you reach, look as good you will not.

For linguists, the many languages and language families provide essential data for the study of universal grammar. Although these languages are diverse in many ways, they are also remarkably similar in many ways. We find that languages from northern Greenland to southern New Zealand, from the Far East to the Far West, all have similar sounds, similar phonological and syntactic rules, and similar semantic systems.

Why Do Languages Change?

Some method should be thought on for ascertaining and fixing our language forever. . . .
I see no absolute necessity why any language should be perpetually changing.

JONATHAN SWIFT (1667–1745)

Stability in language is synonymous with rigor mortis.

ERNEST WEEKLEY (1865–1954)

No one knows exactly how or why languages change. As we have shown, linguistic changes do not happen suddenly. Speakers of English did not wake up one morning and decide to use the word *beef* for 'ox meat,' nor do all the children of one particular generation grow up to adopt a new word. Changes are more gradual, particularly changes in the phonological and syntactic system.

For any one speaker, certain changes may occur instantaneously. When someone acquires a new word, it is not acquired gradually, although full appreciation for all of its possible uses may come slowly. When a new rule enters a speaker's grammar, it is either in or not in the grammar. It may at first be an optional rule, so that sometimes it is used and sometimes it is not, possibly determined by social context or other external factors (see previous chapter), but the rule is either there and available for use or not. What is gradual about language change is the spread of certain changes through an entire speech community.

A basic cause of change is the way children acquire the language. No one teaches a child the rules of the grammar. Each child constructs the grammar of her language alone, generalizing rules from the linguistic input she receives. As discussed in the chapter on language acquisition, the child's language develops in stages until it approximates the adult grammar. The child's grammar is never exactly like that of the adult community because children receive diverse linguistic input. Certain rules may be simplified or overgeneralized, and vocabularies may show small differences that accumulate over several generations.

The older generation may be using certain rules optionally. For example, at certain times they may say "It's I" and at other times "It's me." The less formal style is usually used with children, who, as the next generation, may use only the "me" form of the pronoun in this construction. In such cases the grammar will have changed.

The reasons for some changes are relatively easy to understand. Before television there was no such word as *television*. It soon became a common lexical item. Borrowed words, too, generally serve a useful purpose, and their entry into the language is not mysterious. Other changes are more difficult to explain, such as the Great Vowel Shift in English.

One plausible source of sound change is *assimilation*, an *ease of articulation* process in which one sound influences the pronunciation of an adjacent or nearby sound. For example, vowels are frequently nasalized before nasal consonants because it is easiest to lower the velum to produce nasality in advance of the actual consonant articulation. Once the vowel is nasalized, the contrast that the nasal consonant provided can be equally well provided by the nasalized vowel alone, and the redundant consonant may no longer be pronounced. The contrast between oral and nasal vowels that exists in many languages of the world today (such as French) resulted from just such a historical sound change.

In reconstructing older versions of French, it has been hypothesized that *bol*, 'basin,' *botte*, 'high boot,' *bog*, 'a card game,' *bock*, 'Bock beer,' and *bon*, 'good,' were pronounced [bɔl], [bɔt], [bɔg], [bɔk], and [bɔ̃n], respectively. The nasalized vowel in *bon* resulted from the final nasal consonant. Because of a conditioned sound change that deleted nasal consonants in word-final position, *bon* is pronounced [bɔ̃] in modern French. The nasal vowel alone maintains the contrast with the other words.

Another example from English illustrates how such assimilative processes can change a language. In Old English, word initial [kʲ] (like the initial sound of *cute*), when followed by /i/, was further palatalized to become our modern palatal affricate /tʃ/, as illustrated by the following words:

Old English (c = [kʲ])	Modern English (ch = [tʃ])
ciese	cheese
cinn	chin
cild	child

The process of palatalization is found in the history of many languages. In Twi, the word meaning 'to hate' was once pronounced [ki]. The [k] became first [kʲ] and then finally [tʃ], so that today 'to hate' is [tʃi].

Ease of articulation processes, which make sounds more alike, are countered by the need to maintain perceptibility. Thus sound change also occurs when two sounds are so acoustically similar that there is a risk of confusion. We saw a sound change of /f/ to /h/ in an earlier example that can be explained by the acoustic similarity of [f] to other sounds.

Analogic change is a generalization of rules that reduces the number of exceptional or irregular morphemes. It was by analogy to *plow/plows* and *vow/vows* that speakers started saying *cows* as the plural of *cow* instead of the earlier plural *kine*. In effect, the plural rule became more general.

The generalization of the plural rule continues today with forms such as *yous* (plural of you) used by many speakers in place of the homophonous *you* for singular and plural.

Plural marking continues to undergo analogic change, as exemplified by the regularization of exceptional plural forms. The plural forms of borrowed words like *datum/data, agendum/agenda, curriculum/curricula, memorandum/memoranda, medium/media, criterion/criteria,* and *virtuoso/virtuosi* are being replaced by regular plurals by many speakers: *agendas, curriculums, memorandums, criterias,* and *virtuosos*. In some cases the borrowed original plural forms were considered to be the singular (as in *agenda* and *criteria*), and the new plural (e.g., *agendas*) is therefore a "plural-plural." In addition, many speakers now regard *data* and *media* as nouns that do not have plural forms, like *information*. All these changes are "economy of memory" changes and lessen the number of irregular forms that must be remembered.

The past-tense rule is also undergoing generalization. By analogy to *bake/baked* and *ignite/ignited*, many children and adults now say *I waked last night* (instead of *woke*) and *She lighted the bonfire* (instead of *lit*). These regular past-tense forms are found in today's dictionaries next to the irregular forms, with which they currently coexist. Similarly, in various communities irregular past participles are being replaced by past tense forms. For example, instead of *I have gone* or *I've driven*, speakers of these dialects say *I have went, I've drove*. This simplification of the verb paradigm for irregular verbs is presumably happening on analogy with the regular verb paradigm in which the past tense and the participle forms are the same, for example, *I dance, I danced, I have danced.*

Assimilation and analogic change account for some linguistic changes, but they cannot account for others. Simplification and regularization of grammars occur, but so does elaboration or complication. Old English rules of syntax became more complex, imposing a stricter word order on the language, at the same time that case endings were being simplified. A tendency toward simplification is counteracted by the need to limit potential ambiguity. Much of language change is a balance between the two.

Language contact is also a vehicle of language change, particularly with respect to lexical changes due to borrowing, and also phonological changes such as the introduction of new phonemes. As we saw earlier, /v/ came into English owing to its intimate contact with French following the Norman invasion.

Many factors contribute to linguistic change: simplification of grammars, elaboration to maintain intelligibility, borrowing, and so on. Changes are actualized by children learning the language, who incorporate them into their grammar. The exact reasons for linguistic change are still elusive, although it is clear that the imperfect learning of the adult languages by children is a contributing factor. Perhaps language changes for the same reason all things change: it is the nature of things to change. As Heraclitus pointed out centuries ago, "All is flux, nothing stays still. Nothing endures but change."

Summary

All living languages change. Linguistic change such as **sound shift** is found in the history of all languages, as evidenced by the **regular sound correspondences** that exist between different stages of the same language, different dialects of the same language, and different languages. Languages that evolve from a common source are **genetically related**. Genetically related languages were once dialects of the same language. For example, English, German, and Swedish were dialects of a postulated earlier form of Germanic called **Proto-Germanic**, whereas earlier forms of Romance languages, such as Spanish, French, and Italian, were dialects of Latin. Going back even further in time, earlier forms of Proto-Germanic, Latin, and other languages were dialects of (**Proto-**)**Indo-European**, a postulated ancestor.

All components of the grammar may change. Phonological, morphological, syntactic, lexical, and semantic changes occur. Words, morphemes, phonemes, and rules of all types may be added, lost, or altered. The meanings of words and morphemes may **broaden**, **narrow**, or shift. The lexicon may expand by **borrowing**, which results in **loan words** in the vocabulary. This is very common in **language contact** situations. It also grows through word coinage, blends, compounding, acronyms, and other processes of word formation. On the other hand, the contemporary lexicon may shrink as the frequency of usage of words like *typewriter*, *blackboard*, and *phone booth* fall below a threshold level.

The study of linguistic change is called **historical and comparative linguistics**. Linguists use the **comparative method** to identify regular sound correspondences among the **cognates** of related languages and systematically reconstruct an earlier **protolanguage**. This **comparative reconstruction** allows linguists to peer backward in time and determine the linguistic history of a language family, which may then be represented in a tree diagram similar to Figure 8.5. **Internal reconstruction** uses the same methods applied to different stages of the same language. Where available, written texts are also used to inform linguists about language change.

Recent estimates place the number of languages in the world today (2013) at somewhat less than 7,000 plus a hundred or more sign languages. These languages are grouped into families, subfamilies, and so on, based on their genetic relationships. A vast number of these languages are dying out because in each generation fewer children learn them. However, attempts are being made to preserve dying languages and dialects for the knowledge they bring to the study of Universal Grammar and the cultures in which they are spoken.

Languages may also be classified according to certain characteristics such as a rich versus an impoverished morphology (**synthetic** versus **analytic**), or according to whether their basic word order is Subject-Verb-Object (SVO) like English, or Subject-Object-Verb (SOV) like Japanese, or possibly some other order.

No one knows all the causes of linguistic change. Some sound changes result from assimilation, a fundamentally physiological process of ease of articulation. Others, like the **Great Vowel Shift**, are more difficult to explain. Some grammatical changes are **analogic changes**, generalizations that lead to more regularity, such as *cows* instead of *kine* and *waked* instead of *woke*.

Change comes about through the restructuring of the grammar and lexicon by children learning the language. Grammars may appear to change in the direction of simplicity and regularity, as in the loss of the Indo-European case morphology, but such simplifications may be compensated for by other complexities, such as stricter word order. A balance is always present between simplicity—languages must be learnable—and complexity—languages must be expressive and relatively unambiguous.

References for Further Reading

Aitchison, J. 2001. *Language change: Progress or decay? 3rd ed.* Cambridge, New York, Melbourne: Cambridge University Press.

Anttila, R. 1989. *Historical and comparative linguistics.* New York: John Benjamins.

Baugh, A. C., and T. Cable. 2002. *A history of the English language, 5th ed.* Upper Saddle River, NJ: Pearson Education.

Campbell, L. 2004. *Historical linguistics: An introduction, 2nd ed.* Cambridge, MA: MIT Press.

Comrie, B. (ed.). 1990. *The world's major languages.* New York: Oxford University Press.

Hock, H. H., and B. D. Joseph. 1996. *Language history, language change, and language relationship: An introduction to historical and comparative linguistics.* New York: Mouton de Gruyter.

Lehmann, W. P. 1992. *Historical linguistics: An introduction, 3rd ed.* London, New York: Routledge.

Lewis, M. Paul (ed.), 2009. *Ethnologue: Languages of the world, 16th ed.* Dallas, Tex.: SIL International. (http://www.ethnologue.com/)

Lightfoot, D. 1984. *The language lottery.* Cambridge, MA: MIT Press.

Michel, J-B, et al. "Quantitative analysis of culture using millions of digitized books." *Science,* v. 331, pp 176–182, Jan 14, 2011.

Normile, D. "Experiments probe language's origins and development." *Science,* v. 336, pp 408-411, Apr 27, 2012.

Pyles, T., and J. Algeo. 2005. *The origins and development of the English language, 5th ed.* Boston: Thomson/Wadsworth.

Wolfram, W. 2001. Language death and dying. In Chambers, J. K., Trudgill, P., and Schilling-Estes, N. (eds.), *The handbook on language variation and change.* Oxford, UK: Basil Blackwell.

Exercises

1. Many changes in the phonological system have occurred in English since 449 CE. Below are some Old English words (given in their spelling and phonetic forms) and the same words as we pronounce them today. They are typical of regular sound changes that took place in English. What sound change or changes have occurred in each case?

   Example: OE hlud [xluːd]   →   Mod. Eng. loud

   Changes: (1) The [x] was lost.
               (2) The long vowel [uː] became [aʊ].

	OE		Mod E
a.	crabba [kraba]	→	crab
	Changes:		
b.	fisc [fɪsk]	→	fish
	Changes:		
c.	fūl [fuːl]	→	foul
	Changes:		
d.	gāt [gaːt]	→	goat
	Changes:		
e.	lǣfan [læːvan]	→	leave
	Changes:		
f.	tēþ [teːθ]	→	teeth
	Changes:		

2. The Great Vowel Shift left its traces in Modern English in such meaning-related pairs as:

   (1) serene/serenity [i]/[ɛ]
   (2) divine/divinity [aɪ]/[ɪ]
   (3) sane/sanity [e]/[æ]

   List five such meaning-related pairs that relate [i] and [ɛ] as in example (1), five that relate [aɪ] and [ɪ] as in example (2), and five that relate [e] and [æ] as in example (3).

	[i]/[ɛ]	[aɪ]/[ɪ]	[e]/[æ]
a.			
b.			
c.			
d.			
e.			

3. Sentences **a–g**, taken from Old English, Middle English, and early Modern English texts, illustrate some changes that have occurred in the syntactic rules of English grammar. (Note: In the sentences, the earlier spelling forms and words have been changed to conform to the spelling of Modern English. That is, the OE sentence *His suna twegen mon brohte to þæm cynige* would be written as *His sons two one brought to that king,*

which in Modern English would be *His two sons were brought to the king.*)
Underline the parts of each sentence that differ from Modern English.
Rewrite the sentence in Modern English. State what changes must have
occurred.

Example: It <u>not</u> belongs to you. (Shakespeare, *Henry IV*)

Mod. Eng.: It does not belong to you.

Change: At one time a negative sentence simply had a *not* before the
verb. Today, the word *do,* in its proper morphological form, must
appear before the *not.*

a. It nothing pleased his master.
b. He hath said that we would lift them whom that him please.
c. I have a brother is condemned to die.
d. I bade them take away you.
e. I wish you was still more a Tartar.
f. Christ slept and his apostles.
g. Me was told.

4. Yearbooks and almanacs (including ones online) often publish new-
    words lists. In 2012 several new words, such as *webisode, frenemy*, and
    staycation were said to have entered the English language. Before that,
    new words such as *byte* and *modem* arrived together with the computer
    age. Other words have been expanded in meaning, such as *memory* to
    refer to the storage part of a computer and *crack* meaning a form of
    cocaine. Sports-related new words include *threepeat* and *skybox*; Harry
    Potter's world has donated *apparate* and *muggle*, among others. Some
    fairly recent arrivals came with the new millennium and include *Viagra,
    Sudoku*, and the controversial *fracking* (from 'hydraulic fracturing'
    meaning 'to free oil and gas from rock').

    a. Find five other words or compound words that have entered the lan-
        guage in the last ten years. Describe briefly the source of each word.
    b. Think of three words that might be on the way out. (Hint: Consider
        flapper, groovy, and *slay/slew*. Dictionary entries that say "archaic"
        are a good source.)
    c. Think of three words whose dictionary entries do not say they are
        verbs, but which you've heard or seen used as verbs. Example: "He
        went to piano over at the club," meaning (we guess) 'He went to play
        the piano at the club.'
    d. Think of three words that have become, or are becoming, obsolete as
        a result of changes in technology. Example: *Mimeograph*, a method of
        reproduction, is on the way out because of advances in xerography.
    e. One of the trendy words of the current millennium is *power* as used
        prolifically, if not productively, in new compounds such as *power walk*
        and *power lunch*. Find five or ten such usages and document a refer-
        ence where you observed each usage, such as a magazine article or a
        news report on the radio, Internet, or television.

f. Now that *blog* is a full-fledged word both as a noun and a verb it may become the root for many more words through the attachment of prefixes and suffixes. Some of these stem (pardon the pun) from productive affixes: *reblog,* 'to blog again'; *blogify,* 'to write a blog about something'; *nonblog,* 'writing that isn't a blog, such as this exercise'; *blogness,* 'the quality of being a blog.' Using affixes, make up some "words" and "definitions" with *blog,* say five or ten. Use your imagination. Go bananas! E.g., *blogaroo,* 'a blogger who writes about rodeos,' or *blogorama,* 'a blog with a wide vista.' Email your best creations to one of us authors; we'll publish the cleverest ones whilst enshrining your institution's name in our eleventh edition.

5. Here is a table showing, in phonemic form, the Latin ancestors of ten words in modern French (given in phonetic form):

Latin	French	Gloss
kor	kœr[5]	heart
kantāre	ʃãte	to sing
klārus	klɛr	clear
kervus	sɛr	deer
karbō	ʃarbɔ̄	coal
kwandō	kã	when
kentum	sã	hundred
kawsa	ʃoz	thing
kinis	sãdrə	ashes
kawda/koda[6]	kø[5]	tail

Are the following statements true or false? Justify your answers.

	True	False

a. The modern French word for "thing" shows that a /k/, which occurred before the vowel /o/ in Latin, became [ʃ] in French.   ____   ____

b. The French word for "tail" probably derived from the Latin word /koda/ rather than from /kawda/.   ____   ____

c. One historical change illustrated by these data is that [s] became an allophone of the phoneme /k/ in French.   ____   ____

d. If there were a Latin word *kertus,* the modern French word would probably be [sɛr]. (Consider only the initial consonant.)   ____   ____

6. Here is how to count to five in a dozen languages, using standard Roman alphabet transcriptions. Six of these languages are Indo-European and six are not. Which are Indo-European?

---

[5]œ and ø are front, rounded vowels.

[6]/kawda/ and /koda/ are the words for 'tail' in two Latin dialects.

	L1	L2	L3	L4	L5	L6
a.	en	jedyn	yi	eka	ichi	echad
b.	twene	dwaj	er	dvau	ni	shnayim
c.	thria	tři	san	trayas	san	shlosha
d.	fiuwar	štyri	ssu	catur	shi	arbaʔa
e.	fif	pjeć	wu	pañca	go	chamishsha

	L7	L8	L9	L10	L11	L12
a.	mot	ün	hana	yaw	uno	nigen
b.	hai	duos	tul	daw	dos	khoyar
c.	ba	trais	set	dree	tres	ghorban
d.	bon	quatter	net	tsaloor	cuatro	durben
e.	nam	tschinch	tasŏt	pindze	cinco	tabon

7. The vocabulary of English consists of native words as well as thousands of loan words. Look up the following words in a dictionary that provides etymologies. Speculate how each word came to be borrowed from the particular language.

   Example: Skunk was a Native American term for an animal unfamiliar to the European colonists, so they borrowed that word into their vocabulary so they could refer to the creature.

a. size	h. robot	o. coyote	v. pagoda
b. royal	i. check	p. chocolate	w. khaki
c. aquatic	j. banana	q. hoodlum	x. shampoo
d. heavenly	k. keel	r. filibuster	y. kangaroo
e. skill	l. fact	s. astronaut	z. tomato
f. ranch	m. potato	t. emerald	
g. blouse	n. muskrat	u. sugar	

8. Analogic change refers to a tendency to generalize the rules of language, a major cause of language change. We mentioned two instances, the generalization of the plural rule (*cow/kine* becoming *cow/cows*) and the generalization of the past-tense formation rule (*light/lit* becoming *light/lighted*). Think of at least three other instances of nonstandard usage that are analogic; they are indicators of possible future changes in the language. (Hint: Consider fairly general rules and see whether you know of dialects or styles that overgeneralize them, for example, comparative formation by adding *-er.*)

9. Linguists have noted the "paradox" that *sound change is regular, but produces irregularity*, and *analogic change is irregular, but produces regularity*. Explain what this means, and illustrate your explanation with specific examples. (Hint: Revisit exercises 2 and 8.)

10. Study the following passage from Shakespeare's *Hamlet*, Act IV, Scene iii, and identify every difference in expression between Elizabethan and current Modern English that is evident (e.g., in line 3, *thou* is now *you*).

    HAMLET: A man may fish with the worm that hath eat of a king, and
                    eat of the fish that hath fed of that worm.
    KING: What dost thou mean by this?

> HAMLET: Nothing but to show you how a king may go a progress through the guts of a beggar.
>
> KING: Where is Polonius?
>
> HAMLET: In heaven. Send thither to see. If your messenger find him not there, seek him i' the other place yourself. But indeed, if you find him not within this month, you shall nose him as you go up the stairs into the lobby.

11. Travelers to Spain who know a little Latin American Spanish are often surprised to encounter speakers who appear to have a lisp. That is, they pronounce an expected [s] as [θ], and moreover they pronounce an expected [j] as *ly*, or a palatal lateral whose IPA symbol is [ʎ]. Of course if you've read this book you know that this is a dialectal variation. Consider the following data from two dialects of Spanish:

Dialect 1	Dialect 2	Gloss	Earlier Form (to be completed)
[kasa]	[kaθa]	hunt (noun)	*
[si]	[si]	yes	*
[gajo]	[gaʎo]	rooster	*
[dies]	[dieθ]	ten	*
[pojo]	[pojo]	kind of bench	*
[kaje]	[kaʎe]	street	*
[majo]	[majo]	May	*
[kasa]	[kasa]	house	*
[siŋko]	[θiŋko]	five	*
[dos]	[dos]	two	*
[pojo]	[poʎo]	chicken	*

   a. Find the correspondence sets—there are fourteen of them, for example p-p.
   b. Reconstruct each of the fourteen protosounds: for example, *p.
   c. What, if any, are the sound changes that took place in the two dialects?
   d. Complete the table by filling in the reconstructed earlier form.

12. Here are some data from four Polynesian languages:

Maori	Hawaiian	Samoan	Fijian	Gloss	Proto-Polynesian (to be completed)
pou	pou	pou	bou	post	*
tapu	kapu	tapu	tabu	forbidden	*
taŋi	kani	taŋi	taŋi	cry	*
takere	kaʔele	taʔele	takele	keel	*
hono	hono	fono	vono	stay, sit	*
marama	malama	malama	malama	light, moon	*
kaho	ʔaho	ʔaso	kaso	thatch	*

   a. Find the correspondence sets. (Hint: There are 14: for example, o-o-o-o, p-p-p-b.)

    b. For each correspondence set, reconstruct a protosound. Mention any sound changes that you observe. For example:

o-o-o-o *o

p-p-p-b *p   p → b in Fijian.

    c. Complete the table by filling in the reconstructed words in Proto-Polynesian.

13. Consider these data from two American Indian languages:

Yerington Paviotso = YP	Northfork Monachi = NM	Gloss
mupi	mupi	nose
tama	tawa	tooth
piwɨ	piwɨ	heart
sawaʔpono	sawaʔpono	(a feminine name)
nɨmɨ	nɨwɨ	liver
tamano	tawano	springtime
pahwa	pahwa	aunt
kuma	kuwa	husband
wowaʔa	wowaʔa	indians living to the west
mɨhɨ	mɨhɨ	porcupine
noto	noto	throat
tapa	tape	sun
ʔatapɨ	ʔatapɨ	jaw
papiʔi	papiʔi	older brother
patɨ	petɨ	daughter
nana	nana	man
ʔatɨ	ʔetɨ	bow, gun

    a. Identify each sound correspondence. (Hint: There are ten correspondence sets of consonants and six correspondence sets of vowels: for example, p-p, m-w, a-a, and a-e.)

    b. **(1)** For each correspondence you identified in (a) not containing an m or w, reconstruct a protosound (e.g., for h-h, *h; o-o, *o).

        (2) If the protosound underwent a change, indicate what the change is and in which language it took place.

    c. **(1)** Whenever a *w* appears in YP, what appears in the corresponding position in NM?

        (2) Whenever an *m* occurs in YP, what two sounds may correspond to it in NM?

        (3) On the basis of the position of *m* in YP words, can you predict which sound it will correspond to in NM words? How?

    d. **(1)** For the three correspondences you discovered in (a) involving *m* and *w*, should you reconstruct two or three protosounds?

        (2) If you chose three protosounds, what are they and what did they become in the two daughter languages, YP and NM?

        (3) If you chose two protosounds, what are they and what did they become in the daughter languages? What further statement do you need to make about the sound changes? (Hint: One protosound will become two different pairs, depending on its phonetic environment. It is an example of a conditioned sound change.)

e. Based on the above, reconstruct all the words given in the common ancestor from which both YP and NM descended (e.g., 'porcupine' is reconstructed as *mɨhɨ).

14. The people of the Isle of Eggland once lived in harmony on a diet of soft-boiled eggs. They spoke proto-Egglish. Contention arose over which end of the egg should be opened first for eating, the big end or the little end. Each side retreated to its end of the island, and spoke no more to the other. Today, Big-End Egglish and Little-End Egglish are spoken in Eggland. Below are data from these languages.

a. Find the correspondence sets for each pair of cognates, and reconstruct the proto-Egglish word from which the cognates descended.

b. Identify the sound changes that have affected each language. Use *classes* of sounds to express the change when possible. (Hint: There are three conditioned sound changes.)

Big-End Egglish	Little-End Egglish	Gloss	Proto-Egglish (to be completed)
ʃur	kul	omelet	*
ve	vet	yolk	*
rɔ	rɔk	egg	*
ver	vel	eggshell	*
ʒu	gup	soufflé	*
vel	vel	egg white	*
pe	pe	hard-boiled (obscene)	*

15. Consider the following Latin and Greek words. Each of them has provided a root for many English words. Give three examples of English words derived from each of the Latin and Greek roots below (the roots are in boldface). (Note: The English word need not begin with the root: e.g., *depose* is derived from the Latin *positus*.)

Example: Latin *pater* 'father': English *paternal*, *patricide*, *expatriate*. Note that *paternalistic*, *paternalistically*, and other morphological derivations of *paternal* <u>do not count</u>.

Greek		Latin	
pente	"five"	**acer**	"sharp"
anthropos	"man"	**mater**	"mother"
arche	"beginning"	**bell**um	"war"
pathos	"feeling"	**arbor**	"tree"
morphe	"shape"	**pos**itus	"put, place"
exo	"outside"	**par**	"equal"
sophos	"wise"	**nep**os	"grandson"
gamos	"marriage"	**tac**ere	"to be silent"
logy	"word"	**scrib**ere	"to write"
gigas	"huge, enormous"	**ling**ua	"tongue, language"

16. There are some exceptions to the Adj-Noun order in Modern English, as the examples in column A and B illustrate:

A	B	C
A man alone	*an alone man	a lone man
No man alive	*no alive man	no living man
A lion asleep	*an asleep lion	a sleeping lion

   a. Can you identify a common feature of the adjectives that are grammatical in post-noun position?

   b. Provide some other examples like those in column A.

   c. The expressions in column C have the normal Adj-N order. Do they have the same meaning as their respective items in column A? If not, say how they are different.

9

Language Acquisition

> The capacity to learn language is deeply ingrained in us as a species, just as the capacity to walk, to grasp objects, to recognize faces. We don't find any serious differences in children growing up in congested urban slums, in isolated mountain villages, or in privileged suburban villas.

DAN SLOBIN, *The Human Language Series program 2,* 1994

As we have seen in preceding chapters, language is extremely complex. Yet very young children—before the age of five—already know most of the intricate system that is the grammar of their language. Before they can add small numbers or tie their shoes, children are inflecting verbs and nouns, forming questions, negating sentences, using pronouns appropriately, embedding clauses and effortlessly producing and understanding a limitless number of sentences they never heard before. How children accomplish this prodigious task is the subject of this chapter.

The Linguistic Capacity of Children

> We are designed to walk. . . . That we are taught to walk is impossible. And pretty much the same is true of language. Nobody is taught language. In fact you can't prevent the child from learning it.

NOAM CHOMSKY, *The Human Language Series* program 2, 1994

Clearly, children do not learn a language simply by memorizing sentences. Rather, they acquire a system of grammatical rules of the sort we have been discussing in this book. No one teaches children the rules of grammar or provides them with any kind of explicit language instruction. Parents, unless they are linguists, are generally no more aware of the phonological, morphological, syntactic, and semantic rules of their language than their children. Rather, children extract the rules from the language they hear around them all on their own, in effect "reinventing" the grammar of mature speakers. They don't require any specific kind of environment to do this. Children exposed to different languages under different cultural and social circumstances all develop their native language during a narrow window of time, going through similar, possibly universal, developmental stages. Even deaf children of deaf signing parents acquire signed languages in stages that parallel those of children acquiring spoken languages.

The uniformity of language development in the face of varying environments and (as we will see) impoverished input leads many linguists to believe that children are equipped with an innate template or blueprint for language—which we have referred to as Universal Grammar (UG)—and that this blueprint aids the child in the task of constructing a grammar for her language.

What's Learned, What's Not?

"WHAT'S THE BIG SURPRISE? ALL THE LATEST THEORIES OF LINGUISTICS SAY WE'RE BORN WITH THE INNATE CAPACITY FOR GENERATING SENTENCES."

ScienceCartoonsPlus.com

The **innateness** hypothesis receives its strongest support from the observation that the grammars people ultimately end up with contain many abstract rules and structures that are not directly represented in the linguistic input they receive. In this sense the input to the child is said to be **impoverished** and this argument for the innateness of UG is called the **poverty of the stimulus**.

The principle of structure dependency illustrates one way in which the linguistic input is impoverished. Structure dependency, discussed in chapter 3, refers to the fact that grammatical rules are dependent on hierarchical structure and not on serial order. For example, the rule that moves the auxiliary in English questions, illustrated in (1), must refer to the *main* auxiliary of the sentence and not merely to the *first* auxiliary.

(1) The boy is sleeping. → Is the boy sleeping?

This is clearly shown by introducing a more complex sentence containing a relative clause. We see that moving the main auxiliary, as in (2), produces a grammatical output, while moving the first auxiliary, as in (3), leads to ungrammaticality:

The boy who is sleeping was dreaming.

(2) Was the boy who is sleeping ___ dreaming?
(3) *Is the boy who ___ sleeping was dreaming?

Naturalistic and experimental studies show that young children do not produce sentences such as (3). Presented with simple declarative-question pairs such as (1), children infer the structure-dependent rule, and when tested on the more complex cases, they correctly invert the main auxiliary. The fact that children come up with rules that move the auxiliary of the *main clause* rather than the *first* auxiliary means that they know something about the hierarchical organization of sentences, something they were not provided with directly in the input.

Many grammatical rules rely on the structural difference between main and subordinate clauses. For example, a pronoun can sometimes refer to a following NP as in (1) where *he* can refer to *Billie*. But sometimes pronouns cannot co-refer in this way, as in (2).

(1) When *he* lost the race *Billie* was sad.
(2) *He* was sad when *Billie* lost the race. (ungrammatical as *he* = *Billie*)

The linear relationship between the pronoun and the NP is the same in both sentences, so this cannot be the reason for the difference in grammaticality. Rather, the rule that permits co-reference in (1) but not (2) is structure-dependent (and it is also universal): it states (roughly) that a preceding pronoun in a main clause cannot refer to a NP in a following subordinate clause. As in the case of the question formation rule, when young children are tested on sentences such as (1) and (2) they do not make mistakes. They allow co-reference in (1), but not in (2), showing that they are sensitive to the structural difference between the two sentences and to the structure-dependent pronoun rule.

Children are not given information about structure dependency. Indeed, they are not explicitly informed about constituent structure or any other abstract property of grammar. The input children receive is a sequence of sounds (or signs), not a set of phrase structure trees. Yet children formulate rules that are sensitive to this structure. According to the innateness hypothesis, the child does not need to learn structure dependency or the pronoun rule or any other universal principles of sentence formation such as the rule that heads of categories can take complements. These aspects of grammar are part of the innate blueprint for language.

At the same time, it is clear that some aspects of language are learned. Children acquire the language(s) they hear spoken in their community, not any random language. The child must learn the particular sounds and words of his language as well as those grammatical rules specific to his language as exemplified in the linguistic input, such as word order and movement rules. For example, English-speaking children hear that the subject comes first and that the verb precedes the object inside the VP: that is, they learn that English is an SVO language. Japanese children acquire an SOV language. They learn that the object precedes the verb from hearing mature speakers of Japanese.

English-speaking children must also learn that yes-no questions are formed by moving the auxiliary, while Japanese children learn that to form a yes-no question, the morpheme -*ka* is suffixed to a verb stem.

Tanaka ga sushi o tabete iru.	'Tanaka is eating sushi.'
Tanaka ga sushi o tabete iru**ka**?	'Is Tanaka eating sushi?'

The process of acquiring language is rooted in human biology and supported by linguistic input from the environment.

One of the central goals of linguistic theory is to solve *the logical problem of language acquisition*:

What accounts for the ease, rapidity, and uniformity of language acquisition in the face of impoverished data?

A partial answer is that children are able to acquire a complex grammar quickly and easily without any particular help beyond exposure to the language because they do not start from scratch. Innate principles of UG such as structure dependency and X-bar theory among many others provide them with a significant head start. UG constrains the kinds of grammatical rules children will formulate. It predisposes them to follow a restricted course of development that avoids many grammatical errors and gives rise to uniform developmental stages, as we will discuss in the next section.

The innateness hypothesis also predicts that all languages will conform to UG principles. While we are still far from understanding the full structure of UG, research on different languages provides a way to test any principles that linguists propose. Hypotheses may be revised based on new evidence, as is the case in any science. But there is little doubt that human languages conform to abstract universal principles and that the human brain is specially equipped for acquisition of human language grammars, as we will discuss in the following chapter.

Stages in Language Acquisition

> . . . for I was no longer a speechless infant; but a speaking boy. This I remember; and have since observed how I learned to speak. It was not that my elders taught me words . . . in any set method; but I . . . did myself . . . practice the sounds in my memory. . . . And thus by constantly hearing words, as they occurred in various sentences . . . I thereby gave utterance to my will.
>
> **ST. AUGUSTINE**, *Confessions*, 398 CE

Children do not wake up one morning with a fully formed grammar in their heads. In moving from first words to adult competence children pass through linguistic stages. They begin by babbling, they then acquire their first words, and in just a few months they begin to put words together into sentences.

The earliest studies of language acquisition come from diaries kept by parents. More recent studies include the use of tape recordings, videotapes, and controlled experiments. Linguists record the spontaneous utterances of children and purposefully elicit other utterances to study the children's production and comprehension. Researchers have also invented ingenious experimental techniques for investigating children's comprehension, and even for studying the linguistic abilities of infants, who are not yet speaking.

Children's early utterances may not look exactly like adult sentences, but child language is not just a degenerate form of adult language. The words and sentences that the child produces at each stage of development conform to the set of grammatical rules he has developed to that point. Although child grammars and adult grammars differ in certain respects, they also share many formal properties. Like adults, children have grammatical categories such as NP and VP, rules for building phrase structures and for moving constituents, as well as phonological, morphological, and semantic rules, and they adhere to universal principles such as structure dependency.

From the perspective of the adult grammar, children's utterances often contain grammatical errors, but such "errors" most often reflect the child's current stage of linguistic knowledge and therefore provide researchers with a window into their grammar.

Children are biologically equipped to acquire all aspects of grammar. In the following sections we will look at development in each of the components of language, and we will illustrate the role that Universal Grammar and other factors play in this development.

The Perception and Production of Speech Sounds

> An infant crying in the night:
>
> An infant crying for the light:
>
> And with no language but a cry.
>
> **ALFRED LORD TENNYSON**, *In Memoriam A.H.H.*, 1849

Any notion that a person is born with a mind like a blank slate is belied by a wealth of evidence that newborns react to some subtle distinctions in their environment and not to others. Infants will respond to visual depth and distance distinctions, to differences between rigid and flexible physical properties of objects, and to human faces rather than to other visual stimuli. Infants also show a very early response to different properties of language. Experiments demonstrate that infants will increase their sucking rate—as measured by ingeniously designed pacifiers—when the stimuli (visual or auditory) presented to them are varied, but will decrease the sucking rate when the same stimuli are presented repeatedly. When tested with a preferential listening technique, slightly older infants will turn their heads toward and listen longer to sounds, stress patterns, and words that are familiar to them. On the other hand, they will also respond to novel patterns, showing that they can distinguish the different linguistic elements being tested. These instinctive responses can be used to measure a baby's ability to discriminate and recognize different linguistic stimuli.

A newborn will respond to phonetic contrasts found in human languages even when these differences are not phonemic in the language spoken in the baby's home. A baby hearing a human voice over a loudspeaker saying [pa] [pa] [pa] will slowly decrease her rate of sucking. If the sound changes to [ba] or even [pʰa], the sucking rate increases dramatically. Adults find it difficult to differentiate between the allophones of a phoneme, but for infants it comes naturally. Japanese infants can distinguish between [r] and [l] whereas their parents cannot; babies can hear the difference between aspirated and unaspirated stops even if students in an introductory linguistics course cannot. Babies can discriminate between sounds that are phonemic in other languages and nonexistent in the language of their parents. For example, in Hindi, there is a phonemic contrast between a retroflex *t* [ʈ] (made with the tongue curled back) and the alveolar [t]. To English-speaking adults, these may sound the same; to their infants, they do not.

Infants can perceive voicing contrasts such as [pa] versus [ba], contrasts in place of articulation such as [da] versus [ga], and contrasts in manner of articulation such as [ra] versus [la], or [ra] versus [wa], among many others. However, babies will not react to distinctions that do not correspond to phonemic contrasts in any human language, such as sounds spoken more or less loudly. Furthermore, a vowel that we perceive as [i], for example, is a different physical sound when produced by a male, female, or child, but babies ignore the nonlinguistic aspects of the speech signal just as adults do.

Because infants are born with the ability to perceive just those sounds that are phonemic in some language, it is possible for them to learn any human language they are exposed to. During the first year of life, the infant's job is to uncover the sounds of the ambient language. From around six months, he begins to lose the ability to discriminate between sounds that are not phonemic in his own language as his linguistic environment begins to shape his initial perceptions. Japanese infants can no longer hear the difference between [r] and [l], which do not contrast in Japanese, whereas babies in English-speaking homes retain this perception. They have begun to learn the sounds of the language of their parents. Before that, they appear to know the sounds of human language in general.

Babbling

"Hi & Lois"/King Features Syndicate

The child's linguistic environment shapes not only the child's perceptions of speech sounds but also his productions. Babbling illustrates the readiness of the human mind to respond to linguistic input from a very early stage.

At around six months, the infant begins to babble. The sounds produced in this period include many sounds that do not occur in the language of the household. By the end of the first year the babbles come to include only those sounds and sound combinations that occur in the target language. Babbles begin to sound like words, although they may not have any specific meaning attached to them. At this point English-speaking adults can distinguish the babbles of an English-babbling infant from those of an infant babbling in Cantonese or Arabic. During the first year of life, the infant's perceptions and productions are being fine-tuned to the surrounding language(s).

Studies of babbling in hearing children and deaf children support the view that babbling is a linguistic ability related to the kind of language input the child receives. Four- to seven-month-old hearing infants exposed to spoken language produce a restricted set of phonetic forms. The twelve most frequent consonants in the world's languages make up 95 percent of the consonants infants use in their babbling. The early babbles consist mainly of repeated consonant-vowel sequences, like *mama*, *gaga*, and *dada*. Later babbles are more varied.

At the same age, deaf children exposed to sign language produce a restricted set of signs. They use more than a dozen different hand motions repetitively, all of which are elements of the sign languages used in deaf communities around the world. In each case the forms are drawn from the set of possible sounds or possible gestures found in spoken and signed languages.

The generally accepted view is that humans are born with a predisposition to discover the units that express linguistic meanings, and that at a genetically specified stage in neural development, the infant will begin to produce these units—sounds or gestures—depending on the language input the baby receives. This suggests that babbling is the earliest stage in language acquisition, in opposition to an earlier view that babbling was prelinguistic and merely neuromuscular in origin. The "babbling as language acquisition" hypothesis is supported by recent neurological studies that link babbling to the language centers of the left hemisphere, providing further evidence that the brain specializes for language functions at a very early age.

First Words

From this golden egg a man, Prajapati, was born. . . . A year having passed, he wanted to speak. He said "bhur" and the earth was created. He said "bhuvar" and the space of the air was created. He said "suvar" and the sky was created. That is why a child wants to speak after a year. . . . When Prajapati spoke for the first time, he uttered one or two syllables. That is why a child utters one or two syllables when he speaks for the first time.

HINDU MYTH

Some time after the age of one, the child begins to use the same string of sounds repeatedly to mean the same thing, thereby producing her first words. The age of the child when this occurs varies and has nothing to do with the child's intelligence.

The child's first words may differ from the words of the adult language. The following words of one child, J. P., at the age of sixteen months, illustrate the point:

[ʔaʊ]	'not,' 'no,' 'don't'	[s:]	'aerosol spray'
[bʌʔ]/[mʌʔ]	'up'	[sʲuː]	'shoe'
[da]	'dog'	[haɪ]	'hi'
[iʔo]/[siʔo]	'Cheerios'	[sr]	'shirt,' 'sweater'
[sa]	'sock'	[sæː]/[əsæː]	'what's that?'/'hey, look!'
[aɪ]/[ʌɪ]	'light'	[ma]	'mommy'
[baʊ]/[daʊ]	'down'	[dæ]	'daddy'

What is important is not that these words differ from the adult's, but that they represent a fixed sound-meaning pairing.

Most children go through a stage in which their utterances consist of only one word. This is called the **holophrastic** or "whole phrase" stage because these one-word utterances seem to convey the meaning of an entire sentence. For example, when J. P. says "down" he may be making a request to be put down, or he may be commenting on a toy that has fallen down from the shelf. When he says "cheerios" he may simply be naming the box of cereal in front of him, or he may be asking for some Cheerios. This suggests that children have a more complex mental representation than their language allows them to express. Comprehension experiments confirm the hypothesis that children's productive abilities do not fully reflect their underlying grammatical competence.

It has been claimed that deaf babies develop their first signs earlier than hearing children speak their first words. This has led to the development of Baby Sign, a technique in which hearing parents learn and model for their babies various "signs," such as signs for 'milk,' 'hurt,' and 'mother.' The idea is that the baby can communicate his needs manually even before he is able to articulate spoken words. Promoters of Baby Sign (and many parents) say that this leads to less frustration and less crying. The claim that signs appear earlier than words is controversial. Some linguists argue that what occurs earlier in both deaf and hearing babies are pre-linguistic gestures that lack the systematic meaning of true signs. Baby Sign may be exploiting this earlier manual dexterity, and not indicative of a precocious linguistic development.

Segmenting the Speech Stream

I scream, you scream, we all scream for ice cream.

TRANSCRIBED FROM VOCALS BY TOM STACKS, performing with Harry Reser's Six Jumping Jacks, January 14, 1928

Speech is a continuous stream broken only by breath pauses. The intonation breaks that do exist do not always correspond to word, phrase, or sentence boundaries. The adult speaker can use his knowledge of the lexicon and grammar of a language to impose structure on the speech he hears. But how do babies, who have not yet learned the lexicon or rules of grammar, extract the words from the speech they hear around them? Children are in the same fix that you might be in if you tuned in a foreign-language radio station. You wouldn't have the foggiest idea of what was being said or what the words were. The ability to segment the continuous speech stream into discrete units—words—is one of the remarkable feats of language acquisition.

Studies show that infants are remarkably good at extracting information from continuous speech. They seem to know what kind of cues to look for in the input that will help them to isolate words. One of the cues that English-speaking children use to figure out word boundaries is stress.

As noted in chapter 5 every content word in English has a stressed syllable. (Function words such as *the, a, am, can,* etc. are ordinarily unstressed.) If the content word is monosyllabic, then that syllable is stressed as in *dóg* and *hám.* Bisyllabic content words can be **trochaic**, which means that stress is on the first syllable, as in *páper* and *dóctor,* or **iambic**, which means stress is on the second syllable, as in *giráffe* and *devíce.* The vast majority of English words have trochaic stress. In controlled experiments adult speakers are quicker to recognize words with trochaic stress than words with iambic stress. This can be explained if English-speaking adults follow a strategy of taking a stressed syllable to mark the onset of a new word.

Can children avail themselves of the same strategy? Stress is very salient to infants, and they are quick to acquire the rhythmic structure of their language. Researchers have shown that at just a few months old infants are able to discriminate native and non-native stress patterns. This is shown in production as well. Before the end of the first year their babbling takes on the rhythmic pattern of the ambient language. At about nine months old, English-speaking children prefer to listen to bisyllabic words with initial rather than final stress. And most notably, studies show that infants acquiring English can indeed use stress cues to segment words in fluent speech.

In a series of experiments, seven-and-a-half-month-old infants listened to passages with repeated instances of trochaic words such as *púppy,* and passages with iambic words such as *guitár.* They were then played lists of words, some of which had occurred in the previous passage and others that had not. Experimenters measured the length of time that they listened to the familiar versus unfamiliar words. The results showed that children listened significantly longer (indicated by turning their head in the direction of the loudspeaker) to words that they had heard in the passage, but only when the words had the trochaic pattern (*púppy*). For words with the iambic pattern (*guitár*), the children responded only to the stressed syllable (tár), though the monosyllabic word *tar* had not appeared in the passage. These results suggest that the infants—like adults—are taking the stressed syllable to mark the onset of a new word. Following such a strategy will sometimes lead to errors (for iambic words and unstressed function words), but it provides the child with a way of getting started. This is sometimes referred to as **prosodic bootstrapping**. Infants can use the stress pattern of the language as a start to word learning.

Infants are also sensitive to phonotactic constraints and to the distribution of allophones in the target language. For example, we noted in chapter 6 that in English aspiration typically occurs at the beginning of a stressed syllable—[pʰɛ̃n] (*pen*) versus [opə̃n] (*open*)—and that certain combinations of sounds are more likely to occur at the end of a word rather than at the beginning, for example [rt]. Studies show that nine-month-olds can use this information to help segment speech into words in English.

Languages differ in their stress patterns as well as in their allophonic variation and phonotactics. This means the infant would first need to figure out what stress pattern he is dealing with, or what the allophones and possible sound combinations are, before he could use this information to extract the words of his language from fluent speech. This seems to be a classic chicken and egg problem—he has to know the language to learn the language. A way out of this conundrum is provided by the finding that infants may also rely on statistical properties of the input to segment words, such as the frequency with which particular sequences of sounds occur.

In one study, eight-month-old infants listened to two minutes of speech formed from four nonsense words, *pabiku, tutibu, golabu, babupu*. The words were produced by a speech synthesizer and strung together in three different orders, analogous to three different sentences, without any pauses or other phonetic cues to the word boundaries. Here is an example of what the children heard:

golabupabikututibubabupugolabubabupututibu . . .

After listening to the strings the infants were tested to see whether they could distinguish the "words" of the language, for example *pabiku* (which, recall, they had never heard in isolation before), from sequences of syllables that spanned word boundaries, such as *bubabu* (which the authors refer to as "partwords"). Despite the very brief exposure and the lack of boundary cues, the infants were able to distinguish the words from the partwords. The authors of the study conclude that the children do this by tracking the frequency with which the different sequences of syllables occur: the sequences inside the words (e.g., *pa-bi-ku*) remain the same whatever order the words are presented in, but the sequences of syllables that cross word boundaries will change in the different presentations and hence will occur much less frequently.

Though it is still unclear how much such statistical procedures can accomplish with real language input, which is vastly larger and more varied, this experiment and others like it suggest that babies can use statistical information as well as linguistic structure to extract words from the input. Children may first rely on statistical properties to isolate some words, and then, based on these words, learn the rhythmic, allophonic, and phonotactic properties of the language, which they then use for further segmentation.

Studies that measure infants' reliance on statistics versus stress for segmenting words support this two stage model: younger infants (seven-and-a-half months old) respond to frequency while older infants (nine months old) attend to stress, allophonic, and phonotactic information.

The Acquisition of Phonology

"Baby Blues", Baby Blues Partnership. Reprinted with permission of King Features Syndicate

In terms of his phonology, J. P. is like most children at the one-word stage. The first words are generally monosyllabic with a CV (consonant-vowel) form. The vowel part may be a diphthong, depending on the language being acquired. The phonemic inventory is much smaller than is found in the adult language. It appears that children first acquire the small set of sounds common to all languages regardless of the ambient language(s), and in later stages acquire the less common sounds of their own language. For example, most languages have the sounds [p] and [s], but [θ] is a rare sound. J. P.'s sound system followed this pattern. His phonological inventory at an early stage included the consonants [b], [m], [d], and [k], which are frequently occurring sounds in the world's languages.

In general, the order of acquisition of classes of sounds begins with vowels and then goes by *manner* of articulation for consonants: nasals are acquired first, and then glides, stops, liquids, fricatives, and affricates. Natural classes characterized by *place* of articulation features also appear in children's utterances according to a more or less ordered series: labials, velars, alveolars, and palatals. It is not surprising that *mama* and *dada* are early words for many children.

The distribution and frequency of sounds in a language can also influence the acquisition of certain segments. Sounds that are expected to be acquired late may appear earlier in children's language when they are frequently occurring. For example the fricative [v] is a very late acquisition in English but it is an early phoneme in Estonian, Bulgarian, and Swedish, languages that have several [v]-initial words that are common in the vocabularies of young children.

If the first year is devoted to figuring out the sounds of the target language, the second year involves learning how these sounds are used in the phonology of the language, especially which contrasts are phonemic. When children first begin to contrast one pair of a set (e.g., when they learn that /p/ and /b/ are distinct phonemes due to a voicing difference), they also begin to distinguish between other similar pairs (e.g., /t/ and /d/, /s/, and /z/, and all the other voiceless/voiced phonemic pairs). As we would expect, the generalizations refer to natural classes of speech sounds.

Controlled experiments show that children at this stage can perceive or comprehend many more phonological contrasts than they can produce. The same child who says [wæbɪt] instead of "rabbit," and who does not seem to distinguish [w] and [r], will not make mistakes on a picture identification task in which she is asked to point to either a ring or a wing.

In addition, children sometimes produce different sounds in a way that makes them indiscernible to adult observers. For example, although a child's pronunciation of *wing* and *ring* may seem the same to the adult ear, acoustic analyses of children's utterances show that they are physically different sounds. As a further example, a spectrographic analysis (see chapter 10) of *ephant*, 'elephant,' produced by a three-year-old child, clearly showed an [l] in the representation of the word, even though the adult experimenter could not hear it.

Many anecdotal reports also show the disparity between the child's production and perception at this stage. An example is the exchange between a linguist and his two year old son. At this age the child's pronunciation of 'mouth' is [maʊs].

FATHER:	What does [maʊs] mean?
CHILD:	Like a cat.
FATHER:	Yes, what else?
CHILD:	Nothing else.
FATHER:	It's part of your head.
CHILD:	(*fascinated*)
FATHER:	(*touching A's mouth*) What's this?
CHILD:	[maʊs]

It took the child a few seconds to realize that his word for 'mouse' and his word for 'mouth' were the same. It is not that children do not hear the correct adult pronunciation. They do, but they are unable in these early years to produce it themselves. Another linguist's child (yes, linguists love to experiment on their own children) pronounced the word *light* as *yight* [jaɪt] but would become very angry if someone said to him, "Oh, you want me to turn on the yight." "No no," he would reply, "not yight—yight!"

Therefore, even at this stage, it is not possible to determine the extent of the grammar of the child—in this case, the phonology—simply by observing speech production. It is often necessary to use various experimental and instrumental techniques to reveal the child's underlying competence.

A child's first words show many substitutions of one feature for another or one phoneme for another. In the preceding examples, *mouth* [maʊθ] is pronounced *mouse* [maʊs], with the alveolar fricative [s] replacing the less common interdental fricative [θ]; *light* [laɪt] is pronounced *yight* [jaɪt], with the glide [j] replacing the liquid [l]; and *rabbit* is pronounced *wabbit*, with the glide [w] replacing the liquid [r]. Glides are acquired earlier than liquids, and hence substitute for them. Similarly, alveolars are acquired earlier than interdentals and replace them in production. These substitutions are simplifications of the adult pronunciation. They make articulation easier until the child achieves greater articulatory control.

Children's early pronunciations are not haphazard, however. The phonological substitutions are rule-governed. The following is an abridged lexicon for another child, Michael, between the ages of eighteen and twenty-one months:

[pun]	'spoon'	[maɪtl]	'Michael'
[peɪn]	'plane'	[daɪtər]	'diaper'
[tɪs]	'kiss'	[pati]	'Papi'
[taʊ]	'cow'	[mani]	'Mommy'
[tin]	'clean'	[bərt]	'Bert'
[polər]	'stroller'	[bərt]	'(Big) Bird'

Michael systematically substituted the alveolar stop [t] for the velar stop [k] as in his words for 'cow,' 'clean,' 'kiss,' and his own name. He also replaced labial [p] with [t] when it occurred in the middle of a word, as in his words for 'Papi' and 'diaper.' He reduced consonant clusters in 'spoon,' 'plane,' and 'stroller,' and he devoiced final stops as in 'Big Bird.' In devoicing the final [d] in 'bird,' he created an ambiguous form [bərt] referring both to Bert and Big Bird. No wonder that only parents understand their children's first words!

Michael's substitutions are typical of the phonological rules that operate in the very early stages of acquisition. Other common rules are reduplication—'bottle' becomes [baba], 'water' becomes [wawa]; and the dropping of final consonants—'bed' becomes [be], 'cake' becomes [ke]. These two rules show that the children prefer simple CV syllables.

Of the many phonological rules that children create, no child will necessarily use all rules. Early phonological rules generally reflect natural phonological processes that also occur in adult languages. For example, various adult languages have a rule of syllable-final consonant devoicing (German does—/bʊnd/ is pronounced [bʊnt]—English doesn't). Children do not create bizarre or whimsical rules. Their rules conform to the possibilities made available by Universal Grammar.

The Acquisition of Word Meaning

Suddenly I felt a misty consciousness as of something forgotten—a thrill of returning thought; and somehow the mystery of language was revealed to me. . . . Everything had a name, and each name gave birth to a new thought.

HELEN KELLER, *The Story of My Life*, 1903

In addition to what it tells us about phonological regularities, the child's early vocabulary also provides insight into how children use words and construct word meaning. For J. P. the word *up* was originally used only to mean 'Get me up!' when he was either on the floor or in his high chair, but later he used it to mean 'Get up!' to his mother as well. J. P. used his word for *sock* not only for socks but also for other undergarments that are put on over the feet, such as undershorts. Similarly, a child may use the word *doggie* to refer to any four-legged animal or *daddy* to refer to any adult male. This illustrates how a child may extend the meaning of a word from a particular referent to encompass a larger class.

Eventually children do figure out the adult meanings of words. How do they do this? Most people do not see this aspect of acquisition as posing a great problem. The intuitive view is that children look at an object, the mother says a word, and the child connects the sounds with the object. However, this is not as easy as it seems. As the linguist Lila Gleitman points out:

> A child who observes a cat sitting on a mat also observes . . . a mat supporting a cat, a mat under a cat, a floor supporting a mat and a cat, and so on. If the adult now says "The cat is on the mat" even while pointing to the cat on the mat, how is the child to choose among these interpretations of the situation?[1]

Even if the child succeeds in associating the word *cat* with the animal on the mat he may mistakenly interpret 'cat' as 'Cat,' the name of that particular animal, instead of a type of animal. Upon hearing the word *dog* in the presence of a dog, how does the child know that 'dog' can refer to any four-legged, hairy, barking creature? Should it include poodles, tiny Yorkshire terriers, greyhounds and huge mastiffs, all of which look rather different from one another? What about cows, lambs, and other four-legged mammals? Why are they not 'dogs'? In other words, to learn a word like *cat* or *dog* children have to figure out that the word refers to a class of objects and not just to the object being referred to in a particular situation. The important and very difficult question is: What relevant features define the class of objects we call *dog*, and how does a child acquire knowledge of them? Even if a child succeeds in associating a word with an object, nobody provides explicit information about how to extend the use of that word to all the other objects to which that word refers. In learning the meanings of words, as in other aspects of language acquisition, children are confronted with impoverished data.

It is not surprising, therefore, that children often **overextend** a word's meaning, as J. P. did with the word *sock*. A child may learn a word such as *papa* or *daddy*, which she first uses only for her own father, and then extend its meaning to apply to all men, just as she may use the word *dog* to mean any four-legged creature. On the other hand, children may also use a lexical item in an overly restrictive way. For example, they may first use a word like *bird* to refer only to the family's pet canary without making a connection to birds in the trees outside, as if the word were a proper noun. This is referred

---

[1]Gleitman, L., in Searchinger, G. 1994. The human language series, program 2. Acquiring the Human Language. Video New York: Equinox Film/Ways of Knowing Inc.

to as **underextension**. And just as overextended words eventually hone in on the adult meanings, underextended words will broaden their scope until they match the target language.

The mystery surrounding the acquisition of word meanings has intrigued philosophers and psychologists as well as linguists. We know that all children view the world in a similar fashion and apply the same general principles to help them determine a word's meaning. For example, overextensions are usually based on physical attributes such as size, shape, and texture. *Ball* may refer to all round things, *bunny* to all furry things, and so on. But children will not make overextensions based on color, for example. In experiments they will group objects by shape and give them a name, but they will not assign a name to a group of red objects. Children are predisposed to attach and extend labels to objects in particular ways. In this instance they show a *form over color* preference. Similarly, if an experimenter points to an object and uses a nonsense word like *zav*, saying "that's a zav," the child will interpret the word to refer to the whole object, not to one of its parts or attributes. Given the poverty of stimulus for word learning, principles like the "form over color principle" and the "whole object principle" help the child organize his experience in ways that facilitate word learning. Without such principles, it is doubtful that children could learn words as quickly as they do. Children learn approximately fourteen words a day for the first six years of their lives. That averages to about 5,000 words per year. How many students know 10,000 words of a foreign language after two years of study?

There is also experimental evidence that children can learn the meaning of one class of words—verbs—based on the syntactic environment in which they occur. If you were to hear a sentence such as *John blipped Mary the gloon*, you would not know exactly what John did, but you would likely understand that the sentence is describing a transfer of something from John to Mary. Similarly, if you heard *John gonked that Mary . . .* , you would conclude that the verb *gonk* was a verb of communication like *say* or a mental verb like *think*. The complement types that a verb selects can provide clues to its meaning and thereby help the child. This learning of word meaning based on syntax is referred to as **syntactic bootstrapping**.

The Acquisition of Morphology

"Baby Blues", Baby Blues Partnership. Reprinted with permission of King Features Syndicate

The child's acquisition of morphology provides some of the clearest evidence of rule learning. Children's errors in inflectional morphology reveal that the child acquires the regular rules of the grammar and then over applies them. This **overgeneralization** occurs when children treat irregular verbs and nouns as if they were regular. We have probably all heard children say *bringed*, *goed*, *drawed*, and *runned*, or *foots*, *mouses*, and *sheeps*.

These mistakes tell us much about how children learn language because such forms could not arise through imitation. In fact, children may go through three stages in the acquisition of an irregular form:

Stage 1	Stage 2	Stage 3
broke	breaked	broke
brought	bringed	brought

In stage 1 the child uses the correct term such as *brought* or *broke*. At this point the child's grammar does not relate the form *brought* to *bring*, or *broke* to *break*. The words are treated as separate lexical entries. Stage 2 is crucial. Now the child constructs a rule for forming the past tense and attaches the regular past-tense morpheme to all verbs—*play*, *hug*, and *help*, as well as *break* and *bring*. Children look for general patterns. What they do not know at stage 2 is that there are exceptions to the rule. Now their language is more regular than the adult language. During stage 3 the child learns that there are exceptions to the rule, and then once again uses *brought* and *broke*, with the difference being that these irregular forms will be related to the root forms.

Some studies of the acquisition of morphology are based on children's spontaneous use of language. Other studies rely on experiments that elicit particular forms from children. A classic experimental study of English-speaking children was based on the "wug test" (Berko, 1958). Children were shown a drawing of a nonsense animal like the funny creature shown in the following picture. Each "animal" was given a nonsense name. The experimenter would then say to the child, pointing to the picture, "This is a wug."

Then the experimenter would show the child a picture of two of the animals and say, "Now here is another one. There are two of them. There are two _____."

The child's task was to give the plural form, "wugs" [wʌgz]. Another little make-believe animal was called a "bik," and when the child was shown two biks, he or she again was to say the plural form [bɪks]. The children applied regular plural formation to words they had never heard, showing that they had acquired the plural rule. Their ability to add [z] when the animal's name ended with a voiced sound, and [s] when there was a final voiceless consonant, showed that the children were also using rules based on an understanding of natural classes of phonological segments, and not simply imitating words they had previously heard. Similar elicitations were done for past tense *-ed* and present tense *-s,* among other forms.

More recently, studies of children acquiring languages with richer inflectional morphologies than English reveal that they learn agreement at a very early age. For example, Italian verbs must be inflected for number and person to agree with the subject. This is similar to the English agreement rule "add *s* to the verb" for third-person, singular subjects—*He giggles a lot* but *We giggle a lot*—except that in Italian more verb forms must be acquired. Italian-speaking children between the ages of 1;10 (one year, ten months) and 2;4 correctly inflect the verb, as the following utterances of Italian children show:

Tu leg**gi** il libro.	'You (second person singular) read the book.'
Io vad**o** fuori.	'I go (first person singular) outside.'
Dorm**e** miao dorme.	'Sleeps (third person singular) cat sleeps.'
Leg**giamo** il libro.	'(We) read (first person plural) the book.'

Similar results have been shown for children acquiring other richly inflected languages such as Spanish, German, Catalan, and Swahili. It is rare for them to make agreement errors, just as it is rare for an English-speaking child to say "I goes."

Many languages, including the ones just noted, also have gender and number agreement between the head noun and the article and adjectives inside the noun phrase. Children as young as two years old respect these agreement requirements when producing NPs, as shown by the following Italian examples:

E mi**a** gonn**a**.	'(It) is my (feminine singular) skirt.'
Quest**o** mio bimb**o**.	'This my (masculine singular) baby.'
Guarda **la** mel**a** piccolin**a**.	'Look at the little (feminine singular) apple.'
Guarda **il** top**o** piccolin**o**.	'Look at the little (masculine singular) mouse.'

Experimental studies with 2-year old French-speaking children show that they use gender information on determiners to help identify the subsequent noun, for example, *le ballon* (the-masc. balloon) versus *la banane* (the-fem. banana).

Children also show knowledge of the derivational rules of their language and use these rules to create novel words. In English, for example, we can derive verbs from nouns. From the noun *microwave* we now have a verb *to microwave*; from the noun *e(lectronic) mail* we derived the verb *to email*. Children acquire this derivational rule early and use it often because there are lots of gaps in their verb vocabulary.

Child Utterance	**Adult Translation**
You have to scale it.	'You have to weigh it.'
I broomed it up.	'I swept it up.'
He's keying the door.	'He's opening the door (with a key).'
Give me the big mistaker.	'Give me the big eraser.'

These novel forms provide further evidence that language acquisition is a creative process and that children's utterances reflect their internal grammars, which include both derivational and inflectional rules.

The Acquisition of Syntax

"Doonesbury" 1984 G.B. Trudeau. Reprinted with permission of Universal Press Syndicate

When a child is still in the holophrastic stage, adults listening to the one-word utterances often feel that the child is trying to convey a more complex message. Experimental techniques show that at that stage (and even earlier), children have knowledge of some syntactic rules. In these experiments the infant sits on his mother's lap and hears a sentence over a speaker while seeing two video displays depicting different actions, one of which corresponds to the sentence. Infants tend to look longer at the video that matches the sentence they hear. This methodology allows researchers to tap the linguistic knowledge of children who are using only single words or who are not talking at all. Results show that children as young as seventeen months can understand the difference between sentences such as "Ernie is tickling Bert" and "Bert is tickling Ernie." Because these sentences have all the same words, the child cannot be relying on the words alone to understand the meanings. He must also understand the word-order rules and how they determine the grammatical relations of subject and object. This same preferential looking technique has shown that eighteen-month-olds can distinguish between subject and object *wh*-questions, such as *What is the boy hitting?* and *What hit the boy?* These results and many others strongly suggest that children's syntactic competence is ahead of their productive abilities, which we also see in children's lexical acquisition and the development of other components of grammar. Around the time of their second birthday, children begin to put words together into two-word sentences with clear syntactic and semantic relations. The following utterances illustrate the kinds of patterns that are found in children's utterances at this stage: [2]

---

[2]Many of the examples of child language in this chapter are taken from CHILDES (Child Language Data Exchange System), a computerized database of the spontaneous speech of children acquiring English and many other languages. MacWhinney, B., and C. Snow. 1985. The child language data exchange system. *Journal of Child Language* 12: 271–96.

allgone sock	hi Mommy
bye bye boat	allgone sticky
more wet	it ball
Katherine sock	dirty sock

These early utterances can express a variety of semantic and syntactic relations. For example, noun + noun sentences such as *Mommy sock* can express a subject + object relation in the situation when the mother is putting the sock on the child, or a possessive relation when the child is pointing to Mommy's sock. Two words can also be used to show a subject-locative relation, as in *sweater chair* to mean 'The sweater is on the chair,' or to show attribution as in *dirty sock*. Children often have a variety of modifiers such as *allgone*, *more*, and *bye bye*.

Because children mature at different rates and the age at which children start to produce words and put words together varies, chronological age is not a good measure of a child's language development. Instead, researchers use the child's **mean length of utterances** (MLU) to measure progress. MLU is the average length of the utterances the child is producing at a particular point. MLU is usually measured in terms of morphemes, so words like *boys*, *danced*, and *crying* each have a value of two (morphemes). To compare children acquiring languages with different morphological systems measures such as counting the number of verbs per 100 utterances (VPU) may be more revealing. Children with the same MLU or VPU are likely to have similar grammars even though they are different ages.

In their earliest multiword utterances, children are inconsistent in their use of function words (grammatical morphemes) such as *a* and *the*, subject pronouns like *I* and *we*, auxiliary verbs such as *can* and *is*, and in some languages, verbal inflection. Many (though not all) utterances consist only of open-class or content words, while some or all of the function words, auxiliaries, and verbal inflection may be missing. During this stage children often sound as if they are sending a text message or reading an old-fashioned telegram (which contains only the required words for basic understanding). Such utterances are sometimes called "telegraphic speech," and we call this the **telegraphic stage** of the child's language development.

Cat stand up table.
What that?
He play little tune.
Andrew want that.
Cathy build house.
No sit there.
Ride truck.
Show Mommy that.

It can take many months before children use all the grammatical morphemes and auxiliary verbs consistently. However, the child does not deliberately leave out function words as would an adult sending a tweet. The sentences reflect the child's linguistic capacity at that particular stage of language development.

There is a great deal of debate among linguists about how to characterize telegraphic speech: Do children omit function morphemes because of limitations in their ability to produce longer, more complex sentences, or do they omit these morphemes because their grammar permits such elements to be unexpressed? On the first account, telegraphic speech is due to performance limitations. Since there is an upper limit on the length of utterance a child can produce, and function morphemes are less important to comprehension, they are omitted. On the second view, telegraphic speech is an early grammatical stage similar to adult speech in languages like Italian or Spanish that allow subject pronouns to be dropped, as in *Hablo ingles* '(I) speak English,' or Chinese languages, which lack many types of determiners.

Although children's sentences during the telegraphic stage may lack certain function morphemes, they nevertheless appear to have hierarchical constituent structure and involve syntactic rules similar to those in the adult grammar. For example, children almost never violate the word-order rules of their language. In languages with relatively fixed word order such as English and Japanese, children use the required order (SVO in English, SOV in Japanese) from the earliest stage. In languages with freer word order, like Turkish and Russian, grammatical relations such as subject and object are generally marked by inflectional morphology, such as case markers, and children acquiring case-marking languages quickly learn this morphology. For example, Russian- and German-speaking children mark subjects with nominative case and objects with accusative case with very few errors.

The correct use of word order, case marking, and agreement rules shows that even though children may often omit function morphemes, they are aware of constituent structure and syntactic rules and dependencies, which, as in adult grammar, may be represented with these (simplified non X-bar) phrase structure trees:

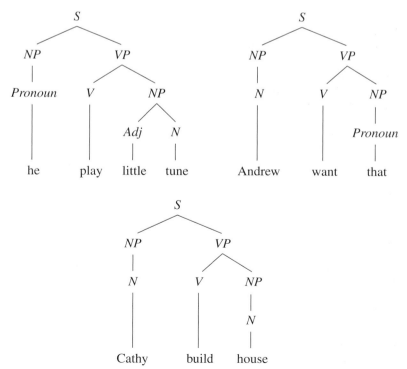

In order to apply morphological and syntactic rules the child must know what syntactic categories the words in his language belong to. But how exactly does the child come to know that *play* and *want* are verbs and *tune* and *house* are nouns? One suggestion is that children first use the meaning of a word to figure out its category. This is called **semantic bootstrapping**. The child may have rules such as "if a word refers to a physical object, it's a noun" or "if a word refers to an action, it's a verb," and so on. However, the rules that link certain meanings to specific categories are not foolproof. For example, the word *action* denotes an action but it is not a verb, *know* is not an action but is a verb, and *justice* is a noun though it is not a physical object. But the rules that drive semantic bootstrapping might be helpful for the kind of words children learn early on, which tend to refer to objects and actions.

Word frames may also help the child to determine when words belong to the same category. Studies of the language that adults use to children show that there are certain frames that occur frequently enough to be reliable for categorization, for example, "you ___ it" and "the ___ one." Most typically, verbs such as *see, do, did, win, fix, turned,* and *get* occur in the first frame, while adjectives like *red, big, wrong,* and *light* occur in the second. If a child knows that *see* is a verb, then he could also deduce that all the other words appearing in the same frame are also verbs. However, this distributional evidence is not foolproof. For example, "it ___ the" can frame a verb, as in *It **hit** the car*, but it can also frame a preposition, as in *I hit it **across** the street*. Nevertheless, like semantic bootstrapping, this evidence may be reliable enough to give the child a head start into the complex task of learning the syntactic categories of words.

The most frequent frames typically consist of function words, determiners such as *the* and *a*, and pronouns like *it* and *one*. This suggests that children can learn from function morphemes in the input even though they omit these elements in their own speech. Indeed, comprehension studies show two-year-olds respond more appropriately to grammatical commands such as *Find the bird* than to commands with an ungrammatically positioned function word as in *Find was bird*. This means that children pay attention to the particular function morphemes and not just to the prosody of the sentence, which is the same in the two commands. Other studies suggest that function morphemes such as determiners help children in word segmentation and categorization.

Sometime between the ages of 2;6 and 3;6, a virtual language explosion occurs. At this point it is difficult to identify distinct stages because the child is undergoing so much development so rapidly. By the age of 3;0, most children are consistent in their use of function morphemes. Moreover, they have begun to produce and understand complex structures, including coordinated sentences and embedded sentences of various kinds, such as the following:

He was stuck and I got him out.
I want this doll because she's big.
I know what to do.
I like to play with something else.
I think she's sick.
Look at the train Ursula bought.
I gon' make it like a rocket to blast off with.
It's too early for us to eat.

Past the age of 3;6 children can generally form grammatical *wh*-questions with the proper Aux inversion, such as *What can I do tomorrow?* They can produce and understand relative clauses such as *This is the lion that chased the giraffe*, as well as other embedded clauses such as *I know that Mommy is home.* They can use reflexive pronouns correctly, such as *I saw myself in the camera.* Somewhat beyond 4;0, depending on the individual, much of the adult grammar has been acquired.

The Acquisition of Pragmatics

"Baby Blues", Baby Blues Partnership. Reprinted with permission of King Features Syndicate

In addition to acquiring the rules of grammar, children must learn the appropriate use of language in context, or pragmatics. The cartoon is funny because of the inappropriateness of the interaction, showing that Zoe hasn't completely acquired the pragmatic "maxims of conversation" discussed in chapter 4.

Context is needed to determine the reference of pronouns. A sentence such as "Surely he loves her anyway" is uninterpretable unless both speaker and hearer understand who the pronouns *he* and *her* refer to. If the sentence were preceded by "I saw John and Mary arguing in the park," then the referents of the pronouns would be clear. Children are not always sensitive to the needs of their interlocutors, and they may fail to establish the referents for pronouns. It is not unusual for a three- or four-year-old (or even older children) to use pronouns out of the blue, like the child who cries to her mother "He hit me" when mom has no idea who did the deed.

The speaker and listener form part of the context of an utterance. The meaning of *I* and *you* depends on who is talking and who is listening, which changes from situation to situation. Younger children (around age two) have difficulty with the "shifting reference" of these pronouns. A typical error that children make at this age is to refer to themselves as "you," for example, saying "You want to take a walk" when they mean 'I want to take a walk.'

Children also show a lack of pragmatic awareness in the way they sometimes use articles. Like pronouns, the interpretation of articles depends on context. The definite article *the*, as in "the boy," can be used felicitously only when it is clear to speaker and hearer what boy is being discussed. In a discourse, the indefinite article *a/an* must be used for the first mention of a new referent, but the definite article (or pronoun) may be used in subsequent mentions, as illustrated following:

A boy walked into the class.
He was in the wrong room.
The teacher directed the boy to the right classroom.

Children do not always respect the pragmatic rules for articles. In experimental studies, three-year-olds may use the definite article for introducing a new referent. In other words, the child tends to assume that his listener knows who he is talking about without having established this in a linguistically appropriate way.

Implicatures are another part of pragmatics that young children have difficulty with. (Implicatures are discussed in chapter 4.) An adult hearing the sentence *Some of the children are playing ball* would infer that not all the children are playing ball. This is because adults follow Grice's conversational maxims, among which is the principle that speakers are maximally informative. If all the children were playing ball, the speaker would say that, even though it is logically true that if *all* the children are playing ball then it is true that *some* of the children are playing ball. Interestingly, children under the age of 7 or so do not seem to get such implicatures. Various experimental studies have shown that when presented with a description of a scenario in which a stronger, more informative term such as *all* would be appropriate, children readily accept a weaker, less informative *some*. For example, in one experiment the child is shown an animated video in which a mouse, who likes vegetables, picks up all the carrots in the display. A puppet who is watching the animation with the child then says "Then mouse picked up some of the carrots." When the child is then asked by the experimenter if this is right, he responds 'yes', while adults in this situation would say" No, he picked up *all* of the carrots." In one sense the child is not wrong in his response—the mouse did pick up some of the carrots—in fact he picked them all up. But adults use pragmatic principles in such cases while children seem to rely more heavily on the literal or logical meaning.

It may take a child several months or years to master those aspects of pragmatics that involve the felicitous use of determiners and pronouns, or the conversational maxims which when violated (usually purposely) result in implicatures. Other aspects of pragmatics are acquired very early. Even in the holophrastic stage children use their one-word utterances with different illocutionary force (see chapter 4). The utterance "up" spoken by J. P. at sixteen months might be a simple statement such as 'The teddy is up on the shelf,' or a request: 'Pick me up.' And as we will discuss below, bilingual children—even very young ones—understand which of their languages to use in different conversational contexts.

The Development of Auxiliaries: A Case Study

We have seen in this chapter that language acquisition involves development in various components—the lexicon, phonology, morphology, and syntax, as well as pragmatics. These different modules interact in complex ways to chart an overall course of language development.

As an example, let us take the case of the English auxiliaries. As noted earlier, children in the telegraphic stage do not typically use auxiliaries such as *can*, *will*, or *do*, and they often omit *be* and *have* from their utterances. Several syntactic constructions in English depend on the presence of an auxiliary, the most central of which are questions and negative sentences. To negate a main verb requires an auxiliary verb (or *do* if there isn't one) as in the following examples:

I don't like this book.
I won't read this book.

An adult does not say "I not like this book."

Similarly, as discussed in chapter 3, English yes-no and *wh* questions are formed by moving an auxiliary to precede the subject, as in the following examples:

Can I leave now?
Do you love me?
Where should John put the book?

Although the two-year-old does not produce auxiliaries, she is able to form negative sentences and questions. During the telegraphic stage, children produce questions of the following sort:

Yes-No Questions	*Wh* questions
I ride train?	What he eat?
Mommy eggnog?	Where Daddy go?
Have some?	What dat train doing?

These yes-no questions have a rising intonation pattern typical of yes-no questions in English, but because there are no auxiliaries, the child cannot use the particular syntactic device for forming questions in English—auxiliary movement. The *wh* questions also lack auxiliaries, but they show that the child knows the grammatical rule that requires *wh*-phrases to move to a fronted position. She also has the pragmatic knowledge to make a request or ask for information, and she has the appropriate prosody, which depends on knowledge of phonology and the syntactic structure of the question. Many components of language must be in place to form an adultlike question.

In languages that do not require auxiliaries to form questions, children appear more advanced. For example, in Dutch and Italian the main verb moves. Because many main verbs are acquired before auxiliaries, Dutch and Italian children produce questions in the telegraphic stage that follow the adult rule:

Dutch

En wat doen ze daar?	and what do they there	'And what are they doing there?'
Wordt mama boos?	becomes mama angry	'Is mommy angry?'
Weet je n kerk?	know you a church	'Do you know a church?'

Italian

Cosa fanno questi bambini?	what do these children	'What are these babies doing?'
Chando vene a mama?	when comes the mommy	'When is Mommy coming?"
Vola cici?	flies birdie	'Is the birdie flying?'

The Dutch and Italian children show us there is nothing intrinsically difficult about syntactic movement rules. The delay that English-speaking children show in producing adultlike questions may simply be because auxiliaries are acquired later than main verbs and because English is idiosyncratic in forming questions by moving only auxiliaries.

The lack of auxiliaries during the telegraphic stage also affects the formation of negative sentences. During this stage the English-speaking child's negative sentences look like the following:

He no bite you.
Wayne not eating it.
Kathryn not go over there.
You no bring choo-choo train.
That no fish school.

Because the auxiliaries are missing, these utterances do not look very adultlike. However, children at this stage understand the pragmatic force of negation. The child who says "No!" when asked to take a nap knows exactly what he means. As children acquire the auxiliaries, they generally use them correctly; that is, the auxiliary usually appears before the subject in yes-no questions, but not always.

Yes-No Questions
Does the kitty stand up?
Can I have a piece of paper?
Will you help me?
We can go now?

***Wh* Questions**
Which way they should go?
What can we ride in?
What will we eat?

The introduction of auxiliaries into the child's grammar also affects negative sentences. We now find correctly negated auxiliaries, though *be* is still missing in many cases.

Paul can't have one.
Donna won't let go.
I don't want cover on it.
I am not a doctor.
It's not cold.
Paul not tired.
I not crying.

The child always places the negation in the correct position in relation to the auxiliary or *be*. Main verbs follow negation and *be* precedes negation. Children never produce errors such as "Mommy dances not" or "I not am going."

In languages such as French and German, which are like Italian and Dutch in having a rule that moves inflected verbs, the verb shows up before the negative marker. French and German children respect this rule, as shown below. (In the German examples *nich* is the baby form of *nicht*.)

French

Veux pas lolo.	want not water	'I don't want water.'
Marche pas.	walks not	'She doesn't walk.'
Ça tourne pas.	that turns not	'That doesn't turn.'

German

Macht nich aua.	makes not ouch	'It doesn't hurt.'
Brauche nich lala.	need not pacifier	'I don't need a pacifier.'
Schmeckt auch nich.	tastes also not	'It doesn't taste good either.'

Though the stages of language development are universal, they are shaped by the grammar of the particular adult language the child is acquiring. During the telegraphic stage, German, French, Italian, and English-speaking children omit auxiliaries, but they form negative sentences and questions in different ways because the rules of question and negative formation are different in the respective adult languages. This tells us something essential about language acquisition: Children are sensitive to the rules of the adult target language at the earliest stages of development. Just as their phonology is quickly fine-tuned to the ambient language(s), so is their syntactic system.

Setting Parameters

Nowhere is the interplay of universal and language-specific properties within acquisition better illustrated than in children's setting of UG parameters.

Children acquire some aspects of syntax very early, even while they are still in the telegraphic stage. Many of these early developments correspond to what we have referred to as the parameters of UG in preceding chapters. One such parameter determines whether the head of a phrase comes before or after its complements: for example, whether the order of the VP is verb-object (VO) as in English or OV as in Japanese. Children produce the correct word order of their language from their earliest multiword utterances, and they understand word order even when they are in the one-word stage of production. According to the parameter model of UG, the child does not actually have to formulate a word-order rule. Rather, he must choose between two already specified values: head first or head last, based on the language he hears around him. The English-speaking child can quickly figure out that the head comes before its complements; a Japanese-speaking child can equally well determine that his language is head-final.

Other parameters of UG involve the verb movement rules. In some languages the verb can move out of the VP to higher positions in the phrase structure tree. We saw this in the Dutch and Italian questions discussed in the last section. In other languages, such as English, verbs do not move (only auxiliaries do). The verb movement parameters provide the child with an option: "my language does/does not allow verb movement." As we saw, Dutch- and Italian-speaking children quickly set the verb movement parameters to the "does allow" value, and so they form questions by moving the verb. English-speaking children never make the mistake of moving the verb, even when they don't yet have auxiliaries. In both cases, the children have set the parameter at the correct value for their language. Even after English-speaking children acquire the auxiliaries and the Aux movement rule, they never overgeneralize this movement to include verbs. This supports the hypothesis that the parameter is set early in development and cannot be undone. In this case as well, the child does not have to formulate a rule of verb movement; he does not have to learn when the verb moves and where it moves to. This is all given by UG. He simply has to decide based on the sentences he hears around him whether verb movement is possible in his language.

The parameters of UG limit the grammatical options to a small well-defined set—is my language head-first or head-last, does my language have verb movement, and so on. Parameters greatly reduce the acquisition burden on the child and contribute to explaining the ease and rapidity of language acquisition.

The Acquisition of Signed Languages

Deaf children who are born to deaf signing parents are naturally exposed to sign language just as hearing children are naturally exposed to spoken language. Given the universal aspects of sign and spoken languages, it is not surprising that language development in these deaf children parallels the stages of spoken language acquisition. Deaf children babble, they then progress to single signs similar to the single words in the holophrastic stage, and finally they begin to combine signs. There is also a telegraphic stage in which the function signs may be omitted. Use of function signs becomes consistent at around the same age for deaf children as function words in spoken languages. The ages at which signing children go through each of these stages are comparable to the ages of children acquiring a spoken language.

We saw earlier that question formation in various spoken languages is a complex phenomenon with many interacting components, some of which are acquired early and others of which show up later in development. In *wh* questions in ASL, the *wh* word can move or it can be left in its original position. Both of the following sentences are grammatical:

_____whq

WHO BILL SEE YESTERDAY?

<u>   </u>whq
BILL SAW WHO YESTERDAY?

(Note: We follow the convention of writing the glosses for signs in uppercase letters.)

There is no Aux movement in ASL, but a question is accompanied by a facial expression with tilted head and furrowed brows. This is represented by the *whq* above the ASL glosses. Such *non-manual markers* are part of the grammar of ASL. It is like the rising intonation we use when we ask questions in English and other spoken languages.

In the acquisition of *wh* questions in ASL, signing children easily learned the rules associated with the *wh* phrase. The children sometimes move the *wh* phrase and sometimes leave it in place, as adult signers do. But they often omit the non-manual marker, an omission that is not grammatical in the adult language.

Sometimes the parallels between the acquisition of signed and spoken languages are striking. For example, some of the grammatical morphemes in ASL are semantically transparent or **iconic**, that is, they look like what they mean; for example, the sign for the pronoun 'I' involves the speaker pointing to his chest. The sign for the pronoun 'you' is a point to the chest of the addressee. As noted earlier, at around age two, children acquiring spoken languages often reverse the pronouns *I* and *you*. Interestingly, at this same age signing children make this same error. They will point to themselves when they mean 'you' and point to the addressee when they mean 'I.' Children acquiring ASL make this error despite the transparency or iconicity of these particular signs, because signing children (like signing adults) treat these pronouns as linguistic symbols and not simply as pointing gestures. As part of the language, the shifting reference of these pronouns presents the same problem for signing children that it does for speaking children.

Deaf children of hearing parents who are not exposed to sign language from birth suffer a severe handicap in acquiring language. They have great difficulty learning a spoken language because normal speech depends largely on auditory feedback. To learn to speak, a deaf child requires extensive training in special schools or programs designed especially for deaf people and they rarely achieve the proficiency that hearing children do, even with intensive oral training. Sadly, it may also be many years before these children encounter a conventional sign language and late learners of sign language do not achieve the same level of competence as children who are exposed early in life. Yet the instinct to acquire language is so strong in humans that these deaf children begin to develop their own manual gestures to express their thoughts and desires. A study of six such children revealed that they not only developed individual signs but joined pairs and formed sentences with definite syntactic order and systematic constraints. Although these "home signs," as they are called, are not fully developed languages like ASL, they have a linguistic complexity and systematicity that could not have come from the input, because there was no input. Cases such as these demonstrate not only the strong drive that humans have to communicate through language, but also the innate basis of language structure.

The Role of the Linguistic Environment: Adult Input

[The acquisition of language] is doubtless the greatest intellectual feat any one of us is ever required to perform.

LEONARD BLOOMFIELD, *Language*, 1933

Children deprived of linguistic input show a clear drive to acquire language and may even create a rudimentary linguistic system, as illustrated by deaf children who create home signs. But there is little doubt that children require a language environment to develop a mature linguistic system. But what exactly is the role of the linguistic input children hear (or see, in the case of sign)? One prominent view, suggested by parameter-setting models of acquisition, is that children use the linguistic data to extract the underlying rules and parameter settings of their language.

Other approaches to understanding language acquisition afford a much more pronounced and formative role to the input provided by adults. This is especially true of early theories of language acquisition which were heavily influenced by behaviorism, a school of psychology prevalent in the 1950s. As the name implies, behaviorism focused on people's directly observable behaviors, rather than on the mental systems underlying these behaviors. Language was viewed as a kind of verbal behavior, and it was proposed that children learn language through imitation, reinforcement, analogy, and similar processes. On this view the adult input and feedback to the child was paramount. B. F. Skinner, one of the founders of behaviorist psychology, proposed a model of language acquisition in his book *Verbal Behavior* (1957). Two years later, in a devastating reply to Skinner entitled *Review of Verbal Behavior* (1959), Noam Chomsky showed that language is a complex cognitive system that could not be acquired by behaviorist principles. In the next section we discuss some of the mechanisms proposed by behaviorists to account for language acquisition.

The Role of Imitation, Reinforcement, and Analogy

CHILD:	My teacher holded the baby rabbits and we patted them.
ADULT:	Did you say your teacher held the baby rabbits?
CHILD:	Yes.
ADULT:	What did you say she did?
CHILD:	She holded the baby rabbits and we patted them.
ADULT:	Did you say she held them tightly?
CHILD:	No, she holded them loosely.

ANONYMOUS ADULT AND CHILD

A common misconception about language acquisition is that children simply listen to what is said around them and imitate the speech they hear. Imitation is involved to some extent of course. An American child hears *milk* and a Mexican child *leche* and each child attempts to reproduce what he hears. But children's early words and sentences show that they are not simply imitating adult speech. Many times the words are barely recognizable to an adult and the meanings are also not always like the adult's.

Moreover, even when children are trying to imitate what they hear, they are unable to produce sentences outside of the rules of their developing grammar. The following are a child's attempts to imitate something the adult has said:

Adult	**Child**
He's going out.	He go out.
That's an old-time train.	Old-time train.
Adam, say what I say:	Where I can put them?
Where can I put them?	

Imitation also fails to account for the fact that children who are unable to speak for neurological or physiological reasons are able to learn the language spoken to them and understand it. When they overcome their speech impairment, they immediately use the language for speaking.

Another proposal in the behaviorist tradition is that children learn to produce correct (grammatical) sentences because adults positively reinforce them when they say something grammatical and negatively reinforce them by correction when they say something ungrammatical. But studies show that parents seldom correct their children, and when they do it is usually for mispronunciations or incorrect reporting of facts and not for "bad grammar." For example, the ungrammatical sentence "Her curl my hair" was not corrected because the child's mother was in fact curling her hair. However, when the child uttered the grammatical sentence "Walt Disney comes on Tuesday," she was corrected because the television program was shown on Wednesday. One researcher concluded somewhat wryly that it is "truth value rather than syntactic well-formedness that chiefly governs explicit verbal reinforcement by parents—which renders mildly paradoxical the fact that the usual product of such a training schedule is an adult whose speech is highly grammatical but not notably truthful."

Adults will sometimes **recast** children's utterances into an adultlike form, as in the following examples:

Child	**Mother**
It fall.	It fell?
Where is them?	They're at home.
It doing dancing.	It's dancing, yes.

In these examples the mother provides the correct model without actually correcting the child. Although recasts are potentially helpful to the child, they are not used in a consistent way. One study of forty mothers of children two to four years old showed that only about 25 percent of children's ungrammatical sentences are recast and that overall, parents recast grammatical sentences as often as bad ones. Because parents focus more on the content than on the form of their children's utterances, and allow many ungrammatical utterances to "slip by" while correcting grammatical ones, a child that relies on recasts to learn grammar would be mightily confused.

Even if adults did correct children's syntax it would still not explain how or what children learn from such adult responses, or how children discover and construct the correct rules. Children do not know what they are doing wrong and are unable to make corrections even when "errors" are pointed out, as shown by the following exchange:

CHILD:	Nobody don't like me.
MOTHER:	No, say "Nobody likes me."
CHILD:	Nobody don't like me.
	(dialogue repeated eight times)
MOTHER:	Now, listen carefully; say "Nobody likes me."
CHILD:	Oh, nobody don't likes me.

It has also been suggested that children put words together to form phrases and sentences by **analogy**, by hearing a sentence and using it as a model to form other sentences. In some sense this must be true. Children must generalize from particular instances to form a general rule. The problem with analogy is that the child must also know when the general rule does not work, as one developmental psycholinguist explains:

[S]uppose the child has heard the sentence "I painted a red barn." So now, by analogy, the child can say "I painted a blue barn." That's exactly the kind of theory that we want. You hear a sample and you extend it to all of the new cases by similarity. . . . In addition to "I painted a red barn" you might also hear the sentence "I painted a barn red." So it looks as if you take those last two words and switch their order. . . . So now you want to extend this to the case of seeing, because you want to look at barns instead of paint them. So you have heard, "I saw a red barn." Now you try (by analogy) a . . . new sentence—"I saw a barn red." Something's gone wrong. This is an analogy, but the analogy didn't work. It's not a sentence of English.[3]

Similarly, based on the sentence "John eats tomatoes" we can say "John eats" with the meaning 'John eats *something*.' But we cannot analogously say, based on the sentence "John grows tomatoes" that "John grows" to mean 'John grows *something*.'

Children do not make syntactic errors of this sort. They may overgeneralize a morphological rule or omit functional elements. But they seem to know enough about syntactic structure not to assign a uniform analysis to sentences with *eat* and *grow* or *paint and see*, each of which has different syntactic properties. Analogy—to the extent it is used by children—must be constrained by the child's knowledge of the general structural principles provided by UG.

The Role of Structured Input

Yet another suggestion is that children are able to learn language because adults speak to them in a special "simplified" language sometimes called **motherese**, or **child-directed speech** (CDS) (or more informally, **baby talk**).

---

[3]Gleitman, L. R., and E. Wanner. 1982. *Language acquisition: The state of the art.* Cambridge, UK: Cambridge University Press.

This hypothesis also places a lot of emphasis on the role of the environment in facilitating language acquisition.

In our culture adults typically talk to young children in a special way. We tend to speak more slowly and more clearly; we may speak in a higher pitch and exaggerate our intonation; and sentences directed to children are generally grammatical. Infants seem to prefer to listen to motherese over normal adult speech. Researchers believe that the exaggerated intonation and other properties may be useful for getting a child's attention and making salient certain features of language.

However, motherese is not syntactically simple. It includes a range of complex sentences such as questions (*Do you want your juice now?*); embedded sentences (*Mommy thinks you should sleep now*); imperatives (*Pat the dog gently!*); and negatives with tag questions (*We don't want to hurt him, do we?*). Moreover, adults do not simplify their language by dropping inflections from verbs and nouns or by omitting function words such as determiners and auxiliaries, though children do this all the time.

Studies show that children's overall language development is not significantly affected by the use of motherese. The child whose mother uses more features of motherese will not develop language any faster than another child whose mother uses fewer features of this mode of speech. Indeed, in many cultures adults do not use a special speech style with children, and there are even communities in which adults hardly talk to babies at all. Nevertheless, children around the world acquire language in much the same way. Adults seem to be the followers rather than the leaders in this enterprise. The child does not develop linguistically because he is exposed to ever more adultlike language. Rather, the adult adjusts his language to the child's increasing linguistic sophistication.

Imitation, reinforcement, and analogy cannot account for language development because they are based on the (implicit or explicit) assumption that what the child acquires is a set of sentences or forms rather than a set of grammatical rules and linguistic structures. Theories that assume that acquisition depends on a specially structured input also place too much emphasis on the environment rather than on the grammar-making abilities of the child. These proposals do not explain the creativity that children show in acquiring language, why they go through the stages they do, or why they make some kinds of "errors" but not others, for example, "It doing dancing" but not "Was the boy who sleeping is dreaming?" They do not address the question of how the child comes to know as much as he does about his language based on varying and impoverished input.

Knowing More Than One Language

He that understands grammar in one language, understands it in another as far as the essential properties of Grammar are concerned. The fact that he can't speak, nor comprehend, another language is due to the diversity of words and their various forms, but these are the accidental properties of grammar.

ROGER BACON (1214–1294)

People can acquire a second language under many different circumstances. You may have learned a second language when you began middle school, or high school, or college. Moving to a new country often means acquiring a new language. Other people live in communities or homes in which more than one language is spoken and may acquire two (or more) languages simultaneously. The term **second language acquisition**, or **L2 acquisition**, generally refers to the acquisition of a second language by someone (adult or child) who has already acquired a first language. This is also referred to as **sequential bilingualism**. **Bilingual language acquisition** refers to the (more or less) simultaneous acquisition of two languages beginning in infancy (or before the age of three years), also referred to as **simultaneous bilingualism**.

Childhood Bilingualism

2009 Tundra Comics

Approximately half of the people in the world are native speakers of more than one language. This means that as children they had regular and continued exposure to those languages. In many parts of the world, especially in Africa and Asia, bilingualism (even multilingualism) is the norm. In contrast, many Western countries (though by no means all of them) view themselves as monolingual, even though they may be home to speakers of many languages. In the United States and many European countries, bilingualism is often viewed as a transitory phenomenon associated with immigration.

Bilingualism is an intriguing topic. People wonder how it's possible for a child to acquire two (or more) languages at the same time. There are many questions, such as: Doesn't the child confuse the two languages? Does bilingual language development take longer than monolingual development? Are bilingual children brighter or does acquiring two languages negatively affect the child's cognitive development in some way? How much exposure to each language is necessary for a child to become bilingual?

Much of the early research into bilingualism focused on the fact that bilingual children sometimes mix the two languages in the same sentences, as the following examples from French-English bilingual children illustrate. In the first example, a French word appears in an otherwise English sentence. In the other two examples, all of the words are English but the syntax is French.

His nose is perdu.   "His nose is lost."
A house pink   "A pink house"
That's to me.   "That's mine."

In early studies of bilingualism, this kind of language mixing was viewed negatively. It was taken as an indication that the child was confused or having difficulty with the two languages. In fact, many parents, sometimes on the advice of educators or psychologists, would stop raising their children bilingually when faced with this issue. However, it now seems clear that some amount of language mixing is a normal part of the early bilingual acquisition—and not an indication of any language problem.

Indeed, various researchers have claimed that language mixing in bilingual children is similar to **codeswitching** used by many adult bilinguals (discussed in chapter 7). In specific social situations bilingual adults may switch back and forth between their two languages in the same sentence, for example, "I put the forks en las mesas" ('I put the forks on the tables'). Codeswitching reflects the grammars of both languages working simultaneously; it is not "bad grammar" or "broken English." Adult bilinguals codeswitch only when speaking to other bilingual speakers and various studies have shown that bilingual children as young as two make contextually appropriate language choices: In speaking to monolinguals the children use one language, and in speaking to bilinguals they mix the two languages.

Theories of Bilingual Development

There is not reason to believe that the underlying principles and mechanisms of language education [in bilinguals] are qualitatively differed from those used by monolinguals.

JÜRGEN MEISEL, *Linguistics 24*, 1986

These mixed utterances raise an interesting question about the grammars of bilingual children. Does the bilingual child start out with only one grammar that is eventually differentiated, or does she construct a separate grammar for each language right from the start? The **unitary system hypothesis** says that the child initially constructs only one lexicon and one grammar. The presence of mixed utterances such as the ones just given is often taken as support for this hypothesis. In addition, at the early stages, bilingual children often have words for particular objects in only one language. For example, a Spanish-English bilingual child may know the Spanish word for 'milk,' *leche*, but not the English word, or she may have the word *water* but not *agua*. This kind of complementarity has also been taken as support for the idea that the child has only one lexicon.

However, careful examination of the vocabularies of bilingual children reveals that although they may not have exactly the same words in both languages, there is enough overlap to make the single lexicon idea implausible. The reason children may not have the same set of words in both languages is that they use their two languages in different circumstances and acquire the vocabulary appropriate to each situation. For example, the bilingual English-Spanish child may hear only Spanish during mealtimes, and so he will first learn the Spanish words for foods. Also, bilingual children initially have smaller vocabularies in each of their languages than the monolingual child has in her one language. This makes sense because a child can only learn so many words a day, and the bilingual child has two lexicons to build. For these reasons the bilingual child may have more lexical gaps than the monolingual child at a comparable stage of development, and those gaps may be different for each language.

The **separate systems hypothesis** says that the bilingual child builds a distinct lexicon and grammar for each language. To test the separate systems hypothesis, it is necessary to look at how the child acquires those pieces of grammar that are different in his two languages. For example, if both languages have SVO word order, this would not be a good place to test this hypothesis. Several studies have shown that where the two languages diverge, children acquire the different rules of each language. Spanish-English and French-German bilingual children have been shown to use the word orders appropriate to each language, as well as the correct agreement morphemes for each language. Other studies have found that children set up two distinct sets of phonemes and phonological rules for their languages.

The separate systems hypothesis also receives support from the study of hearing children of deaf parents who are acquiring both sign and spoken languages. Canadian bilingual children who acquire Langues des Signes Quebecoise (LSQ), or Quebec Sign Language, develop the two languages exactly as bilingual children acquiring two spoken languages. The LSQ/French bilinguals reached linguistic milestones in each of their languages in parallel with Canadian children acquiring French and English. They produced their first words, as well as their first word combinations, at the same time in each language. In reaching these milestones, neither group showed any delay compared to monolingual children.

The LSQ-French bilinguals have semantically equivalent words in the two languages, just as bilinguals acquiring two spoken languages do. In addition, these children, like all bilingual children, were able to adjust their language choice to the language of their addressees, showing that they differentiated the two languages. Like most bilingual children, the LSQ-French bilinguals produced mixed utterances that had words from both languages. What is especially interesting is that these children showed simultaneous language mixing. They would produce an LSQ sign and a French word at the same time, something that is only possible if one language is spoken and the other signed. However, this finding has implications for bilingual language acquisition in general. It shows that the language mixing of bilingual children is not caused by confusion, but is rather the result of two grammars operating simultaneously.

Two Monolinguals in One Head

Although we must study many bilingual children to reach any firm conclusions, the evidence accumulated so far seems to support the idea that children construct multiple grammars from the outset. Moreover, it seems that bilingual children develop their grammars along the same lines as monolingual children. They go through a babbling stage, a holophrastic stage, a telegraphic stage, and so on. During the telegraphic stage they show the same characteristics in each of their languages as the monolingual children. For example, monolingual English-speaking children omit verb endings in sentences such as "Eve play there" and "Andrew want that," and German-speaking children use infinitives as in "S[ch]okolade holen" ('chocolate get-infinitive'). Spanish- and Italian-speaking monolinguals never omit verbal inflection or use infinitives in this way. Remarkably, two-year-old German-Italian bilinguals use infinitives when speaking German but not when they speak Italian. Young Spanish-English bilingual children drop the English verb endings but not the Spanish ones, and German-English bilinguals omit verbal inflection in English and use the infinitive in German. Results such as these have led some researchers to suggest that from a grammar-making point of view, the bilingual child is like "two monolinguals in one head."

The Role of Input

One issue that concerns researchers studying bilingualism, as well as parents of bilingual children, is the relationship between language input and proficiency. What role does input play in helping the child to "separate" the two languages? One input condition that is thought to promote bilingual development is *une personne–une langue* (one person, one language)—as in, Mom speaks only language A to the child and Dad speaks only language B. The idea is that keeping the two languages separate in the input will make it easier for the child to acquire each without influence from the other. Whether this method influences bilingual development in some important way has not been established. In practice this "ideal" input situation may be difficult to attain. It may also be unnecessary. We saw earlier that babies are attuned to various phonological properties of the input language such as prosody and phonotactics. Various studies suggest that this sensitivity provides a sufficient basis for the bilingual child to keep the two languages separate.

Another question is how much input does a child need in each language to become "native" in both? The answer is not straightforward. It seems intuitively clear that if a child hears twelve hours of English a day and only two hours of Spanish, he will probably develop English more quickly and completely than Spanish. In fact, under these conditions he may never achieve the kind of grammatical competence in Spanish that we associate with the normal monolingual Spanish speaker. In reality bilingual children are raised in a variety of circumstances. Some may have more or less equal exposure to the two languages; some may hear one language more than the other but still have sufficient input in the two languages to become "native" in both; some may ultimately have one language that is dominant to a lesser or greater degree. Researchers simply do not know how much language exposure is necessary in the two languages to produce a balanced bilingual, though they are beginning to address this question. For now the assumption is that the child should receive roughly equal amounts of input in the two languages to achieve native proficiency in both.

Cognitive Effects of Bilingualism

Bilingual Hebrew-English-speaking child: "I speak Hebrew and English."

Monolingual English-speaking child: "What's English?"

SOURCE UNKNOWN

Another issue is the effect of bilingualism on intellectual or cognitive development. Does being bilingual make you more or less intelligent, more or less creative, and so on? Historically, research into this question has been fraught with methodological difficulties and has often been heavily influenced by the prevailing political and social climate. Many early studies (pre-1960s) showed that bilingual children did worse than monolingual children on IQ and other cognitive and educational tests. However, when other factors such as schooling and socioeconomic status were controlled for, these differences disappeared. More recent research indicates that bilingual children outperform monolinguals in certain kinds of problem solving. For example, bilingual children are better at accommodating to unpredictable rule changes in sorting games and other tasks. They also seem to have better **metalinguistic awareness**, which refers to a speaker's conscious awareness *about* language rather than *of* language. This is illustrated in the epigraph to this section. Finally, bilingual children have sufficient metalinguistic awareness to speak the contextually appropriate language, as noted earlier.

Whether children enjoy some cognitive or educational benefit from being bilingual seems to depend in part on extralinguistic factors such as the social and economic position of the child's group or community, the educational situation, and the relative "prestige" of the two languages. Studies that show the most positive effects (e.g., better school performance) generally involve children reared in societies where both languages are valued and whose parents were interested in and supportive of their bilingual development.

Second Language Acquisition

In contrast to the bilinguals just discussed, many people are introduced to a second language (L2) after they have achieved native competence in a first language (L1). If you have had the experience of trying to master a second language as an adult, no doubt you found it to be a challenge quite unlike your first language experience.

Is L2 Acquisition the Same as L1 Acquisition?

With some exceptions, adults do not simply pick up a second language. It usually requires conscious attention, if not intense study and memorization, to become proficient in a second language. Again, with the exception of some remarkable individuals, adult second-language learners (L2ers) do not often achieve native-like grammatical competence in the L2, especially with respect to pronunciation. They generally have an accent, and they may make syntactic or morphological errors that are unlike the errors of children acquiring their first language (L1ers). For example, L2ers often make word order errors, especially early in their development, as well as morphological errors in grammatical gender and case. L2 errors may **fossilize** so that no amount of teaching or correction can undo them.

Unlike L1 acquisition, which is uniformly successful across children and languages, adults vary considerably in their ability to acquire an L2 completely. Some people are very talented language learners. Others are hopeless.

Most people fall somewhere in the middle. Success may depend on a range of factors, including age, talent, motivation, and whether you are in the country where the language is spoken or sitting in a classroom five mornings a week with no further contact with native speakers. For all these reasons, many people, including many linguists who study L2 acquisition, believe that adult second language acquisition is something different from first language acquisition. This hypothesis is referred to as the **fundamental difference hypothesis** of L2 acquisition.

In certain important respects, however, L2 acquisition is like L1 acquisition. Like L1ers, L2ers do not acquire their second language overnight; they go through stages. Like L1ers, L2ers construct grammars. These grammars reflect their competence in the L2 at each stage, and so their language at any particular point, though not native-like, is rule-governed and not haphazard. The intermediate grammars that L2ers create on their way to the target have been called **interlanguage grammars**.

Consider word order in the interlanguage grammars of Romance language (e.g., Italian, Spanish, and Portuguese) speakers acquiring German as a second language. The word order of the Romance languages is Subject-(Auxiliary)-Verb-Object (like English). German has two basic word orders depending on the presence of an auxiliary. Sentences with auxiliaries have Subject-Auxiliary-Object-Verb, as in (1). Sentences without auxiliaries have Subject-Verb-Object, as in (2). (Note that as with the child data above, these L2 sentences may contain various "errors" in addition to the word order facts we are considering.)

1. Hans hat ein Buch gekauft.   'Hans has a book bought.'
2. Hans kauft ein Buch.   'Hans is buying a book.'

Studies have shown that Romance speakers acquire German word order in pieces. During the first stage they use German words but the S-Aux-V-O word order of their native language, as follows:

Stage 1:   Mein Vater hat gekauft ein Buch.
        'My father has bought a book.'

At the second stage, they acquire the VP word order Object-Verb.

Stage 2:   Vor Personalrat auch meine helfen.
        in the personnel office [a colleague] me helped
        'A colleague in the personnel office helped me.'

At the third stage they acquire the rule that places the verb or (auxiliary) in second position.

Stage 3:   Jetzt kann sie mir eine Frage machen.
        now can she me a question ask
        'Now she can ask me a question.'

        Ich kenne nich die Welt.
        I know not the world.
        'I don't know the world.'

These stages differ from those of children acquiring German as a first language. For example, German children know early on that the language has SOV word order.

Like L1ers, L2ers also attempt to uncover the grammar of the target language, but with varying success, and they often do not reach the target. Proponents of the fundamental difference hypothesis believe that adult L2ers construct grammars using different principles than those used in L1 acquisition, principles that are not specifically designed for language acquisition, but rather for problem solving used in playing chess or learning math for example. According to this view, L2ers lack access to the specifically linguistic principles of UG that L1ers have to help them.

Opposing this view, others have argued that adults are superior to children in solving all sorts of nonlinguistic problems. If they were using these problem-solving skills to learn their L2, shouldn't they be uniformly more successful than they are? Also, linguistic savants such as Christopher, whom we shall discuss in the next chapter, argue against the view that L2 acquisition involves only nonlinguistic cognitive abilities. Christopher's IQ and problem-solving skills are minimal at best, yet he has become proficient in several languages.

Many L2 acquisition researchers do not believe that L2 acquisition is fundamentally different from L1 acquisition. They point to various studies that show that interlanguage grammars do not generally violate principles of UG, which makes the process seem more similar to L1 acquisition. In the German L2 examples above, the interlanguage rules may be wrong for German, or wrong for Romance, but they are not impossible rules. These researchers also note that although L2ers may fall short of L1ers in terms of their final grammar, they appear to acquire rules in the same way as L1ers.

Native Language Influence in L2 Acquisition

One respect in which L1 acquisition and L2 acquisition are clearly different is that adult L2ers already have a fully developed grammar of their first language. As discussed in chapter 1, linguistic competence is unconscious knowledge. We cannot suppress our ability to use the rules of our language. We cannot decide not to understand English. Similarly, L2ers—especially at the beginning stages of acquiring their L2—seem to rely on their L1 grammar to some extent. This is shown by the kinds of errors L2ers make, which often involve the **transfer** of grammatical rules from their L1. This is most obvious in phonology. L2ers generally speak with an accent because they may transfer the phonemes, phonological rules, syllable structures, stress placement or intonational patterns of their first language to their second language. We see this in the Japanese speaker, who does not distinguish between *write* [raɪt] and *light* [laɪt] because the r/l distinction is not phonemic in Japanese; in the French speaker, who says "ze cat in ze hat" because French does not have [ð]; in the German speaker, who devoices final consonants, saying [hæf] for *have*; and in the Spanish speaker, who inserts a schwa before initial consonant clusters, as in [əskul] for *school* and [əsnab] for *snob*.

Similarly, English speakers may have difficulty with unfamiliar sounds in other languages. For example, in Italian long (or double) consonants are phonemic. Italian has minimal pairs such as the following:

ano	'anus'	anno	'year'
pala	'shovel'	palla	'ball'
dita	'fingers'	ditta	'company'

English-speaking L2 learners of Italian have difficulty in hearing and producing the contrast between long and short consonants. This can lead to embarrassing situations: for example, on New Year's Eve, when instead of wishing people *buon anno* (good year), you wish them *buon ano*.

We also find native language influence in the syntax and morphology. Sometimes this shows up as a wholesale transfer of a particular piece of grammar. For example, a Spanish speaker acquiring English might drop subjects in nonimperative sentences because this is possible in Spanish, as illustrated by the following examples:

Hey, is not funny.
In here have the mouth.
Live in Colombia.

Or speakers may begin with the word order of their native language, as we saw in the Romance-German interlanguage examples.

Native language influence may show up in more subtle ways. For example, people whose L1 is German acquire English yes-no questions faster than Japanese speakers do. This is because German has a verb movement rule for forming yes-no questions that is very close to the English Aux movement rule, while in Japanese there is no syntactic movement in question formation.

The Creative Component of L2 Acquisition

It would be an oversimplification to think that L2 acquisition involves only the transfer of L1 properties to the L2 interlanguage. There is a strong creative component to L2 acquisition. Many language-specific parts of the L1 grammar do not transfer. Items that a speaker considers irregular, infrequent, or semantically difficult are not likely to transfer to the L2. For example, speakers will not typically transfer L1 idioms such as *He hit the roof* meaning 'He got angry.' They are more likely to transfer structures in which the semantic relations are transparent. For example, a structure such as (1) will transfer more readily than (2).

1.   It is awkward to carry this suitcase.
2.   This suitcase is awkward to carry.

In (1) the NP "this suitcase" is in its logical direct object position, while in (2) it has been moved to the subject position away from the verb that selects it.

Many of the "errors" that L2ers do make are not derived from their L1. For example, in one study Turkish speakers at a particular stage in their development of German used S-V-Adv (Subject-Verb-Adverb) word order in embedded clauses (the *wenn* clause in the following example) in their German interlanguage, even though both their native language and the target language have S-Adv-V order:

Wenn	ich	geh	zuruck	ich	arbeit	elektriker	in der Türkei.
if	I	go	back,	I	work (as an)	electrician	in Turkey

(Cf. *Wenn ich **zuruck geh** ich arbeit elektriker*, which is grammatically correct German.)

The embedded S-V-Adv order is most likely an overgeneralization of the verb-second requirement in German main clauses. As we noted earlier, overgeneralization is a clear indication that a rule has been acquired.

Why certain L1 rules transfer to the interlanguage grammar and others don't is not well understood. It is clear, however, that although construction of the L2 grammar is influenced by the L1 grammar, developmental principles—possibly universal—also operate in L2 acquisition. This is best illustrated by the fact that speakers with different L1s go through similar L2 stages. For example, Turkish, Serbo-Croatian, Italian, Greek, and Spanish speakers acquiring German as an L2 all drop articles to some extent. Because some of these L1s have articles, this cannot be caused by transfer but must involve some more general property of language development.

Heritage Language Learners

Heritage language learners are a particular kind of adult language learner. A heritage language learner is someone who was raised with a strong cultural connection to a language through family interaction—for example, a language such as Polish spoken by grandparents who were immigrants—and who decides at some point to study that language more formally, for example, in college. The heritage language learner may have no prior linguistic knowledge of the language, or he may be bilingual to some degree in the heritage language (his weaker language) and the dominant language, that is the language of the broader community, for example, English. Often heritage language learners are exposed to the heritage language in childhood and then switch to another dominant language later in life: for example, when they enter school. At this point they may begin to lose the heritage language—a process known as **language attrition**. On the other hand, the heritage language may be maintained if the speaker continues to use it alongside the dominant language, in his home or community. Sometimes a heritage language learner may speak the language, but be unable to either read or write it because he was educated only in the dominant language.

There has been growing interest in the language abilities of heritage language learners, especially in the extent to which early exposure to a (heritage) language might enhance a person's later ability to become proficient in that language. Preliminary results suggest that the length and manner of exposure to the heritage language in childhood are important determinants of later proficiency. Learners who have consistent exposure to the language until the end of the critical period (roughly puberty) have an advantage over other L2 learners of that language, especially in the areas of phonology and lexicon. Also, studies show that parents' attitude towards the home language and culture correlate with children's later ability in the heritage language.

Is There a Critical Period for L2 Acquisition?

I don't know how you manage, Sir, amongst all the foreigners; you never know what they are saying. When the poor things first come here they gabble away like geese, although the children can soon speak well enough.

MARGARET ATWOOD, *Alias Grace*, 1996

Age is a significant factor in L2 acquisition. The younger a person is when exposed to a second language, the more likely she is to achieve native-like competence.

In a classic study of the effects of age on ultimate attainment in L2 acquisition, researchers tested several groups of Chinese and Korean speakers who had acquired English as a second language. The subjects, all of whom had been in the United States for at least five years, were tested on their knowledge of specific aspects of English morphology and syntax. They were asked to judge the grammaticality of sentences such as:

The little boy is speak to a policeman.
The farmer bought two pig.
A bat flewed into our attic last night.

The study showed that the test results depended heavily on the age at which the person had arrived in the United States. The people who arrived as children (between the ages of three and eight) did as well on the test as American native speakers. Those who arrived between the ages of eight and fifteen did not perform like native speakers. Moreover, every year seemed to make a difference for this group. The person who arrived at age nine did better than the one who arrived at age ten; those who arrived at age eleven did better than those who arrived at age twelve, and so on. The group that arrived between the ages of seventeen and thirty-one had the lowest scores.

Does this mean that there is a critical period for L2 acquisition, an age beyond which it is *impossible* to acquire the grammar of a new language? Most researchers would hesitate to make such a strong claim. Although age is an important factor in achieving native-like L2 competence, it is certainly possible to acquire a second language as an adult. Many teenage and adult L2 learners become proficient, and a few highly talented ones even manage to pass for native speakers. Also, this study looked at the end state of L2 acquisition, after the subjects had been in an English-speaking environment for many years. It is possible that the ultimate attainment of adult L2ers falls short of native competence, but that the process of L2 acquisition is not fundamentally different from L1 acquisition.

It is more appropriate to say that L2 acquisition abilities gradually decline with age and that there are "sensitive periods" for the native-like mastery of certain aspects of the L2. The sensitive period for phonology is the shortest. To achieve native-like pronunciation of an L2 generally requires exposure during childhood. Other aspects of language, such as syntax, may have a larger window.

Some interesting research with heritage language learners provides additional support for the notion of sensitive periods in L2 acquisition. This finding is based on studies into the acquisition of Spanish by college students who had overheard the language as children (and sometimes knew a few words), but who did not otherwise speak or understand Spanish. The *overhearers* were compared to people who had no exposure to Spanish before the age of fourteen. All of the students were native speakers of English studying their heritage language as a second language. These results showed that the overhearers acquired a more native-like accent than the other students did. However, the overhearers did not show any advantage in acquiring the grammatical morphemes of Spanish. Early exposure may leave an imprint that facilitates the later acquisition of certain aspects of language.

Recent research on the neurological effects of acquiring a second language shows that left hemisphere cortical density is increased in bilinguals relative to monolinguals and that this increase is more pronounced in early versus late second-language learners. The study also shows a positive relationship between brain density and second-language proficiency. The researchers conclude that the structure of the human brain is altered by the experience of acquiring a second language. Additionally, a recent Canadian study of elderly adults showed a protective effect of lifelong bilingualism against Alzheimer's disease. Among hundreds of people with probable Alzheimer's the bilinguals showed their first symptoms of the disease five years later than monolinguals.

Summary

When children acquire a language, they acquire the grammar of that language—the phonological, morphological, syntactic, and semantic rules. They also acquire the pragmatic rules of the language as well as a lexicon. Children are not taught language. Rather, they extract the rules (and much of the lexicon) from the language(s) spoken around them.

The ease and rapidity of children's language acquisition and the uniformity of the stages of development for all children and all languages, despite the **poverty of the stimulus** they receive, suggest that the language faculty is innate and that the infant comes to the complex task already endowed with a Universal Grammar. UG is not a grammar like the grammar of English or Arabic, but represents the principles and parameters to which all human languages conform. Language acquisition is a creative process. Children create grammars based on the linguistic input and are guided in this process by UG.

Language development proceeds in stages which are universal. During the first year of life children develop the sounds of their language. They begin by producing and perceiving many sounds that do not exist in their linguistic environment: the **babbling stage**. Gradually their productions and perceptions are fine-tuned to their surroundings. Children's late babbling has all the phonological characteristics of the input language. Deaf children who are exposed at birth to sign languages also produce manual babbling, showing that babbling is a universal first stage in language acquisition that is dependent on the linguistic input received.

At the end of the first year, children utter their first words. During the second year, they learn many more words and they develop much of the phonological system of the language. Children's first utterances are one-word "sentences" (the **holophrastic** stage).

Many experimental studies show that children are sensitive to various linguistic properties such as stress and phonotactic constraints, and to statistical regularities of the input that enable them to segment the fluent speech that they hear into words. One method of segmenting speech is **prosodic bootstrapping**. Other bootstrapping methods can help the child to learn verb meaning based on syntactic context (**syntactic bootstrapping**), or syntactic categories based on word meaning (**semantic bootstrapping**). Distributional evidence such as **word frames** contributes both to syntactic and semantic knowledge.

After a few months the child puts two or more words together. These early sentences are not random combinations of words—the words have definite patterns and express both syntactic and semantic relationships. During the **telegraphic stage**, the child produces longer sentences that often lack function or grammatical morphemes. The child's early grammar still lacks many of the rules of the adult grammar, but is not qualitatively different from it. Children at this stage have correct word order and rules for agreement and case, which show their knowledge of structure.

Children make specific kinds of errors while acquiring their language. For example, they will **overgeneralize** morphology by saying *bringed* or *mans*. This shows that they are acquiring rules of their particular language. Children do not seem to make errors that violate principles of Universal Grammar.

In acquiring the lexicon of the language children may **overextend** word meaning by using *dog* to mean any four-legged creature. As well, they may **underextend** word meaning and use *dog* only to denote the family pet and no other dogs, as if it were a proper noun. Despite these categorization "errors," children's word learning, like their grammatical development, is guided by general principles.

Deaf children exposed to **sign language** show the same stages of language acquisition as hearing children exposed to spoken languages. That all children go through similar stages regardless of language shows that they are equipped with special abilities to know what generalizations to look for and what to ignore, and how to discover the regularities of language, irrespective of the modality in which their language is expressed.

Several learning mechanisms have been suggested to explain the acquisition process. **Imitation** of adult speech, **reinforcement**, and **analogy** have all been proposed. None of these learning mechanisms account for the fact that children create new (and non-adultlike) sentences according to the rules of their language, that they make certain kinds of errors but not others, and that they display knowledge of structures for which there is no evidence in the input. Empirical studies of the **motherese** hypothesis show that grammar development does not depend on the grammaticality of the linguistic input.

Children may acquire more than one language at a time. **Bilingual** children seem to go through the same stages as monolingual children except that they develop two grammars and two lexicons simultaneously. This is true for children acquiring two spoken languages as well as for children acquiring a spoken language and a sign language. Whether the child will be equally proficient in the two languages depends on the input he or she receives and the social conditions under which the languages are acquired.

In **second language acquisition**, L2 learners construct grammars of the target language—called **interlanguage grammars**—that go through stages, like the grammars of first-language learners. Influence from the speaker's first language makes L2 acquisition appear different from L1 acquisition. Adults often do not achieve native-like competence in their L2, especially in pronunciation. The difficulties encountered in attempting to learn languages after puberty may be because there are sensitive periods for L2 acquisition. Some theories of second language acquisition suggest that the same principles operate that account for first language acquisition. A second view suggests that the acquisition of a second language in adulthood involves general learning mechanisms rather than the specifically linguistic principles used by children.

The universality of the language acquisition process, the stages of development, and the relatively short period in which the child constructs a complex grammatical system without overt teaching suggest that the human species is innately endowed with special language acquisition abilities and that language is based in human biology.

All normal children learn whatever language or languages they are exposed to, from Afrikaans to Zuni. This ability is not dependent on race, social class, geography, or even intelligence (within a normal range). This ability is uniquely human.

References for Further Reading

Berko, J. "The child's leaning of English morphology," *Word 14*(1958): 150–177.

Brown, R. 1973. *A first language: The early stages*. Cambridge, MA: Harvard University Press.

Clark, E. 2009. *First language acquisition, 2nd ed.* New York: Cambridge University Press.

Gass, S. and L. Selinker. 2008. *Second language acquisition: An introductory course, 3rd ed.* NJ: Lawrence Erlbaum.

Guasti, M. T. 2004. *Language acquisition: The growth of grammar*. Cambridge, MA: MIT Press.

Hakuta, K. 1986. *Mirror of language: The debate on bilingualism*. New York: Basic Books.

Ingram, D. 1989. *First language acquisition: method, description and explanation*. New York: Cambridge University Press.

Jakobson, R. 1971. *Studies on child language and aphasia*. The Hague: Mouton.

Lust, B. 2006. *Child language: acquisition and growth*. Cambridge, UK: Cambridge University Press.

O'Grady, W. 2005. *How children learn language*. Cambridge, UK: Cambridge University Press.

Ortega, L. 2009. *Understanding second language acquisition*. London: Hodder Education.

Saville-Troike, M. 2005. *Introducing second language acquisition*. Cambridge, UK: Cambridge University Press.

Saxton, M. 2010. *Child language: acquisition and development*. London, UK: Sage Publications Ltd.

White, L. 2003. *Second language acquisition and Universal Grammar*. Cambridge, UK: Cambridge University Press.

Exercises

1. *Baby talk* is a term used to label the word forms that many adults use when speaking to children. Examples in English are *choo-choo* for 'train' and *bow-wow* for 'dog.' Baby talk seems to exist in every language and culture. At least two things seem to be universal about baby

talk: The words that have baby-talk forms fall into certain semantic categories (e.g., food and animals), and the words are phonetically simpler than the adult forms (e.g., *tummy* /tʌmi/ for 'stomach' /stʌmɪk/). List all the baby-talk words you can think of in your native language; then (1) separate them into semantic categories, and (2) try to state general rules for the kinds of phonological reductions or simplifications that occur.

2. In this chapter we discussed the way children acquire rules of question formation. The following examples of children's early questions are from a stage that is later than those discussed in the chapter. Formulate a generalization to describe this stage.

Can I go?	Can I can't go?
Why do you have one tooth?	Why you don't have a tongue?
What do frogs eat?	What do you don't like?
Do you like chips?	Do you don't like bananas?

3. Find a child between two and four years old. Note the age in years; months, and play with the child for about thirty minutes. Keep a list of all words and/or "sentences" that are used inappropriately. Describe what the child's meanings for these words and sentences probably are. Describe the syntactic or morphological errors (including omissions). If the child is producing multiword sentences, write a grammar that could account for the data you have collected.

4. Roger Brown and his coworkers at Harvard University studied the language development of three children, referred to in the literature as Adam, Eve, and Sarah. The following are samples of their utterances during the "two-word stage."

a coat	my stool	poor man
a celery	that knee	little top
a Becky	more coffee	dirty knee
a hands	more nut	that Adam
my mummy	two tinker-toy	big boot

One observation made by Brown was that many of the sentences and phrases produced by the children were ungrammatical from the point of view of the adult grammar. Mark with an asterisk any of the above NPs that are ungrammatical in the adult grammar of English and state the "violation" for each starred item. For example, if one of the utterances were *Lotsa book*, you might say: "The modifier *lotsa* must be followed by a plural noun."

5. In the holophrastic (one-word) stage of child language acquisition, the child's phonological system differs in systematic ways from that in the adult grammar. The inventory of sounds and the phonemic contrasts are smaller, and there are greater constraints on phonotactic rules. (See chapter 6 for a discussion of these aspects of phonology.)

   A. For each of the following words produced by a child, state what the substitution is, and any other differences that result.

Example:

spook   [pʰuk] Substitution: initial cluster [sp] reduced to single consonant; /p/ becomes aspirated, showing that child has acquired the aspiration rule.

(1) don't   [dot]
(2) skip   [kʰɪp]
(3) shoe   [su]
(4) that   [dæt]
(5) play   [pʰe]
(6) thump   [dʌp]
(7) bath   [bæt]
(8) chop   [tʰap]
(9) kitty   [kɪdi]
(10) light   [waɪt]
(11) dolly   [daʊi]
(12) grow   [go]

B. State general rules that account for the children's deviations from the adult pronunciations.

6. Children learn demonstrative words such as *this, that, these,* and *those*; temporal terms such as *now, then,* and *tomorrow*; and spatial terms such as *here, there, right,* and *behind* relatively late. What do all these words have in common? (Hint: See the pragmatics section of chapter 4.) Why might that factor delay their acquisition?

7. We saw in this chapter how children overgeneralize rules such as the plural rule, producing forms such as *mans* and *mouses*. What might a child learning English use instead of the adult words given?

   a. children
   b. went
   c. better
   d. best
   e. brought
   f. sang
   g. geese
   h. worst
   i. knives
   j. worse

8. The following words are from the lexicons of two children ages one year six months (1;6) and two (2;0) years old. Compare the pronunciation of the words to adult pronunciation.

Child 1 (1;6)

soap	[doʊp]	bib	[bɛ]
feet	[bit]	slide	[daɪ]
sock	[kak]	dog	[da]
goose	[gos]	cheese	[tʃis]
dish	[dɪtʃ]	shoes	[dus]

Child 2 (2;0)

light	[waɪt]	bead	[biː]
sock	[sʌk]	pig	[pɛk]
geese	[gis]	cheese	[tis]
fish	[fɪs]	bees	[bis]
sheep	[ʃip]	bib	[bɪp]

a. What happens to final consonants in the language of these two children? Formulate the rule(s) in words. Do all final consonants behave the same way? If not, which consonants undergo the rule(s)? Is this a natural class?

b. On the basis of these data, do any pairs of words allow you to identify any of the phonemes in the grammars of these children? What are they? Explain how you were able to determine your answer.

9. Make up a "wug test" to test a child's knowledge of the following morphemes:

comparative	-er	(as in *bigger*)
superlative	-est	(as in *biggest*)
progressive	-ing	(as in *I am dancing*)
agentive	-er	(as in *writer*)

10. Children frequently produce sentences such as the following:

Don't giggle me.
I danced the clown.
Yawny Baby—you can push her mouth open to drink her.
Who deaded my kitty cat?
Are you gonna nice yourself?

a. How would you characterize the difference between the grammar or lexicon of children who produce such sentences and that of adult English?

b. Can you think of similar, but well-formed, examples in adult English?

11. Many Arabic speakers tend to insert a vowel in their pronunciation of English words. The first column has examples from L2ers whose L1 is Egyptian Arabic; the second column has examples from L2ers whose L1 is Iraqi Arabic (consider [ʧ] to be a single consonant):

L1 = Egyptian Arabic		**L1 = Iraqi Arabic**	
[bilastik]	plastic	[iflo:r]	floor
[θiri:]	three	[ible:n]	plane
[tiransilet]	translate	[ʧilidren]	children
[silaɪd]	slide	[iθri:]	three
[firɛd]	Fred	[istadi]	study
[ʧildiren]	children	[ifrɛd]	Fred

a. What vowel do the Egyptian Arabic speakers insert and where?

b. What vowel do the Iraqi Arabic speakers insert and where?

c. Based on the position of the italicized epenthetic vowel in "I wrote to him," can you guess which list, A or B, belongs to Egyptian Arabic and which belongs to Iraqi Arabic?

Arabic A		**Arabic B**	
kitabta	'I wrote him'	katabtu	'I wrote him'
kitabla	'He wrote to him'	katablu	'He wrote to him'
kitabɪtla	'I wrote to him'	katabtɪlu	'I wrote to him'

12. Following is a list of utterances recorded from Sammy at age two-and-a-half:

    a. Mikey not see him.
    b. Where ball go?
    c. Look Mommy, doggie.
    d. Big doggie.
    e. He no bite ya.
    f. He eats mud.
    g. Kitty hiding.
    h. Grampie wear glasses.
    i. He funny.
    j. He loves hamburgers.
    k. Daddy ride bike.
    l. That's mines.
    m. That my toy.
    n. Him sleeping.
    o. Want more milk.
    p. Read moon book.
    q. Me want that.
    r. Teddy up.
    s. Daddy 'puter.
    t. 'Puter broke.
    u. Cookies and milk!!!
    v. Me Superman.
    w. Mommy's angry.
    x. Allgone kitty.
    y. Here my batball.

    Part One: What stage of language development is Sammy in?

    Part Two: Calculate the number of morphemes in each of Sammy's utterances.

    Part Three: What is Sammy's MLU in morphemes? In words?

    Part Four: **Challenge question:** Deciding the morpheme count for several of Sammy's words requires some thought. For each of the following, determine whether it should count as one or two morphemes and why.

    allgone
    batball
    glasses
    cookies

13. The following sentences were uttered by children in the telegraphic stage (the second column contains a word-by-word gloss, and the last column is a translation of each sentence that includes elements that the child omitted):

	Child's utterance	Gloss	Translation
Swedish	Se, blomster har	look flowers have	'Look, (I) have flowers.'
English	Tickles me		'It tickles me.'
French	Mange du pain	eat some bread	'S/he eats some bread.'
German	S[ch]okolade holen	chocolate get	'I/we get chocolate.'
Dutch	Earst kleine boekje lezen	first little book read	'First, I/we read a little book.'

In each of the children's sentences, the subject is missing, although this is not grammatical in the respective adult languages (in contrast to languages such as Spanish and Italian in which it is grammatical to omit the subject).

  a. Develop two hypotheses as to why the child might omit sentence subjects during this stage. For example, one hypothesis might be "children are limited in the length of sentences they can produce, so they drop subjects."

  b. Evaluate the different hypotheses. For example, an objection to the hypothesis given in (a) might be "If length is the relevant factor, why do children consistently drop subjects but not objects?"

14. Following is a list of overextensions that various children have made. In each case say what the basis is for the overextension. For example, the basis for the overextension of *ball* in example (a) is shape. All the objects in column B are round.

	A	B
a.	*ball*	balls, balloon, marble, grapefruits, oranges, pompoms
b.	*cookie*	cookies, Cheerios, cucumbers
c.	*birdie*	birds, airplanes, flies, bees, kites
d.	*bowwow*	dogs, cows, guinea pigs, cats, hamsters
e.	*truck*	firetruck, garbage truck, bus, van
f.	*dada*	father, policeman, mailman, doctor, men's tie, baseball cap
g.	*moon*	moon, half-moon shaped lemon slice, circular chrome dial on dishwasher, half a Cheerio, hangnail

10

Language Processing and the Human Brain

> No doubt a reasonable model of language use will incorporate, as a basic component, the generative grammar that expresses the speaker-hearer's knowledge of the language; but this generative grammar does not, in itself, prescribe the character or functioning of a perceptual model or a model of speech production.

NOAM CHOMSKY, *Aspects of the Theory of Syntax*, 1965

The Human Mind at Work

Psycholinguistics is the area of linguistics that is concerned with linguistic performance—how we use our linguistic competence—in speech (or sign) production and comprehension. The human brain not only acquires and stores the mental lexicon and grammar, but also accesses that linguistic storehouse to speak and understand language in real time.

How we process knowledge depends largely on the nature of that knowledge. If, for example, language was merely a finite store of fixed phrases and sentences in memory rather than an open-ended system, then speaking might simply consist of finding a sentence that expresses a thought we wished to convey. Comprehension could be the reverse—matching the sounds we hear to a stored string that has been memorized with its meaning. Of course, this is a ridiculous idea! It is not possible because of the creativity of language. In chapter 9, we saw that children do not learn language by imitating and storing sentences, but by constructing a grammar. When we speak, we access our lexicon to find the words, and we use the rules of grammar to construct novel sentences and to produce the sounds that express them. When we listen to speech we also access the lexicon and grammar to assign a structure and meaning to the sequence of words we hear.

The grammar relates sounds and meanings, and contains the units and rules of the language that make speech production and comprehension possible. However, other psychological processes are also used to produce and understand utterances. Various mechanisms enable us to break the continuous stream of speech sounds into linguistic units such as phonemes, syllables, and words in order to comprehend a message and to compose sounds into words in order to produce meaningful speech. Other cognitive mechanisms determine how we pull words from the mental lexicon, and still others explain how we assemble these words into a structural representation.

Ordinarily we have no difficulty understanding or producing sentences in our language. We do it without effort or conscious awareness of the processes involved. However, we have all had the experience of making a speech error, or having a word on the "tip of our tongue," or failing to understand a perfectly grammatical sentence such as **(1)**:

1. The horse raced past the barn fell.

On hearing this sentence many individuals will judge it to be ungrammatical; yet they will judge as grammatical a sentence with the same syntactic structure, such as (2):

2. The bus driven past the school stopped.

Similarly, people will have no problem with sentence (3), which has the same meaning as (1).

3. The horse that was raced past the barn fell.

Conversely, some ungrammatical sentences are easily understandable, such as sentence (4). This mismatch between grammaticality and interpretability tells us that language processing involves more than grammar.

4. *The baby seems sleeping.

A theory of linguistic performance tries to detail the psychological mechanisms that work with the grammar to facilitate language production and comprehension.

Comprehension

"I quite agree with you," said the Duchess; "and the moral of that is—'Be what you would seem to be'—or, if you'd like it put more simply—'Never imagine yourself not to be otherwise than what it might appear to others . . . to be otherwise.'"

"I think I should understand that better," Alice said very politely, "if I had it written down: but I can't quite follow it as you say it."

LEWIS CARROLL, *Alice's Adventures in Wonderland*, 1865

The sentence uttered by the Duchess provides another example of a grammatical sentence that is difficult to understand. The sentence is very long and requires extra resources to process, owing to the multiple negation and the multiple use of *otherwise*. Alice notes that if she had a pen and paper she could "unpack" this sentence more easily. The various breakdowns in performance, such as tip of the tongue phenomena, speech errors, and failure to comprehend tricky sentences, can tell us a great deal about the processes people normally use in speaking and understanding language, just as children's acquisition errors tell us a lot about the mechanisms involved in language development.

The Speech Signal

Understanding a sentence involves analysis at many levels. To begin with, we must comprehend the individual speech sounds we hear. We are not conscious of the complicated processes we use to understand speech any more than we are conscious of the complicated processes of digesting food and utilizing nutrients. We must study these processes deliberately and scientifically. One of the first questions of linguistic performance concerns segmentation of the acoustic signal. To understand this process, some knowledge of the signal can be helpful.

In chapter 5 we described speech sounds according to the ways in which they are produced. These involve the position of the tongue, the lips, and the velum; the state of the vocal cords; whether the articulators obstruct the free flow of air; and so on. All of these articulatory characteristics are reflected in the sound wave itself and so speech sounds can also be described in physical or **acoustic** terms.

Physically, a sound is produced whenever there is a disturbance in the position of air molecules. The ancient philosophers asked whether a sound is produced if a tree falls in the middle of the forest with no one to hear it. This question has been answered by the science of acoustics. Objectively, a sound is produced; subjectively, no sound is heard. In fact, there are sounds we cannot hear because our ears are not sensitive to the full range of frequencies. Many animals, such as dogs, hear a wider range of sounds than humans. *Acoustic phonetics* is concerned only with speech sounds, all of which can be heard by the normal human ear.

When we push air out of the lungs through the glottis, it causes the vocal cords to vibrate; this vibration in turn produces pulses of air that escape through the mouth (and sometimes the nose). These pulses are actually small variations in air pressure caused by the wavelike motion of the air molecules.

The sounds we produce can be described in terms of how fast the variations of the air pressure occur. This determines the **fundamental frequency** of the sounds and is perceived by the hearer as *pitch*. Along with fundamental frequency, when the vocal cords vibrate, they also produce a series of harmonics. A harmonic is a special frequency that is a multiple (2, 3, etc.) of the fundamental frequency. We can also describe the magnitude, or **intensity**, of the variations, which determines the loudness of the sound. The quality of the speech sound—whether it's an [i] or an [a] or whatever—is determined by the shape of the vocal tract when air is flowing through it. This shape modulates the strength of the harmonics into a spectrum of frequencies of greater or lesser intensity, and the particular combination of "greater or lesser" is heard as a particular sound. (Imagine smooth ocean waves with regular peaks and troughs approaching a rocky coastline. As they crash upon the rocks they

FIGURE 10.1 | A spectrogram of the words *heed*, *head*, *had*, and *who'd*, spoken with a British accent (speaker: Peter Ladefoged, February 16, 1973).

From LADEFOGED/JOHNSON. *A Course in Phonetics (with CD-ROM)*, 6E. © 2011 Cengage Learning. Reproduced by permission.

are "modulated" or broken up into dozens of "sub-waves" with varying peaks and troughs. That is similar to what is happening to the glottal pulses as they "crash" through the vocal tract.)

Computer programs can be used to decompose the speech signal into its frequency components. When speech is fed into a computer (from a microphone or a recording), an image of the speech signal is displayed. The patterns produced are called **spectrograms** or more vividly **voiceprints**. A spectrogram of the words *heed*, *head*, *had*, and *who'd* is shown in Figure 10.1.

Time in milliseconds is represented on the *x* axis; frequency (pitch) is represented on the *y* axis. The intensity of each frequency component is indicated by the degree of darkness: the more intense, the darker. Each vowel is characterized by dark bands, called **formants**, which differ in their placement according to the particular vowel. They represent the strongest harmonics (or sub-waves) produced by the shape of the vocal tract. Each vowel has its own formant frequencies, which account for the different vowel qualities you hear. The spectrogram also shows the pitch of the entire utterance (intonation contour) on the line marked P. The striations, or thin vertical lines, indicate a single opening and closing of the vocal cords. When the striations are far apart, the vocal cords are vibrating slowly and the pitch is low; when the striations are close together, the vocal cords are vibrating rapidly and the pitch is high.

By studying spectrograms of many different speech sounds, we can learn a great deal about the basic acoustic components produced by the various shapes of the vocal tract.

Speech Perception

The mice think they are right, but my cat eats them anyways (sic) . . . perception is everything.

TERRY GOODKIND (B. 1948)

Speech is a continuous signal. In natural speech, sounds overlap and influence each other, and yet listeners have the impression that they are hearing discrete units such as words, morphemes, syllables, and phonemes. A central problem of speech perception is to explain how listeners carve up the continuous speech signal into meaningful units. This is referred to as the "segmentation problem."

Another challenge is to understand how the listener manages to recognize particular speech sounds when they are spoken by different people and when they occur in different contexts. For example, how can a speaker tell that a [d] spoken by a man with a deep voice is the same unit of sound as the [d] spoken in the high-pitched voice of a child? Acoustically, they are distinct. Indeed, no two voices are identical in every detail. Similarly, a [d] that occurs before the vowel [i] is somewhat acoustically different from a [d] that occurs before the vowel [u]. Even within a single speaker the physical properties of the "same" sound vary from utterance to utterance depending on the phonological context and even the state of health of the speaker. How does a listener know that two physically distinct instances of a sound are the same? This is called the "lack of invariance problem."

Despite these problems, listeners are usually able to understand what they hear because our speech perception mechanisms are designed to overcome the variability and lack of discreteness in the speech signal. Experimental results show that listeners calibrate their perceptions to control for speaker differences, and can quickly adapt to foreign-accented or distorted speech. When listening to distorted speech, for example, listeners need to hear only two to four sentences to adjust, and can then generalize to words they have never heard before. It takes about a minute to adapt to non-native accents. Similarly, listeners adjust how they interpret timing information in the speech signal as a function of how quickly the speaker is talking. These *normalization* procedures enable the listener to understand a [d] as a [d] regardless of speaker or speech rate. Listeners can exploit various acoustic cues in the signal, as well as relationships among different acoustic elements, to get around the lack of invariance problem. For example, the frequency of the first or lowest formant for /a/ is high relative to /i/ and /u/, though the precise values may differ among speakers. Additionally, certain types of speech sounds have characteristic properties that can be relied upon for identification. Stops have a brief period of silence followed by a burst; fricatives produce high-frequency noise; and vowels are associated with particular formant structures. These acoustic cues help listeners identify phonological units in the signal regardless of speaker.

As we might expect, the units we perceive depend on the language we know, especially its phonemic inventory. For example, the initial consonant in [di], [da], and [du] are physically distinct from one another because of the formant transitions from the consonant to the different vowels—a coarticulation effect. Nevertheless speakers perceive the [d]'s as instances of the same phonological unit, namely the phoneme /d/. This phenomenon is known generally as **categorical perception**: speakers perceive physically distinct stimuli as belonging to the same category because their perceptions are assisted by knowledge of the underlying classificatory system. In the case of language, varying sounds are ascribed to phonemes based on a speaker's knowledge of the phonology of his language. Categorical perception is one of the mechanisms that the speech perception system uses to deal with variability in the signal.

Similarly, speakers of English can perceive the difference between [l] and [r] despite their acoustic similarity because these phones represent distinct phonemes in the language. Speakers of Japanese have great difficulty in differentiating the two because they are allophones of one phoneme in their language. As we saw in our discussion of language development in chapter 9, infants develop these different perceptual biases during the first year of life.

Returning to the segmentation problem, words and syntactic units such as phrases and sentences are seldom surrounded by boundaries such as pauses. Nevertheless, words are obviously units of perception. The spaces between them in writing support this view. How do we find the words and syntactic constituents in the speech stream?

Stress and intonation provide some cues to these units. For example, in English 90% of the words used in conversation begin with a stressed syllable. Experiments have shown that when English listeners hear a stressed syllable, they are likely to treat it as the onset of a new word. Stress and intonation can also cue syntactic constituents. We know that the different meanings of the sentences *He lives in the white house* and *He lives in the White House* can be signaled by differences in their stress patterns. It is also true that syllables at the end of a phrase are longer in duration than at the beginning, and intonation contours mark boundaries of clauses. In addition, listeners use their lexical knowledge to identify words in the signal. This process is called **lexical access**, or word recognition, discussed in detail later.

Bottom-Up and Top-Down Models

I have experimented and experimented until now I know that [water] never does run uphill, except in the dark. I know it does in the dark, because the pool never goes dry; which it would, of course, if the water didn't come back in the night. It is best to prove things by experiment; then you know; whereas if you depend on guessing and supposing and conjecturing, you will never get educated.

MARK TWAIN, *Eve's Diary*, 1906

Language comprehension is very fast and automatic. We understand an utterance as fast as we hear it or read it. Ordinarily, we can process spoken language at a rate of around twenty phonemes per second. A visually impaired person who relies on a sped-up synthetic voice to read written material can comprehend speech at rates near one hundred phonemes per second. To a sighted person, this rate of speech would sound like chipmunks chattering.

Successful language comprehension requires that a lot of operations take place at once—what is called "parallel processing"—including the following sub-operations: segmenting the continuous speech signal into phonemes, morphemes, words, and phrases; looking up the words and morphemes in the mental lexicon; finding the appropriate meanings of ambiguous words; placing them in a constituent structure; choosing among different possible structures when syntactic ambiguities arise; interpreting the phrases and sentences; making a mental model of the discourse and updating it to reflect the meaning of the new sentence; and factoring in the pragmatic context to assist with the other tasks.

To account for this vast amount of mental computation, and owing to the sequential nature of language, psycholinguists believe that listeners make guesses as to what and what not to expect next, thus eliminating unneeded processing. They suggest that perception and comprehension must involve both **top-down processing** and **bottom-up processing**.

Bottom-up processing moves step-by-step from the incoming acoustic (or visual) signal, to phonemes, morphemes, words and phrases, and ultimately to semantic interpretation. Each step of building toward a meaning is based on the sensory data and accompanying lexical information. The listener uses acoustic information to build a phonological representation of words that he can then look up in the lexicon. According to this model the speaker waits until hearing an article followed by a noun and then constructs a noun phrase while awaiting the next word, and so on.

In top-down processing the listener relies on higher-level semantic, syntactic, and contextual information to analyze the acoustic signal. For example upon hearing the determiner *the*, the speaker expects a noun or adjective to be more likely than a verb or preposition. In this instance the listener's knowledge of phrase structure would be the source of information.

Evidence for top-down processing is found in experiments that require subjects to identify spoken words in the presence of noise. Listeners make more errors when the words occur in isolation than when they occur in sentences. Moreover they make more errors if the words occur in nonsense sentences, and they make the most errors if the words occur in ungrammatical sentences. In experiments where subjects are asked to repeat each word of a sentence immediately upon hearing it, they often produce words in anticipation of the input. They can guess what's coming next by having processed the sentence to that point. All these results show that subjects use their knowledge of syntactic and semantic relations to help them narrow down the set of candidate words.

Top-down processing is also supported by a different kind of experiment. Subjects hear recorded sentences in which some part of the signal is removed and a cough or buzz is substituted, such as the bold, underlined "s" in the sentence *The state governors met with their respective legi*s*latures convening in the capital city*. They "hear" the sentence without any phonemes missing, and have difficulty saying where in the word the noise occurred. This effect is called *phoneme restoration*. It appears that subjects can guess that the word containing the cough was *legislatures* and moreover they truly believe they are hearing the [s] even when they're told it's not there. In this case top-down information apparently overrides bottom-up information.

There is also a role for top-down information in segmentation. Sometimes an utterance can be divided in more than one way. For example, the phonetic sequence [grede] in a discussion of meat or eggs is likely to be heard as *Grade A*, but in a discussion of the weather as *grey day*.

In other cases both bottom-up and top-down information may bear on the ultimate decision of what was spoken. Consider the sequence of phonemes /naɪtret/. It is compatible with two segmentations: [naɪtʰret] with an aspirated [tʰ] meaning "nitrate"; and [naɪtret] with an unaspirated [t] meaning "night rate." Bottom-up information such as the phonetic details of pronunciation can signal where the word boundary is. If the first /t/ is heard as aspirated, it must belong to the onset of the second syllable, so the decision is *nitrate*. If it is unaspirated, it must be part of the coda of the first syllable, so the decision is *night rate*.

But top-down information may also weigh in, so that [naɪtʰret] is favored following the word *sodium* or in the context of chemistry whereas [naɪtret] would be more plausible in the context of hotels. If the bottom-up cue is insufficient owing to signal noise, or the top-down cue is vague owing to an indecisive context, then the other cue may weigh more heavily in the final decision.

Lexical Access and Word Recognition

> Oh, are you from Wales?
>
> Do you know a fella named Jonah?
>
> He used to live in whales for a while.
>
> GROUCHO MARX (1890–1977)

Psycholinguists have conducted a great deal of research on *lexical access* or *word recognition*, the process by which listeners obtain information about the meaning and syntactic properties of a word from their mental lexicon. Several different experimental techniques have been used in studies of lexical access.

One technique is to ask whether a string of letters or sounds is or is not a word. Subjects must respond by pressing one button if the stimulus is an actual word, and a different button if it is not, so they are making a **lexical decision**. During these and similar experiments, measurements of *response time* (RT) is taken. The assumption is that the longer it takes to respond to a particular task, the more processing is involved. RT measurements show that lexical access depends to some extent on the word's frequency of usage: more commonly used words such as *car* are responded to more quickly than words that we rarely encounter such as *cad*.

Lexical decision tasks can also provide information about how we use our phonological knowledge in lexical access. Studies show that listeners respond more slowly to "possible" non-words such as *floop* and *plim* than to "impossible" non-words such as *tlat* and *mrock*. The listener can quickly reject the impossible words based on phonotactic knowledge so that a lexical search is unnecessary. That possible and impossible non-words are processed differently is supported by brain imaging studies showing that the same areas of the brain are involved in accessing real words and possible non-words, while different areas respond to impossible non-words.

The speed with which a listener can retrieve a particular word also depends on the size of the word's phonological "neighborhood." A neighborhood is comprised of all the words that are phonologically similar to the target word. A word like *pat* has a dense neighborhood because there are many similar words—*bat, pad, pot, pit,* and so on, while a word like *crib* has far fewer neighbors. Words with larger neighborhoods take longer to retrieve than words from smaller ones because more phonological information is required to single out a word in a denser neighborhood.

Psycholinguists believe that each word in the mental lexicon is associated with a "resting level of activation" which is increased each time the listener accesses the word. Because more frequent words have a higher resting level of activation, listeners show faster RTs to these words in decision tasks.

Words can also be activated by hearing semantically related words. This effect is known as **semantic priming**. A listener will be faster at making a lexical decision on the word *doctor* if he has just heard *nurse* than if he just heard a semantically unrelated word such as *flower*. The word *nurse* is said to *prime* the word *doctor*. When we hear a priming word, related words are "awakened" and become more readily accessible for a few moments. This priming effect might arise because semantically related words are near each other or linked to each other in the mental lexicon.

Morphological priming is kind of semantic priming in which a morpheme of a multimorphemic word primes a related word. For example *sheepdog* primes *wool* as a result of *sheep*. Even when one morpheme is free and the other bound as in *runner*, the free morpheme *run* primes words like *race*. Stranger yet, even in pseudo-multimorphemic words such as *summer,* which does not mean "one who sums," the word "sum" is primed much as *paint* is primed by the word *painter*. These examples suggest that morphological decomposition is taking place automatically based on the phonetics of the word irrespective of the semantics.

Lexical decision techniques can be evaluated alongside results from brain studies to provide a more detailed understanding of the process of lexical access. In some cases electrical brain activity in experimental subjects indicates that lexical access is occurring while RT measurements do not. For example *teach* may prime the related *taught* according to brain activity but not according to RT measurements. This result suggests that lexical decision occurs in stages, and that RT measurements are insensitive to earlier stages, whereas the brain measurements are taken continuously and reflect both earlier and later stages.

Lexical ambiguities also provide important insights into how listeners access the mental lexicon. In certain experimental tasks RTs are longer with ambiguous words than unambiguous ones, suggesting that ambiguous words require more processing resources. Indeed, studies show that listeners retrieve all meanings of an ambiguous word even when the sentence containing the word is biased toward one of the meanings. For example when the word *palm* is heard in *The gypsy read the young man's palm* it primes both the word *hand* and the word *tree* according to RT measurements. The other meaning of *palm* (as in *palm tree*) is apparently activated even though that meaning is not a part of the meaning of the priming sentence. At a subsequent stage of processing—after about 250 milliseconds—the listener makes a decision about which meaning is the intended one based on the information in the rest of the sentence. This means that the initial accessing of a word is strictly bottom-up—every lexical entry that matches the phonological representation is activated—while the subsequent selection of the contextually appropriate meaning is a top-down process. Interestingly, young children do not show priming of all meanings of an ambiguous word, but only the most frequently used meaning. This is most likely because children have more limited processing resources than adults.

Syntactic Processing

Teacher Strikes Idle Kids

Enraged Cow Injures Farmer with Ax

Killer Sentenced to Die for Second Time in 10 Years

Stolen Painting Found by Tree

AMBIGUOUS HEADLINES

Understanding a sentence involves more than merely recognizing its individual words. The listener must also determine the syntactic relations among the words and phrases. This mental process, referred to as **parsing**, is largely governed by the rules of the grammar and strongly influenced by the sequential nature of language.

Listeners actively build a structural representation of a sentence as they hear it. They must therefore decide for each incoming word what its grammatical category is and how it fits into the structure that is being built. Often sentences present "temporary ambiguities" such as a word or words that belong to more than one syntactic category. For example, the string *The warehouse fires . . .* could continue in one of two ways:

1. . . . were set by an arsonist.
2. . . . employees over sixty.

Fires is a noun in sentence (1) and a verb in sentence (2). Experimental studies of such sentences show that both meanings and categories are activated when a subject encounters the ambiguous word. The ambiguity is quickly resolved based on syntactic and semantic context. Disambiguation is usually so fast and seamless that unintentionally ambiguous newspaper headlines such as those at the head of this section are scarcely noticeable except to the linguists who collect them.

Another important type of temporary ambiguity arises in cases in which the grammar permits a constituent to fit into a sentence in two different ways, as illustrated by the following example:

After the child visited the doctor prescribed a course of injections.

When readers encounter the phrase *the doctor* they immediately perceive it as the direct object of the verb *visit*. When they later come to the verb *prescribed,* they must "change their minds" or backtrack, and reanalyze *the doctor* as subject of a main clause instead. Sophisticated laboratory procedures that track the reader's eye movements while he reads can pinpoint difficult regions of the sentence and can see when the reader regresses to an earlier part of the sentence. Sentences that induce this backtracking effect are called **garden path sentences**. The sentence presented at the beginning of this chapter, *The horse raced past the barn fell*, is also a garden path sentence. People naturally interpret *raced* as the main verb, when in fact the main verb is *fell*.

The initial structural choices that lead people astray may reflect general principles that are used by the mental parser to deal with syntactic ambiguity. Two such principles are known as **minimal attachment** and **late closure**.

Minimal attachment says, "Build the simplest structure consistent with the grammar of the language." In the string *The horse raced . . .* , the simpler structure is the one in which *the horse* is the subject and *raced* the main verb; the less simple structure is similar to *The horse that was raced . . .* with *fell* as the main verb.

Late closure says "Attach incoming material to the phrase that is currently being processed," as the following sentence illustrates:

The doctor said the patient will die yesterday.

Readers often experience a garden path effect at the end of this sentence. The reader encounters *yesterday* nearest to the embedded clause *the patient will die,* which is closest to *yesterday*, and immediately tries to work it into the meaning. This fails because *yesterday* conflicts with the future marker *will* so the reader backtracks to attach *yesterday* to the main clause containing *said*.

The syntactic parsing of sentences depends on different sources of information. The parser depends on the grammar to inform it as to how the incoming words can be grouped together into well-formed constituents. In cases of ambiguity there are various structural possibilities to choose from. Principles such as minimal attachment and late closure guide the parser to choose the computationally simplest structure among the different grammatical possibilities. Garden path effects arise when listeners make a strong commitment to the simpler structure and are then "jarred" out of it by some kind of incongruity.

In some cases frequency factors cause the reader to garden path, as illustrated by the following sentence:

The faithful people our church every Sunday.

People occurs much more frequently as a noun than a verb, leading the reader to initially analyze *the faithful people* as an NP, but this does not jibe with the following words, which lack a verb. The reader must backtrack and reanalyze *people* as the main verb meaning "to populate."

Other factors such as prosody, lexical biases, and even visual context can also influence the parser in its structural choices, and may even weaken the effects of the parsing principles. For example, the following sentence is ambiguous: either the actress or the maid can be understood as the one on the balcony:

Someone photographed the maid of the actress who was on the balcony.

Late closure would make *the actress on the balcony* the preferred interpretation. Studies show that placing an intonation pause after *the maid* greatly increases the chances of the listener assigning this meaning. On the other hand a pause after *the actress* increases the likelihood of the interpretation where the maid is on the balcony.

Verb choice may also influence the parser's structural decisions. In a sentence such as (1) the processor is led to parse *the problem* as the direct object of the verb *understood* (minimal attachment) and will have to backtrack when *had no solution* is encountered, while in (2) such a garden path effect is less likely:

(1) Tom understood the problem had no solution.
(2) Tom thought the problem had no solution.

This is because the verb *understand* can be followed by both an NP and a sentence (*Tom understood the story, Tom understood the story was false*), while the verb *think* can be followed by a sentence but not an NP. (*Tom thinks the story is crazy, *Tom thinks the story*). The sentence processor is sensitive to subcategorization information in the lexical entries of verbs and also the frequency of occurrence of different contexts for particular verbs. (Subcategorization is discussed in chapter 3.)

Surprisingly, the parser does not seem to make use of non-linguistic information to make structural decisions. For example you might think that a garden path is less likely in sentence (1) than sentence (2) because real world knowledge tells us that performers are routinely sent flowers and florists routinely *send* them.

(1) The performer sent the flowers was very pleased.
(2) The florist sent the flowers was very pleased.

But this is not the case. Eye-tracking studies have shown that readers garden path equally on these two sentences despite the difference in plausibility.

However, in a different task, when readers are asked to paraphrase the two sentences, they do better with the more plausible *performer sent the flowers* sentence, indicating that non-linguistic context facilitates comprehension at some point, though not at the parsing stage. Sentences that create problems for the parser, such as garden path sentences, tell us a great deal about how the sentence processor operates.

Another striking example of processing difficulty is illustrated by a rewording of a Mother Goose poem. In its original form we have:

This is the dog that worried the cat that killed the rat that ate the malt that lay in the house that Jack built.

No problem understanding that. Now try this equivalent description:

Jack built the house that the malt that the rat that the cat that the dog worried killed ate lay in.

No way, right?

Although the confusing sentence follows the rules of relative clause formation—you have little difficulty with *the cat that the dog worried*—it seems that once is enough; when you apply the same process twice, getting *the rat that the cat that the dog worried killed*, it becomes quite difficult to comprehend but perhaps possible. If we apply the process three times, as in *the malt that the rat that the cat that the dog worried killed ate*, all hope is lost.

The difficulty in parsing this kind of sentence is related to memory constraints. In processing the sentence, you have to keep *the malt* in mind all the way until *ate*, but while doing that you have to keep *the rat* in mind all the way until *killed*, and while doing that . . . It's a form of structure juggling that is difficult to perform; we evidently don't have enough of the right kind of memory capacity to keep track of all the necessary items. Though we have the competence to create such sentences, performance limitations prevent the creation and comprehension of such monstrosities.

Another technique for studying sentence comprehension is the **shadowing task**, wherein subjects are asked to repeat what they hear as promptly as possible. Most subjects manage to do so with a delay of 300 to 800 milliseconds. Fast shadowers often correct speech errors or mispronunciations unconsciously and add inflectional endings if they are absent. Even when they are told that the speech they are to shadow includes errors and they should repeat the errors, they are rarely able to do so. Corrections are more likely to occur when the target word can be predicted from what has been said previously.

These shadowing experiments support extremely rapid use of top-down information; differences in predictability have an effect within about one-quarter of a second. And they also show how rapidly we do grammatical analysis, because some of the errors that are corrected, such as missing agreement inflections, depend on knowing the structural relations of immediately preceding words.

The ability to comprehend what is said to us is a complex psychological process involving the internal grammar, parsing principles such as minimal attachment and late closure, linguistic context, lexical information such as the subcategorization of verbs, prosody, frequency factors, and memory limitations.

Speech Production

> Speech was given to the ordinary sort of men, whereby to communicate their mind; but to wise men, whereby to conceal it.
>
> ROBERT SOUTH, sermon at Westminster Abbey, April 30, 1676

As we saw in the previous sections, the listener's job is to decode the intended meaning of a message from the speech signal produced by a speaker. The speaker's job is the reverse. He must encode an idea into an utterance using speech sounds and words (or signs) organized according to the grammatical structures of the language. It is more difficult to devise experiments that provide information about how the speaker proceeds than to do so for the listener's side of the process. Much of the best information has come from observing and analyzing spontaneous speech, especially speech errors.

Lexical Selection

> Humpty Dumpty's theory, of two meanings packed into one word like a portmanteau, seems to me the right explanation for all. For instance, take the two words "fuming" and "furious." Make up your mind that you will say both words but leave it unsettled which you will say first. Now open your mouth and speak. If . . . you have that rarest of gifts, a perfectly balanced mind, you will say "frumious."
>
> LEWIS CARROLL, Preface to *The Hunting of the Snark*, 1876

In our previous discussion of comprehension, we saw that semantically related words are activated or primed during lexical retrieval. In production we see a similar effect with slips of the tongue or speech errors (see chapter 6), especially word substitution errors. Word substitutions are seldom random; they show that in our attempt to express our thoughts, we may make an incorrect lexical selection based on partial similarity or relatedness of meanings. This is illustrated in the following examples:

Bring me a **pen**. → Bring me a **pencil**.
It stays **light** out late here. → It stays **dark** out late here.
Please set the **table**. → Please set the **chair**.
Are my **tires** touching the curb? → Are my **legs** touching the curb?
I don't know what the term is in **German**. → I don't know what the term is in **Austrian**.

Blends (see chapter 8), in which we produce part of one word and part of another, illustrate how we may select two or more words to express our thoughts and instead of deciding between them, we produce them as "portmanteaus," as Humpty Dumpty calls them. Such blends are illustrated in the following errors:

1. splinters/blisters   →   splisters
2. edited/annotated   →   editated
3. a swinging/hip chick   →   a swip chick
4. frown/scowl   →   frowl

These blend errors are typical in that the segments stay in the same position within the syllable as they were in the target words.

In comprehension, lexical retrieval is affected by the number of words that are phonologically related to the target: what we earlier referred to as "phonological neighborhoods." In production, speakers often make speech errors involving the substitution of a word that is phonologically related to the target but unrelated in meaning, as the following examples show:

Did you feed the **bunny**? → Did you feed the **banana**?
We need a few laughs to break up the **monotony**. → We need a few laughs to break up the **mahogany**.
The flood damage was so bad they had to **evacuate** the city. → The flood damage was so bad they had to **evaporate** the city.

Recall that word incidence also influences lexical access in comprehension—speakers are faster to retrieve more common words. In production, high frequency words are also retrieved more easily than less frequent ones, so speakers come up with *knife* more quickly than *bayonet*, for example. This is shown in studies of speaker hesitations or pauses, which are more common before low frequency words.

Not surprisingly, many of the same factors that influence the listener in comprehension also affect the speaker in production—semantic and phonological relatedness of words, and word frequency. Whether you are speaking or listening you are accessing the same mental lexicon.

Application and Misapplication of Rules

I thought . . . four rules would be enough, provided that I made a firm and constant resolution not to fail even once in the observance of them.

RENÉ DESCARTES, *Discourse on Method*, 1637

Spontaneous errors show that the rules of morphology and syntax are also applied (or misapplied) when we speak. It is difficult to see this process in normal error-free speech, but when someone says *groupment* instead of *grouping, ambigual* instead of *ambiguous*, or *bloodent* instead of *bloody*, it shows that regular rules are applied to combine morphemes and form possible but nonexistent words.

Inflectional rules also surface. The UCLA professor who said **We swimmed in the pool* knows that the past tense of *swim* is *swam*, but he mistakenly applied the regular rule to an irregular form. We also see evidence of the application of morphophonemic rules in production. Consider the *a/an* alternation rule in English. Errors such as *a burly bird* for the intended *an early bird* show that when segmental misordering changes a word beginning with a vowel to a word beginning with a consonant, the indefinite article also changes to conform to the grammatical rule. Clearly, the rule applies, or perhaps reapplies, after the stage at which *early* has slipped to *burly*.

Similarly, an error such as *bin beg*, pronounced [bɪn bɛg] for the intended *Big Ben* [bɪg bɛ̃n] (made by an announcer during the 2012 Olympic Games in London) shows that allophonic rules apply (or reapply) after phonemes are misordered. If the misordering occurred after the phonemes had undergone allophonic rules such as nasalization, the result would have been the phonetic utterance [bɪn bɛ̃g].

Planning Units

We might suppose that speakers' thoughts are simply translated into words one after the other via a semantic mapping process. Grammatical morphemes would be added as demanded by the syntactic rules of the language. The phonetic representation of each word in turn would then be mapped onto the neuromuscular commands to the articulators to produce the acoustic signal representing it.

We know, however, that this is not a true picture of speech production. Although sounds within words and words within sentences are linearly ordered, speech errors or slips of the tongue show that the prearticulation or planning stages involve units larger than the single phonemic segment or even the word, as illustrated by the "U.S. Acres" cartoon. That error is an example of a **spoonerism**, named after William Archibald Spooner, a distinguished dean of an Oxford college in the early 1900s who is reported to have referred to Queen Victoria as "That queer old dean" instead of "That dear old queen," and berated his class of students by saying, "You have hissed my mystery lecture. You have tasted the whole worm," instead of the intended "You have missed my history lecture. You have wasted the whole term."

Indeed, speech errors show that features, segments, words, and phrases may be conceptualized well before they are uttered. This point is illustrated in the following examples of speech errors (the intended utterance is to the left of the arrow; the actual utterance, including the error, is to the right of the arrow):

1. The *h*iring of minority faculty. → The *f*iring of minority faculty.
   (The intended *h* is replaced by the *f* of *faculty*, which occurs later in the intended utterance.)
2. *a*d h*o*c → *o*dd h*a*ck
   (The vowels /æ/ of the first word and /a/ of the second are exchanged or reversed.)
3. *b*ig and *f*at → *p*ig and *v*at
   (The values of a single feature are switched: in *big* [+voiced] becomes [−voiced] and in *fat* [−voiced] becomes [+voiced].)
4. There are many ministers in our church. → There are many churches in our minister.
   (The root morphemes *minister* and *church* are exchanged; the grammatical plural morpheme remains in its intended place in the phrase structure.)
5. salute smartly → smart salutely (heard on *All Things Considered*, National Public Radio (NPR), May 17, 2007)
   (The root morphemes are exchanged, but the *-ly* affix remains in place.)
6. Seymour sliced the salami with a knife. → Seymour sliced a knife with the salami.
   (The entire noun phrases—article + noun—were exchanged.)

In these errors, the intonation contour (primary stressed syllables and variations in pitch) remained the same as in the intended utterances, even when the words were rearranged. In the intended utterance of (6), the highest pitch would be on *knife*. In the misordered sentence, the highest pitch occurred on the second syllable of *salami*. The pitch rise and increased loudness do not therefore depend on the individual words but are determined by the syntactic structure of the sentence. Syntactic structures exist independently of the words that occupy them, and intonation contours can be mapped onto those structures without being associated with particular words.

Errors like those just cited are constrained in interesting ways. Phonological errors involving segments or features, as in (1), (2), and (3), primarily occur in content words, and not in grammatical morphemes, showing the distinction between these lexical classes. In addition, while words and lexical morphemes may be interchanged, grammatical morphemes may not be. We do not find errors like *The boying are sings* for *The boys are singing*. Typically, as example (4) illustrates, the inflectional endings are left behind when lexical morphemes switch and subsequently attach, in their proper phonological form, to the moved lexical morpheme.

Errors like those in (1)–(6) show that speech production operates in real time using the features, segments, morphemes, words, and phrases that exist in the grammar. They also show that when we speak, words are chosen and sequenced ahead of when they are articulated. We do not select one word from our mental dictionary and say it, then select another word and say it.

Planning also goes on at the sentence level. In experimentally controlled settings, speakers take longer to initiate (begin uttering) passive sentences like (1a) than active sentences like (1b). They also take longer to begin speaking subject-object relative clauses (underlined once) like (2a) than object-subject relative clauses (doubly underlined) like (2b).

(1) a. The ball was chased by Nellie.
　　b. Nellie chased the ball.

(2) a. <u>The cat that scratched the dog</u> climbed the tree.
　　b. <u>The cat that the dog chased</u> climbed the tree.

These findings suggest that more planning goes into sentences that have less common word order than into sentences with subject-verb-object word order. Interestingly, however, speakers are more likely to produce a passive sentence after hearing a passive, despite its non-typical word order. In syntactic priming experiments speakers are asked to describe a scene after hearing an unrelated active or passive sentence. Results show that they are more likely to describe the scene using a passive if that is what they have just heard. Researchers believe that once a particular structure has been built, it remains "active" in memory and facilitates the subsequent building of a similar structure.

Speakers must also combine simple sentences into complex structures containing embedded clauses, relative clauses and so on. Studies of speakers' hesitations show that planning for complex structures happens at the beginning of clauses. For example, the initiation time is shorter for producing a simple NP subject such as (1):

(1) The large and raging river . . .

than for a subject NP like (2):

(2) The river that stopped flooding . . . ,

which contains a relative clause, even though both NPs are the same length (in terms of number of syllables).

Pauses occur more often at the beginning of clauses than within them, and speech errors involving exchanges of linguistic units, such as those in (4)–(6) above, happen within clauses and not across clause boundaries. These findings among others support the hypothesis that the clause boundary is the locus of planning in complex sentences, and that sentences are bundled into clause-size units before they are produced.

The comprehension and production of language is an enormously complex process that depends on many aspects of our linguistic knowledge, as well as dedicated processing principles and other cognitive capacities such as memory. Both normal conversational data and experimental data provide the psycholinguist with information about the different units, mechanisms, and stages speakers use to encode an idea into speech and listeners use to decode the speech signal into a linguistic message.

Brain and Language

The human brain is a most unusual instrument of elegant and as yet unknown capacity.

STUART SEATON

Attempts to understand the complexities of human cognitive abilities and especially the acquisition and use of language are as old and as continuous as history itself. What is the nature of the brain? What is the nature of human language? And what is the relationship between the two? Philosophers and scientists have grappled with these kinds of questions over the centuries. But modern advances in brain technology have enabled researchers to study the brain-language connection in ways scarcely imagined in earlier times. The study of the biological and neural foundations of language is called **neurolinguistics**. Neurolinguistic research is often based on data from atypical or impaired language and uses such data to understand properties of human language in general.

The Human Brain

The human brain is unique in that it is the only container of which it can be said that the more you put into it, the more it will hold.

GLENN DOMAN

The brain is the most complex organ of the body. The surface of the brain is the **cortex**, often called "gray matter," consisting of billions of neurons (nerve cells) and glial cells (which support and protect the neurons). The cortex is the decision-making organ of the body. It receives messages from all of the sensory organs, initiates all voluntary and involuntary actions, and is the storehouse of our memories and the seat of our consciousness. It is the organ that most distinguishes humans from other animals. Somewhere in this gray matter resides the grammar that represents our knowledge of language.

The brain is composed of a right and a left **cerebral hemisphere**, joined by the **corpus callosum**, a network of more than 200 million fibers (see Figure 10.2 on the next page). The corpus callosum allows the two hemispheres of the brain to communicate with each other. Without this system of connections, the hemispheres would operate independently. In general, the left hemisphere controls the right side of the body, and the right hemisphere controls the left side. If you point with your right hand, the left hemisphere is responsible for your action. Similarly, sensory information from the right side of the body (e.g., right ear, right hand, right visual field) is received by the left hemisphere of the brain, and sensory input to the left side of the body is received by the right hemisphere. This is referred to as **contralateral** brain function. The following quote from the Bible suggests that the connection between control of the right side of the body and speech has been suspected for a long time.

If I forget thee, O Jerusalem, let my right hand forget her cunning.
If I do not remember thee, let my tongue cleave to the roof of my mouth;
Psalm 137, King James Version

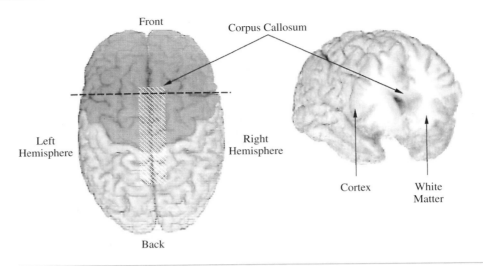

FIGURE 10.2 | Three-dimensional reconstruction of the normal living human brain. The images were obtained from magnetic resonance data using the Brainvox technique. *Left panel* = view from top. *Right panel* = view from the front following virtual coronal section at the level of the dashed line.
Courtesy of Hanna Damásio.

The Localization of Language in the Brain

"Peanuts," United Feature Syndicate, Inc

An issue of central concern has been to determine which parts of the brain are responsible for human linguistic abilities. In the early nineteenth century, Franz Joseph Gall proposed the theory of **localization**, which is the idea that different human cognitive abilities and behaviors are localized in specific parts of the brain. In light of our current knowledge about the brain, some of Gall's

FIGURE 10.3 | Phrenology skull model.

particular views are amusing. For example, he proposed that language is located in the frontal lobes of the brain because as a young man he had noticed that the most articulate and intelligent of his fellow students had protruding eyes, which he believed reflected overdeveloped brain material. He also put forth a pseudoscientific theory called "organology" that later came to be known as **phrenology**, which is the practice of determining personality traits, intellectual capacities, and other matters by examining the "bumps" on the skull.

A disciple of Gall's, Johann Spurzheim, introduced phrenology to America, constructing elaborate maps and skull models such as the one shown in Figure 10.3 in which language is located directly under the eye. Although phrenology has long been discarded as a scientific theory, Gall's view that the brain is not a uniform mass, and that linguistic and other cognitive capacities are functions of localized brain areas, has been upheld by scientific investigation of brain disorders, and, over the past two decades, by numerous studies using sophisticated technologies examining both normal and impaired brain function.

Aphasia

The study of **aphasia** has been an important area of research in understanding the relationship between the brain and language. Aphasia is the neurological term for any language disorder that results from acquired brain damage caused by disease or trauma.

In the second half of the nineteenth century, significant scientific advances were made in localizing language in the brain based on the study of people with aphasia. In the 1860s the French surgeon Paul Broca proposed that language is localized in the left hemisphere of the brain, and more specifically in

FIGURE 10.4 | Lateral (*external*) view of the left hemisphere of the human brain, showing the position of Broca's and Wernicke's areas—two key areas of the cortex related to language processing.

the front part of the left hemisphere (now called **Broca's area**). At a scientific meeting in Paris, he claimed that we speak with the left hemisphere. Broca's finding was based on a study of his patients who suffered language deficits after brain injury to the left frontal lobe.

A decade later Carl Wernicke, a German neurologist, described another variety of aphasia that occurred in patients with lesions in areas of the left temporal lobe, now known as **Wernicke's area**. **Lateralization** is the term used to refer to the localization of function to one hemisphere of the brain. Language is lateralized to the left hemisphere, and the left hemisphere appears to be the language hemisphere from infancy on. Figure 10.4 is a view of the left side of the brain that shows Broca's and Wernicke's areas.

The Linguistic Characterization of Aphasic Syndromes

Most aphasics do not show total language loss. Rather, different aspects of language are selectively impaired, and the kind of impairment is generally related to the location of the brain damage. Because of this damage-deficit correlation, research on patients with aphasia has provided a great deal of information about how language is organized in the brain.

Patients with injuries to Broca's area may have **Broca's aphasia**, as it is often called today. Broca's aphasia is characterized by labored speech and certain kinds of word-finding difficulties, but it is primarily a disorder that affects a person's ability to form sentences with the rules of syntax. One of the most notable characteristics of Broca's aphasia is that the language produced is often **agrammatic**, meaning that it frequently lacks articles, prepositions, pronouns, auxiliary verbs, and other function words. Broca's aphasics also typically omit inflections such as the past tense suffix *-ed* or the third person singular verb ending *-s*. Here is an excerpt of a conversation between a patient with Broca's aphasia and a doctor:

DOCTOR: Could you tell me what you have been doing in the hospital?
PATIENT: Yes, sure. Me go, er, uh, P.T. [physical therapy] none o'cot, speech . . . two times . . . read . . . r . . . ripe . . . rike . . . uh write . . . practice . . . get . . . ting . . . better.
DOCTOR: And have you been going home on weekends?
PATIENT: Why, yes . . . Thursday uh . . . uh . . . uh . . . no . . . Friday . . . Bar . . . ba . . . ra . . . wife . . . and oh car . . . drive . . . purpike . . . you know . . . rest . . . and TV.

Broca's aphasics (also often called **agrammatic aphasics**) may also have difficulty understanding complex sentences in which comprehension depends exclusively on syntactic structure and where they cannot rely on their real-world knowledge. For example, an agrammatic aphasic may have difficulty knowing who kissed whom in questions like:

Which girl did the boy kiss?

where it is equally plausible for the boy or the girl to have done the kissing; or might be confused as to who is chasing whom in passive sentences such as:

The cat was chased by the dog.

in which it is plausible for either animal to chase the other. But they have less difficulty with:

Which book did the boy read?

or

The car was chased by the dog.

where the meaning can be determined by nonlinguistic knowledge. It is implausible for books to read boys or for cars to chase dogs, and aphasic people can use that knowledge to interpret the sentence.

Unlike Broca's patients, people with **Wernicke's aphasia** produce fluent speech with good intonation, and they may largely adhere to the rules of syntax. However, their language is often semantically incoherent. For example, one patient replied to a question about his health with:

I felt worse because I can no longer keep in mind from the mind of the minds to keep me from mind and up to the ear which can be to find among ourselves.

Another patient described a fork as "a need for a schedule" and another, when asked about his poor vision, replied, "My wires don't hire right."

People with damage to Wernicke's area have difficulty naming objects presented to them and also in choosing words in spontaneous speech. They may make numerous lexical errors (word substitutions), often producing **jargon** and **nonsense words**, as in the following example:

The only thing that I can say again is madder or modder fish sudden fishing sewed into the accident to miss in the purdles.

Another example is from a patient who was a physician before his aphasia. When asked whether he was a doctor, he replied:

> Me? Yes sir. I'm a male demaploze on my own. I still know my tubaboys what for I have that's gone hell and some of them go.

The linguistic deficits exhibited by people with Broca's and Wernicke's aphasias point to a **modular** organization of language in the brain. Damage to different parts of the brain results in different kinds of linguistic impairment (e.g., syntactic versus semantic). This supports the hypothesis that the mental grammar, like the brain itself, is not an undifferentiated system, but rather consists of distinct components or modules with different functions.

The kind of word substitutions that aphasic patients produce also tell us about how words are organized in the mental lexicon. Sometimes the substituted words are similar to the intended words in their sounds. For example, *pool* might be substituted for *tool*, *sable* for *table*, or *crucial* for *crucible*. Sometimes they are similar in meaning (e.g., *table* for *chair* or *boy* for *girl*). These errors resemble the speech errors that unimpaired speakers might make, but they occur far more frequently in people with aphasia. The substitution of semantically or phonetically related words tells us that neural connections exist among semantically related words and among words that sound alike. Words are not mentally represented in a simple list but rather in an organized network of connections.

Similar observations pertain to reading. The term **dyslexia** refers to reading disorders. **Acquired dyslexics**—people whose reading ability is impaired due to brain damage—make many word substitutions, such as the following:

Stimulus	Response 1	Response 2
act	*play*	*play*
applaud	*laugh*	*cheers*
example	*answer*	*sum*
heal	*pain*	*medicine*
south	*west*	*east*

The patient was unable to read the stimulus word presented on a card, though his responses were semantically related to the target.

The omission of function words in the speech of agrammatic aphasics shows that this class of words is mentally distinct from content words like nouns. A similar phenomenon has been observed in acquired dyslexia. The patient who produced the semantic substitutions cited previously was also agrammatic and was not able to read function words at all. When presented with words like *which* or *would*, he just said, "No" or "I hate those little words." However, he could read same-sounding nouns and verbs, though with many semantic mistakes, as shown in the following:

Stimulus	Response	Stimulus	Response
witch	*witch*	which	*no!*
hour	*time*	our	*no!*

eye	*eyes*	I	*no!*
hymn	*bible*	him	*no!*
wood	*wood*	would	*no!*

These errors provide evidence that content words and function words are processed in different brain areas or by different neural mechanisms, further supporting the view that both the brain and language are structured in a complex, modular fashion.

Japanese readers provide additional evidence regarding hemispheric specialization. The Japanese language has two main writing systems. One system, *kana*, is based on the sound system of the language; each symbol corresponds to a syllable. The other system, *kanji*, is ideographic; each symbol corresponds to a word. (More about this in chapter 12 on writing systems.) *Kanji* is not based on the sounds of the language. Japanese speakers with left-hemisphere damage are impaired in their ability to read the phonetically based *kana*, whereas ones with right-hemisphere damage are impaired in their ability to read the ideographic *kanji* symbols. Also, experiments with unimpaired Japanese readers show that the right hemisphere is better and faster than the left hemisphere at reading *kanji*, and conversely, the left hemisphere does better with *kana*, though the left hemisphere can read both systems.

Most of us have experienced word-finding difficulties in speaking if not in reading, as Alice did in "Wonderland" when she said:

> "And now, who am I? I will remember, if I can. I'm determined to do it!" But being determined didn't help her much, and all she could say, after a great deal of puzzling, was "L, I know it begins with L."

This **tip-of-the-tongue phenomenon** is not uncommon. But aphasics who suffer from **anomia** have constant word-finding difficulties.

Deaf signers with damage to the left hemisphere show aphasia for sign language similar to the language breakdown in hearing aphasics, even though sign language is a visual-spatial language. Moreover, in paradigms measuring hemispheric activation (some of which we discuss below), one finds that it is the *auditory* cortex of deaf individuals that is activated under certain conditions—the very area we might expect to be the *least* responsive to language in the deaf.

Deaf patients with lesions in Broca's area show language deficits like those found in hearing patients, namely, severely dysfluent, agrammatic sign production. Likewise, those with damage to Wernicke's area have fluent but often semantically incoherent sign language, filled with made-up signs. Although deaf aphasic patients show marked sign language deficits, they have no difficulty producing nonlinguistic gestures or sequences of nonlinguistic gestures, even though both nonlinguistic gestures and linguistic signs are produced by the same "articulators"—the hands and arms. Deaf aphasics also have no difficulty in processing nonlinguistic visual-spatial relationships, just as hearing aphasics have no problem with processing nonlinguistic auditory stimuli.

The language difficulties suffered by aphasics are not caused by any general cognitive or intellectual impairment or loss of motor or sensory controls of the nerves and muscles of the speech organs or hearing apparatus. Aphasics can produce and hear sounds and their other cognitive abilities may be intact. Whatever loss they suffer has to do only with the language faculty (or specific parts of it).

In addition to the evidence provided by deaf aphasics there is also considerable experimental evidence showing that sign language grammar—like spoken language grammar—resides in the left hemisphere. These findings are important because they show that the left hemisphere is lateralized for language—an abstract system of symbols and rules—and not simply for hearing or speech. Language can be realized in different modalities, spoken or signed, but will be lateralized to the left hemisphere regardless of modality.

The kind of selective impairments that we find in people with aphasia has provided important information about the organization of language and other cognitive abilities in the brain, especially grammar and the lexicon. It tells us that language is a separate cognitive module—so aphasics can be otherwise cognitively normal—and also that within language, separate components can be differentially affected by damage to different regions of the brain.

Brain Imaging in Aphasic Patients

Today we no longer need to rely on surgery or autopsy to locate brain lesions. Noninvasive neuroimaging technologies such as computer tomography (CT) scans and **magnetic resonance imaging (MRI)** can reveal lesions in the living brain shortly after the damage occurs. In addition, **positron emission tomography (PET)** scans and **functional MRI (fMRI)** scans can reveal the brain in action by measuring blood flow and oxygen utilization in different areas of the brain during the performance of various linguistic and other cognitive tasks. It is now possible to detect changes in brain activity and to relate these changes to localized brain damage and specific linguistic and nonlinguistic cognitive tasks.

Figures 10.5 and 10.6 show MRI scans of the brains of a Broca's aphasic patient and a Wernicke's aphasic patient. The black areas show the sites of the lesions. Each diagram represents a slice of the left side of the brain.

Dramatic evidence for a differentiated and structured brain is also provided by studies of patients with lesions in regions of the brain other than Broca's and Wernicke's areas. Some patients have difficulty speaking a person's name; others have problems naming animals; and still others cannot name tools. fMRI studies have revealed the shape and location of the brain lesions in each of these types of patients. The patients in each group had brain lesions in distinct, nonoverlapping regions of the left temporal lobe. In a follow-up PET scan study, normal subjects were asked to name persons, animals, or tools. Experimenters found that there was differential activation in the normal brains in just those sites that were damaged in the aphasics who were unable to name persons, animals, or tools.

Further evidence for the separation of cognitive systems is provided by the neurological and behavioral findings that occur after brain damage. Some patients lose the ability to recognize sounds or colors or familiar faces while retaining all other functions. A patient may not be able to recognize his wife

FIGURE 10.5 | Three-dimensional reconstruction of the brain of a living patient with Broca's aphasia. Note area of damage in left frontal region (*dark gray*), which was caused by a stroke.

Courtesy of Hanna Damásio.

FIGURE 10.6 | Three-dimensional reconstruction of the brain of a living patient with Wernicke's aphasia. Note area of damage in left posterior temporal and lower parietal region (*dark gray*), which was caused by a stroke.

Courtesy of Hanna Damásio.

when she walks into the room until she starts to talk. This suggests the differentiation of many aspects of visual and auditory processing.

Other sources of evidence concerning the functional differences between the left and right hemispheres is provided by individuals who have suffered trauma to the brain or have undergone brain surgery for certain medical conditions. For example, a member of the U.S. Congress was shot in the head in an assassination attempt in 2011, with the bullet passing through the left hemisphere of the brain. After a year of courageous recovery, news reports made clear that linguistic ability was still severely compromised and TV images distinctly revealed an asymmetric weakness to the right side of the body. In addition, experimental tests of unimpaired people, such as dichotic listening and event-related potential (ERPs), confirm the left hemisphere's special role in language and the contralateral processing of information by the brain.

Split Brains

It takes only one hemisphere to have a mind.

A. L. WIGAN, *The Duality of the Mind*, 1844

An extreme measure used to help people suffering from intractable epilepsy is a procedure of "splitting the brain" in which a surgeon severs the corpus callosum (see Figure 2.1), the fibrous network that connects the two halves. When this pathway is severed, there is no communication between the "two brains," making it possible to test the functions of each hemisphere without interference from the other.

In people who have undergone **split-brain** surgery, the two hemispheres appear to be independent, and messages sent to the brain result in different responses, depending on which side receives the message. For example, if a pencil is placed in the left hand of a split-brain person whose eyes are closed, the person can use the pencil appropriately but cannot name it because only the left hemisphere can speak. The right brain senses the pencil but the information cannot be relayed to the left brain for linguistic naming because the connections between the two halves have been severed. By contrast, if the pencil is placed in the right hand, the subject is immediately able to name it as well as to describe it because the sensory information from the right hand goes directly to the left hemisphere, where the language areas are located.

Experiments of this sort have provided information on the different capabilities of the two hemispheres. The right brain does better than the left in pattern-matching tasks, in recognizing faces, and in spatial tasks. The left hemisphere is superior for language, rhythmic perception, temporal-order judgments, and arithmetic calculations. According to the psychologist Michael Gazzaniga, "the right hemisphere as well as the left hemisphere can emote and while the left can tell you why, the right cannot."

Studies of split-brain patients have also shown that when the interhemispheric visual connections are severed, visual information from the right and left visual fields becomes confined to the left and right hemispheres, respectively. Because of the crucial endowment of the left hemisphere for language, written material delivered to the right hemisphere cannot be read aloud if the brain is split, because the information cannot be transferred to the left hemisphere. An image or picture that is flashed to the right visual field of a split-brain patient (and therefore processed by the left hemisphere) can be named. However, when the picture is flashed in the left visual field and therefore "lands" in the right hemisphere, it cannot be named.

Dichotic Listening

Dichotic listening is an experimental technique that uses auditory signals to observe the behavior of the individual hemispheres of the human brain. Subjects hear two different sound signals simultaneously through earphones. They may hear *curl* in one ear and *girl* in the other, or a cough in one ear and a laugh in the other. When asked to state what they heard in each ear, subjects are more frequently correct in reporting linguistic stimuli (words, nonsense syllables, and so on) delivered directly to the right ear, but are more frequently correct in reporting nonverbal stimuli (musical chords, environmental sounds, and so on) delivered to the left ear. Such experiments provide strong evidence of lateralization.

Both hemispheres receive signals from both ears, but the contralateral stimuli prevail over the **ipsilateral** (same-side) stimuli because they are processed more robustly. The contralateral pathways are anatomically thicker (think of a four-lane highway versus a two-lane road) and are not delayed by the need to cross the corpus callosum. The accuracy with which subjects report what they hear is evidence that the left hemisphere is superior for linguistic processing, and the right hemisphere is superior for nonverbal information.

These experiments also show that the left hemisphere is not superior for processing all sounds, but only for sounds that are linguistic. The left side of the brain is specialized for language, not sound, as we also noted in connection with sign language research discussed earlier.

Event-Related Potentials

Yet other experimental techniques are also used to map the brain and to investigate the independence of different aspects of language as well as the independence of language from other cognitive systems. **Event-related potentials (ERPs)** are the electrical signals emitted from the brain in response to different stimuli. Researchers can investigate the brain's ERP responses by taping electrodes to different areas of the skull and measuring the responses to different kinds of perceptual and cognitive information. This technique, based upon EEG (electroencephalogram) readings, exploits the fact that the brain is electrically active and that this electrical activity can be measured both for its strength and for its pattern over time.

For example, ERP differences result when the subject hears speech versus non-speech sounds, with a greater response from the left hemisphere to speech. ERP experiments also show variations in timing, pattern, amplitude, and hemisphere of response when subjects hear sentences that are meaningless, such as

The man admired Don's headache of the landscape.

as opposed to meaningful sentences such as

The man admired Don's sketch of the landscape.

Even Jabberwocky sentences—sentences that are grammatical but contain nonsense words, such as Lewis Carroll's *'Twas brillig, and the slithy toves*—elicit an asymmetrical left-hemisphere ERP response, demonstrating that the left hemisphere is sensitive to grammatical structure even in the absence of meaning. Moreover, because ERPs also show the timing of neuronal activity as the brain processes language, they provide insight into the mechanisms that allow the brain to process language quickly and efficiently, on the scale of milliseconds.

These studies also show that the early stages of phonological and syntactic processing do not require the subject's attention but are automatic, very much like reflexes. Experiments show that adults can perform a completely unrelated task while listening to sentences and this task, though requiring considerable attention, will not affect the brain's automatic early syntactic processing. We discuss a number of these studies in more detail in the following section.

Neural Evidence of Grammatical Phenomena

As noted, recent years have seen many technological advances that provide non-invasive methods for studying linguistic and other cognitive functions in the brain. These techniques reveal how the healthy brain reacts to particular linguistic stimuli. For example, researchers observe how the normal brain responds in deciding whether two or more sounds are the same or different, whether a sequence of sounds constitutes a real or possible word, or whether a sequence of words forms a grammatical or ungrammatical sentence. The results of these studies reaffirm earlier findings that language resides in specific areas of the left hemisphere, and demonstrate the neurological reflexes of many of the linguistic categories and constraints posited by linguists.

Neurolinguistic Studies of Speech Sounds

In previous chapters we noted that adults (and infants) perceive speech sounds categorically. Several studies using ERPs and MEGs (magnetoencephalography—the measuring of the magnetic field of the brain) have shown a neural reflex of categorical perception: The brain reacts differently to sounds that are phonemically different (e.g., [t] and [k]) than to sounds that are acoustically distinct (e.g., [p] and [pʰ]) but non-phonemic. The overall patterns of response differ in intensity, speed, and location in the brain.

Another ERP experiment involving the sound system has demonstrated a neurological reflex of the notion *phonotactically permitted* (e.g., *blick versus bnick*). Speakers of French and Japanese showed neurologically distinct response patterns for phonotactically permissible versus impermissible sequences of sounds in their language as well as faster reaction times to the phonotactically correct sequences. Other studies have examined the neurological response to phonotactically permissible and impermissible hand configurations in sign language with similar results.

What these and many other studies show is that the way people discriminate linguistically relevant differences among sounds is both cognitively and neurally distinct from the way we respond to sound differences that are not linguistically relevant. In short, the human brain treats language differently from non-language stimuli.

Neurolinguistic Studies of Sentence Structure

Modern technologies have also been used to examine the brain's response to the syntactic patterns of language. For example, as noted earlier, a number of studies have compared the brain's response to Jabberwocky sentences and sentences using real content words. These studies consistently find that the brain reacts similarly to grammatically well-formed sentences regardless of whether they are anomalous or meaningful. Such findings provide neurological evidence for the separation between syntax and semantics posited by linguists.

Another set of studies has examined brain responses to syntactic dependencies of the sort shown in *wh* questions (see chapter 3). Subjects hear sentences in which the underlying subject or object has been moved to the beginning of the phrase. In the case of a moved subject, the movement is shorter and the basic word order is kept, for example, *Who . . . left the room?* On the other hand, movement from object position involves a longer distance—*Which bagel . . . did Seymour slice __?*—between the moved element (*which bagel*, sometimes called the *filler*) and the position from which it moves (the *gap*). Various studies show that sentences with moved objects elicit longer response times than sentences with moved subjects, providing neural correlates of different *wh* movement transformations (as discussed in chapter 3).

In other studies of *wh* movement researchers have measured the brain's response at the gap site to words that are semantically related to the filler (e.g., *donut* versus *sincerity* from the "Seymour" sentence above). Findings from these studies consistently show increased electrical activity at the gap site when the listener is given a semantically related filler, providing neurological evidence that movement has indeed occurred.

Many neurolinguistic studies have examined the brain's response to ungrammatical sentences, manifested by a type of ERP pattern called a MisMatch Negativity (MMN). Various experiments have found distinct waveforms evoked by different types of ungrammatical sentences: for example, sentences involving violations of phrase structure, C-selection, agreement, etc. It is noteworthy that one can find clear, replicable neurological findings that demonstrate quite specific neural "signatures" for these different kinds of abstract linguistic phenomena.

It is also interesting to observe that the brain responds almost instantly to morphosyntactic violations (e.g., *a boys is running) and does so outside the scope of attention. In one study, the experimenters divided their subjects into groups: one that had to simply listen to phrases, another that had to watch a video while listening to the same phrases, and a third that had to perform a complex auditory task while listening to the phrases. The

MMN response to the syntactic violations was almost immediate, within the first 100–200 milliseconds after hearing the phrase, and the response was equally rapid and strong whether or not the listeners had to perform another task. Particularly striking was the response of those subjects who had to do the auditory task. They had the same strong MMN response, showing that even this complex task requiring considerable attention did not compete with syntactic processing. The results of this study demonstrate that syntactic processing is like a reflex, in being both automatic and attention-free.

In light of the importance that researchers give to the brain's response to ungrammatical sentences, it is reasonable to ask whether ungrammatical strings elicit a strong MMN because they are ungrammatical or simply because they tend to be infrequent. This question was addressed in another study, which used Determiner-Noun agreement as the syntactic feature of interest. Researchers compared responses to the same words in three different conditions: 1) grammatical Det-N strings (e.g., *the car*, used frequently), 2) ungrammatical Det-N combinations (e.g., *a gooses,* heard rarely), and 3) grammatical but extremely rare Det-N combinations (e.g., *an aardvark*). If the MMN is a response to frequency, then the ungrammatical type 2 combinations and the grammatical type 3 combinations should evoke the same response and the same level of response. However, if the MMN is a response to grammaticality, then only the ungrammatical type 2 combinations should give rise to the response. The results showed that grammatical but rare phrases evoked an MMN similar to that of common grammatical strings, and the MMNs to both were extremely rapid (within 200 ms.), leading to the conclusion that the MMN behaves like an "automatic index of grammaticality," and not simply frequency.

Experimental evidence from these various neurolinguistic experiments has provided considerable insight into how the brain processes language, and has also lent empirical support to many of the abstract categories, rules, concepts, and constraints of linguistic theory.

Language and Brain Development

If the brain were so simple we could understand it, we would be so simple we couldn't.

LYALL WATSON

Numerous neurolinguistic studies have found that the way the brain is organized for language and grammar in the adult is already reflected in the brains of newborns and young infants—even before they have entered the period during which language actively develops. Lateralization of language to the left hemisphere is a process that begins very early in life. For example, Wernicke's area is visibly distinctive in the left hemisphere of the fetus by the twenty-sixth gestational week. Moreover, infants show evidence of many of the neural correlates of linguistic categories that we observe in adults.

Left Hemisphere Lateralization for Language in Young Children

"Jump Start" copyright United Feature Syndicate

Everyone loves a smiling baby, but babies' smiles do more than light up a room. They reveal something very important about how the developing brain is organized for language.

In a very intriguing study researchers videotaped smiling babies and babbling babies (producing syllabic sequences like *mamama* or *gugugu*) between the ages of five and twelve months. The videotapes showed that when they were smiling the babies' mouths were opened wider on the left side (the side controlled by the right hemisphere) whereas when they babbled the *right* side of the mouth (controlled by the left hemisphere) was opened wider, indicating greater left hemisphere involvement for language even during the babbling period (see chapter 9).

Many other studies of infants and young children support this conclusion. For example, infants as young as one week old show a greater electrical response in the left hemisphere to language and in the right hemisphere to music, similar to adults. A study measuring brain activation in awake and sleeping 3-month old infants when hearing forward and backward speech showed that different areas of the cortex responded in the two cases.

In the previous chapters we noted that behavioral tests show that infants—like adults—perceive speech sounds categorically. ERP studies have found neurological correlates of categorical perception in infants, just as for adults. These studies show that the infant brain responds differently, and with the same pattern and speed as found in adults, to *phonemic* categories than to non-phonemic acoustic distinctions. Interestingly, this neural pattern occurs even in sleeping babies, showing that the response is automatic and does not require the attention of the infant.

These and similar experiments show that from birth onward, the left hemisphere differentiates between nonlinguistic acoustic processing and the linguistic processing of sounds, and uses the same neural pathways as adults. At birth the left hemisphere is primed to process language, and to do so in terms of the specific localization of language functions we find in the adult brain.

Brain Plasticity

While the left hemisphere is innately predisposed to specialize for language, there is also evidence of considerable *plasticity* (i.e., flexibility) in the system during the early stages of language development. This means that under certain circumstances, the right hemisphere can take over many of the language functions that would normally reside in the left hemisphere.

An impressive illustration of plasticity is provided by children who have undergone a procedure known as **hemispherectomy**, in which one hemisphere of the brain is surgically removed. This procedure is used to treat otherwise intractable cases of epilepsy. In cases of left hemispherectomy after language acquisition has begun, children experience an initial period of aphasia. However, in certain cases, depending on the underlying disease that led to the epilepsy, the child may reacquire a linguistic system that is virtually indistinguishable from that of normal children. They also show many of the developmental patterns of normal language acquisition. UCLA researchers who have studied many of these children hypothesize that the latent linguistic ability of the right hemisphere is "freed" by the removal of the diseased left hemisphere, which may have had a strong inhibitory effect before the surgery.

In adults, however, surgical removal of the left hemisphere inevitably results in severe loss of language function (and so is done only in life-threatening circumstances), whereas adults (and children who have already acquired language) who have had their right hemispheres removed generally retain their language abilities. Other cognitive losses may result, such as those typically lateralized to the right hemisphere. The plasticity of the brain decreases with age and with the increasing specialization of the different hemispheres and regions of the brain.

Despite strong evidence that the left hemisphere is predetermined to be the language hemisphere in most humans, some studies suggest that the right hemisphere also plays a role in the earliest stages of language acquisition. Children with prenatal, perinatal, or childhood brain lesions in the right hemisphere can show delays and impairments in babbling and vocabulary learning, whereas children with early left hemisphere lesions demonstrate impairments in their ability to form phrases and sentences. Also, many children who undergo right hemispherectomy before two years of age do not develop language, even though they still have a left hemisphere.

Various findings converge to show that the human brain is essentially designed to specialize for language in the left hemisphere but that the right hemisphere is involved in early language development. They also show that the brain is remarkably resilient and that if left brain trauma occurs early in life, its normal functions can be taken over by the right hemisphere.

The Critical Period

Under ordinary circumstances a child is introduced to language virtually at the moment of birth. Adults talk to him and to each other in his presence. Children do not require explicit language instruction, but they do need exposure to language to develop normally. Children who do not receive linguistic input during their formative years do not achieve native-like grammatical competence. Moreover, behavioral tests and brain imaging studies show that late exposure to language alters the fundamental organization of the brain for language.

The **critical-age hypothesis** asserts that language is biologically based and that the ability to learn a native language develops within a fixed period, from birth to middle childhood. During this **critical period**, language acquisition proceeds easily, swiftly, and without external intervention. After this period, the acquisition of grammar is difficult and, for most individuals, never fully achieved. Children deprived of language during this critical period show atypical patterns of brain lateralization.

Many species have a critical period for specific, biologically triggered behaviors. For example, during the period from nine to twenty-one hours after hatching, ducklings will follow the first moving object they see, whether or not it looks, quacks and waddles like a duck. Such behavior is not the result of a conscious decision, external teaching, or intensive practice. It unfolds according to what appears to be a maturationally determined schedule that is universal across the species. Similarly, as discussed in chapter 1, certain species of birds develop their bird song within a biologically determined window of time.

Instances of children reared in environments of extreme social isolation constitute "experiments in nature" for testing the critical-age hypothesis. The most dramatic cases are those described as "wild" or "feral" children. A celebrated case, documented in François Truffaut's film *The Wild Child*, is that of Victor, "the wild boy of Aveyron," who was found in 1798. It was ascertained that he had been left in the woods when very young and had somehow survived. In 1920 two children, Amala and Kamala, were found in India, supposedly having been reared by wolves.

Other children have been deliberately isolated from normal social interaction and language. In 1970, a child called Genie in the scientific reports was discovered. She had been confined to a small room under conditions of physical restraint and had received only minimal human contact from the age of eighteen months until nearly fourteen years.

Regardless of the cause of the isolation, none of these children was able to speak or knew any language at the time they were reintroduced into society. This linguistic inability could be simply explained by the fact that these children received no linguistic input, showing that language acquisition, though an innate, neurologically based ability, must be triggered by input from the environment. In the documented cases of Victor and Genie, however, these children were unable to acquire grammar even after years of exposure, and despite the ability to learn many words.

Genie was able to learn a large vocabulary, including colors, shapes, objects, natural categories, and abstract as well as concrete terms, but her grammatical skills never fully developed. The UCLA linguist Susan Curtiss, who worked with Genie for several years, reported that Genie's utterances were, for the most part, "the stringing together of content words, often with rich and clear meaning, but with little grammatical structure." Many utterances produced by Genie at the age of fifteen and later are like those of two-year old children, and not unlike utterances of Broca's aphasia patients, or people with Specific Language Impairment (SLI, discussed below). Some such utterances are:

Man motorcycle have.
Genie full stomach.
Genie bad cold live father house.
Want Curtiss play piano.
Open door key.

Genie's utterances lacked articles, auxiliary verbs like *will* or *can*, the third-person singular agreement marker *-s*, the past-tense marker *-ed*, question words like *who*, *what*, and *where*, and pronouns. She had no ability to form more complex types of sentences such as questions (e.g., *Are you feeling hungry?*). Genie started learning language after the critical period and was therefore never able to fully acquire the grammatical rules of English.

Tests of lateralization (dichotic listening and ERP experiments) showed that Genie's language was lateralized to the *right* hemisphere. Her test performance was similar to that found in split-brain and left hemispherectomy patients, yet Genie was not brain damaged. Curtiss speculates that after the critical period, the usual language areas functionally atrophy because of inadequate linguistic stimulation. Genie's case also demonstrates that language is not the same as communication, because Genie was a powerful nonverbal communicator, despite her limited ability to acquire language.

Chelsea, another case of linguistic isolation, is a woman whose situation also reflects the critical-age hypothesis. She was born deaf but was wrongly diagnosed as retarded. When she was thirty-one her deafness was finally diagnosed and she was fitted with hearing aids. For years she has received extensive language training and therapy and has acquired a large vocabulary. However, like Genie, Chelsea has not been able to develop a grammar. ERP studies of the localization of language in Chelsea's brain have revealed an equal response to language in both hemispheres. In other words, Chelsea also does not show the normal asymmetric organization for language.

More than 90 percent of children who are born deaf or become deaf before they have acquired language are born to hearing parents. These children have also provided information about the critical age for language acquisition. Because most of their parents do not know sign language at the time these children are born, most receive delayed language exposure. Several studies have investigated the acquisition of American Sign Language (ASL) among deaf signers exposed to the language at different ages. Early learners who received ASL input from birth and up to six years of age did much better in the production and comprehension of complex signs and sign sentences than late learners who were not exposed to ASL until after the age of twelve, even though all of the subjects in these studies had used sign for more than twenty years. There was little difference, however, in vocabulary or knowledge of word order.

Another study compared patterns of lateralization in the brains of adult native speakers of English, adult native signers, and deaf adults who had not been exposed to sign language. The nonsigning deaf adults did not show the same cerebral asymmetries as either the hearing adults or the deaf signers. In recent years there have been numerous studies of late learners of sign language, all with similar results.

The cases of Genie and other isolated children, as well as deaf late learners of ASL, show that children cannot fully acquire language unless they are exposed to it within the critical period—a biologically determined window of opportunity during which time the brain is prepared to develop language. Moreover, the critical period is linked to brain lateralization. The human brain is primed to develop language in specific areas of the left hemisphere, but the normal process of brain specialization depends on early and systematic experience with language. Language acquisition plays a critical role in, and may even be *the* trigger for, the realization of normal cerebral lateralization for higher cognitive functions in general, not just for language.

Beyond the critical period, the human brain seems unable to acquire the grammatical aspects of language, even with substantial linguistic training or many years of exposure. However, it is possible to acquire words and various conversational skills after this point. This evidence suggests that the critical period holds for the acquisition of grammatical abilities, but not necessarily for all aspects of language.

The selective acquisition of certain components of language that occurs beyond the critical period is reminiscent of the selective impairment that occurs in various language disorders, in which specific linguistic abilities are disrupted. This selectivity in both acquisition and impairment points to a strongly modularized language faculty. Language is separate from other cognitive systems and is itself an autonomous complex system with various components.

The Modular Mind: Dissociations of Language and Cognition

[T]he human mind is not an unstructured entity but consists of components which can be distinguished by their functional properties.

NEIL SMITH AND IANTHI-MARIA TSIMPLI, *The Mind of a Savant: Language, Learning, and Modularity*, 1995

The modular view of cognition is also supported by various case studies of extraordinary individuals who show deficits in certain cognitive domains alongside normal or superior abilities in other areas. The individuals we discuss below show *dissociations* between their linguistic abilities and other nonlinguistic cognitive abilities. In some cases, their language abilities far outpace the other areas, and in other cases, the reverse is true.

Linguistic Savants

There are numerous cases of intellectually handicapped individuals who, despite their disabilities in certain spheres, show remarkable talents in others. There are superb musicians and artists who lack the simple abilities required to take care of themselves. Such people are referred to as **savants**. Some of the most famous savants are human calculators, who can perform arithmetic computations at phenomenal speed, or calendrical calculators, who can tell you without pause on which day of the week any date in the last or next century falls.

Until recently, most such savants have been reported to be linguistically handicapped. They may be good mimics who can repeat speech like parrots, but they show meager creative language ability. But there are also cases of language savants, people who have acquired the highly complex grammar of their language (as well as other languages in some cases) but who lack nonlinguistic abilities of equal complexity. Laura and Christopher are two such cases.

Laura was a young retarded woman with a nonverbal IQ of 41 to 44. She lacked almost all number concepts, including basic counting principles, and could draw only at a preschool level. She had an auditory memory span limited to three units. Yet, when at the age of sixteen she was asked to name some fruits, she responded with *pears, apples,* and *pomegranates.* In this same period she produced syntactically complex sentences like *He was saying that I lost my battery-powered watch that I loved,* and *She does paintings, this really good friend of the kids who I went to school with and really loved,* and *I was like 15 or 19 when I started moving out of home. . . .*

Laura could not add 2 + 2. She didn't know how old she was or whether 15 is before or after 19. Nevertheless, Laura produced complex sentences with multiple phrases and embedded sentences. She used and understood passive sentences, and she was able to inflect verbs for number and person to agree with the subject of a sentence. She formed past tenses in accord with adverbs that referred to past time. She could do all this and more, but she could neither read nor write nor tell time. She did not know who the president of the United States was or what country she lived in. Her drawings of humans resembled potatoes with stick arms and legs. Yet, in a sentence imitation task, she both detected and corrected grammatical errors.

Laura is but one of many examples of children who display well-developed grammatical abilities, less-developed abilities to associate linguistic expressions with the objects they refer to, and severe deficits in nonlinguistic cognition.

Another linguistic savant, Christopher, has a nonverbal IQ between 60 and 70. He lives in an institution because he is unable to take care of himself. The tasks of buttoning a shirt, cutting his fingernails, or vacuuming the carpet are too difficult for him. However, his linguistic competence is as rich and as sophisticated as that of any native speaker. Furthermore, when given written texts in some fifteen to twenty languages, he translates them quickly, with few errors, into English. The languages include Germanic languages such as Danish, Dutch, and German; Romance languages such as French, Italian, Portuguese, and Spanish; as well as Polish, Finnish, Greek, Hindi, Turkish, and Welsh. He learned these languages from speakers who used them in his presence, or from grammar books. Christopher loves to study and learn languages. Little else is of interest to him. His situation strongly suggests that his linguistic ability is independent of his general intellectual ability.

The question as to whether the language faculty is a separate cognitive system or whether it is derivative of more general cognitive mechanisms is controversial and has received much attention and debate among linguists, psychologists, neuropsychologists, and cognitive scientists. Cases such as Laura and Christopher argue against the view that linguistic ability derives from general intelligence because these two individuals (and others like them) developed language despite other pervasive intellectual deficits. A growing body of evidence supports the view that the human animal is biologically equipped from birth with an autonomous language faculty that is highly specific and that does not derive from general human intellectual ability.

Specific Language Impairment

People like Laura and Christopher have normal or superior linguistic skills though their abilities in other areas are very limited. There are individuals who show the opposite profile: among these are children with **Specific Language Impairment (SLI)**.

Children with SLI have do not have brain lesions, but they nevertheless have difficulties acquiring language or are much slower than the average child. They show no other cognitive deficits, they are not autistic or retarded, and they have no perceptual problems. Only their linguistic ability is affected, and often only specific aspects of grammar are impaired.

Children with SLI have problems with the use of function words such as articles, prepositions, and auxiliary verbs. They also have difficulties with inflectional suffixes on nouns and verbs such as markers of plurality or tense. The following examples from a four-year-old boy with SLI illustrate this:

Meowmeow chase mice.
Show me knife.
It not long one.

An experimental study of several children with SLI showed that they produced the past tense marker on the verb (as in *danced*) about 27 percent of the time, compared with 95 percent by the normal control group. Similarly, the SLI children produced the plural marker -*s* (as in *boys*) only 9 percent of the time, compared with 95 percent by the normal children.

Other studies reveal broader grammatical impairments, involving difficulties with many grammatical structures and operations. However, most investigations of SLI children show that they have particular problems with verbal inflection, especially with producing tensed verbs (*walks, walked*), and also with syntactic structures involving certain kinds of transformational operations, such as *Mother is hard to please*, a rearrangement of *It is hard to please Mother*. In many respects these difficulties resemble the impairments demonstrated by aphasics. In particular, individuals with persistent SLI have been found to have particular problems with *wh* movement, not unlike many agrammatics.

Recent work on SLI children also shows that the different components of language (phonology, syntax, lexicon) can be selectively impaired or spared. For example, in ERP studies of certain children with SLI it was found that they failed to show the expected level of response for syntactic processing, which jibed with their inability to process many syntactic structures normally.

As is the case with aphasia, these studies of SLI provide important information about the nature of language and help linguists develop theories about the underlying properties of language and its development in children. SLI children show that language may be impaired while general intelligence stays intact, supporting the view of a grammatical faculty that is separate from other cognitive systems.

Genetic Basis of Language

Studies of genetic disorders also reveal that one cognitive domain can develop normally along with abnormal development in other domains, and they also underscore the strong biological basis of language. Children with Turner syndrome (a chromosomal anomaly) have normal language and advanced reading skills along with serious nonlinguistic (visual and spatial) cognitive deficits. Similarly, studies of the language of children and adolescents with Williams syndrome reveal a unique behavioral profile in which certain linguistic functions seem to be relatively preserved in the face of visual and spatial cognitive deficits and moderate retardation. In addition, developmental dyslexia and SLI also appear to have a genetic basis. And recent studies of Klinefelter syndrome (another chromosomal anomaly) show quite selective syntactic and semantic deficits alongside intact intelligence.

Epidemiological and familial aggregation studies show that SLI runs in families. One such study is of a large multigenerational family, half of whom are language impaired. The impaired members of this family have a very specific grammatical problem: They do not reliably use verb inflections or "irregular" verbs correctly. They routinely produce sentences such as the following:

She remembered when she hurts herself the other day.
He did it then he fall.
The boy climb up the tree and frightened the bird away.

These and similar results show that a large proportion of SLI children have language-impaired family members, pointing to SLI as a heritable disorder. Studies also show that monozygotic (identical) twins are more likely to both suffer from SLI than dizygotic (fraternal) twins. Thus, evidence from SLI and other genetic disorders, along with the asymmetry of abilities in linguistic savants, strongly supports the view that the language faculty is an autonomous, genetically determined module of the brain.

Summary

Psycholinguistics is concerned with **linguistic performance** or processing, which is the use of linguistic knowledge (competence) in speech production and comprehension.

Comprehension, the process of understanding an utterance, requires the ability to access the mental lexicon to match the words in the utterance to their meanings. Comprehension begins with the perception of the **acoustic speech signal**. The speech signal can be described in terms of the **fundamental frequency**, perceived as pitch; the intensity, perceived as loudness; and the quality, perceived as differences in speech sounds, such as between an [i] and an [a]. The speech wave can be displayed visually as a **spectrogram**, sometimes called a **voiceprint**. In a spectrogram, vowels exhibit dark bands where frequency intensity is greatest. These are called **formants** and result from the emphasis of certain harmonics of the fundamental frequency, as determined by the shape of the vocal tract. Each vowel has a unique formant pattern.

The speech signal is a continuous stream of sounds. Listeners who know the language have the ability to segment the stream into linguistic units and to recognize acoustically distinct sounds as the same linguistic unit.

The perception of the speech signal is necessary but not sufficient for the comprehension of speech. To get the full meaning of an utterance we must access the mental lexicon to retrieve words and **parse** the string into syntactic constituents, because meaning depends on word order and constituent structure in addition to the meaning of individual words. It is likely that we use both **top-down processing** and **bottom-up processing** during comprehension. Top-down processing uses semantic and syntactic information in addition to the lexical and phonological information drawn from the sensory input; bottom-up processing gives primacy to the information contained in the sensory input.

Psycholinguistic studies are aimed at uncovering the units, stages, and processes involved in linguistic performance. Several experimental techniques have proved helpful in understanding **lexical access**. In a **lexical decision** task, subjects are asked to respond to spoken or written stimuli by pressing a button if they consider the stimulus to be a word. The measurement of response times, RTs, shows that it takes longer to retrieve less common words than more common words; longer to retrieve possible non-words than impossible non-words; longer to retrieve words with larger **phonological neighborhoods** than ones with smaller neighborhoods; and longer to retrieve lexically ambiguous words than unambiguous ones. With regard to the latter, studies also show that all meanings of an ambiguous word are initially activated and subsequently the meaning that is most compatible with the semantic and syntactic context is selected, all this conspiring to lengthen the retrieval time.

A word may **prime** another word if the words are semantically, morphologically, or phonologically related. The semantic priming effect is shown by experiments in which a word such as *nurse* is spoken in a sentence, and it is then found that words related to *nurse* such as *doctor* have lower RTs in lexical decision tasks. If an ambiguous word like *mouse* is used in an unambiguous context such as *My spouse has been chasing a mouse*, words related to both meanings of mouse are primed (e.g., *rat* and *computer*). In addition to using behavioral data such as RT, researchers can now use various measures of electrical brain activity to learn about language processing.

To understand a sentence the listener must also break up or **parse** the incoming material into syntactic units. This is done according to the rules of the grammar of the language and also following structural parsing principles that favor simpler structures. Two such principles are **minimal attachment** and

late closure. Other factors such as prosody, frequency of occurrence, and lexical biases can also influence the parser in its structural choices.

Language is filled with **temporary ambiguities**, points at which the sentence can continue in more than one way because of word category ambiguity or different structural possibilities. Usually these ambiguities are quickly resolved and may not be noticed except under experimental conditions.

Occasionally the reader goes down a **garden path**, a structural misanalysis in which he must backtrack and redo the parse. **Eye tracking** techniques can determine the points of a sentence at which readers have such difficulties. These experiments provide strong evidence that the parser has preferences in how it constructs trees. Other sentences, such as multiple center embeddings, are difficulty to parse because of memory constraints.

Another technique is **shadowing**, in which subjects repeat as fast as possible what is being said to them. Subjects often correct errors in the stimulus sentence, suggesting that they use linguistic knowledge rather than simply echoing sounds they hear. Shadowing experiments provide strong evidence of the use of top-down information in sentence processing.

Much of the best information about how speakers produce sentences comes from observing and analyzing spontaneous speech, especially speech errors. Many of the same factors that influence the listener in comprehension also affect the speaker in production. Lexical access is influenced in both cases by semantic and phonological relatedness of words and word frequency.

The production of ungrammatical utterances also shows that morphological, inflectional, and syntactic rules may be wrongly applied or fail to apply when we speak, but at the same time shows that such rules are involved in actual speech production.

The units and stages used in the planning of speech production have been studied by analyzing spontaneously produced speech errors. Speech errors such as **spoonerisms**, in which sounds or words are exchanged or reversed, show that features, segments, words, and phrases may be conceptualized or planned well before they are uttered. Similarly, anticipation errors, in which a sound is produced earlier than in the intended utterance, show that we do not produce one sound or one word or even one phrase at a time. Rather, we construct and store larger units with their syntactic structures specified.

Studies of hesitations and utterance initiation times show certain kinds of complex sentences require more planning and hence greater processing resources. Such studies also suggest that the clause boundary is the locus of planning and that sentences are bundled into clause-size units before they are produced.

The attempt to understand what makes the acquisition and use of language possible has led to research on the brain-mind-language relationship. **Neurolinguistics** is the study of the brain mechanisms and anatomical structures that underlie linguistic competence and performance.

The brain is the most complex organ of the body, controlling motor and sensory activities and thought processes. Research conducted for more than a century has shown that different parts of the brain control different body functions. The nerve cells that form the surface of the brain are called the

cortex, which serves as the intellectual decision maker, receiving messages from the sensory organs and initiating all voluntary actions. The brain of all higher animals is divided into two **cerebral hemispheres**, which are connected by the **corpus callosum**, a network that permits the left and right hemispheres to communicate.

Each hemisphere exhibits **contralateral** control of functions. The left hemisphere controls the right side of the body, and the right hemisphere controls the left side. Despite the general symmetry of the human body, much evidence suggests that the brain is asymmetric, with the left and right hemispheres specialized for different functions. **Lateralization** is the term used to refer to the localization of function to one hemisphere of the brain.

Language is lateralized to the left hemisphere, and the left hemisphere appears to be the language hemisphere from infancy on. Much of the early evidence for language lateralization comes from the study of **aphasia**, which is the neurological term for any language disorder that results from acquired brain damage caused by disease or trauma. For example, lesions in the part of the left hemisphere called **Broca's area** may suffer from **Broca's aphasia**, which results in impaired syntax and **agrammatism**. Damage to **Wernicke's area**, also in the left hemisphere, may result in **Wernicke's aphasia**, in which fluent speakers produce semantically anomalous utterances. Damage to yet different areas can produce **anomia**, a form of aphasia in which the patient has word-finding difficulties.

Deaf signers with damage to the left hemisphere show aphasia for sign language similar to the language breakdown in hearing aphasics, even though sign languages are visual-spatial languages.

Evidence for language lateralization as well as the contralateral control of function is also provided by **dichotic listening** experiments, **split-brain** patients, and neurolinguistic studies of grammatical phenomena. A great deal of neurolinguistic research is centered on experimental and behavioral data from people with impaired or atypical language. By studying people with aphasia and other brain-altered patients, localized areas of the brain can be associated with particular language functions.

Advances in technology have provided a variety of non-invasive methods for studying the living brain as it processes language. By measuring electromagnetic activities (ERPs and MEGs), and through imaging techniques such as CT, MRI, fMRI, and PET scans, both damaged and healthy brains can be observed and evaluated. These studies not only confirm earlier results concerning the lateralization of language to the left hemisphere, but also provide evidence of neural reflexes of various linguistic categories and constraints, such as categorical perception, phonotactic constraints, and *wh* movement. These studies also demonstrate that grammatical processing is automatic and attention-free, like a reflex.

Lateralization of language to the left hemisphere is a process that begins very early in life. Numerous neurolinguistic studies have found that the way the brain is organized for language and grammar in the adult is already reflected in the brains of newborns and young infants. Infants also show evidence of the many of the neural correlates of linguistic categories that we observe in adults.

While the left hemisphere is innately predisposed to specialize for language, there is also evidence of considerable **plasticity** in the system during the early stages of language development. Children who undergo a left **hemispherectomy** experience an initial period of aphasia, but in certain cases, may reacquire a linguistic system like that of normal children. The plasticity of the brain decreases with age and with the increasing specialization of the different hemispheres and regions of the brain.

The **critical-age hypothesis** states that there is a window of opportunity between birth and middle childhood for learning a first language. The imperfect language learning of persons exposed to language after this period supports the hypothesis.

The language faculty is **modular**. It is independent of other cognitive systems with which it interacts. Evidence for modularity is found in the selective impairment of language in aphasia, in children with **specific language impairment (SLI)**, in linguistic **savants**, and in children who learn language past the critical period. The genetic basis for an independent language module is supported by studies of SLI in families and twins and by studies of genetic anomalies associated with language disorders.

References for Further Reading

Ahlsén, E. 2006. *Introduction to neurolinguistics.* Amsterdam: John Benjamins.

Caplan, D. 2001. *Neurolinguistics: The handbook of linguistics*, M. Aronoff and J. Rees-Miller (eds.). London: Blackwell Publishers.

___. 1987. *Neurolinguistics and linguistic aphasiology.* Cambridge, UK: Cambridge University Press.

___. 1992. *Language: Structure, processing, and disorders.* Cambridge, MA: MIT Press.

Carroll, D. W. 2007. *Psychology of language, 5th ed.* Belmont, CA: Wadsworth.

Curtiss, S. 1977. *Genie: A linguistic study of a modern-day "wild child."* New York: Academic Press.

Curtiss, S., and J. Schaeffer. 2005. Syntactic development in children with hemispherectomy: The I-, D-, and C-systems. *Brain and Language* 94: 147–166.

Damásio, H. 1981. Cerebral localization of the aphasias. *Acquired aphasia*, M. Taylor Sarno (ed.). New York: Academic Press, 27–65.

Fernandez, E.M and Cairns, H.S. 2010. *Fundamentals of psycholinguistics.* Oxford, UK: Wiley-Blackwell.

Fromkin, V. A. (ed.). 1980. *Errors in linguistic performance.* New York: Academic Press.

Gazzaniga, M. S. 1970. *The bisected brain.* New York: Appleton-Century-Crofts.

Geschwind, N. 1979. Specializations of the human brain. *Scientific American* 206 (September): 180–199.

Ingram, J. 2007. *Neurolinguistics: An introduction to spoken language processing and its disorders.* Cambridge, U.K.: Cambridge University Press.

Johnson, K. 2003. *Acoustic and Auditory Phonetics, 2nd ed.* Oxford, UK: Blackwell.

Ladefoged, P. 1996. *Elements of acoustic phonetics, 2nd ed.* Chicago: University of Chicago Press.

Lenneberg, E. H. 1967. *Biological foundations of language.* New York: Wiley.

Obler, L. K., and K. Gjerlow. 1999. *Language and brain.* Cambridge, UK: Cambridge University Press.

Patterson, K. E., J. C. Marshall, and M. Coltheart (eds.). 1986. *Surface dyslexia.* Hillsdale, NJ: Lawrence Erlbaum.

Pinker, S. 1994. *The language instinct.* New York: William Morrow.

Poizner, H., E. S. Klima, and U. Bellugi. 1987. *What the hands reveal about the brain.* Cambridge, MA: MIT Press.

Searchinger, G. 1994. The human language series: 1, 2, 3. Videos. New York: Equinox Film/Ways of Knowing, Inc.

Smith, N. V., and I-M. Tsimpli. 1995. *The mind of a savant: Language learning and modularity.* Oxford, UK: Blackwell.

Springer, S. P., and G. Deutsch. 1997. *Left brain, right brain, 5th ed.* New York: W. H. Freeman and Company.

Stromswold, K. 2001. The heritability of language. *Language* 77(4): 647–721.

Traxler, Mathew J. 2012. *Introduction to psycholinguistics.* Oxford, UK: Wiley-Blackwell.

Yamada, J. 1990. *Laura: A case for the modularity of language.* Cambridge, MA: MIT Press.

Exercises

1. Speech errors ("slips of the tongue" or "bloopers") illustrate a difference between linguistic competence and performance, because our recognition of them as errors shows that we have knowledge of well-formed sentences. Furthermore, errors provide information about the grammar. The following utterances are part of the UCLA corpus of more than 5,000 English speech errors. Most of them were actually observed. One is attributed to Dr. Spooner.

   a. For each speech error, state what kind of linguistic unit or rule is involved (i.e., phonological, morphological, syntactic, lexical, or semantic). In (16)–(18), what are the nonlinguistic influences in addition?

   b. State, to the best of your ability, the nature of each error, or the mechanisms that produced it.

   (Note: The intended utterance is to the left of the arrow; the actual utterance to the right.)

   Example: ad hoc → odd hack

   a. phonological vowel segment   **b.** reversal or exchange of segments

   Example: she gave it away → she gived it away

   a. inflectional morphology   **b.** incorrect application of regular past-tense rule to exceptional verb

   Example: When will you leave? → When you will leave?

   a. syntactic rule   **b.** failure to move the auxiliary to form a question

   (1) brake fluid → blake fruid
   (2) drink is the curse of the working classes → work is the curse of the drinking classes (Spooner)

(3) I have to smoke a cigarette with my coffee → . . . smoke my coffee with a cigarette
(4) untactful → distactful
(5) an eating marathon → a meeting arathon
(6) executive committee → executor committee
(7) lady with the dachshund → lady with the Volkswagen
(8) are we taking the bus back → are we taking the buck bass
(9) he broke the crystal on my watch → he broke the whistle on my crotch
(10) a phonological rule → a phonological fool
(11) pitch and stress → piss and stretch
(12) Lebanon → Lemadon
(13) speech production → preach seduction
(14) he's a New Yorker → he's a New Yorkan
(15) I'd forgotten about that → I'd forgot abouten that
(16) It can deliver a large payload → It can deliver a large payroll (spoken by a congressional representative)
(17) He made headlines → He made hairlines (referring to a barber)
(18) I never heard of classes on Good Friday → I never heard of classes on April 9 (spoken by a student when Good Friday fell on April 9 that year)

2. Consider the following ambiguous sentences. Explain each ambiguity, give the most likely interpretation, and state what a computer would have to have in its knowledge base to achieve that interpretation.

Example: A cheesecake was on the table. It was delicious and was soon eaten.
    a. Ambiguity: "It" can refer to the cheesecake or the table.
    b. Likely: "It" refers to the cheesecake.
    c. Knowledge: Tables are not usually eaten.

(1) For those of you who have children and don't know it, we have a nursery downstairs. (Sign in a church)
(2) The police were asked to stop drinking in public places.
(3) Our bikinis are exciting; they are simply the tops. (Bathing suit ad in newspaper)
(4) It's time we made smoking history. (Antismoking campaign slogan)
(5) Do you know the time? (*Hint*: This is a pragmatic ambiguity.)
(6) Concerned with spreading violence, the president called a press conference.
(7) The ladies of the church have cast off clothing of every kind and they may be seen in the church basement Friday. (Announcement in a church bulletin)
(8) She earned little as a whiskey maker but he loved her still.
(9) The butcher backed into the meat grinder and got a little behind in his work.
(10) A dog gave birth to puppies near the road and was cited for littering.
(11) A hole was found in the nudist camp wall. The police are looking into it.

(12) A sign on the lawn at a drug rehab center said, "Keep off the Grass."

The following three items are newspaper headlines:

(13) Red Tape Holds Up New Bridge
(14) Kids Make Nutritious Snacks
(15) Sex Education Delayed, Teachers Request Training

3. Create five sentences containing temporary ambiguities. E.g. *Mary believed the boy was lying*. For each, explain how and when the ambiguity is resolved.

4. Consider the following two headlines:

   Physicists Thrilled To Explain What They Are Doing To People

   Two Sisters Reunited After 18 Years In Checkout Line

   a. What principle explains the unintended, funny interpretations of these headlines?
   b. How might you reorganize the words in the headlines to get rid of the unintended meanings?
   c. Check your local newspapers (or other sources) and see whether you can find similar examples.

5. Some sentences are more likely than others to give rise to a garden path effect even though they have the same structures. This is true of the sentence pairs below. Psycholinguistic experiments show that people misparse the **(a)** sentences less than the **(b)** sentences. Explain why.
   (1) a. The frustrated tourists understood the snow would mean a late start.
   b. The frustrated tourists understood the message would mean they couldn't go.
   (2) a. The ticket agent admitted the airplane had been late taking off.
   b. The ticket agent admitted the mistake had been careless and stupid.
   (3) a. Mary Ann's mother feared the dress would get torn and dirty.
   b. Mary Ann's mother feared the large wolf would escape from its cage.

6. Priming can be used not only by psycholinguists to study how language is organized in the brain, but to tell jokes and annoy your friends. Here are two jokes. Try them out on a number of people and report on what percentage "fall for it." Also, explain why priming is significant in the effectiveness of these jokes and what is primed. It's different in the two cases.

   (1) Begin my asking your friend to respond quickly without thinking as you rapidly say:

   If a soft drink is a coke,
   And a funny story is a joke,
   What do you call the white of an egg?

You'll be amazed at how many people will answer "yolk," whereas the answer is something like "albumin."

(2) Begin by telling your friend: "An airliner crashes, killing all aboard and comes to rest perfectly straddling the international border between the United States and Canada. Where do they bury the survivors?" Record the amount of time spent pondering this question before coming up with an answer. The answer doesn't matter; it may be one country or the other, or both, or simply "I don't know." Also record the percentage of subjects who realize that survivors are not (generally) buried.

7. The Nobel Prize laureate Roger Sperry has argued that split-brain patients have two minds:

> Everything we have seen so far indicates that the surgery has left these people with two separate minds, that is, two separate spheres of consciousness. What is experienced in the right hemisphere seems to lie entirely outside the realm of experience of the left hemisphere. (Sperry, R. W. [1966]. Brain bisection and mechanisms of consciousness. In J. C. Eccles [ed.] *Brain and consciousness experience.* Heidleberg: Springer-Verlag.)

Another Nobel Prize winner in physiology, Sir John Eccles, disagrees. He does not think the right hemisphere can think; he distinguishes between "mere consciousness," which animals possess as well as humans, and language, thought, and other purely human cognitive abilities. In fact, according to him, human nature is all in the left hemisphere.

Write a short essay discussing these two opposing points of view, stating your opinion on how to define "the mind."

8. a. Some aphasic patients, when asked to read a list of words, substitute other words for those printed. In many cases, the printed words and the substituted words are similar. The following data are from actual aphasic patients. In each case, state what the two words have in common and how they differ:

	Printed Word	**Word Spoken by Aphasic**
i.	liberty	freedom
	canary	parrot
	abroad	overseas
	large	long
	short	small
	tall	long
ii.	decide	decision
	conceal	concealment
	portray	portrait
	bathe	bath
	speak	discussion
	remember	memory

b. What do the words in groups **(i)** and **(ii)** reveal about how words are likely to be stored in the brain?

9. The following sentences spoken by aphasic patients were collected and analyzed by Dr. Harry Whitaker. In each case, state how the sentence deviates from normal nonaphasic language.

   a. There is under a horse a new sidesaddle.
   b. In girls we see many happy days.
   c. I'll challenge a new bike.
   d. I surprise no new glamour.
   e. Is there three chairs in this room?
   f. Mike and Peter is happy.
   g. Bill and John likes hot dogs.
   h. Proliferate is a complete time about a word that is correct.
   i. Went came in better than it did before.

10. The investigation of individuals with brain damage has been a major source of information regarding the neural basis of language and other cognitive systems. One might suggest that this is like trying to understand how an automobile engine works by looking at damaged engines. Is this a good analogy? If so, why? If not, why not? In your answer, discuss how a damaged system can or cannot provide information about the normal system.

11. What are the arguments and evidence that have been put forth to support the notion that there are two separate parts of the brain?

12. Discuss the statement: *It only takes one hemisphere to have a mind.*

13. In this chapter, dichotic listening tests in which subjects hear different kinds of stimuli in each ear were discussed. These tests showed that there were fewer errors made in reporting linguistic stimuli such as the syllables *pa*, *ta*, and *ka* when heard through an earphone on the right ear; other nonlinguistic sounds such as a police car siren were processed with fewer mistakes if heard by the left ear. This is a result of the contralateral control of the brain. There is also a technique that permits visual stimuli to be received either by the right visual field, that is, the right eye alone (going directly to the left hemisphere), or by the left visual field (going directly to the right hemisphere). What are some visual stimuli that could be used in an experiment to further test the lateralization of language?

14. The following utterances were made either by Broca's aphasics or Wernicke's aphasics. Indicate which is which by writing a "B" or "W" next to the utterance.

   a. Goodnight and in the pansy I can't say but into a flipdoor you can see it.
   b. Well . . . sunset . . . uh . . . horses nine, no, uh, two, tails want swish.
   c. Oh, . . . if I could I would, and a sick old man disflined a sinter, minter.
   d. Words . . . words . . . words . . . two, four, six, eight, . . . blaze am he.

15. Shakespeare's Hamlet surely had problems. Some say he was obsessed with being overweight because the first lines he speaks in the play when alone on the stage in Act II, Scene 2, are:

> O! that this too too solid flesh would melt,
> Thaw, and resolve itself into a dew;

Others argue that he may have had Wernicke's aphasia, as evidenced by the following passage from Act II, Scene 2:

> Slanders, sir: for the satirical rogue says here
> that old men have grey beards, that their faces are
> wrinkled, their eyes purging thick amber and
> plum-tree gum and that they have a plentiful lack of
> wit, together with most weak hams: all which, sir,
> though I most powerfully and potently believe, yet
> I hold it not honesty to have it thus set down, for you
> yourself, sir, should be old as I am, if like a crab
> you could go backward.

Take up the argument. Is Hamlet aphasic? Argue either case.

16. **Research projects:**
    a. Recently, it's been said that persons born with "perfect pitch" nonetheless need to exercise that ability at a young age or it goes away by adulthood. Find out what you can about this topic and write a one-page (or longer) paper describing your investigation. Begin with defining "perfect pitch." Relate your discoveries to the *critical-age hypothesis* discussed in this chapter.
    b. Consider some of the high-tech methodologies used to investigate the brain discussed in this chapter, such as PET scans, fMRIs and MEGs. What are the upsides and downsides of the use of these technologies on healthy patients? Consider the cost, the intrusiveness, and the ethics of exploring a person's brain weighed against the knowledge obtained from such studies.
    c. Investigate claims that PET scans show that reading silently and reading aloud involve different parts of the left hemisphere.

17. **Article review project**: Read, summarize, and critically review the article that appeared in *Science*, Volume 298, November 22, 2002, by Marc D. Hauser, Noam Chomsky, and W. Tecumseh Fitch, entitled "The Faculty of Language: What Is It, Who Has It, and How Did It Evolve?"

18. As discussed in the chapter, agrammatic aphasics may have difficulty reading function words, which are words that have little descriptive content, but they can read content words such as nouns, verbs, and adjectives.

a. Which of the following words would you predict to be difficult for such a person?

ore	bee	can (be able to)	but
not	knot	may	be
may	can (metal container)	butt	or
will (future)	might (possibility)	will (willingness)	might (strength)

b. Discuss three sources of evidence that function words and content words are stored or processed differently in the brain.

19. The traditional writing system of the Chinese languages (e.g., Mandarin, Cantonese) is ideographic (each concept or word is represented by a distinct character). More recently, the Chinese government has adopted a spelling system called *pinyin*, which is based on the Roman alphabet, and in which each symbol represents a sound. Following are several Chinese words in their character and *pinyin* forms. (The digit following the Roman letters in *pinyin* is a tone indicator and may be ignored.)

木	mu4	tree
花	hua1	flower
人	ren2	man
家	jia1	home
狗	gou3	dog

Based on the information provided in this chapter, would the location of neural activity be the same or different when Chinese speakers read in these two systems? Explain.

20. **Research project**: Dame Margaret Thatcher, a former prime minister of the United Kingdom, has been (famously) quoted as saying: "If you want something said, ask a man . . . if you want something done, ask a woman." (She is also the subject of a major motion picture entitled *The Iron Lady* that won many awards in 2012.) Her remark suggests, perhaps, that men and women process information differently. This exercise asks you to take up the controversial question: *Are there gender differences in the brain having to do with how men and women process and use language?* You might begin your research by seeking answers (try the Internet) to questions about the incidence of SLI, dyslexia, and language development differences in boys and girls.

21. **Research project**: Discuss the concept of *emergence*, namely, that "A major step in the development of language most probably relates to evolutionary changes in the brain," and its relevance to the quoted material below, contrasting the views of Chomsky and Gould as opposed to Pinker.

The linguist Noam Chomsky expresses this view:

> It could be that when the brain reached a certain level of complexity it simply automatically had certain properties because that's what happens when you pack 10^{10} neurons into something the size of a basketball.[1]

The biologist Stephen Jay Gould expresses a similar view:

> The Darwinist model would say that language, like other complex organic systems, evolved step by step, each step being an adaptive solution. Yet language is such an integrated "all or none" system, it is hard to imagine it evolving that way. Perhaps the brain grew in size and became capable of all kinds of things which were not part of the original properties.[2]

Other linguists such as Stephen Pinker, however, support a more Darwinian natural selection development of what is sometimes called "the language instinct":

> All the evidence suggests that it is the precise wiring of the brain's microcircuitry that makes language happen, not gross size, shape, or neuron packing.[3]

---

[1]Chomsky, N., in Searchinger, G. 1994. The human language series 3. Video. New York: Equinox Film/Ways of Knowing, Inc.

[2]Gould, S. J., in Searchinger, G. 1994. The human language series 3. Video. New York: Equinox Film/Ways of Knowing, Inc.

[3]Pinker, S. 1995. *The language instinct.* New York: William Morrow.

11

Computer Processing of Human Language

Man is still the most extraordinary computer of all.

JOHN F. KENNEDY (1917–1963)

Until a few decades ago, language was strictly "humans only—others need not apply." Today, it is common for computers to process language. **Computational linguistics** is a subfield of linguistics and computer science that is concerned with the interactions of human language and computers.

Computational linguistics includes the analysis of written texts and spoken discourse, the translation of text and speech from one language to another, the use of *human* (not computer) languages for communication between computers and people, and the modeling and testing of linguistic theories.

Computers That Talk and Listen

The first generations of computers had received their inputs through glorified typewriter keyboards, and had replied through high-speed printers and visual displays. HAL could do this when necessary, but most of his communication with his shipmates was by means of the spoken words. Poole and Bowman could talk to HAL as if he were a human being, and he would reply in the perfect idiomatic English he had learned during the fleeting weeks of his electronic childhood.

ARTHUR C. CLARKE, *2001: A Space Odyssey*, 1968

The ideal computer is multilingual; it should "speak" computer languages such as Visual Basic and Java, and human languages such as French and Japanese. For many purposes it would be helpful if we could communicate with computers as we communicate with other humans, through our native language. But as of the year 2013, the "computers" portrayed in films and on television as capable of speaking and understanding human language as we do don't exist. (We use 'scare quotes' because nowadays computers are concealed in many everyday objects and we shall use the term *computer* in this general sense.) Even the latest generation of speech-understanding mobile communication devices, while impressive, cannot maintain a drawn-out linguistic interaction.

Computational linguistics is concerned with the interaction between language and computers in all dimensions, from phonetics to pragmatics, from producing speech to comprehending speech, from spoken (or signed) utterances to written forms. **Computational phonetics and phonology** is concerned with processing speech. Its main goals are converting speech to text on the comprehension side, and text to speech on the production side. The areas of **computational morphology**, **computational syntax**, **computational semantics**, and **computational pragmatics**, discussed below, are concerned with higher levels of linguistic processing.

Computational Phonetics and Phonology

The two sides of computational phonetics and phonology are **speech recognition** and **speech synthesis**. Speech recognition is the process of analyzing the speech signal into its component phones and phonemes, and producing, in effect, a phonetic transcription of the speech. Further processing may convert the transcription into ordinary text for output on a screen, or for further processing such as a speech understanding application. (*Note:* Speech recognition is *not* the same as speech understanding, as is commonly thought. Rather, speech recognition is a necessary precursor to the far more complex process of comprehension.)

Speech synthesis is the process of creating electronic signals that simulate the phones and prosodic features of speech and assemble them into words and phrases for output to an electronic speaker, or for further processing as in a language generation application.

Speech Recognition

When Frederic was a little lad he proved so brave and daring,

His father thought he'd 'prentice him to some career seafaring.

I was, alas! his nurs'rymaid, and so it fell to my lot

To take and bind the promising boy apprentice to a pilot—

A life not bad for a hardy lad, though surely not a high lot,

Though I'm a nurse, you might do worse than make your boy a pilot.

I was a stupid nurs'rymaid, on breakers always steering,

And I did not catch the word aright, through being hard of hearing;

Mistaking my instructions, which within my brain did gyrate

I took and bound this promising boy apprentice to a pirate.

GILBERT AND SULLIVAN, *The Pirates of Penzance*, 1879

When you listen to someone speak a foreign language, you notice that it is continuous except for breath pauses, and that it is difficult to segment the speech into sounds and words. It's all run together. In the previous chapter we referred to this as the segmentation problem. The computer also faces this situation when it tries to do speech recognition.

Early speech recognizers were not designed to "hear" individual sounds. Computers were programmed to store the acoustic patterns of entire words or even phrases in their memories, and then further instructed to look for those patterns in any subsequent speech they were asked to recognize. The computers had a fixed, small vocabulary. Moreover, they best recognized the speech of the same person who provided the original word patterns. They would have trouble "understanding" a different speaker, and if a word outside their vocabulary was uttered, the computers were clueless. If the words were run together, recognition accuracy also fell, and if the words were not fully pronounced, say *missipi* for Mississippi, failure generally ensued. Coarticulation effects also muddied the waters. The computers might have [hɪz] as their representation of the word *his*, but in the sequence *his soap*, pronounced [hɪssop], the *his* is pronounced [hɪs] with a voiceless [s]. In addition, the vocabulary best consisted of words that were not too similar phonetically, avoiding confusion between words like *pilot* and *pirate*, which might, as with the young lad in the song, have grave consequences.

Today, many interactive phone systems have a speech recognition component. They will invite you to "press 1 or say *yes*; press 2 or say *no*," or perhaps offer a menu of choices triggered by one or more spoken word responses. Sophisticated mobile phones allow their owners to preprogram complete phrases such as *call my office* or *display the calendar*. These systems have very small vocabularies and so can search the speech signal for anything resembling the acoustic patterns of a keyword and generally get it right.

The more sophisticated speech recognizers that can be purchased for use on a personal computer have much larger vocabularies. To be highly accurate they must adapt to the voice of a specific person, and they must be able to detect individual phones in the speech signal, even when they are fleeting, for a significant meaning difference may ensue. (Compare *The Marines are looking for* **a** *few good men* versus *The Marines are looking for* _____ *few good men,* or the still controversial words of the late Neil Armstrong when he descended from his space capsule onto the surface of the moon. Was it: That's one small step for a man, one giant leap for mankind, or was it: That's one small step for _____ man, one giant leap for mankind?) Adaptation consists in the user making multiple utterances known in advance to the computer, which extracts the acoustic patterns of each phone typical of that user. Later the computer uses those patterns to aid in the recognition process. This is **speaker dependent speech recognition**.

Because no two utterances are ever identical, and because there is generally noise (nonspeech sounds) in the signal, the matching process that underlies speech recognition is statistical. On the phonetic level, the computations may classify some stretch of sound in its input as [l] with 65 percent confidence and [r] with 35 percent confidence. Other factors may be used to help the decision. For example, if the computer is confident that the preceding sound is [d] and begins the word, then [r] is the likely candidate, because no words begin with /dl/ in English. The system takes advantage of its (i.e., the programmer's) knowledge of phonotactic constraints (see chapter 6). If, on the other hand, the sound occurs at the beginning of the word, further information is needed to determine whether it is the phoneme /l/ or /r/. If the following sounds are [up] then /l/ is the one, because *loop* is a word but **roop* is not. If the computer is unable to decide, it may offer a list of choices such as *late* and *rate* and ask the person using the system to decide. The most sophisticated speech recognizers in use nowadays have access to gigantic corpuses of language (we're talking billions of words) and may use the past frequencies of occurrence to assist in a decision. If the choice came down to *look* versus *rook,* the more frequently occurring *look* would be preferred.

Advanced speech recognizers may also utilize syntactic rules to further disambiguate an utterance. If the *late/rate* syntactic context is "It's too _____" the choice is *late* because *too* may be followed by an adjective but not by a noun or verb. Statistical disambiguation based on corpuses of English may also be used. Occurrences of "It's too late . . ." would occur far more frequently than "It's to rate . . ." A statistical model can be built based on such facts that would lead the machine to lend weight to the choice of *late* rather than *rate* in the particular context.

Even these modern systems, with all the computing power behind them, are brittle. They "break" when circumstances become unfavorable. If the user speaks rapidly with lots of coarticulation (*whatcha* for *what are you*), and there is a lot of background noise, recognition accuracy plummets. People do better. If someone mumbles, you can generally make out what they are saying because you have context to help you. In a noisy setting such as a party, you are able to converse with your dance partner despite the background noise because your brain has the ability to filter out irrelevant sounds and zero in on the voice of a single speaker. This effect is so striking it is given a name: the **cocktail party effect**. Computers are not nearly as capable as people in coping with noisy environments, although research directed at the problem is beginning to reap positive (and profitable) results, as the Apple, Inc. "personal assistant" called *Siri,* and other similar systems for use in vocal mobile device communications, are beginning to show.

Speech Synthesis

Machines which, with more or less success, imitate human speech, are the most difficult to construct, so many are the agencies engaged in uttering even a single word—so many are the inflections and variations of tone and articulation, that the mechanician finds his ingenuity taxed to the utmost to imitate them.

SCIENTIFIC AMERICAN, January 14, 1871

Early efforts toward building "talking machines" were concerned with machines that could produce sounds that imitated human speech. In 1779,

Christian Gottlieb Kratzenstein won a prize for building such a machine. It was "an instrument constructed like the vox humana pipes of an organ which . . . accurately express the sounds of the vowels." In building this machine he also answered a question posed by the Imperial Academy of St. Petersburg, Russia: "What is the nature and character of the sounds of the vowels *a, e, i, o, u* [that make them] different from one another?" Kratzenstein constructed a set of "acoustic resonators" similar to the shapes of the mouth when these vowels are articulated and set them resonating by a vibrating reed that produced pulses of air similar to those coming from the lungs through the vibrating vocal cords.

Nearly a century later, a young Alexander Graham Bell, always fascinated with speech and its production, fabricated a "talking head" from a cast of a human skull. He used various materials to form the velum, palate, teeth, lips, tongue, cheeks, and so on, and installed a metal larynx with vocal cords made by stretching a slotted piece of rubber. A keyboard control system manipulated all the parts with an intricate set of levers. This ingenious machine produced vowel sounds, some nasal sounds, and even a few short combinations of sounds.

With the advances in the acoustic theory of speech production and the technological developments in electronics, machine production of speech sounds has made great progress. We no longer have to build physical models of the speech-producing mechanism; we can now imitate the process by producing the physical signals electronically.

Speech sounds can be reduced to a small number of acoustic components. One way to produce synthetic speech is to mix these components together in the proper proportions, depending on the speech sounds to be imitated. It is rather like following a recipe for making soup, which might read: "Take two quarts of water, add one onion, three carrots, a potato, a teaspoon of salt, a pinch of pepper, and stir it all together."

This method of producing synthetic speech would include a recipe that might read:

1. Start with a tone at the same frequency as vibrating vocal cords (higher if a woman's or child's voice is being synthesized, lower for a man's).
2. Emphasize the harmonics corresponding to the formants required for a particular vowel, liquid, or nasal quality.
3. Add hissing or buzzing for fricatives.
4. Add nasal resonances for nasal sounds.
5. Temporarily cut off sound to produce stops and affricates.
6. and so on. . .

All of these ingredients are blended electronically, using computers to produce highly intelligible, more or less natural-sounding speech. Because item (2) is central to the process, this method of speech synthesis is called **formant synthesis**.

Most synthetic speech still has a machinelike quality or accent, caused by small inaccuracies in simulation, and because suprasegmental factors such as changing intonation and stress patterns are not yet fully understood. If not correct, such factors may be more confusing than mispronounced phonemes.

Currently, the chief area of research in speech synthesis is concerned precisely with discovering and programming the rules of rhythm and timing that native speakers apply. Still, speech synthesizers today are no harder to understand than a person speaking a dialect slightly different from one's own, and when the context is sufficiently narrow, as in a synthetic voice reading a weather report (a common application), there are few problems.

An alternative approach to formant synthesis is **concatenative synthesis**. The basic units of concatenative synthesis are recorded units such as phones, diphones, syllables, morphemes, words, phrases, and sentences. A diphone is a transitional unit comprising the last portion of one phone plus the first portion of another, used to smooth coarticulation effects. There may be hundreds or even thousands of these little acoustic pieces. The recordings are made by human speakers. The synthesis aspect is in the assembling of the individual units to form the desired computer-spoken utterance. This would not be possible without the increased computational power now available, and today's synthesizers – especially the ones used in mobile communications – are generally of this type.

The challenge in concatenative synthesis is achieving the fluidity of human speech. This requires electronic fine tuning of speech prosody: that is, duration, intonation, pitch, and loudness, on which naturalness is based. Now, in the second decade of the twenty-first century, near-naturalness has been achieved by the best synthesizers. Still, the units do not always fit together seamlessly, and the perfection of prosodic effects remains elusive, so a human listener often perceives an "accent."

Text-to-Speech

Speak clearly, if you speak at all; carve every word before you let it fall.

OLIVER WENDELL HOLMES, SR. (1809–1894)

To provide input to the speech synthesizer, a computer program called **text-to-speech** converts written text into the basic units of the synthesizer. For formant synthesizers, the text-to-speech process translates the input text into a phonetic representation. This task is like the several exercises at the end of chapter 5 in which we asked you for phonetic transcriptions of written words. Naturally, the text-to-speech process *precedes* the electronic conversion to sound.

For concatenative synthesizers, the text-to-speech process translates the input text into a representation based on whatever units are to be concatenated. For a syllable-based synthesizer, the text-to-speech program would take *The number is 5557766* as input and produce [θə] [nʌ̃m] [bər] [ɪz] [faɪv] [faɪv] [faɪv] [sɛv] [ə̃n] [sɛv] [ə̃n] [sɪks] [sɪks] as output. The "synthesizer" (a computer program) would look up the various syllables in its memory and concatenate them, with further electronic processing supplied for realistic prosody and to smooth over the syllable boundaries. Telephones and mobile devices that attempt to do text-to-speech and announce who's calling, e.g., "unknown caller" or "number not available," often fail on unusual callers ("Mike Krzyzewski") to the point of incomprehensibility if not outright annoyance.

The difficulties of text-to-speech are legion. We will mention two. The first is the problem of words spelled alike but pronounced differently (called heteronyms, see chapter 4). *Read* may be pronounced as [rɛd] in *She has read the book*, but as [riːd] in *She will read the book*. How does the text-to-speech system know which is which? Make no mistake about the answer: the machine must have structural knowledge of the sentence to make the correct choice, just as humans must. Unstructured, linear knowledge will not suffice. For example, we might program the text-to-speech system to pronounce *read* as [rɛd] when the previous word is a form of *have*, but this approach fails in several ways. First, *have* governs the pronunciation at a distance, both from the left and the right, as in *Has the girl with the flaxen hair read the book?* and *Oh, read a lot of books, has he!* The underlying structure needs to be known, namely, that *has* is an auxiliary verb for the main verb *to read*. If we try the strategy "pronounce *read* as [rɛd] whenever *have* is 'in the vicinity,'" we would induce an error in sentences like *The teacher said to have the girl read the book by tomorrow*, where [riːd] is the required pronunciation. Even worse for the linear analysis are sentences like *Which girl did the teacher have read from the book?* where the words *have read* occur next to each other, but the correct version is [riːd]. Of course you know that this occurrence of *read* is [riːd], because you know English and therefore know English syntactic structures. Only through structural knowledge can the heteronym problem be approached effectively. We'll learn more about this in the section on computational syntax later in the chapter.

The second difficulty is inconsistent spelling, which is well illustrated by the first two lines of a longer poem:

I take it you already know

Of tough and bough and cough and dough

Each of the *ough* words is phonetically different, but it is difficult to find rules that dictate when *gh* should be [f] and when it is silent, or how to pronounce the *ou*. Modern computers have sufficient storage capacity to store the recorded pronunciation of every word in a language, its alternative pronunciations, and its likely pronunciations, which may be determined by an extensive statistical analysis. This list may include acronyms, abbreviations, foreign words, proper names, numbers including fractions, and special symbols such as #, &, *, %, and so on. Such a list is helpful—it is like memorizing rather than figuring out the pronunciations—and encompasses a large percentage of items, including the *ough* words. This is the basis of word-level concatenative synthesis. However, the list can never be complete. New words, foreign words, proper names, abbreviations, and acronyms are constantly being added to the English dictionary (e.g., 'obesogenic' in 2012) and their correct pronunciation often cannot be anticipated. The text-to-speech system requires conversion rules for items not in its dictionary, and these must be output by a formant synthesizer or a concatenative synthesizer based on units smaller than the word itself if they are to be spoken. The challenges here are similar to those faced when learning to read aloud, which are considerable and, when it comes to the pronunciation of proper names (try 'Recep Tayyip Ergoğan,' the prime minister of Turkey), or foreign words ('weltanschauungs,' German for "world view philosophy."), utterly daunting.

Speech synthesis has important applications. It benefits visually impaired people in the form of "reading machines," now commercially available, and vocal output of what is displayed on a computer screen. Mute patients with laryngectomies or other medical conditions that prevent normal speech can use synthesizers to express themselves. For example, researchers at North Carolina State University developed a communication system for an individual with so severe a form of multiple sclerosis that he could utter no sound and was totally paralyzed except for nodding his head. Using a head movement for *yes* and its absence as *no*, this individual could select words displayed on a computer screen and assemble sentences to express his thoughts, which were then spoken by a synthesizer. The means of communication utilized by the severely disabled world-renowned physicist Stephen Hawking are legion: try http://singularityhub.com/2010/05/03/how-does-stephen-hawking-talk-video/ to explore them on the Internet.

Computational Morphology

If we wish our computers to speak and understand grammatical English, we must teach them morphology (see chapter 2). We can't have machines going around saying "*The cat is sit on the mat" or "*My five horse be in the barn." Similarly, if computers are to understand English, they need to know that *sitting* contains two morphemes, *sit + ing*, whereas *spring* is one morpheme, and *reinvent* is two but they are *re + invent*, not *rein + vent*.

The processing of word structures by computers is computational morphology. The computer needs to understand the structure of words both to understand the words and to use the words in a grammatically correct way. To process words, the computer is programmed to look for roots and affixes. In some cases this process is straightforward. *Books* is easily broken into *book + s*, *walking* into *walk + ing*, *fondness* into *fond + ness*, and *unhappy* into *un + happy*. These cases, and many like them, are the easy ones, because the spelling is well behaved, and the morphological processes are general. Other words are more difficult, such as *profundity = profound + ity*, *galactic = galaxy + ic*, and *democracy = democrat + y*.

One approach is to place all the morphological forms of all the words in the language into the computer's dictionary. Although today's computers can handle such a high computational load—many millions of forms—there would still be problems because of the generality of the processes. As soon as a new word enters the language, as *blog* did some years ago, a whole family of words is possible: *blogs, blog's, blogging, blogged, reblog*, and *blogable*; and many others are not possible (or seem unlikely – we can't predict): **blogify, *exblog, *disblog*, and so on. The dictionary would be continually out of date.

Moreover, not all forms are predictable. Although *heaten* is not a dictionary word, if you hear it you know, and the computer should know, that it means 'to make hot.' Likewise, compounding is a general process, and it would be impossible to predict all possible compounds of English. When *podcast* was coined from *pod + cast*, no computer could have had it in its dictionary.

The computer needs to have the ability to break words correctly into their component morphemes, and to understand each morpheme and its effect on a word's meaning, and where the word can be placed in a sentence. Computational morphology, then, is a host of interwoven rules, exceptions, and word/morpheme forms, all with the purpose of comprehending the internal structure of words.

One method of morphological analysis is called **stemming**. Here, affixes are detected and repeatedly stripped off the beginnings and ends of words, checking the work against the computer's dictionary. For example, if the word to be analyzed is *befriended*, the computer would recognize and verify the prefix *be-* and the suffix *-ed*, leaving behind the root *friend*, all of which would be verified in a dictionary of words and morphemes. More complex words such as *unsystematically* would be repeatedly broken down into *-ly* (an adverb-former), *-al*, *-atic* (both adjective-formers), *system* (a root word), and *un-* (a negative morpheme).

Difficult problems always remain. If the computer sees *resent*, how does it know if it's the monomorphemic *resent* (with a /z/), or *re + sent*? A broader context is needed, and that is the topic of the next section.

Computational Syntax

Good order is the foundation of all things.

EDMUND BURKE, *Reflections on the Revolution in France*, 1790

To understand a sentence, you must know its syntactic structure. If you didn't know the structure of *dogs that chase cats chase birds*, you wouldn't know whether dogs or cats chase birds. Similarly, machines that understand language must also determine syntactic structure. A **parser** is a computer program that attempts to replicate the structural knowledge that speakers possess. Like us, the parser in a computer uses a grammar to compute the structure of a string of words. Parsers may use structural principles and lexicons similar to those discussed in chapter 3.

For example, a parser may contain the following rules:
(1) A Sentence is (often) a Noun Phrase (or Subject) followed by a Verb Phrase (or Predicate).
(2) A Noun Phrase is (often) a Determiner followed by a Noun.

Suppose the machine is asked to parse *The child found the kittens*. A top-down parser proceeds by first consulting the grammar rules and then examining the input string to see if the first word could begin a Sentence. If the input string begins with a Determiner such as *the*, as in the example, the search is successful, and the parser continues by looking for a Noun, and then a Verb Phrase. If the input string happened to be *child found the kittens*, the parser would be unable to assign it a structure owing to the missing Determiner and would report that the sentence is ungrammatical.

A bottom-up parser takes the opposite tack. It looks first at the input string and finds a Determiner (*the*) followed by a Noun (*child*). Rule 2 tells it that this phrase is a Noun Phrase. It would continue to process *found*, *the*, and *kittens* to construct a Verb Phrase, and would finally combine the two into a Sentence.

Parsers may run into difficulties with words that belong to several syntactic categories. In a sentence like *The little orange rabbit hopped*, the parser might mistakenly assume *orange* is a noun. Later, when the error is apparent, the parser backtracks to the decision point, and retries with *orange* as an adjective. Such a strategy works on confusing but grammatical sentences like *The old man the boats* and *The Russian women loved died*, which cause a garden path effect for humans.

Another way to handle such ambiguous situations is for the computer to try every parse that the grammar allows in parallel. Only parses that finish are accepted as valid. In such a strategy, two parses of *The Russian women loved died* would be explored simultaneously: *Russian* would be an adjective in one and a noun in the other. The adjective parse would get as far as *The Russian women loved* but then fail since *died* cannot occur in that position of a verb phrase. (The parser must not allow ungrammatical sentences such as **The blonde women loved died*.) This parse does not finish because it leaves the word *died* without an analysis. The other parse, when it sees the two nouns *Russian women* together, deduces the presence of a relative clause, which would have been obvious if the word *that* had preceded *women* (but English allows it to be left out). The parser is then able to assign the category of noun phrase to *The Russian women loved*. The sentence is completed with the verb *died*, which can form a verb phrase, and the parse finishes successfully.

People usually handle ambiguity and get to the intended meaning easily, and we do not see much evidence that they are doing lots of extra work to deal with additional possible meanings. Fiendish linguists must toil long and hard to come up with examples like the garden path sentences discussed earlier that confuse the "human parser" and also to devise on-line processing experiments that can detect very small reaction time differences.

Computers may outperform humans in certain cases, however, because they are still semantically naïve. For example, try to figure out all the possible meanings of the sentence *Time flies like an arrow*. A computer parser does it easily. (Hint: Several of the words can belong to more than one syntactic category.) It turns out there are five (at least). The usual sense is 'The way that time flies is the way that an arrow flies' (i.e., quickly). But it can also mean that a particular species of flies, namely "time-flies," are fond of an arrow. Or, it can be a command: '(Please) time (a bunch of) flies in the same way that you would time an arrow!' (e.g., with a stopwatch). Another reading is again a command to time something, but in this case the things to be timed are 'flies (that are) like an arrow.' There is one more (even less plausible) reading: can you find it?[1]

We not only want computers to understand language, we also want them to be able to produce new sentences—ones that are not pre-stored—and this also requires knowledge of the syntactic rules of the grammar. In some cases the programming may be done simplistically. For example, a computer program to generate insults in the style of Shakespeare takes three columns of words, where the first column is a list of simple adjectives, the second a list of hyphenated adjectives, and the third a list of nouns:

---

[1] (Please) time (a bunch of) flies in the same way that an (animate) arrow with a stopwatch would time them.'

Simple Adjectives	Hyphenated Adjectives	Nouns
bawdy	beetle-headed	baggage
churlish	clay-brained	bladder
goatish	fly-bitten	codpiece
lumpish	milk-livered	hedge-pig
mewling	pox-marked	lout
rank	rump-fed	miscreant
villainous	toad-spotted	varlet

The program chooses a word from each column at random to produce a noun phrase insult. Instantaneous insults guaranteed: you goatish, pox-marked bladder; you lumpish, milk-livered hedge-pig.

A less simplistic system might first assign lexical items to the ideas and concepts to be expressed. These, then, must be fit into phrases and sentences that comply with the syntax of the output language. As in parsing, there are two approaches: top-down and bottom-up. In the top-down approach, the system begins with the highest-level categories such as Sentence. Lower levels are filled in progressively, beginning with noun phrases and verb phrases, and descending to determiners, nouns, verbs, and other sentence parts, always conforming to the syntactic rules.

The bottom-up approach begins with the lexical items needed to express the desired meaning, and proceeds to combine them to form the higher-level categories. (Here, too, it is not yet known to what extent human language production employs one or other of these approaches.)

It is not always clear which part of language analysis or language generation is syntactic, and which part is semantic. In considering *time flies like an arrow*, should all of the syntactic parses be presented to a semantic analyzer? Or should both syntactic and semantic analyses occur simultaneously so that the parse in which the arrow does the timing (see footnote 1), which is semantically anomalous, is immediately discarded? Or, as some linguists would have it, should the semantic analysis come first and "drive" the syntactic analysis? These are active areas of recent research both in psycholinguistics and computational linguistics.

Computational Semantics

"Zits", 2001 Zits Partnership. Reprinted with permission of King Features Syndicate

The question of how to represent meaning is one that has been debated for thousands of years, and it continues to engender much research in linguistics, philosophy, psychology, cognitive science, and computer science. In chapter 4 we discussed many of the semantic concepts that a natural language system would incorporate into its operation. For simplicity's sake, we consider computational semantics to be the representation of the meanings of words and morphemes in the computer, as well as the meanings derived from their combinations.

Computational semantics has two chief concerns. One is to produce a semantic representation of language input (speech understanding); the other is to take a semantic representation and produce natural language output that conveys the meaning (speech generation). For example, consider this excerpt from a spoken dialogue system called "The Circuit Fix-It Shop," designed to help a technician repair a faulty circuit:

COMPUTER:	This is the Circuit Fix-It Shop. How may I help you?
TECHNICIAN:	I need to fix the RS111 circuit.
COMPUTER:	I am familiar with that circuit. The LED is supposed to be displaying alternately blinking one and seven.
TECHNICIAN:	Where is the LED?
COMPUTER:	In the middle right of the blue region is the LED.
TECHNICIAN:	No light.
COMPUTER:	What is the switch at when the LED is off?
TECHNICIAN:	The switch is down.
COMPUTER:	You put up the switch.

When in operation the Circuit Fix-It Shop computer must create a semantic representation of the user's input, act on it, and produce another semantic representation, which it then outputs to the user in ordinary language.

To generate sentences, the computer tries to find words that fit the concepts incorporated into its semantic representation. In the Circuit Fix-It Shop system, the computer must decide what to talk about next: the switch, the user, the light, wire 134, or whatever. It needs to choose words corresponding to whether to describe the state of an object in its purview, ask about the state of an object in the user's purview, make a request of the user, tell the user what to do next, and so forth. If the query involves the user, the pronoun *you* is chosen; if the state of the switch is the chief concern, the words *the switch,* or *a switch above the blue light,* are chosen. When the components of meaning are assembled, the syntactic rules that we have seen already are called upon to produce grammatical output.

To achieve **speech understanding**, the computer tries to find concepts in its semantic representation that fit the words and structures of the input. When the technician says *I need to fix the RS111 circuit,* the system recognizes that *I* means the user, that *need* represents something that the user lacks and the computer must provide. It further knows that if fixing is what is needed, it has to provide information about the workings of something. It recognizes *the RS111 circuit* as a circuit with certain properties that are contained in its semantic representation. The system infers that the workings of that particular circuit will be central to the ensuing dialogue.

A computer can represent concepts in numerous ways, none of them perfect or preferable to others. All methods share one commonality: a lexicon of words and morphemes that it is prepared to speak or understand. Such a

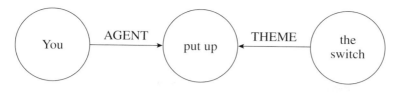

FIGURE 11.1 | Semantic network for *You put up the switch.*

lexicon would contain morphological, syntactic, and semantic information, as discussed in chapters 2, 3, and 4. Exactly how that information is structured depends on the particular applications it is to be suited for.

Many schemes for semantic representation have been developed by computational linguists. One is the use of networks that connect words to their thematic roles (see chapter 4). For example *You put up the switch* might have the representation in Figure 11.1.

This means that the user (*you*) is the agent, or doer, and *put up* is what is to be done, and it is to be done to the theme, which is *the switch.*

Other systems draw on formal logic for semantic representations. *You put up the switch* would be represented in a function/argument form, which is its logical form:

PUT UP (YOU, THE SWITCH)

where PUT UP is a "two-place predicate," in the jargon of logicians, and the arguments are YOU and THE SWITCH. The lexicon indicates the appropriate relationships between the arguments of the predicate PUT UP.

SHRDLU (http://hci.stanford.edu/~winograd/shrdlu/) is an early natural language processing system that used the predicate-argument approach to semantic representation. It demonstrated several semantic abilities, such as being able to interpret questions, draw inferences, learn new words, and even explain its own actions.

More recently question-answering systems such as Wolfram Alpha for computers, and Siri, a personal assistant app for the iPhone operating system, use logic, structured data (e.g., semantic features: see chapter 4), and other advanced techniques to form semantic representations of queries and of natural-language responses to those queries.

Computational Pragmatics

"Baby Blues", Baby Blues Partnership. Reprinted with permission of King Features Syndicate

Pragmatics, as discussed in chapter 4, is the interaction of the "real world" with the language system. In the Circuit Fix-It Shop, the computer knows that there is only one switch, that there is no other switch in the (its) universe, and hence that the determiner *the* is correct for this item. If the human mentioned *a wire*, however, the computer would ask *which wire* because it knows that there are several wires in the circuit. This is simple, computational pragmatics in action.

When a sentence is structurally ambiguous, such as *He saw the boy with a bicycle* ('use a bicycle to see the boy,' or 'see a boy and a bicycle'), the parser will compute each structure. Semantic processing may eliminate some of the structures if they are anomalous (in this case, a bicycle is not a tool for viewing objects, so one parse can be ruled out). *He saw the boy with a telescope* is semantically sensible in both parses and situational—pragmatic—knowledge is needed to determine the intended meaning.

Many natural language processing systems have a knowledge base of contextual and world knowledge. The semantic processing routines can refer to the knowledge base in cases of ambiguity. For example, the syntactic component of the Circuit Fix-It Shop will have two structures for *The LED is in the middle of the blue region at the top*. The sentence is ambiguous. Both meanings are semantically well formed and conceivable. However, the Circuit Fix-It Shop's knowledge base "knows" that the LED is in the middle of the blue region, and the blue region is at the top of the work area, rather than that the LED is in the top of the middle part of the blue region. It uses pragmatic knowledge—knowledge of the world—to disambiguate the sentence.

Another of the many tasks of computational pragmatics is to determine when two expressions refer to the same object: for example, determining the referents of pronouns (see chapter 4). This task of **reference resolution** combines morphological, syntactic, and semantic knowledge, as well as situational context. If the dialogue in the Circuit Fix-It Shop is:

COMPUTER: I am familiar with those circuits. The LED is supposed to be displaying alternately blinking one and seven.

TECHNICIAN: Where is **it**?

the computer must resolve the reference of *it*. The algorithm is to examine previous noun phrases for likely candidates, eliminating them based on both linguistic factors and situation. In this case the two possibilities are *those circuits* and *the LED*, but only the latter matches the singular pronoun.

Computational Sign Language

Research linguists are working on computer algorithms that will recognize sign language much in the same way that speech may be recognized. Signers may sign in front of a camera (like speaking into a microphone) and the computer will attempt to match the sign from a set of prestored signs via visual processing, just as it will attempt to match a sound from a set of prestored acoustic wave forms via audio processing. Visual processing in this case means detecting the shapes and gestures of the hands, their trajectories, and their orientations. These are difficult algorithms to construct and success has so far been limited.

The purpose of this enterprise is twofold. One is to produce a video dictionary of signs. Someone who can imitate a sign but doesn't know its meaning can look it up in the video dictionary just as one uses an ordinary dictionary to look up a written word. Both native and non-native ASL "speakers" could use such a dictionary. The second purpose is to enable a computer to search through ASL videos for a particular sign, just as a search engine like Google searches for certain key words in text documents.

One challenge the ASL dictionary makers must meet is the dialectal variations that signers exhibit. This is analogous to the different spelling systems of American, British, and Australian English, which occasionally challenge the editors of dictionaries. The visual processing system must take into account the nonlinguistic differences of signs to achieve a proper lookup. Once again we see that signed languages share all the advantages and disadvantages that are part of language in general.

Applications of Computational Linguistics

The usefulness of computers in every imaginable language-related field is unquestioned. We have already touched upon several of these in our investigation into the various subfields of computational linguistics, such as natural language interfaces to various kinds of computer programs.

In this section we discuss some of the more common application areas, ranging from the use of computers to test a linguist's grammar for faithfulness to the actual language, to the use of computers to solve language crimes—the field of computational forensic linguistics.

Computer Models of Grammar

I am never content until I have constructed a . . . model of the subject I am studying. If I succeed in making one, I understand; otherwise I do not.

WILLIAM THOMSON (LORD KELVIN), *Molecular Dynamics and the Wave Theory of Light*, 1904

A theory has only the alternative of being right or wrong. A model has a third possibility: it may be right, but irrelevant.

MANFRED EIGEN, *The Physicist's Conception of Nature*, 1973

The grammars used by computers may not be the same as the grammars that linguists construct for human languages, which are models of linguistic competence; nor are they similar, for the most part, to models of linguistic performance. Computers and people are different, and they achieve similar ends differently. Just as an efficient flying machine is not a replica of any bird (at least not yet – there are bird-like aircraft in the development stage), efficient grammars for computers do not resemble human language grammars in every detail.

However, computers may be programmed to model the linguist's description of the (human) grammar of a language. An accurate grammar—one that is a true model of a speaker's competence—should be able to generate all and only the sentences of the language. Failure to generate a grammatical sentence indicates an error in the grammar, as does the generation of a string that speakers consider ungrammatical. Although in actual speech we may produce (technically) ungrammatical strings—sentence fragments, slips of the tongue, and so on—owing to performance, we will judge them to be ill-formed if we notice them. Because grammars are infinite in scope, prodigious amounts of testing are necessary to verify their linguistic description, and that's where computers play an important role.

Computer models of linguists' grammars date back to the 1960s, when programs to test a generative grammar of English were designed by syntacticians at UCLA. Such models are still being developed to test newer theories of grammar. Computational linguists develop computer programs to generate the sentences of a language and to simulate human processing of these sentences using the rules included in various current linguistic theories. The computational models show that it is possible to use a written-down grammar in language production and comprehension that is at least a partially successful description of human competence, but it is still controversial whether such grammars are true models of human language processing.

Frequency Analysis, Concordances, and Collocations

[The professor had written] all the words of their language in their several moods, tenses and declensions [on tiny blocks of wood, and had] emptied the whole vocabulary into his frame, and made the strictest computation of the general proportion there is in books between the numbers of particles, nouns, and verbs, and other parts of speech.

JONATHAN SWIFT, *Gulliver's Travels*, 1726

Jonathan Swift prophesized one kind of application of computers to language: statistical analysis. The relative frequencies (i.e., the "general proportions") of letters and sounds, morphemes, words, word categories, types of phrases, and so on may be swiftly and accurately computed for any **corpus** (body of language data), whether textual or spoken.

A frequency analysis of one million words of written American English reveals the ten most frequently occurring words: *the, of, and, to, a, in, that, is, was,* and *he.* These "little" words accounted for about 25 percent of the words in the corpus, with *the* leading the pack at 7 percent. A similar analysis of *spoken* American English produced somewhat different results. The "winners" were *I, and, the, to, that, you, it, of, a,* and *know,* accounting for nearly 30 percent. This is but one of the differences between spoken and written language demonstrated by corpus analysis. All English prepositions except *to* occur more frequently in written than in spoken English, and not surprisingly, profane and taboo words (see chapter 7) were far more numerous in spoken than written language.

Frequency analyses have been conducted on existing texts (such as the works of Shakespeare or the Bible) and reveal aspects of the authors' styles. For example, by analyzing the various books of the Bible, it is possible to get a sense of who wrote which passages. In a notable study of the Federalist Papers, the authorship of a disputed paper was attributed to James Madison rather than to Alexander Hamilton. This was accomplished by comparing the statistical analyses of the paper in question with those of known works by the two writers.

A **concordance** takes frequency analysis one step further by specifying the location within the text of each word and its surrounding context. A concordance of the paragraph preceding the previous one would not only show that the word *words* occurred five times, but would indicate in which line of the paragraph it appeared, and provide its context. If one chose a "window" of three words on either side for context, the concordance would look like this for *words*:

of one million	**words**	of written American
most frequently occurring	**words**	the, of, and,
These "little"	**words**	accounted for about
percent of the	**words**	in the corpus,
profane and taboo	**words**	(see chapter 7)

A concordance, as you can see, might be of limited usefulness because of its "raw" nature. A way to refine a concordance is through **collocation analysis**. A collocation is the occurrence of two or more words within a short space of each other in a corpus. The point is to find evidence that the presence of one word in the text affects the occurrence of other words. Such an analysis must be statistical and involve large samples to show significant results. In the previous concordance of *words*, there is not enough data to be significant. If we performed a concordance on this entire book, patterns would emerge that would show that *words* and *written*, *words* and *taboo*, and *words* and *of* are more likely to occur close together than, say, *words* and *million*.

A concordance of sounds by computer may reveal patterns in poetry that would be nearly impossible for a human to detect. An analysis of the *Iliad* showed that many of the lines with an unusual number of etas (/i/) were related to youth and lovemaking; the line with the most alphas (/a/) was interpreted as being an imitation of stamping feet, the marching of armies. The use of computers permits literary scholars to more easily study poetic and prosaic features such as assonance, alliteration, meter, and rhythm. Today, computers can do the tedious mechanical work that once had to be done painstakingly with paper and pencil.

Computational Lexicography

Dictionary, n. A malevolent literary device for cramping the growth of a language and making it hard and inelastic.

AMBROSE BIERCE, *The Devil's Dictionary*, 1911

From the first dictionaries of Samuel Johnson to the updated *Oxford English Dictionary* (OED), standard dictionaries are not suitable for computational linguists, who need a wealth of information about individual words and morphemes to accomplish their goals of computer understanding, natural language generation, machine translation, and so on. The field of **computational lexicography**, then, is concerned not only with the making of standard dictionaries but also with the building of electronic dictionaries specifically designed for computational linguists.

Some of the information computational linguists need follows:

- phonemic transcription
- phonetic variants (dialectal, societal)
- syllabification
- syntactic categories
- semantic properties such as *abstract, human, animate,* etc. (see chapter 4)
- number, e.g., *people* is plural, *person* is singular
- gender, e.g., *ship* is female
- c-selection (*murder* requires a direct object)
- s-selection (*murder* requires a human subject and object)
- stylistic level (*ain't* is informal, *rad* is slang, *fuck* is taboo, etc.)
- synonyms, antonyms, possible homophones, etc.

Wordnet is an online dictionary with tens of thousands of entries that attempts to satisfy some of the needs of computational linguists, with emphasis on semantic relationships. Other similar projects are ongoing for European languages (EuroWordNet project), languages of the Balkans (BalkaNet project), and various other language communities.

The Culturomic Revolution

You Ain't Seen Nothin' Yet

RANDY BACHMAN (Title of a rock song, 1974)

Once upon a time a one-million-word corpus of written English was "the cat's meow." Today 361,000 cats have roared to create a 361 billion-with-a-*b*-word corpus of English. The words are drawn from about 5 million books, representing 4% of all books ever published in the English language. Analysis of this corpus, a study termed "culturomics," is producing fascinating insights in the fields of lexicography and grammatical change as well as in many of the social sciences.

Among the astonishing results emanating from this titanic corpus is that the English lexicon, long thought (and perhaps still thought) to contain somewhat under 500,000 words, actually has approximately one million words. How could such a thing come about?

By establishing a (widely accepted) criterion that any sequence of letters that has occurred with a frequency in excess of one in a billion since the 1500s is a word of English, virtually half-a-million "unknown" words such as *slenthem,* 'a type of musical instrument,' are now counted as being in the English lexicon. In fact it is estimated that 52% of the English lexicon—the majority of the words used in English books—consists of lexical "dark matter" undocumented in standard dictionaries.

The culturomics revolution has also produced results on the historical change of irregular verbs. Irregular past-tense verbs live side-by-side with their regular "*-ed*" rivals (e.g., *dove* and *dived*) that threaten to supplant them. Culturomic analysis informs us that in the period between 1800 and 2000 the six irregular past-tense verbs *burn, chide, smell, spell, spill,* and *thrive* (*burnt, chid, smelt, spelt, spilt, throve*) regularized, while at the same time two regular past tense verbs *light/lighted* and *wake/waked* became irregular: *light/lit* and *wake/woke*. A verb's "regularity" is defined via the percentage of instances in which the regular form is used: for example, *chided* went from 10% in 1800 to 90% in 2000. Even the rate of change can be computed from the corpus; *chide* was the fastest-moving verb; *spill* regularized at a constant speed; but *thrive* transitioned in fits and starts. Today the verb moving fastest toward irregularity is *sneak*, with 1% of the English-speaking population sneaking off to use *snuck* instead of *sneaked*.

Yet of further interest to historical linguists, the corpus shows that the regularization of the *t*-irregulars *burnt, smelt, spelt,* and *spilt* originated in the United States. The *-t* irregulars still cling to life in British English but just barely. Each year a population the size of Cambridge adopts *burned* in lieu of *burnt*.

As of this writing we are only scratching the veneer of linguistic possibilities that will arise from the study of vast corpuses. Today 12% of all books (about 15 million) have been digitized and the process is ongoing. Moreover, periodicals have not yet been folded into the corpus. There is a world of fascinating research to look forward to in corpus analysis. (The URL: books.google.com/ngrams/ shows one example of the fascinating information that can be inferred from an analysis of this corpus.)

Twitterology

Our expressiveness and our ease with some words is being diluted so that the sentence with more than one clause is a problem for us, and the word of more than two syllables is a problem for us . . .

RALPH FIENNES (British actor)

Yes, you saw it right! **Twitterology**, the computer analysis of a vast corpus of *microblogs* known as tweets, is becoming a subfield of culturomics.

In the social sciences twitterology is being used for *sentiment analysis* by tabulating the frequency of occurrence of positive emotional words such as *awesome* and *fantastic*, and negative words like *panic* and *fear*. This provides a window into the rhythms of daily life within a community or even within a country.

Intelligence communities such as the CIA use computers to analyze as many as 5 million tweets a day to measure the mood of a region after a major event such as the assassination of Osama bin Laden. And on a more Orwellian note, government agencies gather seemingly meaningless slang and jargon (see chapter 7) to help reveal an author's identity and political leanings along with his or her propensity for opposing the regime in power or committing acts of violence.

On the linguistic front, understanding how dialects (see chapter 7) vary among different regions and demographic groups is being studied by linguists at Carnegie Mellon University via twitterology. The huge corpus reveals such difficult to detect patterns as the wide use of *hella* as a form of emphasis in Northern California, as in, "It's hella cold out there."

Different phonetic spellings reveal distinct patterns of distribution. For example New Yorkers prefer *suttin* to *sumthin* (for *something*) and Californians write *koo* or *coo* for *cool*. Emoticons (see chapter 12), too, differ from region to region and from social group to social group.

The invasiveness of terms from one dialect to another may also be gauged through twitterology. In America such British terms as *bits* (sexy body parts), *snog* (to kiss), *nick* (to steal), and of course the sign-off greeting *cheers* reveal their trip across the "pond" (another Briticism) to take up residence in the former colony. But twitterology plays no favorites and the depth of use in Britain of Americanisms such as *janitor*, *parking lot*, and *teenager* can also be revealed by twitterology.

Interesting though it may be, twitterology is necessarily confined to a very narrow form of communication that's been called trivial and superficial. No less a figure than the linguist Noam Chomsky has warned that "it is not a medium of serious interchange." Undoubtedly, conclusions about language based on twitterology must be carefully drawn. The scientific legitimacy and usefulness of twitterology is, at this writing, an open question to be answered, we presume, within the second decade of this century.

Information Retrieval and Summarization

Hired

Tired

Fired

A CAREER SUMMARY, *source obscure*

Many people use the search features of the Internet to find information. Typically, one enters a keyword, or perhaps several, and magically the computer returns the location of Web sites that contain information relating to that keyword. This process is an example of **information retrieval**. It may be as trivial as finding Web sites that contain the keyword exactly as it is entered, but more often advanced linguistic analysis is applied. Web sites are returned, and even ranked, according to the frequency of occurrence of the keyword, different morphological forms of the keyword, synonyms of the keyword, and concepts semantically related to the keyword. For example, the keyword *bird* might retrieve information based on *bird*, *birds*, *to bird* (verb infinitive), *bird feeders*, *water birds*, *avian*, *sparrow*, *feathers*, *flight*, *migration*, and the basketball great *Larry*.

Companies such as Google turned information retrieval into a multi-billion dollar enterprise, which funded Google's entrance into multiple other fields of information processing, including the production of the huge corpuses that fuel culturomics.

In general, information retrieval is the use of computers to locate and display data gleaned from possibly very large databases. The input to an information retrieval system consists of words, statements, or questions, which the computer analyzes linguistically and then uses the results to sift through the database for pertinent information. Nowadays, complex information retrieval systems identify useful patterns or relationships in corpuses or other computer repositories using advanced linguistic and statistical analyses. The terms **data mining**, *knowledge discovery*, *data analytics*, and *analytics* are all used currently for highly evolved information retrieval systems.

A keyword like *bird* may return more information than could be read in ten lifetimes if a thorough search of the Web occurs. (A search on the day of this writing produced 637 million hits, compared to 200 million three years ago and 122 million seven years ago.) Much of the data would repeat and some information would outweigh other information. Through **summarization** programs, computers can eliminate redundancy and identify the most salient features of a body of information. World leaders, corporate executives, and even university professors—all of whom may wish to digest large volumes of textual material such as reports, newspapers, and scholarly articles—can benefit through summarization processes, providing the material is available in computer-readable form, which is increasingly the case as we plod through the second decade of the twenty-first century.

A typical scenario would be to use information retrieval to access, say, a hundred articles about birds. The articles may average 5,000 words each. Summarization programs, which can be set to reduce an article by a certain amount, say 1/10 or 1/100, are applied. The human reads the final output. Thus 500,000 words can be reduced to 5,000 or 10,000 words containing (it is to be hoped) the most pertinent information, which may then be read in ten or twenty minutes.

Summarization programs range from the simplistic "print the first sentence of every paragraph" to complex programs that analyze the document semantically to identify the important points, often using "concept vectors." A *concept vector* is a list of meaningful keywords whose presence in a paragraph is a measure of the paragraph's significance, and therefore an indication of whether the content of that paragraph should be included in a summarization. The summary document contains concepts from as many of the key paragraphs as possible, subject to length constraints.

Spell Checkers

Take care that you never spell a word wrong . . . It produces great praise to a lady to spell well.

THOMAS JEFFERSON, in a letter to his daughter Martha, 1783

Spell checkers, and perhaps in the future, pronunciation checkers, are applications of computational linguistics that vary in sophistication from mindless, brute-force lookups in a dictionary, to ones with enough intelligence to flag *your* when it should be *you're*, or *bear* when *bare* is intended. One often finds spell checkers as front ends to information retrieval systems, checking the keywords to prevent misspellings from misleading the search. Most e-mail systems also do spell checking, though that feature may be undesirable when texting because of so many nonstandard usages. Moreover, as the following poem reveals, spell checkers cannot replace careful editing:

> I have a spelling checker,
> It came with my PC.
> It plane lee marks four my revue
> Miss steaks aye can knot sea.
>
> A checker is a bless sing,
> It freeze yew lodes of thyme.
> It helps me right awl stiles to reed,
> And aides me when aye rime.
>
> To rite with care is quite a feet
> Of witch won should bee proud,
> And wee mussed dew the best wee can,
> Sew flaws are knot aloud.[2]

Machine Translation

> When I look at any article in Russian, I say: "This is really written in English, but it has been coded in some strange symbols. I will now proceed to decode it."
>
> WARREN WEAVER, in *Machine Translation of Languages*, Locke, W. N., and A. D. Boothe (eds.). 1955.

The need to translate between languages has never been greater than it is in today's global society, and the sheer volume and difficulty of the task makes it eminently suitable for computational assistance.

The first use of computers for natural language processing began in the 1940s with the attempt to develop **automatic machine translation**. At that time translation was treated as if it were deciphering a code, an attitude summed up in the epigraph.

The aim in automatic translation is to input a spoken utterance or a written passage in the **source language** and to receive a grammatical passage of equivalent meaning in the **target language** (the output). In the early days of machine translation, it was believed that this task could be accomplished by entering into the memory of a computer a dictionary of a source language and a dictionary with the corresponding morphemes and words of a target language. The translating program attempted to match the morphemes of the input sentence with those of the target language. Unfortunately, what often happened was a process that early experimenters with machine translation called "language in, garbage out."

Translation is more than word-for-word replacement. Often there is no equivalent word in the target language, and the order of words may differ, as in

---

[2]Journal of Irreproducible Results, "Candidate for a Pullet Surprise" 3 verses beginning "I have a spelling checker," Reprinted by permission from *The Journal of Irreproducible Results,* the science humor magazine, www.jir.com, January/February 1994, reprinted in Vol. 45, No. 5/6, 2000, page 20.

English *the red house* versus Spanish *la casa roja*. There is also difficulty in translating idioms, metaphors, slang, and so on. Human translators cope with these problems because they know the grammars of the two languages and draw on general knowledge of the subject matter and the world to arrive at the intended meanings. But even they fail on occasion, as illustrated by some "garbage out"-type signs posted as "aids" to tourists in non-English-speaking countries:

> The lift is being fixed for the next day. During that time we regret that you will be unbearable. (Bucharest hotel lobby)
> The nuns harbor all diseases and have no respect for religion. (Swiss nunnery hospital)
> All the water has been passed by the manager. (German hotel)
> Because of the impropriety of entertaining guest of the opposite sex in the bedroom, it is suggested that the lobby be used for this purpose. (Hotel in Zurich)
> The government bans the smoking of children. (Sign in Istanbul)

Similar problems are evident in this brief excerpt of the translation of an interview of the entertainer Madonna in the Hungarian newspaper *Blikk*:

> BLIKK: Madonna, let's cut toward the hunt: Are you a bold hussy-woman that feasts on men who are tops?
>
> MADONNA: Yes, yes, this is certainly something that brings to the surface my longings. In America it is not considered to be mentally ill when a woman advances on her prey in a discotheque setting with hardy cocktails present.

Such "translations" represent the difficulties of finding the right words, but word choice is not the only problem in automatic translation. There are challenges in morphology when translating between languages. A word like *ungentlemanliness* is certainly translatable into any language, but few languages are likely to have an exact word with that meaning, so a phrase of several words is needed. Similarly, *mbuki-mvuki* is a Swahili word that means 'to shuck off one's clothes in order to dance.' English does not have a word for that practice, but not for lack of need.

Syntactic problems are equally challenging. English is a language that allows possessive forms of varying syntactic complexity, such as *that man's son's dog's food dish*, or *the guy that my roommate is dating's cousin*. Translating these sentences without a loss of meaning into languages that prohibit such structures requires a great deal of sentence restructuring.

Single word translations between dozens of languages from Afrikaans to Yiddish are readily available on the Internet (translate.google.com), but humans are needed to translate lengthier passages such as newspaper articles with accuracy. Professional translators make copious use of computers to assist their translations, saving them much time and effort, but they are the ultimate arbiters of what is a grammatical, semantically faithful translation.

We have been implicitly discussing translation of written texts. What about the translation of speech from one language to another? On the one side, speech recognition is needed—or "speech-to-text." On the other side, "text-to-speech" is required. The most general machine translation scenario—that of speech-to-speech—encapsulates all of the areas of computational linguistics

FIGURE 11.2 | Logic flow of machine translation of speech.

discussed in this chapter. Diagrammatically, we have a progression like the flowchart in Figure 11.2.

Completely automatic translation of speech at the level of professional human interpreters such as are found in an international setting like the United Nations is still an unachieved if heartily sought after goal.

Computational Forensic Linguistics

Forensic linguistics is a subfield of linguistics that applies to language as used in the legal and judicial fields. It includes authorships studies, interpretation of legal language, language rights and usage in the courtroom, statement analysis (e.g., suicide notes), trademark protection and infringement (McWho?), speaker identification (who left that bomb threat?), text authentication (e.g., questions of plagiarism), legality of lip-reading, and so on.

Computational forensic linguistics is a sub-area that concerns itself with computer applications in forensic linguistics. In this section we will look at three such applications: trademarks, interpreting legal terms, and speaker identification.

Trademarks

> There is a risk that the word "Google" could become so commonly used that it becomes synonymous with the word "search." If this happens, we could lose protection for this trademark, which could result in other people using the word "Google" to refer to their own products, thus diminishing our brand.
>
> QUOTED *IN THE GUARDIAN WEEKLY*, July 21, 2006

Google is not alone in being required to defend its trademarked name in various courts of law. McDonald's has also fought in the courts to defend against the use of the bound morpheme *Mc-* from *McBagel* to *McSleep*. The latter was to be the name of a chain of basic hotels when the subpoenas were served to the Quality Inns International, Inc. In helping to defend the hotel chain, forensic linguist Roger Shuy used a computer to search a huge corpus for words containing the precious morpheme. He found a large number of already accepted usages such as *McMansions, McArt, McCinema,* and *McPrisons,* and based on those data argued that the morpheme *Mc-* had entered the language with its own meaning, 'basic, inexpensive,' and was therefore available to the public at large. The judge did not agree and ruled against the hotel chain because market research showed that the public's perception of the morpheme *Mc-* was nonetheless strongly associated with McDonald's.

Interpreting Legal Terms

A Daniel come to judgment! yea, a Daniel!

WILLIAM SHAKESPEARE, *The Merchant of Venice*, Act IV, Scene 1, c. 1596

The nuances of meaning of legal language have been disputed throughout the entire history of judicial systems. The legal definition of "a pound of flesh" is central to the plot of Shakespeare's play *The Merchant of Venice*.

A recent case hinged on the legitimate use of the word *visa*, not as a credit card trademark, but as a legal term relevant to international travel. The point in question was whether a visa gives a traveler an unconditional right to enter the visa-issuing country, or if it is something subtly, but significantly, different. A computational linguist examined the multimillion-word Bank of England corpus and found seventy-four instances of *visa* and *visas* collocated with common verbs like *issue, refuse, apply for, need*, and *require*, and was able to argue successfully that the meaning of *visa* was, in the mind of the average traveler, *a kind of permit to enter a country*, not *a permit **to request permission to enter a country***, for if that were the case even with a visa a traveler could be denied entry. This finding of one British court continues to have repercussions in the world of international law, though the question is by no means entirely settled.

This analysis and many like it show the usefulness of a corpus-based, computer-driven approach to thorny legal problems. It has become increasingly common for computational forensic linguists to search databases in various, often ingenious ways to make legal points.

Speaker Identification

Good morning. There are three bombs to go off today at three pharmaceuticals in North Carolina. Please be aware. Advise your people or go to their funerals. Goodbye.

TRANSCRIPT OF A VOICE MAIL MESSAGE TO A PHARMACEUTICAL DISTRIBUTION COMPANY IN RALEIGH, **NORTH CAROLINA**

Many crimes involve anonymous recorded messages in which it is important to identify the speaker. **Speaker identification** is the use of computers to assist in such a task, as opposed to **ear witnessing**, which relies on the judgment of human listeners.

Two computational tools are commonly applied to assist in speaker identification. One displays the waveform of an utterance, which shows the amplitude changes of the speech over time; the second displays a spectrogram, discussed in chapter 10, which shows a breakdown of the frequencies of the speech signal over time. Both of these graphical displays can reveal to the eye what the ear may be unsure of hearing, and because of that can be an effective device in a judicial setting.

The bomb threat in the epigraph provides us with a case study. An African American man, born and raised in North Carolina, was accused of leaving the threat. The defense employed a computational forensic linguist as an expert witness to perform a speaker identification analysis. After analyzing many segments of speech, the expert determined that not only was the suspect unlikely to have been the speaker of the bomb threat, but also that there was a high probability that the speaker was not a native speaker of English. Here is an excerpt from the expert witness's report:

> The word "goodbye" occurs in the bomb threat.
> <u>Caller:</u> Inserts an epenthetic vowel so that the pronunciation is "good-a-bye," clearly seen in the waveform and spectrogram. No native speaker of English is likely to have this pronunciation. The caller also pronounces 'bye' with a fully diphthongized /aɪ/—the way foreigners are taught.
> <u>Suspect:</u> His "goodbye" is "goobah," without the /d/ and certainly without the epenthetic vowel. His "bye" is monophthongized and somewhat lengthened as in much speech of the south, black and white.

The expert took exemplars from the suspect, and put the waveforms side by side, as shown in Figure 11.3. The figure on the left is the caller's "goodbye." The figure on the right is the suspect's.

The well-enunciated /d/ of the caller begins at 0.40 seconds with a stop closure (silence) of about 80 milliseconds. (The amplitude is small, but not zero owing to noise.) The epenthetic vowel is seen between 0.52 and 0.64 seconds. At 0.64 seconds the stop closure for the /b/ of *bye* begins. On the right there is no /d/ visible, nor is there an extra vowel. The "gooh" is followed by the stop closure of the /b/ in *bye* at 2.55 seconds. Figure 11.4 is the waveform with its spectrogram beneath it.

FIGURE 11.3 | Waveforms showing the word *goodbye* spoken by a bomb-threat caller (left) and the suspect arrested for that incident (right).

Adobe product screen shot reprinted with permission from Adobe Systems Incorporated

FIGURE 11.4 | Top: waveforms of the word *goodbye*. Bottom: spectrogram of the same utterance.

Adobe product screen shot reprinted with permission from Adobe Systems Incorporated

Recall that the dark bands are the formants, and they occur with vowel sounds. On the caller's side, the near silence of the stop closure of the /d/ is readily apparent in the white space at around 0.40 seconds, and the epenthetic vowel, probably a schwa ([ə]), is clearly visible as a vowel since its first four formants are apparent. The diverging first and second formants at the end of the caller's "good-a-bye" make the diphthong visible.

In the suspect's spectrogram there is no evidence of a /d/ at all, nor of an extra vowel. The only period of silence precedes the stop closure of the /b/ in *bye*. Finally, the flatness of all the formants in the vowel of *bye* indicates a monophthongal sound, quite unlike the caller's.

The suspect was convicted of the crime, but an appeals court reversed the verdict based on the forensic linguistic evidence. After signing a statement not to pursue a false-arrest suit, the suspect was released after serving twenty months in prison.

Summary

Computational linguistics is the study of how computers can process language, thus allowing natural language human-computer interfaces. As well, computers help scholars to analyze literature and language, to translate between languages, to extract useful information from large corpuses, and to assist with criminal and legal affairs.

When communicating with a human being, computers must be capable of **speech recognition**, processing the speech signal into phonemes, morphemes, and words. They also must be able to speak the output. **Speech synthesis** is a two-step process in which a **text-to-speech** program first converts text to phones or other basic units such as words or syllables. **Formant synthesis** simulates the sounds of phones electronically; **concatenative synthesis** is based on assembling prerecorded units such as words to produce complete utterances.

To recognize speech is not to understand speech, and to speak a text does not necessarily mean that the computer knows what it is saying. To either understand or generate speech, the computer must process phonemes, morphemes, words, phrases, and sentences, and it must be aware of the meanings of these units (except for phonemes). The computational linguistics of speech understanding and speech generation has the subfields of **computational phonetics and phonology**, **computational morphology**, **computational syntax**, **computational semantics**, and **computational pragmatics**.

Computational phonetics and phonology relate phonemes to the acoustic signal of speech. It is fundamental to speech recognition and synthesis. Computational morphology deals with the structure of words, so it determines that the meaning of *bird* applies as well to *birds*, which has in addition the meaning of plural. Computational syntax is concerned with the syntactic categories of words and with the larger syntactic units of phrases and sentences. It is further concerned with analyzing a sentence into these components for speech understanding, or assembling these components into larger units for speech generation.

Computational semantics is concerned with representing meaning inside the computer, or **semantic representation**. To communicate with a person, the computer creates a semantic representation of what the person says to it, and another semantic representation of what it wants to say back. In a machine translation environment, the computer produces a semantic representation of the source language input, and outputs that meaning in the target language.

Semantic representations may be based on logical expressions involving predicates and arguments, on **semantic networks**, or on other formal devices to represent meaning.

Computational pragmatics may influence the understanding or the response of the computer by taking into account knowledge that the computer system has about the real world: for example, that there is a unique element in the environment, so the determiner *the* can be used appropriately to refer to it.

There are many applications of computational linguistics. Computational lexicography is the use of computers both to construct "ordinary" dictionaries and to construct electronic dictionaries with far more information, suitable for the goals of language understanding and generation.

Computers may be programmed to model a linguist's grammar of a human language and thus rapidly and thoroughly test that grammar. To analyze a **corpus**, or body of data, a computer can do a frequency analysis of words; compute a **concordance**, which locates words in the corpus and gives their immediate context; and compute a **collocation**, which measures how the occurrence of one word affects the probability of the occurrence of other words. A frequency analysis on a 361-billion-word corpus of English revealed half a million undocumented English words. Such analysis of gargantuan databases of language, called **culturomics**, also reveals many details of language change. **Twitterology** is a subfield of culturomics that focuses on huge corpuses of "tweets."

Computers are also useful for **information retrieval** based on keywords, automatic **summarization**, and **spell checking**.

Soon after their invention, computers were used to try to translate from one language to another. This is a difficult, complex task and the results are often humorous as the computer struggles to translate text (or speech) in the **source language** into the **target language** without loss of meaning or grammaticality.

Other applications of computational linguistics are found in the forensic fields, where computational forensic linguists takes up such legal problems as trademark protection and infringement, in which computers are used to examine huge corpuses to infer how people interpret trademarks such as the *Mc-* in McDonald's; and **speaker identification**, where a computational analysis of speech used in a crime such as a bomb threat can assist in identifying, or exonerating, a suspect.

References for Further Reading

Allen, J. 1987. *Natural language understanding.* Menlo Park, CA: Benjamin/Cummings.

Coulthard, M., and A. Johnson. 2007. *An introduction to forensic linguistics.* New York: Routledge.

Hockey, S. 1980. *A guide to computer applications in the humanities.* London: Duckworth.

Jurafsky, D., and J. H. Martin. 2008. *Speech and language processing, 2nd ed.* Upper Saddle River, NJ: Prentice Hall (Pearson Higher Education).

Michel, J-B, et al. "Quantitative analysis of culture using millions of digitized books." *Science,* v. 331, pp. 176–182, Jan 14, 2011.

Olsson, J. 2008. *Forensic linguistics, 2nd ed.* London: Continuum.

Smith, R., and R. Hipp. 1994. *Spoken natural language dialog systems.* New York: Oxford University Press.

Sowa, J. (ed.). 1991. *Principles of semantic networks.* San Mateo, CA: Morgan Kaufmann.

Stabler, E. P., Jr. 1992. *The logical approach to syntax: Foundations, specifications and implementations of theories of government and binding.* Cambridge, MA: MIT Press.

Weizenbaum, J. 1976. *Computer power and human reason.* San Francisco: W. H. Freeman.

Winograd, T. 1983. *Language as a cognitive process.* Reading, MA: Addison-Wesley.

____. 1972. *Understanding natural language.* New York: Academic Press.

Exercises

1. The use of spectrograms for speaker identification is based on the fact that no two speakers have exactly the same speech characteristics. List some differences you have noticed in the speech of several individuals. Can you think of any reasons for such differences?

2. Using a bilingual dictionary of any target language besides English (translate.google.com will make this easier), attempt to translate the following English sentences by looking up each word:

The children will eat the fish.
Send the professor a letter from your new school.
The fish will be eaten by the children.
Who is the person that is hugging that dog?
The spirit is willing, but the flesh is weak.

a. Have a person who knows (preferably a native speaker) the target language give a correct translation of each sentence. What difficulties are brought to light by comparing the two translations? Mention five of them.

b. Have a different person who knows the target language translate the grammatical translation back into English. What problems do you observe? Are they related to any of the difficulties you mentioned in part (a)?

3. Suppose you were given a manuscript of a play and were told that it is either by Christopher Marlowe or William Shakespeare (both born in 1564). Suppose further that this work, and all works by Marlowe and Shakespeare, were in a computer. Describe how you would use the computer to help determine the true authorship of the mysterious play.

4. Speech synthesis is useful because it allows computers to speak outloud and convey information to persons who are visually impaired. Think of five other uses for speech synthesis in our society.

5. Some advantages of speech recognition are similar to those of speech synthesis. A computer that understands speech does not require a person to use hands and eyes (e.g., a keyboard and mouse) to convey information to the computer. Think of five other possible uses for speech recognition in our society.

6. Play with ELIZA on line. You'll have to search for its website as it changes and the older ones may infect your computer. Ask it questions like "Why am I unhappy?" or ask ELIZA to respond to statements like "My friends all hate me."

a. List five "intelligent" responses to questions or statements that you formulate, and why they are intelligent. For example, if you tell ELIZA "My friends all hate me," ELIZA will respond "Why do you say your friends all hate you?" This is intelligent because it makes sense, it's syntactically correct, the tense is appropriate, and it correctly changed the first-person *me* to the second-person *you*.

b. What are some of the "stock" responses that ELIZA makes? For example, when ELIZA doesn't "understand" you, she says "Please go on."

c. Try to identify some ways in which ELIZA uses your input to formulate its response. For example, if you mention "brother" or "mother," ELIZA will respond with a phrase containing "family member."

7. Let's play "torment the computer." Imagine a fairly good morphological parser. Give it *kindness*, it returns *kind* + *ness*; give it *upchuck*, it returns *up* + *chuck*; but if you give it *catsup* and it returns *cat* + *s* + *up*, you

will scold it. Think of ten more words that are likely to lead to false analyses.

8. A major problem with text-to-speech is pronouncing proper names. Oh, how the telephone companies would like to solve this one! But it is difficult. Open a telephone directory (if you can find one nowadays—it's often called "The White Pages") at random, point at random, and try to pronounce surnames one after another, as they occur alphabetically. How far do you get before you are unsure—not clueless, which you might be if you ran across Duke University's basketball coach *Mike Krzyzewski*—but merely unsure. As we write this exercise, we are doing it. Here is what we got:

> Honeycutt
> Honeywell
> Hong
> Hongtong
> Honig
> Honkanen
> Honnigford
> Honorato
> Honore
> Honour
> Honrine
> Hontz

We think we could do the first four correctly, but there is some doubt regarding the first vowel in *Honig*: is it [o], [ɔ], [a], or even the [ʌ] of *honey*? We also are unsure where to place the primary stress in *Honkanen*, and is the last letter in *Honore* pronounced as in Balzac's first name, and is *Honrine* pronounced to rhyme with *benzine* or *hemline*? Oh, and are all those *h*'s pronounced, or are some silent, as in *honor*? Do this exercise ten times to see the average number of surnames you can pronounce with confidence before becoming unsure. This gives some measure of the vast difficulty facing computers that have to read names.

9. Go to the movies! Rent *2001: A Space Odyssey*, and yes, this is homework if anybody asks. Listen carefully to all the dialogues between the computer HAL and the humans. Write a short paper on the kinds of knowledge you believe HAL had to have to speak and understand as he does. You needn't concern yourselves with HAL's motives, just his use of speech.

10. Access at http://www.natcorp.ox.ac.uk/ the British National Corpus. Choose ten words from the glossary at the back of this book and enter each one, observing in each case how the context of the word jibes with the definition given. For example, we just entered *morphophonemics* and got no hits. That is a highly jargonized term. We fared no better with

twitterology and *culturomics*, unsurprisingly. Then we tried plain old *phonology* and got 175 hits, most of them with the expected meaning. Now you try it, either selecting your own terms or following the suggestions of your instructor.

11. The "culturomics" analysis that the English has nearly one billion lexical items is based on an analysis of documents reaching back some 500 years. Many of those items, like *slenthem* quoted in the text are no longer in use and would not meet the "more than one occurrence per billion words" criterion if documents dating back only 50 or 100 years were measured. Discuss the pros and cons of counting lexical items as belonging to English even if they are obsolete and not in use currently.

12. **Research exercise**: Using Internet search engines and then further sources such as Michel et al., cited in the references to this chapter, discover what you can about "Culturomics" and write an essay expressing whether you think it will be an important field of research for years to come or whether it's a "flash in the pan" in which interest will die quickly. Naturally you will back up your views with cogent arguments drawn from your research.

13. **Research exercise**: Compose an essay or possibly a short talk entitled *Twitterology in Linguistics: Good, Bad, or Irrelevant.*

12

Writing: The ABCs of Language

The Moving Finger writes; and, having writ,
Moves on: nor all thy Piety nor Wit
Shall lure it back to cancel half a Line,
Nor all thy Tears wash out a Word of it.

OMAR KHAYYÁM, *Rubáiyát*, c. 1080 (trans. Edward FitzGerald, 1859)

The palest ink is better than the sharpest memory.

CHINESE PROVERB

Throughout this book we have emphasized the spoken form of language. Grammar is viewed as a system for relating *sound* (sign) and meaning. The human language faculty is biologically and genetically determined and represents a vital evolutionary development.

This is not true of writing, which is a visual system for representing language, including handwriting, printing, and electronic displays of these written forms. (Braille "writing" is a *tactile* system for the visually impaired.) Children learn to speak naturally through exposure to language without formal teaching. To become literate—to learn to read and write—one must make a conscious effort and receive instruction.

Before the invention of writing, useful knowledge had to be memorized. Messengers carried information in their heads. Crucial lore passed from the older to the newer generation through speaking. Even in today's world, many spoken languages lack a writing system, and oral literature still abounds. However, human memory is short-lived, and the brain's storage capacity is limited.

Writing overcomes such limitations and allows communication across space and through time. Writing permits a society to permanently record its literature,

527

its history and science, and its technology. The creation and development of writing systems is therefore one of the greatest human achievements.

The History of Writing

An Egyptian legend relates that when the god Thoth revealed his discovery of the art of writing to King Thamos, the good King denounced it as an enemy of civilization. "Children and young people," protested the monarch, "who had hitherto been forced to apply themselves diligently to learn and retain whatever was taught them, would cease to apply themselves, and would neglect to exercise their memories."

WILL DURANT, *The Story of Civilization*, vol. 1, 1935

There are many legends and stories about the invention of writing. Greek legend has it that Cadmus, Prince of Phoenicia and founder of the city of Thebes, invented the alphabet and brought it with him to Greece. In one Chinese fable, the four-eyed dragon-god Cang Jie invented writing, but in another, writing first appeared as markings on the back of the chi-lin, a white unicorn of Chinese legend. In other myths, the Babylonian god Nebo and the Egyptian god Thoth gave writing as well as speech to humans. The Talmudic scholar Rabbi Akiba believed that the alphabet existed before humans were created, and according to Hindu tradition the Goddess Saraswati, wife of Brahma, invented writing.

Although these are delightful stories, it is evident that uncountable billions of words were spoken before even a single word was written. The invention of writing comes relatively late in human history, and its development was gradual. It is highly unlikely that a particularly gifted ancestor awoke one morning and decided, "Today I'll invent a writing system."

Pictograms and Ideograms

One picture is worth a thousand words.

CHINESE PROVERB

The roots of writing were the early drawings made by ancient humans. Cave art, called **petroglyphs**, have been found in such places as the Chauvet caves in southern France, featured in the 2011 film documentary "Cave of Forgotten Dreams." These can be "read" today although they were created by humans living 30,000 or more years ago. They are literal portrayals of life at that time. We don't know why they were produced; they may be aesthetic expressions rather than pictorial communications. Later drawings, however, are clearly "picture writings," or **pictograms**. Unlike modern writing systems, each pictogram is a direct image of the object it represents. There is a nonarbitrary relationship between the form and meaning of the symbol. Comic strips, minus captions, are pictographic—literal representations of the ideas to be communicated. This early form of writing represented objects in the world directly rather than through the linguistic names given to these objects. Thus they did not represent the words and sounds of spoken language.

FIGURE 12.1 | Six of seventy-seven symbols developed by the National Park Service for use as signs indicating activities and facilities in parks and recreation areas. These symbols denote, from left to right: 'environmental study area,' 'grocery store,' 'men's restroom,' 'women's restroom,' 'fishing,' and 'amphitheater.' Certain symbols are available with a prohibiting slash—a diagonal red bar across the symbol that means that the activity is forbidden.
National Park Service, U.S. Department of the Interior

Pictographic writing has been found throughout the ancient and modern world, from Africa to Oceania to the contemporary world of Internet communications. Email, Instant Messaging, Twittering and other forms of texting make copious use of **emoticons**, which are pictographic symbols such as ☺ and ☹, and which convey specific meanings independent of any language. Pictograms are also found today in international road signs, where the native language of a region might not be understood by all travelers. You do not need to know English to understand the signs used by the U.S. National Park Service (Figure 12.1).

Once a pictogram was accepted as the representation of an object, its meaning was extended to attributes of that object, or concepts associated with it. A picture of the sun could represent warmth, heat, light, daytime, and so on. Pictograms began to represent ideas rather than objects. Such generalized pictograms are called **ideograms** ("idea pictures" or "idea writing").

The difference between pictograms and ideograms is not always clear. Ideograms tend to be less direct representations, and one may have to learn what a particular ideogram means. Pictograms tend to be more literal. For example, the no parking symbol consisting of a black letter P inside a red circle with a slanting red line through it is an ideogram. It represents the idea of no parking abstractly. A no parking symbol showing an automobile being towed away is more literal—more like a pictogram.

Inevitably, pictograms and ideograms became highly stylized and difficult to interpret without knowing the system. To understand the system, one needed to learn the words of the language that the ideograms represented. Thus the ideograms became linguistic symbols. They stood for the words, both meanings and sounds, that represented the ideas. This stage was a revolutionary step in the development of writing systems.

Cuneiform Writing

Bridegroom, let me caress you,
My precious caress is more savory than honey,
In the bed chamber, honey-filled,
Let me enjoy your goodly beauty,
Lion let me caress you

TRANSLATION OF A SUMERIAN POEM WRITTEN IN CUNEIFORM

Much of what we know about writing stems from the records left by the Sumerians, an ancient people of unknown origin, who built a civilization in southern Meso-potamia (modern Iraq) more than 6,000 years ago. They left innumerable clay tablets containing business documents, epics, prayers, poems, proverbs, and so on. So copious are these written records that the Pennsylvania Sumerian Dictionary Project was able to publish an eighteen-volume online dictionary (http://psd .museum.upenn.edu/epsd/index.html) of their written language in 2006.

The writing system of the Sumerians is the oldest one known. They were a commercially oriented people and as their business deals became increasingly complex the need for permanent records arose. They developed an elaborate pictography along with a system of tallies. Some examples are shown here:

| star, sky, God | hand | corn | 5 | oxen[1] | 13 | fish |

Over the centuries the Sumerians simplified and conventionalized their pic-tography. They began to produce the symbols of their written language by us-ing a wedge-shaped stylus that was pressed into soft clay tablets, which quickly hardened in the desert sun to produce enduring records. This form of writing is called **cuneiform**—literally, "wedge-shaped" (from Latin *cuneus*, "wedge"). Here is an illustration of the evolution of Sumerian pictograms to cuneiform:

became   became   star

became   hand

became   fish

The cuneiform symbols in the third column do little to remind us (or the Sumerians) of the meaning represented. As cuneiform evolved, its users began to think of the symbols more in terms of the name of the objects represented than of the object itself. Eventually cuneiform script came to represent words of the language directly, and through them, the meaning. Such a system is called **logo-graphic**, or **word writing**, and the symbols themselves are called **logograms**.

The cuneiform writing system spread throughout the Middle East and Asia Minor. The Babylonians, Assyrians, and Persians made use of it by adapting the cuneiform characters to represent the sounds of the syllables in their own languages. In this way cuneiform evolved into a **syllabic writing** system or **syllabary**.

---

[1]The pictograph for 'ox' evolved, much later, into the letter *A*.

In a syllabic writing system, each syllable in the language is represented by its own symbol, and words are written syllable by syllable. Cuneiform writing was never purely syllabic. A large residue of symbols remained that stood for whole words. The Assyrians retained many word symbols, even though every word in their language could be written out syllabically if it were desired. Thus they could write *mātu*, 'country,' as:

  ma   +   a   +   tu

The Persians (ca. 600–400 BCE) devised a greatly simplified syllabic alphabet for their language, which made little use of word symbols. By the reign of Darius I (521–486 BCE), this writing system was in wide use. The following characters illustrate it:

    da

    di

    fa

    ma

    tu

The Rebus Principle

two bee, oar knot two bee

WILLIAM SHAKESPEARE, *Hamlet*, c. 1600

When a graphic sign no longer has a visual relationship to the word it represents, it becomes a **phonographic symbol**, standing for the sounds that represent the word. A single sign can then be used to represent all words with the same sounds—the homophones of the language. If, for example, the symbol ⊙ stood for *sun* in English, it could then be used in a sentence like *My ⊙ is a doctor*. This sentence is an example of the **rebus principle**.

A rebus is a representation of words by pictures of objects whose names sound like the word. Thus 👁 might represent *eye* or the pronoun *I*. The sounds of the two words are identical, even though the meanings are not. Similarly, 🐝🍃 could represent *belief* (*be* + *lief* = *bee* + *leaf* = /bi/ + /lif/), and 🐝🍃🍃 could be *believes*.

Proper names can also be written in such a way. If the symbol | is used to represent *rod* and the symbol ⚥ represents *man*, then | ⚥ could represent *Rodman*, although nowadays the name is unrelated to either rods or men. Such combinations often become stylized or shortened so as to be more easily written. *Rodman*, for example, might be written in such a system as |⚥ or even ⚥. Jokes, riddles, and advertising use the rebus principle. A popular ice cream company advertises "31derful flavors."

This is not an efficient system because in many languages words cannot be divided into sequences of sounds that have meaning by themselves. It would be difficult, for example, to represent the word *English* (/ɪŋ/ + /glɪʃ/) in English according to the rebus principle. *Eng* by itself does not mean anything, nor does *glish*.

From Hieroglyphics to the Alphabet

"What part of oil lamp next to double squiggle over ox don't you understand?"

Eric Lewis/The New Yorker Collection/www.cartoonbank.com

At the time that Sumerian pictography was flourishing (around 4000 BCE), the Egyptians were using a similar system, which the Greeks later called hieroglyphics (*hiero*, 'sacred,' + *glyphikos*, 'carvings'). These sacred carvings originated as pictography as shown by the following:

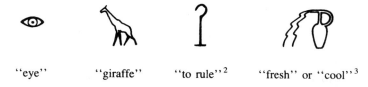

"eye"   "giraffe"   "to rule"[2]   "fresh" or "cool"[3]

Eventually, these pictograms came to represent both the concept and the word for the concept. Once this happened, hieroglyphics became a bona fide logographic writing system. Through the rebus principle, hieroglyphics also became a syllabic writing system.

The Phoenicians, a Semitic people who lived in what is today Lebanon, were aware of hieroglyphics as well as the offshoots of Sumerian writing. By 1500 BCE, they had developed a writing system of twenty-two characters, the West Semitic Syllabary. Mostly, the characters stood for consonants alone. The reader provided the vowels, and hence the rest of the syllable, through knowledge of the language. (Cn y rd ths?) Thus the West Semitic Syllabary was both a **syllabary** and a **consonantal alphabet** (also called **abjad**).

The ancient Greeks tried to borrow the Phoenician writing system, but it was unsatisfactory as a syllabary because Greek has too complex a syllable structure. In Greek, unlike in Phoenician, vowels cannot be determined by context, so Greek required that vowels be specifically written. Fortuitously, Phoenician had more consonants than Greek, so when the Greeks borrowed the system, they used the leftover consonant symbols to represent vowel sounds. The result was **alphabetic writing**, a system in which both consonants and vowels are symbolized. (The word *alphabet* is derived from *alpha* and *beta*, the first two letters of the Greek alphabet.)

Most alphabetic systems in use today derive from the Greek system. The Etruscans knew this alphabet and through them it became known to the Romans, who used it for Latin. The alphabet spread with Western civilization, and eventually most nations of the world had the opportunity to use alphabetic writing.

According to one view, the alphabet was not invented: it was discovered. If language did not include discrete individual sounds, no one could have invented alphabetic letters to represent them. When humans started to use one symbol for one phoneme, they were making more salient their intuitive knowledge of the phonological system of their language.

Modern Writing Systems

... but their manner of writing is very peculiar, being neither from the left to the right, like the Europeans; nor from the right to the left, like the Arabians; nor from up to down, like the Chinese; nor from down to up, like the Cascagians, but aslant from one corner of the paper to the other, like ladies in England.

JONATHAN SWIFT, *Gulliver's Travels*, 1726

[2]The symbol portrays the Pharaoh's staff.
[3]Water trickling out of a vase.

We have already mentioned the various types of writing systems used in the world: word or logographic writing, syllabic writing, consonantal alphabet writing, and alphabetic writing. Most of the world's written languages use alphabetic writing. Even Chinese and Japanese, whose native writing systems are not alphabetic, have adopted alphabetic transcription systems for special purposes such as street signs for foreigners and input for (older) computers.

Word Writing

People separated by a blade of grass cannot understand each other.

CHINESE PROVERB

In a word-writing or logographic writing system, a written character represents both the meaning and pronunciation of each word or morpheme. Such systems are cumbersome, containing thousands of different characters. By contrast all of the entries in an unabridged dictionary may be written using only twenty-six alphabetic symbols and a handful of special characters. It is understandable why word writing gave way to alphabetic systems in most places in the world.

The major exceptions are the writing systems used in China and Japan. The Chinese writing system has an uninterrupted history of 3,500 years. For the most part it is a word-writing system, with each character representing an individual word or morpheme. Longer words are formed by combining two words or morphemes, as shown by the word meaning 'business,' *măimai*, which is formed by combining the words meaning 'buy' and 'sell.' This is similar to compounding in English.

A word-writing system would be awkward for English and other Indo-European languages because of the pervasiveness of inflected verb forms such as *take, takes, taken, took,* and *taking,* and inflected noun forms such as *cat, cats, cat's,* and *cats'.* These are difficult to represent without a huge proliferation of characters. The Chinese languages, on the other hand, have little inflection.

Even without the need to represent inflectional forms, Chinese dictionaries contain tens of thousands of characters—although a person need know "only" about 5,000 to read a newspaper. To make the language more accessible both to young Chinese learning to write, as well as to non-Chinese, the Chinese government has adopted a spelling system using the Roman alphabet called **Pinyin**, which is often used alongside the regular system of characters. By the time of the Summer Olympics of 2008, nearly all public information signs in Beijing, such as the names of streets, parks, restaurants, hotels, and shopping centers, were printed in both systems for the convenience of foreign visitors. It is not the government's intent to replace the traditional writing, which is an integral part of Chinese culture. To the Chinese, writing is an art—**calligraphy**—and thousands of years of poetry, literature, and history are preserved in the old system.

An additional reason for keeping the traditional system is that the unified writing system is a scythe that cuts away the "blade of grass," permitting all literate Chinese to communicate even though their spoken languages are different. This use of written Chinese characters is similar to the use of Arabic numerals, which mean the same thing in every language. For example, the character

5 stands for a different sequence of sounds in English, French, and Finnish. It is *five* /faɪv/ in English, *cinq* /sæk/ in French, and *viisi* /viːsi/ in Finnish, but in all these languages 5 means 'five.' Similarly, the spoken word for 'rice' is different in the various Chinese languages, but the written character is the same. If the writing system in China were to become solely alphabetic, written communication would no longer be possible among the various language communities.

Syllabic Writing

Syllabic writing systems are more efficient than word-writing systems, and they are certainly less taxing on the memory. However, languages with a rich structure of syllables containing many consonant clusters (such as *tr* or *spl*) cannot be efficiently written with a syllabary. To see this difficulty, consider the syllable structures of English:

I	/aɪ/	V	ant	/ænt/	VCC
key	/ki/	CV	pant	/pænt/	CVCC
ski	/ski/	CCV	stump	/stʌmp/	CCVCC
spree	/spri/	CCCV	striped	/straɪpt/	CCCVCC
an	/æn/	VC	ants	/ænts/	VCCC
seek	/sik/	CVC	pants	/pænts/	CVCCC
speak	/spik/	CCVC	sports	/spɔrts/	CCVCCC
scram	/skræm/	CCCVC	splints	/splɪnts/	CCCVCCC

Even this table is not exhaustive; there are syllables whose codas may contain four consonants, such as *strengths* /strɛŋkθs/ and *triumphs* /traɪəmpfs/. With more than thirty consonants and over twelve vowels, the number of different possible syllables is astronomical, which is why English, and Indo-European languages in general, are unsuitable for syllabic writing systems.

Japanese, on the other hand, is more suited for syllabic writing because all its words can be phonologically represented by about one hundred syllables, mostly of the consonant-vowel (CV) type, and there are no underlying consonant clusters. To write these syllables, the Japanese have two syllabaries, each containing forty-six characters, called **kana**. The entire Japanese language can be written using kana. One syllabary, **katakana**, is used for loan words and for special effects similar to italics in European writing. The other syllabary, **hiragana**, is used for native words. Hiragana characters may occur in the same word as ideographic characters, which are called **kanji**, and are borrowed Chinese characters. Thus Japanese writing is part word writing, part syllable writing.

During the first millennium, the Japanese tried to use Chinese characters to write their language. However, spoken Japanese is unlike spoken Chinese. (They are genetically unrelated languages.) A word-writing system alone was not suitable for Japanese, which is a highly inflected language in which verbs may occur in thirty or more different forms. Scholars devised syllabic characters, based on modified Chinese characters, to represent the inflectional endings and other grammatical morphemes. Thus, in Japanese writing, kanji is commonly used for the verb roots, and hiragana symbols for the inflectional markings.

For example, 行 is the character meaning 'go,' pronounced [i]. The word for 'went' in formal speech is *ikimashita*, written 行きました, where the hiragana symbols きました represent the syllables *ki, ma, shi, ta*. Nouns, on the other hand, are not inflected in Japanese, and they can generally be written using Chinese characters alone.

In theory, all of Japanese could be written in hiragana. However, in Japanese, there are many homographs (like *lead* in "lead pipe" or "lead astray"), and the use of kanji disambiguates words that might be ambiguous if written syllabically, similar to the ambiguity of *can* in "He saw that gasoline can explode." In addition, kanji writing is an integral part of Japanese culture, and it is unlikely to be abandoned.

In America in 1821, the Cherokee Sequoyah invented a syllabic writing system for his native language. Sequoyah's script, which survives today essentially unchanged, proved useful to the Cherokee people and is justifiably a point of great pride for them. The syllabary contains eighty-five symbols, many of them derived from Latin characters, which efficiently transcribe spoken Cherokee. A few symbols are shown here:

J gu   Γ hu   ꮼ we   W ta   Ⱨ mi

In some languages, an alphabetic character can be used in certain words to write a syllable. In a word such as *barbecue* (bar-b-q), the single letters represent syllables (*b* for [bi] or [bə], *q* for [kju]).

Consonantal Alphabet Writing

Semitic languages, such as Hebrew and Arabic, are written with alphabets that consist only of consonants. Such an alphabet works for these languages because consonants form the root of most words. For example, the consonants *ktb* in Arabic form the root of words associated with 'write.' Thus *katab* means 'to write,' *aktib* means 'I write,' *kitab* means 'a book,' and so on. Inflectional and derivational processes can be expressed by different vowels inserted into the triconsonantal roots.

Because of this structure, vowels, hence meaning and pronunciation, can be inferred by a person who knows the spoken language, jst lk y cn rd ths phrs, prvdng y knw nglsh. In contrast to Semitic languages like Arabic and Hebrew, however, in English both vowels and consonants are usually crucial, as the Dilbert cartoon illustrates.

Semitic alphabets provide a way to use diacritic marks to express vowels. This is partly out of the desire to preserve the true pronunciation of religious writings, and partly out of deference to children and foreigners learning to read and write. In Hebrew, dots or other small figures are placed under, above, or even in the center of the consonantal letter to indicate the accompanying vowel. For example, ל represents an l-sound in Hebrew writing. Unadorned, the vowel that follows would be determined by context. However, ל (with a tiny triangle of dots below it) indicates that the vowel that follows is [ɛ], so in effect ל the syllable [lɛ]. Yiddish, a Germanic language, is written using a version of the Hebrew alphabet that includes symbols and diacritics for vowel sounds.

The Semitic systems are called consonantal alphabets because only the consonants are fully developed symbols. Sometimes they are considered syllabaries because once the vowel is perceived, the consonantal letter *seems* to stand for a syllable. With a true syllabary, however, a person need know only the phonetic value of each symbol to pronounce it correctly and unambiguously. Once you learn a Japanese syllabary, you can read Japanese in a (more or less) phonetically correct way without knowing any Japanese. This would be impossible for Arabic or Hebrew without the vowel diacritics.

Alphabetic Writing

Alphabetic writing systems are easy to learn, convenient to use, and maximally efficient for transcribing any human language. They are based on the **phonemic principle**, where each letter or letter combination represents a phoneme of the language, and non-phonemic differences, such as the various pronunciations of /p/ discussed in chapter 6, are not represented.

In the twelfth century, an Icelandic scholar developed an alphabetic writing system for the Icelandic language of his day. The orthography he developed was clearly based on the phonemic principle. He used minimal pairs to show the distinctive contrasts. He did not suggest different symbols for voiced and unvoiced [θ] and [ð], nor for [f] or [v], nor for velar [k] and palatal [tʃ], because these pairs are allophones (different pronunciations) of the phonemes /θ/, /f/, and /k/, respectively. The letters of this alphabet represented the distinctive phonemes of Icelandic of that century.

King Seijong of Korea (1397–1450) realized that the same principles held true for Korean when, with the assistance of scholars, he designed a phonemic alphabet. The king was an avid reader and realized that the more than 30,000 Chinese characters used to write Korean discouraged literacy. The fruit of the king's labor was the Korean alphabet called **Hangul**, which today has fourteen consonants (five of which may be long) and ten vowels that may combine further to form eleven diphthongs. (Cf. English /a/ and /ɪ/ that form the diphthong /aɪ/.)

The Hangul alphabet was designed on the phonemic principle. Although Korean has the sounds [l] and [r], Seijong represented them by a single letter because they are allophonic variants of the same phoneme. (See exercise 4, chapter 6.) The same is true for the sounds [s] and [ʃ], and [ts] and [tʃ].

Seijong showed further ingenuity in the design of the characters themselves. The consonants are drawn so as to depict the place and manner of articulation. Thus the letter for /g/ is ᄀ to suggest the raising of the back of the tongue to the velum. The letter for /m/ is the closed figure ▢ to suggest the closing of the lips. Vowels are drawn as long vertical or horizontal lines, sometimes with smaller marks attached to them. Thus ᅵ represents /i/, ᅮ represents /u/, and ᅡ represents /a/. They are easily distinguishable from the blockier consonants.

In Korean writing, the Hangul characters are grouped into squarish blocks, each corresponding to a syllable. The syllabic blocks, though they consist of alphabetic characters, make Korean look as if it were written in a syllabary. If English were written that way, "Now is the winter of our discontent" might have this appearance:

No	i	th	wi te	o	ou	di co te
w	s	e	n r	f	r	s n nt

The space between letters is less than the space between syllables, which is less than the space between words. An example of Korean writing can be found in exercise 9, item 10 at the end of the chapter, or on the Internet (http://think-zone.wlonk.com/Language/Korean.htm).

Many languages have their own alphabets, and each has developed certain conventions for reading and writing. As we have illustrated with English, Icelandic, and Korean, the rules governing the sound system of the language play an important role in the relation between sound and character.

Most European alphabets use Latin (Roman) letters, adding **diacritic marks** to accommodate individual characteristics. For example, Spanish uses the diacritic mark ~ in ñ to represent the palatalized nasal phoneme of *señor*, and German has added a so-called umlaut for certain of its vowel sounds that did not exist in Latin (e.g., in *über*).

Diacritic marks supplement the forty-six kana of the Japanese syllabaries to enable them to represent the more than 100 syllables of the language. Diacritic marks are also used in writing systems of tone languages such as Thai to indicate the tone of a syllable.

Some languages use two letters together—called a **digraph**—to represent a single sound. English has many digraphs, such as *sh* /ʃ/ as in *she*, *ch* /tʃ/ as in *chop*, *ng* as in *sing* (/sɪŋ/), and *oa* as in *loaf* /lof/.

Besides the European languages, languages such as Turkish, Indonesian, Swahili, and Vietnamese have adopted the Latin alphabet. Other languages that have more recently developed a writing system use some of the IPA phonetic symbols in their alphabet. Twi, for example, uses ɔ, ɛ, and ŋ.

Many Slavic languages, especially Russian, use the Cyrillic alphabet, named in honor of St. Cyril. It is derived directly from the Greek alphabet without Latin mediation. See the website at http://www.pbs.org/weta/faceofrussia/reference/cyrillic.html for details.

Many contemporary alphabets, such as those used for Arabic, Farsi (spoken in Iran), Urdu (spoken in Pakistan), and many languages of the Indian subcontinent are ultimately derived from the ancient Semitic syllabaries.

Figure 12.2 shows a coarse time line of the development of the Roman alphabet.

15000 BCE	—	Cave drawings as pictograms
.		
.		
.		
4000 BCE	—	Sumerian cuneiform
3000 BCE	—	Hieroglyphics
1500 BCE	—	West Semitic Syllabary of the Phoenicians
1000 BCE	—	Ancient Greeks borrow the Phoenician consonantal alphabet
750 BCE	—	Etruscans borrow the Greek alphabet
500 BCE	—	Romans adapt the Etruscan/Greek alphabet to Latin

FIGURE 12.2 | Timeline of the development of the Roman alphabet.

Writing and Speech

ALGERNON: But, my own sweet Cecily, I have never written you any letters.

CECILY: You need hardly remind me of that, Ernest. I remember only too well that I was forced to write your letters for you. I wrote always three times a week, and sometimes oftener.

ALGERNON: Oh, do let me read them, Cecily?

CECILY: Oh, I couldn't possibly. They would make you far too conceited. The three you wrote me after I had broken off the engagement are so beautiful, and so badly spelled, that even now I can hardly read them without crying a little.

OSCAR WILDE, *The Importance of Being Earnest*, 1895

The development of writing freed us from the limitations of time and geography, but spoken language is still primary and constitutes the principal concern of most linguists. Nevertheless, writing systems are of interest for their own sake.

The written language reflects, to a certain extent, the elements and rules that together constitute the grammar of the language. The letters of the alphabet largely represent the system of phonemes, although not necessarily in a direct way. The independence of words is revealed by the spaces between them in most writing systems. However, written Japanese and Thai do not require spaces between words, although speakers and writers are aware of the individual words. On the other hand, no writing system shows the individual morphemes within a word in this way, even though speakers know what they are. (The hyphen occasionally serves this purpose in English, as in *ten-speed* or *bone-dry*.)

Languages vary in regard to how much punctuation is used in writing. Some have little or none, such as Chinese. German uses capitalization, a form of punctuation, for all nouns. English uses punctuation to set apart sentences and phrases and to indicate questions, intonation, stress, and contrast.

Consider the difference in meaning between sentences 1 and 2:

1. I don't think I know.
2. I don't think, I know.

In (1), the speaker doesn't know; in (2), the speaker knows. The comma fills in for the pause that would make the meaning clear if spoken.

Similarly, by using an exclamation point or a question mark, the intention of the writer can be made clearer.

3. The children are going to bed at eight o'clock. (a simple statement)
4. The children are going to bed at eight o'clock! (an order)
5. The children are going to bed at eight o'clock? (a question)

In sentences 6 and 7, the use of the comma and quotation marks affects the syntax. In 6 *he* may refer either to John or to someone else, but in sentence 7 the pronoun must refer to someone other than John:

6. John said he's going.
7. John said, "He's going."

The apostrophe used in contractions and possessives also provides syntactic information not always available in the spoken utterance.

8. My cousin's friends (one cousin)
9. My cousins' friends (two or more cousins)

Writing, then, somewhat reflects the spoken language, and punctuation may even distinguish between two meanings not revealed in the spoken forms, as shown in sentences 8 and 9. On the other hand the spoken language may convey meaning that the written language does not. In the normal written version of sentence 10,

10. John whispered the message to Bill and then he whispered it to Mary.

he can refer to either John or Bill. In the spoken sentence, if *he* receives extra stress (called **contrastive stress**), it must refer to Bill; if *he* receives normal stress, it refers to John.

A speaker can usually emphasize any word in a sentence by using contrastive stress. Writers sometimes attempt to show emphasis by using all capital letters, italics, or underlining emphasized words. This is nicely illustrated by the "Garfield" cartoon.

In the first panel we understand Garfield as meaning, 'I didn't do it, someone else did.' In the second panel the meaning is 'I didn't do it, even though you think I did.' In the third, the contrastive stress conveys the meaning 'I didn't do it, it just happened somehow.' In the fourth panel Garfield means, 'I didn't do it, though I may be guilty of other things.' In each case the bold-faced word is contrasted with something else.

"Garfield" 1993 Paws, Inc. Universal Uclick

Although such visual devices can help in English, it is not clear that they can be used in a language such as Chinese. In Japanese, however, this kind of emphasis can be achieved by writing a word in katakana.

The use of italics has many functions in written language. One use is to indicate reference to the italicized word, as in "*sheep* is a noun." A children's riddle, which is sung aloud, plays on this distinction:

Railroad crossing, watch out for cars
How do you spell it without any *r*'s?

The answer is *i-t*. The joke is that the second line, if it were properly written, would be:

How do you spell *it* without any *r*'s?

Written language is more conservative than spoken language. Once a word is spelled and written down, that spelling remains intact, although the word's pronunciation may change over time. When we write we are more apt to obey the prescriptive rules taught in school than when we speak. We may write "it is I" but we say "it's me." Such informalities abound in spoken language. A linguist wishing to describe the language that people regularly use cannot therefore depend on written records alone, except when nothing else is available, as in the study of speaker-less languages (see chapter 8).

Spelling

"Do you spell it with a 'v' or a 'w'?" inquired the judge.

"That depends upon the taste and fancy of the speller, my Lord," replied Sam.

CHARLES DICKENS, *The Pickwick Papers*, 1837

If writing represented the spoken language perfectly, spelling reforms would never have arisen. In chapter 5 we discussed some of the problems in the English orthographic system. These problems prompted George Bernard Shaw to observe that:

[I]t was as a reading and writing animal that Man achieved his human eminence above those who are called beasts. Well, it is I and my like who have to do the writing. I have done it professionally for the last sixty years as well as it can be done with a hopelessly inadequate alphabet devised centuries before the English language existed to record another and very different language. Even this alphabet is reduced to absurdity by a foolish orthography based on the notion that the business of spelling is to represent the origin and history of a word instead of its sound and meaning. Thus an intelligent child who is bidden to spell *debt*, and very properly spells it d-e-t, is caned for not spelling it with a b because Julius Caesar spelt the Latin word for it with a b.[4]

The irregularities between graphemes (letters) and phonemes have been cited as one reason "why Johnny can't read." Homographs such as *lead* /lid/ and *lead* /lɛd/ have fueled the flames of spelling reform movements. Different spellings for the same sound, silent letters and missing letters also are cited as reasons that English needs a new orthographic system. The following examples illustrate the discrepancies between spelling and sounds in English:

Same Sound Different Spelling	Different Sound Same Spelling		Silent Letters	Missing Letters	
/aɪ/	thought	/θ/	listen	use	/juz/
	though	/ð/	debt	fuse	/fjuz/
aye	Thomas	/t/	gnome		
buy			know		
by	ate	/e/	psychology		
die	at	/æ/	right		
hi	father	/a/	mnemonic		
Thai	many	/ɛ/	science		
height			talk		
guide			honest		
			sword		
			bomb		
			clue		
			Wednesday		
			corps		
			autumn		

[4]Shaw, G. B. 1948. Preface to R. A. Wilson, *The miraculous birth of language*. New York: Philosophical Library.

The spelling of most English words today is based on English as spoken in the fourteenth, fifteenth, and sixteenth centuries. Spellers in those times saw no need to spell the same word consistently. Shakespeare spelled his own name in several ways. In his plays, he spelled the first person singular pronoun variously as *I*, *ay*, and *aye*.

After Johannes Gutenberg invented the printing press in the mid-fifteenth century, archaic and idiosyncratic spellings became widespread and more permanent. Words in print were frequently misspelled outright because many of the early printers were not native speakers of English.

Spelling reformers saw the need for consistent spelling that correctly reflected the pronunciation of words. To that extent, spelling reform was necessary, but many scholars became overzealous. Because of their reverence for Classical Greek and Latin, these scholars changed the spelling of English words to conform to their etymologies. Where Latin had a *b*, they added a *b* even if it was not pronounced. Where the original spelling had a *c* or *p* or *h*, these letters were added, as shown by these few examples:

Middle English Spelling		Reformed Spelling
indite	→	indict
dette	→	debt
receit	→	receipt
oure	→	hour

Such spelling habits inspired Robert N. Feinstein to compose the following poem, entitled *Gnormal Pspelling*:[5]

Gnus and gnomes and gnats and such
Gnouns with just one G too much.
Pseudonym and psychedelic
P becomes a psurplus relic.
Knit and knack and knife and knocked
Kneedless Ks are overstocked.
Rhubarb, rhetoric and rhyme
Should lose an H from thyme to time.

Many languages have been the subject of **spelling reforms** in the past hundred years, including Dutch, French, Norwegian, and Russian. The motivation is generally to make spelling easier for children or immigrants, and for the convenience of international communications. As recently as 1996 some German-speaking countries imposed spelling reforms that make spelling less archaic (replacing the traditional ß with ss) and more regular (*rauh* → *rau* ('rough') because of *blau, grau, genau*). As is so often the case, there is much resistance to the imposed changes, which continues to this day.

---

[5]"Gnormal Pspelling" by Robert N. Feinstein from "Son of an Oyster." Copyright © 1986 by Robert N. Feinstein. Reprinted by permission of Roger Lathbury DBA Orchises Press as representative for the estate of Robert N. Feinstein.

Texting

"Blondie" © 2009 King Features Syndicate

Short Message Services (SMS) such as texting, instant messaging (IMing), twittering, and the like are having a growing effect on spelling. Owing to limited space, the words in a text message are often spelled as tersely as comprehension allows. For example, "wat uz tnk of da wy da englsh lang iz evolvn tru da eva incresn yus of txt msgs" (79 keystrokes) for "what do you (all) think of the way the English language is evolving through the ever increasing use of text messages?" (117 keystrokes). Text message spelling is far from standardized. Each person has his own peculiar habits. The need to be understood is paramount, though, and a trick once known only to reading experts has been discovered by the folks who text message: When the letters of a word are scrambled or omitted, retaining the first and last letters is the most important. Try this:

fi yuo cna raed tihs, you porbblay hvae a snees fo txet mssegnig

The rebus principle also pops up in text messaging: *cre8* for 'create' or *1der* for 'wonder.' There is much phonetic spelling: *yusfl* for 'useful' or *thru* for 'through,' and a plethora of acronyms: LOL for 'laugh out loud,' among thousands of others (http://textingabbreviations.blogspot.com/). And even the most tradition-bound spellers may want to step aside and wink at the keystroke-saving *nite* for 'night,' *Wensday* for 'Wednesday,' and so on.

Although some say—these "some" are always saying—that texting and twittering are wrecking the language, in truth the adaptation to mobile communication is yet another example of the enormous creativity that is part of our language competence. And truly, there is nothing in texting that hasn't been done before in the history of writing, from rebuses to logographs to syllabic spelling to acronyms to abbreviations to secret code words (used to deceive nosy parents) and so on. An excellent treatment of the subject is to be found in David Crystal's book *Txtng: The Gr8 Db8*.

The Current English Spelling System

> When our spelling is perfect, it's invisible. But when it's flawed, it prompts strong negative associations.
>
> MARILYN VOS SAVANT

Today's spelling is based primarily on the earlier pronunciations of words. The many changes that have occurred in the sound system of English since then are not reflected in the current spelling, which was frozen due to widespread printed material and scholastic conservatism.

For these reasons, modern English orthography does not always represent what we know about the phonology of the language. The disadvantage is partially offset by the fact that the writing system allows us to read and understand what people wrote hundreds of years ago without the need for translations. If there were a one-to-one correspondence between our spelling and the sounds of our language, we would have difficulty reading the works of Shakespeare and Dickens.

Languages change. It is not possible to maintain a perfect correspondence between pronunciation and spelling, nor is it totally desirable. For instance, in the case of homophones, it is helpful at times to have different spellings for the same sounds, as in the following pair:

The book was red. The book was read.

Lewis Carroll makes the point with humor:

"And how many hours a day did you do lessons?" said Alice.
"Ten hours the first day," said the Mock Turtle, "nine the next, and so on."
"What a curious plan!" exclaimed Alice.
"That's the reason they're called lessons," the Gryphon remarked, "because they lessen from day to day."

There are also reasons for using the same spelling for different pronunciations. A morpheme may be pronounced differently when it occurs in different contexts. The identical spelling reflects the fact that the different pronunciations represent the same morpheme. This is the case with the plural morpheme. It is always spelled with an *s* despite being pronounced [s] in *cats* and [z] in *dogs*. The sound of the morpheme is determined by rules, in this case and elsewhere.

Similarly, the phonetic realizations of the underlined vowels in the following forms follow a regular pattern:

aɪ/ɪ	i/ɛ	e/æ
div**i**ne/div**i**nity	ser**e**ne/ser**e**nity	s**a**ne/s**a**nity
ch**i**ld/ch**i**ldren	obsc**e**ne/obsc**e**nity	prof**a**ne/prof**a**nity
s**i**gn/s**i**gnature	cl**ea**n/cl**ea**nse	hum**a**ne/hum**a**nity

These considerations have led some scholars to suggest that in addition to being phonemic, English has a **morphophonemic orthography**. To read English correctly, morphophonemic knowledge is required. This contrasts with a language such as Spanish, whose orthography is almost purely phonemic.

Other examples provide further motivation for spelling irregularities. The *b* in *debt* may remind us of the related word *debit*, in which the *b* is pronounced. The same principle is true of pairs such as *sign/signal*, *bomb/bombardier*, and *gnosis/prognosis/agnostic*.

There are also different spellings that represent the different pronunciations of a morpheme when confusion would arise from using the same spelling. For example, there is a rule in English phonology that changes a /t/ to an /s/ in certain cases:

democrat → democracy

The different spellings have resulted partly because this rule does not apply to all morphemes, so that *heart + y* is *hearty*, not **hearcy*. Regular phoneme-to-grapheme rules often determine when a morpheme is to be spelled identically and when it is to be changed.

Other subregularities are apparent. A *c* always represents the /s/ sound when it is followed by a *y, i,* or *e*, as in *cynic, citizen,* and *censure*. Because it is always pronounced [k] when it is the final letter in a word or when it is followed by any other vowel (*coat, cat, cut,* and so on), no confusion results. The *th* spelling is usually pronounced as voiced [ð] between vowels as in *rather* or *mother*, and in function words such as *the, they, this,* and *there*. Elsewhere it is mostly the voiceless [θ] though it shows up as [t] in *Thomas, Theresa, Thai* and other "exceptions."

There is another important reason why spelling should not always be tied to the pronunciation of words. Different dialects of English have divergent pronunciations. Cockneys drop their "(h)aitches," and Bostonians and Southerners drop their *r*'s; *neither* is pronounced [niðər], [naɪðər], and [niðə] by Americans, [naɪðə] by the British, and [neðər] by the Irish; some Scots pronounce *night* [nɪxt]; people say "Chicago" and "Chicawgo," "hog" and "hawg," "bird" and "boyd"; *four* is pronounced [fɔː] by the British, [fɔr] in the Midwest, and [foə] in the South; *orange* is pronounced in at least two ways in the United States: [arə̃ndʒ] and [ɔrə̃ndʒ].

Although pronunciations differ across dialects, the common spellings indicate the intended words. It is necessary for the written language to transcend local dialects. With a uniform spelling system, a native of Atlanta and a native of Glasgow can communicate through writing. If each dialect were spelled according to its pronunciation, written communication among the English-speaking peoples of the world would suffer.

Spelling Pronunciations

> For pronunciation, the best general rule is to consider those as the most elegant speakers who deviate least from written words.
>
> SAMUEL JOHNSON (1707–1784)

> Write with the learned, pronounce with the vulgar.
>
> BENJAMIN FRANKLIN, *Poor Richard's Almanack*, mid-eighteenth century

---

Despite the primacy of speech, the written word is often regarded with excessive reverence. The stability, permanency, and graphic nature of writing cause some people to favor it over the more ephemeral and elusive speech. Humpty Dumpty expressed a rather typical attitude when he said, "I'd rather see that done on paper."

Writing has affected speech only marginally, however: most notably in the phenomenon of **spelling pronunciation**. Since the sixteenth century, we find that spelling has to some extent influenced standard pronunciation. The most important of such changes stem from the eighteenth century under the influence and decrees of the dictionary makers and the schoolteachers. The struggle between those who demanded that words be pronounced according to the spelling and those who demanded that words be spelled according to their pronunciation generated great heat in that century. The preferred pronunciations were given in the many dictionaries printed in the eighteenth century, and the "supreme authority" of the dictionaries influenced pronunciation in this way.

Spelling also has influenced pronunciation of words that are used infrequently in daily speech. In many words that were spelled with an initial *h*, the *h* was silent as recently as the eighteenth century. Then, no [h] was pronounced in *honest, hour, habit, heretic, hotel, hospital,* and *herb*. Common words like *honest* and *hour* continued *h*-less, despite the spelling. The other less frequently used words were given a "spelling pronunciation," and the *h* is sounded today. *Herb* is currently undergoing this change. In British English the *h* is pronounced, whereas in American English it generally is not.

Similarly, the *th* in the spelling of many words was once pronounced like the /t/ in *Thomas*. Later most of these words underwent a change in pronunciation from /t/ to /θ/, as in *anthem, author,* and *theater*. Nicknames may reflect the earlier pronunciations: "Ka*t*e" for "Ca*th*erine," "Be*tt*y" for "Eliza*beth*," "Ar*t*" for "Ar*th*ur." *Often* is often pronounced with the *t* sounded, though historically it is silent, and up-to-date dictionaries now indicate this pronunciation as an alternative.

The clear influence of spelling on pronunciation is observable in the way place-names are pronounced. *Berkeley* is pronounced [bərkli] in California, although it stems from the British [baːkli]; *Worcester* [wʊstər] or [wʊstə] in Massachusetts is often pronounced [wurtʃɛstər] in other parts of the country. *Salmon* is pronounced [sæmə̃n] in most parts of the United States, but many Southern speakers pronounce the [l] and say [sælmə̃n].

Although the written language has some influence on the spoken, it does not change the basic system—the grammar—of the language. Indeed, writing, even the deviant writing of abbreviated text messages, and the artistic writing of poets, does not stray far from the grammar that every speaker knows.

Pseudo-writing

Sometimes called "false writing," a pseudo-writing system is based on an artificially constructed alphabet made to look real for such purposes as representing alien dialogue in comic strips. Such alphabets are often **asemic** (meaningless) and unrelated to any actual alphabet or spoken language.

Arguably one of the most bizarre creations ever to undergo printing is the *Codex Seraphinianus* by Italian artist and architect Luigi Serafini. The nearly 400-page book is filled with other-worldly illustrations and thousands of lines of what appear to be alphabetic writing both in printed capital letters and a cursive script. So realistic does this writing seem that when the author himself claimed it was intended to be meaningless and unrelated to any spoken language, scholars nevertheless attempted to decipher it, much as they had done with cuneiform and hieroglyphic writing. Here is a small sample of pseudo-writing from this work. The first are uppercase letters; the second is cursive script:

Serafini L. 2006. *The Codex Seraphinianus.* Milano: Rizzoli, 2006, 384 pp., ISBN 88-17-01389-7.

While it is impossible to say whether authors of pseudo-writing are drawing on their linguistic competence or their artistic muse, or quite likely both, it is clear from "reading" (well, looking at, really) the *Codex Seraphinianus* that it represents the extraordinary capacity of human creativity.

Summary

Writing is a basic tool of civilization. Without it, the world as we know it could not exist. The precursor of writing was "picture writing," which used **pictograms** to represent objects directly and literally. Pictograms are called **ideograms** when the drawings become less literal, and the meanings extend to concepts associated with the objects originally pictured. When ideograms become associated with the words for the concepts they signify, they are called **logograms**. Logographic systems are true writing systems in the sense that the symbols stand for words of a language.

The Sumerians first developed a pictographic writing system to keep track of commercial transactions. It was later expanded for other uses and eventually evolved into the highly stylized (and stylus-ized) **cuneiform** writing. Cuneiform was generalized to other writing systems by application of the **rebus principle**, which uses the symbol of one word or syllable to represent another word or syllable pronounced the same.

The Egyptians also developed a pictographic system known as **hieroglyphics**. This system influenced many peoples, including the Phoenicians, who developed the West Semitic Syllabary. The Greeks borrowed the Phoenician system, and in adapting it to their own language they used the symbols to represent both consonant and vowel sound segments, thus inventing the first alphabet.

There are four types of writing systems: (1) **logographic** (word writing), in which every symbol or character represents a word or morpheme (as in Chinese); (2) **syllabic**, in which each symbol represents a syllable (as in

Japanese hiragana); (3) **consonantal alphabetic**, in which each symbol represents a consonant and vowels may be represented by diacritical marks (as in Hebrew); and (4) **alphabetic**, in which each symbol represents (for the most part) a vowel or consonant (as in English).

Languages change over time, but writing systems tend to be more conservative. In many languages, including English, spelling may no longer accurately reflect pronunciation. This has led to **spelling reforms** in many countries. Also, when the spoken and written forms of the language diverge, some words may be pronounced as they are spelled, sometimes as a result of the efforts of pronunciation reformers.

There are advantages to a conservative spelling system. A common spelling permits speakers whose dialects have diverged to communicate through writing, as is best exemplified in China, where the "dialects" (languages, really) are mutually unintelligible. People are also able to read and understand their language as it was written centuries ago. In addition, despite a certain lack of correspondences between sound and spelling, the spelling often reflects speakers' morphological and phonological knowledge.

The most recent change in the writing habits of people has arisen through the prolific use of **Short Message Services (SMS)** such as instant messaging, which put a premium on minimizing the number of characters used to spell words irrespective of their "proper" spelling, leading to the omission of "superfluous" letters and copious use of all manner of abbreviations such as **acronyms** and **clippings**.

References for Further Reading

Adams, M. J. 1996. *Beginning to read.* Cambridge, MA: MIT Press.

Biber, D. 1988. *Variation across speech and writing.* Cambridge, UK: Cambridge University Press.

Coulmas, F. 1989. *The writing systems of the world.* Cambridge, MA: Blackwell Publishers.

Crystal, David. 2008. *Txtng: The gr8 db8.* London: Oxford University Press.

Cummings, D. W. 1988. *American English spelling.* Baltimore, MD: The Johns Hopkins University Press.

Daniels, P. T., 2001. *Writing systems.* In *The handbook of linguistics*, M. Aronoff and J. Rees-Miller (eds). Hoboken, NJ: Blackwell.

DeFrancis, J. 1989. *Visible speech: The diverse oneness of writing systems.* Honolulu: University of Hawaii Press.

Gaur, A. 1984. *A history of writing.* London: The British Library.

Rogers, H. 2005. *Writing systems: A linguistic approach.* Malden, MA: Blackwell Publishing.

Sampson, G. 1985. *Writing systems: A linguistic introduction.* Stanford, CA: Stanford University Press.

Senner, W. M. (ed.). 1989. *The origins of writing.* Lincoln: University of Nebraska Press.

Serafini L. 2006. *The Codex Seraphinianus.* Milan: Rizzoli.

Exercises

1. **Part One:** "Write" the following words and phrases, using pictograms that you invent:
    a. eye
    b. a boy
    c. two boys
    d. library
    e. tree
    f. forest
    g. war
    h. honesty
    i. ugly
    j. run
    k. Scotch tape
    l. smoke

    Part Two: Which words are most difficult to symbolize in this way? Why?

    Part Three: How does the following statement reveal the problems in pictographic writing? "A grammar represents the unconscious, internalized linguistic competence of a native speaker."

2. A *rebus* is a written representation of words or syllables that uses pictures of objects whose names resemble the sounds of the intended words or syllables. For example, might be the symbol for "eye" or "I" or the first syllable in "idea."

    Part One: Using the rebus principle, "write" the following words:
    a. tearing
    b. icicle
    c. bareback
    d. cookies

    Part Two: Why would such a system be a difficult system in which to represent all words in English? Illustrate with an example.

3. **A.** Construct non-Roman alphabetic letters to replace the letters used to represent the following sounds in English:

    [t r s k w tʃ i æ f n]

    B. Use the letters you created plus the regular alphabet symbols for the other sounds to write the following words in your "new" orthography.
    a. character
    b. guest
    c. cough
    d. photo
    e. cheat
    f. rang
    g. psychotic
    h. tree

4. Suppose the English writing system were a *syllabic* system instead of an *alphabetic* system. Use capital letters to symbolize the necessary syllabic units for the following words, and list your "syllabary." Example: Given the words *mate, inmate, intake,* and *elfin,* you might use A = mate, B = in, C = take, and D = elf. In addition, write the words using your syllabary. Example: *inmate*—BA; *elfin*—DB; *intake*—BC; *mate*—A. (Do not use more syllable symbols than you absolutely need.)

a. childishness	**g.** witness
b. childlike	**h.** lethal
c. Jesuit	**i.** jealous
d. lifelessness	**j.** witless
e. likely	**k.** lesson
f. zoo	

5. In the following pairs of English words, the boldfaced portions are pronounced the same but spelled differently. Can you think of any reason why the spelling should remain distinct? (Hint: *Reel* and *real* are pronounced the same, but *reality* shows the presence of a phonemic /æ/ in *real*.)

	A	B	Reason
a.	I **am**	i**amb**	
b.	g**oose**	pr**oduce**	
c.	f**ashion**	compl**ication**	
d.	New**ton**	or**gan**	
e.	n**o**	kn**ow**	
f.	hy**mn**	**him**	

6. In the following pairs of words, the boldfaced portions are spelled the same but pronounced differently. State some reasons why the spellings of the words in column B should not be changed.

	A	B	Reason
a.	mi**ng**le	lo**ng**	The *g* is pronounced in *longer*.
b.	l**i**ne	ch**i**ldren	
c.	**s**onar	re**s**ound	
d.	**c**ent	mysti**c**	
e.	crumb**le**	bom**b**	
f.	cat**s**	dog**s**	
g.	sta**gn**ant	desi**gn**	
h.	ser**ene**	obsc**eni**ty	

7. Each of the following sentences is ambiguous in the written form. How can these sentences be made unambiguous when they are spoken?

Example: John hugged Bill and then he kissed him.

For the meaning "John hugged and kissed Bill," use normal stress (*kissed* receives stress). For the meaning "Bill kissed John," contrastive stress is needed on both *he* and *him*.

a. What are we having for dinner, Mother?
b. She's a German language teacher.
c. They formed a student grievance committee.
d. Charles kissed his wife and George kissed his wife too.

8. In the written form, the following sentences are not ambiguous, but they would be if spoken. State the devices used in writing that make the meanings explicit.

    a. They're my brothers' keepers.
    b. He said, "He will take the garbage out."
    c. The red book was read.
    d. The flower was on the table.

9. Match the ten samples of writing and the ten languages. There are enough hints in this chapter to get most of them. (The source of these examples, and many others, is *Languages of the World* by Kenneth Katzner, 1975, New York: Funk & Wagnalls.)

a. _____ Cherokee		**1.**	仮に勝手に変えるようなことをすれば.
b. _____ Chinese		**2.**	Κι ὁ νοῦς του ἀγκάλιασε πονετικὰ τὴν Κρήτη.
c. _____ German (Gothic style)		**3.**	«Что это? я падаю? у меня ноги подкашиваются»,
d. _____ Greek		**4.**	וְהָיָה ׀ בְּאַחֲרִית הַיָּמִים נָכוֹן יִהְיֶה הַר
e. _____ Hebrew		**5.**	Saá sáre yi bɛ̩ŋ atɛkyé bí â mpɔ̀torɔ áhyé
f. _____ Icelandic		**6.**	既然必须和新的群众的时代相结合.
g. _____ Japanese		**7.**	*Jℰ�챕 DᎠ JᎦ06 CᏔᎩ CᎧł�286.*
h. _____ Korean		**8.**	Þótt þú langförull legðir sérhvert land undir fót,
i. _____ Russian		**9.**	Pharao's Anblick war wunderbar.
j. _____ Twi		**10.**	스위스는 독특한 체제

10. The following appeared on the safety card of a Spanish airline. Identify each language.

Para su seguridad
For your safety
Pour votre sécurité
Für ihre Sicherheit
Per la Vostra sicurezza
Para sua segurança
あなたの安全のために
Для Вашей безогіасности
Dla bezpieczeństwa
   pasażerów
Za vašu sigurnost
Γιά τήν ἀσφάλειά σας
Kendi emniyetiniz için
من أجل سلامتك

11. Diderot and D'Alembert, the French "Encyclopedists," wrote:

    The Chinese have no alphabet; their very language is incompatible with one, since it is made up of an extremely limited number of sounds. It would be impossible to convey the sound of Chinese through our alphabet or any other alphabet.

Comment on this.

12. Here are several emoticons. See whether you can assign a meaning to each one. There is no one correct answer because they haven't been in the language long enough to become conventionalized. One possible set of answers is printed upside down in the footnote.[6]

   a. >:–(e. :-(o)
   b. :–#   f. :–(O)
   c. 8:—(g. |–)
   d. :D   h. :/)

13. Just as words may be synonyms (*sad*, *unhappy*), so may emoticons. Thus :–> and :–) are both used to mean 'just kidding.'

   A. Try to come up with three instances in which different emoticons have approximately the same meaning.
   B. Emoticons may also be ambiguous, that is, subject to different interpretations. You may have discovered that in the previous exercise. Cite three instances in which a single emoticon may be given two different interpretations.

14. Make up five or ten emoticons, along with their meanings. Don't just look for them on the Internet (where you'll find hundreds of them). Be creative! For example, **3:>8** to mean 'bull!' or 'stubborn.'

15. Punctuate the following with periods, commas, semicolons, and capital letters so that it makes sense:

   that that is is that that is not is not that that is not is not that that is that that is is not that that is not

16. Think of three (or more) "majority rules" sound-spelling correspondences, and then the several exceptions to each one that make learning to read English difficult. In the text we noted words like *brave, cave, Dave, gave, slave*, etc. in which *a* followed by "silent *e*" is pronounced [e], but *have* is exceptional in that the *a* is pronounced [æ]. Another example might be the *ea* spelling in *beak, leak, peak, weak, teak*, where it is pronounced [i], with exceptions such as *steak* or the president's name *Reagan*, where the *ea* is pronounced [e], or the past tense of *read* where it is pronounced [ɛ].

17. Investigate *nushu* using the time-honored template of answering *what, who, where, when*, and *why*. Using the Internet, or any other source, answer the questions:

   a. What is nushu?
   b. Who was involved with nushu?
   c. Where did nushu exist?
   d. When did nushu exist?

---

e. Surprise.   d. Ha, ha.   c. Condescension.   b. My lips are sealed.   a. Annoyance.[9]
h. Not that funny.   g. See no evil.   f. I'm yelling.

    e. Why did nushu exist?

    f. **Speculative:** Can you think of a situation in your own country that might give rise to a nushu-like situation?

18. **Research project**: Investigate the 1996 spelling reform in German-speaking countries.

    a. What are the countries involved?

    b. Are there reasons for the reform movement other than ease of learning and international communications?

    c. What are some of the arguments *against* this spelling reform legislation?

    d. Do you think the spelling reform will "take hold" in this century? Or will there be a return to the traditional system?

    e. Give three reforms other than those mentioned in this book.

19. Spelling rhyme occurs when two words with similar spelling but different pronunciations are rhymed. Words like *move* and *love* are considered to rhyme by many poets; however, there must be a common consonant in the final syllable, in this case [v]. Examine your favorite poems, or the lyrics of your favorite songs, and find five instances of spelling rhyme.

    Example: in the late Michael Jackson's highly popular song *Thriller* we find:

    Creatures crawl in search of <u>*blood*</u>

    To terrorize your <u>*neighborhood*</u>[7]

    where *blood* and *neighborhood* are spelling rhymes.

---

[7]Michael Jackson, *Thriller.* Lyrics written by Rodney Lynn Temperton. Lyrics © Universal Music Publishing Group. Reprinted by permission.

Glossary

AAE Abbreviates **African American English**.[1] See **Ebonics, AAVE**.

AAVE Abbreviates **African American Vernacular English**. See **Ebonics, AAE**.

abbreviation Shortened form of a word: e.g., *prof* from *professor*. See **clipping**.

abjad Consonantal alphabet writing system; the **consonantal alphabet** of such a system.

accent (1) Prominence. See **stressed syllable**; (2) the phonology or pronunciation of a specific **regional dialect**: e.g., Southern accent; (3) the pronunciation of a language by a nonnative speaker: e.g., French accent.

accidental gap Phonological or morphological form that constitutes possible but non-occurring lexical items: e.g., *blick, unsad*.

acoustic Pertaining to physical aspects of sound.

acoustic phonetics The study of the physical characteristics of speech sounds.

acoustic signal The sound waves produced by any sound source, including speech.

acquired dyslexia Loss of ability to read correctly following brain damage in persons who were previously literate.

acronym Word composed of the initials of several words and pronounced as such: e.g., *PET* scan from *positron-emission tomography* scan. See **alphabetic abbreviation**.

active sentence A sentence in which the noun phrase **subject** in d-structure is also the noun phrase subject in s-structure: e.g., *The dog chased the car*. See **passive sentence**.

adjective (Adj) The syntactic category, also lexical category, of words that function as the head of an **adjective phrase**, and that have the semantic effect of qualifying or describing the referents of nouns: e.g., *tall, bright, intelligent*. See **adjective phrase**.

adjective phrase (AP) A syntactic category, also phrasal category, whose head is an adjective possibly accompanied by premodifiers, that occurs inside noun phrases and as complements of the verb *to be*: e.g., *worthy of praise, several miles high, green, more difficult*.

adverb (Adv) The syntactic category, also lexical category, of words that qualify the verb such as manner adverbs like *quickly* and time adverbs like *soon*. The position of the adverb in the sentence depends on its semantic type: e.g., *John will soon eat lunch, John eats lunch quickly*.

affix A **bound morpheme** attached to a stem or root. See **prefix, suffix, infix, circumfix, stem, root**.

affricate A sound produced by a stop closure followed immediately by a slow release characteristic of a **fricative**; phonetically a sequence of stop + fricative: e.g., the *ch* in *chip*, which is [tʃ] and like [t] + [ʃ].

African American (Vernacular) English (AA(V)E) Dialects of English spoken by some Americans of African descent, or by any person raised from infancy in a place where AAE is spoken. See **Ebonics**.

agent The **thematic role** of the noun phrase whose referent does the action described by the verb: e.g., *George* in *George hugged Martha*.

agglutinative language A type of **synthetic language** in which a word may be formed by a root and multiple affixes where the affixes are easily separated and always retain the same meaning.

agrammatic aphasics Persons suffering from **agrammatism**.

---

[1]Bold words in definitions have a separate entry in this glossary, regardless of whether the bold word or term is preceded by the expression *See*.

agrammatism (agrammatic) Language disorder usually resulting from damage to Broca's region in which the patient has difficulty with certain aspects of syntax, especially functional categories. See **Broca's area**.

agreement The process by which one word in a sentence is altered depending on a property of another word in that sentence, such as gender or number: e.g., the addition of *s* to a regular verb when the subject is third-person singular (in English).

allomorph Alternative phonetic form of a **morpheme**: e.g., the [-s], [-z], and [-əz] forms of the plural morpheme in *cats*, *dogs*, and *kisses*.

allophone A predictable phonetic realization of a **phoneme**: e.g., [p] and [pʰ] are allophones of the phoneme /p/ in English.

alphabetic abbreviation A word composed of the initials of several words and pronounced letter-by-letter: e.g., *MRI* from *magnetic resonance imaging*. See **acronym**.

alphabetic writing A writing system in which each symbol typically represents one sound segment.

alveolar A sound produced by raising the tongue to the **alveolar ridge**: e.g., [s], [t], [n].

alveolar ridge The part of the hard palate directly behind the upper front teeth.

ambiguous, ambiguity The terms used to describe a word, phrase, or sentence with multiple meanings.

American Sign Language (ASL) The sign language used by the deaf community in the United States. See **sign languages**.

analogic change A language change in which a rule spreads to previously unaffected forms: e.g., the plural of *cow* changed from the earlier *kine* to *cows* by the generalization of the plural formation rule or by **analogy** to regular plural forms. Also called **internal borrowing**.

analogy The use of one form as an exemplar by which other forms can be similarly constructed: e.g., based on *bow/bows*, *sow/sows*, English speakers began to say *cows* instead of the older *kine*. Analogy also leads speakers to say **brang* as a past tense of *bring* based on *sing/sang/sung*, *ring/rang/rung*, and so on.

analytic Describes a sentence that is true by virtue of its meaning alone, irrespective of context: e.g., *Kings are male*. See **contradiction**.

analytic language A language in which most words contain a single morpheme, and there is little if any word morphology: e.g., there are no plural affixes on nouns or agreement affixes on verbs. Also called **an isolating language**. Vietnamese is an example of an analytic language.

anomalous Semantically ill-formed: e.g., *Colorless green ideas sleep furiously*.

anomaly A violation of semantic rules resulting in expressions that seem nonsensical: e.g., *The verb crumpled the milk*.

anomia A form of **aphasia** in which patients have word-finding difficulties.

antecedent A noun phrase with which a pronoun is **coreferential**: e.g., *the man who is eating* is the antecedent of the pronoun *himself* in the sentence *The man who is eating bit himself.*

anterior A phonetic feature of consonants whose place of articulation is in front of the palato-alveolar area, including **labials**, **interdentals**, and **alveolars**.

antonymic pair Two words that are pronounced the same (i.e., are homonyms) but spelled differently and whose meanings are opposite: e.g., *raise* and *raze*. See **autoantonym**.

antonyms Words that are opposite with respect to one of their semantic properties: e.g., *tall/short* are both alike in that they describe height, but opposite in regard to the extent of the height. See **gradable pair**, **complementary pair**, **relational opposites**.

aphasia Language loss or disorder following brain damage.

approximants Sounds in which the articulators have a near frictional closeness, but no actual friction occurs: e.g., [w], [j], [r], and [l] in English, where the first three are central approximants, and [l] is a lateral approximant.

arbitrary Describes the property of language, including sign language, whereby there is no natural or intrinsic relationship between the way a word is pronounced (or signed) and its meaning.

arc Part of the graphical depiction of a transition network represented as an arrow, often labeled, connecting two nodes. See **node**, **transition network**.

argot The specialized words used by a particular group, such as pilots or linguists: e.g., *morphophonemics* in linguistics.

arguments The various NPs that occur with a verb: e.g., *Jack* and *Jill* are arguments of *loves* in *Jack loves Jill*.

argument structure The various NPs that occur with particular verbs, called its arguments: e.g., **intransitive verbs** take a subject NP only; **transitive verbs** take both a subject and direct object NP.

article (Art) One of several subclasses of determiners: e.g., *the, a*.

articulatory phonetics The study of how the vocal tract produces speech sounds; the physiological characteristics of speech sounds.

asemic Lacking meaning, often used to describe **pseudo-writing**.

aspirated Describes a voiceless stop produced with a puff of air that results when the vocal cords remain open for a brief period after the release of the stop: e.g., the [pʰ] in *pit*. See **unaspirated**.

assimilation rules/assimilation A phonological process that changes feature values of segments to make them more similar: e.g., a vowel becomes [+nasal] when followed by [+nasal] consonant. Also called **feature-spreading rules**.

asterisk The symbol * used to indicate ungrammatical or anomalous examples: e.g., **cried the baby, *sincerity dances*. Also used in historical and comparative linguistics to represent a reconstructed form.

auditory phonetics The study of the perception of speech sounds.

autoantonym A word that has two opposite meanings: e.g., *cleave*, 'to split apart' or 'to cling together.' See **antonymic pair**.

automatic machine translation The use of computers to translate from one language to another. See **source language**, **target language**.

Aux A syntactic category containing **auxiliary verbs** and abstract tense morphemes that function as the **heads** of **sentences** (**S** or **TP** or **IP**). It is **also called INFL**.

auxiliary verb A verbal element, traditionally called a "helping verb," that co-occurs with, and qualifies, the **main verb** in a verb phrase with regard to such properties as tense: e.g., *have, be, will*.

babbling Speech sounds produced in the first few months after birth that gradually come to include only sounds that occur in the language of the household. Deaf children babble with hand gestures.

baby talk A certain **style** of speech that many adults use when speaking to children that includes among other things exaggerated intonation. See **motherese**, **child-directed speech (CDS)**.

back-formation Creation of a new word by removing an affix from an old word: e.g., *donate* from *donation*; or by removing what is mistakenly considered an affix: e.g., *edit* from *editor*.

backtracking The process of undoing an analysis—usually a top-down analysis—when sensory data indicates it has gone awry, and beginning again at a point where the analysis is consistent with the data: e.g., in the syntactic analysis of *The little orange car sped*, analyzing *orange* as a noun, and later reanalyzing it as an adjective. See **top-down processing**.

base Any **root** or **stem** to which an affix is attached.

bidialectal Persons who know two or more **dialects** and speak the one most appropriate to the sociolinguistic context, often mixing the several dialects. See **codeswitching**.

bilabial A sound articulated by bringing both lips together.

bilingualism The ability to speak two (or more) languages with native or near native proficiency, either by an individual speaker (**individual bilingualism**) or within a society (**societal bilingualism**).

bilingual language acquisition The (more or less) simultaneous acquisition of two or more languages before the age of three years such that each language is acquired with native competency.

bilingual maintenance (BM) Education programs that aim to maintain competence in both languages for the entire educational experience.

birdcall One or more short notes that convey messages associated with the immediate environment, such as danger, feeding, nesting, and flocking.

bird song A complex pattern of notes used to mark territory and to attract mates.

blend A word composed of the parts of more than one word: e.g., *smog* from *smoke* + *fog*.

blocked A derivation that is prevented by a prior application of morphological rules: e.g., when *Commun* + *ist* entered the language, words such as *Commun* + *ite* (as in *Trotsky* + *ite*) or *Commun* + *ian* (as in *grammar* + *ian*) were not needed and were not formed.

borrowing The incorporating of a loan word from one language into another: e.g., English borrowed *buoy* from Dutch. See **loan word**.

bottom-up processing Data-driven analysis of linguistic input that begins with the small units like phones and proceeds stepwise to increasingly larger units like words and phrases until the entire input is processed, often ending in a complete sentence and semantic interpretation. See **top-down processing**.

bound morpheme A **morpheme** that must be attached to other morphemes: e.g., *-ly*, *-ed*, *non-*. Bound morphemes are **prefixes**, **suffixes**, **infixes**, **circumfixes**, and some **roots** such as *cran* in *cranberry*. See **free morpheme**.

broadening A semantic change in which the meaning of a word changes over time to become more encompassing: e.g., *dog* once meant a particular breed of *dog*.

Broca, Paul A French neurologist of the nineteenth century who identified a particular area of the left side of the brain as a language center.

Broca's aphasia See **agrammatism**.

Broca's area A front part of the left hemisphere of the brain, damage to which causes **agrammatism** or **Broca's aphasia**. Also called Broca's region.

calligraphy The decorative art of writing or drawing letters, especially Chinese characters.

case A characteristic of nouns and pronouns, and in some languages articles and adjectives, determined by their function in the sentence, and generally indicated by the morphological form of the word: e.g., *I* is in the nominative case of the first-person singular pronoun in English and functions as a subject; *me* is in the accusative case and functions as an object.

case endings Suffixes on a noun based on its grammatical function, such as *'s* of the English genitive case indicating possession: e.g., *Robert's* sheepdog.

case morphology The process of **inflectional morphemes** combining with nouns to indicate the grammatical relation of the noun in its sentence: e.g., in Russian, the inflectional suffix *-a* added to a noun indicates that the noun is an object.

case theory The study of thematic roles or grammatical case in languages of the world.

cause/causative The thematic role of the noun phrase whose referent is a natural force that is responsible for a change: e.g., *the wind* in *The wind damaged the roof*.

cerebral hemispheres The left and right halves of the brain, joined by the **corpus callosum**.

characters (Chinese) The units of Chinese writing, each of which represents a morpheme or word. See **ideogram**, **ideograph**, **logograms**.

Chicano English (ChE) A **dialect** of English spoken by some bilingual Mexican Americans in the western and southwestern United States.

child-directed speech (CDS) The special intonationally exaggerated speech that some adults sometimes use to speak with small children, sometimes called **baby talk**. See **motherese**.

circumfix A **bound morpheme**, parts of which occur in a word both before and after the root: e.g., *ge—t* in German *geliebt*, 'loved,' from the root *lieb*.

classifier A **grammatical morpheme** that marks the semantic class of a noun: e.g., in Swahili, nouns that refer to human artifacts such as beds and chairs are prefixed with the classifiers *ki* if singular and *vi* if plural; *kiti*, 'chair' and *viti*, 'chairs.'

click A speech sound produced by sucking air into the mouth and forcing it between articulators to produce a sharp sound: e.g., the sound often spelled *tsk*.

clipping The deletion of some part of a longer word to give a shorter word with the same meaning: e.g., *phone* from *telephone*. See **abbreviation**.

closed class A category, generally a **functional category**, that rarely has new words added to it: e.g., prepositions, conjunctions. See **open class**.

coarticulation The transfer of **phonetic features** to adjoining segments to make them more alike: e.g., vowels become [+nasal] when followed by consonants that are [+nasal].

cocktail party effect An informal term that describes the ability to filter out background noise and focus on a particular sound source or on a particular person's speech.

coda One or more phonological segments that follow the **nucleus** of a syllable: e.g., the /st/ in /prist/ *priest*.

codeswitching The movement back and forth between two languages or dialects within the same sentence or discourse.

cognates Words in related languages that developed from the same ancestral root, such as English *man* and German *Mann*.

coinage The construction and/or invention of new words that then become part of the lexicon: e.g., *podcast*.

collocation analysis Textual analysis that reveals the extent to which the presence of one word influences the occurrence of nearby words.

comparative linguistics The branch of historical linguistics that explores language change by comparing related languages.

comparative method The technique linguists use to deduce forms in an ancestral language by examining corresponding forms in several of its descendant languages.

comparative reconstruction The deducing of forms in an ancestral language of genetically related languages by application of the **comparative method**.

competence, linguistic The knowledge of a language represented by the mental grammar that accounts for speakers' linguistic ability and creativity. For the most part, linguistic competence is unconscious knowledge.

complement The constituent(s) in a phrase other than the head that complete(s) the meaning of the phrase and which is **C-selected** by the verb. The right sister to the head in the X-bar schema. In the verb phrase *found a puppy*, the noun phrase *a puppy* is a complement of the verb *found*.

complementary distribution The situation in which phones never occur in the same phonetic environment: e.g., [p] and [pʰ] in English. See **allophone**.

complementary pair Two **antonyms** related in such a way that the negation of one is the meaning of the other: e.g., *alive* means *not dead*. See **gradable pair**, **relational opposites**.

complementizer (C) A syntactic category, also functional category, of words, including *that, if, whether*, that introduce an **embedded sentence**: e.g., *his belief that sheepdogs can swim*, or, *I wonder whether sheepdogs can swim*. The head of a complementizer phrase (CP) in the X-bar schema. The complementizer has the effect of turning a sentence into a complement.

complementizer phrase (CP) An X-bar phrase whose specifier may be a preposed wh-word, whose head C may be a complementizer and possibly a preposed Aux, and whose complement is S or TP.

compositional semantics A theory of meaning that calculates the truth values or meanings of larger units by the application of semantic rules to the truth values or meanings of smaller units.

compound A word composed of two or more words, which may be written as a single word or as words separated by spaces or hyphens: e.g., *dogcatcher, dog biscuit, dog-tired*.

computational forensic linguistics A sub-area of **forensic linguistics** that concerns itself with computer applications in matters involving language, the law, and the judicial system.

computational lexicography The building of electronic dictionaries suitable for use by computational linguists.

computational linguistics A subfield of linguistics and computer science that is concerned with the computer processing of human language.

computational morphology The programming of computers to analyze the structure of words.

computational phonetics and phonology The programming of computers to analyze the speech signal into phones and phonemes.

computational pragmatics The programming of computers to take context and situation into account when determining the meanings of expressions.

computational semantics The programming of computers to determine the meanings of words, phrases, sentences, and discourse.

computational syntax The programming of computers to analyze the structures of sentences. See **parse**, **bottom-up processing**, **top-down processing**.

concatenative (speech) synthesis The computer production of speech based on assembling prerecorded human pronunciations of basic units such as phones, syllables, morphemes, words, phrases, or sentences.

concordance An alphabetical index of the words in a text that gives the frequency of each word, its location in the text, and its surrounding context.

conditioned sound change Historical phonological change that occurs in specific phonetic contexts: e.g., the voicing of /f/ to [v] when it occurs between vowels.

connectionism Modeling grammars through the use of networks consisting of simple neuron-like units connected in complex ways so that different connections vary in strength, and can be strengthened or weakened through exposure to linguistic data. For example, in phonology there would be stronger connections among /p/, /t/, and /k/ (the voiceless stops and a natural class) than among /p/, /n/, and /i/. In morphology there would be stronger connections between *play/played* and *dance/danced* than between *play* and *danced*. Semantically, there would be stronger connections between *melody* and *music* than between *melody* and *sheepdog*. Syntactically, there would be stronger connections between *John loves Mary* and *Mary is loved by John* than between *John loves Mary* and *Mary knows John*.

connotative meaning/connotation The evocative or affective meaning associated with a word. Two words or expressions may have the same **denotative meaning** but different connotations: e.g., *president* and *commander-in-chief*.

consonant A speech sound produced with some constriction of the air stream. See **vowel**.

consonantal The phonetic feature that distinguishes the class of obstruents, liquids, and nasals, which are [+consonantal], from other sounds (vowels and glides), which are [−consonantal].

consonantal alphabet The symbols of a **consonantal writing** system.

consonantal writing A writing system of symbols that represent only **consonants**; vowels are inferred from context: e.g., Arabic.

constituent A syntactic unit in a **phrase structure tree**: e.g., *the girl* is a noun phrase constituent in the sentence *the boy loves the girl*.

constituent structure The hierarchically arranged syntactic units such as noun phrase and verb phrase that underlie every sentence.

constituent structure tree See **phrase structure tree**.

content words The nouns, verbs, adjectives, and adverbs that constitute the major part of the vocabulary. See **open class**.

context The discourse preceding an utterance together with the real-world knowledge of speakers and listeners. See **linguistic context**, **situational context**.

continuant A speech sound in which the air stream flows continually through the mouth; all speech sounds except stops and affricates.

contour tones In tone language, tones in which the **pitch** glides from one level to another: e.g., from low to high as in a rising tone.

contradiction Describes a sentence that is false by virtue of its meaning alone, irrespective of context: e.g., *Kings are female*. See **analytic**, **tautology**.

contradictory Mutual negative entailment: the truth of one sentence necessarily implies the falseness of another sentence, and vice versa: e.g., *The door is open* and *The door is closed* are contradictory sentences. See **entailment**.

contralateral Refers to neural signals that travel between one side of the body (left/right) and the opposite **cerebral hemisphere** (right/left).

contrast Different sounds contrast when their presence alone distinguishes between otherwise identical forms: e.g., [f] and [v] in *fine* and *vine*, but not [p] and [pʰ] in [spik] and [spʰik] (two variant ways of saying *speak*). See **minimal pair**.

contrasting tones In tone languages, different tones that make different words: e.g., in Nupe, *bá* with a high tone and *bà* with a low tone mean 'be sour' and 'count,' respectively.

contrastive stress Additional stress placed on a word to highlight it or to clarify the referent of a pronoun: e.g., in *Joe hired Bill and he hired Sam*, with contrastive stress on *he*, it is usually understood that Bill rather than Joe hired Sam.

convention, conventional The agreed-on, although generally arbitrary, relationship between the form and meaning of words.

cooperative principle A broad principle within whose scope fall the various **maxims of conversation**. It states that in order to communicate effectively, speakers should agree to be informative and relevant.

coordinate structure A syntactic structure in which two or more constituents of the same syntactic category are joined by a conjunction such as *and* or *or*: e.g., *bread and butter*, *the big dog or the small cat*, *huffing and puffing*.

coreference The relation between two noun phrases that refer to the same entity.

coreferential Describes noun phrases (including pronouns) that refer to the same entity.

coronals The class of consonants articulated by raising the tip or blade of the tongue, including **alveolars** and **palatals**: e.g., [t], [ʃ].

corpus A collection of language data gathered from spoken or written sources used for linguistic research and analysis.

corpus callosum The nerve fibers connecting the right and left **cerebral hemispheres**.

cortex The approximately ten billion neurons that form the outside surface of the brain; also referred to as gray matter.

count nouns Nouns that can be enumerated: e.g., *one potato, two potatoes*. See **mass nouns**.

cover symbol A symbol that represents a class of sounds: e.g., C for consonants, V for vowels.

creativity of language, creative aspect of linguistic knowledge Speakers' ability to combine the finite number of linguistic units of their language to produce and understand an infinite range of novel sentences.

creole A language that begins as a **pidgin** and eventually becomes the native language of a speech community.

creolization The linguistic *expansion* in the lexicon and grammar, and an increase in the contexts of use, of an existing **pidgin**. See **pidginization**.

critical-age hypothesis The theory that states that there is a window of time between early childhood and puberty for learning a first language, and beyond which first language acquisition is almost always incomplete.

critical period The time between early childhood and puberty during which a child can acquire a native language easily, swiftly, and without external intervention. After this period, the acquisition of the grammar is difficult and, for some individuals, never fully achieved.

C-selection The classifying of verbs and other lexical items in terms of the syntactic category of the complements that they accept (C stands for categorial), sometimes called **subcategorization**: e.g., the verb *find* C-selects, or is subcategorized for, a noun phrase complement.

culturomics A quantitative analysis of a very large corpus of digitized texts, which may reveal previously undocumented words or pinpoint periods of accelerated language change.

cuneiform A form of writing in which the characters are produced using a wedge-shaped stylus, and most notably utilized by ancient civilizations of the Middle East such as the Sumerians.

data mining Complex methods of retrieving and using information from immense and varied sources of data through the use of advanced statistical tools.

declarative (sentence) A sentence that asserts that a particular situation exists. See **interrogative**.

declension A list of the inflections or **cases** of nouns, pronouns, adjectives, and determiners in categories such as grammatical relationship, number, and gender.

deep structure See **d-structure**.

definite Describes a noun phrase that refers to a particular object known to the speaker and listener.

deictic/deixis Refers to words or expressions whose reference relies on context and the orientation of the speaker in space and time: e.g., *I, yesterday, there, this cat*.

demonstrative articles, demonstratives Words such as *this, that, those*, and *these* that function syntactically as articles but are semantically **deictic** because context is needed to determine the referents of the noun phrases in which they occur.

denotative meaning The referential meaning of a word or expression. See **connotative meaning**.

dental A place-of-articulation term for consonants articulated with the tongue against, or nearly against, the front teeth. See **interdental**.

derivation The steps in the application of rules to an underlying form that results in a surface representation: e.g., in deriving a syntactic s-structure from a d-structure, or in deriving a phonetic form from a phonemic form.

derivational affix See **derivational morpheme**.

derivational morpheme A **morpheme** added to a stem or root to form a new stem or word, possibly, but not necessarily, resulting in a change in syntactic category: e.g., *-er* added to a verb like *kick* to give the noun *kicker*.

derived structure Any structure resulting from the application of transformational rules.

derived word The form that results from the addition of a **derivational morpheme**: e.g., *firmly* from *firm* + *ly*.

descriptive grammar A linguist's description or model of the mental grammar, including the units, structures, and rules. An explicit statement of what speakers know about their language. See **prescriptive grammar**, **teaching grammar**.

determiner (Det) The syntactic category, also functional category, of words and expressions, which when combined with a noun form a noun phrase. Includes the articles *the* and *a*, **demonstratives** such as *this* and *that*, quantifiers such as *each* and *every*, etc.

diacritics, diacritic marks Additional markings on written symbols to specify various phonetic properties such as **length, tone, stress, nasalization**; extra marks on a written character that change its usual value: e.g., the tilde ~ drawn over the letter *ñ* in Spanish to represent a palatalized nasal rather than an alveolar nasal.

dialect A variety of a language whose grammar differs in systematic ways from other varieties. Differences may be lexical, phonological, syntactic, and semantic. See **regional dialect, social dialect, prestige dialect**.

dialect area A geographic area defined by the predominant use of a particular language variety, or a particular characteristic of a language variety: e.g., an area where *bucket* is used rather than *pail*. See **dialect, dialect atlas, isogloss**.

dialect atlas A book of **dialect maps** showing the areas where specific dialectal characteristics occur in the speech of the region.

dialect continuum A geographic range of slightly varying **dialects** occurring between two distinct different dialects spoken in different regions of a language area.

dialect leveling Movement toward greater uniformity or decrease in variations among dialects.

dialect map A map showing the areas where specific dialectal characteristics occur in the speech of the region.

dichotic listening Experimental methods for brain research in which subjects hear different auditory signals in the left and right ears.

digraph Two letters used to represent a single sound: e.g., *gh* represents [f] in *enough*.

diphthong A sequence of two vowels run together as a single phonological unit: e.g., [aɪ], [aʊ], [ɔɪ] as in *bite, bout, boy*. See **monophthong**.

direct object The grammatical relation of a noun phrase when it appears immediately below the verb phrase (VP) and next to the verb in deep structure; the noun phrase complement of a transitive verb: e.g., *the puppy* in *the boy found the puppy*.

discontinuous morpheme A **morpheme** with multiple parts that occur in more than one place in a word or sentence: e.g., *ge* and *t* in German *geliebt*, 'loved.' See **circumfix**.

discourse A linguistic unit that comprises more than one sentence.

discourse analysis The study of broad speech units comprising multiple sentences.

discreteness A fundamental property of human language in which larger linguistic units are perceived to be composed of smaller linguistic units: e.g., *cat* is perceived as the phonemes /k/, /æ/, /t/; *the cat* is perceived as *the* and *cat*.

dissimilation rules **Phonological rules** that change feature values of segments to make them less similar: e.g., a fricative dissimilation rule: /θ/ is pronounced [t] following another fricative. In English dialects with this rule, *sixth* /sɪks + θ/ is pronounced [sɪkst].

distinctive Describes linguistic elements that contrast: e.g., [f] and [v] are distinctive segments. Voice is a distinctive phonetic feature of consonants.

distinctive features Phonetic properties of phonemes that account for their ability to contrast meanings of words: e.g., *voice, tense*. Also called **phonemic features**.

ditransitive verb A verb whose complement contains a noun phrase and a prepositional phrase: e.g., *give* in *he gave a cat to Sally*. Some ditransitive verb phrases have an alternative form with two noun phrases in the complement as in *he gave Sally a cat*.

dominate In a **phrase structure tree**, when a continuous downward path can be traced from a node labeled A to a node labeled B, then A dominates B.

downdrift The gradual lowering of the absolute **pitch** of tones during an utterance in a tone language. During downdrift, tones retain their *relative* values to one another.

d-structure Any **phrase structure tree** generated by the phrase structure rules (i.e., by the X-bar schema) of a transformational grammar; the basic syntactic structures of the grammar. Also called **deep structure**. See **transformational rule**.

Dual Language Immersion An education program that enrolls English-speaking children and minority-language students in roughly equal numbers, with the intention of making all students bilingual.

dyslexia A cover term for the various types of reading impairment.

ear witnessing The use of human listeners to identify an unknown speaker of an utterance, as opposed to **speaker identification**, which uses computers to achieve that end.

Early Middle English Vowel Shortening A sound change that shortened vowels such as the first *i* in *criminal*. As a result, *criminal* was unaffected by the **Great Vowel Shift**, leading to word pairs such as *crime/criminal*.

ease of articulation The tendency of speakers to adjust their pronunciation to make it easier, or more efficient, to move the articulators. Phonetic and phonological rules are often the result of ease of articulation: e.g., the rule of English that nasalizes vowels when they precede nasal consonants.

Ebonics An alternative term, first used in 1997, for the various dialects of **African American English**.

embedded sentence A sentence that occurs within a sentence in a **phrase structure tree**: e.g., *You know that **sheepdogs cannot read***.

emoticon A string of text characters that, when viewed sideways, forms a face or figure expressing a particular emotion: e.g., [8,<\ to express 'dismay.' Frequently used in e-mail.

entail One sentence entails another if the truth of the first necessarily implies the truth of the second: e.g., *The sun melted the ice* entails *The ice melted* because if the first is true, the second must be true.

entailment The relationship between two sentences, where the truth of one necessitates the truth of the other: e.g., *Corday assassinated Marat* and *Marat is dead*; if the first is true, the second must be true.

epenthesis The insertion of one or more **phones** in a word: e.g., the insertion of [ə] in *children* to produce [tʃilədrẽn] instead of [tʃildrẽn].

eponym A word taken from a proper name, such as *Hertz* for 'unit of frequency.'

etymology The history of words; the study of the history of words.

euphemism A word or phrase that replaces a **taboo** word or is used to avoid reference to certain acts or subjects: e.g., *powder room* for *toilet*.

euphemism treadmill The process whereby a euphemism takes on the taboo characteristics of the word it replaced, thereby requiring another euphemism: e.g., *cripple—handicapped—disabled—challenged*.

event/eventive A type of sentence that describes activities such as *John kissed Mary*, as opposed to describing states such as *John knows Mary*. See **state/stative**.

event-related brain potentials (ERP) The electrical signals emitted from different areas of the brain in response to different kinds of stimuli.

experiencer The thematic role of the noun phrase whose referent perceives something: e.g., *Helen* in *Helen heard Robert playing the piano*.

extension The referential part of the meaning of an expression; the referent of a noun phrase. See **reference**, **referent**.

false writing See **pseudo-writing**.

feature-changing rules Phonological **rules** that change feature values of segments, either to make them more similar (see **assimilation rules**) or less similar (see **dissimilation rules**).

feature matrix A representation of phonological segments in which the columns represent segments and the rows represent features, each cell being marked with a + or − to designate the presence or absence of the feature for that segment.

feature-spreading rules See **assimilation rules**.

finger spelling In **signing**, hand gestures that represent letters of the alphabet used to spell words for which there is no sign.

flap A speech sound in which the tongue touches the alveolar ridge and withdraws. It is often an allophone of /t/ and /d/ in words such as *writer* and *rider*. Also called **tap**.

fMRI Functional Magnetic Resonance Imaging: scans that can reveal the brain in action by measuring blood flow and oxygen utilization in different cerebral locales during the performance of various linguistic and other cognitive tasks.

folk etymology The process whereby the history of a word is derived from nonscientific speculation or false analogy with another word: e.g., *hooker* for 'prostitute' is falsely believed to be derived from the name of the U.S. Civil War general Joseph Hooker.

forensic linguistics A subfield of linguistics that applies to language as used in legal and judicial matters.

form The phonological or gestural representation of a morpheme or word.

formant In the frequency analysis of speech, a band of frequencies of higher intensity than surrounding frequencies, which appears as a dark line on a **spectrogram**. Individual vowels display different formant patterns.

formant (speech) synthesis The computer production of sound based on the blending of electronic-based acoustic components; no prerecorded human sounds are used.

fossilization A characteristic of second-language learning in which the learner reaches a plateau and seems unable to acquire some property of the L2 grammar.

free morpheme A single **morpheme** that constitutes a word: e.g., *dog*.

free pronoun A pronoun that refers to some object not explicitly mentioned in the sentence: e.g., *it* in *Everyone saw it*. Also called **unbound**. See **bound pronoun**.

free variation Alternative pronunciations of a word in which one sound is substituted for another without changing the word's meaning: e.g., pronunciation of *bottle* as [batəl] or [baʔəl].

frequency effect In **lexical access**, the observation that frequently used words have a shorter response time than less common words.

fricative A consonant sound produced with so narrow a constriction in the vocal tract as to create sound through friction: e.g., [s], [f].

front vowels Vowel sounds in which the tongue is positioned forward in the mouth: e.g., [i], [æ].

function word A word that does not always have a clear lexical meaning but has a grammatical function; function words include conjunctions, **prepositions**, **articles**, auxiliaries, **complementizers**, and pronouns. See **closed class**.

functional category One of the categories of function words, including **determiner**, **Aux**, **complementizer**, and **preposition**. These categories are not lexical or phrasal categories. See **lexical category**, **phrasal category**.

fundamental difference hypothesis The idea that second language acquisition (L2) differs fundamentally from first language acquisition (L1).

fundamental frequency In speech, the rate at which the vocal cords vibrate, symbolized as F_0, called F-zero, perceived by the listener as **pitch**.

fusional languages Synthetic languages in which several meanings are packed into what appears to be a single affix, such as *-amos* in Spanish *hablamos* meaning 'first person, plural, present tense.'

gapping The syntactic process of deletion in which subsequent occurrences of a verb are omitted in similar contexts: e.g., *Bill washed the grapes and Mary, the cherries.*

garden path sentences Sentences that appear at first blush to be ungrammatical, but with further syntactic processing turn out to be grammatical: e.g., *The horse raced past the barn fell.*

geminate A sequence of two identical sounds; a long vowel or long consonant denoted either by writing the phonetic symbol twice as in [biiru], [sakki] or by use of a colon-like symbol [bi:ru], [sak:i].

generate To specify precisely, concisely, and in all particulars: e.g., syntactic rules generate the different kinds of sentence structures of a language.

generative grammar A grammar that accounts for linguistic knowledge by means of rules that generate all and only the grammatical sentences of the language.

generic term A word that applies to a whole class, such as *wombat* in *the wombat lives across the seas, among the far Antipodes.* A word that is ordinarily masculine, when used to refer to both sexes: e.g., *mankind* meaning 'the human race'; the masculine pronoun when used as a neutral form, as in *Everyone should do his duty.*

genetically related Describes two or more languages that developed from a common, earlier language: e.g., French, Italian, and Spanish, which all developed from Latin.

glide A speech sound produced with little or no obstruction of the air stream that is always preceded or followed by a vowel: e.g., [w] in *we*, [j] in *you.*

gloss A word in one language given to express the meaning of a word in another language: e.g., 'house' is the English gloss for the French word *maison.*

glottal/glottal stop A speech sound produced with constriction at the **glottis**; when the air is stopped completely at the glottis by tightly closed vocal cords, a glottal stop is produced.

glottis The vocal cords themselves and/or the opening between the vocal cords.

goal The thematic role of the noun phrase toward whose referent the action of the verb is directed: e.g., *the theater* in *The kids went to the theater.*

gradable pair Two **antonyms** related in such a way that more of one is less of the other: e.g., *warm* and *cool*; more warm is less cool, and vice versa. See **complementary pair**, **relational opposites**.

grammar The mental representation of a speaker's linguistic competence; what a speaker knows about a language, including its phonology, morphology, syntax, semantics, and lexicon. A linguistic description of a speaker's mental grammar.

grammar translation A method of second-language learning in which the student memorizes words and syntactic rules and translates them between the native language and target language.

grammatical, grammaticality Describes a well-formed sequence of words, one conforming to rules of **syntax**.

grammatical case See **case**.

grammatical categories Traditionally called "parts of speech"; also called **syntactic categories**; expressions of the same grammatical category can generally substitute for one another without loss of grammaticality: e.g., **noun phrase**, **verb phrase**, **adjective**, **auxiliary verb**.

grammatical morpheme A **function word** or **bound morpheme** required by the syntactic rules: e.g., *to* and *s* in *he wants to go*. See **inflectional morpheme**.

grammatical relation Any of several structural positions that a noun phrase may assume in a sentence. See **subject**, **direct object**.

graphemes The symbols of an **alphabetic writing** system; the letters of an alphabet.

Great Vowel Shift A sound change that took place in English some time between 1400 and 1600 CE in which seven long vowel phonemes were changed.

Grimm's Law The description of a phonological change in the sound system of an early ancestor of the Germanic languages formulated by Jakob Grimm.

Hangul An alphabet based on the phonemic principle for writing the Korean language designed in the fifteenth century.

head (of a compound) The rightmost word: e.g., *house* in *doghouse*. It generally indicates the category and general meaning of the compound.

head (of a phrase) The central word of a phrase whose lexical category defines the type of phrase: e.g., the noun *man* is the head of the noun phrase *the man who came to dinner*; the verb *wrote* is the head of the verb phrase *wrote a letter to his mother*; the adjective *red* is the head of the adjective phrase *very bright red in the face*.

hemiplegic An individual (child or adult) with acquired unilateral lesions of the brain who retains both hemispheres (one normal and one diseased).

hemispherectomy The surgical removal of a hemisphere of the brain.

heritage language A language with which a person has a strong cultural connection through family interaction, but that isn't learned natively: e.g., Yiddish in a Jewish household.

heteronyms Different words spelled the same (i.e., **homographs**) but pronounced differently: e.g., *bass*, meaning either 'low tone' [bes] or 'a kind of fish' [bæs].

hierarchical structure The groupings and subgroupings of the parts of a sentence into syntactic categories: e.g., *the bird sang* [[[the] [bird]] [sang]]; the groupings and subgroupings of morphemes in a word: e.g., *unlockable* [[un] [[lock][able]]]. Hierarchical structure is generally depicted in a **tree diagram**.

hieroglyphics A writing system used by the Egyptians around 4000 BCE that began as a **pictographic writing** system and evolved over time into a **logographic writing** and **syllabic writing** system.

hiragana A Japanese **syllabary** used to write native words of the language, most often together with ideographic characters. See **kanji**.

historical and comparative linguistics The branch of linguistics that deals with how languages change, what kinds of changes occur, and why they occur.

historical linguistics See **historical and comparative linguistics**.

holophrastic The stage of child language acquisition in which one word conveys a complex message similar to that of a phrase or sentence.

homographs Words spelled identically, and possibly pronounced the same: e.g., *bear* meaning 'to tolerate,' and *bear* the animal; or *lead* the metal and *lead*, what leaders do.

homonyms/homophones Words pronounced, and possibly spelled, the same: e.g., *to*, *too*, *two*; or *bat* the animal, *bat* the stick, and *bat* meaning 'to flutter' as in "bat the eyelashes."

homorganic consonants Two sounds produced at the same place of articulation: e.g., [m] and [p]; [t], [d], [n]. See **assimilation rules**.

homorganic nasal rule A phonological assimilation rule that changes the place of articulation feature of a nasal consonant to agree with that of a following consonant: e.g., /n/ becomes [m] when preceding /p/ as in *impossible*.

hypercorrection Deviations from the "norm" thought by speakers to be "more correct," such as saying *between he and she* instead of *between him and her*.

hyponyms Words whose meanings are specific instances of a more general word: e.g., *red*, *white*, and *blue* are hyponyms of the word *color*; *triangle* is a hyponym of *polygon*.

iambic Stress on the second syllable of a two-syllable word: e.g., *giráffe*.

iconic, iconicity A nonarbitrary relationship between form and meaning in which the form bears a resemblance to its meaning: e.g., the male and female symbols on (some) restroom doors.

ideogram, ideograph A character of a word-writing system, often highly stylized, that represents a concept, or the pronunciation of the word representing that concept.

idiolect An individual's way of speaking, reflecting that person's grammar.

idiom/idiomatic phrase An expression whose meaning does not conform to the **principle of compositionality**, that is, may be unrelated to the meaning of its parts: e.g., *kick the bucket* meaning 'to die.'

ill-formed Describes an ungrammatical or anomalous sequence of words.

illocutionary force The intended effect of a speech act, such as a warning, a promise, a threat, or a bet: e.g., the illocutionary force of *I resign!* is the act of resignation.

imitation A proposed mechanism of child language acquisition, according to which children learn their language by imitating adult speech.

immediately dominate If a node labeled A is directly above a node labeled B in a phrase structure tree, then A immediately dominates B.

implicature An inference based not only on an utterance, but also on assumptions about what the speaker is trying to achieve: e.g., *Are you using the ketchup?* to mean "Please pass the ketchup" while dining in a café.

impoverished data Refers to the incomplete, noisy, and unstructured utterances that children hear, including slips of the tongue, false starts, and ungrammatical and incomplete sentences, together with a lack of concrete evidence about abstract grammatical rules and structure.

individual bilingualism The ability of an individual speaker to speak two (or more) languages with native or near native proficiency. See **bilingualism, societal bilingualism.**

Indo-European The descriptive name given to the ancestor language of many modern language families, including Germanic, Slavic, and Romance. Also called **Proto-Indo-European.**

infinitive An uninflected form of a verb: e.g., (to) *swim.*

infinitive sentence An **embedded sentence** that does not have a tense and therefore is a "to" form: e.g., *sheepdogs to be fast readers* in the sentence *He believes sheepdogs to be fast readers.*

infix A **bound morpheme** that is inserted in the middle of another morpheme: e.g., Tagalog *sulat* 'writing' but *sumulat* 'to write' after insertion of the infix *um.*

INFL Abbreviates "inflection," a term sometimes used in place of **Aux**; the **head** of a sentence (**TP** or **S**).

inflectional affix See **inflectional morpheme.**

inflectional morpheme A bound **grammatical morpheme** that is affixed to a word according to rules of syntax: e.g., third-person singular verbal suffix *-s.*

information retrieval The process of using a computer to search a database for items on a particular topic. See **data mining.**

innateness hypothesis The theory that the human species is genetically equipped with a **Universal Grammar**, which provides the basic design for all human languages.

instrument The thematic role of the noun phrase whose referent is the means by which an action is performed: e.g., *a paper clip* in *Houdini picked the lock with a paper clip.*

intension The inherent, nonreferential part of the meaning of an expression, also called **sense**. See **sense, extension.**

intensity The magnitude of an **acoustic signal**, which is perceived as loudness.

interdental A sound produced by inserting the tip of the tongue between the upper and lower teeth: e.g., the initial sounds of *thought* and *those.*

interlanguage grammars The intermediate grammars that second-language learners create on their way to acquiring the (more or less) complete grammar of the target language.

internal borrowing See **analogic change.**

internal reconstruction The application of the **comparative method** to earlier and later forms of the same language.

International Phonetic Alphabet (IPA) The **phonetic alphabet** designed by the International Phonetic Association to be used to represent the sounds found in all human languages.

International Phonetic Association (IPA) The organization founded in 1888 to further phonetic research and to develop the International Phonetic Alphabet.

interrogative (sentence) A sentence that questions whether a particular situation exists. See **declarative**.

intonation The variation of **pitch** while speaking which is not used to distinguish words, though it may affect meaning.

intransitive verb A verb that must not have (does not **C-select** for) a direct object NP complement: e.g., *sleep, rise.*

IP Inflection Phrase. A term sometimes used in place of **sentence (S)**. A **phrasal category** whose **head** is **Aux**.

ipsilateral Refers to neural signals that travel between one side of the body (left/right) and the same cerebral hemisphere (left/right). See **contralateral**.

isogloss A geographic boundary that separates areas with **dialect** differences: e.g., a line on a map on one side of which most people say *faucet* and on the other side of which most people say *spigot.*

isolating language A language in which most words contain a single morpheme, and there is little if any word morphology: e.g., no plural affixes on nouns or agreement affixes on verbs. Also called an analytic language: e.g., Vietnamese.

jargon Special words peculiar to the members of a profession or group: e.g., *glottis* for phoneticians. See **argot**. Also, the nonsense words sometimes used by Wernicke's aphasics.

kana The characters of either of the two Japanese syllabaries, **katakana** and **hiragana**.

kanji The Japanese term for the Chinese characters used in Japanese writing.

katakana A Japanese **syllabary** generally used for writing loan words and to achieve the effect of italics.

L2 acquisition See **second language acquisition**.

labial A sound articulated at the lips: e.g., [b], [f].

labiodental A sound produced by touching the bottom lip to the upper teeth: e.g., [v].

labio-velar A sound articulated by simultaneously raising the back of the tongue toward the velum and rounding the lips. The [w] of English is a labio-velar glide.

language attrition The gradual loss of heritage language competence owing to lack of use. See **heritage language**.

language contact The situation in which speakers of different languages regularly interact with one another, and especially in which there are many bilingual or multilingual speakers.

language isolate A natural language with no demonstrable genealogical relationship with other living languages.

larynx The structure of muscles and cartilage in the throat that contains the vocal cords and **glottis**; often called the "voice box."

late closure principle A psycholinguistic principle of language comprehension that states: Attach incoming material to the phrase that was most recently processed. E.g., *he said that he slept yesterday* associates *yesterday* with *he slept* rather than with *he said.*

lateral A sound produced with air flowing past one or both sides of the tongue: e.g., [l].

lateralization, lateralized Terms used to refer to cognitive functions localized to one or the other hemisphere of the brain.

lax vowel A vowel produced with relatively less tension in the vocal cords and little tendency to diphthongize: e.g., [ʊ] in *put*, [pʊt]. Most lax vowels do not occur at the ends of syllables, that is, [bʊ] is not a possible English word. See **tense**.

length A prosodic feature referring to the duration of a segment. Two sounds may contrast in length: e.g., in Japanese the first vowel is [+long] in /biːru/ 'beer' but [−long], therefore short, in /biru/ 'building.'

level tones Relatively stable (nongliding) **pitch** on syllables of tone languages. Also called **register tones**.

lexical access The process of searching the mental **lexicon** for a phonological string to determine whether it is an actual word.

lexical ambiguity Multiple meanings of sentences due to words that have multiple meanings: e.g., *He blew up the pictures of his ex-girlfriend*.

lexical category A general term for the word-level syntactic categories of noun, verb, adjective, and adverb. These are the categories of content words like *man, run, large,* and *rapidly,* as opposed to functional category words such as *the* and *and*. See functional category, **phrasal category**, **open class**.

lexical decision A task of subjects in psycholinguistic experiments who on presentation of a spoken or printed stimulus must decide whether it is a word or not.

lexical gap A possible but nonoccurring word; a form that obeys the **phonotactic constraints** of a language yet has no meaning: e.g., *blick* in English.

lexical paraphrases Sentences that have the same meaning due to synonyms: e.g., *She lost her purse* and *She lost her handbag*.

lexical semantics The subfield of semantics concerned with the meanings of words and the meaning relationships among words.

lexicographer One who edits or works on a dictionary.

lexicography The editing or making of a dictionary.

lexicon The component of the grammar containing speakers' knowledge about morphemes and words; a speaker's mental dictionary.

lexifier language The dominant language of a **pidgin** (or **creole**) that provides the basis for the majority of the lexical items in the language.

lingua franca A language common to speakers of diverse languages that can be used for communication and commerce: e.g., English is the lingua franca of international airline pilots.

linguistic competence See **competence, linguistic**.

linguistic context The discourse that precedes a phrase or sentence that helps clarify meaning.

linguistic determinism The strongest form of the **Sapir-Whorf hypothesis**, which holds that the language we speak establishes how we perceive and think about the world.

linguistic performance See **performance, linguistic**.

linguistic relativism A weaker form of the **Sapir-Whorf hypothesis**, which holds that different languages encode different categories, and that speakers of different languages therefore think about the world in different ways. For example, speakers of languages that have fewer color words will be less sensitive to gradations of color.

linguistic sign A sound or gesture, typically a morpheme in a spoken language and a sign in a sign language, that has a form bound to a meaning in a single unit: e.g., *dog* is a linguistic sign whose form is its pronunciation [dag] and whose meaning is *Canis familiaris* (or however we define "dog").

linguistic theory A theory of the principles that characterize all human languages. See **Universal Grammar**.

liquids A class of consonants including /l/ and /r/ and their variants that share vowel-like acoustic properties and may function as syllabic nuclei.

loan translations Compound words or expressions whose parts are translated literally into the borrowing language: e.g., *marriage of convenience* from French *mariage de convenance*.

loan word Word in one language whose origins are in another language: e.g., in Japanese, *besiboru,* 'baseball,' is a loan word from English. See **borrowing**.

localization The hypothesis that different areas of the brain are responsible for distinct cognitive systems. See **lateralization**.

location The thematic role of the noun phrase whose referent is the place where the action of the verb occurs: e.g., *Oslo* in *It snows in Oslo*.

logograms The symbols of a **word-writing** or **logographic writing** system.

logographic writing See **word writing**.

machine translation See **automatic machine translation**.

magnetic resonance imaging (MRI) A technique to investigate the molecular structures in human organs including the brain, which may be used to identify sites of brain lesions.

magnetoencephalogram (MEG) A record of the magnetic field of the brain.

main verb The verb that functions as the head in the highest verb phrase of a sentence: e.g., *save* in *They save money to travel*. See **head of a phrase**.

manner of articulation The way the air stream is obstructed as it travels through the vocal tract. **Stop**, **nasal**, **affricate**, and **fricative** are some manners of articulation. See **place of articulation**.

marked In a gradable pair of antonyms, the word that is *not* used in questions of degree: e.g., *low* is the marked member of the pair *high/low* because we ordinarily ask *How high is the mountain?* not **How low is the mountain?* In a masculine/feminine pair, the word that contains a derivational morpheme, usually the feminine word: e.g., *princess* is marked, whereas *prince* is unmarked. See **unmarked**.

mass nouns Nouns that cannot ordinarily be enumerated: e.g., *milk, water*; **two milks* is ungrammatical except when interpreted to mean 'two kinds of milk,' 'two containers of milk,' and so on. See **count nouns**.

maxim of manner A conversational convention that a speaker's discourse should be brief and orderly, and should avoid ambiguity and obscurity.

maxim of quality A conversational convention that a speaker should not lie or make unsupported claims.

maxim of quantity A conversational convention that a speaker's contribution to the discourse should be as informative as is required, neither more nor less.

maxim of relevance A conversational convention that a speaker's contribution to a discourse should always have a bearing on, and a connection with, the matter under discussion.

maxims of conversation Conversational conventions such as the **maxim of quantity** that people appear to obey to give coherence and sincerity to discourse.

mean length of utterances (MLU) The average number of words or morphemes in a child's utterance. It is a more accurate measure of the acquisition stage of language than chronological age.

meaning The conceptual or semantic aspect of a sign or utterance that permits us to comprehend the message being conveyed. Expressions in language generally have both form—pronunciation or gesture—and meaning. See **extension**, **intension**, **sense**, **reference**.

mental grammar The internalized grammar that a descriptive grammar attempts to model. See **linguistic competence**.

metalinguistic awareness A speaker's conscious awareness *about* language and the use of language, as opposed to linguistic *knowledge*, which is largely unconscious. This book is very much about metalinguistic awareness.

metaphor Nonliteral, suggestive meaning in which an expression that designates one thing is used implicitly to mean something else: e.g., *The night has a thousand eyes*, to mean 'One may be unknowingly observed at night.'

metathesis The phonological process that reorders segments, often by transposing two sequential sounds: e.g., the pronunciation of *ask* /æsk/ in some English dialects as [æks].

metonym, metonymy A word substituted for another word or expression with which it is closely associated: e.g., *gridiron* to refer to the game of American football.

mimetic Similar to imitating, acting out, or miming.

minimal attachment principle The principle that in comprehending language, listeners create the simplest structure consistent with the grammar: e.g., *the horse raced past the barn* is interpreted as a complete sentence rather than a noun phrase containing a relative clause, as if it were *the horse* (that was) *raced past the barn*.

minimal pair (or set) Two (or more) words that are identical except for one phoneme that occurs in the same position in each word: e.g., *pain* /pen/, *bane* /ben/, *main* /men/.

modal An **auxiliary verb** other than *be*, *have*, and *do*, such as *can*, *could*, *will*, *would*, or *must*.

modularity (modular) The organization of the brain and mind into distinct, independent, and autonomous parts that interact with each other.

monogenetic theory of language origin The belief that all languages originated from a single language. See **Nostratic**.

monomorphemic word A word that consists of one morpheme.

monophthong Simple vowel: e.g., [ɛ] in [bɛd]. See **diphthong**.

monosyllabic Having one syllable: e.g., *boy*, *through*.

morpheme Smallest unit of linguistic meaning or function: e.g., *sheepdogs* contains three morphemes, *sheep*, *dog*, and the function morpheme for plural, *s*.

morphological parser A process, often a computer program, that uses rules of word formation to decompose words into their component morphemes.

morphological rules Rules for combining morphemes to form stems and words.

morphology The study of the structure of words; the component of the grammar that includes the rules of word formation.

morphophonemic orthography A writing system, such as that for English, in which morphological knowledge is needed to read correctly: e.g., in *please/pleasant* the *ea* represents [i]/[ɛ].

morphophonemic rules Rules that specify the pronunciation of morphemes; a morpheme may have more than one pronunciation determined by such rules: e.g., the plural morpheme /z/ in English is regularly pronounced [s], [z], or [əz].

motherese See **child-directed speech (CDS)**.

Move Sometimes called "Move X" or "Move α (alpha)"; relocates elements placed by the X-bar schema (the phrase structure rules) to different parts of the structure to help account for sentence relatedness such as a declarative sentence and the corresponding yes-no question.

naming task An experimental technique that measures the response time between seeing a printed word and saying that word aloud.

narrowing A semantic change in which the meaning of a word changes in time to become less encompassing: e.g., *deer* once meant 'animal.'

nasal (nasalized) sound Speech sound produced with an open nasal passage (lowered velum), permitting air to pass through the nose as well as the mouth: e.g., /m/. See **oral sound**.

nasal cavity The passageways between the throat and the nose through which air passes during speech if the velum is open (lowered). See **oral cavity**.

natural class A class of sounds characterized by a phonetic property or feature that pertains to all members of the set: e.g., the class of stops. A natural class may be defined with a smaller feature set than that of any individual member of the class.

negative polarity item (NPI) An expression that is grammatical in the presence of negation, but ungrammatical in simple affirmative sentences: e.g., *any* in *James does not have any money* but **James has any money*.

Neo-Grammarians A group of nineteenth-century linguists who claimed that sound shifts (i.e., changes in phonological systems) took place without exceptions.

Neo-Grammarian hypothesis The claim that sound shifts (i.e., changes in phonological systems) take place without exceptions.

neurolinguistics The branch of linguistics concerned with the brain mechanisms that underlie the acquisition and use of human language; the study of the neurobiology of language.

neutralization Phonological processes or rules that obliterate the contrast between two phonemes in certain environments: e.g., in some dialects of English /t/ and /d/ are both pronounced as voiced flaps between vowels, as in *writer* and *rider*, thus neutralizing the voicing distinction so that the two words sound alike.

node A labeled branch point in a phrase structure tree; part of the graphical depiction of a transition network represented as a circle, pairs of which are connected by arcs. See **arc**, **phrase structure tree**, **transition network**.

noncontinuant A sound in which air is blocked momentarily in the oral cavity as it passes through the vocal tract. See **stops**, **affricate**.

nondistinctive features Phonetic features of phones that are predictable by rule: e.g., aspiration in English.

nonphonemic features See **nondistinctive features**.

nonredundant A phonetic feature that is distinctive: e.g., stop, voice, but not aspiration in English.

nonsense word A permissible phonological form without meaning: e.g., *slithy*.

Nostratic A hypothetical language that is postulated as the first human language.

noun (N) The syntactic category, also lexical category, of words that can function as heads of noun phrases, such as *book, Jean, sincerity*. In many languages nouns have grammatical alternations for number, case, and gender and occur with determiners.

noun phrase (NP) The syntactic category, also phrasal category, of expressions containing some form of a noun or pronoun as its head, and which functions as the subject or as various objects in a sentence.

nucleus That part of a syllable that has the greatest acoustic energy; the vowel portion of a syllable: e.g., /i/ in /mit/ *meet*.

obstruents The class of sounds consisting of nonnasal stops, fricatives, and affricates. See **sonorants**.

onomatopoeia/onomatopoeic Words whose pronunciations suggest their meanings: e.g., *meow, buzz*.

onset One or more phonemes that precede the syllable **nucleus**: e.g., /pr/ in /prist/ *priest*.

open class The class of lexical content words; a category of words that commonly adds new words: e.g., nouns, verbs.

Optimality Theory The hypothesis that a universal set of ranked phonological constraints exists, where the higher the constraint is ranked, the more influence it exerts on the language: e.g., in English, one constraint is the following: *Obstruent sequences may not differ with respect to their voice feature at the end of a word.*

oral cavity The mouth area through which air passes during the production of speech. See **nasal cavity**.

oral sound A non-nasal speech sound produced by raising the velum to close the nasal passage so that air can escape only through the mouth. See **nasal sound**.

orthography The written form of a language; spelling.

overextension The broadening of a word's meaning in language acquisition to encompass a more general meaning: e.g., using *dog* for any four-legged animals including cats or horses.

overgeneralization Children's treatment of irregular verbs and nouns as if they were regular: e.g., *bringed, goed, foots, mouses*, for *brought, went, feet, mice*. This shows that the child has acquired the regular rules but has not yet learned that there are exceptions.

palatal A sound produced by raising the front part of the tongue to the palate.

palate The bony section of the roof of the mouth behind the **alveolar ridge**.

paradigm A set of forms derived from a single root morpheme: e.g., *give, gives, given, gave, giving*; or *woman, women, woman's, women's*.

paradox A sentence to which it is impossible to ascribe a truth value: e.g., *this sentence is false*.

parallel processing The ability of a computer to carry out several tasks simultaneously as a result of the presence of multiple central processors.

parameters The small set of alternatives for a particular phenomenon made available by Universal Grammar. For example, Universal Grammar specifies that a phrase must have a head and possibly complements; a parameter states whether the complement(s) precedes or follows the head.

paraphrases Sentences with the same truth conditions; sentences with the same meaning, except possibly for minor differences in emphasis: e.g., *He ran up a big bill* and *He ran a big bill up*. See **synonymy**.

parsing The act of determining the grammaticality of sequences of words according to rules of syntax, and assigning a linguistic structure to the grammatical ones.

parser A computer program that determines the grammaticality of sequences of words according to whatever rules of syntax are stored in the computer's memory, and assigns a linguistic structure to the grammatical ones.

participle The form of a verb that occurs after the auxiliary verbs *be* and *have*: e.g., *kissing* in *John is kissing Mary* is a present participle; *kissed* in *John has kissed many girls* is a past participle; *kissed* in *Mary was kissed by John* is a passive participle.

passive sentence A sentence in which the verbal complex contains a form of *to be* followed by a verb in its participle form: e.g., *The girl was kissed by the boy*; *The robbers must not have been seen*. In a passive sentence, the direct object of a transitive verb in d-structure functions as the subject in s-structure. See **active sentence**.

performance, linguistic The *use* of linguistic competence in the production and comprehension of language; behavior as distinguished from linguistic knowledge: e.g., linguistic competence permits one-million-word sentences, but linguistic performance prevents this from happening.

performative sentence A sentence containing a performative verb used to accomplish some act. Performative sentences are affirmative and declarative, and are in first-person, present tense: e.g., *I now pronounce you husband and wife*, when spoken by a justice of the peace in the appropriate situation, is an act of marrying.

performative verb A verb, certain usages of which result in a **speech act**: e.g., *resign* when the sentence *I resign!* is interpreted as an act of resignation.

person deixis The use of terms to refer to persons whose reference relies entirely on context: e.g., pronouns such as *I, he, you* and expressions such as *this child*. See **deictic**, **time deixis**, **place deixis**, **demonstrative articles**.

petroglyph A drawing on rock made by prehistoric people.

pharynx The tube or cavity in the vocal tract above the glottis through which the air passes during speech production.

phone A phonetic realization of a **phoneme**.

phoneme A contrastive phonological **segment** whose phonetic realizations are predictable by rule.

phonemic features Phonetic properties of phonemes that account for their ability to contrast meanings of words: e.g., *voice, tense*. Also called **distinctive features**.

phonemic principle The principle that underlies alphabetic writing systems in which one symbol typically represents one phoneme.

phonemic representation The phonological representation of words and sentences prior to the application of phonological rules.

phonetic alphabet Alphabetic symbols used to represent the phonetic segments of speech in which there is a one-to-one relationship between each symbol and each speech sound.

phonetic features Phonetic properties of segments (e.g., voice, nasal, alveolar) that distinguish one segment from another.

phonetic representation The representation of words and sentences after the application of phonological rules; symbolic transcription of the pronunciation of words and sentences.

phonetic similarity Refers to sounds that share most phonetic features.

phonetics The study of linguistic speech sounds, how they are produced (**articulatory phonetics**), how they are perceived (**auditory** or perceptual **phonetics**), and their physical aspects (**acoustic phonetics**).

phonetic transcription The "spelling" of a word in terms of the individual phones it contains with a **phonetic alphabet** as opposed to ordinary orthography: e.g., [fənɛɹɪk] for *phonetic*.

phonographic symbol A symbol in a writing system that stands for the sounds of a word.

phonological rules Rules that apply to phonemic representations to derive phonetic representations or pronunciation.

phonology The sound system of a language; the component of a grammar that includes the inventory of sounds (phonetic and phonemic units) and rules for their combination and pronunciation; the study of the sound systems of all languages.

phonotactics/phonotactic constraints Rules stating permissible strings of phonemes within a syllable: e.g., a word-initial nasal consonant may be followed only by a vowel (in English). See **possible word**, **nonsense word**, **accidental gap**.

phrasal category The class of syntactic categories that comprise the root of an X-bar structure including NP, VP, AP, PP, and AdvP. See **lexical category**, **functional category**.

phrasal semantics See **sentential semantics**.

phrase structure rules Principles of grammar that specify the constituency of syntactic categories and of phrase structure trees: e.g., NP → Det $\bar{\text{N}}$, or VP → $\bar{\text{V}}$ NP in the X-bar schema.

phrase structure tree A tree diagram with syntactic categories at each node that reveals both the linear and hierarchical structure of phrases and sentences.

phrenology A pseudoscience of examining bumps on the skull to determine personality traits and intellectual ability. Its contribution to neurolinguistics is that its methods were highly suggestive of the modular theory of brain structure.

pictogram A symbol in a writing system that resembles the object represented in a direct way; a nonarbitrary form of writing.

pictographic writing A method of writing that utilizes **pictograms**, or literal representations of words.

pidgin A simple but rule-governed language developed for communication among speakers of mutually unintelligible languages, often based on one of those languages called the **lexifier language**. See **substrate languages**.

pidginization The process of the creation of a pidgin that involves a simplification of the grammars of the impinging languages and a reduction of the number of domains in which the language is used. See **creolization**, **pidgin**.

Pinyin An alphabetic writing system for Mandarin Chinese using a Western-style alphabet to represent individual sounds.

pitch The **fundamental frequency** of sound perceived by the listener.

pitch contour The intonation of a sentence.

place deixis The use of terms to refer to places whose reference relies entirely on context: e.g., *here, there, behind, next door*. See **deictic**, **time deixis**, **person deixis**, **demonstrative articles**.

place of articulation The part of the vocal tract at which constriction occurs during the production of consonants. See **manner of articulation**.

plosives Oral, or non-nasal, stop consonants, so called because the air that is stopped explodes with the release of the closure.

polyglot A person who speaks several languages.

polymorphemic word A word that consists of more than one **morpheme**.

polysemous/polysemy Describes a single word with several closely related but slightly different meanings: e.g., *face*, meaning 'face of a person,' 'face of a clock,' 'face of a building.'

polysynthetic language Language with an extraordinarily rich morphology, in which a single word may carry the semantic content of an entire sentence.

positron emission tomography (PET) Method to detect changes in brain activities and relate these changes to localized brain damage and cognitive tasks.

possessor The thematic role of the noun phrase to whose referent something belongs: e.g., *the dog* in *The dog's tail wagged furiously.*

possible word A string of sounds that obeys the **phonotactic constraints** of the language but has no meaning: e.g., *gimble.* Also called a **nonsense word**.

poverty of the stimulus See **impoverished data**.

pragmatics The study of how context and situation affect meaning; the study of extra-truth-conditional meaning.

predicate A cover term for verbs, adjectives, and common nouns.

predictable feature A nondistinctive, noncontrastive, redundant phonetic feature: e.g., aspiration in English voiceless stops, or nasalization in English vowels.

prefix An **affix** that is attached to the beginning of a morpheme or stem: e.g., *in-* in *inoperable.*

preposition (P) The syntactic category, also functional category, that heads a prepositional phrase: e.g., *at, in, on, up.*

prepositional object The grammatical relation of the noun phrase complement that occurs immediately following the prepositional head in a **prepositional phrase (PP)** in d-structure: e.g., *skis* in *on skis.*

prepositional phrase (PP) The syntactic category, also phrasal category, consisting of a prepositional head and a noun phrase complement: e.g., *with a key, into the battle, over the top.*

prescriptive grammar Rules of grammar brought about by grammarians' attempts to legislate what speakers' grammatical rules should be, rather than what they are. See **descriptive grammar, teaching grammar**.

prestige dialect The dialect usually spoken by people in positions of power, and the one deemed correct by prescriptive grammarians: e.g., RP (received pronunciation) (British) English, the dialect spoken by the English royal family.

presupposition Implicit assumption about the world required to make an utterance meaningful or relevant: e.g., "some tea has already been taken" is a presupposition of *Take some more tea!*

primes The basic formal units of sign languages that correspond to phonological elements of spoken language.

priming An experimental procedure that measures the response time between hearing a word and grasping the meaning of that word, as a function of whether the participant has heard a related word previously. See **semantic priming**.

principle of compositionality A principle of semantic interpretation that states that the meaning of a word, phrase, or sentence depends on both the meaning of its components (morphemes, words, phrases) and how they are combined structurally.

productive Refers to **morphological rules** that can be used freely and apply to all forms to create new words: e.g., the addition to an adjective of *-ish* meaning 'having somewhat of the quality,' such as *newish, tallish, incredible-ish.*

pro-form A word that replaces another word or expression found elsewhere in discourse, or understood from the situational context. Pronouns are the best known pro-forms, but words like *did* may function as "pro-verb phrases" as in *John washed three sheepdogs and Mary did too.*

proper name A word or words that refer to a person, place, or other entity with a unique reference known to the speaker and listener. Usually capitalized in writing: e.g., Nina Hyams, New York, Atlantic Ocean.

prosodic bootstrapping The learning of word or phrase segmentation by infants inferred from the stress pattern of a language.

prosodic feature The duration (**length**), **pitch**, or loudness of speech sounds.

Proto-Germanic The name given by linguists to the language that was an ancestor of English, German, and other Germanic languages.

Proto-Indo-European (PIE) See **Indo-European**.

protolanguage The earliest identifiable language from which genetically related languages developed.

pseudo-writing (systems) artificially constructed alphabets or scripts that appear to be linguistic but are generally **asemic** and unrelated to any actual alphabet or spoken language.

psycholinguistics The branch of linguistics concerned with **linguistic performance**, language acquisition, and speech production and comprehension.

rebus principle In writing, the use of a **pictogram** for its phonetic value: e.g., using a picture of a bee to represent the verb *be* or the sound [bi].

recast The repetition with "corrections" of a child's utterance by an adult. E.g., the child says *I holded the rabbit*, and the adult corrects by saying *You mean you held the rabbit.*

recursive rule A **phrase structure rule** that repeats its own category on its right side: e.g., VP → VP PP, hence permitting phrase structures of potentially unlimited length, corresponding to that aspect of speakers' **linguistic competence**.

reduced vowel A vowel that is unstressed and generally pronounced as schwa [ə] in English.

redundant Describes a nondistinctive, nonphonemic feature that is predictable from other feature values of the segment: e.g., [+voice] is redundant for any [+nasal] phoneme in English because all nasals are voiced.

reduplication A morphological process that repeats or copies all or part of a word to produce a new word: e.g., *wishy-washy, teensy-weensy, hurly-burly.* Also used in some languages as an inflectional process: e.g., Samoan *manao/mananao*, 'he wishes/they wish.'

reference That part of the meaning of a noun phrase that associates it with some entity. That part of the meaning of a declarative sentence that associates it with a **truth value**, either true or false. Also called **extension**. See **referent, sense**.

reference resolution In **computational pragmatics**, the computer algorithms that determine when two expressions have the same referent: e.g., identifying the referents of pronouns; also the mental process determining the referent of a pronoun or other kind of deictic word or phrase.

referent The entity designated by an expression: e.g., the referent of *John* in *John knows Sue* is the actual person named John; the referent of *Raleigh is the capital of California* is the truth value *false*. Also called **extension**.

reflexive pronoun A pronoun ending with -*self* that generally requires a noun-phrase antecedent within the same S: e.g., *myself, herself, ourselves, itself.*

regional dialect A dialect spoken in a specific geographic area that may arise from, and is reinforced by, that area's integrity. For example, a Boston dialect is maintained because large numbers of Bostonians and their descendants remain in the Boston area. See **social dialect**.

register A stylistic variant of a language appropriate to a particular social setting. Also called **style**.

register tones In tone languages, level tones; high, mid, or low tones.

regular sound correspondence The occurrence of different sounds in the same position of the same word in different languages or dialects, with this parallel holding for a significant number of words: e.g., [aɪ] in non-Southern American English corresponds to [aː] in Southern American English. Also found between newer and older forms of the same language.

relational opposites A pair of **antonyms** in which one describes a relationship between two objects and the other describes the same relationship when the two objects are reversed: e.g., *parent/child, teacher/pupil; John is the parent of Susie* describes the same relationship as *Susie is the child of John*. See **gradable pair**, **complementary pair**.

retroflex sound A sound produced by curling the tip of the tongue back behind the alveolar ridge: e.g., the pronunciation of /r/ by many speakers of English.

rime The **nucleus** + **coda** of a syllable: e.g., the /en/ of /ren/ *rain*.

root The **morpheme** that remains when all affixes are stripped from a complex word: e.g., *system* from *un* + *system* + *atic* + *ally*.

rounded vowel A vowel sound produced with pursed lips: e.g., [o].

rules of syntax Principles of grammar that account for the grammaticality of sentences, their hierarchical structure, their word order, whether there is structural ambiguity, etc. See **phrase structure rules**, **transformational rules**.

SAE See **Standard American English**.

Sapir-Whorf hypothesis The proposition that the structure of a language influences how its speakers perceive the world around them. It is often presented in its weak form, **linguistic relativism**, and its strong form, **linguistic determinism**.

savant An individual who shows special abilities in one cognitive area while being deficient in others. Linguistic savants have extraordinary language abilities but are deficient in general intelligence.

second language acquisition The acquisition of another language or languages after first language acquisition is under way or completed. Also called **L2 acquisition**.

segment (1) An individual sound that occurs in a language; (2) the act of dividing utterances into sounds, morphemes, words, and phrases.

semantic bootstrapping The learning of word categories inferred from the words' meanings: e.g., a word whose meaning is a person, place, or thing would be considered a noun.

semantic features Conceptual elements by which a person understands the meanings of words and sentences: e.g., "female" is a semantic feature of the nouns *girl* and *filly*; "cause" is a semantic feature of the verbs *darken* and *kill*.

semantic network A network of **arcs** and **nodes** used to represent semantic information about sentences.

semantic priming The effect of being able to recognize a word (e.g., *doctor*) more rapidly after exposure to a semantically similar word (e.g., *nurse*) than after exposure to a semantically more distant word. The word *nurse* primes the word *doctor*.

semantic properties See **semantic features**.

semantic representation A symbolic system suitable for the characterization of the meaning of natural language utterances in a computer: e.g., logic-based expressions or **semantic networks**.

semantic rules Principles for determining the meanings of larger units like sentences from the meanings of smaller units like noun phrases and verb phrases.

semantics The study of the linguistic meanings of morphemes, words, phrases, and sentences.

sense The inherent part of an expression's meaning that, together with context, determines its referent. Also called **intension**. For example, knowing the sense or intension of a noun phrase such as *the president of the United States in the year 2010* allows one to determine that Barack Obama is the referent. See **intension, reference**.

sentence (S) A syntactic category of expressions consisting minimally of a **noun phrase (NP)** followed by a **verb phrase (VP)** in **d-structure**. Also called a **TP (tense phrase)**. The head of S is the category **Aux**, which may be empty except for tense.

sentential semantics The subfield of semantics concerned with the meanings of syntactic units larger than the word.

Separate Systems Hypothesis A proposal that a bilingual child builds a distinct lexicon and grammar for each language being acquired.

sequential bilingualism The acquisition of a second language by someone (adult or child) who has already acquired a first language.

shadowing task An experiment in which subjects are asked to repeat what they hear as rapidly as possible as it is being spoken. During the task, subjects often unconsciously correct "errors" in the input.

short message service The exchange of limited-character communication between mobile phones that includes many types of abbreviated written forms.

sibilants The class of sounds that includes alveolar and palatal **fricatives** and **affricates**, characterized acoustically by an abundance of high frequencies perceived as "hissing," e.g., [s], [ʧ].

sign A single gesture (possibly with complex meaning) in any of the sign languages used by the deaf.

sign languages The languages used by deaf people in which linguistic units such as morphemes and words as well as grammatical relations are formed by manual and other body movements.

simultaneous bilingualism Refers to the (more or less) simultaneous acquisition of two languages beginning in infancy (or before the age of three years).

sisters In a phrase structure tree, two categories that are directly under the same node: e.g., V and the direct object NP are sisters inside the verb phrase.

situational context Knowledge of who is speaking, who is listening, what objects are being discussed, and general facts about the world we live in, used to aid in the interpretation of meaning.

slang Words and phrases used in casual speech, often invented and spread by close-knit social or age groups, and fast-changing.

slip of the tongue An involuntary deviation of an intended utterance. See **spoonerism**. Also called **speech error**.

social dialect A dialect spoken by members of a group delineated by socioeconomic class, racial background, place of origin, or gender, and perpetuated by the integrity of the social class. See **regional dialect**.

societal bilingualism The mutual abilities of a community to speak two (or more) languages with native or near native proficiency. See **bilingualism, individual bilingualism**.

sociolinguistic variable A linguistic phenomenon, such as double negation in English, whose occurrence varies according to the social context of the speaker.

sonorants The class of sounds that includes **vowels, glides, liquids**, and **nasals**; non-obstruents. See **obstruents**.

sound change See **sound shift**.

sound shift Historical phonological change. Also called **sound change**.

sound symbolism The notion that certain sound combinations occur in semantically similar words: e.g., *gl* in *gleam, glisten, glitter*, which all relate to vision.

source The thematic role of the noun phrase whose referent is the place from which an action originates: e.g., *Mars* in *Mr. Wells just arrived from Mars.*

source language In automatic machine translation, the language being translated. See **target language**, **automatic machine translation**.

speaker dependent speech recognition A computer system that best processes the speech of particular known users, who train the system to their voices in advance.

speaker identification The use of computers to assist in matching a voice recording by an unknown person to a known person.

specific language impairment (SLI) Difficulty in acquiring language faced by certain children with no other cognitive deficits.

specifier The category of the left sister of $\overline{X}$ in the X-bar schema: e.g., a **determiner** in an NP. It is a modifier of the head and is often optional.

spectrogram A visual representation of speech decomposed into component frequencies, with time on the horizontal axis, frequency on the vertical axis, and intensity portrayed on a gray scale—the darker, the more intense. Also called **voiceprint**.

speech act The action or intent that a speaker accomplishes when using language in context, the meaning of which is inferred by hearers: e.g., *There is a bear behind you* may be intended as a warning in certain contexts, or may in other contexts merely be a statement of fact. See **illocutionary force**.

speech error An inadvertent deviation from an intended utterance that often results in ungrammaticality, nonsense words, anomaly, etc. See **slip of the tongue**, **spoonerism**.

speech recognition In computer processing, the ability to analyze speech sounds into phones, phonemes, morphemes, and words; the transcription of speech.

speech synthesis An electronic process that produces speech either from acoustically simulated sounds or from prerecorded units. See **formant synthesis**, **concatenative synthesis**.

speech understanding Computer processing for interpreting speech, one part of which is **speech recognition**.

spelling pronunciation Pronouncing a word as it is spelled, irrespective of its actual pronunciation by native speakers: e.g., pronouncing *Wednesday* as "wed-ness-day."

spelling reform The attempt by governments or academic institutions to change the spellings of words to more accurately reflect their current pronunciations.

spell-out rules Rules that convert abstract inflectional morphemes such as tense, agreement, and possessive into phonetically realized affixes: e.g., [+pst] into -*ed*.

split brain The result of an operation for epilepsy in which the **corpus callosum** is severed, thus separating the brain into its two hemispheres; split-brain patients are studied to determine the role of each hemisphere in cognitive and language processing.

spoonerism A **speech error** in which phonemic segments are reversed or exchanged: e.g., *you have hissed my mystery lecture* for the intended *you have missed my history lecture*; named after the Reverend William Archibald Spooner, a nineteenth-century Oxford don.

S-selection The classifying of verbs and other lexical items in terms of the semantic category of the head and complements that they accept, e.g., the verb *assassinate* S-selects for a human subject and a prestigious, human NP complement.

s-structure The structure that results from applying transformational rules to a **d-structure**. It is syntactically closest to actual utterances. Also called **surface structure**. See **transformational rule**.

standard The **dialect** (regional or social) considered to be the norm.

Standard American English (SAE) An idealized dialect of English that some prescriptive grammarians consider the proper form of English.

state/stative A type of sentence that describes states of being such as *Mary likes oysters*, as opposed to describing events such as *Mary ate oysters*. See **event/eventive**.

stem The base to which an affix is attached to create a more complex form that may be another stem or a word. See **root**, **affix**.

stemming In **computational morphology**, the analysis of words into their component morphemes by the recursive stripping off of affixes.

stops [–continuant] sounds in which the airflow is briefly but completely stopped in the oral cavity: e.g., [p], [n], [g].

stress, stressed syllable A syllable with relatively greater length, loudness, and/or higher pitch than other syllables in a word, and therefore perceived as prominent. Also called **accent**.

stress-timed language A language in which at least one syllable of a word receives primary stress. English is such a language.

structural ambiguity The phenomenon in which the same sequence of words has two or more meanings accounted for by different phrase structure analyses: e.g., *He saw a boy with a telescope*.

structure dependent (1) A principle of Universal Grammar that states that the application of **transformational rules** is determined by phrase structure properties, as opposed to structureless sequences of words or specific sentences; (2) the way children construct rules using their knowledge of syntactic structure irrespective of the specific words in the structure or their meaning.

style A situation dialect: e.g., formal speech, casual speech; also called **register**.

subcategorization See **C-selection**.

subject The grammatical relation of a noun phrase to a S(entence) when it appears immediately below that S in a phrase structure tree: e.g., *the zebra* in *The zebra has stripes*.

subject-verb agreement The addition of an **inflectional morpheme** to the main verb depending on a property of the noun phrase subject, such as number or gender. In English, it is the addition of *s* to a verb when the subject is third-person singular present tense: e.g., *A greyhound runs fast* versus *Greyhounds run fast*.

substrate languages The language(s) of the indigenous people in a language contact situation that contribute(s) to the lexicon and grammar of a pidgin or creole but in a less obvious way than the **superstrate language**.

suffix An **affix** that is attached to the end of a morpheme or stem: e.g., *-er* in *Lew is taller than Bill*.

summarization The computer scanning of a text and condensation to its most salient points.

superstrate language The language that provides most of the lexical items of a pidgin or creole, typically the language of the socially or economically dominant group. Also called **lexifier language**. See **substrate languages**.

suppletive forms A term used to refer to **inflected morphemes** in which the regular rules do not apply: e.g., *went* as the past tense of *go*.

suprasegmentals Prosodic features: e.g., length, tone.

surface structure See **s-structure**.

syllabary The symbols of a syllabic writing system.

syllabic A phonetic feature of those sounds that may constitute the nucleus of syllables; all vowels are syllabic, and liquids and nasals may be syllabic in such words as *towel, button, bottom*.

syllabic writing A writing system in which each syllable in the language is represented by its own symbol: e.g., **hiragana** in Japanese.

syllable A phonological unit composed of an **onset**, **nucleus**, and **coda**: e.g., *elevator* has four syllables: *el e va tor*; *man* has one syllable.

syllable-timed language A language in which the syllables have approximately the same loudness, length, and pitch, as opposed to a **stress-timed language**. French, for example, is such a language.

synonyms Words with the same or nearly the same meaning: e.g., *pail* and *bucket*.

synonymy (synonymous) Having the same meaning in all contexts. More technically, in the semantic component of the grammar, two sentences are synonymous if they **entail** each other: e.g., *the cat ate the rat; the rat was eaten by the cat*. See **paraphrases**.

syntactic bootstrapping The learning of word meaning inferred from syntax: e.g., when a child hears *John glouted Mary a clibe* he realizes that *glout* is a verb and likely means the transferring of something from one person to another.

syntactic category/class See **grammatical categories**.

syntax The rules of sentence formation; the component of the mental grammar that represents speakers' knowledge of the structure of phrases and sentences.

synthetic language Language in which words often contain multiple morphemes: e.g., English and Indo-European languages in general.

T (tense) A categorial label sometimes used in place of **Aux**. The syntactic category that is the head of **TP (tense phrase)** or **sentence (S)**. Also, for English, past or present, indicating the time frame of a sentence.

taboo Words or activities that are considered inappropriate for "polite society," e.g., *cunt, prick, fuck* for vagina, penis, and sexual intercourse, respectively.

tap A speech sound in which the tongue quickly touches the alveolar ridge, as in some British pronunciations of /r/. Also called **flap**.

target language In automatic machine translation, the language into which the source language is translated. See **source language**, **automatic machine translation**.

tautology A sentence that is true in all situations; a sentence true from the meaning of its words alone: e.g., *Kings are not female*. Also called **analytic**.

teaching grammar A set of language rules written to help speakers learn a foreign language or a different dialect of their language. See **descriptive grammar, prescriptive grammar**.

telegraphic speech Utterances of children that may omit **grammatical morphemes** and/or **function words**: e.g., *He go out* instead of *He is going out*.

telegraphic stage The period of child language acquisition that follows the two-word stage and consists primarily of **telegraphic speech**.

tense A **phonetic feature** that distinguishes similar pairs of vowels. Vowels that are [+tense] are somewhat longer in duration and higher in tongue position and pitch than the corresponding [–tense] (lax) vowel: e.g., in English [i] is a high front tense vowel whereas [ɪ] is a high front lax vowel. See **lax vowel**. Also a term sometimes used in place of **Aux**, and usually abbreviated **T**, it is the syntactic category that is the head of **TP (tense phrase)** or **sentence (S)**.

text-to-speech A computer program that converts written text into the basic units of a speech synthesizer, such as phones for **formant synthesizers**, or diphones, disyllables, etc. for **concatenative synthesizers**.

thematic role The semantic relationship between the verb and the noun phrases of a sentence, such as **agent, theme, location, instrument, goal, source**.

theme The thematic role of the noun phrase whose referent undergoes the action of the verb: e.g., *Martha* in *George hugged Martha*.

theta assignment The ascribing of thematic roles to the syntactic elements in a sentence.

time deixis The use of terms to refer to time whose reference relies entirely on context: e.g., *now, then, tomorrow, next month*. See **deictic, deixis, demonstrative articles, person deixis, place deixis**.

tip of the tongue phenomenon The difficulty encountered from time to time in retrieving a particular word or expression from the mental lexicon. Anomic aphasics suffer from an extreme form of this problem. See **anomia**.

tone The contrastive **pitch** of syllables in **tone languages**. Two words may be identical except for such differences in pitch: e.g., in Thai *naa* [naː] with falling pitch means 'face,' but with a rising pitch means 'thick.' See **register tones, contour tones**.

tone language A language in which the **tone** or **pitch** on a syllable is phonemic, so that words with identical segments but different tones are different words: e.g., Mandarin Chinese, Thai.

top-down processing Expectation-driven analysis of linguistic input that begins with the assumption that a large syntactic unit such as a sentence is present, and then analyzes it into successively smaller constituents (e.g., phrases, words, morphemes), which are ultimately compared with the sensory or acoustic data to validate the analysis. If the analysis is not validated, the procedure backs up to the previously validated point and then resumes. See **bottom-up processing, backtracking**.

topicalization A transformation that moves a syntactic element to the front of a sentence: e.g., deriving *Greyhounds I love very much* from *I love greyhounds very much*.

TP (tense phrase) A term sometimes used in place of **sentence (S)**, especially in the X-bar schema, where it is a phrasal category whose head is **Aux**.

transcription, phonemic The phonemic representation of speech sounds using phonetic symbols, ignoring phonetic details that are predictable by rule, usually given between slashes: e.g., /pæn/, /spæn/ for *pan*, *span* as opposed to the phonetic representation [pʰæn], [spæn].

transcription, phonetic The representation of speech sounds using phonetic symbols between square brackets. It may reflect nondistinctive predictable features such as aspiration and nasality: e.g., [pʰat] for *pot* or [mæ̃n] for *man*.

transfer of grammatical rules The application of rules from one's first language to a second language that one is attempting to acquire. The "accent" that second-language learners have is a result of the transfer of first language phonetic and phonological rules.

transformational rule, transformation A syntactic rule that applies to an underlying phrase structure tree of a sentence (either **d-structure** or an intermediate structure already affected by a transformation) and derives a new structure by moving, deleting or inserting elements: e.g., the transformational rules of *wh-* movement and *do* insertion relate the deep structure sentence *John saw who* to the surface structure *Who(m) did John see*.

transformationally induced ambiguity A situation in which different **d-structures** are mapped into the same **s-structure** by one or more transformations: e.g., the ambiguous *George loves Laura more than Dick* may be transformationally derived from the d-structure *George loves Laura more than Dick <u>loves Laura</u>* or *George loves Laura more than <u>George loves</u> Dick*, with the underlined words being deleted under identity by a transformation in either case.

transition network A graphical representation that uses nodes connected by labeled arcs to depict syntactic and semantic relationships. See **node, arc**.

transitional bilingual education (TBE) Educational programs in which students receive instruction in both English and their native language, for example Spanish, and the native language support is gradually phased out over two or three years.

transitive verb A verb that C-selects an obligatory noun-phrase complement: e.g., *find*.

tree diagram A graphical representation of the linear and hierarchical structure of a phrase or sentence. A **phrase structure tree**.

trill A speech sound in which part of the tongue vibrates against part of the roof of the mouth: e.g., the /r/ in Spanish *perro*, 'dog,' is articulated by vibrating the tongue tip behind the alveolar ridge; the /r/ in French *rouge*, 'red,' may be articulated by vibrations at the uvula.

trochaic Stress on the first syllable of a two-syllable word: e.g., *páper*.

truth conditions The circumstances that must be known to determine whether a sentence is true, which are therefore part of the meaning, or **sense**, of declarative sentences.

truth-conditional semantics A theory of meaning that takes the semantic knowledge of when sentences are true and false as basic.

truth value TRUE or FALSE; used to describe the truth of declarative sentences in context; the **reference** of a declarative sentence in **truth-conditional semantics**.

twitterology The computer analysis of short electronic textual communications known as tweets.

umlaut A **diacritic mark** (¨) written over a vowel, as ä, ö, ü, to indicate a sound different from that of the letter without the diacritic, used in written German among other languages.

unaspirated Phonetically voiceless stops in which the vocal cords begin vibrating immediately upon release of the closure: e.g., [p] in *spot*. See **aspirated**.

unconditioned sound change Historical phonological change that occurs in all phonetic contexts: e.g., the **Great Vowel Shift** of English in which long vowels were modified wherever they occurred in a word.

underextension The narrowing of a word's meaning in language acquisition to a more restrictive meaning: e.g., using *dog* for only the family pet and not for other dogs.

ungrammatical Describes structures that fail to conform to the rules of grammar.

uninterpretable Describes an utterance whose meaning cannot be determined because of **nonsense words**: e.g., *All mimsy were the borogoves.*

Unitary System Hypothesis A proposal that a bilingual child initially constructs only one lexicon and one grammar for both (or all) languages being acquired.

Universal Grammar (UG) The innate principles and properties that pertain to the grammars of all human languages.

unmarked The term used to refer to that member of a gradable pair of antonyms used in questions of degree: e.g., *high* is the unmarked member of high/low; in a masculine/feminine pair, the word that does not contain a derivational morpheme, usually the masculine word: e.g., *prince* is unmarked, whereas *princess* is marked. See **marked**.

uvula The fleshy appendage hanging down from the end of the **velum** (soft palate).

uvular A sound produced by raising the back of the tongue to the **uvula**.

velar A sound produced by raising the back of the tongue to the soft palate, or **velum**.

velum The soft palate; the part of the roof of the mouth behind the hard palate.

verb (V) The syntactic category, also lexical category, of words that can be the head of a verb phrase. Verbs denote actions, sensations, and states: e.g., *climb, hear, understand.*

verb phrase (VP) The syntactic category of expressions that contain a verb as its head along with its complements such as noun phrases and prepositional phrases: e.g., *gave the book to the child.*

verbal particle A word identical in form to a preposition which, when paired with a verb, has a particular meaning. A particle, as opposed to a preposition, is characterized syntactically by its ability to occur next to the verb, or transposed to the right: e.g., *out,* in *spit out* as in *He spit out his words,* or *He spit his words out.* Compare with *He ran out the door* versus **he ran the door out,* where *out* is a preposition.

Verner's law The description of a conditioned phonological change in the sound system of certain Indo-European languages wherein voiceless fricatives were changed when the preceding vowel was unstressed. It was formulated by Karl Verner as an explanation to some of the exceptions to **Grimm's law**.

vocal tract The oral and nasal cavities, together with the vocal cords, glottis, and pharynx, all of which may be involved in the production of speech sounds.

vocalic A phonetic feature that distinguishes vowels and liquids, which are [+vocalic], from other sounds (obstruents, glides, nasals), which are [–vocalic]. The feature is little used in contemporary linguistic literature.

voiced sound A speech sound produced with vibrating vocal cords.

voiceless sound A speech sound produced with open, nonvibrating vocal cords.

voiceprint A common term for a **spectrogram**.

vowel A sound produced without significant constriction of the air flowing through the **oral cavity**.

well-formed Describes a grammatical sequence of words, one conforming to rules of syntax. See **grammatical**, **ill-formed**.

Wernicke, Carl Neurologist who showed that damage to specific parts of the left cerebral hemisphere causes specific types of language disorders.

Wernicke's aphasia The type of aphasia resulting from damage to **Wernicke's area**.

Wernicke's area The back (posterior) part of the left brain that if damaged causes a specific type of aphasia. Also called Wernicke's region.

wh questions Interrogative sentences beginning with one or more of the words who(m), what, where, when, and how, and their equivalents in languages that do not have wh-words, such as quién in Spanish: ¿A quién le gusta? 'Who(m) do you like?'

word frames Lexical contexts often used by adults such as the _ one that assist a child learning language to categorize words, in this case adjectives.

word writing A system of writing in which each character represents a word or morpheme of the language: e.g., Chinese. See **ideograph**, **logographic writing**.

X-bar theory A universal schema specifying that the internal organization of all phrasal categories (i.e., NP, PP, VP, TP (S), AP, AdvP) can be broken down into three levels: e.g., NP, $\overline{\text{N}}$, and N.

yes-no question An interrogative sentence that inquires as to whether a certain situation is true or not: e.g., *Is the boy asleep?*

Index